Inhaled Medicines

Inhaled Medicines

Optimizing Development Through Integration of In Silico, In Vitro, and In Vivo Approaches

Edited by

STAVROS KASSINOS
Computational Sciences Laboratory (UCY-CompSci), Mechanical and Manufacturing Engineering, University of Cyprus, Nicosia, Cyprus

PER BÄCKMAN
Emmace Consulting AB, Lund, Sweden

JOY CONWAY
Respiratory Sciences, Centre for Health and Life Sciences, Brunel University, London, United Kingdom

ANTHONY J. HICKEY
Engineered Systems, RTI International, Research Triangle Park, NC, United States

ELSEVIER

ACADEMIC PRESS
An imprint of Elsevier

Academic Press is an imprint of Elsevier
125 London Wall, London EC2Y 5AS, United Kingdom
525 B Street, Suite 1650, San Diego, CA 92101, United States
50 Hampshire Street, 5th Floor, Cambridge, MA 02139, United States
The Boulevard, Langford Lane, Kidlington, Oxford OX5 1GB, United Kingdom

British Library Cataloguing-in-Publication Data
A catalogue record for this book is available from the British Library

Library of Congress Cataloging-in-Publication Data
A catalog record for this book is available from the Library of Congress

ISBN: 978-0-12-814974-4

For Information on all Academic Press publications
visit our website at https://www.elsevier.com/books-and-journals

Publisher: Andre Gerhard Wolff
Acquisitions Editor: Glyn Jones
Editorial Project Manager: Megan Ashdown
Production Project Manager: Maria Bernard
Cover Designer: Christian J. Bilbow

Typeset by MPS Limited, Chennai, India

Contents

List of contributors

Elham Amini
Department of Pharmaceutics, College of Pharmacy, University of Florida, Gainesville, FL, United States

Per Bäckman
Emmace Consulting AB, Lund, Sweden

Erica Bäckström
Drug Metabolism and Pharmacokinetics, Research and Early Development, Respiratory & Immunology, BioPharmaceuticals R&D, AstraZeneca, Gothenburg, Sweden

Martyn Biddiscombe
National Heart and Lung Institute (NHLI), Imperial College London & Royal Brompton Hospital, London, United Kingdom

Britta Bonn
Drug Metabolism and Pharmacokinetics, Research and Early Development, Respiratory and Immunology (R&I), BioPharmaceuticals R&D, AstraZeneca, Gothenburg, Sweden

Jens Markus Borghardt
Drug Discovery Sciences, Research DMPK, Boehringer Ingelheim Pharma GmbH & Co. KG, Biberach, Germany

Joy Conway
Brunel University London, London, United Kingdom; Southampton NIHR Biomedical Research Centre for Respiratory and Critical Care, Southampton, United Kingdom; University of Southampton, Southampton, United Kingdom

Anne Haaije de Boer
Department of Pharmaceutical Technology and Biopharmacy, Faculty of Science and Engineering, University of Groningen, Groningen, The Netherlands

Martin Donnelley
Adelaide Medical School and Robinson Research Institute, University of Adelaide, Adelaide, SA, Australia

Zachary Enlo-Scott
Institute of Pharmaceutical Science, King's College London, London, United Kingdom

Ben Forbes
Institute of Pharmaceutical Science, King's College London, London, United Kingdom

Markus Fridén
Drug Metabolism and Pharmacokinetics, Research and Early Development, Respiratory & Immunology, BioPharmaceuticals R&D, AstraZeneca, Gothenburg, Sweden; Translational PKPD Group, Department of Pharmaceutical Biosciences, Uppsala University, Uppsala, Sweden

Mark Gardner
Australian Cancer Research Foundation Image X Institute, University of Sydney, Sydney, NSW, Australia

Anthony J. Hickey
RTI International, Research Triangle Park, NC, United States

Anneke Himstedt
Drug Discovery Sciences, Research DMPK, Boehringer Ingelheim Pharma GmbH & Co. KG, Biberach, Germany; Department of Clinical Pharmacy, Institute of Pharmacy, University of Hamburg, Hamburg, Germany

Guenther Hochhaus
Department of Pharmaceutics, College of Pharmacy, University of Florida, Gainesville, FL, United States

Eric A. Hoffman
Department of Radiology, The University of Iowa, Iowa City, IA, United States; Roy J. Carver Department of Biomedical Engineering, The University of Iowa, Iowa City, IA, United States; Department of Internal Medicine, The University of Iowa, Iowa City, IA, United States

Stavros Kassinos
Computational Sciences Laboratory (UCY-CompSci), Mechanical and Manufacturing Engineering, University of Cyprus, Nicosia, Cyprus; Department of Mechanical and Manufacturing Engineering, University of Cyprus, Nicosia, Cyprus; Respiratory Hub (UCY RespiHub), University of Cyprus, Nicosia, Cyprus

Pantelis Koullapis
Department of Mechanical and Manufacturing Engineering, University of Cyprus, Nicosia, Cyprus; Respiratory Hub (UCY RespiHub), University of Cyprus, Nicosia, Cyprus

Ching-Long Lin
Department of Mechanical Engineering, The University of Iowa, Iowa City, IA, United States; Department of Radiology, The University of Iowa, Iowa City, IA, United States; Roy J. Carver Department of Biomedical Engineering, The University of Iowa, Iowa City, IA, United States

Hans Lundbäck
Emmace Consulting AB, Lund, Sweden

Kaye Morgan
School of Physics and Astronomy, Monash University, Clayton, VIC, Australia

Bo Olsson
Emmace Consulting AB, Lund, Sweden

David Parsons
Adelaide Medical School and Robinson Research Institute, University of Adelaide, Adelaide, SA, Australia; Respiratory and Sleep Medicine, Women's and Children's Hospital, North Adelaide, SA, Australia

Matthew Perry
Medicinal Chemistry, Research and Early Development, Respiratory and Immunology (R&I), BioPharmaceuticals R&D, AstraZeneca, Gothenburg, Sweden

Fotos Stylianou
Department of Mechanical and Manufacturing Engineering, University of Cyprus, Nicosia, Cyprus; Respiratory Hub (UCY RespiHub), University of Cyprus, Nicosia, Cyprus

Mårten Svensson
Emmace Consulting AB, Lund, Sweden

Magda Swedrowska
Institute of Pharmaceutical Science, King's College London, London, United Kingdom

Josué Sznitman
Department of Biomedical Engineering, Technion-Israel Institute of Technology, Haifa, Israel

Kyrre Thalberg
Inhalation Product Development, Pharmaceutical Technology & Development, Operations, AstraZeneca Gothenburg, Sweden; Emmace Consulting AB, Medicon Village, Lund, Sweden

Omar Usmani
National Heart and Lung Institute (NHLI), Imperial College London & Royal Brompton Hospital, London, United Kingdom

Introduction

With many excellent texts already available on the subject of inhalation therapies, this volume has a unique perspective that we hope will complement the existing literature. This book emerged largely as the product of COST Action MP1404—"SimInhale" and to some degree it reflects the philosophy that underpinned the SimInhale network. Over the last 30 years, but primarily during the last decade, we have witnessed a leap in the capabilities and sophistication of *in silico* methods for predicting aerosol deposition and drug pharmacokinetics in the lung. Three-dimensional computational Fluid Particle Methods (3D-CFPD) in particular are now capable of providing estimates of drug deposition not only at the airway generational level, but also in the central airways at least, even at the level of individual bronchi. Yet, the impact of this unprecedented computational power has had limited impact on the development and approval cycle of inhaled pharmaceutical products. This text argues that the impact of 3D-CFPD has been limited by the lack of a closer integration with the two other pillars of product development, *in vivo* and *in vitro* methods. Furthermore, while the evolution of sophisticated 3D-CFPD brings new capabilities and expectations to the foreground, *in vivo* and *in vitro* methods have not remained static. On the contrary, methods continue to be improved and streamlined leading to improvements in our understanding of the underlying physical and physiological processes that determine the fate of inhaled drugs.

In the last section of the book, we synthesize a vision of the field of inhalation over the next decade, in which a significant advance is achieved by greater integration of *in vivo*, *in vitro*, and *in silico* methods. However, to reach the point where the value of such a synthesis can be appreciated, the book takes the reader through a journey that looks at the latest developments and enduring gaps in our understanding of the processes that determine the fate, and ultimately the efficacy and safety, of inhaled drugs. The opening chapter of the book provides a short perspective commentary placing the current state of the art in inhalation in the context of its historical development. The second chapter is devoted to the key physicochemical attributes of active pharmaceutical ingredient (API). This chapter provides the stage upon which the remaining chapters project a picture of the current state of the art in inhaled drug delivery addressing the critical features of therapeutic aerosols. Chapters 3–5 provide a critical review of the three main types of inhalation devices, nebulizers, metered dose inhalers and dry powder inhalers, offering an expert perspective on the strengths and limitations of each type of device and the prospects for future development. Chapters 6 and 7 discuss the current status of *in vitro* and *in silico* methods, presenting the current state of the art from several different points of view, for example, from the perspective of achieving regulatory approval for bioequivalence or from the perspective of obtaining a quantitatively accurate estimate of generational deposition in the vast expanse of the human lung. The discussion evolves around how *in vitro* and *in silico* tools can help achieve targeted delivery, not only in the standard healthy lung, but also more appropriately in the lungs of population segments whose airways diverge due to disease, age, or sex determinants. Chapters 8 through 12 focus the reader on the airway epithelium where the fate of the drug once it has been deposited is scrutinized. The discussion offers a timely perspective on the increasing appreciation of the role of dissolution and drug release in the wider context of the competing mechanisms that determine the drug fate. The current state of understanding of the physicochemical and physiological processes that underpin these competing mechanisms is presented, leading to a discussion of physiologically based pharmacokinetic modeling. Chapter 13 marks a shift in perspective, turning the focus on clinical diagnostics and imaging as the tools that allow the *in vivo* assessment of drug delivery and fate. The current limitations to imaging resolution and access to the peripheral lung are critically discussed. Chapter 14 extends and concludes the discussion of *in silico* methods begun in Chapter 7, offering examples of the application of state-of-the-art AI tools and methods, illustrating their increasing use both in preclinical and clinical population studies. Building on the foundation of the preceding chapters, Chapter 15 offers a vision for the future where a synthesis of *in vivo*, *in vitro*, and *in silico* methods will achieve sufficient integration to allow concurrent leverage in the service of efficient product development. Each would complement the others and offer a roadmap for overcoming some of the current obstacles to rapid development. The pace of discovery in pulmonary biology and disease is accelerating through the application of the molecular/cellular tools of genomics, transcriptomics, proteomics, and metabolomics combined with machine learning and AI to identify new drug candidates. In this context, the closing paragraph of the chapter could very well be adopted as the message of this book: "we have reached the point where coordinated effort in a spirit of openness and cooperation among academia and industry-based researchers, as well as closer consultation with regulatory agencies, provide the best hope for continued progress in inhalation therapies" sufficient to support rapid new drug discovery efforts.

STAVROS KASSINOS
Computational Sciences Laboratory (UCY-CompSci),
Mechanical and Manufacturing Engineering, University of Cyprus, Nicosia, Cyprus

PER BÄCKMAN
Emmace Consulting AB, Lund, Sweden

ANTHONY J. HICKEY
Engineered Systems, RTI International,
Research Triangle Park, NC, United States

CHAPTER 1

Historical perspective — Disruptive technologies and strategies

Anthony J. Hickey[1] and Joy Conway[2]
[1]RTI International, Research Triangle Park, NC, United States
[2]University of Southampton, Southampton, United Kingdom

The evolution of inhaled medicines in recorded history can be traced back to the Indus Valley and China 5000 years ago with inhalation of smokes of stromonium alkaloids and ephedra [1]. There have been some excellent reviews of developments in the intervening period leading to modern developments in the period following since the middle of the 20th century [2,3]. In keeping with the intent of this volume to guide the reader to critical issues in inhaled pharmaceutical research and development, the approach to the topic taken here is to focus on the disruptive technologies and the evolution of modern methods and treatment strategies.

In this regard, the major developments have occurred in dosage forms, aspects of characterization and biopharmaceutical considerations. In addition, the diseases that were primarily the target for therapy, asthma and chronic obstructive pulmonary disease are now expanding to include a wide range of other pulmonary and systemic diseases.

1.1 Dosage forms

1.1.1 Metered dose inhalers

In the mid-1950s metered dose inhaler technology was developed at 3M Pharmaceuticals [4]. The key to the success of this dosage form was the combination of small, metered dose valves and the ability to use the vapor pressure of chlorofluorocarbon propellants (CFCs) as the propulsive force through flash evaporation of small respirable droplets. The discovery in 1973 of the atmospheric ozone depletion resulting from CFC emissions led to the Montreal Protocol, an international agreement, to phase out the CFCs for all applications including medical use [5,6]. Development of hydrofluoroalkane or hydrofluorocarbon (HFA or HFC) alternative propellants was largely driven by the phase out of CFC propellants and resulted in the first product a corticosteroid (Qvar, beclomethasone dipropionate, 3M Pharmaceuticals) appearing in the late 1990s and the first broncholdilator, albuterol sulfate in 2003 (GSK) [7—9].

Inhaled Medicines
DOI: https://doi.org/10.1016/B978-0-12-814974-4.00003-1

As the transition to HFA formulations progressed it became evident that the number of formulation options was even more restricted than had been the case with CFC formulations. Creating a formulation strategy that was generalizable to a variety of drugs was a challenge and the initial approved products required significant formulation optimization. In recent years the development of co-suspension technology (Budesonide, Glycopyrrolate, Bevespi®, AstraZeneca) is a major step towards a solution to the formulation constraints usually experienced [10].

As concerns about global warming potential increase there is some pressure to phase out HFAs and a new series of propellants are under development.

1.1.2 Dry powder inhalers

In the 1960s and 1970s alternative strategies for the delivery of aerosol particles emerged both as a proprietary strategy (Spinhaler, Cromlyn Sodium, Intal®, Pfisons) [11] and as an alternative to metered dose inhalers for those who were for whatever reason reluctant or incapable of using them (Rotahaler, Albuterol Sulfate, Ventolin®, GSK) [12]. These products were not a huge market success but offered a different platform from which to consider aerosol delivery. At the time of CFC phase out discussions, there was a concurrent interest in the delivery of the products of biotechnology, which were not suitable for conventional routes of administration. Consequently, in the early 1990s the focus returned to the potential of dry powder inhaler technology most obviously for insulin products, such as Exubera® (Pfizer/Nektar), which was finally approved in the United States in 2006 [13].

There were a number of dosage form advances as the emphasis was placed on improving the technology. The first step was to move from pre-metered unit dose devices (capsule based) to multidose devices the earliest of which, in the 1980s, was the Turbuhaler originally developed for the delivery of terbutaline (Astrazeneca) [14]. There was significant market uptake for this device particularly for the combination product with budesonide, Pulmocort® [15].

During the early 2000s the advent of new potent drugs and technologies led to dry powder inhalers finally becoming a commercial success led by Advair®/Seretide® Diskus and the first inhaled therapy for Chronic Obstructive Pulmonary Disease, tiotropium (Handihaler, Spiriva®, Boehringer Ingelheim) [16,17].

Throughout the period of new drug and inhaler technology development there had been a significant focus on new formulation approaches. Initial products consisted of micronized (attrition milled) particles that were manipulated to overcome forces of particle interaction by including in carrier particle blends (Intal® and Ventolin®) or through controlled loose aggregates (Turbuhaler) [18]. The focus on stabilizing proteins in dry powders led to exploration of spray drying technology [19,20]. The concept of low-density particles emerged from spray drying engineering with the advantage of producing respirable particles that can be easily dispersed [21]. A similar technology resulted in a dry powder antibiotic form of Tobramycin (PulmoSpheres®, Novartis) [22].

It should be noted that there have been numerous published technologies intended to modify the release rate of drugs or for specific targeting e.g. macrophages, in the lungs. This topic alone would justify an independent review. However, very few of these technologies have resulted in commercial products. Indeed, most modulation of the drug disposition and effect has been achieved through modifying the drug itself during the discovery effort. Therefore, this topic is considered beyond the scope of this historical review, while it is acknowledged it may be important in the future.

1.1.3 Nebulizers

Technology for the delivery of aqueous droplets by Bernoulli, or Venturi, effect from a nebulizer is arguably one of the older technologies for the delivery of solutions of drugs [19,23]. As these devices are uniquely regulated in the United States as separate medical instruments from the drug solution, they exist in a wide variety and are considered a relatively inexpensive commodity item. While the alternative method of ultrasonic aerosol generation has existed for decades, it is a slightly less efficient approach and has generally been less popular the jet nebulizers [23]. The desire to preserve expensive drug, increase the efficiency of delivery and reduce the time of delivery, which would help with patient compliance, was a significant impetus for the development of alternative technologies.

The need to deliver products of biotechnology, potentially expensive potent drugs, initiated the interest in vibrating mesh technologies, which have since been developed to one of the most popular methods of delivering nebulized drugs [24]. The advent of these systems has also allowed for specific nebulizers and drugs to be dispensed together which moves nebulizers closer to regulation as a combined drug product. The delivery of large dose antibiotics, efficiently and over relatively short periods has also benefited from the development of vibrating mesh systems [25].

1.1.4 Soft mist inhalers

Soft mist inhalers represent a unique approach to progressing from metered dose inhalers and dry powder inhalers in terms of metered systems. This product is exemplified by the tiotropium (Spiolto Respimat®, Boehringer Ingelheim®) product, which is based on forcing the drug solution through a silica-based orifice system impinging flows to generate the aerosol [26]. This has been a remarkably successful new technology since its approval in Europe in 2015.

1.1.5 Other considerations

As new technologies related to aerosol delivery and inhaler design are developed there is a growing need to consider components that will assist in patient compliance and adherence. The first step in this direction was the requirement for counters on all metered devices, which began as a universal demand at the turn of the Millennium [27–29]. This has since been followed by a variety of electronic systems that report to both the patient and the clinician. Moreover, these systems can be used for immediate and long-term monitoring of therapy through apps on hand held devices which parallel developments in fitness monitoring [30]. These developments have yet to meet their full potential but the future is clear from the speed of adoption for lifestyle monitoring systems for other aspects of life.

1.2 Characterization

1.2.1 In vitro testing

The performance characteristics of greatest importance for inhalers, as identified by pharmacopoeias and regulatory guidance documents, are delivered dose and aerodynamic particle size distribution (APSD) [31,32]. The latter is a unique characteristic of aerosols and there is only one way to determine practically in a manner that meets the requirements for regulatory approval and this is by a principle known as inertial impaction. Simply stated inertial impaction occurs when the mass of a particle is such that as it approaches a barrier to flow its inertia (mass and linear velocity) propels it toward the object on which it impacts. Particles with smaller mass are more likely to relax into the direction of the airflow on which they are carried and pass around the obstacle. Particles with higher linear velocity, and therefore inertia, tend to impinge on a collection surface and by sequentially increasing the velocity a series of particle sizes can be collected on a device, which is known as a cascade impactor [33,34].

The principle of cascade impaction which is a semi-empirical phenomenon based on Stokes' law has been known for some time and was originally developed for capturing ambient aerosols following the detonation of conventional and, subsequently, nuclear weapons in the 1940s and 1950s [35]. Their value was soon realized by those studying atmospheric physics, industrial hygiene and inhalation toxicology. Their adoption for characterization of pharmaceutical aerosol was approximately concurrent with the development of the early inhaler technologies. However, by the late 1980s it was evident that there were some important characteristics of inhaled aerosols that differed from atmospheric aerosols. Firstly, atmospheric aerosols were on a short time scale of minutes or hours steady state aerosols that could be sampled at almost any flow rate and through any sampling inlet from atmosphere provided the cascade impactor was calibrated at that flow rate and particles were sufficiently small to pass through the inlet without deposition. Secondly, it was always the case with ambient aerosols that a sample was taken, as collection of the entire aerosol was both physically impossible and given the nature of locational sampling undesirable.

In contrast, pharmaceutical aerosols are not steady state (with the possible exception of nebulized droplets) entitites and it is important that the entire dose is sampled and subjected to chemical analysis. At the end of the 1980s significant attention was given to the flow rate of sampling for relevance to human effort and to the adoption of a standard inlet [32]. Both of these items were central to the ability to compare data from one laboratory to the next and to establish the quality and uniformity of performance. At the turn of the decade from the 1980s to 1990s a standard inlet was adopted by the United States Pharmacopoeia and as the effect of flow rate on performance of dry powder inhalers in particular was noted three flow rates were settled on as relevant for testing of 30, 60 and 90 L/min, representing weak (sedentary), intermediate and strong inhalation effort [31].

The observation that there was a limited correlation between cascade impaction data for particles collected <3 μm in aerodynamic diameter and experimental data on lung deposition for a number of different inhaler devices was encouraging with respect to the prospects of developing predictive models [36].

1.2.1.1 Sampling inlet configuration and airflow rate

The sampling inlet adopted was frequently referred to as the 'throat' although there was no evidence that it behaved as an anatomical human oropharynx [37]. However, in time the notion that it should reflect deposition in a human oropharynx gained popularity among those searching for an in vitro predictor or lung deposition. In the 2000s Warren Finlay at the University of Alberta was the first to explore the possibility of a cascade impactor, sampling inlet in which deposition would approximate that of a human throat [38,39].

As inlet considerations were evolving another obvious consideration that would need attention was beginning to be addressed in some laboratories, namely that inspiratory flow is not a step function constant volumetric flow rate as defined by a vacuum pump but is in fact a flow cycle exemplified by acceleration and deceleration or continuous flow variations [40]. The combination of instruments designed to deliver variable inspiratory flow rates with physiological throat casts has been shown to bring our in vitro estimates of lung deposition as close as they have every been to actual predictions [41].

1.2.2 Lung deposition

1.2.2.1 Modeling

As in vitro methods have improved lung deposition modeling has improved dramatically. Extensive analytical modeling appeared between the 1940s and 1990s in the field of atmospheric exposure and industrial hygiene that informed considerations of drug deposition but was not adopted widely by the industry or those in academia focused on pharmaceutical technology [42,43]. At the end of the last Millennium the adoption of computational fluid dynamics both for flow path optimization in devices and for lung deposition modeling linked the two aspects of inhaled medicines in a manner that has promoted its mainstream application [44]. The common approach now seems to be one of combining CFD and analytical approaches to iterate towards greater predictive capacity and to formally link device performance to expectations of biological targeting [45].

1.2.2.2 Imaging

The value of models is gauged by their ability to predict lung deposition and is only as good as our practical knowledge of lung deposition as measured by imaging technologies. Two dimensional planar imaging, using gamma scintigraphy, has been common practice as a diagnostic tool for over a half century [46]. It became the tool of choice for studying the deposition of pharmaceutical aerosols in the 1970s and 1980s and has been used to evaluate all currently marketed products. There are many considerations with respect to the importance of this method [47]. Tissue overlay, attenuation and, ultimately, resolution make this method somewhat insensitive. Nevertheless, qualified researchers in this field are sufficiently well versed in the technology to extract helpful information and have been able, by considering regions of interest, to make broad claims as to measures of deposition site for correlation with subsequent pharmacokinetic and pharmacodynamics interpretation [48]. Three-dimensional methods have been the subject of increasing imagining research since the turn of the Millennium in terms of transitioning to development tools. Single Photon Emitted Computer Tomography (SPECT) and positron emission tomography (PET) have been the subject of extensive development [49]. The approach to interpretation of the data has also expanded to allow for many more regions of interest to be identified, almost to the level of airway branching numbers, through a onion layer approach [50].

1.3 Biopharmaceutics

1.3.1 Pharmacokinetics

Following the disposition of drugs from the lungs has been part of inhaled product development activities for many years. Early product assessments gave little attention to pharmacokinetics as the drugs were delivered in such low doses to the lungs that plasma concentrations were difficult to detect. As analytical methods improved, most notably with the development of high performance liquid chromatography and subsequently with the shift from standard detection methods such as ultra-violet to mass spectrometry detection, sensitivity and limits of detection were reduced dramatically. The ability to follow drug disposition as a function of dose rendered this the most sensitive biological approach to assessing differences in product performance or for generic products differences between innovator and generic alternate products.

As it has been acknowledged that the pharmacokinetics may be the first, and perhaps most important, biological measure of drug performance the approach to studying the data has also evolved [51,52]. It is possible to conduct analysis in a model independent fashion using the raw data, but where complex patterns of disposition are involved this may make data interpretation difficult. Classical pharmacokinetic models call for the overlay of mathematical transformations in which compartments may be inferred for which there may, or may not, be physiological equivalents [53]. In recent years, physiological models are beginning to yield more physically accurate depictions of drug disposition [54]. From a regulatory standpoint, the adoption of population pharmacokinetics in clinical trials now renders interpretation of direct relevance to this important step in establishing the biological performance of an inhaled therapeutic agent [55].

1.3.2 Pharmacodynamics

Clinical endpoints vary from one disease to another. Consequently, there is no general approach to establishing these measures of efficacy that are the desired outcome for the clinician and the patient.

Unfortunately, therapeutic outcomes are rarely good measures of the quality or performance of an aerosol product. The primary commercially available therapeutic categories of drug employed are beta$_2$-adrenergic agonists (BAA), anticholinergics (AC) and corticosteroids (CS) used in the treatment of asthma and chronic obstructive pulmonary disease [56]. BAA and AC drugs are delivered in doses that are so far above their therapeutic dose (along the pharmacological plateau) that the will be effective regardless of a wide disparity in patient pulmonary function due to age, gender or disease state. CS therapy involves stabilizing on daily doses given for a period of time and so any variability in response to an instantaneous dose is averaged over the entire dosing period. Consequently, the challenge is to identify sensitive measures of efficacy that do vary with dose delivered.

Since the majority of the work on inhaled aerosols has focused on asthma and chronic obstructive pulmonary disease, the Forced Expiratory Volume at 1 s (FEV$_1$) has been employed as a measure of pulmonary function in response to drug therapy [57]. However, as interest in the use of therapeutic aerosols has expanded the question has arisen as to whether a broader view of the pulmonary function tests should be taken and whether biomarkers can be identified such as sputum eosinophils, exhaled gas (NO), C-reactive protein or other metrics for infectious disease such as secreted proteins or toxins [58].

1.3.3 Diseases

In modern times asthma was the first disease to be treated with inhaled therapy [59]. The nature of the disease being localized to the airways and its high incidence worldwide made it a clear therapeutic and commercial target. It took almost a half-century for the same approach to be taken to chronic obstructive pulmonary disease despite the localized nature of disease and the severity of disease globally. At this point asthma and COPD are the most significant diseases being treated with aerosol therapy.

As the technology and drug portfolio has evolved many other diseases have become targets for aerosol therapy. Cystic fibrosis is significant among these for the range of treatments that are now available including Mucolytics (sodium chloride and acetylcysteine) DNAse (Dornase®, Genentech), tobramycin (TOBI®, Novartis) and a revival of gene therapy driven by the possibility of gene editing [60,61]. Each of these approaches treats different aspect of disease. Mucolytics hydrate mucus and DNAse clips leukocyte DNA that contributes to thickening of mucus and both make mucus less viscous and more mobile. Tobramycin treat the primary *Pseudomonas aeruginosa* infection that complicates the disease and causes severe local inflammation. Gene therapy or editing can be employed to correct the Cystic Fibrosis Transmembrane Receptor (CFTR) defects that give rise to a chloride imbalance and result in a thickening of mucus in the lungs [61].

In the late 1980s and early 1990s several organizations began to develop inhaled insulin to treat diabetes by regulating circulating glucose. The first such product, Exubera® (Pfizer/Nektar) was approved in 2006 and voluntarily withdrawn from the market after one year [13]. The second product Afrezza® (Mannkind) was approved in 2014 [62]. There is no question that the drive to develop inhaled insulin had an enormous stimulus particularly on dry powder inhaler development the extent of which would be hard to measure.

Unique inhaler development was required for the delivery of drugs for the treatment of disorders of the brain. One of the first evaporation condensation devices the Staccato® (Alexza Pharmaceuticals) is in development for a number of drugs. Adasuve® (loxapine) for the treatment of schizopherenia and bipolar disorder was approved in 2012 [63]. A supercritical fluid manufacturing method was employed for the preparation of dihydroxyergotamine for inclusion in an HFA metered dose inhaler (Levadex®, MAP Pharma now Allergan) [64]. Approval of this product has been anticipated for over five years.

There are many other diseases for which inhaled therapy may be potentially useful ranging from tuberculosis [65] and non-tuberculous mycobacterial [66] treatment to the delivery of drugs to treat pulmonary arterial hypertension [67] and idiopathic pulmonary fibrosis [68]. There continues to be a bright future for inhaled therapy as technology evolves and new disease applications are identified.

While new developments are occurring there is increasing interest in promoting the development of generic products. The challenge that is being addressed by pharmaceutical scientists is connecting many of the items discussed earlier, in vitro testing, modeling and imaging of lung deposition and pharmacokinetics to allow sufficiently accurate prediction to facilitate product development while meeting regulatory requirements [69–71].

1.4 Conclusion

The history of inhaled therapy is probably as long as man since it is not beyond the realms of possibility to think that inhalation of smokes and vapors has always soothed lung disorders. This can certainly be traced back to the beginning of recorded civilization. In modern times there have been areas in which disruptive technologies and scientific observations have rapidly advanced our ability to treat or evaluate treatment of disease. This chapter has dealt with important developments that have arisen over a period of approximately 60 years. During this time new inhalers have been developed that have advanced in formulation, metering system and aerosol generation. In addition, our understanding and ability to measure in vitro aerosol properties, to predict and measure lung deposition has also improved. We have advanced our ability to understand the disposition of drugs from the lungs and continue to improve our measures of therapeutic outcome. There is no question that with the continued demand for new therapies for diseases that are currently treated with aerosols and for diseases for which aerosol therapy would be beneficial a bright future of inhaled medicines is assured.

References

[1] M. Sanders, Inhalation therapy: an historical review, Prim. Care Respir. J. 16 (2007) 71–81.
[2] M. Sanders, Pulmonary drug delivery: an historical overview, in: H. Smyth, A. Hickey (Eds.), Controlled Pulmonary Drug Delivery, Springer, New York, 2011, pp. 51–73.
[3] S. Stein, C. Thiel, The history of therapeutic aerosols: a chronological review, J. Aerosol Med. Pulm. Drug. Deliv. 30 (2017) 20–41.
[4] C. Thiel, From Susie's question to CFC free: an inventor's perspective on forty years of MDI development and regulation, Respir. Drug. Deliv. V. 1 (1996) 115–124.
[5] M. Molina, F. Rowland, Stratospheric sink for chlorofluoromethanes: chlorine atom-catalysed destruction of ozone, Nature 249 (1974) 810–812.
[6] G. Velders, S. Anderson, J. Daniel, D. Fahey, M. McFarland, The importance of the Montreal Protocol in protecting the environment, PNAS 104 (2007) 4814–4819.
[7] R. Hawkesworth, A. Sykes, M. Faris, T. Mant, T. Lee, Albuterol HFA is as effective as albuterol CFC in preventingt exercise-induced bronchoconstriction, Ann. Allergy, Asthma Immunol. 88 (2002) 473–477.
[8] C. Leach, The CFC to HFA transition and its impact on pulmonary drug development, Respir. Care 50 (2005) 1201–1208.
[9] C. Leach, G. Colice, A pilot study to assess lung deposition of HFA-beclomethasone and CFC-beclomethasone from a pressurized metered dose inhaler with and without add-on spacers and using varying breathold times, J. Aerosol Med. Pulmonary Drug. Deliv. 23 (2010) 355–361.
[10] G. Ferguson, A. Hickey, S. Dwivedi, Co-suspension delivery technology in pressurized metered-dose inhalers for multi-drug dosing in the treatment of respiratory diseases, Respir. Med. 124 (2018) 16–23.
[11] A. Edwards, The discovery of cromlyn sodium and its effect on research and practice in allergy and immunology, J. Allergy Clin. Immunol. 115 (2005) 885–888.
[12] C. Marasco, Salbutamol, Chem. Eng. N. 83 (2005) 3.
[13] L. Profit, Exubera (inhaled insulin): an evidence-based review of it effeciveness in the management of diabetes, Core Evid. 1 (2005) 89–101.

[14] C. Johnsen, E.R. Weeke, Turbuhaler: a new device for dry powder terbutaline inhalation, Allergy 43 (1988) 392–395.
[15] A. Jones, C. Langdon, P. Lee, S. Lingham, J. Nankani, R. Follows, et al., Pulmicort turbuhaler once daily as initial prophylactic therapy for asthma, Respir. Med. 88 (1994) 293–299.
[16] M. Littner, J. Ilowite, D. Tashkin, M. Friedman, C. Serby, S. Menjoge, et al., Long-acting bronchodilatation with once-daily dosing of tiotrpium (Spiriva) in stable chronic obstructive lung disease, Am. J. Respir. Crit. Care Med. 161 (2000) 1136–1142.
[17] H. Nelson, Advair: combination treatment with fluticasone dipropionate/salmeterol in the treatment of asthma, J. Allergy Clin. Immunol. 107 (2001) 397–416.
[18] A. Hickey, Complexity in pharmaceutical powders for inhalation: a perspective, KONA (2017). Available from: https://doi.org/10.14356/kona.2018007.
[19] A. Lefebvre, Atomization and Sprays, Hemisphere Publishing Corporation (Taylor and Francis Group), New York, 1989.
[20] R. Vehring, Pharmaceutical particle engineering via spray drying, Pharm. Res. 25 (2007) 999–1022.
[21] D. Edwards, J. Hanes, G. Caponetti, J. Hrkach, A. Ben-Jebrai, M. Eskew, et al., Large porous particles for pulmonary drug delivery, Science 276 (1997) 1868–1872.
[22] D. Geller, J. Weers, S. Heuerding, Development of an inhaled dry-powder formulation of tobramycin using PulmoSphere technology, J. Aerosol Med. Pulmonary Drug. Deliv. 24 (2011) 175–182.
[23] R. Niven, A. Hickey, Atomization and nebulizers, in: A. Hickey (Ed.), Inhalation Aerosols, Physical and Biological Basis for Therapy, second ed., Informa Healthcare, New York, 2007, pp. 253–283.
[24] R. Dhand, Nebulizers that use a vibrating mesh or plate with multiple apertures to generate aerosol, Respir. Care 47 (2002) 1406–1416.
[25] A. Coates, O. Denk, K. Leung, N. Ribeiro, J. Chan, M. Green, et al., Higher tobramycin concentration and vibrating mesh technology can shorten antibiotic treatment time in cystic fibrosis, Pediatric Pulmonol. 46 (2011) 401–408.
[26] K. Lyseng-Williamson, G. Keating, Tiotropium respimat soft mist inhaler: a guide to its use in chronic obstructive pulmonary disease (COPD) in the EU, Drug. Ther. Perspect. (2014). Available from: https://doi.org/10.1007/s40267-0114-0181-x.
[27] U. F. a. D. Administration, Integration of dose-counting mechanism into metered dose inhaler products *Guidance for Industry/Federal Register*: United States Government, March 2003.
[28] I. Kaur, B. Aggarwal, J. Gogtay, Integration of dose counters in pressurized metered-dose inhalers for patients with asthma and chronic obstructive pulmonary disease: review of evidence, Expert. Opin. Drug. Deliv. 12 (2015) 1301–1310.
[29] S. Stein, P. Sheth, P. Hodson, P. Myrdal, Advances in metered dose inhaler technology: hardware development, AAPS PharmSciTech 15 (2014) 326–338.
[30] K. Huckvale, C. Morrison, J. Ouyang, A. Ghaghda, J. Car, The evolution of mobile apps for asthma: an updated systematic assessement of content and tools, BMC Med. 13 (2015) 58.
[31] U. F. a. D. Administration, Metered dose inhaler and dry powder inhaler drug products-quality considerations, Draft Guidance for Industry, Federal Register (Vol. 04/19/18): United States Government, 2018.
[32] U.S. Pharmacopeia, General Chapter <601> Aerosols, nasal sprays, metered dose inhalers, and dry pwoder inhalers, vol. 34, United States Pharmacopeia: USP Rockville, MD, 2011, pp. 218–239.
[33] J. Lodge, T. Chan, Cascade Impactor, American Industrial Hygiene Association, Akron, OH, 1986.
[34] T. Tougas, J. Mitchell, S. Lyapustina, Good Cascade Impactor Practices, AIM and EDA for Orally Inhaled Products, Springer, New York, NY, 2013.
[35] K. May, A personal note on the history of the cascade impactor, J. Aerosol Sci. 13 (1982) 37–47.
[36] S. Newman, H.-K. Chan, In vitro/In vivo comparisons in pulmonary drug delivery, J. Aerosol Med. Pulmonary Drug. Deliv. 21 (2008) 77–84. Available from: https://doi.org/10.1089/jamp.2007.0643.
[37] J. Mitchell, M. Nagel, Cascade impactors for the size characterization of aerosols from medical inhalers: their uses and limitations, J. Aerosol Med. 16 (2004) 341–377.

[38] C. Ruzycki, L. Golshahi, R. Vehrig, W. Finlay, Comparison of in vitro deposition of pharmaceutical aerosols in an idealized child throat with in vivo deposition in the upper respiratory tract of children, Pharm. Res. 31 (2014) 1525–1535.
[39] Y. Zhang, K. Gilbertson, W. Finlay, In vivo-in vitro comparison of deposition in three mouth-throat models with Qvar and Turbuhaler inhalers, J. Aerosol Med. 20 (2007) 227–235.
[40] P. Byron, M. Hindle, C. Lange, P. Longest, D. McRobbie, M. Oldham, et al., In vivo-in vitro correlations: predicting pulmonary drug deposition from pharmaeutical aerosols, J. Aerosol Med. Pulm. Drug. Deliv. 23 (S2) (2010) S59–S69.
[41] B. Olsson, L. Borgstom, H. Lundback, M. Svensson, Validation of a general in vitro approach for prediction of total lung deposition in healthy adults for pharmaceutical inhalation products, J. Aerosols Med. Pulmonary Drug. Deliv. 26 (2013) 355–369.
[42] J. Heyder, J. Gebhart, G. Rudolf, C. Schiller, W. Stahlhofen, Deposition of particles in the human respiratory tract in the size range 0.005-15um, J. Aerosol Sci. 17 (1986) 811–825.
[43] G. Rudolf, A mathematical model for the deposition of aerosol particles in the human respiratory tract, J. Aerosol Sci. 15 (1984) 195–199.
[44] P. Longest, L. Holbrook, In silico models of aerosol delivery to the respiratory tract- development and applications, Adv. Drug. Deliv. Rev. 64 (2012) 296–311.
[45] P. Longest, K. Bass, R. Dutta, V. Rani, M. Thomas, A. El-Achwah, et al., Use of computational fluid dynamics deposition modeling in respiratory drug delivery, Expert. Opin. Drug. Deliv. 16 (2019) 7–26.
[46] S. Newman, G. Pitcairn, P. Hirst, A brief history of gamma scintigraphy, J. Aerosol Med. 14 (2004) 139–145.
[47] T. Fok, H. Kirpalanim, M. Al-Essa, S. Monkman, Estimation of pulmonary depostion of aerosol using gamma scintigraphy, J. Aerosol Med. 12 (1999) 9–15.
[48] S. Newman, K. Steed, G. Hooper, A. Kallen, L. Borgstrom, Comparison of gamma scintigraphy and a pharmacokinetic technique for assessing pulmonary deposition of terbutaline sulfate delivered by pressurized metered dose inhaler, Pharm. Res. 12 (1995) 231–236.
[49] J. Conway, Lung imaging-two dimensional gamma scintigraphy, SPECT, CT and PET, Adv. Drug. Deliv. Rev. 64 (2012) 357–368.
[50] T. Martonen, J. Schoeter, J. Fleming, 3D In silco modeling of the human respiratory system for inhaled drug delivery and imaging analysis, J. Pharm. Sci. 96 (2007) 603–617.
[51] H. Derendorf, R. Nave, A. Drollmann, F. Cerasoli, W. Wurst, Relevance of pharmacokinetics and pharmacodynamics of inhaled corticosteroids to asthma, Eur. Respir. J. 28 (2006) 1042–1050.
[52] J. Padden, D. Skoner, G. Hochhaus, Pharmacokinetics and pharmacodynamics of inhaled glucocorticoids, J. Asthma 45 (S1) (2008) 13–24.
[53] S. Suarez, A. Hickey, Pharmacokinetic and pharmacodynamic aspects of inhaled therapeutic agents, in: T. Martonen (Ed.), Medical Applications of Computer Modeling: The Respiratory System, WIT Press, Southampton UK, 2001, pp. 225–304.
[54] J. Borghardt, B. Weber, A. Staab, C. Kraft, Pharmacometric models for characterizing the pharmacokinetics of orally inhaled drugs, AAP J. 17 (2015) 853–870.
[55] P. Bäckman, S. Arora, W. Couet, B. Forbes, W.D. Kruijf, A. Paudel, Advances in experimental and mechanistic computational models to understand pulmonary exposure to inhaled drugs, Eur. J. Pharm. Sci. 113 (2018) 41–52.
[56] A. Hickey, Pulmonary drug delivery: pharmaceutical chemistry and aerosol technology, in: B. Wang, L. Hu, T. Siahaan (Eds.), Drug Delivery, Principles and Applications, Second ed., John Wiley and Sons, New York, 2016, pp. 186–206.
[57] J. Peat, A. Woolcock, K. Cullen, Rate of decline of lung function in subjects with asthma, Eur. J. Respir. Dis. 70 (1987) 171–179.
[58] N. Snell, P. Newbold, The clinical utility of biomarkers in asthma and COPD, Curr. Opin. Pharmacol. 8 (2008) 222–235.
[59] M. Dolovich, R. Ahrens, D. Hess, P. Anderson, R. Dhand, H. Rau, et al., Device slection and outcomes of aerosol therapy: evidence-based guidelines: American College of Chest Physicians/ American College of Asthma, Allergy and Immunology, Chest 127 (2005) 335–371.

[60] L. Garcia-Contreras, A. Hickey, Pharmaceutical and biotechnological aerosol for systic fibrosis therapy, Adv. Drug. Deliv. Rev. 54 (2002) 1491–1504.
[61] R. Stribling, E. Brunette, D. Liggitt, K. Gaensler, R. Debs, Aerosol gene delivery in vivo, PNAS 89 (1992) 11277–11281.
[62] D. Klonoff, Afrezza inhaled insulin, J. Diabetes Sci. Technol. 8 (2014) 1071–1073.
[63] D. deBerardis, M. Fornaro, L. Orsilino, F. Iasevoli, C. Tomasetti, A. deBartolomei, et al., The role of inhaled loxapine in the treatment of acute agitation in patients with psychiatric disorders: a clinical review, Int. J. Mol. Sci. 18 (2017) 349.
[64] A. Chua, S. Silberstein, Inhaled drug therapy development for the treatment of migraine, Expert. Opin. Pharmacother. 17 (2016) 1733–1743.
[65] A. Hickey, P. Durham, A. Dharmadhikari, E. Nardell, Inhaled drug treatment for tuberculosis: past progress and future prospects, J. Controlled Release 240 (2016) 127–134.
[66] K. Olivier, P. Shaw, T. Glaser, D. Battacharyya, M. Fleshner, C. Brewer, et al., Inhaled amikacin for treatment of refractory pulmonary nontuberculous mycobacterial disease, Ann. Am. Thorac. Soc. 11 (2014) 30–35.
[67] M. Hoeper, M. Schwarze, S. Ehlerding, A. Adler-Schuermeyer, E. Spiekerkoetter, J. Niedermeyer, et al., Long-term treatment of prmiary pulmonary hypertension with aerosolized iloprost, a prostacyclin analogue, N. Engl. J. Med. 342 (2000) 1866–1870.
[68] K. Diaz, S. Skaria, K. Harris, M. Solomita, S. Lau, K. Bauer, et al., Delivery and safety of inhaled interferon-gamma in idiopathic pulmonary fibrosis, J. Aerosol Med. Pulmonary Drug. Deliv. 25 (2012) 79–87.
[69] W. Adams, R. Ahrens, M.-L. Chen, D. Christopher, B. Chowdhury, D. Conner, et al., Demonstrating bioequivalence of locally acting orally inhaled drug products (OIPs): Workshop summary report, J. Aerosol Med. Pulm. Drug. Deliv. 23 (2010) 1–29.
[70] J. Hastedt, P. Backman, A. Clark, W. Doub, A. Hickey, G. Hochhaus, et al., Scope and relevance of a pulmonary biopharmaceutical classification system AAPS/FDA/USP Workshop March 16-17th, 2015 in Baltimore, MD, AAPS Open. 2 (2016) 1.
[71] G. Apiou-Sbirlea, S. Newman, J. Fleming, R. Siekmeier, S. Ehrmann, G. Scheuch, et al., Bioequivalence of inhaled drugs: fundamentals, challenges and perspectives, Ther. Deliv. 4 (2013) 343–367.

CHAPTER 2

The API

Britta Bonn[1] and Matthew Perry[2]
[1]Drug Metabolism and Pharmacokinetics, Research and Early Development, Respiratory and Immunology (R&I), BioPharmaceuticals R&D, AstraZeneca, Gothenburg, Sweden
[2]Medicinal Chemistry, Research and Early Development, Respiratory and Immunology (R&I), BioPharmaceuticals R&D, AstraZeneca, Gothenburg, Sweden

2.1 Introduction

2.1.1 Inhalation of drugs

The deliberate inhalation of pharmacologically active substances has a long history going back at least as far as the discovery of the effects of tobacco smoke around 1000 years ago [1]. The physiological effects of recreational inhalation arise because the lung provides a highly permeable route enabling molecules to enter the systemic circulation rapidly and without first-pass metabolism, giving an almost immediate effect through interaction with their target proteins.

For pharmaceuticals, inhalation has been used for four categories of drugs:

1. Inhaled gaseous anesthetics.
2. Compounds requiring rapid access to systemic circulation to exert an immediate effect, typically on the CNS.
3. Compounds that are unable to access the systemic circulation through oral administration, this has been used for peptides, nucleotides and related large molecules.
4. Compounds intended to act topically in the lung, often with the intention to minimize systemic exposure and any related side-effects.

In general, absorption of molecules from the lung to the systemic circulation is rapid; even the peptide hormone insulin is absorbed rapidly with a plasma C_{max} at only 12–17 minutes post inhalation [2]. In this chapter we will focus discussion on the fourth category of molecules, those intended to exert a local effect in the lung for which rapid absorption is not a benefit but a challenge to overcome.

2.2 Considerations for designing inhaled molecules

Introducing the design of the inhaled active pharmaceutical ingredient (API), we first want to discuss the important considerations and desirable properties of the API followed by describing drivers and compound physico-chemical properties in Section 2.4. We can describe strategies for designing molecules suitable for inhaled route of delivery in terms of

Inhaled Medicines
DOI: https://doi.org/10.1016/B978-0-12-814974-4.00006-7

physico-chemical properties, but, as described by [3], assessing inhaled pharmacokinetics is accompanied by a list of challenges: (1) dosage form – different material preclinically compared to final product may influence pharmacokinetic profile, (2) lung dose amount – not all of an inhaled dose reaches the lung and this makes for uncertainty over the dose estimate, (3) exposure measurements – lung concentrations can be measured in preclinical species but not in man, (4) Lung retention – lack of understanding of what is really required in terms of concentration over time and how to predict for man, (5) PKPD - requires knowledge of unbound concentrations in lung or even in the relevant compartment of the lung, e.g. epithelium, alveolar region etc., rather than systemically; these are difficult to measure. An additional consideration for inhaled drug programs, in contrast to oral drug delivery, is that the capacity of devices limits the dose (Chapter 5.4.2). This has consequences on the properties of the drug and requires a high potency for the target.

2.2.1 Maximizing free drug concentration in the lung

In designing compounds to modify disease by acting on a pharmacological target in the lung the aim will be to achieve high free concentrations of drug locally. Free drug concentration here refers to molecules being accessible to interact with the target receptor, enzyme, ion channel, etc. By administration of the drug topically to the lung *via* inhalation it is possible to achieve high concentrations at time of dosing, however, it is important to appreciate the difference between total concentrations and the free drug concentrations accessible for the target. High local concentrations also involve a risk for lung irritancy, and this must be assessed during the development of a new inhaled drug. Additionally, the drug needs sufficient lung residency and duration of action to achieve the required pharmacological effect that translates to a suitable dosing regimen. The level of lung retention needed will, of course, be different, depending of the nature of the target and the drug mechanism, i.e. "hit and run" or coverage required over the entire dosing interval. The intrinsic lung retention of the drug will also contribute to a delayed absorption and lower systemic C_{max}, as discussed in the next section. Among the approaches to achieve lung retention, described below, both slowly dissolving particles and trapping in intracellular compartments will reduce the free concentration accessible to the target and during the design process these properties need to be optimized and balanced against each other. Obviously, this needs to be assessed in combination with the potency of the drug and requirements for a pharmacological effect; this highlights the need to build PKPD understanding and knowledge about the target location. Once again, this puts an emphasis on the need for highly potent molecules.

2.2.2 Minimizing systemic exposure

In addition to the need for achieving high local concentrations in the lung another driver for considering inhaled delivery is to minimize the systemic exposure and systemic side effects. Depending on the risks associated with the target/compound class this could either be C_{max} related or dependent on total exposure. High systemic C_{max} is directly related to rapid absorption into the circulation; to avoid this, molecules should be designed to reduce the rate of pulmonary absorption. Modulation of absorption rates through the lung can both enhance duration of action in the lung and reduce systemic C_{max}. Factors that affect the absorption rate are the dissolution rate of solid particles and the permeability of the compound. Modifying physico-chemical properties to reduce permeability (i.e. increase polarity) may, however, also result in decreased plasma protein binding, which will in turn be counter-productive in reducing free C_{max}.

The total systemic exposure of a drug is made up from both the pulmonary absorbed drug and also from any swallowed portion of the inhaled drug, typically greater than 50% of the total dose will end up in the gastrointestinal tract. The oral contribution to the systemic exposure may be minimized by designing molecules with low oral bioavailability. High clearance from the system, in the sense of high blood clearance (CLb) will also help to minimize systemic exposure. Deliberate incorporation of metabolic liabilities within the molecule will contribute to this, for example in the design of fluticasone furoate (**2**) [4] and vilanterol (**25**) [5]. All the foregoing considerations are the complete opposite of the design principles for an oral drug. Drug interactions are typically less of a concern for inhaled drugs than systemically active ones due to low doses and overall low systemic exposures. If designing highly metabolized molecules however, it is preferable to have multiple routes of metabolism to avoid the risk of interactions with other co-administered drugs acting as inhibitors of a specific metabolic enzyme. An example of an inhaled molecule with multiple routes of metabolism is demonstrated by the β_2-agonist formoterol (**27**) which undergoes both oxidative metabolism and glucuronidation/sulfation in man [6].

2.2.3 Multiple simultaneous processes

In order to build understanding of PKPD relationships and the behavior of the inhaled API multiple processes need to be considered. First, the inhaled administration will result in regional deposition within the lung and, depending on the properties/chemotype of the molecule, there can be different spatial patterns for the lung residency. It is critical to understand where the target resides to support rational design of your drug. If, as is normal, the compound is intended for administration as a dry powder or a suspension then once a particle has landed in the lung the solid material needs to dissolve before the drug can act on its target. Dissolution rate is affected by the compound properties and is one of the factors that can be modified during the design process [7]. Solid particles are also subject to mucociliary clearance from the upper airways, the primary innate defense mechanism of the lung against pathogens and inhaled particles [8]. Consequently, for inhaled drugs, part of the dose will be cleared from the lung without exerting any pharmacological effect and will enter the GI tract where it may then be absorbed to the systemic circulation. These different processes each add additional levels of complexity which need to be considered when designing drugs for inhalation and predicting the clinical outcomes.

2.3 Physicochemical properties of pulmonary drugs

There are a relatively limited number of targets for which inhaled delivery has been used successfully and, depending on the types of molecule that are required to modulate the target, different strategies have been used to obtain retention. As described above, the properties of inhaled drugs for pulmonary conditions are further affected by the desire to minimize systemic exposure, so both high clearance and low oral bioavailability (of the proportion of the inhaled dose that will reach the gastrointestinal tract through both swallowed dose and from mucociliary clearance) are required. These combined requirements mean that the property-space for inhaled drugs differs significantly from that of oral drugs (Fig. 2.1).

Inspection of Fig. 2.1A shows that inhaled drugs have a much wider range of properties than those identified by Lipinski et al. in their seminal paper on the properties for oral drugs [9] with both highly lipophilic and highly hydrophilic molecules being commonplace; many of the latter also have multiple charges as well as large numbers of hydrogen bond donors and acceptors. Molecular weights are often well beyond 500, particularly for compounds currently in development.

2.4 Drivers for pulmonary absorption and retention

Examination of Fig. 2.1B shows that inhaled drugs for different target classes vary much more in their properties than drugs within any given class. In part this relates to the types of molecule required to interact with target, however an additional factor is the location of the target. Inhaled antibacterial drugs are typically targeting bacteria within the lung lumen, and thus do not need to cross the lung epithelium, though, of course, entry to the bacterial cell may be required. Drugs, such as β-adrenergic agonists and muscarinic antagonists, that target receptors in the cell membrane of smooth muscle in the major airways, can exert their action without needing to cross lipid membranes. Drugs for which the target is intracellular, for example steroids targeting the glucocorticoid receptor, or drugs for any kinase targets, need to be able to generate sufficient intracellular concentrations to produce an effect and thus require cell permeability.

2.4.1 Overview of factors which drive local targeting in the lung

Most inhaled drugs are delivered as dry powders or through nebulization of either solutions or suspensions. Consideration of the processes that a drug molecule will undergo *en route* to the systemic circulation highlights opportunities for the designer to

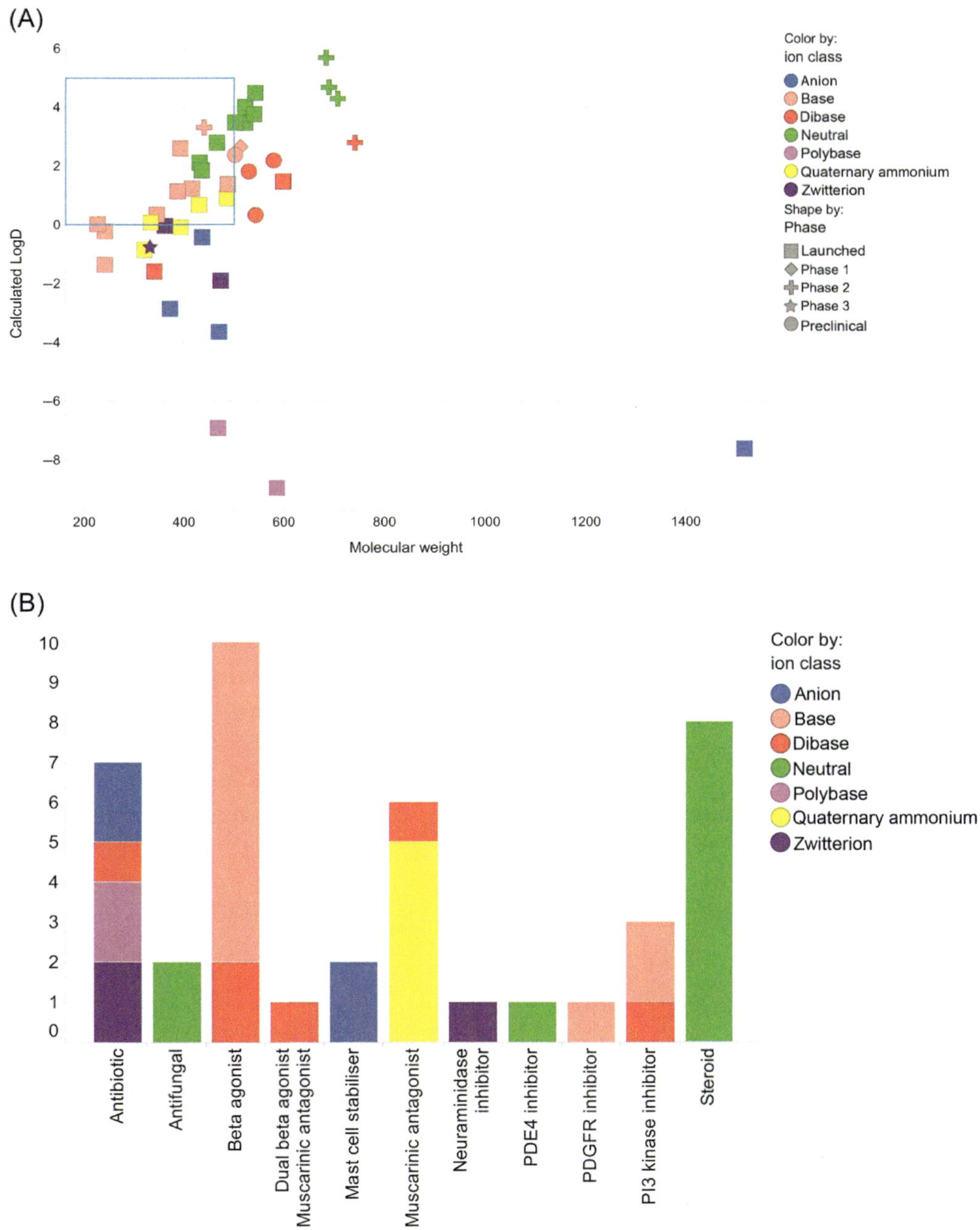

Figure 2.1 Physicochemical properties of launched and candidate inhaled drugs targeting the lung. (A) Calculated LogD and molecular weight. Blue box corresponds to property space within the guidelines defined by Lipinski et al. (B) Therapeutic category and ion class.

affect the process to prolong the effect. The inhaled material will land within the lung and, if administered as a solid, then dissolve to give a solution in the lung lining fluid; nebulized solutions bypass this step. From the lining fluid the drug can cross the epithelial membrane into the epithelial cells. Once in the cells the drug will partition into the subcellular components or migrate on to the next layer of cells. This transcellular migration will continue down a concentration gradient until the molecule reaches the capillaries of the systemic circulation from where it will then be distributed throughout the body and cleared by the liver and/or kidneys. At some point a drug molecule may encounter a target protein whereupon it can bind and exert its effect before subsequently dissociating and returning to the surrounding medium. Each of these processes has a rate that is determined by the physicochemical properties of the drug and each can be modulated to affect the overall rate of clearance from the lung and the pharmacodynamic effect. A schematic of these different processes is presented in Fig. 2.2.

Once in a cell, drug can partition into the subcellular organelles as well as the cell membrane. Factors that affect this partitioning are lipophilicity, which results in concentration into membranes and the presence of basic centers, particularly weak bases. Lung tissue is rich in acidic organelles, such as lysosomes, and these can concentrate basic molecules and subsequently act as a depot slowly releasing the drug. Basic centers also promote residence of molecules in phospholipid membranes; this is particularly beneficial if the target is membrane-bound.

The interaction of the drug with its target presents a final opportunity for an extended effect. If the rate of dissociation from the target is slow, then extended duration of action may be seen based not on pharmacokinetic duration but pharmacodynamic duration. This type of effect is most likely to be seen for very potent molecules,

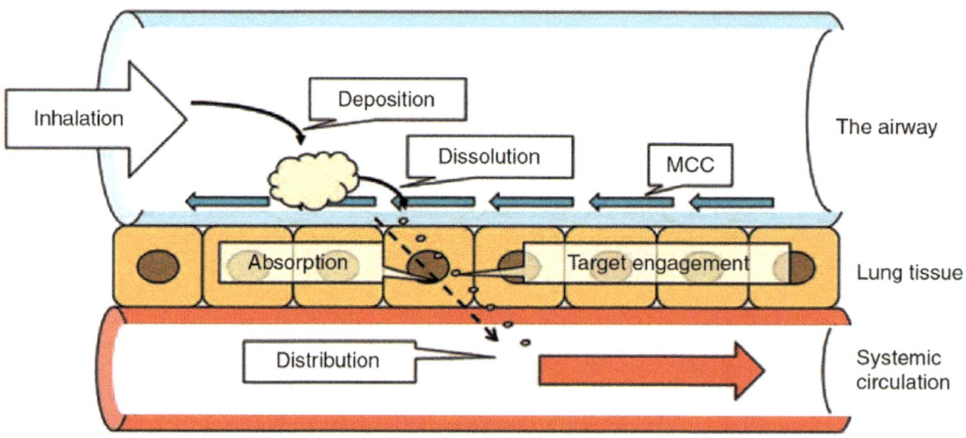

Figure 2.2 Schematic of particle deposition, dissolution, mucociliary clearance, absorption into airway tissue, target engagement and diffusion in to systemic circulation.

though in practice this is not easy to achieve [10]. Highly membrane-bound drugs with membrane resident targets, like long-acting β_2-agonists and muscarinic antagonists, benefit from rebinding to the target being significantly faster than loss of drug from the membrane to achieve a similar effect.

2.4.2 Dissolution rate limited absorption

The rate of dissolution of solid particles is affected by a combination the thermodynamics of dissolution of the material in lung lining fluid, the strength of the crystal packing forces in the solid particles and the particle size (since dissolution rate is proportional to surface area). In general, most molecules dissolve rapidly in the lung and only for compounds of extremely low solubility, typically with high lipophilicity and/or high crystallinity (reflected in high melting points) is an effect seen giving increased lung retention from solubility [11–13]. The case where solubility-driven lung retention has been applied most notably and successfully is the class of steroidal glucocorticosteroids. These molecules are inherently lipophilic and therefore poorly water soluble, they are also extremely potent, meaning that only low doses are required to drive an effect, which is important if concentrations of dissolved drug will always be low. The highly lipophilic nature of steroids means that they can readily cross cell membranes to access their intracellular targets. Examples of inhaled steroids and their associated properties are given in Table 2.1 and Fig. 2.3.

From the data in Table 2.1 it can be seen that, in addition to the low solubility, at least some of the drugs used as inhaled steroids have long residence times on the glucocorticoid receptor; this may contribute to their duration of effect – see Section 2.4.5 below. The low solubility of fluticasone furoate (**2**) has also been shown to deliver prolonged duration after intranasal administration [20], an administration route with many similarities to inhalation.

Steroids are not the only class of inhaled drug where low solubility has been used to drive lung retention, however. Antifungal drugs have been investigated for inhaled administration relying on this mechanism, thus the established oral antifungal itraconazole (**9**) (Fig. 2.4), known to be of high lipophilicity and extremely low solubility (LogP 5.7, 1.4–7.0 nM, [21,22]), was studied for inhaled use, albeit with high daily doses (2.8–35 mg, [23,24]). A newer antifungal agent, PC945 (**10**) (Fig. 2.4) has been designed for inhaled administration [25] and is currently being investigated in a phase 2 clinical trial at a lower dose (5 mg) [26]. Although data for lipophilicity and solubility have not been published for **10**, the structural similarity to itraconazole and calculated LogD 5.3, [27] suggest that it too will have extremely low solubility. Progress of PC945 in development will be an indicator as to the applicability of this method of obtaining drug retention in lung beyond steroids Fig. 2.4.

Table 2.1 Data for inhaled steroids.

Compound	Drug	MW	LogP	Solubility μM	Relative receptor affinity	T½ of drug-receptor complex h
1	Fluticasone propionate	500.6	4.5[a]; 3.7[d]	0.0020[a] 0.0010[b] 0.00026[e]	1775[c]	10.5[c]
2	Fluticasone furoate	538.6	4.1[d]		2989[c]	
3	Budesonide	430.5	3.7[a]	0.033[a]	855[c]	5.1[c]
4	Mometasone furoate	521.4	5.1[d]		2244[c]	
5	Beclomethasone 17-propionate	465.0	4.3[a]	0.033[e]	1345[c]	7.5[c]
6	Beclomethasone dipropionate	521.0	4.7[a]	0.00025[e]	[f]	
7	Triamcinolone acetonide	434.5	3.5[a]	0.048[e]		
8	Ciclesonide	540.7		0.92	1212[g,h]	

[a]Ref[14].
[b]Ref.[15].
[c]Ref.[16].
[d]Ref.[17].
[e]Ref.[18].
[f]Beclomethasone dipropionate is a prodrug for the monopropionate.
[g]Ciclesonide is a prodrug, the affinity value refers to that of the active metabolite desisobutyryl-ciclesonide.
[h]Ref.[19].

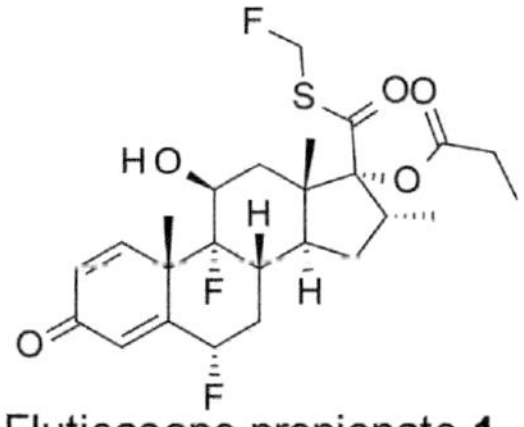
Fluticasone propionate **1**

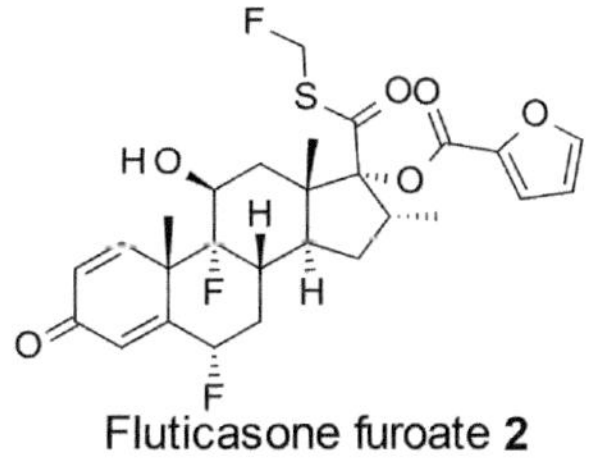
Fluticasone furoate **2**

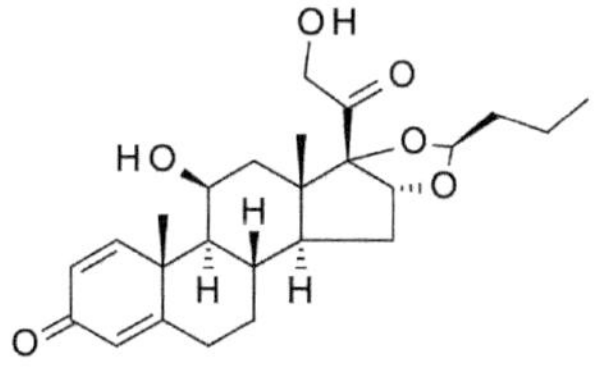
Budesonide **3**

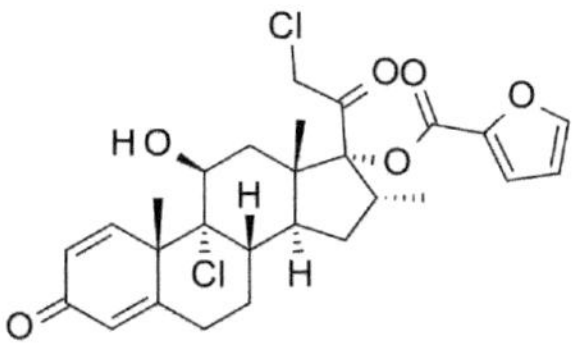
Mometasone furoate **4**

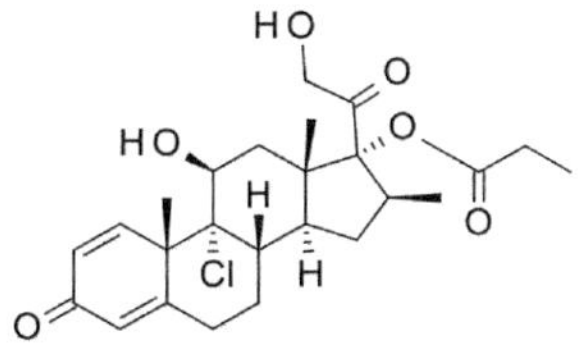
Beclomethasone 17-propionate **5**

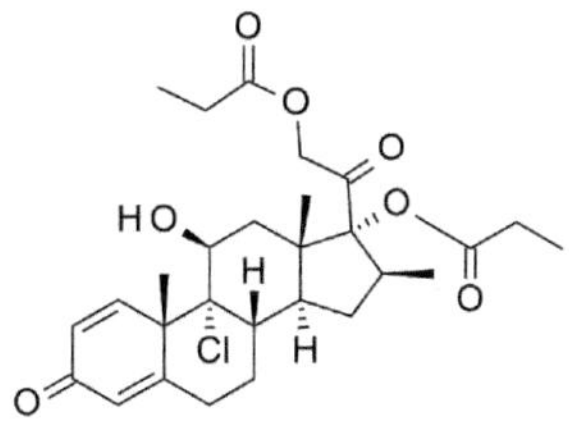
Beclomethasone dipropionate **6**

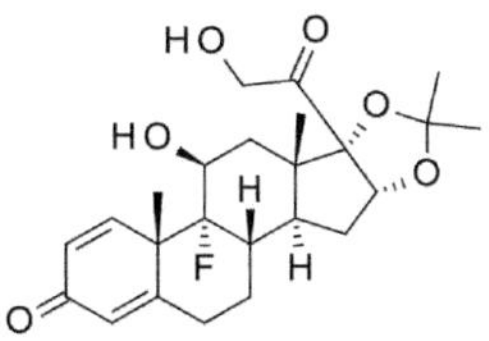
Triamcinolone acetonide **7**

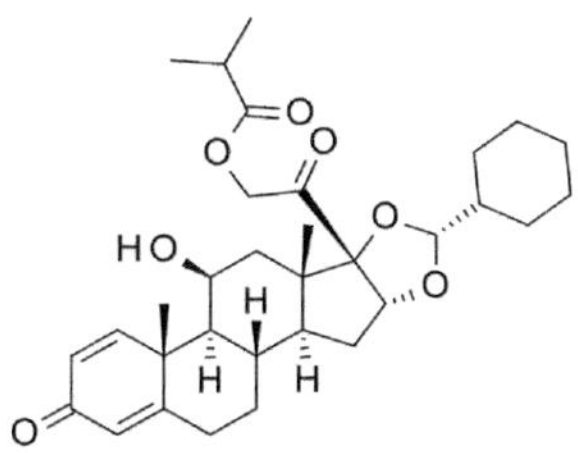
Ciclesonide **8**

Figure 2.3 Inhaled corticosteroids.

2.4.3 Permeability limited retention

Membrane permeability is governed principally by polarity, with molecules needing to be able to cross the highly lipophilic lipid barrier, thus charged molecules and ones with multiple hydrogen bond donors (NH & OH) are typically poorly permeable. Many antibiotics have been taken to clinical trials to treat pulmonary infections by local delivery to the lung [28] with six in clinical use today colistimethate sodium **12**, amikacin **13**, tobramycin **14**, aztreonam lysine **15**, levofloxacin **16** (all for treating infections in cystic fibrosis patients (CF)) and pentamidine **17** (used to treat tuberculosis, principally in immunocompromised patients) (Fig. 2.5). The compounds investigated have not been designed for inhalation, but rather existing compounds have been evaluated *via* inhalation for the treatment of respiratory infections. Of the six compounds marketed, only levofloxacin is orally bioavailable, the others are all highly polar and have poor passive permeability.

Three fluoroquinolone antibiotics, including ciprofloxacin **18** (Fig. 2.5), though not **16**, were evaluated in rats for their behavior after nebulized administration to the lung

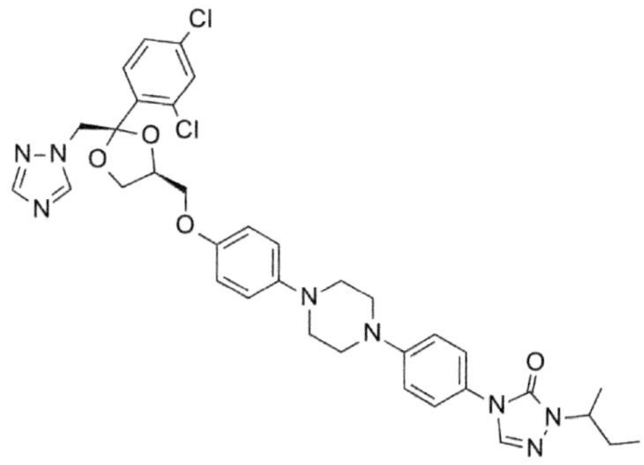

Itraconazole **9**

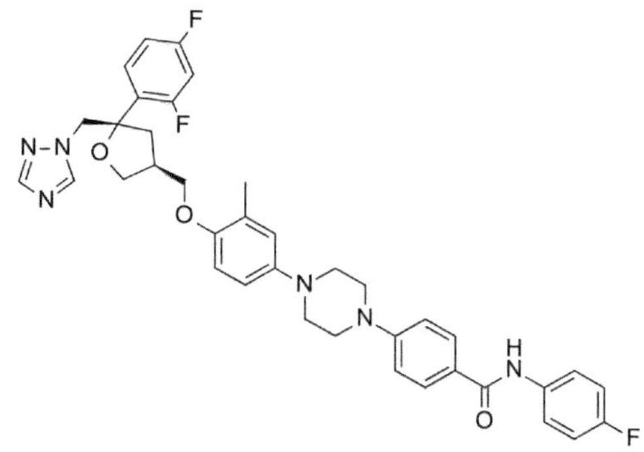

PC-945 **10**

Figure 2.4 Inhaled antifungal agents.

[29]. Ciprofloxacin is currently in preregistration for inhaled administration to bronchiectasis patents [30]. These studies revealed that some lung targeting was achieved, but that this was probably a consequence of efflux transporters in the lung and that there was no difference in the distribution of the drug between inhaled and IV administration. In contrast, similar studies with the much more polar molecules colistin sulfate (**12**), the prodrug form of the active agent colistin (**11**) [31], **13** [32], **14** [33], and **15** [34] have shown very significant lung targeting, with concentrations in pulmonary epithelial lining fluid (ELF) between 200 (**14**) and 1800 (**12**) times greater than those achieved *via* IV administration. These significantly increased lung concentrations are almost certainly a consequence of the poor permeability of the molecules through the lung epithelium. It should be noted that doses for inhaled antibiotics are typically high by inhalation standards, ranging from 80 mg b.i.d. (**12**) to as high as 500 mg q.d. (**13**).

In a series of platelet-derived growth factor receptor inhibitors, it was shown that the most important factor to obtain duration after inhaled administration was for the compound to have low permeability [35]. Low permeability alone, however, was not sufficient and the pKa of a basic amine was also important, with pKa > 8.5 being optimal. This led to the identification of **19** for further profiling (Fig. 2.6). The authors speculate that the low permeability of their molecules allows the compound time to partition into lung tissue rather than simply being absorbed rapidly into systemic circulation.

2.4.4 Tissue targeting through increased basicity

Basic centers are common in inhaled drugs and the role of basicity in modulating lung residence has been investigated [3]. These authors showed that, over a range of chemotypes, lung retention was longest for molecules with two basic centers, shorter for monobases and shortest for neutral and acidic molecules (Fig. 2.7).

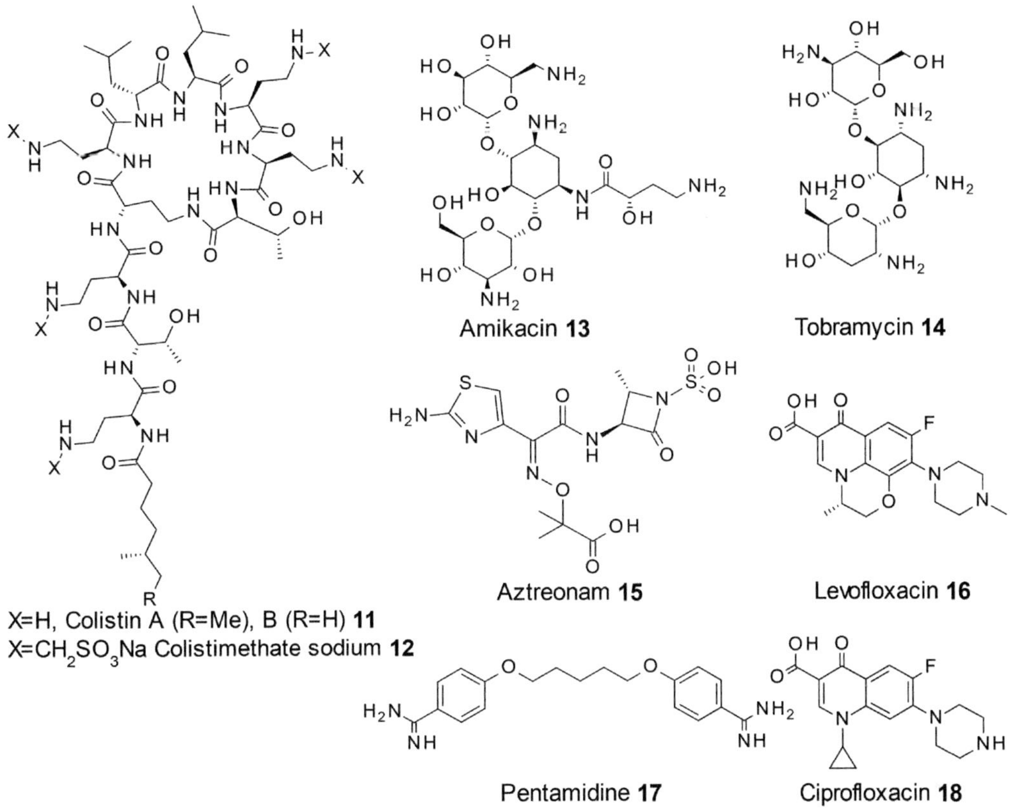

Figure 2.5 Antibiotics administered clinically *via* inhalation. Note: Colistin is administered as a mixture of colistins A, B and C; colistimethate sodium consists of a mixture of colistins which have been methylsulfonalyated on four amino groups.

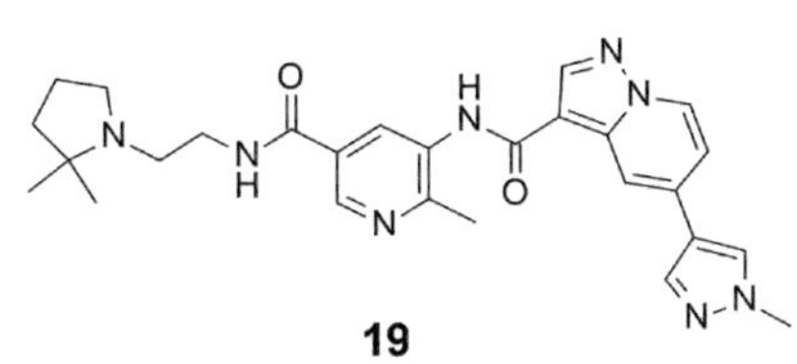

19

Figure 2.6 Low permeability and basic PDGFR inhibitor.

These principles were applied in the β_2-agonist field by AstraZeneca scientists, who described work leading to long-acting β_2-agonists where lipophilic compounds incorporating a second basic center were shown to have very long duration of action leading to the identification of two clinical candidates AZD3199 (**20**) and AZD9708 (**21**) (Fig. 2.8) [36–40]. Further work in a series of PI3 kinase inhibitors showed that the second pKa of the molecule was critical for this dibase effect, with molecules

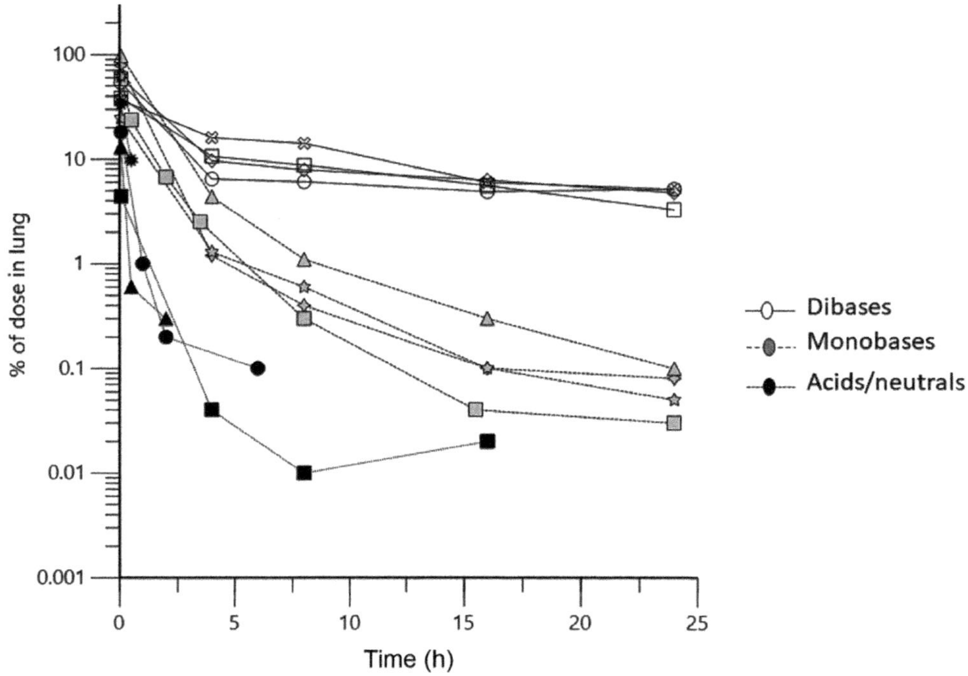

Figure 2.7 Influence of basicity on lung retention of drugs administered as solutions by IT dosing to rats.

where the weaker base had pKa < 5 behaving as monobases, whilst those with this pKa > 6 exhibited extended duration (compound **22** (Fig. 2.8)) [41]. This was attributed to trapping of the more basic molecules as dications in lysosomes (pH 4.5–5 [42]) providing a reservoir of compound. Although no details of the design process for the inhaled M3 agonist revefenacin (**23**) (Fig. 2.8) have been described, it fits the same pattern of a lipophilic dibase and is thus likely to derive duration from these properties. The pattern of lipophilic dibases is also characteristic of dual muscarinic antagonist β_2-agonist (MABA) drugs that are under development currently [43]. The most advanced example of these is batefenterol (**24**); this molecule also illustrates the large size (MW 740) typical of this class of bifunctional agent (Fig. 2.8).

2.4.5 Duration through extended pharmacology

Second and third generation β_2-agonists are characterized by significantly longer duration of effect than the early compounds. Binding to an exosite has been proposed as a driver for the behavior observed with salmeterol (**25**) [44–46] and vilanterol (**26**) [47]. The key behavior of salmeterol, and other long-acting β_2-agonists, is that of reassertion, whereby the compound can be antagonized by an inhibitor (sotalol) and then,

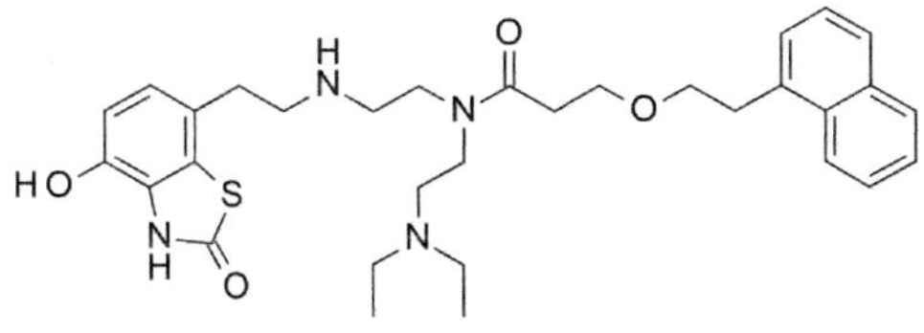

AZD3199 **20**

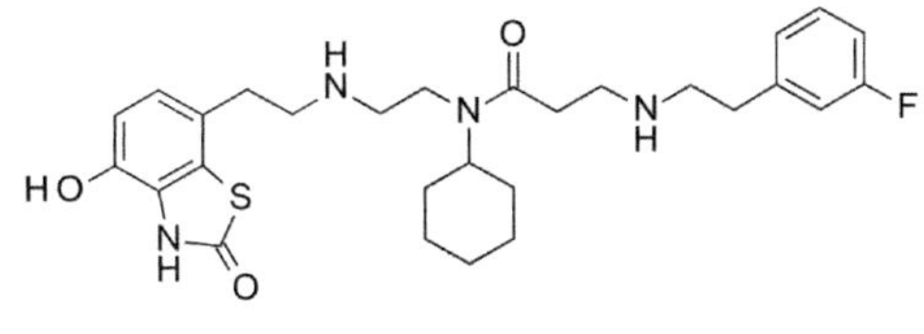

AZD9708 **21**

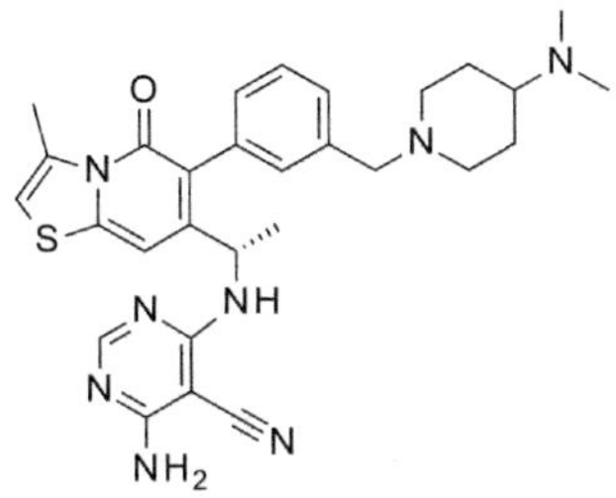

22

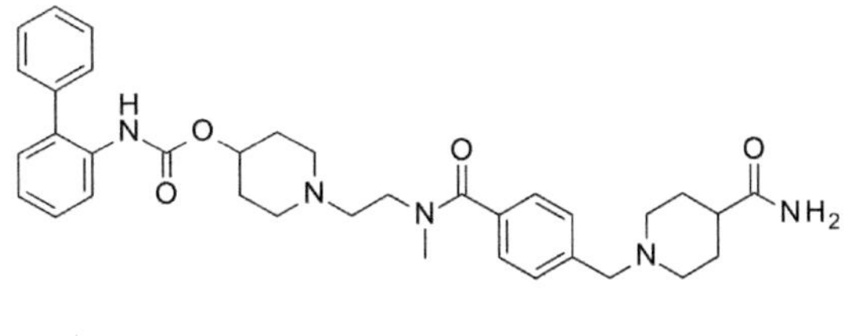

Revefenacin **23**

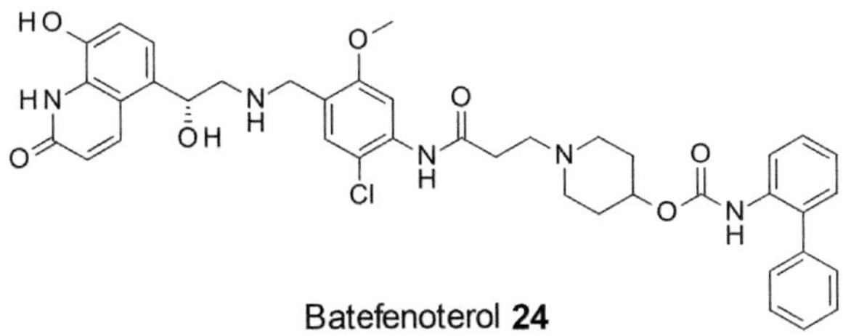

Batefenoterol **24**

Figure 2.8 Lipophilic dibasic molecules for inhalation.

after washing away the antagonist, reassert activity. The exosite model has been challenged [48,49] and alternative hypotheses proposed to account for the reassertion based on lipophilicity of the compounds. Other β_2-agonists, such as formoterol (**27**) [50], indacaterol (**28**) [51], have been shown to exhibit long duration and reassertion without fitting the pharmacophore for the proposed exosite, which can therefore not be regarded as essential for this property. In these latter cases lipophilicity driving membrane residence provides the depot for the molecules, which are thus still present after the hydrophilic antagonist has been washed off and so are able to rebind and reassert activity (Fig. 2.9).

It is instructive to compare the twice-daily second generation β_2-agonist drugs (**25**, **27**) with the once-daily third-generation (**26**, **28**, **29**) Table 2.2.

The third-generation β_2-agonist vilanterol (**26**) was designed to have very low systemic exposure [5] through targeting low oral bioavailability and rapid metabolic deactivation, in addition to rapid onset and high selectivity. This was so successful that, although the duration was similar to salmeterol, dosing at a ten-fold higher level was possible without side-effects, meaning that extended coverage could be obtained in practice.

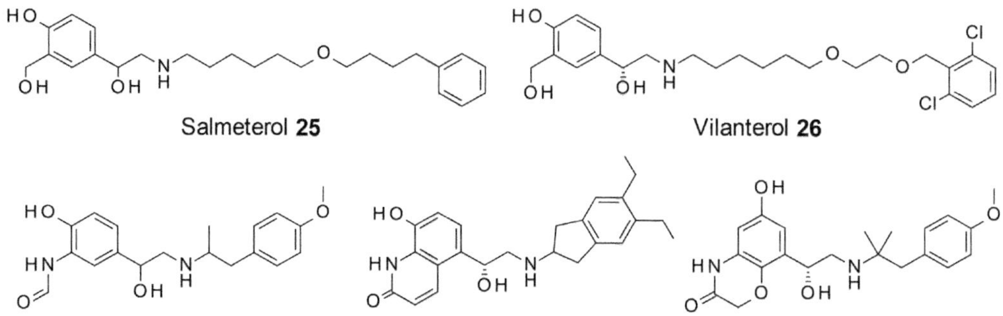

Figure 2.9 β_2-agonist drugs for inhalation.

Table 2.2 Data for inhaled β_2-agonists.

Compound	Drug	β_2 pEC$_{50}$	MW[a]	LogD
25	Salmeterol	9.6[b]	415	2.0[c]
26	Vilanterol	9.4[b]	486	1.3[d]
27	Formoterol	9.4[b]	344	0.3[c]
28	Indacaterol	8.0[e]	392	2.7[c]
29	Olodaterol	8.9[f]	386	1.2[f]

[a]Free base.
[b]Ref.[5].
[c]Ref.[52].
[d]Internal AstraZeneca measurement; method as Hendrickx et al.
[e]Ref.[51].
[f]Ref.[53].

The design of indacaterol (**28**) was intentionally targeted at long duration through lipophilicity, however there was also a desire to ensure rapid onset of action and high intrinsic activity [51]. **28** was identified as having the desired balance of properties and gave 24 h coverage in animal models.

The design of olodaterol (**29)** [53], in contrast to **26**, did inot prioritize metabolic clearance, though oral bioavailability was very low (3% in rats). **29** is more lipophilic than **27**, but less so than **25** or **28** and similar to **26**, nevertheless 24 h duration in patients has been demonstrated [54]. An additional feature of **29** is that it exhibits extended residence time on the β_2 receptor and it may be that combination of the two effects of membrane-binding and long residence on the receptor drive the observed duration of effect.

The once-daily muscarinic M3 antagonist, tiotropium (**30**) has been proposed to achieve duration through a long residence time on the receptor [55]. The relevance of this effect to the duration of tiotropium in the physiological setting has been challenged, however [56], and other muscarinic antagonists, like glycopyrronium (**31**), that

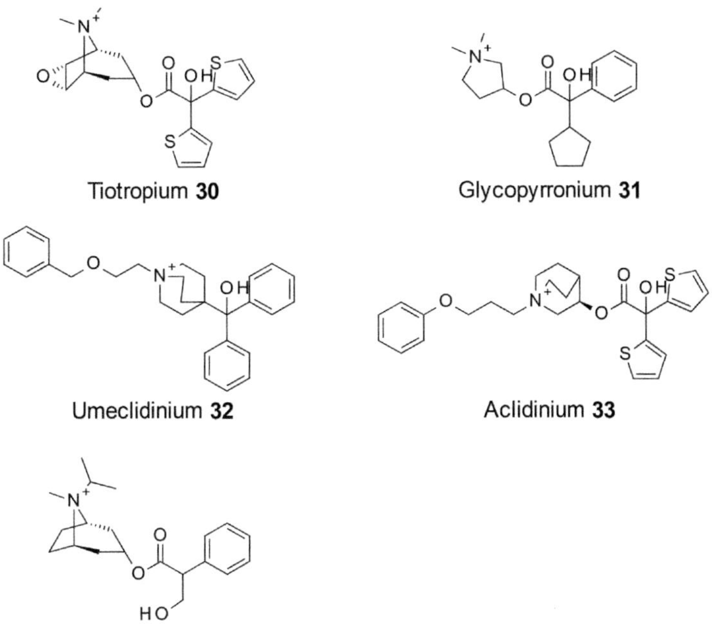

Figure 2.10 Inhaled muscarinic M_3 antagonists.

have shorter receptor residencies are still able to achieve 24 h duration. Thus, it is entirely possible that other mechanisms are involved. A study comparing marketed inhaled muscarinic antagonists (tiotropium (**30**), glycopyrronium (**31**), umeclidinium (**32**) and aclidinium (**33**) (Fig. 2.10)) [57] showed that all four had much longer tissue residence on human bronchiolar rings than the short-acting compound ipratropium (**34**). **30** and **32** appeared to show longer residence than **31** or **33**, consistent with the once-daily and twice-daily administration of the agents. A human pharmacokinetic study of **30** revealed an extremely large volume of distribution for the compound of up to 2700 L (corresponding to c.38 L/kg), indicative of very high tissue binding [58]. This high tissue binding, potentially in membranes, will provide a reservoir of compound for prolonged activity and can contribute to the long duration observed.

2.4.6 Pro-drugs/esterification

The prodrug laninamivir octanoate (**35**) has been launched as a targeted inhaled influenza neuraminidase inhibitor with long duration [59]. The design of the prodrug was based on the hypothesis that a lipophilic molecule would have slower clearance from lung to plasma and provide a reservoir of active drug through slow hydrolysis [60]. The lung targeting of laninamivir octanoate is in marked contrast to the structurally

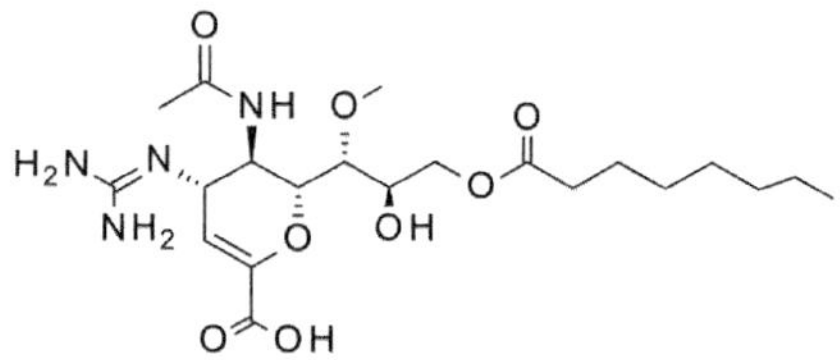

Laninamivir octanoate **35**

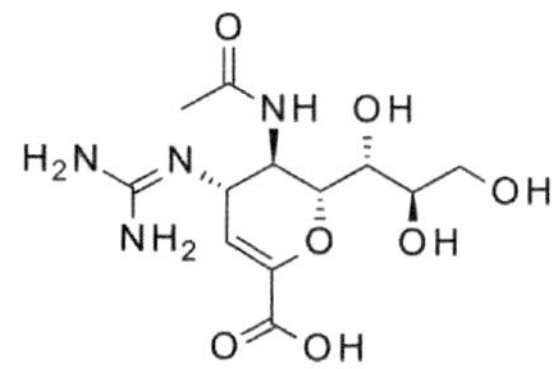

Zanamivir **36**

Figure 2.11 Inhaled neuraminidase inhibitors.

related earlier compound zanamivir (**36**), which is administered by inhalation to obtain systemic activity in order to overcome low oral bioavailability [61] (Fig. 2.11).

In a similar manner, fatty-acid esterification has been proposed as a mechanism that prolongs retention and duration of action in the lung for budesonide (**3**) [62]. This process involves the formation of an ester (typically oleate) from free budesonide within the airway epithelium, which then can be subsequently cleaved by lipases to the active drug. This recycling of budesonide has been shown to prolong duration of action in preclinical studies by comparison to studies in the presence of an esterification blocker, or in comparison with similar corticosteroids that cannot form esters.

2.4.7 Comparison of retention methods

In a recent paper, GSK scientists described a fascinating comparison of the pharmacokinetic and pharmacodynamic behavior between two similar PI3Kδ inhibitors where one (GSK2292767A, **37**), derived retention from low solubility, whilst the other (nemiralisib, **38**), derived retention from a basic center [63]. In this case, the advantage appeared to be with the basic molecule over the compound with solubility driven retention, since the duration of effect in patients was longer for **38** than **37**, with only **38** showing an effect for 24 h post administration. This difference, whilst clearly of great interest, particularly for inhaled kinase inhibitors and other intracellular targets, should not be taken to indicate that it will apply for all target classes and locations (Fig. 2.12).

The PDE4 inhibitor CHF6001 (**39**) (Fig. 2.13) is currently in phase two clinical trials for COPD. In the design of this molecule the project team targeted low permeability for their candidate [64] and this has shown impressive lung retention with a duration of effect extending over 24 h. The exact driving force for this long duration, however is unclear since the molecule also has an extended pharmacology with an estimated dissociation half-life of >24 h. Additionally, given the high lipophilicity (measured LogD 4.5) solubility is likely to be low and thus may also contribute to the duration of effect.

A group from GSK developed a QSAR model based on results from 17 marketed drugs and 82 internal clinical candidates in isolated perfused rat lung studies for the

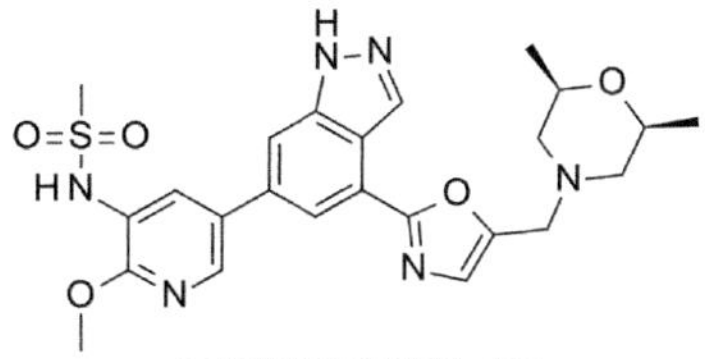

GSK2292767A **37**

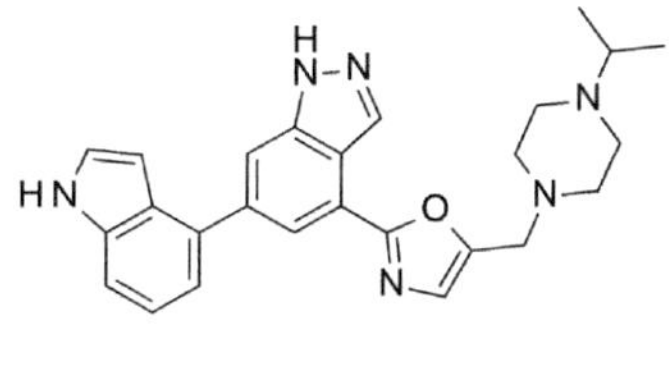

Nemiralisib **38**

Figure 2.12 Inhaled PI3Kδ inhibitors from GSK.

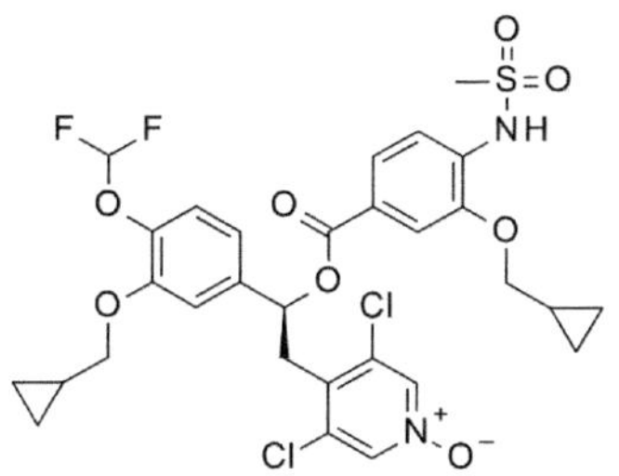

CHF6001 **39**

Figure 2.13 Inhaled PDE4 inhibitor CHF6001.

prediction of pulmonary absorption [65]. The measurements were of the percentage of dissolved dose that was found in the lung perfusate 20 minutes after dosing. This model identified two groups of compounds, low lipophilicity soluble molecules and a second group of much more lipophilic compounds. For the first group of compounds, permeability and tissue binding were identified as the key parameters affecting absorption. For the more lipophilic group of compounds, which were dosed as suspensions, in contrast, solubility was the decisive factor. The authors also identify that compounds with very low absorption were those where subsequent problems with accumulation were observed.

2.4.8 Conclusions

There are a variety of methods that have been used successfully to enable drugs to be administered by inhalation to treat lung conditions. The requirements are different from those for oral drugs and molecular size is not a limitation, whilst lipophilicity limits are more flexible than for oral administration. It is up to the team working on any given project to determine which will be most appropriate for their target. In many cases, the chemotype used as starting point will provide a strong lead towards the most appropriate method to obtain duration – thus any pharmacophoric requirement for a base will naturally lead to a strategy involving targeting some form of base-driven retention, whilst neutral, highly lipophilic molecules are more likely to be suitable for a low-solubility method and highly polar molecules may well be able to drive duration through low permeability. The location of the target with respect to both the lung physiology and to the cell itself is critical and needs to be accounted for in the selection of a candidate molecule. Location within the different generations of the lung can be targeted by selection of particle size and properties, as discussed in Chapters 3–5. The properties of the different generations of the lung also vary, so the upper airways have relatively thick walls with normal cell membranes and present a much larger barrier to the permeation of small molecules than the very thin membranes of the alveoli where gas exchange occurs. Beyond the lung generation there are also impacts of the location of the target cells in the tissue, so bacteria and macrophages are found in the lung lumen, adrenergic and muscarinic receptors are found on the cell walls of the bronchial sub-epithelium whilst other targets are found within cells in the sub-epithelium and thus create additional challenges for molecules to reach their site of action. Going to the cell level intracellular targets require membrane permeability for the drug to access the target; in contrast membrane-bound targets may well favor drugs that have high affinities for membranes, such as lipophilic amines.

Although long target residence time seems not yet to have been unequivocally established as a viable strategy, it is conceptually very attractive and, if the opportunity arises, one worth investigating. Whatever method of lung retention is opted for, the desirability of high potency will be a constant.

References

[1] J. Goodman, Tobacco in History and Culture: An Encyclopedia, Thomson Gale, 2005.

[2] K. Rave, E. Potocka, A.H. Boss, M. Marino, D. Costello, R. Chen, Pharmacokinetics and linear exposure of AFRESATM compared with the subcutaneous injection of regular human insulin, Diabetes, Obes. Metab. 11 (7) (2009) 715–720. Available from: https://111/11111/j.1463-1326.2009.01039.x.

[3] A.E. Cooper, D. Ferguson, K. Grime, Optimisation of DMPK by the inhaled route: challenges and approaches, Curr. Drug. Metab. 13 (4) (2012) 457–473. Available from: https://111/10.2174/138920012800166571 22299825.

[4] K. Biggadike, et al., X-ray crystal structure of the novel enhanced-affinity glucocorticoid agonist fluticasone furoate in the glucocorticoid receptor – ligand binding domain, J. Med. Chem. 51 (12) (2008) 3349–3352. Available from: https://111/10.1021/jm800279t.

[5] P.A. Procopiou, et al., Synthesis and structure – activity relationships of long-acting β_2 adrenergic receptor agonists incorporating metabolic inactivation: an antedrug approach, J. Med. Chem. 53 (11) (2010) 4522–4530. Available from: https://111/10.1021/jm100326d.

[6] J. Rosenborg, P. Larsson, K. Tegnér, and G. Hallström, Mass balance and Metabolism of [3H] Formoterol in Healthy Men after Combined i.v. and oral administration–mimicking inhalation, Drug. Metab. Dispos., 27 (10) (1999) 1104–1116 10497135.

[7] M. Sakagami, H. Li, J. Venitz, In vivo-relevant transwell dish-based dissolution testing for orally inhaled corticosteroid products, Pharm. Res. 36 (7) (2019) 95. Available from: https://111/10.1007/s11095-019-2635-2.

[8] X.M. Bustamante-Marin, L.E. Ostrowski, Cilia and mucociliary clearance, Cold Spring Harb. Perspect. Biol. 9 (4) (2017) a028241. Available from: https://10.1101/cshperspect.a028241 27864314.

[9] C.A. Lipinski, F. Lombardo, B.W. Dominy, P.J. Feeney, Experimental and computational approaches to estimate solubility and permeability in drug discovery and development settings, Adv. Drug. Deliv. Rev. 23 (1−3) (1997) 3−25. Available from: https://111/10.1016/S0169-409X(96)00423-1.

[10] G. Dahl, T. Akerud, Pharmacokinetics and the drug−target residence time concept, Drug. Discov Today 18 (15−16) (2013) 697−707. Available from: https://111/10.1016/J.DRUDIS.2013.02.010.

[11] G. Hochhaus, R.J. Gonzalez-Rothi, A. Lukyanov, H. Derendorf, H. Schreier, T. Dalla Costa, Assessment of glucocorticoid lung targeting by ex-vivo receptor binding studies in rats, Pharm. Res. 12 (1) (1995) 134–137 7724475.

[12] G. Hochhaus, H. Möllmann, H. Derendorf, R.J. Gonzalez-Rothi, Pharmacokinetic/pharmacodynamic aspects of aerosol therapy using glucocorticoids as a model, J. Clin. Pharmacol. 37 (10) (1997) 881−892. Available from: https://111/10.1002/j.1552-4604.1997.tb04262.x 9505979.

[13] R.M. Jones, N. Neef, Interpretation and prediction of inhaled drug particle accumulation in the lung and its associated toxicity, Xenobiotica 42 (1) (2012) 86−93. Available from: https://111/10.3109/00498254.2011.632827 22106935.

[14] R. Brattsand, What factors determine anti-inflammatory activity and selectivity of inhaled steroids?, Eur. Respir. Rev. 7 (50) (1997) 356–361.

[15] L.Z. Benet, F. Broccatelli, T.I. Oprea, BDDCS applied to over 900 drugs, AAPS J. 13 (4) (2011) 519−547. Available from: https://111/10.1208/s12248-011-9290-9.

[16] A. Valotis, P. Högger, Human receptor kinetics and lung tissue retention of the enhanced-affinity glucocorticoid fluticasone furoate, Respir. Res. 8 (1) (2007) 54. Available from: https://111/10.1186/1465-9921-8-54.

[17] C.F. Stratton, D.J. Newman, D.S. Tan, Cheminformatic comparison of approved drugs from natural product versus synthetic origins, Bioorg. Med. Chem. Lett. 25 (21) (2015) 4802−4807. Available from: https://111/10.1016/J.BMCL.2015.07.014.

[18] S. Edsbäcker, Uptake, retention, and biotransformation of corticosteroids in the lung and airways, in: R.P. Schleimer, P.M. O'Byrne, S.J. Szefler, R. Brattsand (Eds.), Inhaled Steroids in Asthma: Optimising Effects in the Airways, Marcel Dekker, Inc, New York, 2001, pp. 213−245.

[19] M. Stoeck, et al., In vitro and in vivo anti-inflammatory activity of the new glucocorticoid ciclesonide, J. Pharmacol. Exp. Ther. 141 (3) (2004) 369−376. Available from: https://111/10.1124/jpet.103.059592 14064201.

[20] D. Baumann, C. Bachert, P. Högger, Dissolution in nasal fluid, retention and anti-inflammatory activity of fluticasone furoate in human nasal tissue *ex vivo*, Clin. Exp. Allergy 39 (10) (2009) 1540−1550. Available from: https://111/111/j.1365-2222.2009.03306.x.

[21] J. Heykants, et al., The clinical pharmacokinetics of itraconazole: an overview, Mycoses 32 (17) (1989) 67−87. Available from: https://111/1111/j.1439-0507.1989.tb02296.x 6250585.

[22] T.M. Deshpande, H. Shi, J. Pietryka, S.W. Hoag, A. Medek, Investigation of polymer/surfactant interactions and their impact on itraconazole solubility and precipitation kinetics for developing spray-dried amorphous solid dispersions, Mol. Pharm. 15 (3) (2018) 962−974. Available from: https://111/10.1021/acs.molpharmaceut.7b00902.

[23] O. Holz, et al., Efficacy and safety of inhaled calcium lactate PUR118 in the ozone challenge model - a clinical trial, BMC Pharmacol. Toxicol. 16 (1) (2015) 21. Available from: https://111/10.1186/s40360-015-0021-1 26265479.

[24] Pulmatrix, Pulmatrix Announces Positive Top-Line Results from Parts 1 and 2 of the 3-Part Phase 1/1b Clinical Trial of Pulmazole - an Inhaled Dry-Powder iSPERSETM Formulation of Itraconazole - Jun 25, 2018. [Online]. Available: <https://ir.pulmatrix.com/2018-06-25-Pulmatrix-Announces-Positive-Top-Line-Results-from-Parts-1-and-2-of-the-3-Part-Phase-1-1b-Clinical-Trial-of-Pulmazole-an-Inhaled-Dry-Powder-iSPERSE-TM-Formulation-of-Itraconazole>, 2018 (accessed 03.01.19).

[25] T. Colley, et al., In vitro and in vivo antifungal profile of a novel and long-acting inhaled azole, PC945, on Aspergillus fumigatus infection, Antimicrob. Agents Chemother. 61 (5) (2017) e02280−16.

[26] NCT03905447, The Effect of Early Treatment of PC945 on Aspergillus Fumigatus Lung Infection in Lung Transplant Patients. - Full Text View - ClinicalTrials.gov. [Online]. Available: <https://clinicaltrials.gov/ct2/show/NCT03905447?term=NCT03905447&rank=1>, 2019 (accessed 29.05.19).

[27] ACD/LogD, Advanced Chemistry Development, Inc, Toronto.
[28] J.A. Biller, Inhaled antibiotics, Curr. Opin. Pulm. Med. 21 (6) (2015) 596–601. Available from: https://111/10.1097/MCP.0000000000000216.
[29] A.V.L. Gontijo, et al., Biopharmaceutical characterization of nebulized antimicrobial agents in rats: 1. Ciprofloxacin, moxifloxacin, and grepafloxacin, Antimicrob. Agents Chemother. 58 (7) (2014) 3942–3949. Available from: https://111/AAC.01722-17/AAC.02818-14 24798283.
[30] S. Chorepsima, K.S. Kechagias, G. Kalimeris, N.A. Triarides, M.E. Falagas, Spotlight on inhaled ciprofloxacin and its potential in the treatment of non-cystic fibrosis bronchiectasis, Drug. Des. Devel. Ther. 12 (2018) 4059–4066. Available from: https://111/10.2147/DDDT.S168014 30568427.
[31] A.V.L. Gontijo, N. Grégoire, I. Lamarche, P. Gobin, W. Couet, S. Marchand, Biopharmaceutical characterization of nebulized antimicrobial agents in rats: 2. Colistin, Antimicrob. Agents Chemother. 58 (7) (2014) 3950–3956. Available from: https://111/AAC.01722-17/AAC.02819-14 24798284.
[32] S. Marchand, et al., Biopharmaceutical characterization of nebulized antimicrobial agents in rats: 6. Aminoglycosides, Antimicrob. Agents Chemother. 62 (10) (2018) e01261-18, Available from: https://111/10.1128/AAC.01261-18.
[33] S. Marchand, N. Grégoire, J. Brillault, I. Lamarche, P. Gobin, W. Couet, Biopharmaceutical characterization of nebulized antimicrobial agents in rats: 3. Tobramycin, Antimicrob. Agents Chemother. 59 (10) (2015) 6646–6647. Available from: https://111/10.1128/AAC.01647-15 26239992.
[34] S. Marchand, N. Grégoire, J. Brillault, I. Lamarche, P. Gobin, W. Couet, Biopharmaceutical characterization of nebulized antimicrobial agents in rats. 4. Aztreonam, Antimicrob. Agents Chemother. 60 (5) (2016) 3196–3198. Available from: https://111/10.1128/AAC.00165-16 26926626.
[35] D.E. Shaw, et al., Optimization of platelet-derived growth factor receptor (PDGFR) Inhibitors for duration of action, as an inhaled therapy for lung remodeling in pulmonary arterial hypertension, J. Med. Chem. 59 (17) (2016) 7901–7914. Available from: https://111/10.1021/acs.jmedchem.6b00703.
[36] M.J. Stocks, et al., Design driven HtL: the discovery and synthesis of new high efficacy β2-agonists, Bioorg. Med. Chem. Lett. 21 (13) (2011) 4027–4031. Available from: https://111/10.1016/J.BMCL.2011.04.135.
[37] S. Connolly, et al., Design-driven LO: the discovery of new ultra long acting dibasic β2-adrenoceptor agonists, Bioorg. Med. Chem. Lett. 21 (15) (2011) 4612–4616. Available from: https://111/10.1016/J.BMCL.2011.05.097.
[38] L. Alcaraz, et al., From libraries to candidate: the discovery of new ultra long-acting dibasic β2-adrenoceptor agonists, Bioorg. Med. Chem. Lett. 22 (1) (2012) 689–695. Available from: https://111/10.1016/J.BMCL.2011.10.049.
[39] M.J. Stocks, et al., Discovery of AZD3199, an inhaled ultralong acting (beta)2 receptor agonist with rapid onset of action, ACS Med. Chem. Lett. 5 (4) (2014) 416–421. Available from: https://111/10.1021/ml4005232 24900851.
[40] L. Bjermer, P. Kuna, C. Jorup, T. Bengtsson, J. Rosenborg, Clinical pharmacokinetics of AZD3199, an inhaled ultra-long-acting β2-adrenoreceptor agonist (uLABA), Drug Des. Devel. Ther. 9 (2015) 753–762. Available from: https://111/10.2147/DDDT.S66049.
[41] M.W.D. Perry, et al., Design and synthesis of soluble and cell-permeable PI3Kδ inhibitors for long-acting inhaled administration, J. Med. Chem. 60 (12) (2017) 5057–5071.
[42] J.A. Mindell, Lysosomal acidification mechanisms, Annu. Rev. Physiol. 74 (2012) 69–86.
[43] N.C. Ray, L. Alcaraz, Muscarinic antagonist-β-adrenergic agonist dual pharmacology molecules as bronchodilators: a patent review, Expert. Opin. Ther. Pat. 19 (1) (2009) 1–12. Available from: https://111/10.1517/13543770802630331.
[44] A.T. Nials, M.J. Sumner, M. Johnson, R.A. Coleman, Investigations into factors determining the duration of action of the β2-adrenoceptor agonist, salmeterol, Br. J. Pharmacol. 108 (2) (1993) 507–515. Available from: https://111/10.1111/j.1476-5381.1993.tb1283.

[45] D. Jack, A way of looking at agonism and antagonism: lessons from salbutamol, salmeterol and other β-adrenoreceptor agonists, Br. J. Clin. Pharmacol. 31 (1991) 501–514.

[46] R.A. Coleman, M. Johnson, A.T. Nials, C.J. Vardey, Exosites: their current status, and their relevance to the duration of action of long-acting β2-adrenoceptor agonists, Trends Pharmacol. Sci. 17 (9) (1996) 324–330. Available from: https://111/10.1016/0165-6147(96)10040-7.

[47] R.J. Slack, et al., In vitro pharmacological characterization of vilanterol, a novel long-acting β2-adrenoceptor agonist with 24-hour duration of action, J. Pharmacol. Exp. Ther. 344 (1) (2013) 218–230. Available from: https://111/10.1124/jpet.112.198481. 23131596.

[48] R.P. Austin, et al., QSAR and the rational design of long-acting dual D2-receptor/β2-adrenoceptor agonists, J. Med. Chem. 46 (2003) 3210–3220. Available from: https://111/10.1021/jm020886c.

[49] G.P. Anderson, A. Lindén, K.F. Rabe, Why are long-acting beta-adrenoceptor agonists long-acting?, Eur. Respir. J. 7 (3) (1994) 569–578 7912202.

[50] G.P. Anderson, Formoterol: pharmacology, molecular basis of agonism, and mechanism of long duration of a highly potent and selective β2-adrenoceptor agonist bronchodilator, Life Sci. 52 (26) (1993) 2145–2160. Available from: https://111/10.1016/0024-3205(93)90729-M.

[51] F. Baur, et al., The identification of indacaterol as an ultralong-acting inhaled β_2-adrenoceptor agonist, J. Med. Chem. 53 (9) (2010) 3675–3684. Available from: https://111/10.1021/jm400966v.

[52] R. Hendrickx, et al., Identification of novel substrates and structure–activity relationship of cellular uptake mediated by human organic cation transporters 1 and 2, J. Med. Chem. 56 (18) (2013) 7232–7242. Available from: https://111/10.1021/jm400966v.

[53] T. Bouyssou, et al., Discovery of olodaterol, a novel inhaled β2-adrenoceptor agonist with a 24 h bronchodilatory efficacy, Bioorg. Med. Chem. Lett. 20 (4) (2010) 1410–1414. Available from: https://111/10.1016/J.BMCL.2009.12.087.

[54] P.M. O'Byrne, et al., Prolonged bronchoprotection against inhaled methacholine by inhaled BI 1744, a long-acting β2-agonist, in patients with mild asthma, J. Allergy Clin. Immunol. 124 (6) (2009) 1217–1221. Available from: https://111/10.1016/J.JACI.2009.08.047.

[55] P. Casarosa, et al., Functional and biochemical rationales for the 24-hour-long duration of action of olodaterol, J. Pharmacol. Exp. Ther. 337 (3) (2011) 600–609. Available from: https://111/10.1124/jpet.111.179259. 21357659.

[56] D.A. Sykes, et al., The influence of receptor kinetics on the onset and duration of action and the therapeutic index of NVA237 and tiotropium, J. Pharmacol. Exp. Ther. 343 (2) (2012) 520–528. Available from: https://111/10.1124/jpet.112.194456 22854200.

[57] E. Naline, et al., Comparison of the in vitro pharmacological profiles of long-acting muscarinic antagonists in human bronchus, Pulm. Pharmacol. Ther. 49 (2018) 46–53. Available from: https://111/10.1016/J.PUPT.2018.01.003.

[58] D. Türck, et al., Pharmacokinetics of intravenous, single-dose tiotropium in subjects with different degrees of renal impairment, J. Clin. Pharmacol. 44 (2) (2004) 163–172. Available from: https://111/10.1177/0091270003261315.

[59] K. Toyama, H. Furuie, H. Ishizuka, Intrapulmonary pharmacokinetics of laninamivir, a neuraminidase inhibitor, after a single nebulized administration of laninamivir octanoate in healthy Japanese subjects, Antimicrob. Agents Chemother. 62 (1) (2018) e01722-17, Available from: https://111/10.1128/AAC.01722-17.

[60] T. Honda, S. Kubo, T. Masuda, M. Arai, Y. Kobayashi, M. Yamashita, Synthesis and in vivo influenza virus-inhibitory effect of ester prodrug of 4-guanidino-7-O-methyl-Neu5Ac2en, Bioorg. Med. Chem. Lett. 19 (11) (2009) 2938–2940. Available from: https://111/10.1016/J.BMCL.2009.04.067.

[61] L.M.R. Cass, C. Efthymiopoulos, A. Bye, Pharmacokinetics of zanamivir after intravenous, oral, inhaled or intranasal administration to healthy volunteers, Clin. Pharmacokinet. 36 (Suppl. 1) (1999) 1–11.

[62] S. Edsbäcker, R. Brattsand, Budesonide fatty-acid esterification: a novel mechanism prolonging binding to airway tissue. Review of available data, Ann. Allergy, Asthma Immunol. 88 (6) (2002) 609–616. Available from: https://111/10.1016/S1081-1206(10)61893-5.

[63] M. Begg, et al., Relationship between pharmacokinetics and pharmacodynamic responses in healthy smokers informs a once daily dosing regimen for nemiralisib, J. Pharmacol. Exp. Ther. 369 (3) (2019) 337–344, Available form: https://111/10.1124/jpet.118.255109 30886125.

[64] E. Armani, et al., Novel class of benzoic acid ester derivatives as potent PDE4 inhibitors for inhaled administration in the treatment of respiratory diseases, J. Med. Chem. 57 (3) (2014) 793–816. Available from: https://111/10.1021/jm401549m.

[65] C.D. Edwards, C. Luscombe, P. Eddershaw, E.M. Hessel, Development of a novel quantitative structure-activity relationship model to accurately predict pulmonary absorption and replace routine use of the isolated perfused respiring rat lung model, Pharm. Res. 33 (11) (2016) 2604–2616. Available from: https://111/10.1007/s11095-016-1983-4. 27401409.

CHAPTER 3

Devices and formulations: General introduction and wet aerosol delivery systems

Anne Haaije de Boer[1] and Kyrre Thalberg[2,3]
[1]Department of Pharmaceutical Technology and Biopharmacy, Faculty of Science and Engineering, University of Groningen, Groningen, The Netherlands
[2]Inhalation Product Development, Pharmaceutical Technology & Development, Operations, AstraZeneca Gothenburg, Sweden
[3]Current address: Emmace Consulting AB, Medicon Village, Lund, Sweden

3.1 General introduction

An overview of the history of inhaled medicines in relation to the contents of this book is given in Chapter 1. The early history is strongly connected with the evolution of aerosol delivery principles and devices with their specific drug formulations. This evolution has resulted in the existence of three main classes of aerosol delivery devices: wet aerosol systems, propellant driven metered dose inhalers and dry powder inhalers (Fig. 3.1). Their principles of operation, diversity and performances are described in the Chapters 3, 4, and 5 respectively. Each of the three classes has different design possibilities and within all classes different subgroups exist. They all share the same purpose of transferring a drug formulation into a suitable aerosol for inhalation. The desired aerosol properties may depend on various factors, of which the specific target area for the drug and the flow rate at which the drug is inhaled are most important.

Which delivery system to use for a particular type of drug may depend on the dose level, the frequency of administration, the cost per dose, drug stability and physicochemical nature, including its solubility in water and various solid-state properties. Also, the ability of the patient to use the delivery system appropriately plays a role in the choice. To evaluate the performance of a pulmonary drug delivery system, the relevant properties of the aerosol produced need to be measured. Measurement must be performed using the inspiratory conditions at which the inhaler is intended to deliver its aerosol to the patient. The aerosol characterization principles are basically the same for all three classes of delivery systems but the conditions used to operate these principles may vary due to the differences in inspiratory conditions and physical aerosol properties. They refer to flow rate, breathing pattern, inhaled volume, inhalation time,

Inhaled Medicines
DOI: https://doi.org/10.1016/B978-0-12-814974-4.00011-0

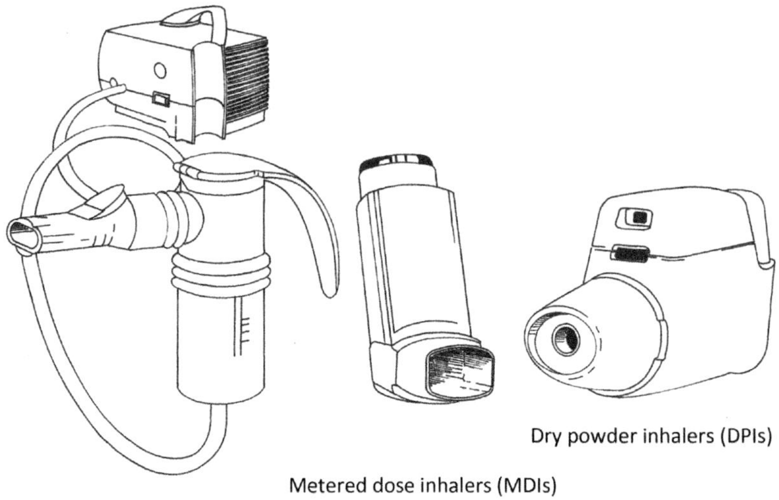

Figure 3.1 Examples from the three main classes of aerosol delivery devices.

air temperature and/or relative humidity. The most relevant aerosol property to lung deposition is the aerodynamic size distribution [1]. In the literature, performance evaluation studies based on achieved clinical effect can be found, but *in vitro* measurement is more accurate as it excludes the influence of patient variables. Proper evaluation of *in vitro* determined aerosol data from literature requires that measurement principle and conditions, as well as the manner in which the data are processed and defined, are precisely known. Different measuring principles and definitions make (comparative) evaluation complex and it is the purpose of this paragraph to summarize very briefly the different measuring techniques and various data presentation methods used. Also, some pitfalls are discussed that may be encountered when using values from literature.

Size measurement of aerosols is most frequently performed with cascade impactors (CIs), laser diffraction apparatus (LDAs) and time of flight (TOF) particle size analyzers (Fig. 3.2). Their principles of operation have been described before [1–4] and they produce fundamentally different diameters. They also have different conditions at which they need to be operated and this may limit or prevent their use for certain inhaler types. CIs and TOFs are based on particle's inertia and yield aerodynamic particle diameters [1,2]. In contrast, LDAs measure the forward light diffraction of particles in a laser beam and its scientific principle has been described by Mie [3]. Correct use of the Mie theory requires that the complex refractive index of the particles is precisely known, and in many cases the Fraunhofer approximation theory is more practicable [4]. Selection of technique depends on the purpose and the required accuracy for the type of aerosol to be tested [5]. Different techniques may yield different results for the same aerosol [6,7]

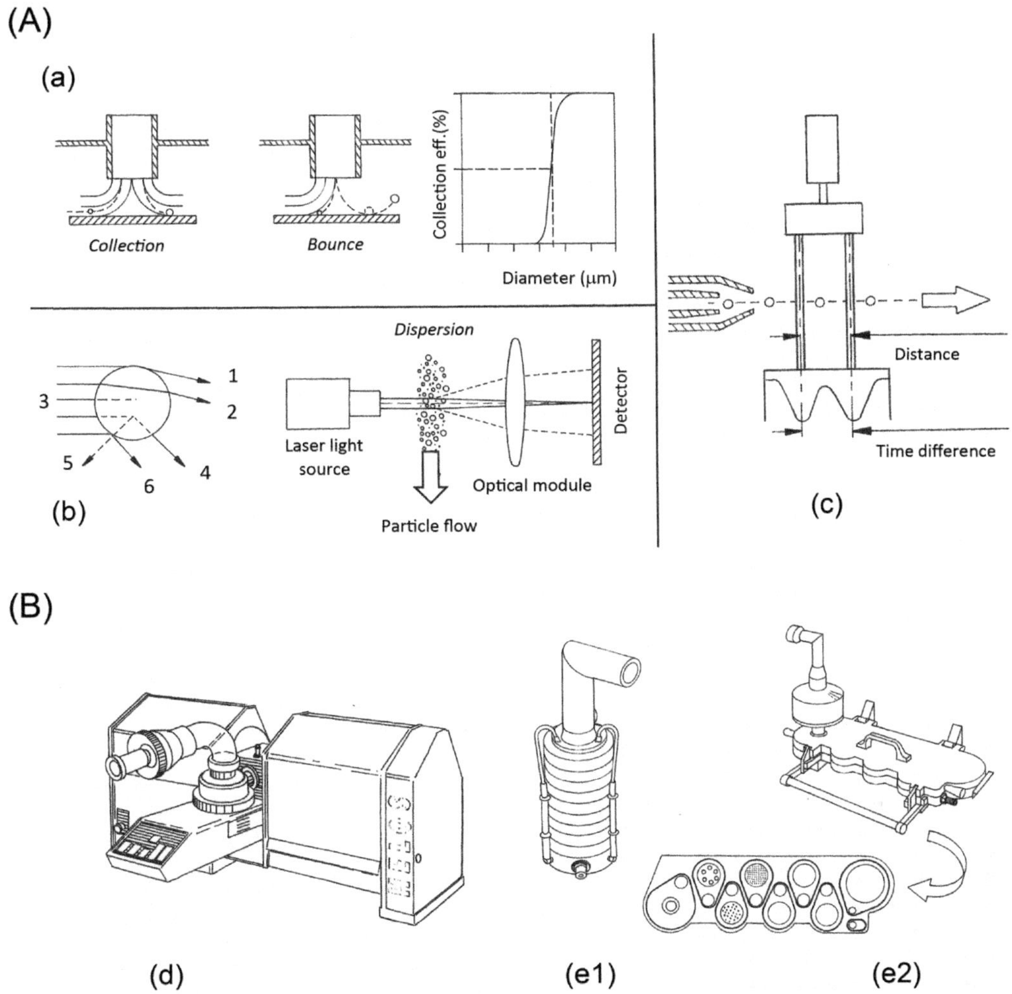

Figure 3.2 (A) The measuring principles of cascade impactor (a), laser diffraction (b) and time of flight (c) analysis. Impactor analysis relies on inertial deposition of particles on a collection plate, time of flight on the traveling time of particles between two laser beams in an accelerated gas stream and laser diffraction on deflection of light around a particle respectively, as described more in detail in the Refs. [1–4]. All three principles depend on the particle size, but also other particle properties are involved and they are different for different techniques. (B) Examples of the arrangements for aerosol characterization with laser diffraction technique (d), stacked impactor stages (e1), as for the Andersen impactor, and impactor stages in the same plane (e2), as for the Next Generation Impactor (NGI) respectively.

and this may be due to the particle properties, the air temperature and relative humidity [7,8] the amount of aerosol tested [9] or the flow rate and use of ancillary parts, such as a pre-separator or type of induction port [10,11]. Because of this latter aspect, size analyzers like CIs should not be combined randomly with casts of the human (adult or pediatric) throat. It is better to perform the size analysis experiments and deposition studies in an artificial throat or cast separately.

Inhaled drug aerosols can be wet or dry. Liquid aerosol particles are mostly transparent, isotropic, homogeneous, and spherical almost immediately after their formation due to the effect of the surface tension. Particles from diluted aqueous drug solutions also have unit, or near-unit density. This makes them suitable for laser diffraction measurement as the Lorenz-Mie theory for LDA includes the assumption that particles are spherical, isotropic and homogeneous. Hence, the laser diffraction diameter approaches the aerodynamic diameter of such particles. Solid particles, in contrast, are mostly irregularly shaped and non-transparent with densities ranging as much as from <0.1 to 1.5 g/cm^3, depending on how they were prepared. Spray dried solid particles may approach sphericity, but they often have corrugated surfaces to reduce interparticle attraction [12]. All these differences in properties and behavior related to the physical state can considerably influence the size measurement [13].

Significant changes in the size distribution may furthermore occur in the brief moment between aerosol generation and measurement, or deposition. These changes too depend on the properties of the drug formulation and the principle of aerosol generation, making either dry or wet particles. In addition to influencing the aerosol measurement, they can affect the aerosol transport through, deposition in, respectively distribution over the human airways considerably. Such changes include for instance rapid evaporation of non-aqueous solvents, growth of wet particles by coalescence (merging) or by moisture uptake of both wet and dry (hygroscopic) particles e.g. [14,15].

In the literature most data are from CI analysis. CI data are usually processed into the mass fractions of aerosol particles within the desired size fraction, referred to as the fine particle dose (FPD). For comparative use, FPDs are often expressed as percent of the mass of the total drug dose and then referred to as fine particle fractions (FPFs). Although this is theoretically incorrect, as fractions have a value between 0 and 1, the FPF expressed as percentage has widely been accepted in the literature. Using FPF for defining an aerosol may seem quite straightforward, but there exist many different definitions for FPF. Unfortunately, these definitions are not always given, and also FPFs having different definitions are without correction compared with each other in the literature e.g. [16,17]. In early *in vitro* deposition studies, often the mass fractions of drug derived from the lower impactor stages were summed and presented as fraction smaller than the upper-class limit of the highest impactor stage taken into consideration. Because different impactors were used, and these impactors were operated at different flow rates, this resulted in a variety of different size fractions with the upper-class limit between approximately 4.5 and 6.5 μm e.g. [17–20]. Currently, with an increasing interest in the pulmonary route for the administration of systemically acting drugs, 3 μm is rather considered as the preferred upper limit for FPF because larger particles may not effectively reach the most peripheral airways [21], particularly at flow rates higher than 50 L/min. Hence, FPFs in the narrow size fraction 1–3 μm seem more relevant for drugs that need to travel deep.

Different references may be used for the computation of FPF. FPF has been presented as percent of label claim and as percent of delivered dose; the latter being meaningful only when also the delivered dose, or the inhaler retention is given. Confusion in this respect may come from the change in the label claim from measured dose to delivered dose in the period when combination products with corticosteroids (ICSs) and bronchodilators (LABAs) were introduced to the market. For instance, devices measuring 200 μg ICS and 6 μg LABA were re-labeled into 160/4.5 μg. This increased FPF of the same product significantly and makes direct comparison of old and new data impossible. FPF in development and performance studies has also been expressed as percentage of nominal dose (what should be measured) and weighed dose (what has been measured).

The FPF does not discriminate between the considerable differences that may exist within the same narrow size fraction (e.g. 1–5 μm: Fig. 3.3). All three distributions in Fig. 3.3 have exactly the same volume (equals mass) fraction within the size range 1–5 μm (FPF = 49%) and the same geometric standard deviation (GSD = 3.5), but the mass median aerodynamic diameters (MMADs) of neighboring distributions differ by a factor 2 (1, 2 and 4 μm respectively). Based on what is known from deposition studies with monodisperse particles e.g. [21] this must result in significant differences in lung distribution for all three aerosols in spite of having the same FPF. It may also result in different deposition efficiencies as the predominant deposition mechanisms for C and A are different, being primarily inertial impaction and sedimentation (for C) and sedimentation and diffusion (for A) respectively e.g. [1]. Therefore, they may have different sensitivity to the flow rate at which they are inhaled. Hence, comparison on the basis of FPF alone for the same inspiratory flow maneuver is arguable; in addition, the

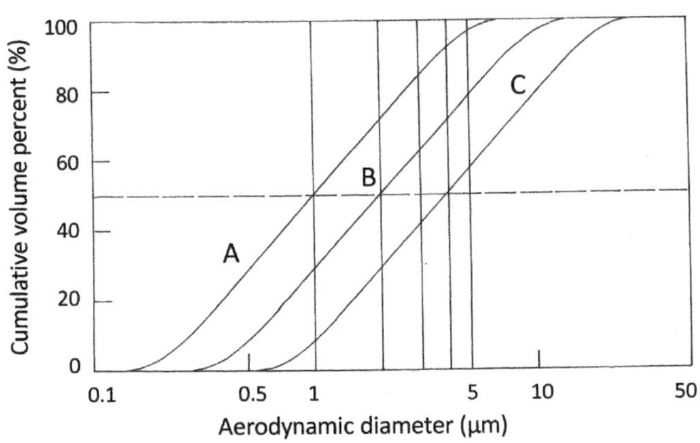

Figure 3.3 Three different size distributions with exactly the same volume (mass) fraction within the narrow size range 1–5 μm and the same geometric standard deviation, but completely different mass median aerodynamic diameters of 1 μm (A), 2 μm (B) and 4 μm (C) respectively.

MMAD and the GSD should be considered. Neither the MMAD alone is characterizing an aerosol adequately, because it does not give information about the range of the size distribution. Theoretically, the mass fraction for an aerosol with an MMAD of 3 μm (as arithmetic mean of 1 and 5 μm) within the desired narrow size range 1–5 μm can vary as much as from 0% to 100%: 0% being the result of submicron particles that are partly agglomerated into some larger clusters >5 μm.

It is often assumed that knowing the FPF and MMAD of an inhalation aerosol in combination with the inhaled flow rate is sufficient to predict the lung deposition of the inhaled drug. This is a misconception. Even when inhalers deliver aerosols with exactly the same FPF and MMAD at the same flow rate, considerable differences in lung deposition may occur for different reasons. Firstly, the same flow rate may result in different aerosol velocities due to different cross sections for the inhaler mouthpieces. In fact, the flow pattern of the aerosol cloud into the oral cavity is usually very complex, particularly when the air flow from the mouthpiece has tangential components, as from cyclone, whirl chamber, helical channel or classifier types of dispersion principles. These differences can result in considerable differences in mouth and throat deposition [22–24]. In addition, FPF as measured *in vitro* with CI analysis may not be representative for the *in vivo* situation. During *in vitro* testing, a constant flow rate is adjusted through the inhaler, whereas patients generate a great variety of different inspiratory flow curves that reach a peak value relatively fast and slant down much slower [25,26]. Particularly for dry powder inhalers, this can influence the entire dose emission process, including the emptying of the dose (measuring) compartment, the dispersion performance and the retention behavior, all affecting the FPF. It has furthermore been found for some DPIs that FPF particularly depends on the first phase of inhalation, as defined with the flow increase rate (FIR) to the peak inspiratory flow rate (PIFR) [25]. The performance of some inhalers is even more dependent on FIR than on the PIFR above a certain threshold value for the latter [27,28]. Finally, the lung distribution of a particular aerosol depends on the volume of air in which the aerosol is dispersed. Only aerosol particles released in the first 0.5–1 L of inhaled air can penetrate the alveolar region by convective transport.

3.2 Wet aerosol delivery systems

3.2.1 Introduction

Although inhalation of therapeutic gases and vapors dates back to at least 4.000 BCE, the rationale for inhalation became first clear in the 18th century when it was understood that drug delivery to the lungs is only possible via the 'windpipe' [29]. Not much later, spraying of thermal waters and spas became popular, although this technique remained long highly ineffective until the end of the 19th and the beginning of the 20th century due to inappropriate droplet sizes [30]. Several events in this period, including continuous outbreaks of White Plague (tuberculosis), strongly strengthened the awareness of the benefits of drug delivery via the pulmonary route. From this period on, nebulization technique has received several boosts for improvement. Particularly the recognition of the clinical effect of adrenaline for the treatment of asthma patients in the early 20th century and the need for nebulization systems for warfare during World War I and II accelerated the advancement of the technique. Handheld glass-constructed nebulizers with rubber squeeze balls became popular before electric compressors were made available for jet (venturi-type) aerosol generation principles and in 1949 a first ultrasonic nebulizer using a piezo-electric technique was presented [30]. In the past four decades, various alternative wet aerosol generation principles have been developed for pulmonary drug delivery (e.g. Electrospray, impinging jet aerosolization, vibrating mesh technology and Rayleigh break-up). Also, chip technology has been added to devices to adapt the aerosol delivery to the breathing pattern of the individual patient, or even control the inhalation maneuver of the patient [31]. These principles increase the lung deposition and aim to add to the efficacy of the therapy. It is the purpose of this chapter to present and discuss the state-of-the-art technique for aqueous based aerosol production.

3.2.2 Jet nebulizers

Modern jet nebulizers exist in a wide variety of different designs but their basic principle of operation is the same. They are by far the most common type of nebulizer used worldwide [32] and consist of a two-fluid nozzle utilizing a compressed air flow for the aerosolization of the drug solution or suspension. Nearly all currently marketed devices have nozzles consisting of co-axial tubes (Fig. 3.4). Compressed air passes

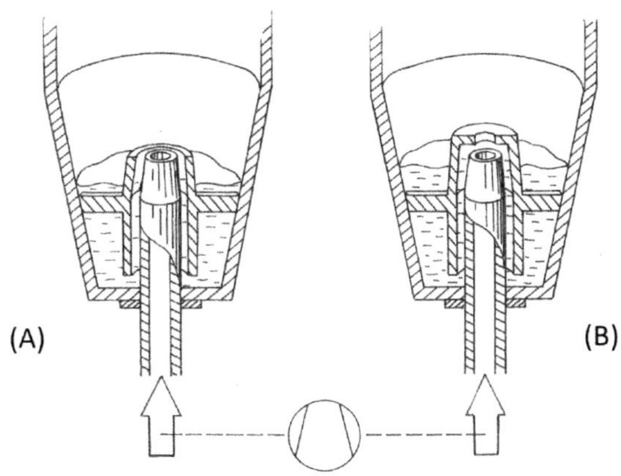

Figure 3.4 Two-fluid nozzles with external (A) and internal (B) fluid mixing. Of the two co-axial tubes, the inner tube is used for a pressurized air flow from a compressor or a pressurized gas (air, oxygen, or nitrogen) supply system; the outer tube, closely surrounding the inner tube to create an annular capillary, is for the drug solution (suspension) from the reservoir cup.

through the inner tube surrounded by the liquid pipe and is forced through a narrow opening in the immediate vicinity of the tip of the liquid pipe. The narrowing increases the air velocity and reduces the local pressure according to Bernoulli's principle of energy conservation. This results in sub-atmospheric pressure at the tip of the liquid tube causing the liquid to be pushed up through the capillary from a reservoir.

Internally mixing nozzles have a higher liquid flow rate than externally mixing types [33]. An effect on the liquid flow may also come from transfer of momentum between the high velocity gas stream and the low velocity liquid jet. Shearing effects as a result of the extreme difference in gas and liquid velocity cause disruption of the liquid jet into ligaments and subsequently into droplets (Fig. 3.5). Instead of using pressurized air, the aerosolization process can be driven with oxygen, as in exacerbations of chronic obstructive pulmonary disease (COPD), but it has been shown that this can lead to an increase in transcutaneous partial pressure of carbon dioxide ($PtCO_2$; [34]), which is a measure of the adequacy of ventilation [35].

The droplet formation process with a two-fluid nozzle involves complex phenomena which are not yet fully understood and it may depend on the nozzle design [36]. However, the size distribution of the droplets obtained for a particular liquid relates to the gas and liquid flow rate [37]. The size range can be extremely wide between 15 and 500 μm [38]. For this reason, a baffle is positioned at a short distance from the nozzle to reduce the droplet size from the jet (by inertial impaction) to a range suitable for inhalation (Fig. 3.5). Large droplets impact with the baffle and are returned to the liquid reservoir by the force of gravity. Only droplets in the desired aerodynamic size range for inhalation can bypass the baffle and leave the nebulizer cup.

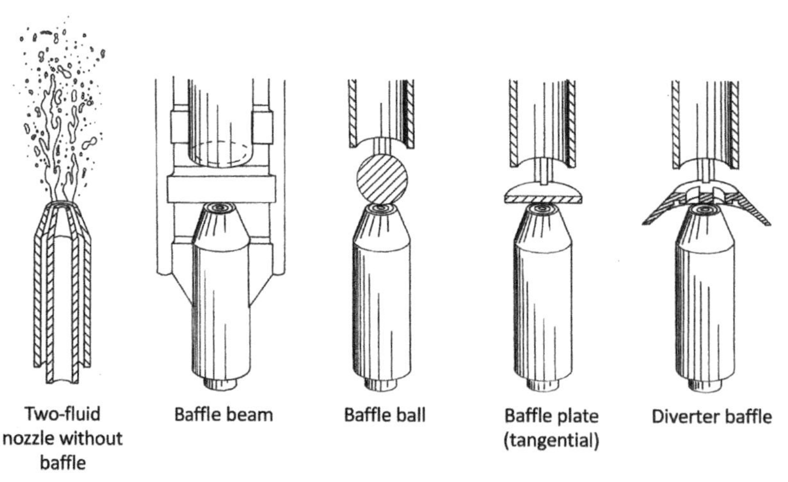

Figure 3.5 Different baffle designs for two-fluid nozzles collecting large droplets and returning them to the liquid reservoir. With a plate and diverter, the collected liquid is directed effectively away from the nozzle exit hole.

Well-designed and appropriately-positioned baffles may reduce the droplet size to less than 5–10 μm having a median diameter between 1 and 4 μm. The output rate of a jet nebulizer depends on the liquid flow rate from the nozzle and the return flow from the baffle which is a function of its design, its distance to the nozzle and the gas flow rate determining the droplet velocity. These variables determine the effective cutpoint of the baffle and the fraction of aerosolized liquid returned to the reservoir can be as high as 93%–99% of the nozzle output [32]. This recirculation increases the nebulization time and results in substantial liquid evaporation which leads to an increase in the drug concentration during the nebulization process [39]. This also has an effect on the droplet size distribution [40].

Two-fluid nozzles for the aerosolization of inhalation drugs are typically operated at an air flow rate between 2 and 8 L/min, depending on the type of compressor used. The pressure required for this flow rate depends on the specific nebulizer design as different nozzles have different resistances to air flow [41]. Increasing the flow rate, by increasing the pressure, results in a higher output rate and shifts the particle size distribution of the aerosol to smaller droplets, mainly as it affects the cut-off diameter and efficiency of the baffle. Often a higher air flow rate is used than recommended to increase the output rate and shorten the nebulization time, but this is likely to affect the efficacy of the therapy due to a change in drug distribution over the lungs.

The constant nozzle flow rate between 2 and 8 L/min (33 and 267 mL/s) contributes to significant aerosol losses to the environment during periods of exhalation. The breathing rates of adults are between 12 and 20 min^{-1} and the normal inhalation time : exhalation time (I : E) ratio is approximately 2 : 3. Consequently, exhalation duration varies roughly between 1.8 s (at rate 20 min^{-1}) and 3 s (at rate 12 min^{-1}). In this period a volume of 60 (respectively 480) mL to 100 (respectively 800) mL aerosol is produced at a nozzle flow rate of 2 (respectively 8) L/min. For the high nozzle flow rate, this is considerably more than a nebulizer cup with a volume of approx. 150 mL can store. Consequently, loss of about 2/3 of the aerosolized dose to the environment is possible [32]. The small volume of the nebulizer cup in combination with the high aerosol generation rate also promotes particle coalescence and intensive droplet-wall contact. The first aspect increases the droplet size, the second contributes to a high residual volume from large droplets adhering onto the inner walls of the nebulizer in case of poor wettability (high contact angle). They add to the drug residue in the dead volume of the nebulizer cup, varying in the range between 1 and 3 mL [33]. New cups are often hydrophobic by thin fat layers from the injection molding process and exhibit good wettability first after rinsing with hot water and liquid detergent [40].

To reduce the environmental exposure to the aerosol, corrugated tubes may be connected to the expiration side of the nebulizer [42]. They increase the storage volume for the aerosol. Alternatively, collection bags or so-called conservation devices can be used [32], with or without a one-way valve that opens to the patient only during inhalation. Also, open-vent nebulizers exist that make use of the low-pressure area in the nozzle region. This low pressure draws air from the environment that is conducted past the aerosol generation zone to lower the particle concentration and support the aerosol release from the nebulizer cup. More advanced systems are the breath-enhanced (or breath-assisted) nebulizers and breath-actuated nebulizers (BANs) [33,42]. They have a valve system that allows air to flow into the nebulizer cup only during moments of inhalation in order to increase the amount of aerosol delivered to the lungs. During exhalation, this valve (conducting the air in a similar way to the nozzle region as an open-vent valve) closes, and a second valve in the mouthpiece opens to release the exhaled air into the free space. This exhalation valve usually has a filter to remove remaining aerosol particles from the exhaled air. BANs interrupt the aerosol generation during periods of exhalation. This can be done manually by interrupting the pressurized air flow to the two-fluid nozzle, or automatically by a normally closed valve that is triggered to open by the inhaled air flow to restore the aerosol production (trigger point at approx. 15 L/min for the AeroEclipse, Trudell Medical International). This reduces aerosol waste to the environment, but it increases the total nebulization time.

The performance of jet nebulizers depends further on a large number of variables, including the properties of the drug solution (or suspension), the breathing maneuver of the patient and various environmental conditions. Several studies have been undertaken to investigate the effect of most of these variables on the nebulizer output rate and aerodynamic particle size distribution of the aerosol and some examples are given in Section 3.5.

3.2.3 Ultrasonic nebulizers

Ultrasonic nebulizers, also referred to as high frequency vibration nebulizers [43], have been in use since their introduction in 1949. In the most basic design, they consist of a piezoelectric crystal submersed in the drug solution (Fig. 3.6). By applying an alternating electric field to the piezoelectric transducer, a high frequency mechanical vibration (generally 1–3 MHz: [42]) is obtained that causes oscillatory pressure disturbances (sound waves) in the liquid contacting the transducer [44].

The energy of the ultrasonic vibration is focussed on the surface of the drug solution. Different explanations exist for the mechanism(s) of droplet generation due to these sound waves that are referred to as cavitation and acoustic streaming, as has been explained elsewhere, e.g. [44]. Similar to jet nebulizers, ultrasonic nebulizers produce polydisperse aerosols, but for many ultrasonic devices, the size distribution is slightly narrower [45]. The median size of the droplets is inversely proportional with two-thirds of the power of the acoustic frequency [32]. Because the aerosol generation process does not involve a gas flow, the droplets are either transported towards the exit of

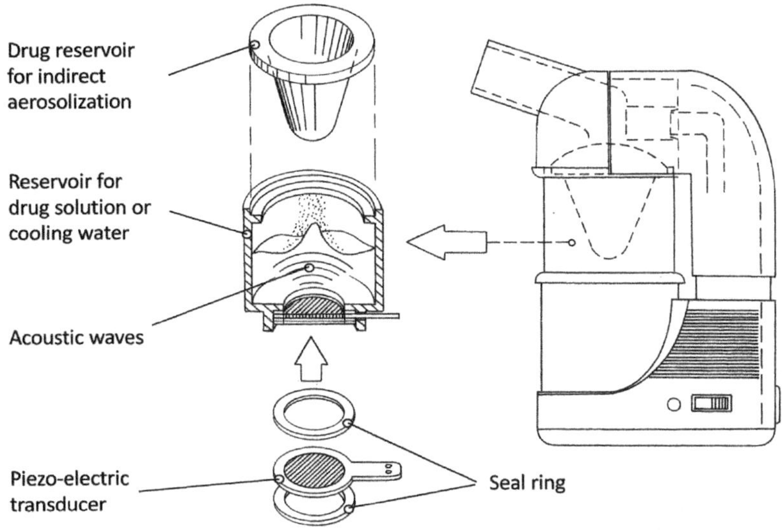

Figure 3.6 The principle of an ultrasonic nebulizer. The piezo-electric transducer creates oscillating acoustic waves in the liquid in contact with the transducer placed in the reservoir bottom. The liquid may either be the drug solution (direct nebulization) or cooling water when the drug solution is placed in a second inner reservoir surrounded by the cooling water (indirect nebulization).

the nebulizer by the inhaled air stream of the patient, or by a current of air from an internal fan. In the case of insufficient air flow, droplets coalesce and become larger. Most ultrasonic nebulizers require longer aerosolization times as their output rate is generally lower than that of jet nebulizers. The high frequency oscillations of the fluid molecules have unwanted effects that may be problematic for heat-sensitive drugs. To solve this problem, some nebulizers have a construction with two concentric tanks (e.g. Omron NE-U17, Omron Healthcare) of which the largest tank contains cooling water and the smaller inner tank the drug solution (Fig. 3.6). For this concept, the efficacy of droplet generation may be affected by the filling degree of the tank with cooling water. Other difficulties and limitations of ultrasonic nebulization include the inefficient aerosolization of high-viscosity liquids and suspensions [43] and large residual volumes [42]. In a study with increasing concentration of tobramycin, it was found that a drug concentration of 10%, corresponding with a viscosity of 2.6 mPa.s, may be maximal for an ultrasonic nebulizer [39]. Because of all these limitations and inefficiencies ultrasonic nebulization has never been widely adopted.

3.2.4 Mesh nebulizers

Mesh nebulizers are devices with small liquid reservoirs for the drug solution which has contact with a thin membrane having multiple small tapered holes (mesh). Basically, two different types of mesh nebulizers can be distinguished [42]: those having a horn in the liquid reservoir connected to a piezoelectric transducer (passive mesh nebulizers) and those with the membrane connected to the piezo transducer (active mesh nebulizers) (Fig. 3.7).

By activating the transducer, a high frequency vibration is applied either to the horn or to the mesh. This introduces pressure waves in the liquid and as a result, the drug solution is forced through the tapered pores at the pressure peaks, similarly to a piezoelectric ink-jet printer [46]. Various mechanisms of droplet formulation through a mesh have been proposed, as summarized and discussed for instance by [47]. Most meshes are constructed of a metal alloy or ceramic material to guarantee sufficient rigidity, durability and inertia towards the drugs and solvents [48]. Because the pores in the membranes can be made with carefully controlled diameters, more or less monodisperse aerosols are obtained. As a result of the large number of pores in the membrane, the output rate of mesh nebulizers is relatively high, but careful maintenance of the mesh according to the instructions for cleaning is required. For passive mesh nebulizers, the mesh can cheaply and easily be replaced as it is not connected to the piezoelectric transducer. The high rigidity of the mesh increases the risk of resonance and when the resonant frequency of the mesh differs from the frequency of the piezoelectric transducer, inconsistent aerosolization may occur [48]. Therefore, some nebulizers do not have a flat mesh, but a domed one because of a higher mechanical integrity. A domed mesh also (slightly) increases the distance between individual droplets at a certain distance from the pores.

Mesh inhalers have several advantages. They are small, relatively silent and portable and the aerosol generation process with a mesh requires low energy (from small

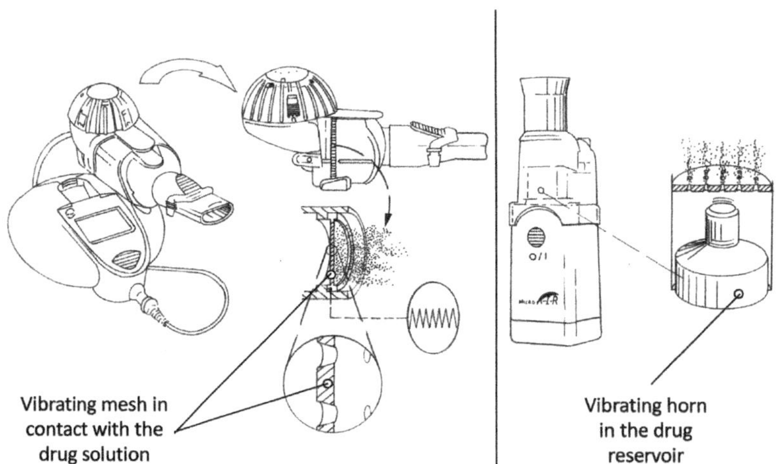

Figure 3.7 Vibrating mesh nebulizers with the drug solution or suspension either in direct contact with the vibrating mesh (active vibrating mesh), as for the Pari e-Flow, or with a vibrating horn in the liquid reservoir (passive vibrating mesh), as for the Omron NE U22.

batteries, having a long lifespan). The aerosolization process can be adjusted to specific requirements by changing the mesh size, cup volume and output rate [42]. They enable chip-controlled adaption of the aerosol delivery to the breathing maneuver of the patient (see paragraph 'breath control and breath adapted aerosol delivery'). They also have several specific drawbacks and limitations however. Only low viscosity drug solutions can be aerosolized effectively [49] whereas drug suspensions bear the risk of clogging the small pores of the mesh. Regarding stability of aqueous drug formulations, and cleaning (and disinfection) of the device, the same limitations and patient burden exist as for jet and ultrasonic nebulizers. Mesh nebulizers are also vulnerable to malfunction, particularly when maintenance is insufficient or incorrect. Gowda et al. [50] reported a high incidence (30%) of random and spontaneous interruptions of the aerosolization process with the Aerogen Solo (Aerogen) used for mechanical ventilation. Insufficient or inadequate compliance with the cleaning and disinfection procedures for a mesh nebulizer (Pari e-Flow Rapid) during use at home by cystic fibrosis (CF) patients has been reported in at least two different studies [51,52]. Partial clogging of holes appeared not to change the size distribution of the aerosol significantly but to reduce the output rate of the nebulizer. This was explained with a much higher resistance of the partially clogged pores which increases with decreasing square of the diameter and stops the liquid flow rather than reducing it. Design details and performance specifications of various active and passive mesh nebulizers can be found elsewhere in the literature [42,53,54].

3.2.5 Other principles and innovations

Different principles exist for the generation of fine drug aerosols in addition to the jet, ultrasonic and vibrating mesh nebulizers described in the previous paragraphs. They include Rayleigh break-up of liquid jets and droplet formation by impinging jets and by electrospray. Neither of these principles is new, but for the generation of drug aerosols they have found new applications in innovative devices of which most are to date the only ones of their kind.

3.2.5.1 The AERx platform and Medspray Ecomyst and aqueous droplet inhaler (ADI)

Rayleigh break-up is applied in the AERx (Aradigm) and Medspray nebulizers. In contrast with vibrating mesh inhalers, pressure is applied for these devices to force the drug solution through an array of equally sized micron- or submicron-holes in a thin membrane. The basic principle for the break-up of liquid jets from such nozzle holes into droplets of uniform size has first been described by Lord Rayleigh [55] but a better understanding of the break-up mechanism was obtained after the effect of viscosity of the liquid was taken into consideration by Weber [56]. Theoretically, the droplet size of pure water at room temperature is 1.95 times the diameter of the nozzle, unless small satellite droplets are formed and evaporation or droplet coalescence occurs for closely arranged nozzles.

The AERx platform has a dosage package that consists of three different layers (Fig. 3.8), including a bottom layer with a collapsible 45 μL blister for the drug solution, a lid layer and a nozzle layer with 2.5 μm holes [57]. The blister package is inserted in a delivery device and emptied by a piston that is actuated by the inhalation maneuver. The actuator presses against the blister with a pressure of approx. 23×10^5 N/m^2 (23 bar) to open a channel in the lid layer and extrude the drug solution through that channel towards a distribution chamber underneath the nozzle patch and through the nozzle holes (Fig. 3.8). For the first-generation device, heating of the aerosol was applied to reduce the droplet size being initially approximately 5 μm.

By controlling the depth of the stroke of the piston, dose adjustability can be achieved [58]. This enables dose delivery as required, as for instance needed in diabetes control. Aradigm has different delivery devices for the same blister technology of which the Essence is the latest, having simple mechanical elements only, instead of electrochemical parts. Therefore, no batteries are needed. The Essence device initiates aerosol release early during the inhalation maneuver and regulates the flow rate at 30–40 L/min. Recent information from Aradigm mentions 300–450 submicrometer-sized holes,

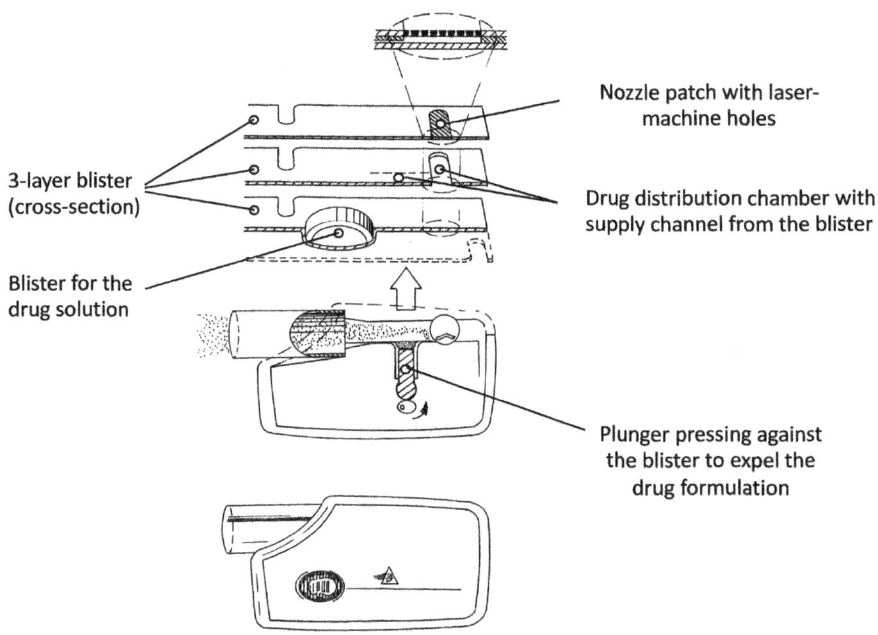

Figure 3.8 The AERx device with the disposable single dose strip that consists of three different layers. The bottom layer has the collapsible blister for the drug solution. It is covered by a lidding layer having a distribution chamber for the drug solution underneath the nozzle patch in the top layer, connected to the blister.

making heating of the aerosol unnecessary, and an aerosol extrusion time of 2.5 s for a 50 μL blister [59]. It is claimed that the emitted dose is approx. 57% of the dose loaded in the blister and that approx. 90% of the nearly monodisperse aerosol particles is smaller than 4.95 μm.

Medspray nozzles based on Rayleigh break-up are applied in the Ecomyst and Aqueous Droplet Inhaler, ADI (co-developed with Pharmaero). The principle of droplet formation is basically the same as that for the AERx devices, requiring a pressure of 20–50 bar depending on the viscosity of the drug solution (1–5 mPa.s). The Ecomyst is a multi-dose inhaler with a design and mode of operation similar to an MDI. It has a container for >200 doses and a preservative-free pump system (Aero Pump) to press a volume of 25 μL from a metering chamber through the nozzles [60]. The nozzle holes of the Medspray membrane have a diameter of 1.8 μm, which theoretically results in droplets of approx. 3.6 μm. However, turbulences in the nozzle region, influenced by the inhaled air stream, cause some droplet collision and merging. This process of coalescence can increase the droplet size from the Ecomyst to a mass median diameter between 5 and 6 μm (GSD = 1.4). To achieve good lung deposition with these droplets, the resistance of the inhaler is high in order to limit the inhaled flow rate to approx. 15 L/min. This results in a predicted lung deposition of >50% of the metered dose based on Next Generation Impactor data [60]. The ADI has the same nozzle technology as the Ecomyst device but uses a pre-filled 1 mL glass syringe for containing the drug formulation. The ADI has a disposable mouthpiece and a (one month) re-usable spring-loaded drive for emptying of the syringe through the nozzle holes. Both nebulizers in which the Medspray nozzles are applied were developed for the aerosolization of drug solutions and Medspray has a device for drug suspensions in development.

3.2.5.2 The Respimat soft mist inhaler

The Respimat soft mist inhaler makes use of impinging jets, as shown schematically in Fig. 3.9. The mechanism of droplet formation using this principle has been investigated since the 1950 s [61]. Upon impingement of the two jets that are placed at an angle towards each other a thin liquid sheet is formed that breaks up in droplets at its circumference. It has been shown that droplet formation is related to two different Reynolds numbers (based on the jet diameter and sheet thickness respectively) and the Weber number, which is a function of the jet velocity, and the density and surface tension of the drug solution [62]. Li and Ashgriz distinguished two major breakup regimens characterized by capillary instability and Kelvin-Helmholz instability respectively. In the capillary instability regimen, disturbances in the local momentum force on the edge of the water sheet can exceed the local surface tension force. This causes thickenings of the water sheet on the edge that develop into droplets which move, attached to water ligaments, to the tip of the sheet where they are released due to capillary instability of the jet formed at the tip. The ligaments further disintegrate into small droplets after

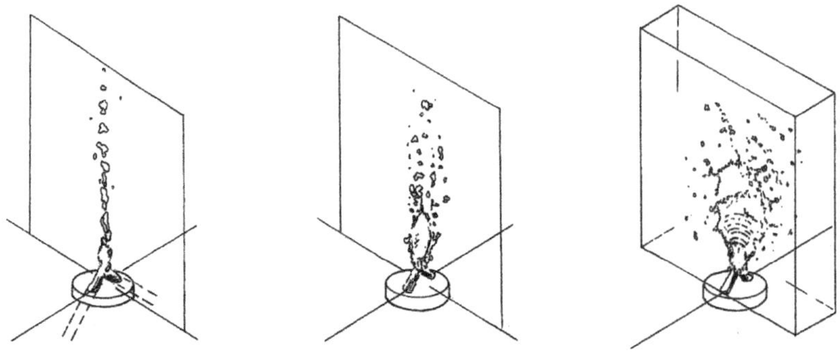

(A) Jet velocity 2.25 m/s (B) Jet velocity 4.50 m/s (C) Jet velocity 7.90 m/s

Figure 3.9 Liquid sheets formed by two impinging nozzles. With increasing jet velocity, the liquid sheet transforms from stable into smooth (A: jet velocity is 2.25 m/s) and ruffled (B: 4.50 m/s) in the capillary instability regimen, to an open-rim and turbulent sheet in the Kelvin-Helmholz regimen (C: 7.90 m/s).

detachment from the sheet. In the open-rim and turbulent sheet regimens interaction of the liquid sheet with the surrounding air results in waves on the sheet surface which cause the sheet to become unstable and break up into ligaments and droplets [63]. This regimen, obtained at high jet velocity, is most preferred for small droplet formation [64].

The Respimat with impinging jets has a small metering chamber for the drug solution. A volume of 135 μL is forced by mechanical power from a coiled spring through a 'Uniblock housing' to the two opposing nozzles (Fig. 3.10) [65]. The Uniblock has a filtering function that prevents blockage of the nozzles. The mist is released at a low velocity of 0.8 m/s [66,67] and the fine particle fraction varies between approx. 65% for an aqueous drug solution to 80% for a drug solution in ethanol.

3.2.5.3 Electrospray or electro hydro dynamic atomization (EHDA)

Electro Hydro Dynamic Atomization (EHDA) is an aerosolization technique widely used for ionization in mass spectroscopy, thin film formation and particle engineering. It is also referred to as electrospray and the technique has been explored for therapeutic aerosol delivery [68]. With an experimental set-up, it could be shown that near-monodisperse particles in the size range 1.6–4.6 μm can be produced (SD = 1.18–1.29) [69] but the technique has many disadvantages and limitations and currently no inhaler developments based on this principle are known.

3.3 Breath control and breath adapted aerosol delivery (AAD)

Effective drug delivery to the lungs with nebulizers depends not only on the aerodynamic size distribution of the aerosol, but also on the patient's inhalation maneuver and

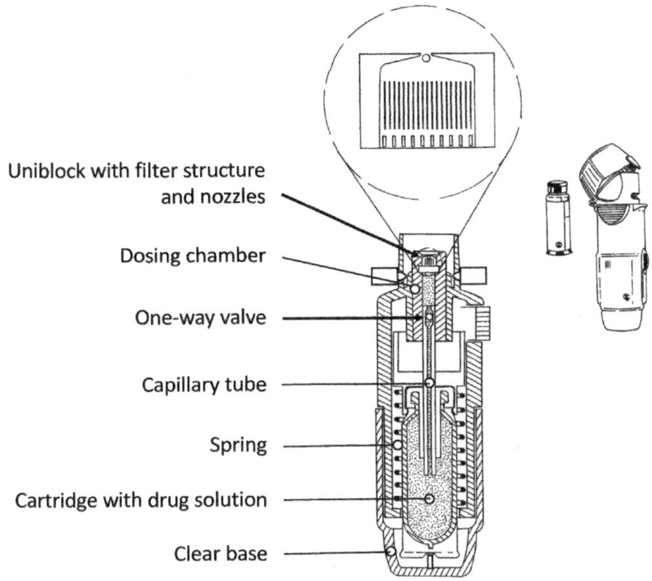

Figure 3.10 Schematic presentation of the Respimat soft mist inhaler. The nozzle openings at the top of the Uniblock release two very thin liquid films that collide in its immediate vicinity and form the aerosol as a soft mist. For more details about the precise working mechanism of the Respimat, a reference is made to Zierenberg [65].

the timing of aerosol delivery relative to the inhalation maneuver [70]. The principle of breath activation for the aerosol production with BAN has already been described for jet nebulizers. It minimizes aerosol waste to the environment but it does not affect the way in which the aerosol is inhaled. Different systems have been developed to influence the patient's breathing maneuver and/or adapt the aerosol production to that maneuver. AKITA (developed by Inamed and currently owned by Vectura) is a system for controlled and personalized aerosol delivery to be used in combination with conventional nebulizers. The device measures the flow rate, inhaled volume and breath-holding period of a patient and stores the data on a smart card [71]. This enables optimization of the breathing pattern of patients on an individual basis and to program the compressor of the Akita correspondingly. This compressor delivers the jet pressure for the aerosolization process at the start of the inhalation maneuver. In addition, it also delivers a predetermined constant flow rate at which the aerosol is inhaled and controls the inhalation time on the basis of the inhaled volume. During inhalation, the patient receives feedback on the time remaining for each breath and number of breaths remaining for the prescribed dose. Akita can be used with jet, ultrasonic and vibrating mesh nebulizers [72]. Different studies have shown an improvement in (peripheral) lung deposition achieved with the Akita nebulizer system compared to uncontrolled nebulization [73,74]. However, Reychler et al. [75] concluded from a randomized crossover scintigraphic comparison study that the amount of drug delivered to the peripheral lung is independent of the inhalation mode with Akita.

The development and evolution of Adaptive Aerosol Delivery (AAD) for improved aerosol delivery to the lungs has been described by Denyer and Dyche [70]. AAD was originally introduced to the market for the HaloLite (MedicAid) nebulizer in 1997. It was developed to minimize the waste of aerosol to the environment, reduce variability in drug delivery, improve the patient's adherence to the therapy and increase the compliance with the instructions for correct use [76]. The system constantly measures the breathing pattern of the patient in order to predict the duration of the next inhalation and to deliver aerosol only during the first half of this inhalation (Fig. 3.11). The volume of air inhaled during the second half of the inhalation period without aerosol production is used to transport the aerosol towards the peripheral

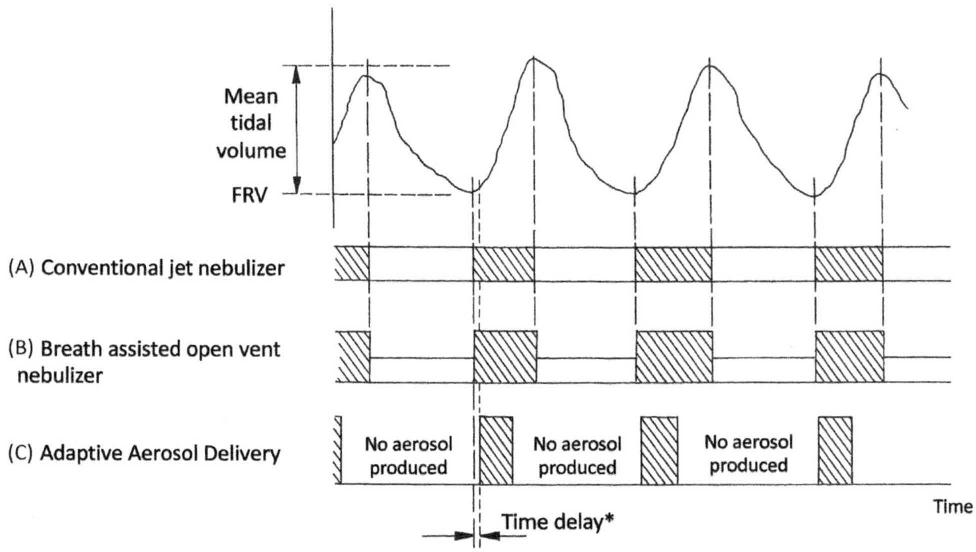

Aerosol fraction delivered to the lungs
Aerosol fraction returned to the nebulizer cup and/or wasted to the environment

Figure 3.11 Drug delivery to the lungs with the principle of adaptive aerosol delivery (C) compared with delivery via a conventional jet nebulizer (A) and a breath-assisted open vent nebulizer (B). The top graph shows the in- and exhalation pattern during tidal breathing. For the conventional jet nebulizer, the largest fraction of aerosol produced is lost to the environment or returned to the reservoir cup during exhalation (about 2/3). For the breath-assisted open vent an increased fraction is inhaled by air flushing of the nebulizer cup during the inhalation phase. With AAD, aerosol production is stopped during periods of exhalation and first re-started after a short time delay corresponding with an inhalation flow rate of 0.15 L/s. Different AAD inhalation modes are possible as described by Denyer and Dyche [70].

airways. The AAD system was improved twice for the Prodose (jet) nebulizer and I-neb (passive mesh vibrating) nebulizer respectively, and can now be operated with two different breathing modes [70]: the tidal breathing mode (TBM) and Target Inhalation Mode (TIM). TBM is for normal breathing and the TIM mode for slow inhalation at approximately 20 L/min. This enables increasing the inhalation period initially to 3 s and the aerosol delivery time to 2 s which is extended to 8 s inhalation and 7 s aerosol delivery during the course of the nebulization process. The TIM mode shortens the total treatment time and increases the deep lung deposition due to strongly reduced inertial upper tract deposition at 20 L/min.

3.4 Drug formulations for wet aerosol generation

Many drug formulations for nebulization are quite straightforward and they are not fundamentally different for different types of wet aerosol generation principles. They are simply aqueous solutions or suspensions of the drug in the desired concentration or particle size distribution respectively. Only a few drug formulations have been approved for the administration with a particular type of nebulizer and many nebulization liquids are prepared locally, such as inhaled antibiotics and solutions (dilutions) for provocation tests. Also, formulations developed for injection are frequently used for nebulization (e.g. colistin sulfate and colistimethate sodium) [77]. Preparation of the formulation should be made with sterile water and often water for injection is used for local preparations.

Different excipients may be added to the drug solution or suspension e.g. [78]. For instance, the use of ethanol as co-solvent may be necessary. Solutions (and suspensions) for nebulization must be isotonic and sodium chloride is mostly used to adjust the tonicity. Particularly patients with bronchial hyperresponsiveness are sensitive to hypo- or hyperosmotic solutions which can lead to bronchoconstriction [79]. Also, the pH has to be controlled within certain limits, as a low value may be harmful to the lung epithelial cilia and result in bronchoconstriction too. Especially asthmatic patients are sensitive to acid aerosols [80]. Mostly, hydrochloric acid and sodium hydroxide are used to balance the pH. Drug suspensions often require surfactants (e.g. Polysorbate 80) for their stabilization and to prevent microbial growth during storage of multidose preparations, preservatives such as benzalkonium chloride and chlorobutanol may be required. It has to be noted that such preservatives have a negative influence on the ciliary beat frequency and that this influence is highly concentration dependent [81]. In aqueous drug formulations, particularly *Pseudomonas* growth is a risk. Stabilizers for the drug, like the chelating agent disodium edetate, can remove traces of metal ions to inhibit oxidation. Finally, an electrolyte may be desired to suppress electrostatic charges that inhibit the drug output rate of vibrating mesh inhalers due to reduced liquid passage through the pores of the mesh [78].

Drugs for nebulization (and injection) are often lyophilized and stored as a dry powder in glass vials to increase their shelf life. They are delivered with vials of sterile water (1–3 mL). First briefly before the administration (nebulization) a solution is made. Buffer salts may be needed for the reconstitution of the lyophlisate [82]. For frequently nebulized colistimethate sodium, only freshly prepared solutions can be used because polymyxine E is rapidly formed after dissolution of the drug. Polymyxine E is toxic to the lung. Also, reconstituted bronchoconstrictor agents, like methacholine chloride in the concentrations 0.25–25 mg/mL, have a relatively short shelf life of no longer than 2 weeks in the refrigerator (the concentration 0.025 mg/mL must be freshly prepared like colistimethate sodium). The amount of solution needed may be different for different nebulizers and depends on the volume of the nebulization cup, the residual volume when sputtering starts and the amount of evaporation during the nebulization process. In some cases, larger volumes may be needed. There may be incompatibilities between excipients and drugs in nebulization solutions and this has particularly been investigated for ipratropium bromide [79]. Patients also mix different drug solutions together for simultaneous nebulization to save time for the administration of their medication [83,84]. Both groups reported that mixing of many nebulizer solutions and/or suspensions is possible without provoking incompatibilities and that in case of failure, the excipients are often the reason. Burchett et al. [83] developed a compatibility guide for respiratory therapists to show which combinations are safe, and which are to be avoided respectively. Particularly Dornase Alpha shows impaired activity after mixing with all other drug solutions for nebulization.

In addition to incompatibilities between drug-drug and drugexcipient mixtures there are limitations to some physical properties of the drug solutions and suspensions. Key properties for efficacy of the nebulization process are the temperature, concentration, surface tension and viscosity [82]. During nebulization all these properties change due to solvent evaporation and this affects the droplet size distribution. Evaporation results in a temperature drop for jet nebulizers (generally less than 10°C in 10 min nebulization time); for ultrasonic nebulizers an increase due to the input of acoustic energy with 20°C in the same time lapse is possible. This may be critical for highly thermolabile drugs. A higher drug concentration may be desired, as this reduces the nebulization time, and, thus, the burden of the patient. For tobramycin sulfate, normally given in a concentration between 4% and 5%, an increase up to 20% is possible for aerosolization with a jet nebulizer [39]. However, at a concentration >20% the higher drug output rate per ml drug solution (in mg/mL) is more than counterbalanced by a lower droplet aerosolization rate (in mL/s). Severe foam development in the medication cup is another reason for limiting the drug concentration, for drugs like colistimethate sodium.

A special group of formulations for nebulization are the liposomal drug formulations. Liposomal formulations can carry lipophilic drugs that are poorly soluble in water and they have a high potential for the prevention of local irritation [85]. This makes them for instance suitable for pulmonary delivery of hydrophobic antibiotics and chemotherapeutic agents in the treatment of lung infections and lung cancer respectively [86]. The small size of liposomes (around 100 nm) enables them to pass though leaks in tumor blood vessels and accumulate in local tissue to release the encapsulated drug. The stability of liposomes is an aspect of concern however, and different studies have been undertaken to investigate their survival rate during the nebulization process with different nebulizer types. Some of these studies were reviewed by Rudokas et al. [86], who concluded that jet nebulizers and vibrating mesh nebulizers are to be preferred over ultrasonic devices.

Because of a deficient regulation for nebulizers, device and formulation combinations are used randomly rather frequently. This may lead to an inefficient therapy because the output rate and droplet size distribution of such combinations are often not known. Moreover, regulatory guidelines for nebulizer testing are inadequate for predicting relative performance between devices and a revision of the test protocols has strongly been recommended [87].

3.5 The performance of nebulizers

Many different aerosolization principles and different design solutions for these principles (nebulizer devices) exist. The huge number of combinations with drug solutions and suspensions make it impossible to present a good overview of nebulizer performances. Examples of marketed devices within all aforementioned categories are given by Carvalho and McConville [68]. Only a few performance examples are presented hereafter to indicate the range of performance characteristics that can be achieved. It is furthermore important to recognize the likelihood of changes in the initial size distribution of the aerosol post-droplet generation, due to evaporation and droplet coalescence. Both depend on the circumstances under which the aerosol is released from the aerosol generator into the inhaled air stream. The aerosol properties may also change during the nebulization process due to an increase in drug and excipient concentration, and briefly before, respectively during dry running (sputtering) of the process. This requires that wet aerosol data should be presented only in combination with the conditions established for the measurement.

In order to give an impression of the size range that can be covered with nebulizers, a reference is made to a study of Cohen et al. [88]. For targeting large and small airways with adenosine monophosphate (AMP), they used a Microcirrus and Pari TIA nebulizer to produce aerosols with MMADs of 1.1 and 9.9 μm respectively. Usually, AMP is administered with the DeVilbiss 646 nebulizer yielding an MMAD of 3.9 μm. This extreme difference in MMADs confirms the need to use the approved or recommended types of nebulizers for the administration of inhalation drugs. For instance, approval for the administration of the tobramycin solution TOBI was given with the Pari LC Plus jet nebulizer [89]. Various studies have shown also the extreme effect of the type of nebulizer (jet, ultrasonic or mesh), or jet nebulizer/compressor combination on the delivered dose and output rate for a particular type of drug e.g. [40,45,90–93].

General conclusions for jet nebulizers are:

1. that the MMAD can vary over a wide range from <1 μm to >10 μm under the same testing and operating conditions for the same drug,
2. that changing the compressor, or the suction conditions, affects the delivered dose and size distribution of the aerosol, and
3. that there may be a great difference in accuracy of delivered dose to the patient, treatment times and wastage between conventional (constant-output), breath-enhanced and breath-actuated (dosimetric) jet nebulizers; the latter two types yielding considerably higher lung doses.

Pitance et al. [94] however, showed that aerosol delivery to the lung with a conventional non-vented nebulizer may also strongly be improved by using a corrugated tube-like extension on the exhalation side (blocking the vent inlet). They reported an even higher lung dose than with a vented (breath-enhanced) jet nebulizer. It should furthermore be noted that differences found *in vitro* do not always result in significant differences in total lung deposition, or regional deposition patterns for the drug [95]. This makes it possible to select an equivalent compressor for a particular type of jet nebulizer when the approved or recommended compressor is not available [41] by defining the acceptable range of variance in a nebulizer's MMAD and output.

The performance of ultrasonic nebulizers has not been well documented. Of the few available studies, a majority focussed on drug inhalation during mechanical (pediatric) ventilation e.g. [96] or on drug stability [97]. In comparative studies with jet nebulizers [98] or Mesh nebulizers [99], ultrasonic nebulizers showed comparable output rate, MMAD and delivered dose for tobramycin solutions, but this may vary with the devices used for the study and the type of drug solution. Heating of the drug solution during ultrasonic nebulization is an aspect that needs careful consideration as it may inactivate thermolabile drugs [100]. Systematic *in vitro* (comparative) evaluation studies of vibrating mesh nebulizers are relatively scarce too e.g. [101,102,106] and the outcomes of such studies depend strongly on how they were tested (stand-alone, or in a set-up for mechanical ventilation, with or without face mask, etc.) and the properties of the drug formulation used for the experiments. Most studies have been performed in animals [103] or in patients [104,105], in comparison with other types of nebulizers, and reported differences in residual volumes, delivery time, clinical parameters and/or lung dose. They lack *in vitro* output rate and particle size data. Najlah et al. [107] showed that, in contrast with jet nebulizers, the aerosolization efficacy of drug suspensions with vibrating mesh nebulizers depends strongly on the size of the suspended particles. Delivery of aerosols to pediatric and ventilated patients with nebulizers has its own specific challenges. It requires the use of interfaces like face masks that may have considerable effect on the efficiency of aerosol delivery to the lungs [108]. Performance data depend entirely on the combination of aerosol generator and interface used, which should be carefully paired [109]. Aspects to consider in this respect have been reviewed by DiBlasi [110].

3.6 Discussion and future perspectives

Nebulizers have the advantage that high drug doses can be administered, almost without limitation. Particularly when the drug is water soluble, drug formulation can be extremely simple compared to that for MDIs and DPIs. This makes nebulization suitable for fast drug efficacy testing and special treatment regimens for hospitalized patients. Nebulization is also attractive as a replacement for painful injection. However, nebulization has several disadvantages too. Most nebulizers need pressurized gas or electricity, which may not always be available at the appropriate time. Nebulization is a time-consuming process that includes proper (daily) cleaning and often also disinfection of the apparatus. Aqueous drug solutions (and suspensions) have a limited shelf life and often require storage in a refrigerator. Hence, the necessity to reconstitute a drug solution from powder and sterile water prior to each inhalation contributes to the burden for the patient. It also produces a dangerous and mixed waste of needles and glassware (broken and polluted ampoules). This all makes patients who need to use a nebulizer less mobile. On the long term, this high burden may become at the cost of the adherence to the therapy and the compliance with the instructions for good maintenance of the equipment. Therefore, nebulization is less appropriate for the treatment of chronic diseases. For hospital use, disposable nebulizer cups have been developed to eliminate the need for cleaning and disinfection, but studies have shown that such disposable cups may exhibit various malfunctions (spraying of large droplets, leaking drug solution and exhibiting air leaks). This causes poor reproducibility in output rate and particle size distribution [111].

Although many drugs are considered suitable for nebulization, approved or recommended drug-nebulizer combinations are scarce. This tempts physicians and patients to use jet and compressor combinations that happen to be available in the region, or are least expensive, often without knowing the consequences of their choice for the output (rate) and particle size distribution. This all makes the efficacy of the therapy highly uncertain. For all these reasons, future use of classic (jet and ultrasonic) nebulization may be limited primarily to use in hospitals. The development of battery-operated vibrating mesh nebulizers with reduced nebulization time reduced the burden of the patient to certain extent (Fig. 3.12), but also the maximal drug dose to be administered, whereas it did not bring a solution for limited drug stability. Dry powder inhalers seem superior regarding all these aspects.

Vibrating mesh nebulizers are still in development. Compared to classic jet and ultrasonic nebulizers, they are relatively small (portable), fast, silent and they may show

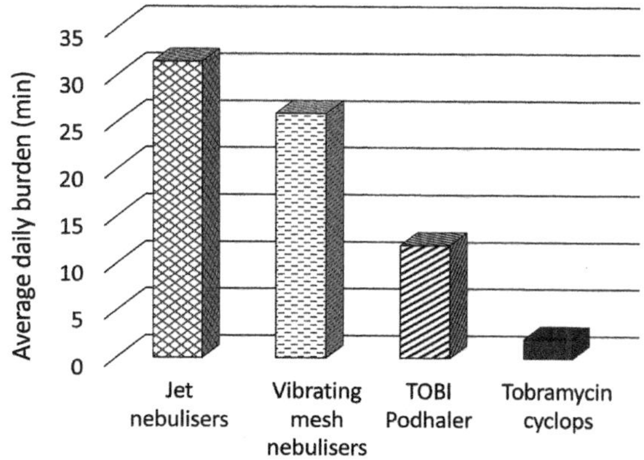

Figure 3.12 The daily burden of therapy (in minutes) for the patient using different administration devices for the administration of inhaled antibiotics; figure partly based on Weers [112]. Values for jet and vibrating nebulizers have been averaged for a number of different devices, ranging from 22 to 46 minutes and 21 to 31 minutes respectively; Podhaler and Cyclops are dry powder inhalers with four capsules and a single dose compartment to be inhaled per dose respectively.

improved drug delivery to the lungs thanks to the possibilities of breath control, and a breath adapted aerosolization process. This all makes them more efficient and patient friendly than classic jet and ultrasonic nebulizers. Further improvement may be expected, although drug stability (in solution) and cleaning need remain a hurdle to overcome for chronic use. Despite several limitations regarding viscosity, drug (e.g. protein) sensitivity to shear stress and suspension particle size, new aerosolization principles like Rayleigh break-up and impinging jets are being developed for various new and old drugs too. They may have future competition from yet investigational systems, like surface acoustic wave (SAW) microfluid atomization and capillary aerosol generation (CAG) [68]. Similar to electro-hydrodynamic atomization (EHDA), these new principles have specific pros and cons and their success may be limited to the administration of specific classes of drug, like proteins (SAW), thermolabile drugs (CAG) and drugs yielding an appropriate viscosity and conductivity in dissolution (EHDA).

References

[1] W.C. Hinds, Aerosol Technology. Properties, Behaviour, and Measurement of Airborne Particles, John Wiley & Sons, New York, 1982 (Chapters 3, 5, 11).

[2] S.W. Stein, P.B. Myrdal, B.J. Gabrio, D. Obereit, T.J. Beck, Evaluation of a new aerodynamic particle sizer spectrometer for size dispersion measurements of solution metered dose inhalers, J. Aerosol Med. 16 (2) (2003) 107–119.

[3] G. Mie, Beiträge zur Optik trüber Medien, speziell kolloidaler Metallösungen, Annalen der Phys. 4 (25) (1908) 24–25.

[4] A. Annapragada, E. Adjei, An analysis of the Fraunhofer Diffraction method for particle size distribution analysis and its application to aerosolized sprays, Int. J. Pharm. 127 (1–2) (1996) 219–227.

[5] A.H. de Boer, D. Gjaltema, P. Hagedoorn, M. Schaller, W. Witt, H.W. Frijlink, Design and application of a new modular adapter for laser diffraction characterization of inhalation aerosols, Int. J. Pharm. 249 (1–2) (2002) 233–245.

[6] J.P. Mitchell, M.W. Nagel, K.J. Wiersema, C.D. Doyle, Aerodynamic Particle size analysis of aerosols from pressurized metered-dose inhalers: comparison of Andersen 8-stage cascade impactor, Next Generation Pharmaceutical Impactor, and Model 3321 Aerodynamic Particle Spectrometer, AAPS PharmSciTech 4 (4) (2003) 1–9.

[7] J.C. Waldrep, A. Berlinski, R. Dhand, Comparative analysis of methods to measure aerosol generated by a vibrating mesh nebulizer, J. Aerosol Med. 20 (3) (2007) 310–319.

[8] W.H. Finlay, K.W. Stapleton, Undersizing of droplets from a vented nebulizer caused by aerosol heating during transit through an Anderson impactor, J. Aerosol Sci. 30 (1) (1999) 105–109.

[9] F. Grasmeijer, P. Hagedoorn, H.W. Frijlink, A.H. de Boer, Characterisation of high dose aerosols from dry powder inhalers, Int. J. Pharm. 437 (1–2) (2012) 242–249.

[10] N.C. miller, A.M. Purrington, A cascade impactor entry port for MDI sprays with collection characteristics imitating a physical model of the human throat, Pharm. Res. 13 (3) (1966) 391–397.

[11] C. Guo, S.R. Gillespie, J. Kauffman, W.H. Doub, Comparison of delivery characteristics from a combination metered-dose inhaler using the Andersen cascade impactor and the Next Generation Pharmaceutical Impactor, J. Pharm. Sci. 97 (8) (2008) 3321–3334.

[12] R. Vehring, Pharmaceutical particle engineering via spray drying, Pharm. Res. 25 (5) (2008) 999–1022.

[13] A.H. de Boer, D. Gjaltema, P. Hagedoorn, H.W. Frijlink, Characterization of inhalation aerosols: a critical evaluation of cascade impactor analysis and laser diffraction technique, Int. J. Pharm. 249 (1–2) (2002) 219–231.

[14] P. Worth Longest, M. Hindle, Condensational growth of combination drug-excipient submicrometer particles for targeted high efficiency pulmonary delivery: comparison of CFD predictions with experimental results, Pharm. Res. 29 (3) (2012) 707–721.

[15] Y.-J. Son, P.W. Longest, G. Tian, M. Hindle, Evaluation and modification of commercial dry powder inhalers for the aerosolization of a submicrometer excipient enhanced growth (EEG) formulation, Eur. J. Pharm. Sci. 49 (2013) 390–399.

[16] L.S. Hill, A.L. Slater, A comparison of the performance of two modern multidose dry powder asthma inhalers, Resp. Med. 92 (1998) 105–110.

[17] K.J. Smith, H.-K. Chan, K.F. Brown, Influence of flow rate on aerosol particle size distributions from pressurized and breath-actuated inhalers, J. Aerosol Med. 11 (4) (1998) 231–245.

[18] D. Prime, A.C. Grant, A.L. Slater, R.N. Woodhouse, A critical comparison of the dose delivery characteristics of four alternative inhalation devices delivering salbutamol: pressurized metered dose inhaler, *Diskus* inhaler, *Diskhaler* inhaler, and *Turbuhaler* inhaler, J. Aerosol Med. 12 (2) (1999) 75–84.

[19] W.E.S. Kamin, T. Genz, S. Roeder, G. Scheuch, T. Trammer, T. Juenemann, et al., Mass output and particle size distribution of glucocorticosteroids emitted from different inhalation devices depending on various inspiratory parameters, J. Aerosol Med. 15 (1) (2002) 65–73.

[20] R. Guchardi, M. Frei, E. John, J.S. Kaerger, Influence of fine lactose and magnesium stearate on low dose dry powder inhaler formulations, Int. J. Pharm. 348 (1–2) (2008) 10–17.

[21] O.S. Usmani, M.F. Biddiscombe, P.J. Barnes, Regional lung deposition and bronchodilator response as a function of β_2-agonist particle size, Am. J. Respir. Crit. Care Med. 172 (2005) 1497–1504.

[22] W.H. DeHaan, W.H. Finlay, *In vitro* monodisperse aerosol deposition in a mouth and throat with six different inhalation devices, J. Aerosol Med. 14 (3) (2001) 361–367.

[23] W.H. DeHaan, W.H. Finlay, Predicting extrathoracic deposition from dry powder inhalers, J. Aerosol Sci. 35 (2004) 309–331.

[24] Z.L. Wang, B. Grgic, P. Eng, W.H. Finlay, A dry powder inhaler with reduced mouth-throat deposition, J. Aerosol Med. 19 (2) (2006) 168–174.

[25] J.P. de Koning, Dry powder inhalation, Technical Physiological Aspects, Prescribing Use, Thesis Univ. Gron., Groningen (2001). Available from: https://www.rug.nl/research/portal/files (Chapter 3).

[26] B.L. Laube, H.M. Janssens, F.H.C. de Jongh, S.G. Devadason, R. Dhand, P. Diot, et al., What the pulmonary specialist should know about the new inhalation therapies, Eur. Resp. J. 37 (2011) 1308–1331.
[27] A.H. de Boer, G.K. Bolhuis, D. Gjaltema, P. Hagedoorn, Inhalation characteristics and their effects on *in vitro* drug delivery from dry powder inhalers. Part 3: the effect of flow increase rate (FIR) on the *in vitro* drug release from the Pulmicort 200 Turbuhaler, Int. J. Pharm. 153 (1–2) (1997) 67–77.
[28] M.L. Everard, S.G. Devadason, P.N. Le. Souéf, Flow early in the inspiratory manoeuvre affects the aerosol particle size distribution from a Turbuhaler, Resp. Med. 91 (1997) 624–628.
[29] M. Sanders, Inhalation therapy: an historical review, Prim. Care Resp. J. 16 (2) (2007) 71–81.
[30] J.-F. Dessanges, A history of nebulization, J. Aerosol Med. 14 (1) (2001) 65–71.
[31] R. Dhand, Intelligent nebulizers in the age of the internet: the I-neb adaptive aerosol delivery (AAD) system, I Aerosol Med. Pulm. Drug. Deliv. 23 (Suppl. 1) (2010). iii-v.
[32] C. O'Callaghan, P.W. Barry, The science of nebulised drug delivery, Thorax 52 (Suppl. 2) (1997) S31–S44.
[33] D.R. Hess, Nebulizers: principles and performance, Resp. Care 45 (6) (2000) 609–622.
[34] G. Bardsley, J. Pilcher, S. McKinstry, P. Shirtcliffe, J. Berry, J. Fingleton, et al., Oxygen versus air-driven nebulizers for exacerbations of chronic obstructive pulmonary disease: a randomised controlled trial, BMC Pulm. Med. 18 (157) (2018) 1–9.
[35] P. Eberhard, The design, use, and results of transcutaneous carbon dioxide analysis: current and future directions, Anesth. Analg. 105 (2007) S48–S52.
[36] P.D. Hede, P. Bach, A.D. Jensen, Two-fluid spray atomisation and pneumatic nozzles for fluid bed coating/agglomeration purposes: a review, Chem. Engr Sci. 63 (4) (2008) 3821–3842.
[37] S. Mandato, E. Rondet, G. Delaplace, A. Barkouti, L. Galet, P. Accart, et al., Liquids' atomization with two different nozzles: modelling of the effects of some processing and formulation conditions by dimensional analysis, Powd Technol. 224 (2012) 323–330.
[38] O. Nerbrink, M. Dahlbäck, A.-C. Hansson, Why do medical nebulizers differ in their output and particle size characteristics? J. Aerosol Med. 9 (4) (1994) 259–276.
[39] P.P.H. Le Brun, A.H. de Boer, D. Gjaltema, P. Hagedoorn, H.G.M. Heijerman, H.W. Frijlink, Inhalation of tobramycin in cystic fibrosis. Part 2: optimization of the tobramycin solution for a jet and ultrasonic nebulizer, Int. J. Pharm. 189 (1–2) (1999) 215–225.
[40] A.H. de Boer, P. Hagedoorn, H.W. Frijlink, The choice of compressor for the aerosolization of tobramycin (TOBI®) with the PARI LC PLUS® reusable nebuliser, Int. J. Pharm. 268 (1–2) (2003) 59–69.
[41] T.S. Standaert, S. Elwood Bohn, M.L. Aitken, B. Ramsey, The equivalence of compressor-flow relationships with respect to jet nebulizer aerosolization characteristics, J. Aerosol Med. 14 (1) (2001) 31–42.
[42] A. Ari, Jet, ultrasonic, and mesh nebulizers: an evaluation of nebulizers for better clinical outcomes, Eurasian J. Pulmonol. 16 (2014) 1–7.
[43] A.R. Martin, W.H. Finlay, Nebulizers for drug delivery to the lungs, Expert. Opin. Drug. Deliv. 12 (6) (2014) 889–900.
[44] L.Y. Yeo, J.R. Friend, M.P. McIntosh, E.N.T. Meeusen, D.A. Morton, Ultrasonic nebulization platforms for pulmonary drug delivery, Expert. Opin. Drug. Deliv. 7 (6) (2010) 663–679.
[45] P.P.H. Le Brun, A.H. de Boer, D. Gjaltema, P. Hagedoorn, H.G.M. Heijerman, H.W. Frijlink, Inhalation of tobramycin in cystic fibrosis. Part 1: the choice of a nebulizer, Int. J. Pharm. 189 (1–2) (1999) 205–214.
[46] J.S. Lass, A. Sant, M. Knoch, New advances in aerosolised drug delivery: vibrating membrane nebuliser technology, Expert. Opin. Drug. Deliv. 3 (5) (2006) 693–702.
[47] E.A. Chemmalasseri, Numerical Modelling of Droplet Formation in Mesh Nebulizers (thesis), University of Delft, The Netherlands, 2012.
[48] J.N. Pritchard, D. von Hollen, R.H.M. Hatley, Nebulizers, in: A.J. Hickey, S.R.P. de Rocha (Eds.), Pharmaceutical Inhalation Aerosol Technology, third ed., CRC Press, Boca Raton, FL, 2019 (Chapter 20).

[49] J.N. Pritchard, Nebulized drug delivery in respiratory medicine: what does the future hold? Ther. Deliv. 8 (6) (2017) 391–399.
[50] A.A. Gowda, A.D. Cuccia, G.C. Smaldone, Reliability of vibrating mesh technology, Resp. Care 26 (1) (2017) 65–69.
[51] B.L. Rottier, C.J.P. van Erp, T.S. Sluyter, H.G.M. Heijerman, H.W. Frijlink, A.H. de Boer, Changes in performance of the Pari eFlow® Rapid and Pari LC Plus™ during 6 months use by CF patients, J. Aerosol Med. Pulm. Drug. Deliv. 22 (3) (2009) 263–269.
[52] M. Baravalle-Einaudi, N. Dufeu, C. Dupont, L. Vecellio, B. Delaisi, A. Carsin, et al., Vibrating-mesh nebulizer maintenance by CF patients: results from a French study, Pulm. Pharmacol. Therapeutics 44 (2017) 57–60.
[53] L. Vecellio, The mesh nebuliser: a recent technical innovation for aerosol delivery, Breathe 2 (3) (2006) 253–260.
[54] J.N. Pritchard, R.H.M. Hatley, J. Denyer, D. von Hollen, Mesh nebulizers have become the first choice for new nebulized pharmaceutical drug developments, Ther. Deliv. 9 (2) (2018) 121–136.
[55] J.W.S. Rayleigh, On the instability of jets, Proc. Lond. Math. Soc. 10 (1) (1878) 4–13.
[56] C. Weber, Disintegration of liquid jets, Z. Angew. Math. Mech. 11 (1931) 136–159.
[57] J. Schuster, R. Rubsamen, P. Lloyd, J. Lloyd, The AERx™ asrosol delivery system, Pharm. Res. 14 (3) (1997) 354–357.
[58] J. Thipphawong, B. Otulana, P. Clauson, J. Okikawa, S.J. Farr, Pulmonary insulin administration using the AERx® insulin diabetes system, Diabetes Technol. Ther. 4 (2) (2002) 499–504.
[59] Aradigm, AERx Essence® pulmonary delivery device: AERx® system 'unplugged.' www.aradigm.com/docs (accessed December 2019).
[60] W. de Kruijff, Development of a propellant-free metered dose inhaler, I Aerosol Med. Pulm. Drug. Deliv. 30 (3) (2017). A-23.
[61] M.F. Heidmann, R.J. Priem, J.C. Humphrey, A Study of Sprays Formed by Two Impinging Jets, Technical note 3825, National Advisory Committee for Aeronautics, Washington, DC, 1957.
[62] R. Li, N. Ashgriz, Characteristics of liquid sheets formed by two impinging jets, Phys. Fluids 18 (087104) (2006) 1–13.
[63] Y. Xia, L. Khezzar, S. Bojanampati, A. Molki, Breakup of water sheets formed by two impinging jets, Hindawi Int. J. Chem. Eng. (2019) 1–8. ID 9514848.
[64] H. Wachtel, Respiratory drug delivery, in: A. Dietzel (Ed.), Microsystems for Pharmatechnology: Manipulation of Fluids, Particles, Droplets, and Cells, Springer, Heidelberg, 2016, p. 257.
[65] B. Zierenberg, Optimizing the *in vitro* performance of Respimat, J. Aerosol Med. 12 (Suppl. 1) (1999) S19–S24.
[66] D. Hochrainer, H. Höltz, C. Kreher, L. Scaffidi, M. Spallek, H. Wachtel, Comparison of the aerosol velocity and spray duration of Respimat® Soft Mist™ inhaler and pressurized metered dose inhalers, J. Aerosol Med. 18 (3) (2005) 273–282.
[67] R.N. Dalby, J. Eicher, B. Zierenberg, Development of Respimat® Soft Mist™ inhaler and its clinical utility in respiratory disorders, Med. Devices: Evid. Res. 4 (2011) 145–155.
[68] T.C. Carvalho, J.T. McConville, The function and performance of aqueous aerosol devices for inhalation therapy, J. Pharm. Pharmacol. 68 (5) (2016) 556–578.
[69] J.C. IJsebaert, K.B. Geerse, J.C.M. Marijnissen, J.-W.J. Lammers, P. Zanen, Electro-hydrodynamic atomization of drug solutions for inhalation purposes, J. Appl. Physiol. 91 (2001) 2735–2741.
[70] J. Denyer, T. Dyche, The Adaptive Aerosol Delivery (AAD) technology: past, present, and future, J. Aerosol Med. Pulm. Drug. Deliv. 23 (Suppl. 1) (2010) S1–S10.
[71] W.D. Bennett, Controlled inhalation of aerosolised therapeutics, Expert. Opin. Drug. Deliv. 2 (4) (2005) 763–767.
[72] A. Fischer, J. Stegemann, G. Scheuch, R. Siekmeier, Novel devices for individualized controlled inhalation can optimize aerosol therapy in efficacy, patient care and power of clinical trials, Eur. J. Med. Res. 14 (Suppl. IV) (2009) 71–77.
[73] P. Brand, H. Beckmann, M. Maas Enriquez, T. Meyer, B. Müllinger, K. Sommerer, et al., Peripheral deposition of α1-protease inhibitor using commercial inhalation devices, Eur. Respir. J. 22 (2003) 263–267.

[74] C. Vogelmeier, P. Kardos, T. Hofmann, S. Canisius, G. Scheuch, B. Muellinger, et al., Nebulised budesonide using a novel device in patients with oral steroid-dependent asthma, Eur. Respir. J. 45 (2015) 1273–1282.
[75] G. Reychler, A.-S. Aubriot, V. Depoortere, F. Jamar, G. Liistro, Effect of drug targeting nebulization on lung deposition: a randomized crossover scintigraphic comparison between central and peripheral delivery, Respir. Care 59 (10) (2014) 1501–1507.
[76] J. Denyer, K. Nikander, N.J. Smith, Adaptive Aerosol Delivery (AAD®) technology, Expert. Opin. Drug. Deliv. 1 (1) (2004) 165–176.
[77] M. Gurjar, Colistin for lung infection: an update, J. Intensive Care 3 (3) (2015) 1–12.
[78] S. Hou, J. Wu, X. Li, H. Shu, Practical, regulatory and clinical considerations for development of inhalation drug products, Asian J. Pharmacol. Sci. 10 (6) (2015) 490–500.
[79] J.S. Mann, P.H. Howarth, S.T. Holgate, Bronchoconstriction induced by ipratropium bromide in asthma: relation and hypotonicity, Br. Med. J. (Clin. Res. Ed.) 289 (6443) (1984) 469.
[80] J.R. Balmes, J.M. Fine, D. Christian, T. Gordon, D. Sheppard, Acidity potentiates bronchoconstriction induced by hypoosmolar aerosols, Am. Rev. Respir. Dis. 138 (1) (1988) 35–39.
[81] S.G. Romeijn, J.C. Verhoef, E. Marttin, F.W.H.M. Merkus, The effect of nasal drug formulations on ciliary beating *in vitro*, Int. J. Pharm. 135 (1–2) (1996) 137–145.
[82] H. Steckel, F. Eskandar, Factors affecting aerosol performance during nebulization with jet and ultrasonic nebulizers, Eur. J. Pharm. Sci. 19 (2003) 443–455.
[83] D.K. Burchett, W. Darko, J. Zahra, J. Noviasky, L. Probst, A. Smith, Mixing and compatibility guide for commonly used aerosolized medications, Am. J. Health-Syst Pharm. 67 (2010) 227–230.
[84] W. Kamin, F. Erdnüss, I. Kramer, Inhalation solutions – which ones may be mixed? Physico-chemical compatibility of drug solutions in nebulizers – update 2013, J. Cyst. Fibros. 13 (2014) 243–250.
[85] M. Zaru, S. Mourtas, P. Klepetsanis, A.M. Fadda, S.G. Antimisiaris, Liposomes for drug delivery to the lungs by nebulization, Eur. J. Pharm. Biopharm. 67 (2007) 655–666.
[86] M. Rudokas, M. Najlah, M.A. Alhnan, A. Elhissi, Liposome delivery systems for inhalation: a critical review highlighting formulation issues and anticancer applications, Med. Princ. Pract. 25 (Suppl. 2) (2016) 60–72.
[87] R.H.M. Hatley, S.M. Byrne, Variability in delivered dose and respirable delivered dose from nebulizers: are current regulatory testing guidelines sufficient to produce meaningful information? Med. Devices: Evid. Res. 10 (2017) 17–28.
[88] J. Cohen, D.S. Postma, W.R. Douma, J.M. Vonk, A.H. de Boer, N.T.H. ten Hacken, Particle size matters: diagnostics and treatment of small airways involvement in asthma, Eur. Respir. J. 37 (2011) 532–540.
[89] V.B. Pai, M.C. Nahata, Efficacy and safety of aerosolized tobramycin in cystic fibrosis, Pediatric Pulmonol. 32 (2001) 314–327.
[90] M.M. Clay, D. Pavia, S.P. Newman, S.W. Clarke, Factors influencing the size distribution of aerosols from jet nebulizers, Thorax 38 (1983) 755–759.
[91] P.W. Barry, C. O'Callaghan, Drug output from nebulizers is dependent on the method of measurement, Eur. Respir. J. 12 (1998) 463–466.
[92] J.L. Rau, A. Ari, R.D. Restrepo, Performance comparison of nebulizer designs: constant-output, breath-enhanced and dosimetric, Respir. Care 49 (2) (2004) 174–179.
[93] K. Leung, E. Louca, A.L. Coates, Comparison of breath-enhanced to breath-actuated nebulizers for rate, consistency, and efficiency, Chest 126 (5) (2004) 1619–1627.
[94] L. Pitance, G. Reychler, T. Leal, H. Reychler, G. Liistro, J. Montharu, et al., Aerosol delivery to the lung is more efficient using an extension with a standard jet nebulizer than an open-vent jet nebulizer, J. Aerosol Med. Pulm. Drug. Deliv. 26 (4) (2013) 208–214.
[95] S.P. Newman, G.R. Pitcairn, G. Hooper, M. Knoch, Efficient drug delivery to the lungs form a continuously operated open-vent nebulizer and low pressure compressor system, Eur. Respir. J. 7 (1994) 1177–1181.
[96] A. Berlinski, J.R. Willis, Albuterol delivery by 4 different nebulizers placed in 4 different positions in a pediatric ventilator *in vitro* model, Respir. Care 58 (7) (2013) 1124–1133.

[97] A.Y. Ip, T. Arakawa, H. Silvers, C.M. Ransone, R.W. Niven, Stability of recombinant consensus interferon to air-jet and ultrasonic nebulization, J. Pharm. Sci. 84 (10) (1995) 1210–1214.

[98] M.J. Asmus, G. Milavetz, A.I. Tice, M.E. Teresi, *In vitro* characteristics of tobramycin aerosol from ultrasonic and jet nebulizers, Pharmacother 21 (5) (2001) 534–539.

[99] K.M. Pedersen, V.N. Handlos, L. Heslet, H.G. Kristensen, Factors influencing the *in vitro* deposition of tobramycin aerosol: a comparison of an ultrasonic nebulizer and a high-frequency vibrating mesh nebulizer, J. Aerosol Med. 19 (2) (2006) 175–183.

[100] R.W. Niven, A.Y. Ip, S. Mittelman, S.J. Prestrelski, T. Arakawa, Some factors associated with the ultrasonic nebulization of proteins, Pharm. Res. 12 (1) (1995) 53–59.

[101] L.E.A. Hardaker, R.H.M. Hatley, *In vitro* characterization of the I-neb Adaptive Aerosol Delivery (AAD) system, J. Aerosol Med. Pulm. Drug. Deliv. 23 (Suppl. 1) (2010) S11–S20.

[102] J.B. Michotte, E. Staderini, D. Le Pennec, J. Dugernier, R. Rusu, J. Roeseler, et al., *In vitro* comparison of a vibrating mesh nebulizer operating in inspiratory synchronized and continuous nebulization modes during noninvasive ventilation, J. Aerosol Med. Pulm. Drug. Deliv. 29 (4) (2016) 328–336.

[103] K.H. Chang, S.-H. Moon, J.Y. Oh, Y.-S. Yoon, N. Gu, C.-Y. Lim, et al., Comparison of salbutamol delivery efficiency for jet versus mesh nebulizer using mice, Pharmaceutics 11 (192) (2019) 1–12.

[104] N. Murayama, K. Murayama, Comparison of the clinical efficacy of salbutamol with jet and mesh nebulizers in asthmatic children, Hindawi Pulm. Med. (2018). 1648652.

[105] M. Knoch, M. Keller, The customised electronic nebuliser: a new category of liquid aerosol drug delivery systems, Expert. Opin. Drug. Deliv. 2 (2) (2005) 377–390.

[106] C.-Y. Liu, H.-K. Ko, J.B. Fink, G.-H. Wan, C.-C. Huang, Y.-C. Chen, et al., Size distribution of colistin delivery by different type nebulizers and concentrations during mechanical ventilation, Pharmaceutics 11 (459) (2019) 1–10.

[107] M. Najlah, J. Parveen, M.A. Ahmed, A. Faheem, D.A. Phoenix, K.M. Taylor, et al., The effects of suspension particle size on the performance of air-jet, ultrasonic and vibrating-mesh nebulizers, Int. J. Pharm. 461 (102) (2014) 234–241.

[108] A. Ari, A.D. de Andrade, M. Sheard, B. AlHamad, J.B. Fink, Performance comparisons of jet and mesh nebulizers using different interfaces in simulated spontaneously breathing adults and children, J. Aerosol Med. Pulm. Drug. Deliv. 28 (4) (2015) 281–289.

[109] K.K. El Taoum, J. Xi, J.W. Kim, A. Berlinski, *In vitro* evaluation of aerosols delivered via the nasal route, Respir. Care 60 (7) (2015) 1015–1025.

[110] R.M. DiBlasi, Clinical controversies in aerosol therapy for infants and children, Respir. Care 60 (6) (2015) 894–916.

[111] G.F. Alvine, P. Rodgers, K.M. Fitzsimmons, R.C. Ahrens, Disposable jet nebulizers. How reliable are they? Chest 101 (1992) 316–319.

[112] J. Weers, Inhaled antimicrobial therapy – Barriers to effective treatment, Adv. Drug. Deliv. Rev. 85 (2015) 24–43.

CHAPTER 4

Metered dose inhalers (MDIs)

Anne Haaije de Boer[1] and Kyrre Thalberg[2,3]
[1]Department of Pharmaceutical Technology and Biopharmacy, Faculty of Science and Engineering, University of Groningen, Groningen, The Netherlands
[2]Inhalation Product Development, Pharmaceutical Technology & Development, Operations, AstraZeneca Gothenburg, Sweden
[3]Current address: Emmace Consulting AB, Medicon Village, Lund, Sweden

4.1 Introduction

Metered dose inhalers (MDIs), also referred to as pressurized metered dose inhalers (pMDIs) to emphasize the difference with dry powder inhalers (DPIs), deliver metered amounts of a drug solution, or suspension, that contain a single drug dose. The principal solvent (or dispersion medium) for MDI formulations is an organic propellant, a propellant mixture, or a mixture of propellant(s) and one or more co-solvent(s). The propellant (mixture) has a low boiling point and is compressed into a liquid that is contained in a small pressure vessel (canister). Upon release of a metered amount of propellant (mixture) with the desired drug dose from the pressurized canister, rapid propellant evaporation occurs. This disrupts the liquid jet into small droplets and creates the aerosol. MDIs are much smaller and more convenient devices to use than nebulizers and they are relatively cheap. These advantages explain why they are widely used for the treatment of asthma and COPD, but they are also relatively inefficient in delivering the drugs to the lungs, partly due to patient errors. These errors have been the subject of various studies and the primary concerns include poor coordination (of inhalation and dose actuation) and inhaling too quickly or too slowly [1]. With the emission of propellant, a greenhouse gas, into the air, MDIs are also harmful to the environment. For these reasons MDIs underwent a series of technological advancements since they were first introduced to the market as drug aerosol delivery devices in 1956 by Riker Laboratories Inc., currently 3 M [2]. In addition, various add-on devices were developed and design modifications were made to improve and ease the drug administration with MDIs. In the following paragraphs the basic design of MDIs, their aerosol generation principle, their pros and cons, and their performance (with and without add-on devices) are explained and discussed.

Inhaled Medicines
DOI: https://doi.org/10.1016/B978-0-12-814974-4.00001-8

4.2 Basic MDI design, manufacturing and working principle

The basic design of an MDI has been described before (e.g. Refs. [1,3,4]). The key components of an MDI (Fig. 4.1) are:

- a pressure reservoir (canister) that contains the drug formulation with one or more propellants and (mostly) small amounts of a co-solvent and one or more excipients,
- a dose metering chamber with a valve (lock) system, and
- an actuator including the canister-containing body with the mouthpiece and atomizing nozzle.

All these components may influence the aerosol formation process and, by that, the drug delivery to the respiratory airways (e.g. Refs. [3,5–7]). For each of these key components different design solutions exist. It is, therefore, the purpose of this paragraph to explain their properties and working principles, how they are manufactured and what effects design and production may have on their performance.

4.2.1 The canister

The canister is the bulk reservoir for the drug formulation which is under pressure [8,9]. As long as there is liquid in the reservoir, the pressure remains the same, being the saturation pressure of the liquid mixture in the canister which depends on the temperature however. Early reservoirs for the drug formulation were plastic coated glass vials [2], but currently preferred canisters are deep-drawn aluminum containers, with or without inner coating [10]. Compared to glass vials they are more compact, less fragile, lightproof, and also lighter than stainless-steel [3]. MDI canisters have standard volumes within the range from 10 to 22 mL and their wall thickness depends on the pressure inside. Coating of the inner side of the canister wall (and components of the metering

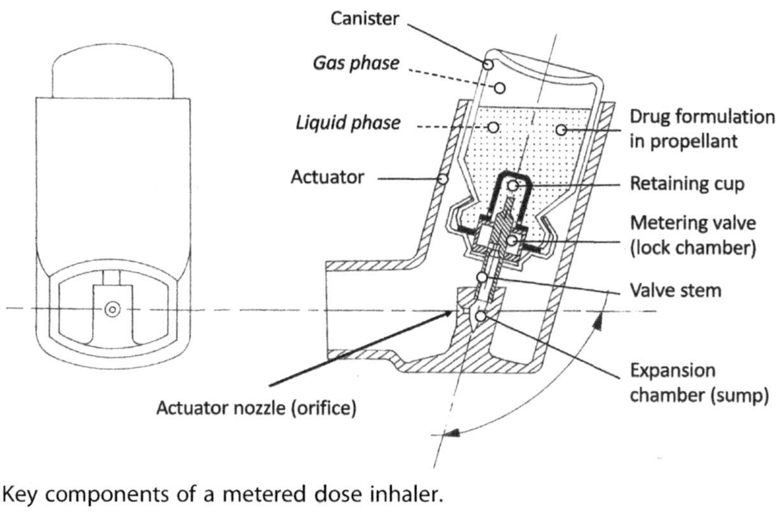

Figure 4.1 Key components of a metered dose inhaler.

valve) may be necessary for different reasons. It may prevent degradation of the drug due to interaction with the canister wall, reduce drug adhesion or particle deposition onto the canister wall and eliminate corrosion of the canister material in acid formulations. These undesired phenomena all contribute to poor stability and/or inconsistent dose delivery. Different coating techniques and materials are available and the choice depends largely on the type of drug formulation. Very often, fluorocarbon polymers with a high ratio of fluorine to carbon are used, including perfluoroalkoxyalkylene (PFA) and polytetrafluoroethylene (PTFE). These materials are chemically inert and have favorable surface energy performance. To improve their adhesion to the canister wall and the components of the metering valve, fluorocarbon polymers may be combined with non-fluorocarbon polymers (e.g. polyamides), but also epoxy-phenol resins are used for coating and some canisters have a thin glass inner lining. The different coating techniques include standard metal plate coating prior to shaping the material into the components or spraying, dipping and electrostatic dry-powder coating followed by curing for already formed components. Curing requires high temperatures up to 400°C to which only robust canisters can be subjected. Recently, a gentler gas plasma technique has been developed. This technique is carried out in vacuum and does not include exposure to very high temperatures ($<75°C$ for metal surfaces and $<45°C$ for polymeric surfaces). The technique creates an ultra-thin protective layer against degradation, deposition and corrosion and appears to be ideal for uniform treatment of components with complex shapes.

Different studies have been undertaken to quantify the drug-canister material interactions, reveal the relevant variables and understand the underlying mechanisms [11,12]. Traini et al. [12] used a previously presented surface component approach (SCA) for the stability of colloidal particles in MDI formulations based on two types of interactions: an apolar Lifshitz-van der Waals component and a polar Lewis acid-base component [13]. A profound difference in adhesion between different drugs and different canister materials exists and polymer coating of the aluminum canister wall significantly reduces the force of interaction. They used water-free propellant in their experiments because it is known that traces of water can have significant effect on the propellant polarity and, thereby, on the particle adhesion. It has also been suggested that the surface morphology (roughness) of the canister wall plays an important role in the particle adhesion [11].

Not only the design and material selection for the canisters are relevant, equally important is the impact of the manufacturing strategy on the performance of the MDI, particularly the filling of the canisters. Basically, two different methods exist: cold filling and pressure filling [14,15]. The basic steps of both methods are different and they also meet different formulation requirements. For cold filling, first a solution or suspension of the drug in a suitable liquid is made at room temperature. Meanwhile the propellant (or propellant mixture) is transferred to a pre-cooled vessel to make it liquid. Next, the propellant is mixed with the drug solution or suspension and the cooled mixture is dispensed into open canisters that are closed after filling with a head that contains the valve system for metering of single doses from the bulk reservoir. The valve-holding head is crimped into place with a rubber seal and the canisters are weighed to check for the correct amount of formulation. Finally, the canisters are submersed in water to warm the MDI to room temperature for a leakage test.

Pressure filling has two different routes, single-step and two-step, and uses pressure instead of low temperature. With the single-step procedure, the drug formulation and propellant are mixed under pressure and the pressurized mixture is forced through the valve system into the canister in reverse direction with the valve-holding head already crimped to the canister. With the two-step procedure, the drug solution or suspension is metered into the open canister before the valve-holding head is placed and crimped into position. Next, the propellant is driven under pressure in reverse direction through the valve into the canister. With the two-step pressure method, mixing of the drug solution or suspension occurs in the drug reservoir container. Pressure filling has the same checks on filling accuracy and leakage as cold filling. Although pressure filling is most prevalent in the manufacturing industry, cold filling is more versatile and has certain advantages compared to pressure filling [14]. Cold filling enables filling of both drug solution and drug suspension formulations. The technique is particularly suitable for highly concentrated (thick) suspensions and checking of the homogeneity after mixing with propellant before it is transferred to the canisters. The cooling of drug suspensions can also be used to control the crystallization of the drug, and by that, the particle size of the suspension. In contrast, single-step pressure filling is inappropriate for highly concentrated suspensions and there is no check on mixing with the propellant within the small container into a homogenous formulation. Many aspects of the filling process are critical to the MDI performance and they should be carefully monitored or controlled. They have been reviewed by Vallorz et al. [15].

4.2.2 The metering chamber with valves

Fig. 4.2 shows the principle of operation of an MDI metering chamber with two valves positioned at the bottom of the canister when the MDI is held in the correct upright position. The assembly is meant to separate an amount of liquid from the bulk reservoir that contains sufficient drug in solution or suspension for a single dose in reproducible manner. This requires that the concentration of drug (in solution or suspension) in the sampled volume is representative of the drug concentration in the bulk formulation. At rest, the top valve in Fig. 4.2 is open and there is communication between the bulk formulation in the canister and the metering chamber (A). In this condition, the metering chamber is filled with liquid and the bottom valve is closed. When the canister is pressed down, the hollow valve stem being blocked by the sump is pressed against the elastic force of a metal spring into the canister body. This closes the top valve and disconnects

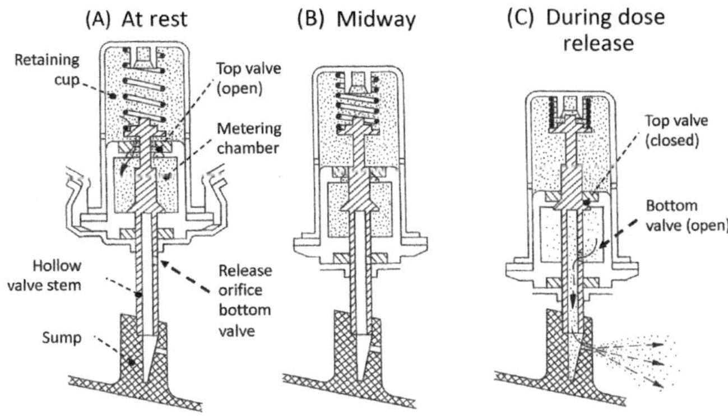

Figure 4.2 The principle of operation of a metering valve. At rest (A) the metering chamber is communicating with the bulk volume of the drug solution, or suspension, in the canister (or in the retaining cup: see text). When the MDI container is pressed, first the communication between the metering chamber and the bulk volume of the drug solution is ended [(B) midway situation] and next, communication between the metering chamber and the valve stem is established (C) to release the contents of the metering chamber.

the metering chamber from the canister with the bulk formulation (B). Further pressing to the position as shown in figure (C) opens the bottom valve which enables communication between the metering chamber and the ambient air having a much lower pressure than the propellant (mixture) in the metering chamber. This results in emptying of the chamber through the sump, having a small expansion chamber, and the spray orifice, and in rapid evaporation of the propellant(s). Several metered-dose valve designs are available, which are essentially lock systems, but their basic mechanism of action is the same [16]. They usually have a volume in the range from 25 to 100 μL [17]. It has been reported that the volume of the metering chamber in the range from 25 to 63 μL does not have a major effect on the particle size distribution of the aerosol for suspension formulations in HFA-227 propellant [5], although it may have an influence on other plume characteristics [18], as will be discussed below.

Metering chambers must meet several other criteria in addition to reproducible drug dose measuring [1], including a low leakage rate during storage, low moisture transmission to the drug formulation in the canister and metering valve, a low actuation force and low extractables and leachables.

Many MDI concepts also have a retaining cup between the metering chamber and bulk reservoir (Fig. 4.1). Such retaining cups contain the next few doses of drug. They may hold as many as four or more doses and they are refilled from the main reservoir through an opening in the base when the MDI is held in the position as during dose administration [16]. Their purpose is to prevent formulation from draining out of the metering chamber by the force of gravity when the MDI is held upside down and the filling opening of the metering chamber is facing the earth. The retaining cup eliminates 'loss of prime' (see

Section 4.5: The performance of MDIs) when the inhaler is used after a long storage period and also improves consistency of delivered dose at the end of the MDI's life cycle [1].

With the transition from CFC- to HFA-propellants (see Section 4.3) several design modifications and new seal materials became desired or necessary to meet the requirements of the new propellants and co-solvents. Challenges to deal with included reduction of loss of prime and imperfect sampling of flocculating suspension formulations, minimizing drug accumulation in restricted corners as a result of vibration during transportation and drug uptake on valve components, and elimination of drug degradation and the generation of unwanted particles [1].

These challenges have resulted in a series of improvements of the conventional valve design and currently different valve concepts are in use. Changes in the materials used for various valve components were driven by increased regulatory requirements on dosing uniformity and extractables and leachables levels. Pre-extracted ethylene propylene diene monomer (EPDM) rubber components have been introduced for the valve seals and thermoplastic elastomers for the canister sealing gasket to reduce these levels, but also other materials are available [10]. Further investigations are made to reduce drug uptake and swelling of the seal materials after exposure to the formulation. Elastomer swelling can cause deviation of the metering volume of the valve and changes in the friction of the moving stem.

4.2.3 The actuator and aerosol generation

The actuator of a MDI is an angled tube-like plastic part that comprises a housing for the canister (conduit) and a mouthpiece part with the sump (Fig. 4.1). Mostly, the angle between central axes of the conduit and the mouthpiece-part is larger than 90 degrees, but there are also 90 degrees concepts. The mouthpiece has a blocking point for the valve stem, referred to as sump, that has a small expansion chamber and an atomizing orifice (also, actuator or spray nozzle) through which the liquid dose is released and transformed into an aerosol. Actuators exist in different sizes to house canisters of different volumes and usually the mouthpiece has a dust cap [10]. The precise design of the sump with expansion chamber and atomizing nozzle has a great effect on the particle size distribution of the aerosol (e.g. Refs. [1,18,19]).

Since the introduction of the first MDIs to the market in 1956, the actuator design has been modified quite significantly. Originally, the conduit was much shorter and the mouthpiece section much longer [18]. The elongation of the conduit was meant to prevent accidental release of doses. The shortening of the mouthpiece reduced the size of the MDI to the benefit of a better portability, but it also reduced the lung dose as the result of a higher oropharyngeal deposition and it has a negative effect on the ability of patients to coordinate inhalation correctly with MDI actuation. Therefore, it introduced the need for an add-on device to compensate for the decline in performance, as will be discussed in Section 4.4. Different mouthpiece designs are in use and it has been described that a round shape widens the patient's mouth in order to open the pathway for the aerosol [20]. This reduces drug deposition on the tongue and teeth and leaves a greater part of the delivered dose for deposition in the lungs. However, the most essential actuator part for successful aerosol delivery to the lungs is the sump with the atomizing orifice. Atomization of the drug suspension or solution after releasing the contents from the metering chamber is the result of rapid evaporation of the propellant(s). The precise atomization mechanism has long been unclear, except for what is known from investigations by the automotive, chemical and nuclear industries about flash evaporation [21]. Flash evaporation is the phenomenon occurring when a saturated liquid stream passes through a narrowing, such as a throttle valve. The narrowing increases the local velocity which results in a decrease in pressure, as governed by Bernoulli's law of energy conservation. This sudden pressure drop causes the saturated liquid to boil instantaneously. A similar event takes place in the narrow atomizing orifice, although evaporation starts already after the pressure decreases in the valve stem and it continues into the expansion chamber of the sump (e.g. Ref. [18]). The evaporation process in these regions results in the formation of vapor cavities in the liquid and expansion of the total volume. When the gas-liquid mixture passes through the atomizing orifice, the pressure decreases further and flash evaporation starts to contribute to the droplet formation (Fig. 4.3). The rapid

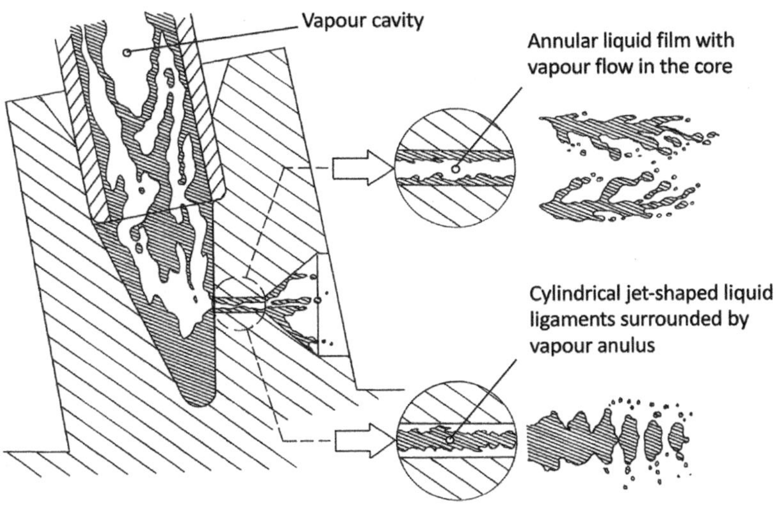

Figure 4.3 Proposed mechanism(s) for the droplet formation process as described by Lewis [18], Dunbar et al. [21], Clark [22], and Gavtash et al. [25]. Flash evaporation starts in the valve stem, creating vapor cavities, and is propagated in the sump and atomizing orifice due to sudden pressure drops as a consequence of a volume expansion (in the stem) and the increase in velocity (in the narrow atomizing orifice) respectively. This may result in the formation of an annular liquid film or jet-shaped liquid ligaments in the atomizing orifice from which droplets are liberated, depending on how the vapor-liquid distribution in the atomizing orifice is established.

Table 4.1 Properties of propellants.

Propellant	CFC 11	CFC 12	CFC 114	HFA 134a	HFA 227
Density of liquid (g/cm^3)	1.49	1.33	1.47	1.23	1.41
Viscosity (mPa.s)				0.21	0.27
Boiling point (°C)	22.8	−29.8	3.6	−26	−16
Vapor pressure (kPa)	89	566	182	572	390
Dipole moment (D)	0.46	0.51	0.50	2.06	0.93
Water solubility (ppm)[a]	130	120	110	2220	610
Log P (ethanol/H_2O)	2.0	2.2	2.8	1.1	2.1
Spec. heat cap. (kJ/kg.°K)				1.40	1.15
Atmospheric life time (years)	50	102	300	33	18.8
Global warming potential[b]	4000	8500	9300	2900	1300

HFA data from Solvay data sheet; CFC data from Myrdal et al. (2014) [30].
[a]At 30°C for the HFAs and 25°C for the CFCs.
[b]Relative to CO_2, being 1.

propellant evaporation has two unfavorable side effects. Firstly, both the vapor and residual liquid (aerosol droplets) are cooled to the saturation temperature (boiling point) of the propellant (mixture) at ambient pressure. For the HFA propellants (134a and 227), this is considerably below room temperature (see Table 4.1). The temperature shock is unpleasant for the patient and may cause a sudden cessation of the inhalation maneuver. Secondly, the rapid expansion of the gas volume causes the aerosol to leave the atomizing orifice of a conventional MDI at a high velocity of about 30 m/s [18] (see also Section 4.5).This increases the droplet deposition by inertial impaction in the oropharyngeal region and upper airways.

Various studies into the mechanism(s) of droplet formation in MDIs can be found in the literature (e.g. Refs. [21,22]). It has been found that the key parameters are the geometry and size of the atomizing orifice and the vapor pressure of the propellant (mixture). This knowledge has been used to develop the Modulite concept, in which also the volume of the metering chamber is considered [17]. According to this concept, the particle size distribution and plume speed can be controlled by varying these key variables. For a given HFA-propellant, the vapor pressure can be altered by adding non-volatile agents, such as ethanol, glycerol and polyethylene glycol (e.g. PEG 400).

Versteeg and Hargrave [23] showed that there is also an effect of the state of flow inside the MDI valve and expansion chamber on the nature of the external spray downstream of the atomizing orifice. Therefore, the design of the entire valve-nozzle combination is of great relevance to the atomization process.

Atomizing orifices have diameters typically in the range between 0.14 and 0.6 mm and a channel length of 0.6–0.7 mm [18]. There are limitations to the size and to the accuracy of manufacturing for very narrow nozzles that can be achieved with conventional molding techniques. Nozzle diameters smaller than 0.2 mm have to be prepared by laser-drilling. The relationship between the initial particle size distribution of the spray and the size of the atomizing orifice depends on the drug formulation. Generally, orifices with smaller diameters deliver finer particles at a lower spray velocity [18]. They also increase the atomization time and reduce the plume temperature [24]. In different studies empirical relationships between the atomizing orifice diameter and the fine particle fraction have been presented (e.g. Refs. [1,18]). Also, a theoretical model to predict the aerosol droplet size from MDIs has been published [25]. The model is based on two different presumed liquid precursor geometry variants being (1) cylindrical jet-shaped liquid ligaments surrounded by vapor annulus and (2) annular liquid film with vapor flow in the core (see Fig. 4.3). Numerical solutions of dispersion equations were used to predict the accession of instabilities in the liquid precursor surfaces and the size of the produced droplets. The predicted data seem to indicate that in addition to the vapor pressure of the propellant, also its viscosity and surface tension are relevant to the droplet formation process. The data presented showed fair agreement between both theoretical models, but the agreement obtained between either of these models and some measured data from literature was found to depend on the experimental data set used. This suggests that the droplet formation process may vary between MDI types and that the aerosolization of the drug formulation may be more complex than assumed. For instance, it has been suggested that the spray is pre-atomized on the basis of the observation that liquid ligaments are absent [21]. Measured data from literature for Sauter mean diameter as function of the aerosol emission time also show great variation suggesting that there is a variable presence of small numbers of very large particles (10–20 μm) in the spray.

The entire atomization process of a single dose has a duration in the range from <100 to 500 ms, depending on the volume of the metering chamber and the diameter (and length) of the atomizing orifice [21]. The duration also depends on the formulation and it has been reported that short spray durations are typically for formulations with a mass fraction of HFA 134a propellant >80% [26]. Such sprays have poor quality with unsteady peak exit velocity and changeable spray density. In the first 1–2 ms after opening of the release valve, the liquid entering the valve stem is completely evaporated [23]. In the next 5–10 ms, a spray of a vapor-liquid mixture is formed, followed by a fully developed spray in the next phase of dose emission. In this spray, fine droplets are in the core, and larger droplets at the edges of the spray. This observation of larger droplets at a longer distance from the central axis of the spray cone is confirmed by others (e.g. Ref. [21]) for CFC propellants, but not for HFA 134a. Other observations include ellipsoid and asymmetrical spray patterns in the vertical direction [7]. They were influenced by the atomizing orifice size, although no logical correlation could be obtained, and asymmetrical spray patterns were consistent with regional differences in particle size distribution. Various authors also have reported the observation of pulsations in spray density and cone angle occurring at a high frequency of 700 [21] to (500-)1000 Herz [23]. The large droplets appear to have a noticeable radial flow component and it has been suggested that this is the result of a rotating flow pattern in the atomizing orifice [23]. At the end of the atomization process the propellant runs out and the aerosol density gradually decreases to zero whereas the proportion of large droplets increases.

Observations as discussed above indicate that both temporal and spatial variations exist in the properties of the aerosols from MDIs. The effect is enhanced by ongoing evaporation downstream of the atomizing orifice. It has the consequence that the location of sampling for particle size analysis affects the outcome of the measurement. For instance, Dunbar et al. [21] measured volume mean diameters in the center of the spray for an HFA 134a propellant-only aerosol of 7 μm at a distance of 25 mm from the atomizing orifice versus 4 μm at a distance of 100 mm. According to Martin et al. [27] the rate of change in droplet volume as the result of evaporation, as derived from image analysis, is constant. They also found that the droplet evaporation is not significantly dependent on the relative humidity (RH between 10% and 100% at 37°C), nor is it different between pure propellant (HFA 227), or propellant with 15% ethanol and also with 0.2% sorbitol trioleate (see par. 4.3 for the explanation) They used rather large droplets from a needle with inner diameter of 2.5 mm for their experiments however, and they warned that their findings may not be valid for much smaller droplets (as from a MDI) nor for HFA 134a propellant having a much higher vapor pressure than HFA 227. Earlier it was reported by Lange and Finlay [28] that it is the absolute mole fraction of water vapor in the air, rather than the air temperature or the relative humidity, that affects the droplet evaporation of MDI sprays. They hypothesized that the effect of a high water vapor pressure is not droplet growth by condensation, but an interaction of the water molecules with the surfactant in the formulation causing a reduction in the evaporation rate of the propellant. A high water content may also have a strong effect on the particle morphology. Lange and Finlay [28] studied the morphology and solid phase of beclomethasone dipropionate dry particles from a solution in a mixture of HFA propellants 134a and 127 with different amounts of ethanol as co-solvent. Air humidification had no effect on the solid phase of the drug particles, being amorphous, but drying at low RH% resulted in solid spheroidal particles versus drying at RH% (above a critical threshold value) in highly porous particles. The critical threshold value for the RH% was found to depend on the amount of ethanol in the formulation and not on the type of propellant. In contrast with Lange and Finlay [28], Ivey et al. [29] did explain their findings with water condensation or ice deposition on the droplets during particle formation. Not only timely changes in droplet size occur, also spray distribution asymmetry may occur which has been related to droplet evaporation and sedimentation processes (e.g. Ref. [7]).

4.3 Drug formulations for MDIs

The formulation in an MDI is either a suspension or a solution. It consists of the drug and a suitable propellant, or propellant mixture, comprising the bulk of the formulation. Additionally, there can be some excipients in the formulation to improve overall product performance [30]. These excipients include volatile and non-volatile co-solvents for the drug, surfactants, suspension stabilizers, bulking agents and lubricants for the valve. Most marketed products are suspension formulations. For suspensions, the drug particles have to exhibit the correct aerodynamic particle size distribution to enable effective deposition in the target area. To prepare the drug in the correct aerodynamic size distribution for MDI suspensions, the same basic techniques can be used as applied for dry powder formulations. They include micronisation, controlled solvent crystallization, spray drying, spray-freeze drying, particle formation from liquid dispersion systems and super critical fluid processing. Explaining all these techniques in detail lies beyond the scope of this paragraph. A brief description of various techniques is given in chapter 5 about dry powder inhalers. For more detailed information the reader is directed to Chow et al. [31] for particle engineering in pulmonary drug delivery, Shoyele and Cawthorne [32] for particle engineering of biopharmaceuticals, and Myrdal et al. [30] for suspension formulations.

Poor physical stability is the major concern for suspension formulations [10]. Different processes, similar as defined for emulsions, may occur that deteriorate the uniformity of the suspension. They are referred to as creaming and flocculation. Although literature is not clear about the definitions for both phenomena, creaming is mostly considered as the migration of the dispersed phase under the influence of buoyancy. Particles rise through the medium or sink to the bottom (sedimentation), depending on their size, density relative to that of the continuous phase and viscosity of the continuous phase. In the state of creaming, particles are clustered but they remain to be identified as single entities. Therefore, creaming is reversible (e.g. by shaking the MDI). Flocculation occurs when the particles start clumping together to form larger entities. Small particles in the micron range inherently interact with each other to form agglomerates due to the relatively high co- and adhesive attraction forces compared with separation forces, such as the force of gravity. To reduce, or overcome the particle-particle interactions, ethanol and/or surfactants may be added to the formulation. Wu and da Rocha [33] showed with colloidal force microscopy that the forces of cohesion between salbutamol particles suspended in HFA can be reduced by 50% when less than 10% ethanol is added to the continuous phase. With a surfactant designed especially for HFA propellants, the cohesion force could be reduced even further. For improved stability of suspension MDIs also the use of hollow porous particles is beneficial [34]. The hollow structure of such particles prepared by spray drying, enables the propellant (mixture) to permeate into the particles' hollow spaces. This brings the particle density more in agreement with that of the continuous phase, which contributes to suspension homogeneity and, thus, dose uniformity [30].

Such particles have aerodynamic diameters within the respirable range (1–3 μm), although they are geometrically larger due to their low apparent density. In MDI formulations such particles consist of phospholipid and calcium chloride and they are carrier particles for the drug crystals that are associated with their large surface area. Therefore, these co-suspensions have greatly improved stability compared with suspensions of drug particles alone. This makes them perfectly suitable for double- and triple-therapy (fixed dose) products as the carrier particles with the drug crystals attached on their surface can be inhaled. The technique, developed by Pearl Therapeutics can handle doses up to about 100 μg per actuation [30], but it shows the same efficacy at the lower level down to 300 ng per actuation [34]. It has been shown that the co-suspensions exhibit generally efficient drug delivery to the lungs with fine particle fractions of more than 60% over the entire dose range. Some other techniques to reduce particle-particle interaction forces in MDI suspensions have been listed by da Rocha et al. [10].

The major constituent of drug formulations for MDIs is propellant or a propellant mixture. Propellants must be toxicologically safe, non-flammable, compatible with the drug formulated either as solution or suspension and they must have appropriate boiling points and densities [3,30]. They are stored in the MDI canister and contain the energy for atomization of the formulation upon actuation. Within the canister the compressed propellant is present in the liquid as well as in the gas phase. The saturated vapor pressure (gas phase) keeps the pressure in the canister the same throughout the MDI's lifetime for as long as there remains some liquid in the canister and providing that the temperature is kept constant. Exposing the MDI to extreme temperature changes increases the variability in spray characteristics. For a good stability of suspensions, the density of the propellant should approach that of the drug particles. For suspension MDIs the drug must be completely insoluble in the liquid components of the formulation in order to prevent Ostwald ripening [35]. This process of particle enlargement in suspensions affects the size distribution of the aerosol and becomes more likely when the size distribution is wider and the temperature variations to which the MDI is exposed become more frequent and more extreme. The presence of surfactants in the formulation may influence the Ostwald ripening process by increasing the solubility of the drug [36].

The first propellants used for MDIs were chlorofluorocarbon (CFC) compounds. Most important was dichlorofluoromethane (R-12 or CFC-12), but also CFC-114 (dichloro tetrafluoroethane) and C-11 (trichlorofluoromethane) with higher boiling points were used, mainly to adapt the vapor pressure and to facilitate the preparation of the formulation [3]. All three CFCs contributed significantly to the depletion of the ozone layer however and in 1987 an international treaty was agreed upon in Montreal (Montreal Protocol) that intended to terminate the manufacture of all CFCs, including those used in MDIs, per 1996 in the industrial, and 2010 in developing countries. The treaty was enforced in 1989 and in the same year a consortium (International Pharmaceutical Aerosol Consortium for Toxicity Testing: IPACT I) was formed by the pharmaceutical industry for toxicological testing of a potential CFC replacement candidate HFA 134a (tetrafluoroethane). One year later, a second consortium (IPACT II) followed to study the toxicity of a second candidate HFA 227 (heptafluoropropane). HFA 134a is meant to replace CFC-12 and both HFA-propellants have thermodynamic and physical properties closely resembling those of the chlorofluorocarbons. Positive opinions about the use of both HFA-propellants by the Committee for Proprietary Medicinal Products (CPMP) in 1994 and 1995 led to the development of new MDI formulations, as previously used excipients (as well as hardware components) were not compatible with the HFA propellants [30]. The vapor pressures and some other physical properties of most frequently used CFC and HFA propellants are presented in Table 4.1. Only a few CFC-MDIs remained permitted, till today, for products having no acceptable alternatives.

For some drugs, a mixture of propellants, or that of a propellant and a co-solvent (mostly ethanol, with the exception of Atrovent HFA which contains water as co-solvent) is used. Co-solvents either enhance the solubility of the drug [37] or that of other excipients (surfactant) in the MDI formulation [10], modify the dissolution behavior of the aerosol particles after deposition in the lungs [38], and/or influence the particle size distribution [39]. This shows that the role of the co-solvents can be quite complex and includes negative effects too which have been described quite in detail by da Rocha et al. [10] and the reader is directed to their overview for more detailed information.

Theoretically, the vapor pressure (P) of a gas mixture is given by Raoult's law:

$$P = x_a{}^*P_a + x_b{}^*P_b$$

Where x_a and x_b are the mole fractions of the components a and b in the mixture, P_a and P_b are the partial vapor pressures of the mixture components a and b respectively.

Deviations from Raoult's law do exist however, and Vervaet and Byron [40] showed that mixtures of HFA with ethanol exhibit a positive deviation for both HFA 134a and HFA 227: the vapor pressure remains almost the same up to 0.3 mol fraction of ethanol. A positive deviation is the result of a weaker interaction between ethanol and propellant molecules than either the ethanol-ethanol or propellant-propellant molecular interaction. This might explain why Martin et al. [27] could not observe an effect of the addition of ethanol (up to 15%) on the evaporation rate of HFA 227. A higher drug solubility does not always result in a higher respirable mass. Gupta et al. [37] prepared different BDP concentrations (approx. 0.3−1.2%) on the basis of the maximal solubility of this drug in HFA 134a-ethanol mixtures with 5−20% ethanol respectively. They found an almost linearly decreasing fine particle fraction (between approx. 55% and 25%) versus an increasing throat deposition (between 20% and 45%), both with increasing ethanol concentration (from 5% to 20%). The net result of the increasing drug concentration and decreasing respirable mass, results in a maximum in the respirable mass for the formulation with 10−15% ethanol. Findings like these should not be generalized however, as they may depend on the drug formulation. The effect of ethanol and surfactant on the size distribution of the aerosol for HFA 227 formulations according to Saleem et al. [39], is not related to the droplet evaporation rate but to the mechanism of droplet formation and they claimed different mechanisms for both excipients.

Not only the particle size distribution of the aerosol varies with the liquid composition of the MDI formulation, but also the plume temperature depends on the type of propellant and/or the presence of co-solvent [24,41]. A low temperature is the result of heat extraction from the inhaled air stream and the MDI hardware around the atomizing orifice that is necessary for the evaporation of the propellant. The lower the boiling point, the colder the plume may become, although the design of the MDI hardware (e.g. atomizing nozzle opening and metering volume) has an influence too. For instance, delivery though a narrow orifice decreases the mass ratio of (cold) aerosol to (warm) air and yields a warmer plume than delivery through a wide orifice. A larger propellant volume yields a colder plume as it requires more evaporative heat and also has a higher heat capacity. Obviously, the temperature is lowest in the proximity of the atomizing orifice as the heat transfer from warmer plume-surrounding air takes time [24]. A highly relevant plume characteristic to aerosol deposition is also its velocity [41]. A high velocity increases the momentum of the aerosol and a high momentum is associated with inertial impaction in the oropharynx. Therefore, the force of impaction of the spray ('spray force') onto an object facing the mouthpiece opening of the MDI is a good predictive measure for oropharyngeal drug deposition from an MDI. Gabrio et al. [41] concluded from measuring 28 marketed products that CFC-containing MDIs generally have higher spray forces than HFA-containing devices. Nevertheless, they found that the atomizing orifice diameter is more determinative than the type of propellant.

With the EU ratification of the Kigali Amendment to the Montreal Protocol in September 2018, a further global phasedown of hydrofluorocarbons as powerful greenhouse gasses has been initiated. This might include a complete ban of the HFAs currently used for MDIs and considering the growing pressure on European governments to take more action in stopping the climate change, it could happen in the short term. Potential strategies for dealing with this problem are presented and discussed by da Rocha et al. [10].

Various excipients in concentrations much lower than those of the propellant(s) and co-solvent(s) may be used, or be unintendedly present in MDI formulations. They are for instance surfactants and other suspension aids (e.g. polyethylene and propylene glycol), but there may also be leachables and extractables that are rather unwanted. Different interactions between drugs, propellants and surfactants have been investigated. They include primarily drug-drug particle interaction studies (e.g. Ref. [42]), drug-propellant interaction studies (e.g. Ref. [43]) and drug-surfactant interaction studies (e.g. Ref. [40]). The interactions are generally quite specific for a particular type of drug, drug combination, or drug formulation and have limited general value. They are also rather complex with the involvement of the influences of multiple components of the MDI formulation. For instance, Michael et al. [44] reported that the agglomeration behavior of drugs depends on the physical and chemical properties of both the drug substances and the suspension media. They found larger agglomerates (flocs) for salmeterol xinafoate compared with fluticasone propionate and both drugs formed larger agglomerates in HFA 134a compared with CFC 113. Agglomerates containing particles of both drugs were stronger compared to agglomerates of both drugs alone and their size depended on the dispersion medium. The interaction between two or more drugs has become particularly interesting since the acknowledgment of the benefits of combination therapies such as inhaled corticosteroid with a long-acting beta-agonist: ICS-LABA (e.g. Ref. [45]) and the positive recommendation of fixed-dose triple therapy, i.e. IC + LABA with a muscarinic antagonist: ICS-LABA-LAMA (e.g. Ref. [46]). The most common approach used for development of such combination MDIs is to use suspension formulations [30]. A good overview of the state of the art regarding drug-surfactant-propellant interactions in HFA formulations in the transition period from CFC to HFA propellants has been written by Vervaet and Byron [40]. A concern of particular interest is the presence of small amounts of leachables and extractables in the formulation, such as (for instance) silicone oil, a common valve lubricant for MDIs [1]. Its effect has been subject of various studies (e.g. Refs. [47,48]). Berry et al. [47] reported for low- and high-silicon valves that small amounts of respectively (approximately) 20 and 140 μg of the silicon oil from these valves may leach into a formulation of micronised corticosteroid in HFA 227 (with <5% ethanol w/w). They observed (using glass canisters) that silicon oil leads to a more rapid flocculation which potentially decreases the drug content uniformity (μg drug per actuation). They measured (with cascade impactor analysis) a great effect on the fine particle dose, which appeared to be on average 22.6% (range 13.0%–27.9%) lower for an MDI with high silicone oil content compared with an MDI with low silicone oil content. This decrease was accompanied with an increase in MMAD. They found no evidence for crystal growth, but hypothesized that silicon oil is promoting particle agglomeration. Laser diffraction analysis did not provide evidence for an effect of silicone oil on droplet evaporation rate. Fallon et al. [48] performed a similar study with a corticosteroid formulation in HFA 134a, using considerably higher amounts of silicone oil (up to 550 μg). They found only a small increase in particle size between 0 and 200 μg but did not mention the presence of a surfactant in the formulation. At silicone oil concentrations above 200 μg a further increase in particle size became even less pronounced and this non-linear behavior is confirmed by a study of Sherwood et al. [49]. A review on regulatory, safety and scientific aspects regarding extractables and leachables has been written by Markovic [50], who presented also strategies for their identification, quantification and monitoring.

4.4 Special MDI types and add-on devices for MDIs

The strong points and weaknesses of MDIs have been described in the past (e.g. Ref. [51]) and the disadvantageous performance properties were the driving force for the development of various add-on devices, like mouthpiece adapters (spacers and aerosol holding chambers) and dose counters, and the introduction of breath actuated MDIs. They are meant to provide solutions for:

1. high oropharyngeal deposition as the result of the fast-moving aerosol cloud, driven by gas (propellant) expansion,
2. loss of drug dose for inhalation due to poor synchronization between dose activation and inhalation ('hand-lung coordination problem'),
3. premature stopping of the inhalation maneuver when experiencing the unpleasant feeling of the cold spray in the mouth and throat area ('cold Freon effect'), and
4. continuing to use the MDI after the labeled number of doses have been taken due to the absence of a dose counter for the indication of the number of doses left in the canister.

The use of mouthpiece adapters is recommended by many national and international guidelines, as they basically provide solutions for most of shortcomings mentioned above. However, mouthpiece adapters and other add-on devices eliminate the portability advantage of the MDI [18]. They reduce the patient's freedom of movement and the increased inconvenience may eventually become at the cost of patient's adherence to the therapy. They also influence the drug delivery with MDIs quite significantly, except for the dose counters, and this makes them relevant to this chapter.

4.4.1 Mouthpiece extensions: Spacers and valved holding chambers (VHCs)

Different names are used for the mouthpiece extensions in literature, including spacers (e.g. Ref. [52]), (valved) holding chambers (VHCs) (e.g. Ref. [53]) and, mostly when used for the treatment of small animals, aerosol chambers. Originally spacers were simple tubular-like mouthpiece extensions (e.g. Refs. [54,55]) They had an open end and provided improvement only for the cold Freon effect and oropharyngeal deposition by increasing the distance between the atomizing nozzle and the patient's mouth. This gives more time for heat transfer between the inhaled air stream, having room temperature, and the cold droplets, as well as for droplet evaporation making the inhaled particles smaller. The increased traveling distance for the aerosol also slows down the particle velocity. Nearly all currently used MDI mouthpiece extensions have more complex designs with one or two valves, and some of them offer the possibility to use them in combination with a face mask. VHCs are meant to fire a dose into the device which traps and holds the aerosol for at least a few seconds. This eliminates the hand-lung coordination problem, adds some time for the aerosol to acclimate to the room temperature and for the aerosol particles to evaporate and become smaller. It also gives time to the patient to inhale the aerosol slowly, or in a few subsequent breaths. The one-way valve at the mouthpiece side prevents accidental exhalation through the VHC and the presence of this valve is the most significant difference between a spacer and a VHC.

VHCs are usually made of plastic (polycarbonate) and many of them have an antistatic coating to reduce electrostatic attraction and adhesion of aerosol particles on the inner surface. An early metal VHC of steel for children, with separate inlet and outlet valves for unidirectional flow through the chamber (Nebuhaler), was presented in 1995 [56]. It was shown that in a steel VHC, the time in which the aerosol concentration decreases by 50% is at least three times longer than in a plastic version of the same type (> 30s versus 9s). Currently, the Vortex (Pari) aluminum antistatic VHC is the only metal VHC available [57]. In developing countries cold drink (500 mL) plastic bottles can be a good alternative for expensive and unaffordable commercially available VHCs [58]. To solve the VHC portability problem for school children, collapsible paper VHCs have been proposed [59]. They are labeled for one-week use before they need to be disposed in connection with bacterial growth. Many examples of home-made VHCs exist, including toilet-paper rolls, and it has been claimed with a literature search that no clinically relevant differences are to be expected between delivery of a rapid bronchodilator via a home-made spacer and via a commercially available device [60]. This suggests that significant differences in delivered dose and in aerosol properties from different VHCs, as discussed in the next paragraph, do not necessarily result in differences in clinical effect.

The instructions for maintenance and cleaning are nearly the same for VHCs made of plastic, and those made of plastic (or metal) with an antistatic coating. Prior to first use, as well as once every week during use, the completely disassembled VHC must be washed by hand and soaked in diluted household detergent for 15 minutes while agitating gently. Next, the parts have to be placed in a vertical position for drip drying and to be re-assembled after it has been assured that all parts are completely dry. Rinsing with clean water should be discouraged for VHCs without antistatic coating as the inner surface of all parts has to be coated with surfactant. Neither may dish towels be used for all types of VHCs. It has been found that the type of detergent is not critical, nor its dilution, as long as the detergent is ionic. Detergent coating may increase the fine particle dose of salbutamol by nearly 40% [61]. The obtained improvement depends on the drug formulation and the ambient relative air humidity however, as shown by Rottier et al. [62].

VHCs have different shapes, sizes and volumes, varying from 140 mL (Philips Respironics OptiChamber Diamond) to 700 mL (GSK Volumatic): see Fig. 4.4. They have an opening on both ends for inserting the MDI mouthpiece, and releasing the aerosol respectively. Some VHCs are MDI-specific regarding the shape of the

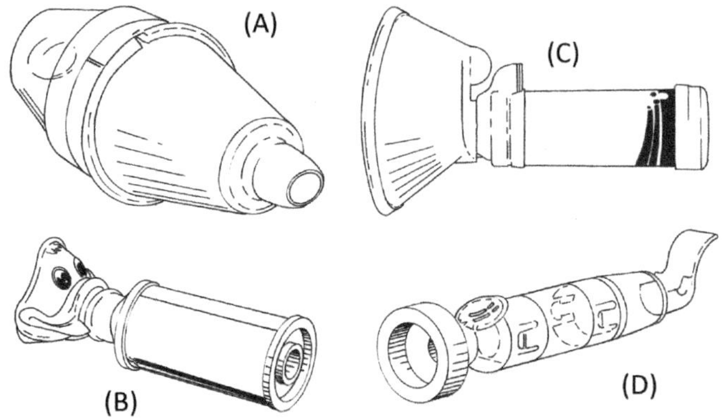

Figure 4.4 Different designs for Valved Holding Chambers (VHCs) resulting in different shapes and volumes as shown for Volumatic, GSK (A), Vortex aluminum VHC with baby face mask, Pari (B), AeroChamber Plus Flow-Vu with face mask, Trudell Medical (C) and Babyhaler, GSK (D) respectively.

mouthpiece opening; some are for general purpose having a soft rubber MDI-adapter. The aerosol release opening has a mouthpiece for the patient and a one-way valve preventing exhalation through the chamber. Reverse flow devices are special types of spacers (e.g. Refs. [55,63]). In such devices, the aerosol from the MDI is fired away from the patient into a small chamber or collapsible bag.

4.4.2 Face masks

Most spacer mouthpieces can adapt a face mask which is beneficial to young children who find mouthpieces difficult to use [63]. They need to use the smallest holding chambers as children have a low tidal flow rate and a small tidal volume [56]. The Global Initiative for Asthma consider MDI-VHC combinations with face masks as the preferred delivery systems for drug administration to children <4 years with asthma [64]. This does not include neonates however, as most new-born children appear to be unable to generate sufficient negative inspiratory pressure to open the valve of a VHC [65]. Very much in this respect depends on correct fitting of the face mask [66]. Even a small leak of less than 0.2 cm^2 along the circumference of the mask can decrease the pressure in the mask downstream of the valve and reduce the delivered dose both substantially [67]. Hence, a good design and appropriate size are crucial. Key issues for mask design have been presented and discussed by Morton and Mitchell [68]. Sanders and Bruin [69] highlighted the important points for optimal spacer use.

4.4.3 Breath actuated MDIs

A different approach for overcoming the hand-lung coordination problem is with a breath actuated MDI. Such breath actuated inhalers, also referred to as BAI-MDIs (e.g. Ref. [70]), have a design that includes a spring contacting the bottom of the

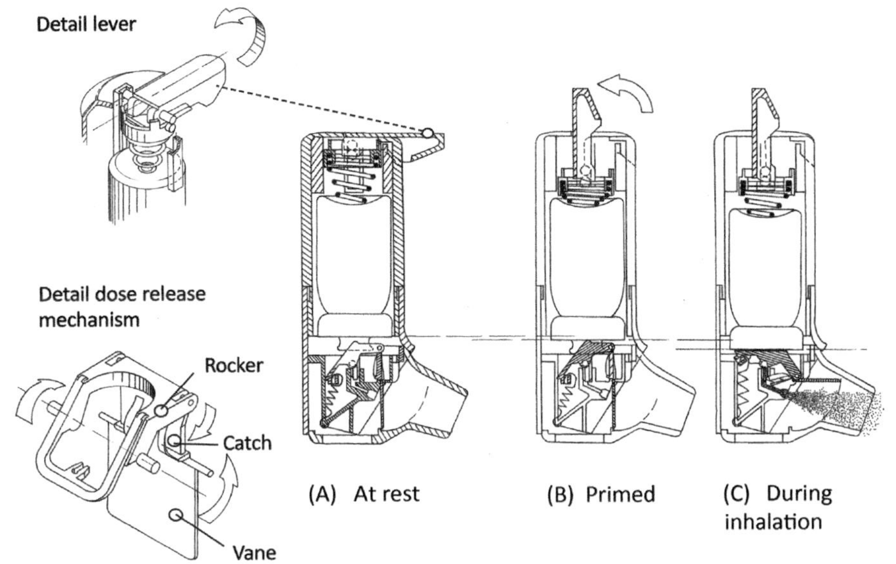

Figure 4.5 The working principle of a breath actuated MDI showing the device at rest (A), after priming (B) and during inhalation (C). See the text for a more detailed explanation.

canister and a dose release system as shown in Fig. 4.5. The dose release system of a BAI-MDI consists of three tiltable parts, being a rocker, a catch and a vane (Fig. 4.5). Priming of the MDI (Fig. 4.5B) equals compression of the spring with a lever on top of the MDI against the canister bottom when it is held in the upright position. This causes the top of the canister to make contact with the rocker. When the patient inhales, the vane opens the mouthpiece channel. This causes the catch to move aside and the rocker to tilt by the pressure of the loaded spring (Fig. 4.5C). Because the distance between the pivot point to the top of the rocker in the tilted position is shorter than that in the starting position, the canister is pressed further down to discharge the contents of the metering chamber. This automatic dose release during inhalation eliminates the need to synchronize both actions actively. A small spring, attached to the rear end of the rocket, brings it back in the starting position after the lever has been reset to remove the load of the spring on top of the canister.

The first breath actuated MDI on the market was the Autohaler (Riker) in 1970. The device was noisy and required a high flow rate to open the vane [3]. The advanced second generation Autohaler (3 M Pharmaceuticals) has a valve switch point of less than 30 L/min and is much more convenient to use. Even patients with severe inspiratory limitation are able to actuate the Autohaler on their first or second attempt [71]. More devices according to the same principle followed the Autohaler [3]. They include so-called breath coordinated inhalers, which either control the inhaled flow rate, or allow air to flow past the triggering mechanism only when the MDI is depressed.

A high preference for the use of breath actuated MDIs is reported from a study with elderly subjects [70], mainly because they are easier to use [72]. In accordance with that, the percentage correct use in both studies appeared much higher for BAI-MDIs than for conventional MDIs. Ruggins et al. [73] showed that also acutely wheezing children in the range of ages between 4 and 13 years are capable of operating the Autohaler successfully in terms of switching the valve to release a dose. They observed only 1% failure against 26% failure with a dry powder inhaler (Rotahaler). They also reported that not all patients benefit from a clinically significant improvement with the Autohaler and mentioned a concern about glottic closure after firing a dose.

4.4.4 MDIs with reduced plume velocity

Attempts to decrease the plume velocity from MDIs are known [3], referring to Spacehaler (Celltec Medeva), Tempo (Map Pharmaceuticals) and BronchoAir (BronchoAir Medizintechnik). These devices use different principles to reduce the forward momentum of the spray. The Tempo has been used for pulmonary delivery of an investigational orally inhaled dihydroergotamine (mesylate). It showed good tolerability [74] and fast and consistent absorption via the lung [75]. This device has also been in development for treatment of type 1 and type 2 diabetes, but to date no publications about this development can be found in the scientific literature. The principle of operation of BronchoAir has been described by Steckel and Müller [76]. They could show that the improvement in delivered fine particle fraction with the BronchoAir depends on the type of formulation and that for some formulations a conventional MDI with appropriate VHC may be better.

4.4.5 Dose counters

Dose counters do not contribute to the quality of the MDI performance during normal life time but they may positively influence the therapy, as by knowing the number of doses left in the device, patients are less likely to forget timely replacement of a device that starts 'running empty' [77]. A confusing factor for patients in this respect is the excess formulation (in volume frequently equal to at least 20–30 doses) in the MDI canister [1]. In a questionnaire among fifty asthmatic children regarding their methods for determining the residual doses in their MDI, the often-recommended canister flotation method was regarded as ineffective, whereas in nearly one-third of the time obstruction of the valve stem with water was reported [78]. Hence, 74% did not know how many actuations were left in their canisters and all reported to use their MDI until it can no longer be heard that a dose is released. Rubin et al. [78] also measured under laboratory conditions that CFC-containing MDIs typically contain 86% more actuations than labeled, versus 52% more for HFA-containing MDIs. In a study with 17 patients, 15 subjects reported never to float their canister, but to shake it, 1 subject test-fired a dose and 1 subject reported to notice a change in the taste of the aerosol [79]. In a study of the same authors with 100 participants, between 155 and 289 doses (on average 224) were derived from a 200 dose MDI before it was considered empty [79]. Counters indicating the number of doses left are relatively new to MDIs, but the innovation has greatly increased since the issuing of a guidance document for their introduction onto MDIs by the FDA in 2003, as reported by Stein et al. [1], who also summarized the key requirements from this document. Since the start of this millennium, dose counters have already evolved from add-on to build-in (device-integrated) systems. Early studies have shown that patient satisfaction with MDIs having dose counters is very high, up to 95% [80], and it has been confirmed that they improve the adherence to the therapy. Price et al. [81] compared respiratory-related emergency department (ED) visit rates in (120,709) patients with asthma, COPD, or both, using salbutamol MDIs with, versus MDIs without dose counters. They reported that the ED visit incidence rate during a 1-year period was 45% lower in the MDI with dose counter cohort (93,980 subjects) than in the MDI without dose counter cohort (26,729 subjects). Dose counters also appear to be useful for controlling the adherence to the therapy, which for children is frequently overestimated by their parents [82].

4.5 The performance of MDIs

Therapies with inhalation systems depend on inhaler performance and inhaler use. Numerous studies can be found about *in vitro* MDI performance, with or without VHCs, using different inspiratory and environmental conditions and spray characterization principles. Also, numerous studies on the clinical efficacy of MDIs with and without add-on devices exist and the number of variables (referring to MDI types, formulations, add-on devices, conditions and patient groups) is simply too large to present a complete overview. MDI performance concerns various aspects, including the stability of the drug formulations, the consistency of delivered dose and the characteristics of the released aerosol. Because of the differences in the properties between CFC and HFA propellants that affect all of these performance aspects, great care should be taken in considering findings obtained with CFC-containing MDIs also true for HFA-containing devices. Many studies from before the propellant transition period may be of lower significance to currently used MDIs. An example is given by Barry and O'Callaghan [83] who tested the delivered fine particle mass (FPM $<5\,\mu m$) from two different salbutamol MDIs using two different VHCs: Nebuhaler (AstraZeneca) and AeroChamber (Trudell Medical). The salbutamol MDIs ($100\,\mu g$) differed in the type of formulation, being a CFC-MDI (Ventolin, Allen & Hanburys) and a HFA-MDI (Airomir, 3 M Pharmaceuticals) respectively. They found more than twice the delivered FPM from the Airomir compared with the Ventolin via the Nebuhaler versus a 1.7 times higher FPM via the AeroChamber. When the Nebuhaler was coated with static dissipative paint, the difference between the FPMs from both MDIs via the VHCs almost dissipated too, in spite of a difference in plume velocity: 3.1 m/s for the Airomir and 5.3 m/s for the Ventolin. Without VHC, Barry and O'Callaghan [83] measured the highest FPM (46.3 μg) and smallest MMAD (5.2 μm) for the Ventolin, versus 37.2 μg and 5.7 μm for the AeroChamber.

It has been well documented that some early CFC-only MDIs delivered aerosols with high plume velocities of greater than 30 m/s [84]. As a consequence, reported oropharyngeal depositions from MDIs were initially high, even up to approximately 80–90% of the delivered dose [85,86] and total lung depositions were generally very low within the range from 2.5% to 15% for the standard devices with only a few exceptions, mostly for salbutamol [87]. Newman and Newhouse [55] compared the total lung and oropharyngeal deposition from MDIs, with and without VHC, of ^{99}Tc labeled drugs presented in eight different MDI studies in the period 1989–1995. On average, the use of a VHC in these studies reduced oropharyngeal deposition from 67.0% (range 47.0–79.5%) to 15.4% (range 6.3–31.8%). This 51.6% difference did not equate the increase in total lung deposition however, which improved (on average) only from 15.0% (range 8.8–25.9%) to 20.8% (range 9.3–34.3%). In a paired comparison, some VHCs resulted even in a lower total lung deposition compared with the MDI alone and the lack of agreement must be contributed to losses in the VHC by sedimentation of large particles and inertial impaction of particles traveling fast. The smaller the volume of the VHC, the greater these losses seem to be [55]. Comparable data were presented by Steckel and Müller [76]. They referred to König [88], who concluded from reviewing 'recent studies' that the use of a spacer or VHC for the administration of a bronchodilator does not seem to have an advantage over an MDI alone for adults and older children.

Several performance and handling issues are the same for CFC and HFA MDIs in spite of the advances made in drug formulation and device design that accompanied the CFC-HFA propellant transition. HFA propellants have not provided a solution for the co-ordination problem, nor did they consistently reduce the high plume velocity and increase the plume temperature. Some HFA 134a sprays are even colder than CFC 11/12 formulations, as the temperature depends also on the metered volume, the diameter of the atomizing orifice and whether there are excipients in the formulation that increase its boiling point or not [24]. The results presented by Brambilla et al. [24] seem in agreement with those of Gabrio et al. [41], who also showed that neither all HFA 134 formulations have lower impaction force compared with CFC formulations, as this too depends more strongly on the actuator orifice design. A greater effect from the CFC to HFA transition process has been reported for the particle size in the aerosol of inhaled steroids [9]. For BDP, a reduction in average particle diameter from 3.5 to 4.0 μm for CFC-BDP (with the drug in suspension) to 1.1 μm for HFA-BDP (which is rather a solution) could be achieved as measured with CI technique [89]. This increased the respirable fraction significantly and in a study with healthy volunteers, a lung deposition with HFA-BDP of 55–60% (of the actuator dose) was found with only 29–30% of the dose deposited in the oropharynx [89]. In comparison, lung deposition with a CFC-BDP was only 4–7% versus 90–94% deposition in the oropharynx. Also, the distribution pattern of the drug from both MDIs appeared to be different, with the drug spread evenly over the entire lung for the HFA-BDP and drug primarily delivered to the central airways, with very little penetration into the peripheral airways for the CFC-BDP. The data could be confirmed in a study with asthmatics and another study in healthy volunteers [90]. Not all HFA-MDIs deliver the same fine aerosol however. For fluticasone dipropionate HFA, a median diameter of 2.8 μm has been reported from laser diffraction measurement [91] versus 3.5 μm for CFC-budesonide. This is a difference by only 0.7 μm. In the same study by de Vries et al. [91], a volume median diameter of 1.9 μm for HFA-BDP and HFA-ciclesonide was presented. This is slightly larger compared with the diameters mentioned by Leach [89] for HFA-BDP (1.1 μm) and for HFA-ciclesonide (1.0 μm) from cascade impactor analysis respectively [9]. Comparing data obtained with different measuring principles is arguable however. The laser diffraction measurements were conducted at a distance of approx. 40 mm from the atomizing orifice, whereas the distances for the aerosol to travel before it reaches the stages of an impactor are much longer. De Vries et al. [91] found only a negligible effect of flow rate (20–40 L/min), relative humidity of the ambient air (35–70%) and the number of doses taken from the MDI on the size distribution in the aerosol for all four devices tested. However, they did measure a gradually decreasing metered drug mass between the first and last dose of the labeled contents for fluticasone HFA suspension MDIs with 125 and 250 μg per actuation. It decreased from 106% (first) to 63% (last) and from 104% (first) to 78% (last) of the labeled drug dose for the 125 and 250 μg MDI respectively. In contrast, delivered drug dose from a 50 μg/actuation fluticasone MDI of the same brand (Flixotide, GSK) remained constant. Also, the plume velocity may slow down with the number of doses delivered from a MDI, although considerable differences between MDIs exist in the extent of velocity decrease [92]. For some devices, the decrease is only measurable at short distance (50 mm) from the atomizing nozzle, whereas at a much longer distance (200 mm), the velocity remains the same over the entire labeled dose range. Velocities presented by Dal Negro et al. [92] at short distance from the atomizing nozzle, vary within the range from 25 to 65 m/s. For comparison, the previously mentioned Spacehaler has a plume velocity of only 2 m/s [93]. In a study with ^{99m}Tc-labeled beclomethasone dipropionate a much higher lung dose from Spacehaler (23% of metered dose) was reported compared to administration with a conventional MDI (12.8%) [94]. However, no difference in lung distribution pattern could be shown. The reduction in oropharyngeal deposition from the Spacehaler was more substantial (from 73.6% for the conventional MDI to 27.9%). The discrepancy between the great reduction in oropharyngeal deposition and only marginal improvement of lung deposition can be explained with a much higher retention around the atomizing nozzle for the Spacehaler (48.0% versus 12.4%). Equivalent bronchodilator effects were achieved with the Spacehaler compared to a conventional MDI with Volumetic in asthma patients with reversible obstructive airway disease [93].

Two characteristic and unfavorable performance aspects of MDIs are 'loss of prime' (LOP) and 'rise, or fall of dose' (e.g. Refs. [10,16]). Loss of prime is an aspect of concern for new devices or MDIs that are not used on a regular basis and are left to rest for considerable time (days to weeks) in between. On the first actuation of new devices, or on dose actuation following a long period of disuse, a (very) low dose may be delivered because propellant has drained somehow from the metering chamber. The risk depends on the valve design and the presence of a retaining cup. When the metering chamber is filled with formulation again, the MDI should operate as required. Rise, or fall of dose (also referred to as loss of dose) is a phenomenon confined to suspension formulations and its occurrence depends also on the design of the valve system and the tendency of the formulation to cream. A rapid creaming results in inhomogeneity of the formulation and when the time between shaking the canister and firing a dose is too long, the refill of the metering chamber (or retaining cup) may either be primarily propellant alone or contain too many drug particles. This depends on the position of the opening of the metering chamber, or that of the retaining cup, and whether creaming results in sedimentation, or not. When loss or fall occurs on a regular basis, the drug concentration in the bulk supply changes significantly and drug doses at the end of the MDI's lifetime may become either too high, or too low.

The aforementioned example regarding loss of dose indicates that MDI performance relies strongly on good formulation stability and correct inhaler use. Many aspects concerning the drug stability and consistency of delivered dose have already been addressed in the previous paragraphs about devices and formulations. They are only partly the same for CFC- and HFA-containing MDIs. It may be clear that suspension formulations cause the greatest concerns, particularly since the list of surfactants, used as suspension stabilizers, that are compatible with HFA propellants and FDA-approved for MDI formulations, is short. Most of them require the use of a co-solvent to enhance their solubility [10]. Many of the undesirable instabilities can be explained by the physical and chemical properties of the dispersed powder in the liquid propellant system. A review providing detailed understanding of these properties has been written by O'Donnell and Williams [95]. Methods for evaluating the physical and chemical particle stability in suspension-based MDIs were presented by Ooi et al. [43] and D'Sa and Chan [96].

Different studies have shown that incorrect use of MDIs is highly prevalent and persistent, and failure percentages (on at least one, or more handling steps) vary in the approximate range between 70% and 90%. Training may decrease error use, as shown in a British study, from 86% during the first score test, via 78% during a second, to 66%

during a third test respectively [97], which is still disturbingly high. However, physicians and nurses may not be the best instructors as they showed only 28% and 15% correct use in a Spanish study versus 9% for patients [98]. From a similar study held in the Toronto Hospital, Canada, it was concluded that medical personnel responsible for monitoring and instructing patients in optimal inhaler use, have insufficient skills with these devices themselves [99]. They never receive formal training in the use of inhalation devices and their knowledge and practical skills are roughly proportional with the time a system has been in clinical use. Giraud and Roche [100] found evidence that MDI misuse results in decreased asthma stability. General practitioners measured an asthma instability score (AIS) based on adverse events among 4078 adult asthmatics using MDIs for their therapy who produced 3955 useful questionnaires. They computed 71% misuse, of which 47% was due to poor hand-lung co-ordination. Asthma was significantly less stable in misusers (AIS = 3.93) than in correct users (AIS = 2.86).

Because of poor hand-lung co-ordination in most patients, many national and international guidelines recommend to use MDIs only in combination with VHCs, particularly for neonatal and pediatric patients [101]. Alternatively, breath-actuated MDIs can solve the co-ordination problem, but they seem better suited for adult patients because they provide no solution for the adverse effects from a high plume velocity and a cold spray. In a comparative evaluation study with 18 asthma patients using a standard MDI and a breath-actuated (BAI-) MDI (Autohaler) it was found that (10) patients having good co-ordination did not benefit from the BAI-MDI: their lung depositions and bronchodilator effects from both devices were equivalent: 18.6% for MDI versus 17.3% for BAI-MDI [102]. In contrast, for (8) patients with poor co-ordination, the lung deposition improved significantly from using the BAI-MDI (yielding a lung deposition of 20.8%) compared with the conventional MDI (7.2%). Remarkably, differences in oropharyngeal deposition were relatively small between all inhalations (using both devices), varying from 59% to 71%. Also, noteworthy, patients showing good co-ordination with a conventional MDI performed less good when they were extra trained how to use their inhaler optimally. Their lung deposition decreased from 18.6% to 12.8%. The performances of VHCs have quite extensively been studied, either in comparison with the performances of the MDIs alone, or in a comparative evaluation of different VHC designs. It is not the objective of this paragraph to give a complete survey however and reference is made to only a few studies to draw the readers' attention to the many effects that may be expected with VHCs, with or without face masks. In a comparative *in vitro* evaluation study with 7 different spacer designs it was found that the FPM from a VHC depends on its volume and on the drug type [103]. The largest VHCs in this study (Fisonair, Nebuhaler and Volumatic) delivered a significantly higher dose of disodium cromoglycate compared with the smaller devices. In a follow-up study the AeroChamber (145 mL), Babyhaler (330 mL) and Volumatic (700 mL) were compared [52]. In this follow-up study with BDP, Salmeterol Xinafoate and Fluticasone dipropionate MDIs, not the largest VHC (Volumatic) delivered the highest FPM, but the Babyhaler (on average 37% of the FPM from the MDI), in spite of a greater variability in delivered dose for the Babyhaler than for both other VHCs. No significant effect of the flow rate (20 versus 60 L/min) on FPM was reported. In contrast, a delay of 20 s between dose activation and inhalation substantially decreased FPM delivered via the VHC. Delivered FPM after 20 s delay for BDP (50 μg), Salmeterol Xinafoate (25 μg) and Fluticason dipropionate (50 μg) was only 15.2%, 17.2% and 7.6% of the label claim for the Babyhaler (as best performing VHC), versus 6.6%, 8.4% and 7.6% for the Aerochamber (as worst performing VHC) respectively. Dalby et al. [104] and Slator et al. [105] concluded that the effect of flow rate may depend on the type of VHC and whether the VHC is antistatic, or not, respectively. Using a two-level, three factor full-fractional design of experiments to assess the influence of VHC type, flow rate and inhalation delay on MDI performance characteristics it was found that the inhalation delay has the greatest influence of all variables on most output parameters [106]. Inhalation flow rate and time delay interact with each other in the breathing pattern through a VHC and Csonka and Lethtimäki [53] investigated its effect on the delivered dose from two different VHC designs using a breathing simulator. They measured an increasing delivered dose from a salbutamol MDI to a filter via an Optichamber Diamond (140 mL) and a Babyhaler (350 mL) using increasing tidal volumes (from 30 to 200 mL). They also reported that the effect of tidal volume is greater than that of the respiratory rate (25 versus 50 min^{-1}) and found, in contrast with the previously mentioned data of Barry and O'Callaghan [52,103], the highest output for the smallest VHC for all test conditions. A review manuscript specifically about the differences between small versus large, and conductive versus non-conductive VHCs respectively, has been written by Dissayanake and Suggett [107]. They concluded that significant *in vitro* performance differences exist, but also that literature regarding the performance of a large number of different VHCs is substantially contradictory. This suggests that unrecognized factors have played a significant role in the performance of the MDI-VHC combinations tested. It could be the shape of the VHC rather than its volume, the design of the valve [108], the type of construction or coating material [109,110], or the ambient air conditions. The relative humidity of the air may have a great effect of the delivered dose from a VHC, the magnitude of the effect for the same VCH being dependent on the drug formulation [62]. Dissayanake and Suggett [107] also mentioned a lack of clinical studies of adequate scale and design to decide whether *in vitro* differences result in meaningful differences in clinical effect. Lipworth and Clark [111] compared salbutamol plasma concentrations in healthy volunteers from lung deposition via a small VHC (Aerochamber) and two larger ones (Nebuhaler and Volumatic) with that from the MDI alone. They measured the highest peak plasma level (C_{max} after 5 min) from Nebuhaler (8.87 ng/mL), versus 6.54 ng/mL (Volumatic), 5.51 ng/mL (Aerochamber) and 4.37 ng/mL for the MDI, an increase from lowest (MDI) to highest (Nebuhaler) by a factor 2.0. The depositions from the Nebuhaler and Volumatic were significantly higher compared to the deposition from the MDI without spacer, but these differences did not significantly change heart rate and tremor. Only plasma potassium level was significantly higher from Nebuhaler than from the MDI without VHC. Lipworth and Clark [111] also argued that the difference made by a VHC is not in the lung deposition, but in that in the oropharynx. The reduction in upper airways deposition leads to less systemically available drug [112] and this may permit to give higher doses [113]. Finally, whether the dose from a VHC as measured *in vitro* is delivered effectively to small children indeed, depends also on the face masks used and how well the children co-operate with the procedure of aerosol administration (e.g. Ref. [114]). Various studies have shown that the face mask is a key factor in this procedure and for a child with a crying breathing pattern the amount of drug administered may be smaller than 1% of the labeled dose [115].

4.6 Discussion and future perspectives

The future of MDIs may depend very much on the outcomes of the climate debate and the political willingness and decisiveness to take action in limiting the climate change. Global warming is a major concern and it has in a number of European countries already led to drastic proposals and decisions. One of them is the ratification of the Kigali amendment to the Montreal Protocol by the European Union (September 2018), which is meant to bring about a global phasedown of the HFA propellants. This may also affect the use of HFAs in MDIs and make expensive toxicity testing, drug reformulation and device re-design programs for alternative propellants necessary again as required earlier for the CFC-HFA transition. Alternative propellants may be available in hydrofluoroolefins [10], but DPI development has made considerable advancements too and seems to have much greater potential as suitable alternative for MDIs compared to when the CFC-HFA transition took place. Not to mention that various alternative and highly innovative wet aerosol delivery principles have become available in the past two decennia as well. Limitations of MDIs that are difficult to overcome are the low dose range and the stability of the drug formulation, particularly when they are suspensions. This makes formulation of high dose biopharmaceuticals, like proteins and vaccines, for MDIs almost impossible as they need high amounts of excipients (sugars) for their stabilization, often more than 75% of the total mass (e.g. Ref. [116]). The number of recent protein and peptide formulation studies for MDIs is very low anyway and confined mostly to suspension stability studies (e.g. Refs. [117,118]). This may testify to the difficulties encountered in development of (high dose) biopharmaceuticals for MDIs. The hand-lung co-ordination problem seems to have found solutions in breath-actuated devices and the use of VHCs, but for pediatric patients BAI-MDIs are not suitable because of the high flow rate needed for valve switching and dose activation, whereas aerosol delivery via VHCs is very inefficient. Decreasing the trigger flow rate for BAI-MDIs makes them very instable and sensitive to uncontrolled movement. Antistatic coatings have improved the performance of VHCs, but mostly they deliver only a fraction of the dose from the MDI to the patient, particularly when face masks are involved. This is a serious disadvantage for expensive drugs. Studies focusing on understanding the mechanisms of particle deposition in VHCs making use of computational fluid dynamics may direct the approach for improvement of VHC design (e.g. Refs. [108,119]) and mark the onset of advanced MDI efficacy however.

References

[1] S.W. Stein, P. Sheth, P.D. Hodson, P.B. Myrdal, Advances in metered dose inhaler technology: hardware development, AAPS PharmSciTech 15 (2) (2014) 326–338.

[2] S.W. Stein, C.G. Thiel, The history of therapeutic aerosols: a chronical review, J. Aerosol Med. Pulm. Drug. Deliv. 30 (1) (2017) 20–41.

[3] S.P. Newman, Principles of metered-dose inhaler design, Resp. Care 50 (9) 1177–1190.

[4] H.D.C. Smyth, Propellant-driven metered-dose inhalers for pulmonary drug delivery, Expert. Opin. Drug. Deliv. 2 (1) (2005) 53074.

[5] J. Berry, S. Heimbecker, J.L. Hart, J. Sequeira, Influence of the metering chamber volume on the aerodynamic particle size of a metered dose inhaler, Drug. Dev. Ind. Pharm. 29 (8) (2003) 865–876.

[6] H. Smyth, G. Brace, T. Barbour, J. Gallion, J. Grove, A.J. Hickey, Spray pattern analysis for metered dose inhalers: effect of actuator design, Pharm. Res. 23 (7) (2006) 1591–1596.

[7] H. Smyth, A.J. Hickey, G. Brace, T. Barbour, J. Gallion, J. Grove, Spray pattern analysis for metered dose inhalers I: orifice size, particle size and droplet motion, Drug. Dev. Ind. Pharm. 32 (2006) 1033–1041.

[8] G.A. Johnson, V.R. Gutti, S.K. Loyalka, K.A. O'Beirne II, S.K. Cochran, H.M. Dale, et al., Albuterol metered dose inhaler performance under hyperbaric pressures, Undersea Hyperbaric Med. 36 (1) (2009) 55–63.

[9] C.L. Leach, The CFC to HFA transition and its impact on pulmonary drug development, Resp. Care 50 (9) (2005) 1201–1208.

[10] S.R.P. da Rocha, B. Bharatwaj, R.S. Heyder, L. Yang, Pressurized metered-dose inhalers, in: A.J. Hickey, S.R.P. de Rocha (Eds.), Pharmaceutical Inhalation Aerosol Technology, third ed., CRC Press, Boca Raton, FL, 2019 (Chapter 18).

[11] P.M. Young, R. Price, D. Lewis, S. Edge, D. Traini, Under pressure: predicting pressurized metered dose inhaler interactions using the atomic force microscope, J. Colloid Interface Sci. 262 (2003) 298–302.

[12] D. Traini, P.M. Young, P. Rogueda, R. Price, The use of AFM and surface energy measurements to investigate drug-canister material interactions in a model pressurized metered dose inhaler formulation, Aerosol Sci. Technol. 40 (4) (2006) 227–236.

[13] D. Traini, P. Rogueda, P. Young, R. Price, Surface energy and interparticle force correlation in model pMDI formulations, Pharm. Res. 22 (5) (2005) 816–825.

[14] R. Errington, Inhalation manufacturing: cold fill, pressure fill, and finding the right partner, ONdrugDelivery 37 (2012) 30–32.

[15] E. Vallorz, P. Sheth, P. Myrdal, Pressurized metered dose inhaler technology: manufacturing, AAPS PharmSciTech 20 (177) (2019) 1–10.

[16] R.K. Schultz, Drug delivery characteristics of metered-dose inhalers, J. Allergy Clin. Immunol. 96 (1995) 284–287.

[17] D. Ganderton, D. Lewis, R. Davies, B. Meakin, G. Brambilla, T. Church, Modulite: a means of designing the aerosols generated by pressurized metered dose inhalers, Resp. Med. (2002) S3–S8. 96 Suppl.

[18] D. Lewis, Metered-dose inhalers: actuators old and new, Exp. Opin. Drug. Deliv. 4 (3) (2007) 235–245.

[19] J.W. Ivey, R. Vehring, Understanding pressurized metered dose inhaler performance, Exp. Opin. Drug. Deliv. 12 (6) (2015) 901–916.

[20] J. Elvecrog, Metered dose inhalers in a CFC-free future, Pharm. Tech. Eur. 9 (1997) 52.

[21] C.A. Dunbar, A.P. Watkins, J.F. Miller, An experimental investigation of the spray issued from a pMDI using laser diagnostic techniques, J. Aerosol Med. 10 (4) (1997) 351–368.

[22] A.R. Clark, Metered Atomisation for Respiratory Drug Delivery (thesis), Loughbogough University of Technology, 1991. http://creativecommons.org/licenses/by-nc-nd/2.5/.

[23] H.K. Versteeg, G.K. Hargrave, Near-orifice spray and valve flow regime of a pharmaceutical pressurized metered dose inhaler, in: Proceedings 18th ILASS Europe Conference, Zaragoza, Spain, 2012.

[24] G. Brambilla, T. Church, D. Lewis, B. Meakin, Plume temperature emitted from metered dose inhalers, Int. J. Pharm. 405 (1–2) (2011) 9–15.

[25] B. Gavtash, H.K. Versteeg, G. Hargrave, B. Myatt, D. Lewis, T. Church, et al., Transient aerodynamic atomization model to predict aerosol droplet size of pressurized metered dose inhalers (pMDI), Aerosol Sci. Technol. 51 (8) (2017) 998–1008.

[26] D. Ju, J. Shrimpton, A. Hearn, The effect of reduction of propellant mass fraction on the injection profile of metered dose inhalers, Int. J. Pharm. 391 (1–2) (2010) 221–229.

[27] A.R. Martin, D.Y. Kwok, W.H. Finlay, Investigating the evaporation of metered-dose inhaler formulations in humid air: single droplet experiments, J. Aerosol Med. 18 (2) (2005) 218–224.

[28] C.F. Lange, W.H. Finlay, Overcoming the adverse effect of humidity in aerosol delivery via pressurized metered-dose inhalers during mechanical ventilation, Am. J. Respir. Crit. Care Med. 161 (2000) 1614–1618.

[29] J.W. Ivey, P. Bhambri, T.K. Church, D.A. Lewis, M.T. MdDermott, S. Elbayomy, et al., Humidity affects the morphology of particles emitted from beclomethasone dipropionate pressurized metered dose inhalers, J. Pharm. 520 (1–2) (2017) 207–215.

[30] P.B. Myrdal, P. Sheth, S.W. Stein, Advances in metered dose inhaler technology: formulation development, AAPS PharmSciTech 15 (2) (2014) 434–455.

[31] A.H.I. Chow, H.H.Y. Tong, P. Chattopadhyay, B.Y. Shekunov, Particle engineering for pulmonary drug delivery, Pharm. Res. 24 (3) (2007) 411–437.

[32] S.A. Shoyele, S. Cawthorne, Particle engineering techniques for inhaled biopharmaceuticals, Adv. Drug. Deliv. Rev. 58 (2006) 1009–1029.

[33] L. Wu, S.R.P. da Rocha, Biocompatible and biodegradable copolymer stabilizers for hydrofluoroalkane dispersion: a colloidal probe microscopy investigation, Langmuir 23 (2007) 12104–12110.

[34] R. Vehring, D. Lechuga-Ballesteros, V. Joshi, B. Noga, S.K. Dwivedi, Cosuspensions of microcrystals and engineered microparticles for uniform and efficient delivery of respiratory therapeutics from pressurized metered dose inhalers, Langmuir 28 (2012) 15015–15023.

[35] P.W. Voorhees, The theory of Ostwald ripening, J. Stat. Phys. 38 (1/2) (1985) 231–253.

[36] C. Mbah, C.O. Ozuo, Effect of surfactants on the solubility and intrinsic dissolution rate of sparfloxacin, Pharmazie 66 (3) (2011) 192–194.

[37] A. Gupta, S.W. Stein, P.B. Myrdal, Balancing ethanol cosolvent concentration with product performance in 134a-based pressurized metered dose inhalers, J. Aerosol Med. 16 (2) (2003) 167–174.

[38] F. Buttini, M. Miozzi, A.G. Balducci, P.G. Royall, G. Brambilla, P. Colombo, et al., Differences in physical chemistry and dissolution rate of solid particle aerosols from solution pressurized inhalers, Int. J. Pharm. 465 (1–2) (2014) 42–51.

[39] I.Y. Saleem, H.D.C. Smyth, Tuning aerosol particle size distribution of metered dose inhalers using cosolvents and surfactants, Biomed. Res. Int. (2013). Article ID 574310.

[40] C. Vervaet, P.R. Byron, Drug-surfactant-propellant interactions in HFA-formulations, Int. J. Pharm. 186 (1–2) (1999) 13–30.

[41] B.J. Gabrio, S.W. Stein, D.J. Velasquez, A new method to evaluate plume characteristics of hydrofluoroalkane and chlorofluorocarbon metered dose inhalers, Int. J. Pharm. 186 (1–2) (1999) 3–12.

[42] D. Traini, P.M. Young, P. Rogueda, R. Price, *In vitro* investigation of drug particulates interactions and aerosol performance of pressurised metered dose inhalers, Pharm. Res. 24 (1) (2007) 125–135.

[43] J. Ooi, S. Gaisford, B.J. Boyd, P.M. Young, D. Traini, Isothermal calorimetry: a predictive tool to model drug-propellant interactions in pressurized metered dose systems, Int. J. Pharm. 461 (102) (2014) 301–309.
[44] Y. Michael, M.J. Snowden, B.Z. Chowdhry, I.C. Ashurst, C.J. Davies-Cutting, T. Riley, Characterisation of the aggregation behaviour in a salmeterol and fluticasone propionate inhalation aerosol system, Int. J. Pharm. 221 (1–2) (2001) 165–174.
[45] I. Mayers, R. Damant, Role of combination inhaled corticosteroids and long acting beta agonists in the treatment of adult asthma, Issues Emerg. Health Technol. 68 (2005) 1–4.
[46] S. Langham, J. Lewis, N. Pooley, N. Embleton, J. Langham, M.K. Han, et al., Single-inhaler triple therapy in patients with chronic obstructive pulmonary disease: a systematic review, Respir. Res. 20 (242) (2019). Available from: doi.org/10.1186/512931-org-1213-9.
[47] J. Berry, L. Kline, V. Naini, S. Chaudry, J. Hart, J. Sequeira, Influence of the valve lubricant on the aerodynamic particle size of a metered dose inhaler, Drug. Dev. Ind. Pharm. 30 (3) (2004) 267–275.
[48] J.K. Fallon, I.D. Peyron, A.J. Hickey, Effects of direct spiking of silicone oil into a model pMDI formulation, Drug. Dev. Ind. Pharm. 39 (5) (2013) 681–686.
[49] J.K. Sherwood, S. Alex, G. Salama, L. Obenauer-Kutner, S. Huyck, J. Berry, et al., Particle size coarsening induced by valve silicone in a metered dose inhaler, Drug. Dev. Ind. Pharm. 33 (2) (2007) 155–162.
[50] I. Markovic, Evaluation of safety and quality impact of extractable and leachable substances in therapeutic biologic protein products: a risk-based perspective, Expert. Opin. Drug. Deliv. 6 (5) (2007) 487–491.
[51] M. Keller, Innovations and perspectives of metered dose inhalers in pulmonary drug delivery, Int. J. Pharm. 186 (1–2) (1999) 81–90.
[52] P.W. Barry, C. O'Callaghan, A comparative analysis of the particle size output of beclomethasone dipropionate, salmeterol xinafoate and fluticasone propionate metered dose inhalers used with the Babyhaler, Volumatic and Aerochamber spacer devices, Br. J. Clin. Pharmacol. 47 (1999) 357–360.
[53] P. Csonka, L. Lehtimäki, Valved holding chamber drug delivery is dependent on breathing pattern and device design, Eur. Respir. J. Open. Res. 5 (2019). Available from: https://doi.org/10.1183/23120541.00158-2018.
[54] F. Morén, Drug deposition of pressurized inhalation aerosols I. Influence of actuator tube design, Int. J. Pharm. 1 (1978) 205–212.
[55] S.P. Newman, M.T. Newhouse, Effect of add-on devices for aerosol drug delivery: deposition studies and clinical aspects, J. Aerosol Med. 9 (10) (1996) 55–70.
[56] H. Bisgaard, A metal aerosol holding chamber devised for young children with asthma, Eur. Respir. J. 8 (1995) 856–860.
[57] V. Voeurng, V. Andrieu, H. Bun, J.-P. Reynier, J.-C. Dubus, A new small volume holding chamber for asthmatic children: comparison with Babyhaler spacer, Pediatr. Allergy Immunol. 17 (2006) 629–634.
[58] H.J. Zar, M.J. Asmus, E.G. Weinberg, A 500-ml plastic bottle: an effective spacer for children with asthma, Pediatr. Allergy Immunol. 13 (2002) 217–360.
[59] J.L. Goodwin, L.B. Gerald, J.L.H. Johnson, J.K. Gerald, Use of a disposable valved-holding chamber (spacer) in a school-based asthma trial, J. Allergy Immunol. Pract. 6 (2018) 307–309.
[60] C.E. Rodriguez-Martinez, M. Sossa, J.M. Lozano, Commercial versus home-made spacers in delivering bronchodilator therapy for acute therapy in children, Cochrane Database Syst. Rev. 2 (2008). Available from: https://doi.org/10.1002/14651858.CD005536.pub2.
[61] F. Piérart, J.H. Wildhaber, I. Vrancken, S.G. Devadason, P.N. Le Souëf, Washing plastic spacers in household detergent reduces electrostatic charge and greatly improves delivery, Eur. Respir. J. 13 (1999) 673–678.
[62] B.L. Rottier, Improving Drug Delivery to the Lungs. Chapter 4: High air humidity increases delivered total and fine particle dose of inhaled corticosteroids from valved holding chambers. Thesis University of Groningen, the Netherlands, 2012.
[63] G. Anderson, N. Johnson, A. Mulgirigama, B. Aggarwal, Use of spacers for patients treated with pressurized metered dose inhalers: focus on the VENTOLIN Mini Spacer, Exp. Opin. Drug. Deliv. 15 (4) (2018) 419–430.

[64] GINA Report Global Strategy for Asthma Management and Prevention, Global Initiative for Asthma, 2017. Available at: http://ginasthmaorg/gina-reports, 2017.

[65] C. Herbes, A.M. Concalves, G.C. Motta, D.A. dos Santos Ventura, M. Colvero, S.L. Amantéa, Metered-dose inhaler therapy with spacers: are newborns capable of using this system correctly? Ped Pulmonol. 54 (2019) 1417–1421.

[66] H.M. Janssens, H.A.W.M. Tiddens, Facemasks and aerosol delivery by metered dose inhaler – valved holding chamber in young children: a tight seal makes the difference, J. Aerosol Med. 29 (Suppl. 20) (2007) S59–S65.

[67] J.E. Esposito-Festen, B. Ates, F.J.M. van Vliet, A.F.M. Verbraak, J.C. de Jongste, H.A.W.M. Tiddens, Effect of facemask leak on aerosol delivery from a pMDI-spacer system, J. Aerosol Med. 17 (1) (2004) 1–6.

[68] R.W. Morton, J.P. Mitchell, Design of facemasks for delivery of aerosol-based medication via pressurized metered dose inhaler with valved holding chamber: key issues that affect performance, J. Aerosol Med. 20 (Suppl. 1) (2007) S29–S45.

[69] M. Sanders, R. Bruin, A rationale for going back to the future: use of disposable spacers for pressurised metered dose inhalers, Hindawi Pulm. Med. (2015). Article ID 176194.

[70] K.R. Chapman, L. Love, H. Brubaker, A comparison of breath-actuated and conventional metered-dose inhaler inhalation techniques in elderly subjects, Chest 104 (1993) 1332–1337.

[71] R.J. Fergusson, J. Lenney, G.J.R. McHardy, G.K. Crompton, The use of a new breath-actuated inhaler by patients with severe airflow obstruction, Eur. Respir. J. 4 (1991) 172–174.

[72] J. Lenney, J.A. Innes, G.K. Crompton, Inappropriate inhaler use: assessment of use and patient preference of seven inhalation devices, Respir. Med. 94 (2000) 496–500.

[73] N.R. Ruggins, A.D. Milner, A. Swarbrick, An assessment of a new breath actuated inhaler device in acutely wheezy children, Arch. Dis. Child. 68 (1993) 477–480.

[74] S.B. Shrewsbury, R.O. Cook, G. Taylor, C. Edwards, N.M. Ramadan, Safety and pharmacokinetics of dihydroergotamine mesylate administered via a novel (Tempo) inhaler, Headache 48 (3) (2008) 355–367.

[75] D.J. Kellerman, A. Forst, D.L. Combs, S. Borland, S. Kori, Assessment of the consistency of absorption of dihydroergotamine following oral inhalation: pooled results from four clinical studies, J. Aerosol Med. Pulm. Drug. Deliv. 26 (5) (2013) 297–306.

[76] H. Steckel, B.W. Müller, Metered-dose inhaler add-on devices: an in vitro evaluation of the BronchoAir inhaler and several spacer devices, J. Aerosol Med. 11 (3) (1998) 133–142.

[77] N. Sander, S.J. Fusco-Walker, J.M. Harder, B.E. Chipps, Dose counting and the use of pressurized metered-dose inhalers: running on empty, Ann. Allergy Asthma Immunol. 97 (2006) 34–38.

[78] B.K. Rubin, L. Durotoye, How do patients determine that their metered-dose inhaler is empty? Chest 126 (2004) 1134–1137.

[79] S. Holt, A. Holt, M. Weatherall, M. Masoli, R. Beasley, Metered dose inhalers: a need for dose counters, Respirology 10 (2005) 105–106.

[80] J. Given, H. Taveras, H. Iverson, M. Lepore, Prospective, open-label assessment of albuterol sulfate hydrofluoroalkane metered-dose inhaler with new integrated dose counter, Allergy Asthma Proc. 34 (1) (2013) 42–51.

[81] D.B. Price, A. Rigazio, M.B. Small, T.J. Ferro, Historical cohort study examining comparative effectiveness of albuterol inhalers with and without integrated dose counter for patients with asthma or chronic obstructive pulmonary disease, J. Asthma Allergy 9 (2016) 145–154.

[82] M. Reznik, P.O. Ozuah, Measurement of inhaled corticosteroid adherence in inner-city, minority children with persistent asthma by parenteral report and integrated dose counter, Hindawi J. Allergy, 2012. Article ID 570850.

[83] P.W. Barry, C. O'Callaghan, In vitro comparison of the amount of salbutamol available for inhalation from different formulations used with different spacer devices, Eur. Respir. J. 10 (1997) 1345–1348.

[84] S.P. Newman, S.W. Clarke, Bronchodilator delivery from Gentlehaler, a new low-velocity pressurized aerosol inhaler, Chest 103 (1993) 1442–1446.

[85] S.P. Newman, A.B. Millar, T.R. Lennard-Jones, F. Morén, S.W. Clarke, Improvement of pressurised aerosol deposition with Nebuhaler spacer device, Thorax 39 (1984) 935–941.

[86] C.L. Leach, P.J. Davidson, R.J. Boudreau, Improved airway targeting with the CFC-free HFA-beclomethasone metered-dose inhaler compared with CFC-beclomethasone, Eur. Respir. J. 12 (1998) 1346–1353.
[87] R. Pauwels, S. Newman, L. Borgström, Airway deposition and airway effects of antiasthma drugs delivered from metered-dose inhalers, Eur. Respir. J. 10 (1997) 2127–2138.
[88] P. König, Spacer devices used with metered-dose inhalers, breakthrough or gimmick? Chest 88 (2) (1985) 276–284.
[89] C.L. Leach, Improved delivery of inhaled steroids to the large and small airways, Respir. Med. 92 (Suppl. A) (1998) 3–8.
[90] C.L. Leach, P.J. Davidson, B.E. Hasselquist, R.J. Boudreau, Lung deposition of hydrofluoroalkane-134a beclomethasone is greater than that of chlorofluorocarbon beclomethasone, Chest 122 (2002) 510–516.
[91] T.W. de Vries, B.L. Rottier, D. Gjaltema, P. Hagedoorn, H.W. Frijlink, A.H. de Boer, Comparative *in vitro* evaluation of four corticosteroid metered dose inhalers: consistency of delivered dose and particle size distribution, Respir. Med. 103 (2009) 1167–1173.
[92] R.W. Dal Negro, P. Longo, O. Villanis Ziani, L. Bonadiman, P. Turco, Instant velocity and consistency of emitted cloud change by the different levels of canister filling with metered dose inhalers (MDSs), but not with soft mist inhalers (SMIs): a bench study, Multidisciplinary, Respir. Med. 12 (13) (2017) 1–6.
[93] K.A. Gunawardena, T. Sohal, J.I. Jones, F.C. Upchurch, G.K. Crompton, The Spacehaler for delivery of salbutamol: a comparison with the standard metered-dose inhaler plus Volumatic spacer device, Respir. Med. 91 (1997) 311–316.
[94] S.P. Newman, K.P. Steed, G. Hooper, J.I. Jones, F.C. Upchurch, Improved targeting of beclomethasone dipropionate (250 μg metered dose inhaler) to the lungs of asthmatics with the Spacehaler, Respir. Med. 93 (1999) 424–431.
[95] K.P. O'Donnell, R.O. Williams, Pulmonary dispersion formulations: the impact of dispersed powder properties on pressurized metered dose inhaler stability, Drug. Dev. Ind. Pharm. 39 (3) (2013) 413–424.
[96] D. D'Sa, H.K. Chan, A review of methods for evaluating particle stability in suspension based pressurized metered dose inhalers, Curr. Pharm. Des. 21 (27) (2015) 3955–3965.
[97] A. Hardwell, V. Barber, T. Hargadon, E. McKnight, J. Holmes, M.L. Levy, Technique training does not improve the ability of most patients to use pressurized metered-dose inhalers (pMDIs), Prim. Care Respir. J. 20 (1) (2011) 92–96.
[98] V. Plaza, J. Sanchis, CESEA Group, Medical personnel and patient skill in the use of metered dose inhalers: a multicentric study, Respiration 65 (1998) 195–198.
[99] N.A. Hanania, R. Wittman, S. Kesten, K.R. Chapman, Medical personnel's knowledge of and ability to use inhaling devices, metered dose inhalers, spacing chambers, and breath-actuated dry powder inhalers, Chest 105 (1994) 111–116.
[100] V. Giraud, N. Roche, Misuse of corticosteroid metered-dose inhaler is associated with decreased asthma stability, Eur. Respir. J. 19 (2002) 246–251.
[101] W. Vincken, M.L. Levy, J. Scullion, O.S. Usmani, P.N.R. Dekhuijzen, C.J. Corrigan, Spacer devices for inhaled therapy: why use them, and how? Eur. Respir. J. Open. Res. 4 (2018). Available from: https://doi.org/10.1183/23120541.00065-2018.
[102] S.P. Newman, A.W. Weisz, N. Talace, S.W. Clarke, Improvement of drug delivery with a breath actuated pressurised aerosol for patients with poor inhaler technique, Thorax 46 (1991) 712–716.
[103] P.W. Barry, C. O'Callaghan, Inhalational drug delivery from seven different spacer devices, Thorax 51 (1996) 835–840.
[104] R.N. Dalby, S. Somaraju, V.S. Chavan, D. Jarvis, Evaluation of aerosol drug output from the OptiChamber and AeroChamber spacers in a model system, J. Asthma 35 (2) (1998) 173–177.
[105] L. Slator, D. von Hollen, D. Sandell, R.H.M. Hatley, *In vitro* comparison of the effect of inhalation delay and flow rate on the emitted dose from three valved holding chambers, J. Aerosol Med. Pulm. Drug. Deliv. 27 (1) (2014) S-37–S-43.
[106] X. Liu, C. Guo, B. Chowdhury, P. Starke, S. Limb, P. Peri, et al., Valved holding chambers and *in vitro* metered dose inhaler performance: effects of flow rate and inhalation delay, J. Aerosol Med. Pulm. Drug. Deliv. 30 (6) (2017) 399–410.

[107] S. Dissanayake, J. Suggett, A review of the *in vitro* and *in vivo* valved holding chamber (VHC) literature with a focus on the AeroChamber Plus Flow-Vu anti-static VHC, Ther. Adv. Respir. Dis. 12 (2018) 1–14.

[108] S. Sarkar, S.P. Peri, B. Chaudhuri, Investigation of multiphase multicomponent aerosol flow dictating pMDI-spacer interactions, Int. J. Pharm. 529 (1–2) (2017) 264–274.

[109] J. Anhøj, H. Bisgaard, B.J. Lipworth, Effect of electrostatic charge in plastic spacers on the drug delivery of HFA-salbutamol in children, Br. J. Clin. Pharmacol. 47 (1999) 333–336.

[110] J.H. Wildhaber, G.W. Waterer, G.L. Hall, Q.A. Summers, Reducing electrostatic charge on spacer devices and bronchodilator response, Br. J. Clin. Pharmacol. 50 (2000) 277–280.

[111] B.J. Lipworth, D.J. Clark, Early lung absorption profile of non-CFC salbutamol via small and large volume plastic spacer devices, Br. J. Clin. Pharmacol. 46 (1998) 45–48.

[112] M. Hindle, H. Chrystyn, Relative bioavailability of salbutamol to the lung following inhalation using metered dose inhalation methods and spacer devices, Thorax 49 (1994) 549–553.

[113] P.H. Brown, A.P. Greening, G.K. Crompton, Large volume spacer devices and the influence of high dose beclomethasone dipropionate on hypothalamo-pituitary-adrenal axis function, Thorax 48 (1993) 233–238.

[114] G.C. Smaldone, E. Berg, K. Nikander, Variation in pediatric aerosol delivery: importance of facemask, J. Aerosol Med. 18 (3) (2005) 354–363.

[115] K. Nikander, E. Berg, G.C. Smaldone, Jet nebulizers versus pressurized metered dose inhalers with valved holding chambers: effects of the facemask on aerosol delivery, J. Aerosol Med. 20 (Suppl. 1) (2007) S46–S58.

[116] V. Carli, L. Menu-Bouaouiche, P. Cardinael, L. Benissan, G. Coquerel, Immunoglobulin G particles manufacturing by spray drying process for pressurised metered dose inhaler formulations, Ann. Pharm. Fr. 76 (4) (2018) 291–298.

[117] E. Cocks, S. Somavarapu, O. Alpar, D. Greenleaf, Influence of suspension stabilisers on the delivery of protein-loaded porous poly (DL-lactide-co-glycolide) (PLGA) microparticles via pressurised metered dose inhaler, Pharm. Res. 31 (8) (2014) 2000–2009.

[118] Z. Huang, H. Wu, B. Yang, L. Chen, Y. Huang, G. Quan, et al., Anhydrous reverse micelle nanoparticles: new strategy to overcome sedimentation instability of peptide-containing pressurized metered-dose inhalers, Drug. Deliv. 24 (1) (2017) 572. 538.

[119] N. Ogrodnik, V. Azzi, E. Sprigge, S. Fiset, E. Matida, Nonuniform deposition of pressurized metered-dose aerosol in spacer devices, J. Aerosol Med. Pulm. Drug. Deliv. 29 (6) (2016) 490–500.

CHAPTER 5

Dry powder inhalers (DPIs)

Anne Haaije de Boer[1] and Kyrre Thalberg[2,3]
[1]Department of Pharmaceutical Technology and Biopharmacy, Faculty of Science and Engineering, University of Groningen, Groningen, The Netherlands
[2]Inhalation Product Development, Pharmaceutical Technology & Development, Operations, AstraZeneca Gothenburg, Sweden
[3]Current address: Emmace Consulting AB, Medicon Village, Lund, Sweden

5.1 Introduction

The history of dry powder inhalers and the arguments for their development have been described before [1,2]. Strong motives for their large-scale introduction in the 1960s–1980s were the desire to reduce patient burden (as from using time consuming nebulization: Chapter 3) and to minimize handling errors (as from using MDIs: Chapter 4). A recent interest in the pulmonary route for high dose (e.g. antibiotics) and systemically acting drugs, such as levodopa and loxapin, and the desire to improve the stability of inhaled medication further boosted device and formulation development from the 1990s on. DPIs are also appreciated for improving the adherence to the therapy [3] and increasing the safety of pulmonary antibiotic delivery because they are less prone to contamination with specific pathogenic germs compared to nebulizers [4]. DPIs can easily (and cheaply) be disposable which makes them highly appropriate for vaccination (e.g. against measles, influenza, COVID-19 and tuberculosis) for which the pulmonary route seems particularly suitable [5–7]. Many new DPI applications are technology-driven since certain benefits of particle engineering techniques for inhalation powders have been acknowledged [8]. An abundance of different techniques and formulations can be found in the literature and they may be needed for the stabilization of biomolecules and vaccines, or be desired for improvement of the dispersion process when using poorly designed inhalers. However, they have disadvantages of their own. Most particle engineering processes increase the mass and/or volume of powder to be inhaled, depending on how they are prepared and the amounts of excipients used for their preparation. This may increase the number of inhalations needed for the administration of a single (high) drug dose and, therefore, such formulation techniques should preferably not be used unless strictly needed. It is not the purpose of this chapter to sum up all the different particle engineering, or drug stabilization processes for new biopharmaceuticals however, but to discuss DPI technology (design and performance) in perspective of effective drug delivery to the lungs. Still much can be improved to achieve optimal efficacy for dry powder inhalation, not only by designing more

Inhaled Medicines
DOI: https://doi.org/10.1016/B978-0-12-814974-4.00005-5

powerful DPIs, but also by making the devices more versatile in order to reduce the number of different inhalers to be used for different inhalation drugs by the same patient. Patients with asthma, chronic obstructive pulmonary disease, cystic fibrosis, or severe and persistent lung infections (e.g. tuberculosis) all use more than one drug for their therapies. They may need different inhalers for the administration with different designs and handling procedures, and this is known to increase errors in inhaler use, whereas it may become easily at the cost of patient compliance and adherence. Therefore, inhalers that can effectively deliver all drugs prescribed for a particular disease to the patient are strongly desired.

5.2 DPI design: general description and considerations

Nearly all DPIs comprise three primary functional parts: a powder formulation for the drug, a dose (measuring) system for the powder formulation and a powder dispersion principle as shown in Fig. 5.1 [9]. These parts are assembled with a central housing having a mouthpiece and a control function for the dose activation too. Basic DPI design must be simple and comprise a minimal number of parts for different reasons. It minimizes molding costs and simplifies parts assembly, which is important for making the inhaled medication (and vaccination programs) affordable and available to all patients, particularly in developing countries. It also facilitates simple inhaler handling (preparation and use), which is to the benefit of patient compliance with the instructions and adherence to the therapy. Additionally and only when needed, various secondary parts can be added to the basic design, such as a dose counter, feedback signals to the patient about

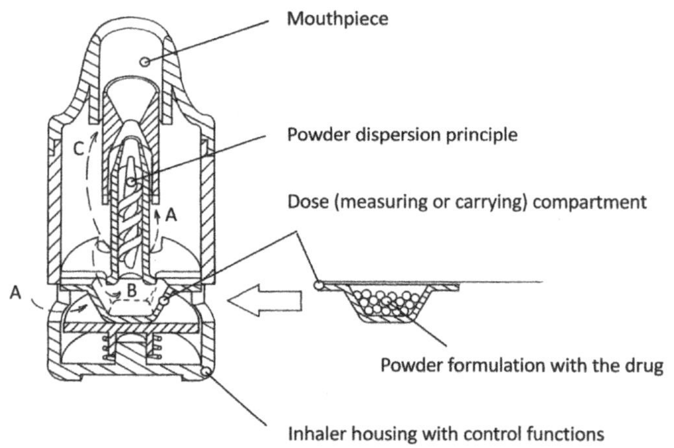

Figure 5.1 Schematic presentation of an imaginary dry powder inhaler with the primary functional parts: a powder formulation containing the drug, a dose (measuring or carrying) compartment, a powder dispersion principle, a mouthpiece (with or without bypass flow) and a central housing with control functions. In this figure, (A) is the air inlet to the central chamber that splits into a partial flow through the dose compartment and the dispersion principle (B) and a partial bypass flow towards the mouthpiece (C).

performance and a desiccant compartment. Because they are not directly relevant to lung deposition of the drug, they will not be discussed in this chapter.

The most important functions of a DPI are:

- Delivering a consistent drug amount to the patient as an appropriate aerosol for deposition in the target area,
- Requiring a minimal number of simple steps for taking a dose to improve the adherence to the therapy (stimulating intuitive operation),
- Protecting the drug formulation (dose) from the environment (air humidity, light and dust),
- Preventing waste of powder after the DPI has been activated for inhalation,
- Delivering the entire dose preferably within the first 0.5–1 L of inhaled air for systemically acting drugs to facilitate aerosol transport to the intermediate and deep lung,
- Be mechanically stable (device and formulation) with a reliable operating mechanism,
- Limiting the range of achievable flow rates through the device (having a medium to high resistance).

For special patient groups (e.g. children and patients with a severely impaired lung function), additional functions or deviating specifications may be desired (e.g. Refs. [10,11]) and for some applications (e.g. hygroscopic drug formulations, rescue medication, vaccines and antibiotics) disposable DPIs may be desired [12]. Different choices can be made for each of the primary parts of a DPI and their design possibilities depend strongly on the drug dose. Low dose drugs in the μg-range are generally processed in a different manner than high dose drugs in the mg-range. Different types of formulations require different dose (metering) and powder dispersion principles and incompatibilities between these primary functional DPI parts have to be avoided. This will all be explained and discussed in the next paragraphs, starting with the aerosol particle manufacturing techniques that have to produce particles in the desired aerodynamic size distribution for inhalation.

5.3 Aerosol particle manufacturing techniques for DPIs

5.3.1 Micronization

Micronization using a jet mill is the traditional way for size reduction of a crystalline active pharmaceutical ingredient (API) to the inhalable size range. The process and the equipment used were developed more than a hundred years ago and are thus off patent. Nitrogen is the preferred milling gas for pharma applications and eliminates the risk for dust explosions. Most common is to use a spiral jet mill (Fig. 5.2) also called a micronizer or a pancake mill [13]. In brief, the drug particles are accelerated to high velocity and collide with each other and with the walls due to the action of the "jets", which leads to rapid size reduction. At the same time the particles are subjected to the centrifugal action of the circulating gas and cannot reach the centrally placed outlet

Figure 5.2 Spiral jet mill (in open position). The stainless steel of the upper and lower mill parts is coated by a layer of titanium nitride to prevent abrasion.

Figure 5.3 Micronized salbutamol sulfate (left) and micronized budesonide (right).

until they have been sufficiently size reduced. The basic principles of spiral jet mills are thus well understood [14,15]. Spiral jet mills have no moving parts, which makes the equipment small, cheap and easy to operate. Alternative jet mill designs such as the fluidized bed opposed jet mill [16], in which a classifier wheel rotating at high speed separates out the fine particles, are also used for production of inhalable particles.

Micronization by jet milling is a continuous process and can be operated in batch sizes from less than a gram up to several kg/hour. The resulting powder consists of fractured irregular particles (Fig. 5.3) which are notoriously sticky and prone to electrostatic charging. Micronized powders hence need to be formulated. Another disadvantage is that the micronization process is very harsh and leads to formation of significant amounts of amorphous material [17]. Some kind of conditioning of the resulting powder is therefore needed in order to ensure stability of the API and the formulated drug product. Moreover, micronization is unsuitable for most biomolecules.

Micronization can also be applied to a mixture of materials, typically an API and a so-called "coating agent", with the aim to cover or coat the API, thereby obtaining improved dispersibility and better flowability of the resulting powder [18,19]. An alternative process able to coat micron-sized particles is mechanofusion [20].

5.3.2 Spray drying and related techniques

Spray drying is the main bottom up technique for production of inhaled particles. It is extensively used both in the food (e.g. dry milk) and pharma industry (e.g. spray dried lactose for tableting), which means that the process is well established [21,22]. A spray drier is schematically shown in Fig. 5.4 and examples of spray dried particles for inhalation are shown in Fig. 5.5.

Spray drying is in many ways complementary to micronization. It can be utilized for APIs that cannot be crystallized and for biomolecules like peptides and proteins [23]. The possibility to include additives directly in the particles enables functionalities such as humidity protection and stabilization of the amorphous state to be designed into the particles [24,25].

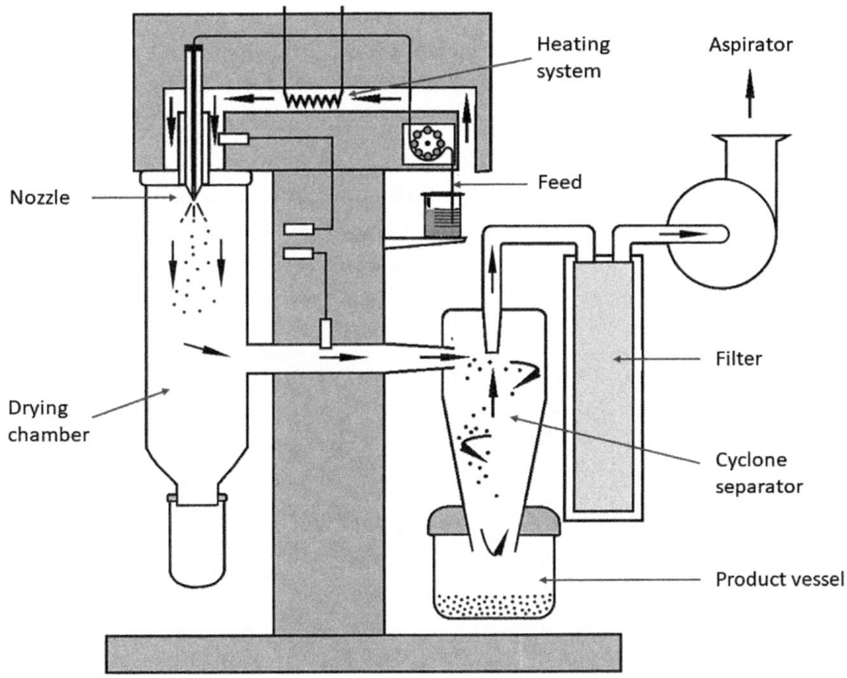

Figure 5.4 Schematic picture of a spray drier.

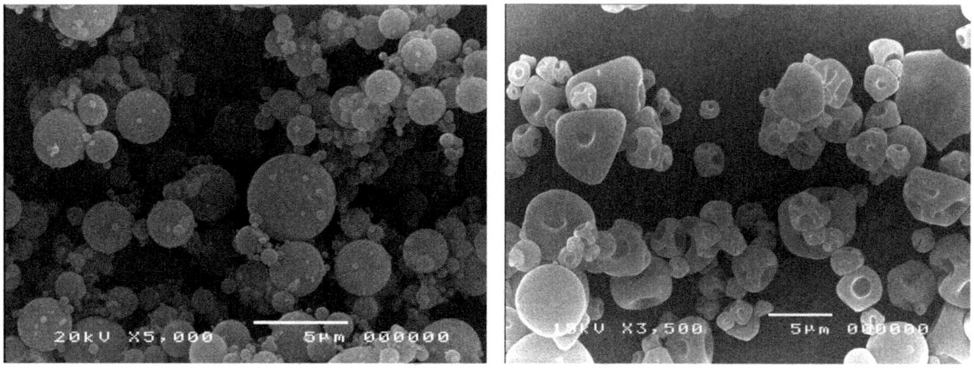

Figure 5.5 Spray dried particles consisting of mannitol (left) and insulin (right).

Additives used for spray drying and stabilization of biomolecules comprise sugars such as trehalose, sucrose, raffinose and amino acids such as leucine [24]. The main principle behind stabilization with the sugars is to achieve an amorphous glass with a high glass transition temperature, Tg, relative to room temperature, thus ensuring physical stability of the formulation [26]. Different explanations are given for the stabilization mechanism provided by the sugars, including water replacement and bulking. The objective is to preserve the three-dimensional structure of the biopharmaceuticals in the dry state. By embedding them in a solid matrix that has certain properties of a liquid, such as the absence of a rigid (crystal) structure, denaturation can be prevented and the conformation of the biopharmaceutical can be maintained.

The use of additives also enables optimization of the morphology of spray dried particles, e.g. to reduce powder cohesivity. Leucine is typically used in this context. By varying the amount of leucine in the feed to the spray drier, particle morphology can be significantly affected and thereby interparticle interactions [27].

The use of spray drying for production of dry powders for inhalation is becoming increasingly popular. One reason for this is that spray dried particles can be used without carrier particles, which means that higher drug doses to the lungs can be achieved, see further Section 5.4.3.

Highly porous particles can be produced using spray drying technology. Such particles have a small aerodynamic size [28], and can therefore be inhaled in spite of a larger geometric size. One way to produce porous particles is by spray drying an emulsion consisting of aqueous phase and fluorocarbon such as perfluorooctyl bromide [29]. The particles are referred to as PulmoSphere or AeroSphere depending on whether they contain drug or not (Fig. 5.6). AIR technology, purchased by Alkermes, is a method for manufacturing of large, but still inhalable, porous particles with geometric diameter in the range of 10 µm [28]. A technology developed by Prosonix Ltd., UK (now Circassia), employs spray drying in combination with ultrasound to initiate crystallization during the droplet drying stage, thereby enabling crystalline API particles with a rounded shape [30].

Figure 5.6 Porous particles: PulmoSphere Tobramycin, Novartis.

Spray freeze drying is a process where droplets are sprayed directly into liquid nitrogen [31]. In this way the droplets are frozen and the water is thereafter removed by freeze drying. The process typically results in highly porous particles (Fig. 5.7). In addition to opportunities, there are also challenges associated with spray drying for production of inhalable particles, such as:

Low production capacity

High cost for large scale equipment

Scale up while maintaining particle size

Spray dried amorphous particles are highly sensitive to moisture

The latter point requires humidity to be tightly controlled in production and handling of the powders. The doses must furthermore be protected from moisture in the inhaler, e.g. by filling into Aluminum blisters or similar, and the dose needs to be taken short after blister punching.

Supercritical techniques have been intensely researched for production of pharmaceutical particles [32]. An attractive aspect is the possibility to control polymorphs and get nice crystal shapes. For inhaled particles, work has focused on the SEDS technology (Solution Enhanced Dispersion by Supercritical fluids) [32]. An example of such particles is given in Fig. 5.8. Also, for this technique, however, a lot of challenges exist, including scale up, cost of equipment and environmental aspects. Additionally, it should be noted that particles with smooth surfaces may not necessarily be a benefit, as they give rise to larger area of contact between particles, thus rendering the powders more cohesive and, hence, more difficult to handle and disperse (see further Section 5.4.1).

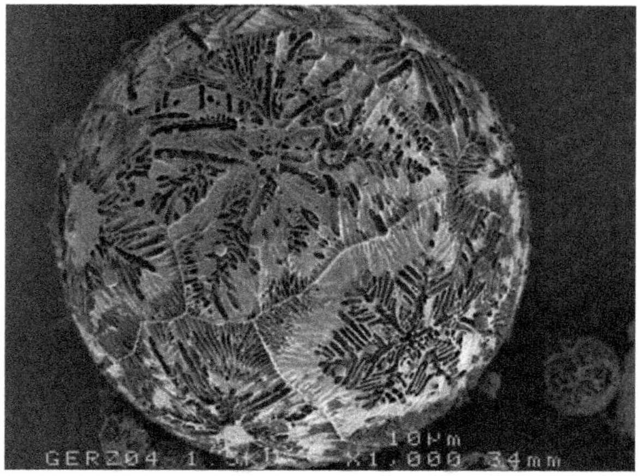

Figure 5.7 Spray-freeze dried particle of inulin.

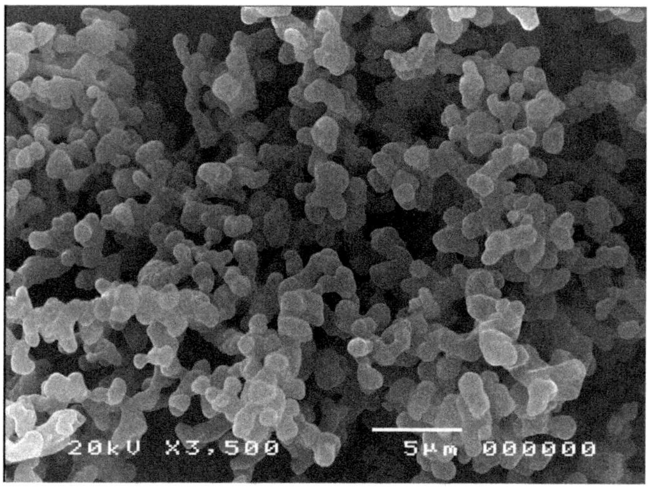

Figure 5.8 Budesonide particles produced using supercritical precipitation technology (SEDS).

5.4 Powder formulations for DPIs

5.4.1 Introduction

Irrespective of the manufacturing technique used for their preparation, particles in the suitable aerodynamic size range for inhalation (preferably 1–5 μm) are very cohesive. It is important for the inhalation expert to understand the basic physics and variables that control the particle-particle interaction forces, as they have to be exceeded for appropriate aerosol generation during inhalation. These forces are theoretically the same for all types of inhalation powders. They may, however, differ in their order of magnitude due to differences in physical and chemical particle properties and the process conditions at which the powders were prepared, as they determine particle density, shape, degree of crystallinity and surface rugosity. It is not the purpose of this paragraph to enter deeply in the basic theory of interparticle interactions as this has extensively been done by others. (e.g. Refs. [33–36]). It is the objective to present the effects of the various particle properties, process variables and their interactions on the magnitude of these forces and how this affects dispersion. In the following paragraphs, a review of studies on the effects of these variables and interactions on the dispersibility of the powders is given.

The most important attraction forces between particles in a powder are the Van der Waals forces. They are relatively weak electromagnetic forces based on (induced) dipoles or temporally polarized molecules (e.g. Ref. [37]). On a macroscale, cohesive and adhesive Van der Waals forces can be distinguished for particles of the same, and of different nature (chemical composition) respectively. Whether Van der Waals forces result in adhesion (or cohesion) between particles, or not, depends on the magnitude of separation forces, which for a powder at rest are confined to gravitational forces [34]. The magnitude of Van der Waals forces between two particles is affected by at least four factors: the chemical nature (composition) of the particles, the contact area between the particles, the distance between the particles and the presence of particle surface impurities (including water of adhesion). The contact area and distance depend on the size and shape (distributions), the surface texture (rugosity), and the type and conditions of the powder preparation process(es) exerting external forces on the particles. Excipients, like lactose carrier particles (see Section 5.4.2) mostly contain small amounts of impurities on their surface, like peptides, proteins, salts [38]. Particle surface roughness either increases or decreases the van der Waals force, depending on the scale of the rugosity [39]. Small particles adhering to the surface of large particles may also contribute to high rugosity [40]. Particle shape (e.g. plate or sphere) may affect the size of a single contact point, but also influence the powder packing and flowability. A change in powder packing (porosity) results in a change of the co-ordination number, i.e. the number of contact points per particle in the powder [41], and hence affects the adhesion strength within a powder agglomerate [42]. Mixing of particles can have a combined effect of influencing the powder packing, decreasing the distance between individual particles and increasing the contact area [43]. Particle-particle and particle-wall collisions during mixing are associated with 'press-on forces' that may flatten sub-microscopic surface discontinuities. These forces can also increase the contact area between particles by plastic particle deformation (e.g. Ref. [44]) (Fig. 5.9).

Mixing also has an effect on the break-up of natural agglomerates of drug and excipient fines, as well as on the formation of new, small agglomerates that are coherent enough to act as larger particles during dispersion [45]. This is beneficial, because an increase in particle diameter decreases the ratio of attraction to separation forces during inhalation, which improves dispersion [8]. A prerequisite for this to be an advantage is that the agglomerates are (aerodynamically) smaller than 5 μm, or that they are further dispersed

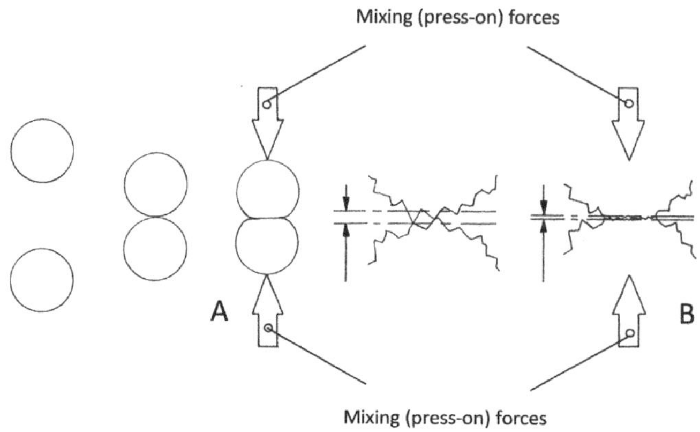

Figure 5.9 Possible effects of particle-particle, or particle -wall collisions during the mixing process on the contact surface area between particles. Such repeatedly occurring collision forces can result in flattening of the particle surface by plastic deformation (A) or decreasing the effective distance between two particles (B) by changing the scale of the particle's surface rugosity.

into smaller entities before they leave can the DPI, as in classifier-based DPIs [46]. This benefit is also one of the reasons for the preparing highly porous particles that have a small aerodynamic, but large geometric diameter [28]. The state-of-the-art knowledge regarding all these aspects is discussed in the next paragraphs.

In addition to the Van der Waals forces, capillary and electrostatic forces can act between particles [36]. These forces decrease dispersibility and should thus be kept to a minimum. Even though electrostatic forces may be temporary, they can increase Van der Waals forces permanently by changing the particle contact area (as the result of plastic deformation). Capillary forces can transform into solid bridges due to crystallization of solid material that is dissolved in the adsorbed water layers when they are removed, e.g. by heating or changing the relative humidity to which the powder is exposed [47].

5.4.2 Low dose formulations: adhesive mixtures

Two major aspects prevent the use of most inhalation drugs without further processing into a suitable powder formulation: a low dose level and the extremely poor flow properties of micronized particles. Many drugs are administered in the μg-range and dilution is required to ensure reproducible dosing. Micronized inhalation drug particles are thus often mixed with coarse carrier crystals in the size range 60–250 μm, which act not only as a diluent, but also improve the flowability of the formulation. During the blending process, the fine drug particles adhere to the surface of the much larger carrier particles. Such an adhesive mixture (also called ordered mixture, interactive mixture, or carrier-based formulation) is the most common dry powder formulation type. The carrier material should be pharmaceutically inert, chemically and physically stable, and preferably non-hygroscopic. Carriers, like any other excipients for inhalation, need to go through an extensive program of toxicity and safety studies, including administration via the inhaled route, with significant associated costs and risk of delays in the development programs [48]. This obviously constitutes a hurdle to the introduction of new excipients. By tradition, therefore, lactose monohydrate is the most common carrier material, although other materials have been investigated - in particular mannitol [49]. A range of carrier grades for inhalation use are commercially available, see some examples in Fig. 5.10.

During inhalation, the API must detach from the carrier and be dispersed into the airstream in order to reach to the lungs. The interaction between the micronized drug and the carrier is, however, highly complex, as discussed in the previous paragraph. Table 5.1

Figure 5.10 SEM images of carriers used for inhalation, Left: Inhalac 70 (Meggle GmbH, Germany), Center: Respitose SV003 (DFE Pharma, Germany), Right: Parteck mannitol carrier (Merck KGaA, Germany). Note the differences in magnification.

Table 5.1 Carrier particle properties and other formulation properties known to affect the performance of adhesive mixtures for inhalation. From ref. [50].

	Carrier	Drug	Process	Additive	Other
Property	Size	Content	Mixing time	Fine excipient-material	CAB[a]
	Surface roughness	Material	Mixing intensity	Fine excipient-amount	Storage humidity
	Shape	Size	Press-on-force	Coating agent	
	Grade	Shape	Processing pressure		
	Material	Crystal form			
	Surface energy	Mechanical props.			
	Carrier milling	Surface energy			
	Crystal form	Surface roughness			
	Amorphous content				
	Surface chemistry				

[a]Cohesive-adhesive balance, described in the text below.

From reference F. Grasmeijer, N. Grasmeijer, P. Hagendoorn, H.W. Frijlink, A.H. De Boer, Recent advances in the fundamental understanding of adhesive mixtures for inhalation. Curr. Pharm. Des. 21 (2015) 5900–5914.

lists properties of the carrier, the drug, the mixing process, and the additive reported to affect the performance of an adhesive mixture [50]. To obtain a robust and reliable performance of the DPI product, all these properties need to be controlled.

5.4.2.1 Mixing

The two main processes for manufacturing of adhesive mixtures are (i) low shear mixing using a tumbling mixer, and (ii) high shear mixing using an impeller type mixer [51]. A primary goal of the process is to achieve blend homogeneity of the batch at the dose level. Technically, the requirement for content uniformity is often expressed in terms of a relative standard deviation (RSD) of the API content for a number of samples sampled throughout the batch. An RSD of <5% is generally considered as acceptable, e.g. in development work. The break-up of API agglomerates has been identified as the rate-limiting step in the preparation of adhesive mixtures [52]. It takes more time in a low shear mixer, which is why relatively long mixing times are used. For high shear mixers, a few minutes of mixing is usually enough to ensure content uniformity. Prolonged mixing in a high shear mixer may give rise to the generation of fine particles ('fines') by attrition of the coarse carrier crystals and to the creation of amorphous regions at the carrier surfaces [53,54]. Amorphisation influences drug-to-carrier interaction and the mixture stability negatively and is, therefore, highly unwanted.

Fig. 5.11 shows SEM pictures of a selection of adhesive mixture formulations. They all display a similar pattern with the fine API particles predominantly adhered to the carrier particle surfaces.

5.4.2.2 Drug load and surface coverage ratio

Adhesive mixture technology allows drugs to be formulated as low as a few micrograms per dose [55]. The upper dose level is however limited. The dose to the patient can be increased either by increasing the total amount of powder delivered per inhalation, or by an increase in the formulation drug load, but there is a limit to how much powder

Figure 5.11 SEM images of adhesive mixtures consisting of 2% salbutamol sulfate (SBS) and Respitose SV003 (Left), 4% Budesonide (Bud) and Respitose SV003 (Center), and 4% Bud with 1% magnesium stearate and Respitose 003 (Right). Note the differences in magnification.

a patient can inhale without cough or other discomfort. This depends very much on the size and the chemical nature of the particles inhaled, but is normally between 50 and 100 mg of inhaled powder. The maximum drug payload in the mixture is in the range from 5% to 10% w/w, depending on the carrier type used. Hence, the maximum API dose is approximately 5 mg of API per inhalation (i.e. in 50 mg powder) using adhesive mixture technology. However, the higher the drug load, the poorer the powder flow [56]. High drug loads could thus result in difficulties in handling and filling the formulation as well as in emptying the full dose from the inhaler [57]. Hence, drug concentrations in adhesive mixtures are generally less than 2.5% [58]. A way to achieve higher drug loads is to use carriers which themselves are aggregates of e.g. lactose crystals and thus possess cavities and clefts which are larger than the size of the API [59]. During blending, the drug particles find shelter and gather in the cavities without compromising powder flow and ease of handling of the formulation. Inhalac 70 (Fig. 5.10) is an example of this type of carrier.

The drug load of the adhesive mixture not only affects the powder flow; it also affects the dispersibility of the formulation. Several investigations have reported an increase in fine particle fraction (FPF) when the drug load is increased [60–63]. From an industry perspective, however, it is desirable to achieve constant dispersibility over a wide range of API load, as this will be required for dose finding studies.

The available surface area of the carrier particles and the drug load together determine what is known as the 'blend state', i.e. the arrangement of the particles in the carrier-fines unit. The notion of a surface coverage ratio, SCR, is here useful [64,65]. A carrier covered with a close-packed monolayer of API particles gives an SCR value of 1. Above SCR 1, multilayers of fine particles start to form, or alternatively, small clusters of fine-particles adhering to the carrier surfaces. At high SCR values, there is a risk for formation of large aggregates of API only, co-existing with the carrier-fines units, which in turn means inhomogeneous formulation and hence product failure. The behavior is schematically outlined in Fig. 5.12. The 'blend state map' can differ significantly between different carrier grades [65,66].

5.4.2.3 Formulation factors affecting adhesive mixture dispersibility

Despite more than three decades of research and development on dry powders for inhalation, there is still a lack of adequate characterization methods for many of the critical parameters listed in Table 5.1. While the size distribution is often well controlled both for the micronized API and for the carrier, quantitative information on shape and surface roughness is normally lacking. These parameters affect the contact area between API and carrier, and hence the magnitude of the particle interactions. The blending process may alter the particle properties, especially in the case of high shear mixing. The API itself influences the dispersibility of the adhesive blend. It is for example known that salbutamol sulfate (SBS) gives a fair fine particle fraction (FPF) in most systems while beclomethasone dipropionate (BDP) generally yields low FPF values [60,67].

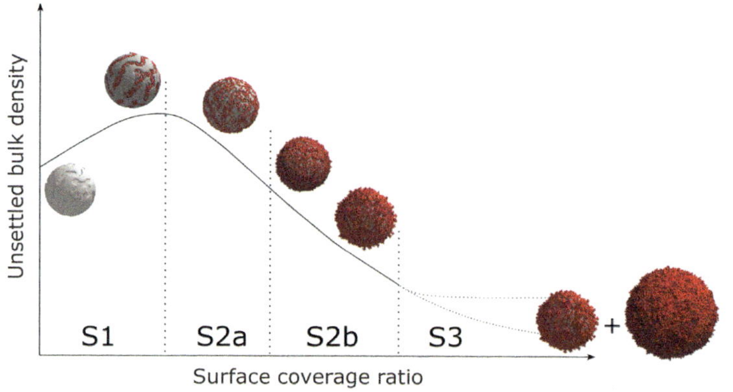

Figure 5.12 Representation of a blend state map. The different blend states S1-S3 are illustrated together with the trends in unsettled (poured) bulk density. S1: API fines are gathering in cavities and clefts of the carrier. S2a: API is adhered to the outer carrier surfaces. S2b: responsive adhered layer. S3: large agglomerates of drug only co-exist with the carrier-fines units. Further details are given in references [59,65].

The interaction force between the API and the carrier is a key factor to the performance of the adhesive mixture and consequently, to therapeutic effect. For a strong adhesive force between API and carrier, the detachment of the drug from the carrier during aerosolization will be limited, leading to a low FPF. On the other hand, the interaction should not be too weak either, as this increases the risk for segregation of the formulation during filling and handling of the inhaler. Direct measurement of the force between API and carrier can be performed using atomic force microscopy (AFM) [68]. However, a limitation is that only very few particles are measured, and it can be questioned whether obtained AFM data really represent the batch. The Cohesive-Adhesive Balance (CAB) technique is a way to assess the relative magnitudes of the API-API, the API-carrier, and the carrier-carrier interactions for specific combinations of an API and a carrier [69]. A CAB value above 1 indicates that the drug is cohesive and prone to API-API interaction, while a value below 1 indicates a propensity for adhesive behavior (i.e. drug-carrier interaction). In the literature, some fair to good correlations between CAB and powder performance in terms of FPF have been reported [70]. However, CAB data are obtained from AFM measurement on single particles, and they do not take account of the effect of the mixing process on the interaction forces in the mixture. Process-induced changes may significantly alter the interactions in the final formulation. Besides, interaction force (including the effect of mixing) and detachment efficacy (during inhalation) do not relate uniquely to each other for a particular API-carrier combination. Various additional effects influence the detachment propensity of a particle with a defined interaction force, such as for instance its position on the carrier surface. Most detachment forces act less effectively on API particles hiding within carrier surface irregularities than on API particles attached on the surface. Hence, the detachment and dispersion by a DPI is highly complex and cannot be captured solely by measurement of forces between the particles measured under standard conditions. Therefore, it is hard to draw any general predictions about formulation performance during dispersion from CAB analysis.

5.4.2.4 Addition of lactose fines

In order to increase the fine particle fraction of the API, fine excipient particles, typically less than 10 μm, can be incorporated in the adhesive mixture. This can be done either by using a carrier grade containing fine particles (intrinsic fines), or by addition of a fine excipient grade in the mixing step (extrinsic fines). Milled lactose carriers contain significant amounts of fine particles while sieved grades most often have a narrow size distribution with a low fine particle content. Still the amount can be significant in comparison to the API load also for sieved grades, e.g. see Fig. 5.10B and [60]. Several investigations have been undertaken to clarify the mechanism behind the 'fines effect', as has been reviewed by Jones and Price [40]. It seems however difficult to attribute reported observations to one single mechanism. Various additional variables play a role as well, such as the particle size distributions of the API and the added fines, the amount of added fines and the surface structure of the carrier lactose. Addition of coarse lactose fines (CLF, $d_{50} \cong 4$ μm) were seen to give a better effect on FPF than addition of fines lactose fines (FLF, $d_{50} \cong 2$ μm) at all investigated flow rates [45]. Similar findings have been reported by Adi et al., studying addition of both lactose and glucose fines to adhesive mixtures [71,72].

5.4.2.5 Coating agents

Additives that serve to coat the other mixture constituents, so called "coating agents" or "force control agents", are today commonly used in adhesive mixtures. These agents are lubricant type materials, often with a prior use in pharmaceutical tableting, e.g. magnesium stearate (MgSt) and sodium stearyl fumarate (PRUV). The amino acid leucine (L-leucine) is seen to act in a similar way. MgSt has been shown to enhance the dispersibility of the API [53,61], and has been approved for use in several DPI products [73]. It can also improve the physical stability of the adhesive mixture [74], primarily because addition of MgSt renders the formulation less moisture sensitive. The use of MgSt may thus omit the need for desiccant in the dry powder inhaler.

Different processes can be used to add the coating agent to the formulation. The most common way is to pre-blend the carrier with coating agent prior to addition of the API. A comprehensive study illustrating the smearing mechanism of MgSt was performed by Tai et al. using a Turbula mixer [75]. Fig. 5.13 displays a TOF-SIMS image of lactose carrier particles coated with MgSt in a high shear mixer. The overall size and shape of the carrier particles remain unchanged during the coating process.

Figure 5.13 TOF-SIMS image of carrier particles (Respitose SV003) coated with 1% MgSt in a high shear mixer. Red color refers to lactose, green to MgSt.

When adding coating agents to the adhesive mixture, it is critical to select the right parameters, both for the coating process and for the subsequent mixing process. If the wrong parameters are selected, there may be no improvement in drug dispersibility, and even a reduction in FPF may result. Fig. 5.14 illustrates the effect of mixing time on the FPF of adhesive mixtures containing (top) leucine and MgSt (bottom).

Mechanofusion and the Cyclomix are intense processing techniques that have been investigated for carrier particle coating and it has been reported that they can provide significant improvements in powder flow [76]. However, to our knowledge, such processes have not been applied for any inhaled product on the market. Besides improving the dispersibility and physical stability of DPI products, coating agents can provide an enhanced degree of control of some additional formulation properties. The explanation for this is that the additives are smeared out onto the complex, irregular and often contaminated lactose surfaces, thereby rendering them smoother and more uniform, and additionally that electrostatic charging effects are reduced.

5.4.2.6 Spheronized formulations

The adhesive mixture is the standard formulation type for low dose DPI products. However, formulations consisting of fine particles only also exist, e.g. in Pulmicort Turbuhaler and Asmanex Twisthaler. Such formulations consist of micronized particles,

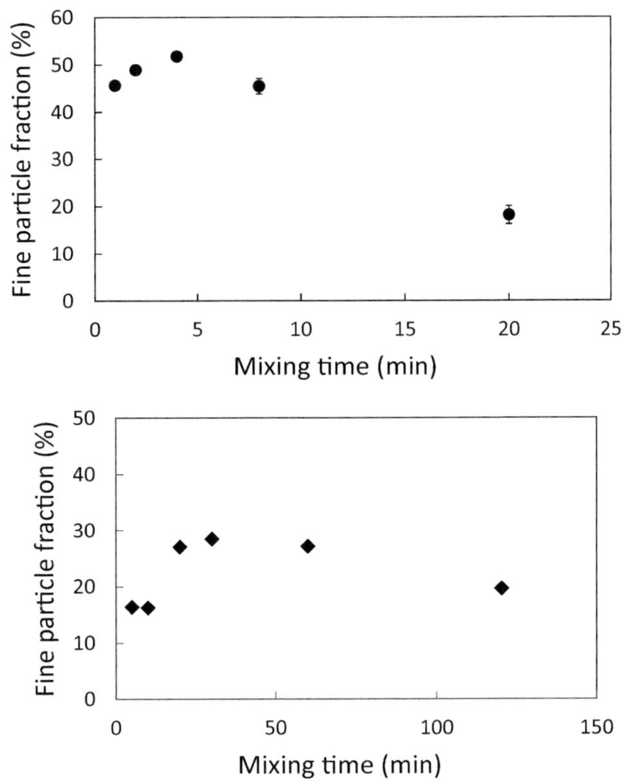

Figure 5.14 Fine particle fraction as a function of mixing time for adhesive mixtures containing, Top: 5% budesonide, 1% leucine (left) and LactoHale LH100, Bottom: 8% BDP, 1% MgSt and Respitose SV003. For the latter study, see [53].

either pure or mixed with a fine particle excipient, usually lactose monohydrate (for reasons discussed previously). As stated above, micronized powders are challenging to handle and tend to form lumps and aggregates when subject to handling, e.g. in a powder filling system. The natural tendency to aggregate can however be utilized in a 'spheronization' process, in which spherical agglomerates of controlled size and density (Fig. 5.15) are formed by a process which combines sieving and dry granulation steps. The 'spheronization' process dramatically improves powder flow, thus enabling high speed filling of the powder. The agglomerate strength of the spheres must however be low, and specifically designed devices with the ability to break up the agglomerates must be used in order to ensure efficient dispersion during inhalation.

5.4.3 High dose formulations

There is not a unique definition for the term high dose formulation or a high dose inhaler as 'high dose' can refer to the drug mass as well as to the powder mass to be

Figure 5.15 Light micrograph of a 'spheronized' powder formulation.

delivered to the patient. Often powder doses that cannot be administered in a single breath are considered high doses, but they may contain only small drug amounts because of the formulation technology used. The ambiguity is the consequence of the formulation processes used, such as spray drying and adhesive mixture preparation, in which drug and excipient(s) are incorporated within the same single particulate unit. In adhesive mixtures this is a physically stable 'carrier-fines unit' and from co-spray drying it is frequently an inseparable solid dispersion of drug and excipient(s) in the same particle. Recently, it has been proposed to consider drug doses <2.5 mg as low and drug doses >2.5 mg as high [58]. The underlying reasoning is that 2.5 mg is about the maximal drug amount for a single breath dose that can be processed into an adhesive mixture because of mixture stability reasons.

High drug doses for inhalation are for instance antibiotics [77] and various systemically acting drugs, including levodopa [78,79], loxapine [80] and insulin [81]. They vary from a few (e.g. insulin), to several tens and possibly hundreds of milligrams (e.g. antibiotics). The maximal powder dose that patients can handle has never systematically been investigated, but it is known that it depends on the chemical nature of the drug. Tolerability can be affected by the nature of the counterion, as has been shown for colistin [82] and the aerosol deposition pattern. Substantial particle deposition on the mechanical cough receptors in the throat should be avoided [83]. Whether these receptors are triggered or not, depends largely on the size distribution of the inhaled particles and the velocity at which they enter the throat. However, some patients find inhalation of high powder doses also burdensome when the cough receptors are not triggered and in order to avoid choking, chest tightness and couch, the use of excipients should be minimized in order not to increase the inhaled powder mass significantly further. Minimizing the use of excipients and avoiding to increase the powder volume by making low density particles may also prevent that multiple inhalations for a single dose are needed. However, refraining from using abundant amounts of excipient, in particular the pore forming agents to increase particle porosity for improved dispersion, has the consequence that the powder properties largely depend on those of the drug itself. This affects particularly the flow properties and the dispersibility of the powder. Therefore, the inhaler design needs to meet the demands for correct powder handling in this respect.

For high dose DPI's, individual doses are normally pre-metered into capsule, blisters or other types of powder compartments because of issues with dose metering in multi dose reservoir devices. The extreme cohesiveness of micronized drug formulations in the absence of large carrier crystals makes not only dispersion difficult, but also reproducible gravity filling of small cavities impossible. In addition, large powder quantities containing multiple doses cannot be stored in a relatively large multi-dose reservoir. Movements while carrying the DPI around change the powder density significantly and deteriorate the accuracy of dose metering even further. Also, soft spherical free-flowing pellets are distorted in a relatively large multi-dose reservoir. The necessity of pre-metering reduces the need of powder formulation primarily to particle formulation or engineering. Engineering aims to control or tailor particle shape, particle surface composition and rugosity and particle density in addition to the particle size distribution. All these particle properties influence dispersion for reasons explained in previous paragraphs. Particle engineering may also serve other purposes such as improving the drug stability, increasing wettability and the dissolution rate, controlling the drug release pattern, prolong the particles' residence times in the lungs, e.g. by escaping macrophage clearance, enhancing the absorption, etc. Except for improving the dispersion performance, these formulation purposes are not further discussed in this chapter as they are not relevant to controlling the aerosol delivery to the respiratory tract. Also, liposomal dry powder formulations are disregarded because of their low drug load. (e.g. Refs. [84,85]).

Engineered particles (Section 5.3) for formulations with and without excipients are eminently appropriate for high dose drugs and can be found in the literature. Particles prepared by spray drying can be spherical or irregular, have different morphologies, exhibit internal and external voids, be layered or have composite shells, contain embedded nanoparticles or small air bubbles (solid foams) among many other forms. They can also have enriched surfaces by compounds that reduce the interparticle forces, thereby acting as dispersion enhancers. Such compounds include lipids (e.g. Ref. [86]), trileucine (e.g. Ref. [87]), L-leucine (e.g. Ref. [88]) and magnesium stearate (e.g. Ref. [89]). Dispersion enhancers can also be co-micronized with drugs for the same effect, as has been shown for magnesium stearate (e.g. Ref. [90]) and L-leucine (e.g. Ref. [91]). The advantage of using dispersion enhancers for dispersion improvement is that required excipient concentrations are low (generally less than 5%), whereas for magnesium stearate a positive effect on the stability of the powder has been reported (e.g. Ref. [92]). Most dispersion enhancers have not been approved for inhalation yet however, except for magnesium stearate which is co-processed with various low dose drugs for marketed products already (e.g. Refs. [93,94]).

Spray drying can also be used to create highly porous particles. The benefits of such particles for inhalation were first recognized by Edwards et al. [28]. They reported at least two-fold improved dispersion for large porous particles compared to non-porous high-density particles, using a simple capsule inhaler. They also mentioned the advantage of avoiding phagocytic clearance from the lungs. A concept for low-density particle preparation, originally developed by Alliance Pharmaceuticals, has further evolved into the PulmoSphere and the Aerosphere Technologies (Fig. 5.6). The technology has been applied for developing dry powder antibiotic formulations, including Tobramycin [95] and Ciprofloxacin [96]. For the administration of these powders the Turbospin capsule DPI is used, also referred to as Podhaler for Tobramycin PulmoSphere, brand name TOBI, and T-326 for Ciprofloxacin PulmoSphere.

A disadvantage of large porous particles for high dose drugs is their large volume and they can also contain high mass percentages of excipients. An increase in geometric diameter from 3.5 to 8.5 μm (2.4x) alone, as reported by Edwards et al. [28], results theoretically in an increase in the powder volume by a factor 14 (2.4^3), if the packing density of the particles remains the same. This is without an additional contribution to the volume from the excipients used. PulmoSphere particles have drug contents of 54% and 65% for tobramycin (free base) and ciprofloxacin respectively, and drug contents in many particle-engineered powders in literature are even considerably lower (e.g. Ref. [97]). This has the consequence that multiple inhalations may be necessary for the inhalation of a single dose which may adversely impact on adherence to the therapy. Hence, developing more efficient inhalers may be a better route to the delivery of higher doses, particularly if the drug is an antibiotic. Considering that minimum inhibitory concentrations (MICs) need to be achieved throughout the entire lung, the inhalation of huge amounts of powder will be necessary to prevent bacterial resistance development in the most distal airways, where the surface area is largest and drug concentration (in mg/m^2) is lowest.

5.5 The dry powder inhaler device

5.5.1 The dose (metering) system

Basically, three different concepts of dose (metering) systems exist for dry powder inhalers: single dose compartments like capsules, blisters or other types of small containers (Figs. 5.16 and 5.17), multiple unit-dose containers like blisters on a disk or strip (Fig. 5.18) and dose metering cavities deriving a desired volume of powder from a storage chamber (reservoir) (Fig. 5.19). The primary functions of the dose (metering) system are:

- Carrying, or metering the volume of drug formulation (powder) that contains the amount of drug for a single dose,

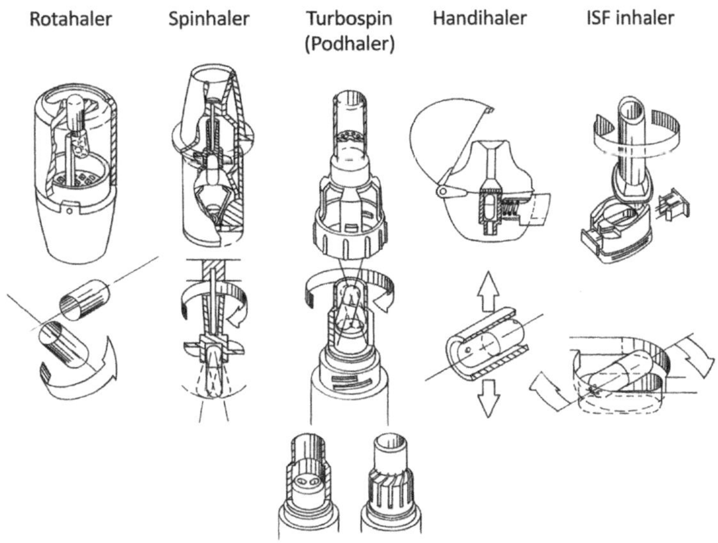

Figure 5.16 Examples of single dose compartment inhalers making use of hard gelatin or hydroxypropyl methylcellulose (HPMC) capsules. All devices depicted have their own opening or piercing system for the capsules and specific capsule motion in the inhaled air stream. Capsule halves in the Rotahaler are separated from each other and the capsule bottom containing the powder starts rattling in the inhaler chamber to release its contents upon inhalation. All other DPIs have different piercing mechanisms to perforate the capsule wall either on one (Spinhaler) or both ends (Turbospin, Handihaler and ISF Inhaler). Capsules in the Spinhaler and Turbospin are made to wiggle during rotation along their longitudinal axis; those in the Handihaler jump up and down primarily in the narrow channel in which they are placed and capsules in the ISF Inhaler start spinning in a disk-shaped chamber.

- Enabling complete powder entrainment from the dose (metering) compartment during inhalation,
- Protecting the drug formulation from environmental influences, such as humidity, light and dust; if necessary, a desiccant compartment may be added,
- Protecting the drug formulation from mechanical damage (e.g. segregation of adhesive mixtures or distortion of soft pellets) during normal inhaler use.

In addition, the design of the dose (metering) compartment should make opening (for pre-filled dose carrying containers) or displacement (for dose metering cavities) possible in a simple action by the patient. After opening, waste of the powder from the compartment upon holding the inhaler in tilted position must be prevented. The design of a dose metering compartment must furthermore ensure that at least part of the inhaled air stream is directed through the compartment for entrainment of the complete powder mass. This requires that the partial flow rate through the powder compartment is sufficiently high and that the exit holes of the compartment are sufficiently large.

To meet the prerequisites for consistent dose delivery, the type of dose (metering) compartment must be compatible with the powder formulation. Capsules are the oldest and most widely used type of drug container for single doses of inhalation powder. Mostly size number 3 is used and various compositions and manufacturing processes are being used. To administer their contents to the patient, capsules are usually (one- or two-sided) pierced with one or more pins immediately prior to inhalation. During inhalation the pierced capsule starts spinning, wiggling, vibrating or tumbling to release the powder. The holes through which the powder has to be discharged are extremely small however, which limits the size of pellets or the carrier particles in adhesive mixtures. Too large particles can lead to an incompatibility between the powder formulation and the device by blocking the discharge holes. Also, when the powder is too cohesive, emptying of pierced capsules may be problematic [98].

Traditionally, hard gelatin capsules are used, but they become brittle if they lose moisture when they are stored under low humidity conditions or exchange water with the drug formulation (e.g. Ref. [99]). This generally results in loose shell flaps around the perforation hole(s) that hinder the emptying of the capsule during inhalation. Severe capsule damage around the perforation hole(s) may even result in complete capsule fragmentation, and the inhalation of shell fragments, when the capsule starts to rotate or spin violently during inhalation. Therefore, preference is often given to hydroxypropyl methylcellulose (HPMC, or Hypromellose) capsules since they became available for inhalation around 2000 [100]. HPMC is less brittle, in spite of a lower moisture content (6% versus 14% for gelatin at 50% RH). Studies into the piercing and fragmentation of inhalation capsules were performed by Birchard et al. [99] and Martinelli et al. [101].

Wauthoz et al. [102] studied the delivered dose, fine particle dose and capsule retention for formoterol-lactose mixtures with the low-resistance Axahaler (based on the RS01 device, Plastiape, Italy) using different capsule types and brands. They found significant differences in aerodynamic performance between the capsules which they attributed to differences in water content and the proportion of capsule fragmentation around the perforation holes. Their data seem to confirm those presented earlier for capreomycin oleate formulations by Schoubben et al. [103], who showed that the differences to be found between different capsules types may furthermore depend on the type of formulation and inhaler used. Saleem et al. [104] contributed differences in aerosolization performance of a carrier-based salbutamol-lactose (1:50) mixture from HMPC capsules to differences in the amount of lubricant used to remove the capsule halves during production from the mold pins.

Disadvantages of capsules in addition to a high drug retention [105] and the risk of fragmentation, are a poor protection of the drug against moisture uptake from the air [106] and a long dose emission time [107]. Even for particle engineered powders, designed to ensure efficient and reproducible delivery to the lungs, effective emptying of capsules using an inhaler like the Turbospin (T-326) may require a minimum inhaled volume of 1.4 L at a flow rate of 45 L/min or higher [108]. It has also been reported that capsules for inhalation were mistaken by patients for oral capsules (and the other way around). Patients may get confused in this respect, when the color codes of the different capsules that they use are insufficiently discriminating, when manufacturers suddenly decide to change the color code, or when the patient receives capsules from a different manufacturer (using different colors). Particularly older patients with vision loss have great propensity for this error and the risk of mixing up capsules has increased since preference policies were started in several countries and patients receive different brands of the same medication, depending on which is cheapest at the moment of dispensing. This is a strong rationale for pre-loaded inhalers. Currently, also blisters and plastic dose compartments or tubs are used for carrying single drug doses (Fig. 5.17).

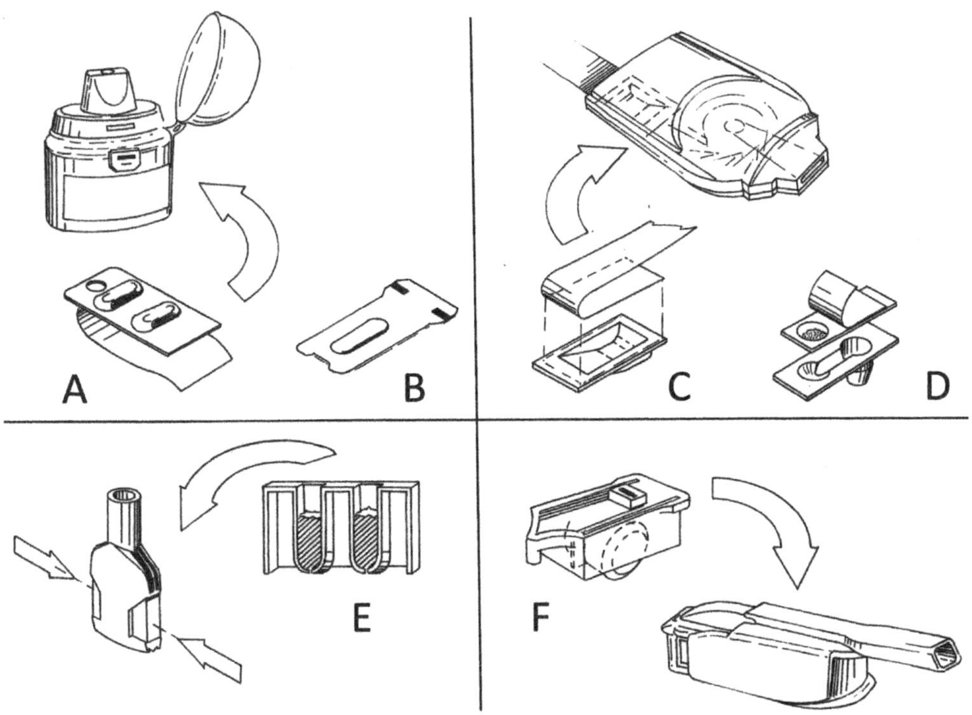

Figure 5.17 Examples of single dose compartment inhalers making use of blisters (A, B, as for the Elpenhaler and Exubera inhaler respectively), single plastic cups (C, D and F as for the Cyclops, Conix One and Dreamboat respectively), and pre-filled compartments in a slide (E, Twincaps inhaler). Regarding the inhalers, only the Elpenhaler, Cyclops, Twincaps and Dreamboat are shown. The compartments for the Elpenhaler, Cyclops and Conix One are sealed with a peelable lidding foil.

Multiple unit-dose inhalers mostly utilize blister cups in a long strip of aluminum laminate or blister cups in a disk. They are sealed with an aluminum lidding foil and provide good moisture protection. Cold formed aluminum blisters are bound to maximal ratios regarding their width and depth however. They also have rounded corners and are vulnerable to deformation when subjected to local pressure. This can make blisters aerodynamically less appropriate for powder entrainment [109], resulting in incomplete emptying. Peeling off the lidding foil may have preference above perforation as it prevents that fragments of lidding foil from local rupture become a barrier in the way out for the drug formulation. This leaves high powder residues in the blister cup. The number of blister cups in a disk is quite limited (e.g. GSK Diskhaler). The number of blisters on a strip with an automatic dual winding system for the blister strip and lidding foil can be much higher but the transport mechanism for such devices is considerably more complex (e.g. GSK Diskus and Ellipta: Fig. 5.18).

Powder containers (reservoirs) in multi-dose inhalers carry between 50 and 200 doses. They have a dose metering system to be operated by the patient. They require drug formulations with good to excellent flow properties, like adhesive mixtures, which contain generally free-flowing lactose size fractions. Soft spherical pellets have good flow properties too, but they are mechanically instable and likely to become an unstructured powder mass when the inhaler is dropped or treated violently. Therefore, they are less suitable for multi-dose inhalers when the drug

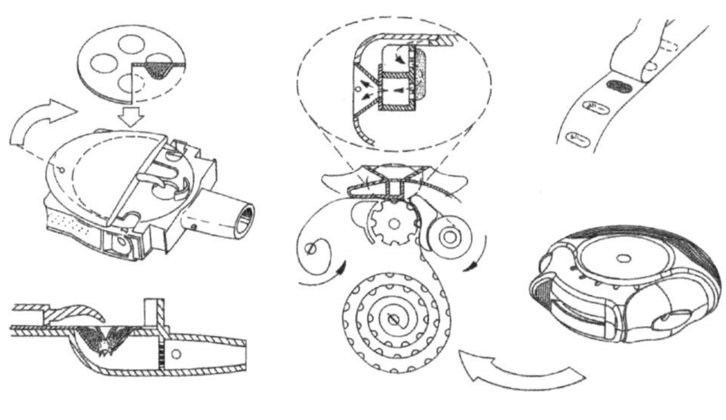

Figure 5.18 Examples of blisters on a disk (as for the Diskhaler) and on a strip (as for the Diskus) respectively. The disk can be rotated to arrange one of the blisters in line with the passageway for the inhaled air stream after which both lidding foil and blister film are perforated (bottom left). The blister strip in the Diskus is transported with a complex winding system that separates blister strip and lidding foil in the vicinity of the mouthpiece (center). The open blister is placed against a chamber with a partition that separates the chamber into a section that communicates with the air supply channel and a section opening towards the mouthpiece. Both chamber sections also have an opening towards the blister (center top).

dose, and by that, the total mass of powder in the container is high, which results in high forces of impact. Different dose metering principles are known (Fig. 5.19). They all have a volumetric metering cavity corresponding to a powder mass containing a single drug dose. The cavity is placed underneath the powder container and is filled when the inhaler is kept in the correct position by the force of gravity. For well-designed dose metering principles, filling can still be accurate when the inhaler is held oblique at angles less than 45 degrees from the right position. Accurate filling may also be supported by a puff of air through the powder bed as for the Spiromax, formerly referred to as Airmax [110].

DPIs like the Genuair (AstraZenenca) and NEXThaler (Chiesi) have a slide with a single powder metering cavity that is in open connection with the powder container while the inhaler is not activated. A multi-dose DPI for low dose drugs that does not contain adhesive mixtures, but soft spherical pellets from mixtures of micronized drug and micronized excipient (see Fig. 5.15) is the Turbuhaler (AstraZeneca). The dose metering system of this inhaler is basically the same as that for adhesive mixtures with a drug reservoir. It has a rotating disk with five filling positions, each consisting of multiple small holes. The formulation has been spheronized to enable rapid filling of the reservoirs (see Fig. 5.15). Once in contact with the dosing disk, the spheres are forced into the small holes by a series of successive scrapers being in contact with the disk when the patient activates dose metering.

For single-dose and multiple unit-dose inhalers, consistent dose delivery depends on the performance of the filling technique and the efficiency of dose entrainment from the dose (measuring) compartment during inhalation. The most appropriate type of

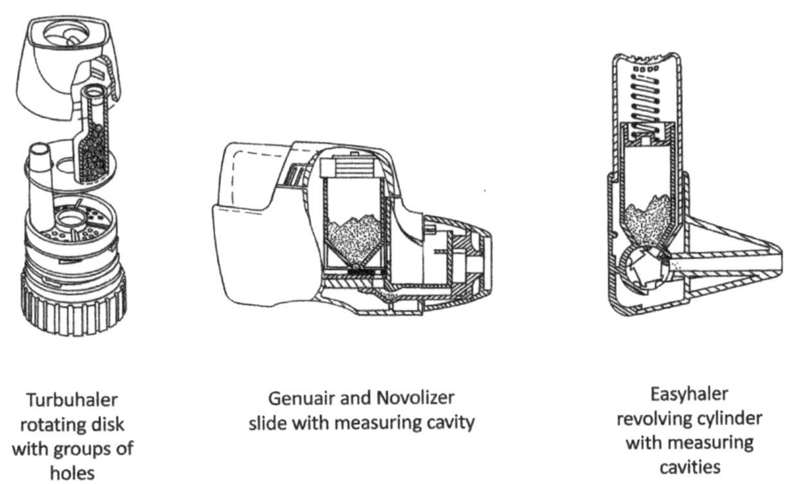

Figure 5.19 Examples of multi-dose reservoir inhalers with a metering disk, slide or cylinder.

filling apparatus for a particular drug formulation depends on the dose weight and the type of formulation. Filling of capsules is most standard and several methods of precise powder dosing into capsules have been reviewed by Edwards [111]. Recent advancements in the dosing of challenging (highly cohesive) powders in the mg-range in capsules were reported by Stranzinger et al. [112] and Wagner et al. [113]. Not much in the literature can be found about dosing in powder containers for multi-dose inhalers or in single dose compartments of multiple-unit dose DPIs. Some of the techniques used are proprietary and confidential information and many of them have challenges of their own, often related to the specific properties of the drug formulation [114]. Eskandar et al. [115] showed that the Omnidose vacuum technique (Harro Hoefliger, Germany) is suitable for reproducible metering of very low doses in the range of 1−5 mg. The technique is for instance used to fill the single dose compartments for the Twincer and Cyclops DPI devices [116,117]. A special feature of the vacuum filling technique is that it compacts cohesive powders into small pellets. This may exclude its use for capsule inhalers with small piercing pins or multidose inhalers with small air passage ways transporting the drug formulation from the dose compartment.

The consistency of delivered dose for the combination of adhesive mixtures and dose metering slides or cylinders depends also largely on the ability of the drug formulation to withstand segregation. The carrier size fractions used to prepare adhesive mixtures are often quite wide, ranging from 10 to 250 μm (or more). Some formulations also contain considerable amounts of fine excipient particles (<10 μm) to improve the separation of the drug and carrier particles during inhalation. Wide, or bimodal size carrier distributions increase the risk of segregation, which likely changes the apparent powder density and, thus, the mass of powder in the same volume. With a constant metering volume this can result in a variable drug dose over the life span of the multi-dose DPI. Detachment of drug particles from the carrier crystals in the drug reservoir as a result of rough inhaler handling (e.g. shaking, dropping or vibration) is another potential risk. Liberated drug particles may adhere onto inhaler parts or accumulate in dead corners of the container and become 'lost' for administration to the patient. Fine drug and carrier particles may also end up between moving parts of multi-dose inhalers and increase the friction between these parts to the point where operating the dose metering principle by the patient is no longer possible. These examples show that there must be a good balance between the requirements on physical formulation stability, dispersion and inhaler functioning. For pre-filled dose compartments (e.g. capsules and blisters) the risk of segregation is shifted to the filling process.

Finally, incompatibility of the dose (metering) principle with the dispersion principle must be avoided. Some dispersion principles have a limited powder payload, like powder circulation and classifier chambers. Because there is a certain residence time for the powder in such chambers, they may become overloaded when the powder dose is larger than the payload limit and dropped in the chamber as a whole. This results in the release of insufficiently dispersed particles [116]. A good balance between the loading and unloading rate of the disperser is, thus, needed but it must not prevent that the total drug dose is released in the first 0.5−1 L of inhaled air.

5.5.2 The powder dispersion principle

Adequate powder dispersion requires that the interaction forces between the individual particles in the inhalation powder are exceeded to obtain an aerosol with primary particles in the correct aerodynamic size distribution. However, complete dispersion of fine cohesive powders is difficult with separation forces arising from fluid energy [118]. Common fluid energy dispersers such as eductors, nozzles, Venturis and capillary tubes are inappropriate for complete dispersion of cohesive powders, even at operating pressures of a few hundred kPa. Particularly the detachment of drug particles from carrier crystals in adhesive mixtures is difficult. Particles with diameters smaller than 10 μm cannot effectively be removed by drag forces generated during inhalation and about ten times as much force is required to remove 98% of particles from a surface as that required for 50% removal [119]. Unfortunately, many DPIs do not have a distinct dispersion principle and the range of pressures to operate them is limited to what most patients can achieve, which is only approximately 2−8 kPa.

From a theoretical viewpoint three variables exist for optimizing the powder dispersion process during inhalation: (a) the type of dispersion force, (b) the magnitude of the dispersion force and (c) the duration of the force, or the number of repetitions at which a separation force is applied. For the type of force, a selection can be made from drag, lift, and inertial forces such as acceleration or centrifugal forces (Fig. 5.20).

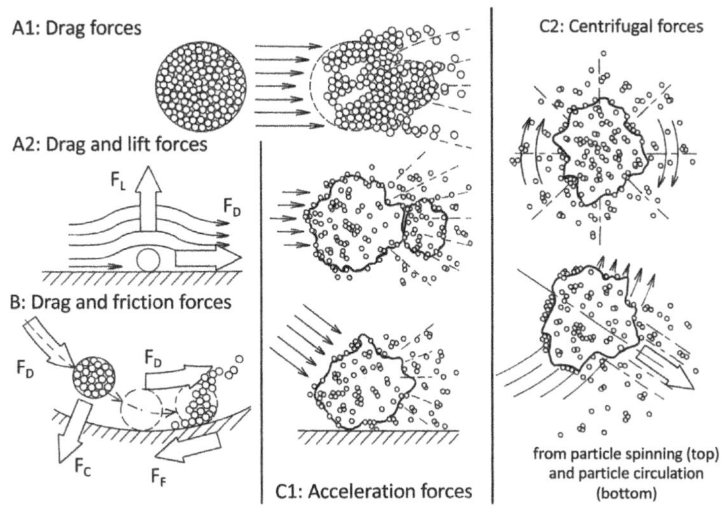

Figure 5.20 Schematic presentation of dispersion forces utilized by dry powder inhalers (see text for the descriptions).

Drag forces may occur as the result of a sudden change in flow direction for the particle-laden air, a narrowing or widening of the passageway for the air stream that causes an acceleration, or in regions of high turbulence. These examples result in a (at least temporary) difference in the velocity (and/or flow direction) between the air and particles in that air stream due to a difference in inertia (Fig. 5.20.A1). It creates an air flow along the particle surface resulting in a drag force (F_D) acting on the particle, which may be a drug particle attached to a carrier crystal (Fig. 5.20.A2). As the air flow is deflected over the particle, its velocity is increased according to the law of energy conservation, and also a lift force (F_L) is created. The resulting combined drag and lift forces may detach the adhering particle from the carrier surface, as in the dispersion of adhesive mixtures. However, drag forces acting on inhalation particles are relatively small and proportional to the first power of the diameter (Stokes' law). A more effective application of the drag force is in a combined action with a friction force (Fig. 5.20.B). Particles circulating in a disk-shaped chamber or being dragged through a spiral-shaped channel by the air flow slide along the cylindrical wall of the circulation chamber or channel, respectively, by the combined action of a drag and centrifugal force. This results in a friction force opposing the drag force, which gives rise to particle disruption by internal shear when the particle is a soft agglomerate.

Inertial forces are generally more effective for powder dispersion as they are proportional with the particle mass and, thus, with the third power of the particle diameter [46]. They can be divided into acceleration forces and centrifugal forces and there are different manners of generating them, including particle-particle or particle-wall collision, (carrier) particle spinning and rotation or circulation. Particle-particle collision may be the result of rapid acceleration of the air stream in which the particles are suspended. When the aerosol consists of particles with different diameters, they will have different stopping distances [119] as small particles accelerate (or decelerate) faster than large particles. This is shown in Fig. 5.20.C1 for particles in a decelerating air stream causing the largest particle with highest inertia to collide with a smaller particle. Upon collision of a 'carrier-fines' particle against an inhaler wall, the carrier particle is rapidly decelerated to a much lower, or even zero velocity and inertial forces are exerted to all fine particles adhering to its surface. These forces are proportional with particle momentum which provides the largest adhering particles the greatest opportunity for detachment. However, to make particle detachment successful, the force has to act in a direction that takes the drug particle away from the carrier surface and repeated collision may be necessary in order to release sufficient drug particles.

Particles circulating in a disc-shaped circulation chamber, or passing through a spiral-shaped channel, are subjected to centrifugal forces (Fig. 5.20.C2 bottom picture). They may also start rotating around their own central axis (Fig. 5.20.C2 top figure). This spinning creates centrifugal separation forces acting on the small particles attached to the surface of a coarser carrier crystal and internal disruption forces of soft spherical pellets.

Circulation chambers (Fig. 5.21) have theoretically the additional advantage of a classifying ability, similar to a fluid energy mill or a wind sifter. Depending on its specific design, particles stay in circulation for as long as the centrifugal force is larger than the drag force which needs to bring the particles to the outlet opening around the central axis of the chamber. By designing the circulation chamber correctly for the conditions (range of pressure drops) at which it is used, a theoretical cut-off point can be created that approaches the upper size range for inhalation. Such classifiers can be designed to retain carrier particles completely and release drug particles only, but they can also be modified to discharge the entire powder dose in a desirable time span [46].

There may exist several complicating factors to dispersion. Carrier and drug particles in adhesive mixtures are not spherical and drug particles are not all single entities as often assumed in simulation studies (e.g. Refs. [59,120]). In adhesive mixtures, lactose carrier particles are either largely Tomahawk, or wedge-shaped (for sieved products), or highly irregular (for milled products) and they have multiple surface discontinuities. Drug particles are present on their surface both as single entities and as small agglomerates and most of them are accumulated in the carrier surface discontinuities. Consequently, drug distribution over the carrier surface is not homogeneous [50]. This can have a dramatic effect on the dispersion behavior, depending on the inhaler type used. Both the degree of agglomeration and distribution over the carrier surface are difficult to predict as outcome of the mixing process and also difficult to measure, because of the presence of lactose fines and the lack of good characterization methods, although recently some successful attempts have been made (e.g. Ref. [121]). Drug particles and agglomerates accumulated in carrier surface discontinuities find shelter from drag and lift types of dispersion forces. In contrast,

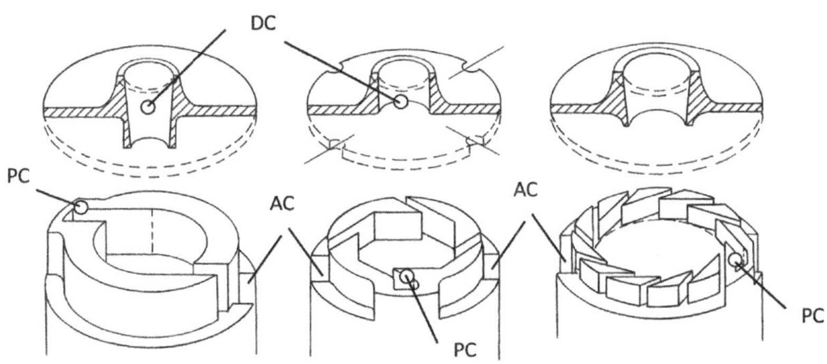

A. Basic classifier B. Genuair classifier C. Cyclops classifier

Figure 5.21 Different classifier concepts for different types of powder formulations and/or dose weights. The basic classifier (A) is designed for research on adhesive mixtures and enables complete carrier retention for analysis of residual drug. PC: Powder supply Channel, AC: Air supply Channel and DC: aerosol Discharge Channel.

accumulation facilitates detachment by inertial forces when the drug agglomerates are coherent and act as a much larger particle being subjected to a much higher detachment force than the single entities that comprise the agglomerate. It makes, under circumstances, granular carriers appropriate for DPIs generating inertial dispersion forces. This is opposite to what has been concluded for many capsule inhalers.

Most capsule inhalers do not really have distinct dispersion principles as separate parts. Discharge and dispersion often occur in the same process step. Coates et al. [122] reported that the dispersion performance of the Aerolizer capsule DPI depends largely on the powder release through the small holes in the spinning capsule. They found that dispersion of mannitol powder at 60 L/min from a pierced capsule increases from 59% to 76%, and throat retention decreases from 14% to 6% compared to when the powder is loaded into the DPI outside the capsule and does not have to pass through the perforation holes. In follow-up studies they showed that most modifications, e.g. changing the voidage of the grid structure and mouthpiece length [123] or mouthpiece geometry [124], has a minor effect on the flow field and dispersion efficacy, although it may influence the drug retention. Only the air inlet size was found to affect dispersion by changing the flow turbulence and particle impaction velocities, but the effect depends on the flow rate [125]. The effect of design modifications on the same capsule device has also been investigated by Shur et al. [126]. They showed that increasing the Cyclohaler resistance by narrowing the inlet channels in different ways to match the resistance of the Handihaler, is insufficient to attain comparable aerosolization performance. This contradicts the simplified conception of Laube et al. [107] that dispersion is a function of the product of the patient's inhalation flow rate and the DPI resistance. A dispersion improvement achieved by Shur et al. [126] with the Cyclohaler, was related to a similarity in air flow rate through the capsule DPIs and the impact velocity of the carrier-based particles. This confirms that the mechanism of action of the dispersion principle is important and not its resistance to air flow, although both may be related to each other. The effect of Handihaler mouthpiece modification on the dispersion has been reported by Son et al. [127]. Benque and Khinast [128] recently studied the complex capsule motion in an Aerolizer DPI and observed that collisions of the capsule with the surrounding inhaler walls during spinning contribute to the discharge of the powder.

5.5.3 Parts incompatibility

DPIs are drug delivery devices for which each of the primary functional parts, including the drug formulation, as described in Section 5.2 has many different design solutions with different features and properties. This means that with only a few functional parts a great number of different combinations is possible. However, well designed individual inhaler components may not be compatible with each other when combined in the same device, or may not be compatible with a certain formulation concept. Inappropriate combinations will yield a mismatch that makes the DPI fail to perform as desired. Some examples have already been given in the previous sections, like the finding in various studies of the positive effect of a certain mass percent of fine excipient particles in adhesive mixtures on the dispersion of inhalation mixtures, mostly when using capsule based inhalers (e.g. Refs. [129,130]). This finding has more or less been adapted as a general conception for the preparation of adhesive mixtures. However, fine excipient particles have a negative effect on dispersion in classifier-based DPIs like the Novolizer [131]. Therefore, combinations of drug formulations that have high contents of excipient fines and classifier-based dispersion principles are to be considered a mismatch. Also, in contrast with capsule inhalers, the dispersion of adhesive mixtures with the Novolizer and Genuair improves when a very coarse granular excipient is used as drug carrier. These examples emphasize that the interplay between inhalers and drug formulations is complex and that the device and formulation must be designed and developed simultaneously and in conjunction with each other to avoid incompatibilities. It also indicates that the outcomes of formulation and dispersion studies have to be evaluated in consideration of all variables (and their interactions). Several examples of interactive factors, e.g. the effect of drug load and flow rate, on the performance of inhalation formulations have been reviewed by Grasmeijer et al. [45,50]. They showed, for instance, that the effect of carrier excipient size on the dispersion of mixtures with a drug can be negligible, negative, or positive, depending on other factors involved.

Mismatches can also arise between DPIs and individual patients or patient groups. Patients need to be able to perform the necessary inspiratory flow maneuver to obtain effective drug delivery to the lungs. Failure in this respect may for instance be the result of insufficient flow rate, inhaled volume or inhalation time. In contrast with what is often claimed in literature, this is not dependent on the inhaler resistance alone. It may also be related to the dispersion principle, the type of powder formulation and the dose release pattern. Patients may have different sensitivity towards throat deposition, resulting either in cough reflexes, local side effects, or both. Such patients may benefit from using a high resistance DPI that prevents the generation of high flow rates, as this reduces inertial deposition in the throat region. They may also prefer a DPI that delivers carrier-free aerosols which prevents the oropharyngeal deposition of (not fully dispersed) drug-carrier units.

5.6 DPI performance

The number of DPI-drug-formulation combinations is almost endless and giving a complete summary of their performance characteristics is impossible. Abundant in vitro deposition studies have been published, and although comparative evaluation between studies is hindered by the use of different impactors, being operated at different flow rates, and different expressions as well as definitions for the fine particle fraction (see Chapter 3), they witness that performance has strongly been improved in the past 30 years (Fig. 5.22).

Progress in delivered fine particle fraction (FPF) has particularly been achieved from particle engineering which is mostly applied for high dose drugs. The delivered FPF to the lung depends not only on the efficacy of the powder dispersion or the properties of the drug formulation however. It is also affected by the extent to which the dose (measuring) system is emptied, and fine particles are lost by adherence onto inhaler walls and by deposition in the oropharynx. Total inhaler retention of several new devices, which may be as high as 35% (Fig. 5.23), or more for capsule inhalers, particularly at flow rates lower than 60 L/min [105], has in many cases been not been decreased compared to classic DPIs with adhesive mixtures. Also, oropharyngeal depositions are still high, in spite of the absence of large carrier crystals, onto which high drug fractions remain attached when they deposit in this region. This is largely due to the low resistance of most currently used inhalers, also for newly developed particle engineered powders which enables the patient to inhale at high flow rates. Several studies have shown a considerable effect of the inspiratory flow curve on the performance of DPIs. Some DPIs are more sensitive to the peak flow rate (Fig. 5.24), others to the acceleration to the peak flow [132,133], whereas the duration of the inhalation maneuver can be relevant to DPIs releasing the aerosol relatively slowly [105,108]. This sensitivity to different flow parameters makes it likely that significant differences in performance can exist between operating the DPI with real life inhalation curves and at a constant flow rate during cascade impactor analysis respectively. This aspect has so far insufficiently been investigated.

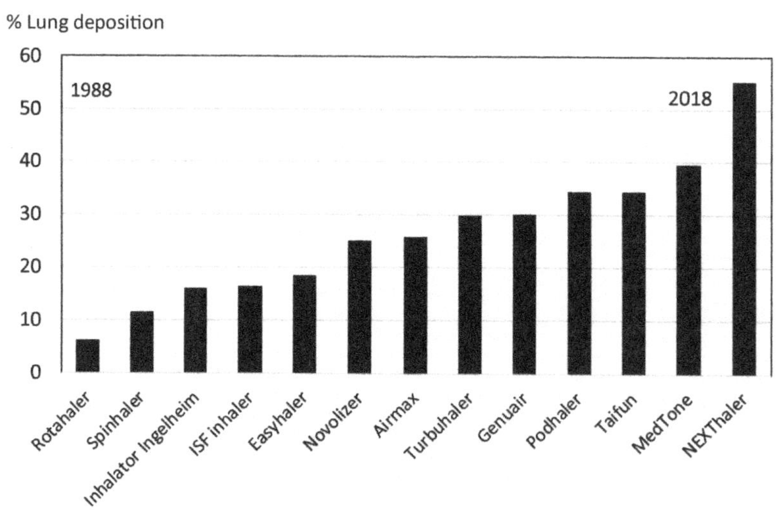

Figure 5.22 Improvement in lung deposition from DPIs at on average 59 (range 30–90) L/min in the past 30 years as measured with radiolabel studies presented in the scientific literature.

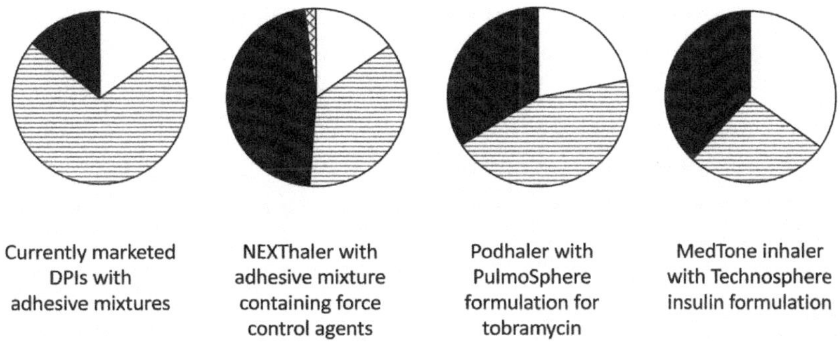

Figure 5.23 Deposition fractions of radiolabeled drugs for different DPIs. The graph representing currently marked DPIs shows mean values of four different DPIs with adhesive mixtures (Easyhaler, Airmax, Novolizer) and a ring tablet (MAGHaler). The NEXThaler contains an adhesive mixture with MgSt as dispersion aid; the Podhaler a PulmoSphere formulation (for tobramycin) and the MedTone inhaler a Technosphere formulation (for insulin). All DPIs were operated at 60 L/min, except for the MedTone at 27 L/min. White sectors represent inhaler retentions, sectors with horizontal stripes represent oropharyngeal depositions, black sectors lung depositions and sectors with grid pattern exhaled fractions (all as percent of label claim).

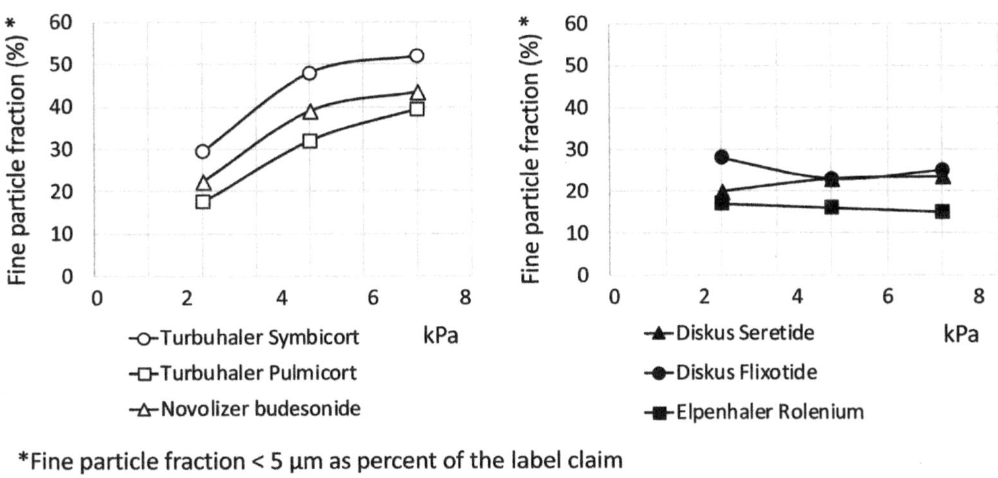

Figure 5.24 Different types of DPIs delivering an increasing FPF with increasing flow rate (left) and delivering more or less the same FPF at all flow rates (right) respectively.

Basically, two different types of DPIs can be distinguished; those delivering an increasing fine particle dose (FPD) with increasing flow rate, and those delivering more or less the same FPD at all flow rates (Fig. 5.24). The latter type has long been considered most favorable (e.g. Ref. [134]), as it suggests a patient effort-independent lung deposition. This conception does not take account of the effect of flow rate on lung deposition however. At a higher flow rate the oropharyngeal and upper airways deposition increases at the cost of intermediate and peripheral lung deposition (e.g. Ref. [135]). A higher FPD at a higher flow rate can at least partly compensate for these losses and improve the therapy.

It must be considered that DPIs with the same total lung deposition may not yield the same clinical effect for the same drug, as differences in the flow rates at which these DPIs are operated can result in different drug distributions. Drug distribution is furthermore influenced by the rate of aerosol release. Particles released in the beginning of inhalation travel deepest and particles released at the end of inhalation remain in the central and intermediate airways. All these differences make it impossible to use in vitro performance data as predictor for lung deposition and therapeutic effect, unless all effects involved are carefully considered.

Intra and inter-patient variability also plays a complex role. It has been shown that the in vitro variability in delivered dose from a DPI may be much higher than that of an MDI, whereas *in vivo* the opposite can be true due to a difference in use between both types of devices reflecting the inter-patient variability [136]. Incorrect inhaler use is one of the reasons for a high inter-patient variability and it has a major effect on performance. Sanchis et al. [137] compared data from 144 studies on inhaler use and computed an overall prevalence of errors of 70% for both DPIs and MDIs. One third of DPI errors relates to incorrect preparation and for instance tilting of the inhaler instead of keeping it at level reduced the delivered dose to an extent depending on the type of DPI [138]. Using multiple devices for the therapy increases the number of errors and the increase is greater for a combination of a DPI and an MDI than for two (or more) DPIs [139]. This is a strong rationale for having all medication for a particular therapy in the same (type of) device.

5.7 Discussion and future perspectives

In the past two decades, most attention in DPI development has been given to formulation improvement by means of particle engineering (e.g. by spray drying and spray-freeze drying) and exploring technologies (e.g. mechanofusion, sugar glass stabilization), and using excipients (e.g. MgSt, leucine) that are new to inhalation. Primary objectives were to improve dispersion for a higher lung deposition efficiency with dry powder inhalation, and to open the door to pulmonary administration of biopharmaceuticals, antibiotics and vaccines as dry powder. Improved delivery efficiency and long-term stability are two major prerequisites for expensive new drugs and one-off administration (e.g. for most vaccines). If vaccination fails, the vaccinee will have no protection. In comparison, limited energy has been put in the design of new device concepts. Most of the new particle engineered powders were developed for delivery to the patient with first generation capsule inhalers (e.g. Tobramycin and Ciprofloxacin PulmoSphere particles in the Turbospin) and only a few new device concepts have been introduced to the market, or in the literature since the millennium change. Novel devices are for instance the Exubera inhaler and the MedTone DPI for insulin, and the Twincer platform and Orbital for high dose antibiotics respectively. The Exubera is meanwhile (2007) withdrawn from the market, and the MedTone is (2020) facing an uncertain future because the inhaled insulin sales volume fails to meet the expectations (e.g. Ref. [140]). In contrast, the Twincer platform and Orbital still have to find their way to the patient. Also new compared to the DPI concept based on the use of capsules, are the Diskus, Ellipta, Genuair, NEXThaler and Spiromax. They are more successful on the market, but they cannot be considered novel developments for improved powder dispersion. The Diskus and Ellipta are devices with a new concept for transport and opening of pre-metered single dose compartments (blisters on a strip). The Genuair and NEXThaler are an improvement and a modification of the Novolizer concept respectively, and the Spiromax is an old device (Airmax) brought to the market again with new name. There are a few more new developments, but neither of them was designed to increase lung delivery, as they mostly lack an effective dispersion principle.

The success and efficacy of pulmonary drug delivery depend, however, not on delivered fine particle dose alone. At least evenly important are the patient's compliance with the instruction and adherence to the therapy. Handling has to be simple and preferably self-intuitive to minimize the risk of inhaler errors, and should include a minimal number of handling steps. Also, the number of inhalations per dose needs to be minimized. If these conditions are not met, the patient may consider inhalation burdensome and difficult to perform correctly, and skip administrations or even completely stop the therapy. Particularly, for chronic use of inhaled antibiotics, this may bring the patient in danger when it results in resistance development by the lung bacteria that need to be eradicated or kept under control. Good compliance and adherence can, however, not be achieved with formulation development. Some formulation concepts may even have an unfavorable effect on these aspects when they result in increased powder masses and/or volumes to be inhaled, particularly when it leads to multiple inhalations for a single dose. For this reason, particle engineering should aim at minimizing the amount of excipients in high dose formulations, as well as keeping the powder porosity as low as possible.

Currently, particularly with the latest developments, dry powder inhalation can in most ways compete well with drug administration via nebulizers or MDIs. Lung depositions up to 40–50% of the label claim can be achieved (Figs. 5.22 and 5.23) and a further increase may be expected when particle engineering and (future) device innovation can be fused for a harmonious interplay. This is best achieved with simultaneous development as the requirements for formulations and device parts need to be adjusted to one another. The focus in device development has to be put on ease of operation to exclude errors and minimize the burden of the patient. Pre-filled single, or multiple dose compartments that need not to be placed in the inhaler device by the patient may have the preference, particularly for the elderly, and design of special devices for specific patient groups (e.g. children) may help to optimize the therapy. In addition, delivery efficiency should be improved by designing innovative dispersion principles which are highly efficient already at low flow rates to minimize oropharyngeal deposition. More efficient dispersion principles may make high excipient contents, and formulation technologies that increase the powder volume for dispersion enhancement, less necessary. As a consequence, higher drug doses can be given and the number of inhalations per dose can be minimized.

DPIs can carry higher drug doses and provide mostly better stability to the drug formulation than MDIs. Compared to nebulizers, they are much smaller whereas dose delivery is much faster, which substantially reduces the daily burden of the patient. DPIs require no auxiliary energy and can be disposable for one-off applications, such as vaccinations. All these advantages in combination with an improved performance expectation make DPIs eminently suitable for delivery of many new biopharmaceuticals, antibiotics and vaccines. The next section, which is the last one of this chapter, deals with in silico simulations of dose delivery from inhalers. This relatively novel area has the potential to further enhance the development of inhalers and their interplay with formulations, in particular as regard the DPI area.

5.8 *In silico* simulation of pulmonary delivery systems

In silico simulations for the study of different pulmonary delivery systems is a rapidly expanding area. It brings together experts in the fields of chemical engineering and pharmaceutical sciences with the aim to improve fundamental understanding of the interplay between formulations and devices which in turn can be used to develop better products. Most effort in this area has been dedicated to dry powder systems, therefore a high-level overview is placed at the end of this chapter. As is obvious, there are huge challenges associated with the aim of capturing the behavior of billions of very fine particles or droplets which are aerosolized in complex devices at highly turbulent airflows.

Computational Fluid Dynamics (CFD) is an established tool for simulation of air flow and is commonly applied in the field of device development [141]. Still, the description of turbulence is a challenge, although significant progress has been made over the years [142]. When it comes to simulation of aerosols, the challenges are even bigger. Firstly, the computational power today is not sufficient to simulate the movement of all particles (or droplets) generated in a typical drug inhalation. It is today feasible to track up to about 10^5 particles using Discrete Element Method (DEM) within reasonable computational time. This is comparable to the number of carrier particles in one dose from an adhesive mixture. However, the number of fine particles in a 100 μg API dose is more than 10 million, and a high dose of 10 mg corresponds to billions of particles. The second challenge is also related to the limitations of computational power as only a few milliseconds of real time behavior can be simulated for micron-sized inhalable particles.

A third challenge is how to provide an adequate description of the particles. To date, only spherical particles have been simulated. This is a fair assumption for droplet generating devices, but far from reality for DPI formulations. While the size and the density of dry particles can be captured in simulations, particle shape and surface rugosity, which are critical to powder dispersion (see Section 5.4.1), are extremely difficult to assess experimentally. This means that it is virtually impossible to select appropriate material properties for the simulations.

From the above it is obvious that several short-cuts need to be taken in order to simulate pulmonary drug delivery systems, and that only approximate behavior can be obtained. Nevertheless, simulation work can contribute to the advancement of inhalation science, by providing information of what can happen inside a device during the dosing event and how this is affected by changes in device geometry, air flow rate, etc. Fig. 5.25 illustrates particle assemblies which are used in simulations. It should be noted that "fines" and "fine particles" in this section refer to API particles.

The remainder of this section is an overview of DPI simulation work. Few studies have been performed on simulating pMDI devices and nebulizers, some of which are described in other parts of this book. For detailed information on underlying physical equations, simulation methodology etc., we refer to review articles by Wong et al. [143], Yang et al. [144] and Sommerfeld et al. [142], and references therein.

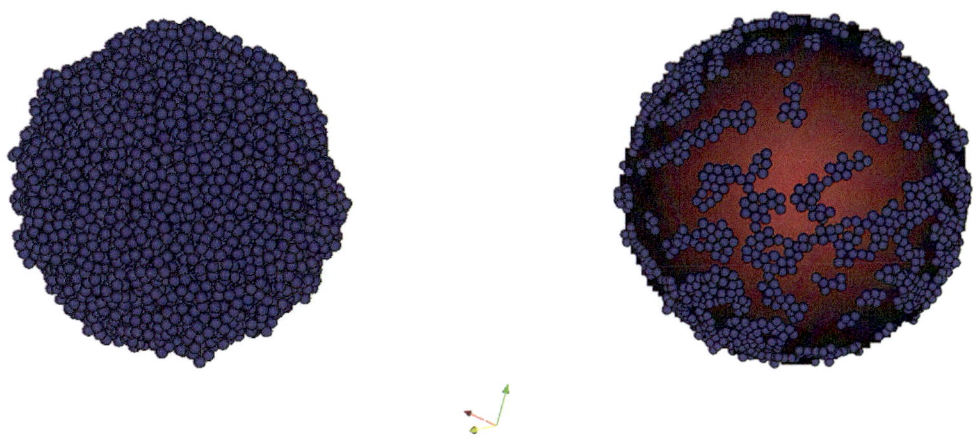

Figure 5.25 Fine particle agglomerate (left) and 'carrier-fines unit' (right) used for in silico simulations.

5.8.1 Simulation of dry powder inhalers

As is obvious from this chapter, dry powder inhalers are complex products and still quite poorly understood. Simulation tools bring the opportunity to study dose emptying from the dosing compartment, powder dispersion and the travel of particles throughout the DPI, all in an integrated approach. As a first step, the often highly turbulent air flow inside the inhaler must be handled adequately. Reported work ranges from the use of a basic Reynolds-averaged Navier-Stokes description (RANS) to more advanced turbulence modeling such as Large Eddy Simulations (LES) [145], and the Lattice-Boltzmann Model (LBM) to resolve the airflow around a 'carrier-fines' unit [142,146]. An important but sometimes neglected aspect in simulating the dose from a DPI is that a realistic flow profile with a relevant rise (acceleration) time should be used and not just a constant air flow rate.

Various approaches have been applied for the description of particles and for the coupling between particles and air-flow. Tracking of single particles can be performed within the CFD code itself, so-called Lagrangian tracking [142]. This may provide useful information about particle trajectories inside the device, such as traveling velocities, frequency and magnitude of wall collisions, and how this is affected by changes in device geometry [123,124,147]. An example relating to the Cyclohaler device is provided in Fig. 5.26. Lagrangian particle tracking however relies on one-way coupling,

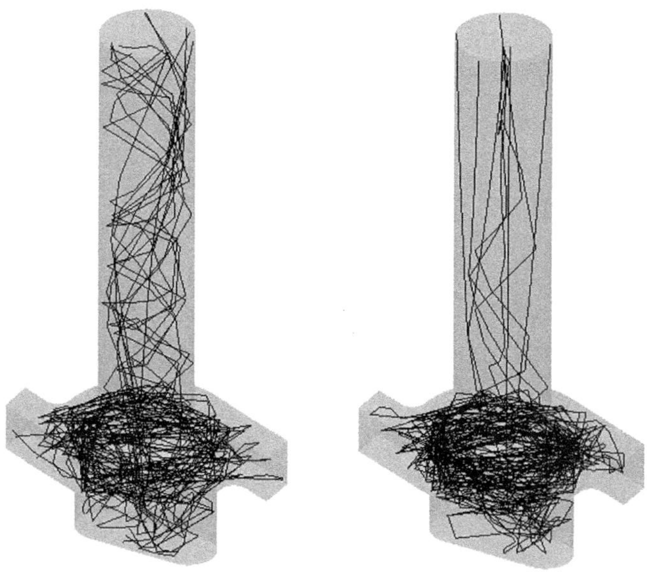

Figure 5.26 Calculated carrier particle trajectories at 70 L/min through a capsule-based inhaler (A) without grid, (B) with grid, i.e. the Cylcohaler. *From reference Y. Cui, S. Schmalfus, S. Zellnitz, M. Sommerfeld, N. Urbanetz, Towards the optimisation and adaptation of dry powder inhalers. Int. J. Pharm. 470 (2014) 120–132, reproduced with permission.*

i.e. the particles are impacted by the air flow but not vice versa. The particles are furthermore tracked one at the time, i.e. neglecting interactions between particles, which poses a major limitation. To take the formulation fully into account, the CFD simulation needs to be combined with a code which takes the behavior of the particles into account, such as the Discrete Element Method (DEM). Coupled CFD-DEM simulations have been applied both to adhesive mixtures and to formulations consisting only of (aggregates of) fine particles.

A complete simulation of the dosing event including all particles is still not feasible, not even for spherical particles. For adhesive mixtures, 'multi-scale' modeling is a way to circumvent this hurdle. This approach separates the 'micro-scale' simulations, which capture the behavior of fine particles and 'carrier-fines units', e.g. upon drag and collisions, from 'macro-scale' simulation of the carrier particles in the device geometry. As these simulations operate at different time-scales, micro-models can be combined with macro-models in a relatively straightforward way. Starting from basic experiments of carrier-fines units impacting a wall, Tong et al. [148] were able to derive models for fine particle release, wall retention and remaining fine particles on the carrier as function of impact velocity and collision angle. In the subsequent macro-scale simulation, the number and magnitude of carrier collisions were tracked in the Aerolizer device. By combining this information with the micro-scale output functions, the fine particle fraction from the device could be estimated.

A further development of multi-scale simulations using fully coupled CFD-LES-DEM was presented by van Wachem et al. [149]. The set-up included micro-models for fines release due to wall and carrier particle collisions as well as from drag forces. An example of a micro-model output is given in Fig. 5.27 and two snapshots from a macro-scale simulation of a cavity type inhaler are shown in Fig. 5.28. Due to the

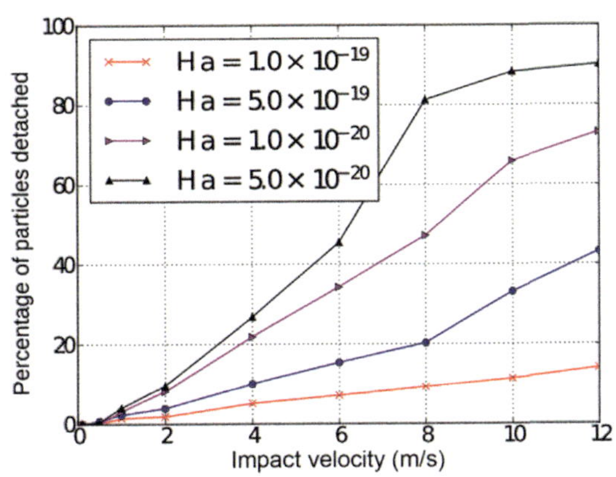

Figure 5.27 Micro-model output showing the fraction of released fine particles (API) versus relative impact velocity for collisions between two carrier-fines units. Four different values for the Hamaker constants (Ha) were simulated, representing different levels of the interaction between fines and carrier.

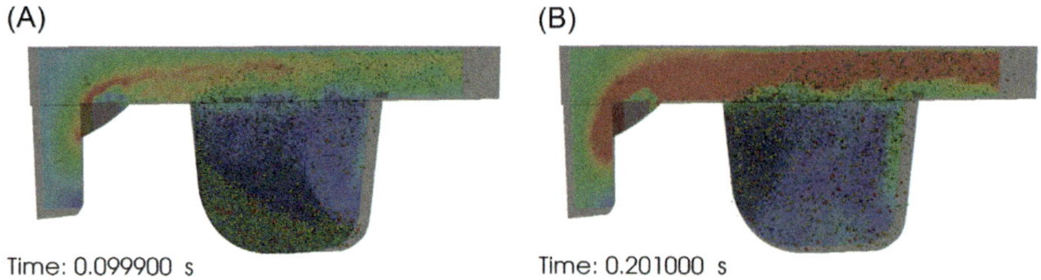

Figure 5.28 Snapshots from CFD-DEM simulation of dose emptying from a cavity-shaped device after approx. (A) 100 ms, (B) 200 ms. Red color indicates high air velocity, blue indicates low. The air flow applied was 60 L/min with a rise time of 240 ms.

multi-scale approach, the entire dose (10 mg of powder) could be simulated, using a realistic flow profile. The validity of the model was assessed by comparison to experimental data, using two formulations and two very different devices, each operated at two air flow rates [150]. By the adoption of an apparent surface energy (or alternatively: apparent Hamaker constant) to account for the interaction between the fines and the carrier, performance trends could be correctly modeled, but in order to get a quantitative prediction of the FPF, the use of a distribution in apparent surface energy was required. This finding is not surprising, considering the polydispersity and heterogeneity of both API and carrier particles in real DPI systems.

The dispersion of formulations consisting of fine particles only can be approached by realizing that fine powders always form aggregates of some kind. Simulation studies of aggregate breakage was pioneered by Thornton and co-workers [151]. Several studies have combined experimental studies performed at different impaction angles with DEM simulations [152–154], which in turn was used to study de-aggregation in the commercial Aerolizer device [155]. However, in total only 8 agglomerates were simulated, which is just a tiny fraction of the dose. To date, a multi-scale simulation approach for fine powder formulations (i.e. without carrier) which takes the complete dose into account, and with full coupling between the air flow and the powder, is still lacking. However, a way to handle aggregates, including the formation of satellite aggregates upon collisions has been envisaged by Bruchmüller and co-workers [156].

Not only the dispersion of fine particles from the device in terms of the fine particle fraction is of interest in simulation studies. Of equal importance would be to predict the extent of fine particles (API) retained in the device and hence not delivered to the patient (see Section 5.6). An attempt to qualitatively capture device deposition was done in [149], and is shown in Fig. 5.29. For quantitative prediction, a better description of the device surfaces would however be required, and both fine particle deposition onto device surfaces and fine particle re-suspension into the air flow need to be considered.

To conclude this section, simulation studies of inhaled drug delivery systems is a rapidly growing area and the level of sophistication is continuously increasing. The ultimate

Figure 5.29 Deposition pattern of fine particles in the "screenhaler" prototype device, bottom view. For more information, see Ref. [149].

goal is to gain improved fundamental understanding of inhaled systems, which in turn should enable the development of more efficient devices and products. However, there are still significant challenges to overcome with an obvious risk that simulated results are flawed. A main challenge is the lack of adequate characterization tools for powders and particles, which means that key particle properties cannot be correctly ascribed *in silico*. The use of apparent properties, such as an apparent surface energy [150] seems to provide a route around this challenge and towards more quantitative predictions. The topic of in silico studies is taken up again in Chapters 7 and 15 where simulation methods used for predicting the fate of the delivered dose are discussed.

References

[1] A.H. De Boer, P. Hagedoorn, M. Hoppentocht, F. Buttini, F. Grasmeijer, H.W. Frijlink, Dry powder inhalation: past, present and future, Expert. Opin. Drug. Deliv. 14 (4) (2017) 499–512.

[2] S.W. Stein, C.G. Thiel, The history of therapeutic aerosols: a chronological review, J. Aerosol Med. Pulm. Drug. Deliv. 30 (1) (2017) 20–41.

[3] K. Hamed, V. Conti, H. Tian, E. Loefroth, Adherence to tobramycin inhaled powder vs inhaled solution in patients with cystic fibrosis: analysis of US insurance claims data, Patient Prefer. Adherence 11 (2017) 831–838.

[4] P. Opitz, C. Schwarz, R. Fischer, M. Hogardt, Dry powder inhalation devices are a safe alternative to nebulizers regarding contamination with CF specific pathogenic germs, J. Cyst. Fibros. 14 (Suppl. 2) (2015) S75.

[5] W.F. Tonnis, A.J. Lexmond, H.W. Frijlink, A.H. De Boer, W.L.J. Hinrichs, Devices and formulations for pulmonary vaccination, Expert. Opin. Drug. Deliv. 10 (10) (2013) 1383–1397.

[6] D.E. Griffin, Current progress in pulmonary delivery of measles, Expert. Rev. Vaccines 13 (6) (2014) 751–759.

[7] J. Tomar, W.F. Tonnis, H.P. Patil, A.H. De Boer, P. Hagedoorn, R. Vanbever, et al., Pulmonary immunization: deposition site is of minor relevance for influenza vaccination but deep lung deposition is crucial for hepatitis B vaccination, Acta Pharm. Sin. B 9 (6) (2019) 1231–1240.

[8] J.G. Weers, D.P. Miller, Formulation design of dry powders for inhalation, J. Pharm. Sci. 104 (2015) 3259–3288.

[9] H.W. Frijlink, A.H. De Boer, Dry powder inhalers for pulmonary drug delivery, Exp. Opin. Drug. Deliv. 1 (1) (2004) 67–86.

[10] A.J. Lexmond, T.J. Kruizinga, P. Hagedoorn, B.L. Rottier, H.W. Frijlink, A.H. De Boer, Effect of inhaler design variables on paediatric use of dry powder inhalers, PLoS One 9 (6) (2014) e0099304.

[11] A.J. Lexmond, P. Hagedoorn, H.W. Frijlink, B.L. Rottier, A.H. De Boer, Prerequisites for a dry powder inhaler for children with cystic fibrosis, PLoS One 12 (8) (2017) e0183130.

[12] A.H. De Boer, P. Hagedoorn, The role of disposable inhalers in pulmonary drug delivery, Exp. Opin. Drug. Deliv. 12 (1) (2015) 143–157.

[13] N. Midoux, N.P. Hosek, P.L. Pailleres, L.J.R. Authelin, Micronization of pharmaceutical substances in a spiral jet mill, Powder Technol. 104 (1999) 113–120.

[14] J.R. Müller, F. Polke, R. Schädel, Spiral jet mills: hold up and scale up, Int. J. Miner. Proc. 44–45 (1996) 315–326.
[15] R. MacDonald, D. Rowe, E. Martin, L. Gorringe, The spiral mill cut size equation, Powder Technol. 299 (2016) 26–40.
[16] L.W. Chan, C.C. Lee, P.W.S. Heng, Ultrafine grinding using a fluidized bed opposed jet mill: effects of feed load and rotational speed of classifier wheel on particle shape, Drug. Dev. Ind. Pharm. 28 (8) (2002) 939–947.
[17] L.E. Briggner, G. Buckton, K. Bystrom, P. Darcy, The use of iso-thermal calorimetry in the study of changes in crystallinity induced during the processing of powders, Int. J. Pharm. 105 (1994) 125–135.
[18] S. Mangal, H. Park, R. Nour, N. Shetty, A. Cavallaro, D. Zemlyanov, et al., Correlations between surface composition and aerosolization of jet-milled dry powder inhaler formulations with pharmaceutical lubricants, Int. J. Pharm. 568 (2019) 118504.
[19] Q. Zhou, B. Armstrong, I. Larson, P. Stewart, D. Morton, Improving powder flow properies of a cohesive lactose monohydrate powder by intensive mechanical dry coating, J. Pharm. Sci. 99 (2) (2010) 969–981.
[20] Q.T. Zhou, L. Qu, I. Larson, P.J. Stewart, D.A.V. Morton, Improving aerosolization of drug powders by reducing powder intrinsic cohesion via a mechanical dry coating approach, Int. J. Pharm. 394 (2010) 50–59.
[21] K. Masters, Spray Drying Handbook, fifth ed., Longman Group Ltd, Harlow, Essex, UK, 1991.
[22] A. Al-Khattawi, A. Bayly, A. Phillips, D. Wilson, The design and scale-up of spray dried particle delivery systems, Exp. Opin. Drug. Deliv. 15 (2018) 47–63.
[23] K. Ståhl, M. Claesson, P. Lilliehorn, H. Lindén, K. Bäckström, Biomolecules can survive spray drying if good conditions are used, Int. J. Pharm. 233 (2002) 227–237.
[24] R. Vehring, Pharmaceutical particle engineering via spray drying, Pharm. Res. 25 (2008) 999–1022.
[25] L. Li, S. Sun, T. Parumasivam, J.A. Denman, T. Gengenbach, P. Tang, et al., L-Leucine as an excipient against moisture on *in vitro* aerosolization performances of highly hygroscopic spray-dried powders, Eur. J. Pharm. Biopharm. 102 (2016) 132–141.
[26] P.J. Skrdla, P.D. Floyd, P.C. Dell'Orco, The amorphous state: first-principles derivation of the Gordon-Taylor equation for direct prediction of the glass transition temperature of mixtures; estimation of the crossover temperature of fragile glass formers; physical basis of the "Rule of 2/3", PCCP 19 (31) (2017) 20523–20532.
[27] A.L. Feng, M.A. Boraey, M.A. Gwin, P.R. Finlay, P.J. Kuehl, R. Vehring, Mechanistic models facilitate efficient development of leucine containing microparticles for pulmonary drug delivery, Int. J. Pharm. 409 (2011) 156–163.
[28] D.A. Edwards, J. Hanes, G. Caponetti, J. Hrkach, A. Ben-Jebria, M.L. Eskew, et al., Large porous particles for pulmonary drug delivery, Science 276 (5320) (1997) 1868–1871.
[29] S. Duddu, S. Sisk, Y. Walter, T. Tarara, K. Trimble, A. Clark, et al., Improved lung delivery from a passive dry powder inhaler using an engineered PulmoSphere powder, Pharm. Res. 19 (5) (2002) 689–695.
[30] G. Ruecroft, D. Parick, Sonocrystallization particle engineering for inhaled medicines, J. Pharm. Pharmacol. 62 (10) (2010) 1470–1471.
[31] S. Wanning, R. Süverkrüp, A. Lamprecht, Pharmaceutical spray freeze drying, Int. J. Pharm. 488 (2015) 136–153.
[32] J. Fages, H. Lochard, J.-J. Letourneau, M. Sauceau, E. Rodier, Particle generation for pharmaceutical applications using supercritical fluid technology, Powder Technol. 141 (2004) 219–226.
[33] S. Moser, K. Sommer, Calculation of Van der Waals forces in adhering systems, Powder Technol. 17 (1977) 191–195.
[34] P.J. Stewart, Particle interactions in pharmaceutical systems, Pharm. Int. (1968) 146–149.
[35] J. Visser, Van der Waals and other cohesive forces affecting powder fluidization, Powder Technol. 58 (1989) 1–10.
[36] A.J. Hickey, N.M. Concessio, M.M. van Oort, R.M. Platz, Factors influencing the dispersion of dry powders as aerosols, Pharm. Technol. 18 (8) (1994) 58–62.

[37] E.N. Hiestand, Dispersion forces and plastic deformation in tablet bond, J. Pharm. Sci. 74 (1985) 768–770.
[38] A.H. De Boer, P. Hagedoorn, D. Gjaltema, J. Goede, K.D. Kussendrager, H.W. Frijlink, Air classifier technology (ACT) in dry powder inhalation Part 2. The effect of lactose carrier surface properties on the drug-to-carrier interaction in adhesive mixtures for inhalation, J. Pharm. 260 (102) (2003) 201–216.
[39] Y. Kawashima, T. Serigano, T. Hino, H. Yamamoto, H. Takeuchi, Effect of surface morphology of carrier lactose on dry powder inhalation property of pranlukast hydrate, Int. J. Pharm. 172 (1–2) (1998) 179–188.
[40] M. Jones, R. Price, The influence of fine excipient particles on the performance of carrier-based dry powder inhalation formulations, Pharm. Res. 23 (2006) 1665–1674.
[41] H. Leuenberger, The application of percolation theory in powder technology, Adv. Powder Technol. 10 (4) (1999) 323–352.
[42] S.C. Das, S. Ravindra Babu Behara, J.B. Bulitta, D.A. Morton, I. Larson, P.J. Stewart, Powder strength distributions for understanding de-agglomeration of lactose powders, Pharm. Res. 29 (2012) 2926–2935.
[43] M. Hertel, E. Schwarz, M. Kobler, S. Hauptstein, H. Steckel, R. Scherliess, The influence of high shear mixing on ternary dry powder inhaler formulations, Int. J. Pharm. 534 (1–2) (2017) 242–250.
[44] F. Podczeck, J.M. Newton, Development of an ultracentrifuge technique to determine the adhesion and friction properties between particles and surfaces, J. Pharm. Sci. 84 (9) (1995) 1067–1071.
[45] F. Grasmeijer, A.J. Lexmond, M. van den Noort, P. Hagedoorn, A.J. Hickey, H.W. Frijlink, et al., New mechanisms to explain the effects of added lactose fines on the dispersion performance of adhesive mixtures for inhalation, PLoS One 9 (1) (2014) e87825.
[46] A.H. De Boer, P. Hagedoorn, D. Gjaltema, J. Goede, H.W. Frijlink, Air classifier technology in dry powder inhalation Part 1. Introduction of a novel force distribution concept (FDC) explaining the performance of a basic air classifier on adhesive mixtures, Int. J. Pharm. 260 (1–2) (2003) 187–200.
[47] G. Henning, S. Torben, Granulation, Encyclopedia of Pharmaeutical Technology, Marcel Dekker, New York, 1997, pp. 121–144.
[48] C. Abrantes, D. Duarte, C. Reis, An overview of pharmaceutical excipients: safe or not safe? J. Pharm. Sci. 105 (2016) 2019–2026.
[49] M. Telko, A. Hickey, Dry powder inhaler formulation, Respir. Care 50 (9) (2005) 1209–1227.
[50] F. Grasmeijer, N. Grasmeijer, P. Hagendoorn, H.W. Frijlink, A.H. De Boer, Recent advances in the fundamental understanding of adhesive mixtures for inhalation, Curr. Pharm. Des. 21 (2015) 5900–5914.
[51] W. Kaialy, On the effects of blending, physicochemical properties, and their interactions on the performance of carrier-based dry powders for inhalation — a review, Adv. Colloid Interface Sci. 235 (2016) 70–89.
[52] D. Nguyen, A. Rasmuson, B.I. Niklasson, K. Thalberg, Mechanistic time scales in adhesive mixing investigated by dry particle sizing, Eur. J. Pharm. Sci. 69 (2015) 19–25.
[53] K. Thalberg, S. Åslund, M. Skogevall, P. Andersson, Dispersibility of lactose fines as compared to API in dry powders for inhalation, Int. J. Pharm. 504 (2016) 27–38.
[54] S. Pazesh, M. Heidarian Höckerfelt, J. Berggren, T. Bramer, G. Alderborn, Mechanism of amorphisation of micro-particles of griseofulvin during powder flow in a mixer, J. Pharm. Sci. 102 (2013) 4036–4045.
[55] F. Grasmeijer, P. Hagedoorn, H.W. Frijlink, A.H. De Boer, Drug content effects on the dispersion performance of adhesive mixtures for inhalation, PLoS One 8 (8) (2013) e71339.
[56] K. Thalberg, D. Lindholm, A. Axelsson, Comparison of different flowability tests for powders for inhalation, Powder Technol. 46 (2006) 206–213.
[57] E. Guenette, A. Barrett, D. Kraus, R. Brody, L. Harding, G. Magee, Understanding the effect of lactose particle size on the properties of DPI, Int. J. Pharm. 380 (2009) 80–88.
[58] I. Sibum, P. Hagedoorn, A.H. De Boer, H.W. Frijlink, F. Grasmeijer, Challenges for pulmonary delivery of high dose powder doses, Int. J. Pharm. 548 (2018) 325–336.

[59] J. Rudén, G. Frenning, T. Bramer, K. Thalberg, J. An, G. Alderborn, Linking carrier morphology to the powder mechanics of adhesive mixtures for dry powder inhalers via a blend-state model, Int. J. Pharm. 561 (2019) 148–160.
[60] K. Thalberg, E. Berg, M. Fransson, Modeling dispersion of dry powders for inhalation. The concepts of total fines, cohesive energy and interaction parameters, Int. J. Pharm. 427 (2012) 224–233.
[61] R. Guchardi, M. Frei, E. John, J.S. Kaerger, Influence of fine lactose and magnesium stearate on low dose dry powder inhaler formulations, Int. J. Pharm. 348 (2008) 10–17.
[62] M. Louey, S. Razia, P. Stewart, Influence of physico-chemical carrier properties on the in vitro aerosol deposition from interactive mixtures, Int. J. Pharm. 252 (2003) 87–98.
[63] P. Young, S. Edge, D. Traini, M. Jones, R. Price, D. El-Sabawi, et al., The influence of dose on the performance of dry powder inhalation systems, Int. J. Pharm. 296 (2005) 26–33.
[64] B. Dickhoff, A.H. De Boer, D. Lambregts, H.W. Frijlink, The effect of carrier surface and bulk properties on drug particle detachment from crystalline lactose carrier particles during inhalation, as function of carrier payload and mixing time, Eur. J. Pharm. Biopharm. 56 (2003) 291–302.
[65] J. Rudén, G. Frenning, T. Bramer, K. Thalberg, G. Alderborn, Relationships between surface coverage ratio and powder mechanics of binary adhesive mixtures for dry powder inhalers, Int. J. Pharm. 541 (2018) 143–156.
[66] M.R. Tamadondar, L. de Martin, K. Thalberg, I. Niklasson Bjoern, A. Rasmuson, The influence of particle interfacial energies and mixing energy on the mixture quality of the dry-coating process, Powder Technol. 338 (2018) 313–324.
[67] H. Steckel, P. Marefka, H. te Wierik, R. Kammelar, Effect of milling and sieving on functionality of dry powder inhalation products, Int. J. Pharm. 309 (2006) 51–59.
[68] C. Weiss, P. McLoughlin, H. Cathcart, Characterisation of dry powder inhaler formulations using atomic force microscopy, Int. J. Pharm. 494 (2015) 393–407.
[69] P. Begat, D.A. Morton, J. Staniforth, R. Price, The cohesive-adhesive balance in dry powder inhaler formulations 1: Direct quantification by atomic force microscopy, Pharm. Res. 21 (2004) 1591–1597.
[70] J.C. Hooton, M. Jones, R. Price, Predicting the behavior of novel sugar carriers for dry powder inhaler formulations via the use of a cohesive–adhesive force balance approach, J. Pharm. Sci. 96 (2006) 1288–1297.
[71] H. Adi, I. Larson, H. Chiou, P. Young, D. Traini, P. Stewart, Agglomerate strength and dispersion of salmeterol xinafoate from powder mixtures for inhalation, Pharm. Res. 23 (2006) 2556–2565.
[72] H. Adi, I. Larson, J.P. Stewart, Influence of the polydispersity of the added fine lactose on the dispersion of salmeterol xinafoate from mixtures for inhalation, Eur. J. Pharm. Sci. 36 (2009) 265–274.
[73] J. Shur, R. Price, D. Lewis, P.M. Young, G. Woollam, D. Singh, et al., From single excipients to dual excipient platforms in dry powder inhaler products, Int. J. Pharm. 514 (2016) 374–383.
[74] M. Keller, R. Müller-Walz, Dry powder for inhalation. US patent 6645466, 2003.
[75] T. Tay, S. Das, P. Stewart, Magnesium stearate increases salbutamol sulphate dispersion: what is the mechanism? Int. J. Pharm. 383 (2010) 62–69.
[76] Q. Zhou, B. Armstrong, I. Larson, P. Stewart, D. Morton, Improving powder flow properties of a cohesive lactose monohydrate powder by intensive mechanical dry coating, J. Pharm. Sci. 99 (2) (2009) 969–981.
[77] S. Das, I. Tucker, P. Stewart, Inhaled dry powder formulations for treating tuberculosis, Curr. Drug. Deliv. 12 (2015) 26–39.
[78] R.A. Hauser, S.H. Isaacson, A. Ellenbogen, B.E. Safirstein, D.D. Truong, S.F. Komjathy, et al., Orally inhaled levodopa (CVT-301) for early morning OFF periods in Parkinson's disease, Parkinsonism Relat. Orders 64 (2019) 175–180.
[79] M. Luinstra, W. Rutgers, T. van Laar, F. Grasmeijer, A. Begeman, V. Isufi, et al., Pharmacokinetics and tolerability of inhaled levodopa from a new dry-powder inhaler in patients with Parkinson's disease, Ther. Adv. Chronic Dis. 10 (2019) 1–10.
[80] S. Selim, R. Riesenberg, J. Cassella, J. Kunta, E. Hellriegel, M.A. Smith, et al., Pharmacokinetics and safety of single-dose inhaled loxapine in children and adolescents, J. Clin. Pharmacol. 57 (10) (2017) 1244–1257.

[81] S. White, D.B. Bennett, S. Cheu, P.W. Conley, D.B. Guzek, S. Gray, et al., EXUBERA: pharmaceutical development of a novel product for pulmonary delivery of insulin, Diabetes Technol. Ther. 7 (6) (2005) 896–906.

[82] E.M. Westerman, A.H. De Boer, P.P.H. Le Brun, D.J. Touw, H.W. Frijlink, H.G.M. Heijerman, Dry powder inhalation of colistin sulfomethate in healthy volunteers: a pilot study, Int. J. Pharm. 335 (1–2) (2007) 41–45.

[83] S.B. Mazzone, An overview of the sensory receptors regulating cough, Cough 1 (2) (2005). Available from: https://doi.org/10.1186/1745-9974-1-2.

[84] S.P. Shah, A. Misra, Development of liposomal amphotericin B dry powder inhaler formulation, Drug. Deliv. 11 (4) (2004) 247–253.

[85] I. Khatib, D. Khanal, J. Ruan, D. Cipolla, F. Dayton, J.D. Blanchard, et al., Ciprofloxacin nanocrystals liposomal powders for controlled drug release via inhalation, Int. J. Pharm. 566 (1–2) (2019) 641–651.

[86] G. Pilcer, T. Sebti, K. Amighi, Formulation and characterization of lipid-coated tobramycin partices for dry powder inhalation, Pharm. Res. 23 (5) (2006) 931–940.

[87] D. Lechuga-Ballesteros, C. Charan, C.L.M. Stults, C.L. Stevenson, D.P. Miller, R. Vehring, et al., Trileucine improves aerosol performance and stability of sprey-dried powders for inhalation, J. Pharm. Sci. 97 (1) (2008) 287–302.

[88] M.A.M. Momin, B. Ragnekar, S. Sinha, C.-Y. Cheung, G.M. Cook, S.C. Das, Inhalable dry powder of bedaquiline for pulmonary tuberculosis: in vitro physicochemical characterization, antimicrobial activity and safety studies, Pharmaceutics 11 (2019) 502.

[89] C. Parlati, P. Colombo, F. Buttini, P.M. Young, H. Adi, A.J. Ammit, et al., Pulmonary spray dried powders of tobramycin containing sodium stearate to improve aerosolization efficiency, Pharm. Res. 26 (5) (2009) 1084–1092.

[90] M. Lau, P.M. Young, D. Traini, Investigation into the manufacture and properties of inhalable high-dose dry powders produced by comilling API and lactose with magnesium stearate, AAPSPharmSciTech 18 (6) (2017) 2248–2259.

[91] M. Luinstra, F. Grasmeijer, P. Hagedoorn, J.R. Moes, H.W. Frijlink, A.H. De Boer, A levodopa dry powder inhaler for the treatment of Parkinson's disease patients in off periods, Eur. J. Pharm. Biopharm. 97 (2015) 22–29.

[92] M. Lau, P.M. Young, D. Traini, Co-milled API-lactose systems for inhalation therapy: impact of magnesium stearate on physico-chemical stability and aerosolization performance, Drug. Dev. Ind. Pharm. 43 (6) (2017) 980–988.

[93] F. Buttini, G. Brambilla, D. Copelli, V. Sisti, A.G. Balducci, R. Bettini, et al., Effect of flow rate on in vitro aerodynamic performance of NEXThaler in comparison with Diskus and Turbohaler dry powder inhalers, J. Aerosol Med. Pulm. Drug. Deliv. 29 (2) (2016) 167–178.

[94] R. Wilson, A. Templeton, C. Leemereise, R. Eames, E. Banham-Hall, E.M. Hessel, et al., Safety, tolerability, and pharmacokinetics of a new formulation of nemiralisib administered via a dry powder inhaler to healthy individuals, Clin. Ther. 41 (6) (2019) 1214–1220.

[95] M.T. Newhouse, P.H. Hirst, S.P. Duddu, Y.H. Walter, T.E. Tarara, A.R. Clark, et al., Inhalation of a dry powder tobramycin PulmoSphere formulation in healthy volunteers, Chest 124 (2003) 360–366.

[96] H. Stass, J. Nagelschmitz, S. Willmann, H. Delezen, A. Gupta, S. Baumann, Inhalation of a dry powder ciprofloxacin formulation in healthy subjects: a phase I study, Clin. Drug. Investig. 33 (2013) 419–427.

[97] D.M. Silva, R. Palenco, D. Traini, V. Sencadas, Development of ciprofloxacin-loaded poly(vinyl alcohol) dry powder formulations for drug delivery, Int. J. Pharm. 547 (1–2) (2018) 114–121.

[98] J.H. Bell, P.S. Hartley, J.S.G. Cox, Dry powder aerosols I: a new powder inhalation device, J. Pharm. Sci. 60 (10) (1971) 1559–1563.

[99] J.V. Birchall, B.E. Jones, A. Morrissey, B.E. Jones, A comparison of the puncturing properties of gelatin and Hypromellose capsules for use in dry powder inhalers, Drug. Dev. Ind. Pharm. 34 (8) (2008) 870–876.

[100] M.M. Al-Tabakha, HPMC capsules: current status and future prospects, J. Pharm. Pharm. Sci. 13 (3) (2010) 428–442.

[101] F. Martinelli, A.G. Balducci, A. Rossi, F. Sonvico, P. Colombo, F. Buttini, Pierce and inhale' design in capsule based dry powder inhalers: effect of capsule piercing and motion on aerodynamic performance of drugs, Int. J. Pharm. 487 (1–2) (2015) 197–204.

[102] N. Wauthoz, I. Hennia, S. Ecenarro, K. Amighi, Impact of capsule type on aerodynamic performance of inhalation products: a case study using formoterol-lactose binary and ternary blend, Int. J. Pharm. 553 (1–2) (2018) 47–56.

[103] A. Schoubben, P. Blasi, A. Giontella, S. Giovagnoli, Powder, capsule and device: an imperative ménage à trois for respirable dry powders, Int. J. Pharm. 494 (1–2) (2015) 40–48.

[104] I.Y. Saleem, F. Diez, B.E. Jones, N. Kayali, L. Polo, Investigation on the aerosol performance of dry powder inhalation Hypromellose capsules with different lubricant levels, Int. J. Pharm. 492 (1–2) (2015) 258–263.

[105] V. Chavan, R. Dalby, Effect of rise in simulated inspiratory flow rate and carrier particle size on powder emptying from dry powder inhalers, AAPS Pharmsci. 2 (2) (2000). Article 10.

[106] A.S. Barham, F. Tewes, A.M. Healy, Moisture diffusion and permeability characteristics of hydroxypropylmethylcellulose and hard gelatin capsules, Int. J. Pharm. 478 (1–2) (2015) 796–803.

[107] B.L. Laube, H.M. Janssens, F.H.C. de Jongh, S.G. Devadason, R. Dhand, P. Diot, et al., What the pulmonary specialist should know about the new inhalation therapies, Eur. Resp. J. 37 (2011) 1308–1331.

[108] P.J. McShane, J.G. Weers, T.E. Tarara, A. Haynes, P. Durbha, D.P. Miller, et al., Ciprofloxacin dry powder for inhalation (ciprofloxacin DPI): technical design and features of an efficient drug-device combination, Pulm. Pharmacol. Ther. 50 (2018) 72–79.

[109] A.H. De Boer, P. Hagedoorn, R. Woolhouse, E. Wynn, Computational fluid dynamics (CFD) assisted performance evaluation of the Twincer disposable high-dose dry powder inhaler, J. Pharm. Pharmacol. 64 (2012) 1316–1325.

[110] G.W. Canonica, J. Arp, J.R. Keegstra, H. Chrystyn, Spiromax, a new dry powder inhaler: dose consistency under simulated real-world conditions, J. Aerosol Med. Pulm. Drug. Deliv. 28 (5) (2015) 309–319.

[111] D. Edwards, Applications of capsule dosing techniques for use in dry powder inhalers, Ther. Deliv. 1 (1) (2010) 195–201.

[112] S. Stranzinger, E. Faulhammer, O. Scheibelhofer, V. Calzolari, S. Biserni, A. Paudel, et al., Study of a low-dose capsule filling process by dynamic and static tests for advanced process understanding, Int. J. Pharm. 540 (1–2) (2018) 22–30.

[113] B. Wagner, T. Brinz, S. Otterbach, J. Khinast, Rapid automated process development of a continuous capsule-filling process, Int. J. Pharm. 546 (1–2) (2018) 154–165.

[114] O.A.A. Pinzon, Modelling of Dosator Filling and Discharge (thesis), University of Greenwich, The Wolfson Centre for Bulk Solids Handling, UK, 2012.

[115] F. Eskandar, M. Lejeune, S. Edge, Low powder mass filling of dry powder inhalation formulations, Drug. Dev. Ind. Pharm. 37 (1) (2011) 24–32.

[116] A.H. De Boer, P. Hagedoorn, E.M. Westerman, P.P.H. Le Brun, H.G.M. Heijerman, H.W. Frijlink, Design and in vitro performance testing of multiple air classifier technology in a new disposable inhaler concept (Twincer) for high powder doses, Eur. J. Pharm. Sci. 28 (2006) 171–178.

[117] M. Hoppentocht, O.W. Akkerman, P. Hagedoorn, H.W. Frijlink, A.H. De Boer, The Cyclops for pulmonary delivery of aminoglycosides: a new member of the Twincer family, Eur. J. Pharm. Biopharm. 90 (2015) 8–15.

[118] G. Calvert, M. Ghadiri, R. Tweedie, Aerodynamic dispersion of cohesive powders: a review of understanding and technology, Adv. Powder Technol. 20 (2009) 4–16.

[119] W.C. Hinds, Aerosol Technology, Properties, Behavior, and Measurement of Airborne Particles, 104–126, John Wiley & Sons, New York, 1982, pp. 127–132. and.

[120] Y. Cui, M. Sommerfeld, Forces on micron-sized particles randomly distributed on the surface of larger particles and possibility of detachment, Int. J. Multiph. Flow. 72 (2015) 39–52.

[121] A.L. Fussell, F. Grasmeijer, H.W. Frijlink, A.H. De Boer, H.L. Offerhaus, CARS microscopy as a tool for studying the distribution of micronised drugs in adhesive mixtures for inhalation, J. Raman Spectrosc. 45 (2014) 495–500.

[122] M.S. Coates, D.F. Fletcher, H.-K. Chan, J.A. Raper, The role of capsule on the performance of a dry powder inhaler using computational and experimental analysis, Pharm. Res. 22 (6) (2005) 923–932.
[123] M.S. Coates, D.F. Fletcher, H.-K. Chan, J.A. Raper, Effect of design on the performance of a dry powder inhaler using computational fluid dynamics, Part 1: Grid structure and mouthpiece length, J. Pharm. Sci. 93 (11) (2004) 2863–2876.
[124] M.S. Coates, H.-K. Chan, D.F. Fletcher, H. Chiou, Influence of mouthpiece geometry on the aerosol delivery performance of a dry powder inhaler, Pharm. Res. 24 (8) (2007) 1450–1456.
[125] M.S. Coates, H.-K. Chan, D.F. Fletcher, J.A. Raper, Effect of design on the performance of a dry powder inhaler using computational fluid dynamics, Part 2: air inlet size, J. Pharm. Sci. 95 (6) (2006) 1382–1392.
[126] J. Shur, S. Lee, W. Adams, R. Lionberger, J. Tibbats, R. Price, Effect of device design on the *in vitro* performance and compatibility for capsule-based dry powder inhalers, AAPS J. 14 (4) (2012) 667–676.
[127] Y.-J. Son, P. Worth Longest, G. Tian, M. Hindle, Evaluation and modification of commercial dry powder inhalers for the aerosolization of a submicrometer excipient enhanced growth (EEG) formulation, Eur. J. Pharm. Sci. 49 (3) (2013) 390–399.
[128] B. Benque, J.G. Khinast, Understanding the motion of hard-gel capsules in dry powder inhaler, Int. J. Pharm. 567 (1–2) (2019) p118481.
[129] P. Lucas, K. Anderson, J. Staniforth, Protein deposition from dry powder inhalers: fine particle multiplets as performance modifiers, Pharm. Res. 15 (1998) 562–569.
[130] J. Shur, H. Harris, M.D. Jones, J.S. Kaerger, R. Price, The role of fines in the modification of the fluidization and dispersion mechanism within dry powder inhaler formulations, Pharm. Res. 25 (7) (2008) 1631–1640.
[131] A.H. De Boer, H.-K. Chan, R. Price, A critical view on lactose-based drug formulation and device studies for dry powder inhalation: which are relevant and what interactions to expect? Adv. Drug. Deliv. Rev. 64 (2012) 257–274.
[132] A.H. De Boer, G.K. Bolhuis, D. Gjaltema, P. Hagedoorn, Inhalation characteristics and their effects on the in vitro drug delivery from dry powder inhalers: Part 3: The effect of flow increase rate (FIR) on the in vitro drug release from the Pulmocort 200 Turbuhaler, Int. J. Pharm. 153 (1–2) (1997) 67–77.
[133] M.L. Everard, S.G. Devadason, P.N. Le Souëf, Flow early in the inspiratory manoeuvre affects the aerosol particle size distribution from a Turbuhaler, Respir. Med. 91 (10) (1997) 624–628.
[134] M.B. Dolovich, R. Dhand, Aerosol drug delivery: developments in device design and clinical use, Lancet 377 (2011) 1032–1045.
[135] O.S. Usmani, M.F. Biddiscombe, P.J. Barnes, Regional lung deposition and bronchodilator response as a function of β_2-agonist particle size, Am. J. Respir. Crit. Care Med. 172 (2005) 1497–1504.
[136] L. Borgström, T. Bengtsson, E. Derom, R. Pauwels, Variability in lung deposition of inhaled drug, within and between asthmatic patients, with a pMDI and a dry powder inhaler, Turbuhaler, Int. J. Pharm. 193 (1–2) (2000) 227–230.
[137] J. Sanchis, I. Gich, S. Pedersen, Systemic review of errors in inhaler use, has patient technique improved over time? Chest 150 (2) (2016) 394–406.
[138] T. Kondo, T. Tanigaki, H. Yokoyama, M. Hibino, S. Tajiri, K. Akazawa, et al., Impact of holding position during inhalation on drug release from a reservoir-, blister- and capsule-type dry powder inhaler, J. Asthma 54 (8) (2017) 792–797.
[139] J. van der Palen, J.J. Klein, C.L.A. van Herwaarden, G.A. Zielhuis, E.R. Seydel, Multiple inhalers confuse asthma patients, Eur. Respir. J. 14 (1999) 1034–1037.
[140] J. Oleck, S. Kassam, J.D. Goldman, Commentary: why was inhaled insulin a failure in the market? Pharm. Ther. 29 (3) (2016) 180–184.
[141] J.H. Ferziger, M. Peric, Computational Methods for Fluid Dynamics, third edition, Springer, Berlin, 2012.
[142] M. Sommerfeld, Y. Cui, S. Schmalfuss, Potential and constraints for the application of CFD combined with Lagrangian particle tracking to dry powder inhalers, Eur. J. Pharm. Sci. 128 (2019) 299–324.

[143] W. Wong, D.F. Fletcher, D. Traini, H.-K. Chan, P.M. Young, The use of computational approaches in inhaler development, Adv. Drug. Deliv. Rev. 64 (2012) 312–322.
[144] J. Yang, C.-Y. Wu, M. Adams, Numerical modelling of agglomeration and deagglomeration in dry powder inhalers: a review, Curr. Pharm. Des. 21 (2005) 5915–5922.
[145] G. Mallouppas, B. van Wachem, Large eddy simulations of turbulent particle-laden channel flow, Int. J. Multiph. Flow. 54 (2013) 65–75.
[146] Y. Cui, S. Schmalfus, S. Zellnitz, M. Sommerfeld, N. Urbanetz, Towards the optimisation and adaptation of dry powder inhalers, Int. J. Pharm. 470 (2014) 120–132.
[147] M. Ariane, M. Sommerfeld, A. Alexiadis, Wall collision and drug-carrier detachment in dry powder inhalers: using DEM to devise a sub-scale model for CFD calculations, Powder Technol. 334 (2018) 65–75.
[148] Z. Tong, H. Kamiya, A. Yu, H.-K. Chan, R. Yang, Multi-scale modelling of powder dispersion in a carrier-based inhalation system, Pharm. Res. 32 (2015) 2086–2096.
[149] B. van Wachem, K. Thalberg, J. Remmelgas, I. Niklasson Björn, Simulation of dry powder inhalers: combining micro-scale, meso-scale and macro-scale modeling, AIChE J. 63 (2017) 501–516.
[150] D. Nguyen, J. Remmelgas, I. Niklasson Björn, B. Van Wachem, K. Thalberg, Towards quantitative prediction of the performance of dry powder inhalers by multi-scale simulations and experiments, Int. J. Pharm. 547 (2018) 31–43.
[151] C. Thornton, L. Liu, How does agglomerates break? Powder Technol. 143–144 (2004) 110–116.
[152] S. Adi, Z. Tong, H.-K. Chan, R. Yang, A. Yu, Impact angles as an alternative way to improve aerosolisation of powders for inhalation? Eur. J. Pharm. Sci. 41 (2010) 320–327.
[153] Z. Tong, S. Adi, R. Yang, H.-K. Chan, A. Yu, Numerical investigation of the de-agglomeration mechanisms of fine powders on mechanical impaction, J. Aerosol Sci. 42 (2011) 811–819.
[154] W. Wong, D.F. Fletcher, D. Traini, H.-K. Chan, J. Crapper, P.M. Young, Particle aerosolization and break-up in dry powder inhalers: evaluation and modelling of impaction effects for agglomerated systems, J. Pharm. Sci. 100 (2011) 2744–2754.
[155] Z. Tong, B. Zheng, R. Yang, A. Yu, H.-K. Chan, CFD-DEM investigations of the dispersion mechanisms in commercial dry powder inhalers, Powder Technol. 240 (2013) 19–24.
[156] J. Bruchmüller, B. van Wachem, S. Gu, K.H. Luo, Modelling discrete fragmentation of brittle particles, Powder Technol. 208 (2011) 731–739.

CHAPTER 6

In vitro methods to study dose deposition

Bo Olsson, Hans Lundbäck and Mårten Svensson
Emmace Consulting AB, Lund, Sweden

6.1 Introduction

In the two last decades an impressive amount of evidence has been gathered to show that *in vitro* methods to study dose deposition of inhaled medication can provide clinically relevant information about inhaler performance if conducted under patient realistic conditions. Unfortunately, much of this information is not in the public domain due to reluctance from the industry to publish what is judged to be privileged business data. In this chapter we will try to both share our own experiences in the field and review literature data. We will restrict this chapter to *in vitro* methods that study dose deposition and that we think have clinical relevance. This means that we will focus on *in vitro* methods involving realistic inhalation flow rate versus time profiles and realistic aerosol interaction with the mouth-throat region, which, as will be described, is a powerful determinant of the total lung dose. Depending on the physiochemical/biopharmaceutical properties of the compound of interest and the question to be answered, this may warrant *in vitro* methods of simpler or more advanced complexity. In some simple contexts, total lung deposition may adequately be addressed by an *in vitro* estimate of total lung deposited dose. In more complex cases, regional lung deposition must be considered, which necessitates *in silico* lung deposition modeling, briefly discussed at the end of this chapter, and in detail in Chapters 7 and 14.

6.2 The lung dose

"Dose" is an ambiguous concept, especially for locally acting compounds and particularly for inhaled medicines. For starters, all modern inhaled medicines are delivered via a device in which part of the pre-metered or device-metered "dose" is retained upon use. The "dose" leaving the device, often named delivered dose or emitted dose (aka, dose to the patient, inhaled dose) is typically dependent on the flow-time profile, i.e., the user's inhalation maneuver (and handling). Different territories apply different regulatory rules

Inhaled Medicines
DOI: https://doi.org/10.1016/B978-0-12-814974-4.00010-9

for the definition of the label claimed dose for different types of inhalation products, which could be either the pre-metered or the delivered dose. During the inhalation, the upper airways (nasal or oral) filters out part of the aerosol leaving the remainder to reach the lung. Upper airway deposition is also known as the extra-thoracic dose. Most of the aerosol reaching the lung will deposit there during the inhalation, breath hold or exhalation period. We call this the initial lung dose or initial thoracic dose. Some of the aerosol will however escape lung deposition and be exhaled. The sum of the extra-thoracic and thoracic dose could be called the body dose. Following deposition, various non-absorptive clearance mechanisms may prevent part of the initial lung dose of the active pharmaceutical ingredient (API) from reaching and traversing the lung epithelium to appear in the blood. Of particular relevance for low solubility compounds (and potentially also for poorly permeable compounds) is the mucociliary escalator which translocates some of the initial lung deposition from the conducting airways to the larynx where it is swallowed into the gastro-intestinal tract (GI, from which it may partially be absorbed into the systemic circulation). Some compounds are partially converted before being absorbed into the blood. Thus, chemical/enzymatic degradation and/or activation may also compete with the absorption process. The pulmonary bioavailable dose may thus be significantly smaller than the initial lung deposited dose through these non-absorptive clearance mechanisms. Importantly, the lung is a very heterogeneous organ and the regional distribution of the deposited dose not only affects pulmonary bioavailability but, of course, also the local concentration at the target (which typically is also heterogeneously distributed within the lung, assuming a local target). Disregarding the finer details, most scintigraphic imaging methods estimate the initial (regional) lung deposition whereas pharmacokinetic methods (with proper procedures to prevent/minimize contributions from buccal and GI absorption) estimate the pulmonary bioavailable dose. Scintigraphic and pharmacokinetic methods thus estimate different aspects of the "lung dose" and should be viewed as complementary rather than competing. When comparing *in vitro* and *in vivo* measures it is important to acknowledge which "lung doses" are being compared.

6.3 Realistic *in vitro* testing

Using pure *in vitro* methods, the best one can achieve are crude estimates of where "the particle has landed". One-dimensional (1D, Chapter 7) or three-dimensional (3D, i.e., computational fluid particle dynamics, CFPD, Chapter 7) *in silico* methods may address deposition sites in much finer detail and physiologically-based pharmacokinetic (PBPK, Chapter 12) models may address what happens after the particle has landed. These *in silico* methods must be informed with relevant input. This chapter will describe and discuss *in vitro* methods that aim to provide data that are clinically relevant, either on their own or, more powerfully, when coupled with *in silico* post processing methods. To denote this class of *in vitro* methods we will use the term *realistic* methods.

The concept for a realistic estimation of the total lung dose is very simple and naturally follows from the lung acting as a filter-in-series (Fig. 6.1A). The inhaled aerosol is filtered by the mouth-throat (MT) in which part of the dose is deposited. The remainder reaches the lung where it may deposit. Experience from *in silico* modeling and technical studies show that deposition in the mouth-throat is small during exhalation and many *in vivo* studies show that in general very little is exhaled for typical pharmaceutical products (but note that some solution pMDIs produce submicron aerosols that may have high exhaled fractions). Thus, deposition in the lung is normally very efficient and for now is assumed to be complete *for the fraction of the aerosol that gets there.* From this assumption it follows that total lung deposition (TLD) equals the delivered dose minus MT deposition. Thus, TLD can be estimated *in vitro* by determining the delivered dose and the MT deposition, or simply, by determining the dose that exits an MT model (Fig. 6.1B). Whether or not such an estimated lung dose has clinical relevance hinges on whether or not the dose delivered *in vitro* equals the dose delivered and inhaled *in vivo* and if the MT deposition equals that occurring *in vivo*. The strategy for maximizing *in vivo* and *in vitro* equality is simply to mimic *in vitro* all factors that affect the delivered

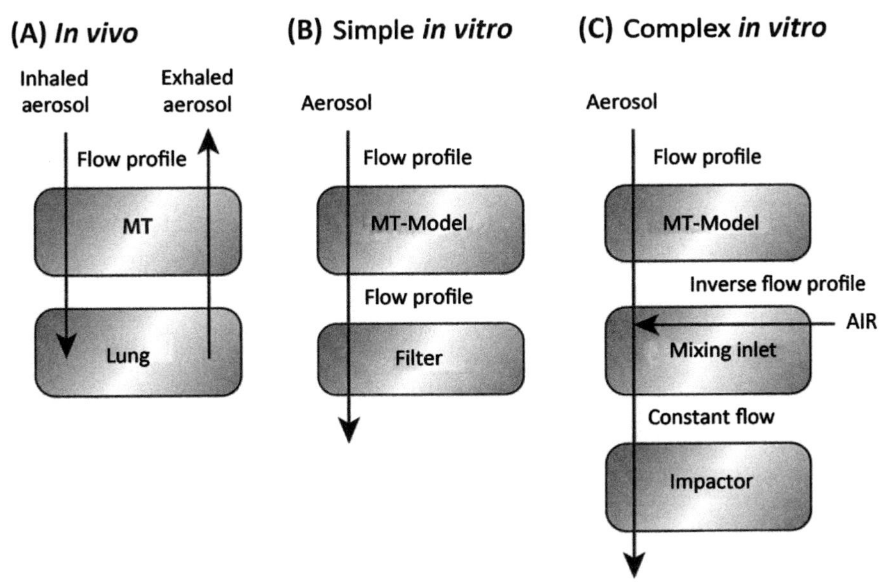

Figure 6.1 Conceptual illustration of *in vitro* emulation of the *in vivo* inhalation process for determination of the (initial) total lung dose. (A) *In vivo*, (B) simple *in vitro*: filter dose taken as estimate of lung dose, (C) Complex *in vitro*: a mixing inlet supplied with the inverse flow profile allows constant impactor flow to obtain the particle size distribution that via *in silico* post-processing may estimate the regional lung deposition. See text for further details.

dose and the MT deposition *in vivo*. Most important among these factors are thought to be device handling, inhalation flow-time profile, and geometry and surface properties of the physical MT model. (Other factors that are thought to be of lesser importance or which address special situations are relative humidity and temperature, electrostatics, coordination, rigidity of MT model, one-MT-model-fits-all-devices-or-not, etc.)

Fig. 6.1B illustrates the *in vitro* approach to estimate (initial) TLD. Technically, as is evident, it is a very simple procedure. The flow profile can be directly applied to the device through the MT model and a downstream filter using a computer-controlled piston, choke valve or other gadget. A determination of the amount of compound captured by the filter provides the estimate of the initial lung dose. By also determining the amount captured by the MT model an estimate of the delivered dose is obtained. Alternatively, measurements may be done with and without the MT model in place to obtain a lung dose estimate in the former case and an estimate of the delivered dose in the latter case.

For compounds with complete pulmonary bioavailability, the dose absorbed into lung tissue is the same as the initial lung deposited dose. If the problem at hand is to estimate this, then the *in vitro* approach sketched in Fig. 6.1B may be used, which is discussed in more detail below.

For compounds with incomplete pulmonary bioavailability, e.g. due to mucociliary clearance, the initial total lung deposition may be of insufficient value to predict *in vivo* performance. The dose available for tissue absorption and target occupancy will then be lower than the initial lung dose. Estimating the bioavailable lung dose then requires use of the more complex *in vitro* setup sketched in Fig. 6.1C in order to measure the aerodynamic particle size distribution (APSD) of the aerosol exiting the MT model which is needed for in-silico modeling of the regional lung deposition. Of course, if the problem at hand is to estimate regional lung deposition, this more complex approach is also needed for compounds with complete pulmonary bioavailability. Measuring the APSD exiting an MT model is described in more detail below.

6.3.1 Realistic versus pharmacopeial *in vitro* testing

Pharmacopeial methods were developed for quality control (QC) purposes with the aim to ensure that commercial batches are therapeutically equivalent to the batches used in the pivotal clinical trials. This may seem quite similar to the aim of the realistic methods to produce clinically relevant data, but is in fact quite different. QC methods focus on being able to detect differences of batch attributes assumed to have some clinical relevance, but without needing to know exactly how and to what extent. The realistic methods, on the other hand, focus on being able to measure attributes of known clinical relevance. Thus, for QC methods aiming to *control* the "lung dose" attribute it is sufficient to compare a defined set of impactor stage depositions, obtained in a standardized way, usually with a square-wave flow profile, to preset limits. This gives the possibility to use a relevant flow rate and stage groupings that contain size ranges relevant for the chosen flow rate. The "fine particle dose", defined in the European Pharmacopoeia as the mass of API in particles smaller than 5 μm, is commonly used as a QC attribute for "lung dose", and is frequently cited in the literature. This is of course not optimal since it completely disregards inhalation flow rate, known to be an important determinant of lung deposition. To obtain an *estimate* of the clinically relevant attribute "lung dose", realistic methods aim to emulate the conditions which produce the "lung dose" (and then catch it) when the device is used by a (typical) patient.

A more practical difference between QC and realistic methods is perhaps that the latter tolerates higher complexity and cost since the primary use is research and not routine.

6.4 Realistic estimation of the (initial) total lung dose

This section describes in more detail the approach sketched in Fig. 6.1B. It relies on being able to record and replay a realistic inhalation flow-time profile through the inhaler and MT model and then quantify the amount of API that escaped deposition in the MT model and was collected downstream the model. Collection may be on a high-efficiency filter, preferably with low flow resistance. If knowledge of the APSD of the aerosol exiting the MT model is desired in addition to the quantity, the much more complex method sketched in Fig. 6.1C is required, which is described in the next section. This section addresses recording of realistic inhalation profiles (flow rate *vs* time), realistic MT models, and replaying the inhalation profile in the analytical setup.

6.4.1 Recording and replaying patient realistic inhalation profiles

For realistic testing of medical inhalers, independently of type of inhaler, the flow profile used to withdraw the dose from the inhaler should simulate that from a representative patient group. Therefore, appropriate test profiles should be collected from a representative cohort of patients or healthy volunteers (HV), using the same type of inhalation device as used in e.g., a clinical study or if possible, collected during the particular study. A sufficient number of subjects should be tested so that a (statistically) relevant range of flow profiles and if desired 'average profile(s)' can be estimated [1–4]. Unfortunately, it is not common that full inhalation profiles are published. If published at all, it is most common to include some calculated flow parameters such as peak inspiratory flow rate (PIFR), flow acceleration, time to PIFR, inhaled volume (IV), inhalation time, and the flow resistance of the device. As also discussed in Chapters 3–5, it depends on the type of device and usage which of these attributes are most meaningful.

For standard press-and-breath pressurized metered dose inhalers (pMDIs), which require a synchronization between the mechanical fire action and the start of the inhalation, the time difference between these actions is also of interest.

Breathing profiles of human subjects can be recorded in different ways and so far no method has emerged as an established standard. It is important to understand the function of the inhaler and its characteristics and in detail monitor how the recording is done and flow data is collected (e.g., time resolution) so that, later in the analytical lab, the replayed flow profile is sufficiently similar to that *in vivo*, with regard to amplitude, shape of the profile and inhaled volume. For inhalers that invoke a significant pressure drop, it should be clarified if the flow rate refers to that entering the inhaler or exiting the mouthpiece. Further, the flow measuring system should not add significant resistance to the system since this may lead to misleading profiles.

One method is to place a sensor measuring the differential pressure (dp) adjacent to the exit of the inhaler mouthpiece during the testing. By separately establishing the relation between dp and flow rate for the setup and device in question, the air flow profiles can be calculated from the dp versus time data, or the pressure drop data could be used directly for replaying the flow profile. Care should be taken to ensure that the dp-sensor is not interfering with the air stream and also not interfering with the usage of the inhaler. Alternatively, a flow meter may be connected in series with the inhaler, either upstream or downstream the inhaler. If drug is delivered from the device the placement must be upstream to avoid interference between the aerosol and flow meter. Care should be taken that the flow meter is not generating a significant pressure drop compared to that generated by the inhaler itself. The human interaction with the setup may be different from that with the inhaler alone, especially if the setup is much bulkier or heavier than the inhaler, and important handling information could be lost. The shape and size of the mouthpiece may affect the inhalation maneuver so for a downstream meter it may be important to use a mouthpiece on the meter that is similar to that of the inhaler. For an upstream meter, it may be challenging to achieve a slim and leak tight connection between the meter and the air intakes of the inhaler, especially if the air intake is located close to the mouthpiece and if the inhaler has multiple air intakes. If recording of a flow profile is the only output parameter of interest, it is possible to just connect a proper air flow resistance between the meter and the inhaler mouthpiece. Care should then be taken that the relation between under pressure and flow rate is similar to that of the inhaler.

Of all gas flow-meter principles available that perform suitably in normal environments, currently differential pressure pneumotachometers, e.g., multi-laminar flow elements and mass flow meters (hot wire anemometers) dominate in inhalation research. Rotameters have earlier been used extensively and are simple to use, but cannot record dynamic processes such as an inhalation profile. Meters using multi-laminar flow elements provide a signal that is directly proportional to the volumetric flow rate and the flow range is adaptable via various sizes and numbers of the laminar flow elements. Mass flow meters are also widely used measuring systems with high accuracy and easy handling and maintenance. Modern mass flow meters have insignificant flow resistance and may also report the instantaneous volumetric flow rate, which is nearly always the parameter of interest. Both flow meter systems have the ability to measure very rapid changes in flow rate (milliseconds).

Compared to a DPI, recording of the inhalation profiles for standard pMDIs involves another challenge. The time between the start of the inhalation flow profile and the press event on the device canister must be measured to be able to realistically replay the device handling in a correct manner. One technical solution to this challenge is to record the inhalation maneuver by high speed camera and at the same time record the inhalation profile as described above. The relation between the start of inhalation and the start of the finger press event may be determined by including a visual flow sensitive wane in the flow stream close to the device and observe when this reacts and when the canister is pressed down. The determined time difference (positive of negative) can at replay be combined with the corresponding inhalation flow profile. Other solutions are also possible, for instance Olsson et al. [1] developed a recording system for pMDIs, as schematically shown in Fig. 6.2. In this study the

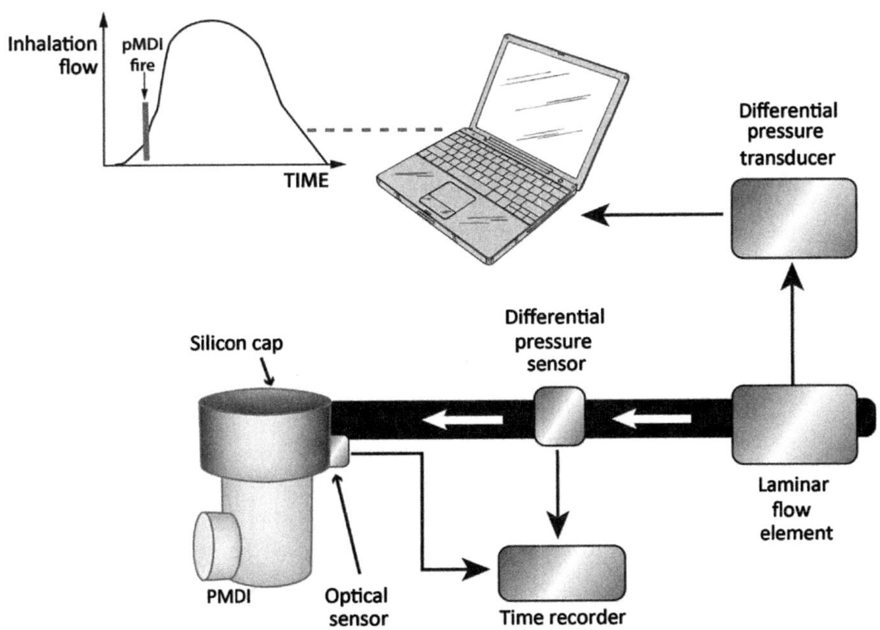

Figure 6.2 Setup for measuring a test subject's flow profile and their coordinated actuation time using a standard pMDI. *Adapted from B. Olsson, L. Borgström, H. Lundbäck, M. Svensson, Validation of a general in vitro approach for prediction of total lung deposition in healthy adults for pharmaceutical inhalation products, J. Aerosol Med. Pulm. Drug. Deliv. 26 (2013) 355–369.*

pMDI was equipped with a soft silicone cap that apart from allowing an undisturbed press motion by subject's finger also included a flow inlet for all incoming air flow to the device. Moreover, an optical sensor that reacted on canister actuation motion was also mounted on the silicon adapter. In the flow stream into the device both a laminar flow element and a small differential pressure sensor was placed. The laminar flow element records the complete inhalation flow profile and the differential pressure sensor was used to measure the start of the profile. Furthermore, by incorporating both the differential pressure sensor and the optical sensor into the same sampling software (time recorder) the coordination between the start of the inhalation profile and subject's press on canister could be recorded.

To successfully replay a chosen flow profile through an inhaler without causing bias from the expected profile, several aspects have to be considered. It is of course necessary to compare the replayed profile to the recorded one, which means it must be measured. When recording the profile, it is vital that the flow resistance of the test inhaler as well as of the flow meter are considered. Usually, the applied and resulting profiles will differ due to decompression of the air in the system. It is therefore likely that the applied profile must be tweaked in order for the resulting profile to mimic the recorded one, especially if the peak pressure drop is high and when large dead volumes are present in the system. In such cases, great demands are put upon the flow profile generating piston or bellow system. Compensation for and tuning of a distorted flow profile is usually done manually by refining the applied profile by iterated calculations until the desired output flow profile is achieved.

Replay of an inhalation profile in combination with the coordination time for the actuator press event of a pMDI canister (as described above), requires a mechanical fire station that can be synchronized with the replay of the inhalation profile. An example of such a gadget was described in Olsson et al. [1].

6.4.1.1 Literature profile models

Realistic inhalation profiles for some dry powder inhalers (DPIs), pMDIs and nebulizers have been published by Azouz et al., and cover various clinical conditions [2–5]. If no profiles are available for a specific DPI, condition and/or patient group, recently developed formulas by Delvadia et al. based on the flow resistance of the DPI could be used [6–8]. They generated formulas for medium, weak and strong profiles for different flow resistances and different degrees of training and suggested that such calculated data would be applicable to any type of inhaler [8]. Sandell refined and generalized the PIFR prediction formulas developed by Delvadia et al. based on 16 published studies, including 10 different DPIs [9]. It should be noted that specific characteristics of the inhaler and/or user instructions could render the above mentioned generalizations inapplicable.

6.4.2 Physical mouth-throat models

As discussed above, MT deposition is together with delivered dose the major determinant of TLD. In order to emulate human MT deposition in a physical model of the region it is obviously important that the major features affecting deposition are realistically mimicked in the model. Since it may not be obvious exactly which these features are and since they are likely to vary for different types of aerosols, a wise strategy would be to create a physical model with as much detail as possible. Swift, probably the first to realize the importance of realistic MT models, manufactured hollow plastic models made from rubber casts of the mouth-throat region of a few diseased adults and children [10,11]. These casts were generously shared with colleagues in the respiratory community, which crucially helped us and coworkers at Astra Draco (now AstraZeneca) to understand the reason why Turbuhaler® gave about twice as high lung deposition compared to the contemporary CFC pMDI [12,13]. Impactor tests using pharmacopeial type inlet throats had given similar lung deposition estimates for both products due to similar throat depositions. The realistic models of Swift demonstrated much higher MT deposition for the pMDI, which finally explained the clinical outcome.

The Alberta Idealized Throat (AIT, available from Copley Scientific, UK), on the other hand, began as a CFD grid developed on the principles of using simple geometric shapes to incorporate average dimensions of the essential geometric features thought to govern aerosol dynamics in the mouth-throat region [14]. Dimensions were derived by combining data from casts, imaging studies, literature, and direct observations of living subjects. Experimentally, the AIT has been shown to reproduce well the average population values for published *in vivo* deposition studies in which mono-disperse aerosols were inhaled tidally through wide mouthpieces [15]. MT deposition in the AIT has also been compared to *in vivo* study results for a DPI [16]. Further development has resulted in an idealized Child MT replica [17] and an idealized replica of the nasal airways of infants [18]. The child model has shown comparable results to *in vivo* deposition for a pMDI and a DPI [19].

The oropharyngeal consortium (OPC) was a collaboration between scientists from GlaxoSmithKline, AstraZeneca, Sanofi-Aventis and The Hammersmith Hospitals (London, UK) to derive representative MT models of adults [20–22]. Briefly, 80 magnetic resonance images (MRI) were obtained from 20 healthy volunteers inhaling from two mouthpiece geometries, each with two different air flow resistance. Using objective methods (both statistical and experimental), three models, later designated Small, Medium and Large, were selected from the 80 MRI scans to represent the adult population (available from Emmace Consulting, Sweden). *In vitro* deposition for two different budesonide DPIs was determined for these MT models in a pilot study and compared with lung deposition in adult volunteers for the same DPIs [23]. The results supported the hypothesis that lung deposition could be directly predicted by the amount of drug that penetrated the MT models, with no post-processing of the data. The general *in vitro* approach for predicting total lung deposition using these MT models was validated by Olsson et al. using nine different pharmaceutical inhalation products, including DPIs, pMDIs with and without spacers, and dosimetric nebulizers, delivering either the medium-to-high solubility compounds budesonide or AZD4818 (solubility ≥ 25 μg/mL) [1], Fig. 6.3. Importantly, total lung deposition (pulmonary BA using PK with charcoal block) in healthy adults was determined in parallel with the *in vitro* determinations using the same batches. It was shown that the amount of drug escaping filtration in the medium MT model predicted the typical total lung deposition in the subjects in the absence of significant exhaled mass and mucociliary clearance, and that combinations of three MT models and three realistic flow profiles reflected between-subject variation in lung deposition.

The group at Virginia Commonwealth University (VCU) used the anatomical literature, including the published OPC data [22], to design physical models of small, medium, and large versions of the mouth-throat, trachea and main bronchi. Combining the three models with three realistic flow profiles they showed for Budelin Novolizer that the fraction of budesonide recovered from components downstream the MT model compared well with the mean and range of total lung deposition measured in a scintigraphic study on an earlier version of Budelin Novolizer conducted ten years before [6]. In a next paper the group compared similarly derived in-vitro estimates (using the medium model) of total lung deposition with mean scintigraphic results for five further dry powder inhalers (DPI) [24]. For four of these DPIs the match was good, but again the *in vivo* studies had been reported many (6–19) years before the *in vitro* study was performed. All five compounds

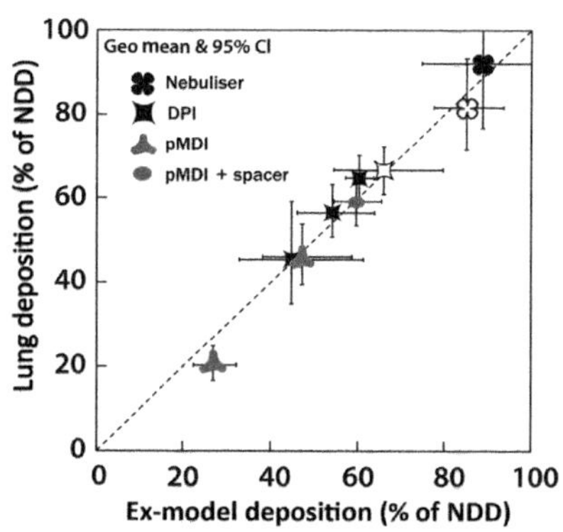

Figure 6.3 Lung deposition versus *in vitro* ex-MT model deposition for medium MT and medium flow profiles for pMDIs, pMDI + spacer, DPIs, and dosimetric nebulizers. Solid symbols, budesonide; open symbols, AZD4818. Geometric mean and 95% confidence interval for the mean are shown. Dashed line is the identity line. NDD = nominal delivered dose for each product. *Adapted from B. Olsson, L. Borgström, H. Lundbäck, M. Svensson, Validation of a general in vitro approach for prediction of total lung deposition in healthy adults for pharmaceutical inhalation products, J. Aerosol Med. Pulm. Drug. Deliv. 26 (2013) 355–369.*

had medium to high solubility. Wei et al. [25] extended their methodology to combine realistic inhalation profiles and MT models with APSD determination using a constant flow impactor through use of a mixing inlet along the same way as reported by Olsson et al. [1,23]. The VCU MT models are available from RDD Online, USA.

In a recent study the group in Virginia compared the AIT, OPC, and VCU MT models using a DPI, a pMDI and a soft mist inhaler (SMI) [26]. Older scintigraphic lung deposition data were available in the literature for these or similar (SMI) products. The standard QC inlet throat (USP) was included in the comparison. They found that MT deposition was dependent on both the flow condition and MT geometry for all the inhalers, while the deposition rank order was independent of both factors. The overall ranking was $USP < OPC_L < AIT < VCU_L < VCU_M < OPC_M < VCU_S < OPC_S$ (where the subscripts refer to Large, Medium and Small versions of the model groups). All model groups (VCU, OPC, AIT, and USP) produced *in vitro* TLD comparable with *in vivo* TLD for the DPI, where flow conditions dominated aerosol deposition. Only the VCU and OPC models produced good correlations for the MDI, where MT geometry dominated deposition. *In vitro* tests with the SMI at 15−45 L/min underestimated MT deposition and overestimated lung deposition with all MT models except OPC_S, although testing at higher flow rates showed good agreement with *in vivo* results. The authors concluded that while realistic *in vitro* tests may produce results that correspond to drug deposition *in vivo*, MT model selection was most important for the MDI and SMI, but much less important than inhalation strength for the DPI.

For all these MT models to have a chance of realistically capture the deposition occurring in the human MT region it is imperative that a particle on contact with a wall surface sticks to the surface. The surfaces of the human MT region are moist, and to emulate this, a wet and sticky coating must be applied to the interior surface of the MT model. The coating must be non-volatile to evade evaporation during the experiment. Various methods have been used, such as filling the MT model with glycerol-Brij35 aqueous solution, and let it drip-dry before the test [1], coating with Tween 20-methanol [16], glycerol:methanol mixture or silicone fluid [24]. Fig. 6.4 shows a typical experimental set-up for *in vitro* lung dose testing of inhalers using clinically realistic flow profiles, replayed using a breath simulator [8].

The Data usage section below describes how realistic *in vitro* estimates of the initial total lung dose may be utilized for gauging bioequivalence of test and reference inhalers, and limitations thereof.

6.5 Realistic estimation of the regional lung dose

This section describes in more detail the approach sketched in Fig. 6.1C. In addition to the requirements for estimating the initial total lung dose it requires the ability to divorce a realistic flow-time profile in the device and MT replica from the constant flow rate required in

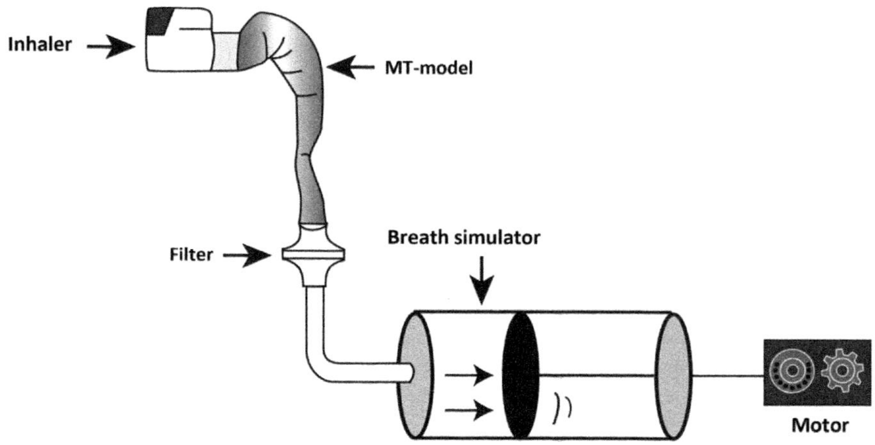

Figure 6.4 Experimental set-up with realistic MT model with an integral filter at the outlet. The dose withdrawal is performed by a piston generating realistic flow profiles. *Adapted from R.R. Delvadia, X. Wei, P.W. Longest, J. Venitz, P.R. Byron, In vitro tests for aerosol deposition. IV: Simulating variations in human breath profiles for realistic DPI testing, J. Aerosol Med. Pulm. Drug. Deliv. 29 (2) (2016) 196–206.*

an impactor to maintain known cut-off sizes of the impactor stages. The measured APSD is chiefly useful as input to deposition modeling, as discussed below.

Estimation of the regional distribution of lung deposition requires knowledge of the parameters that determine deposition in the lung, their values, and a deposition model. The parameters can conveniently by grouped into properties of the breath maneuver, the aerosol properties, and the respiratory tract properties. Their values may either be experimentally determined or be hypothesized from the relevant literature or past experiences. Although the simplest deposition models could in principle be coded into a spreadsheet, in practice modeling is performed by more advanced *in silico* methods. This is the subject of Chapters 7 and 14 and will not be dealt with here but in a cursory way (at the end of this chapter). From an *in vitro* point of view, the most important contribution to the input data needed by the models is the APSD of the aerosol. It is important to realize that the APSD is modified both by the inhalation maneuver and by the interaction of the aerosol with the mouth-throat. Hence, the most relevant data for modeling is the APSD of an aerosol generated with a realistic flow-time profile exiting a realistic MT model. However, realism can be further improved by taking into consideration the timing of the aerosol bolus within the breath profile (i.e., the dose release process), methods for which are described below.

6.5.1 Measuring the size distribution of an aerosol exiting a realistic mouth-throat model

The set-up and procedure for determining the APSD of an aerosol exiting an MT model is complicated by the incompatible flow requirements for the device and MT model on the one hand and the impactor on the other (currently, there exist no viable alternatives to using an impactor for the APSD determination since a chemical analysis is mandated by the fact that nearly all aerosols of interest have a heterogeneous composition). The device and MT should be subjected to a realistic flow-time profile at the same time as the impactor must be operated at a constant volumetric flow rate in order to collect defined size fractions. Various methods to reconcile these opposing requirements have been tried. A pioneering approach was to separate the aerosol generation from the analysis by using a large semi-closed volume as a buffer [27–29]. Another approach was to sample only a fraction of the aerosol using a constant sampling flow. Both these methods suffer from size dependent losses and other analytical problems.

The ingenious so-called mixing-inlet invention by Miller et al. [30] solved these problems (available from RDD Online, USA and Copley Scientific, UK). This works by establishing a constant flow rate in the impactor and then balancing this exactly by addition of pressurized air in the mixing inlet thereby creating zero flow through the device. The pressurized air supply is then choked by the inverse of the intended flow profile. This forces the intended profile to flow through the device in order to uphold the air flow mass balance dictated by the constant impactor flow (Fig. 6.1C). A convenient way to choke the pressurized air supply to the mixing inlet is to temporarily draw the pressurized air into a computer-controlled piston coupled in line with the mixing inlet. The computer may be programmed to move the piston such that the intended flow-time profile is created through the device, given that the piston has a volume in excess of the inhaled volume and that the PIFR is lower than the constant impactor flow rate, see Fig. 6.5. There are of course several key design considerations of which only a few will be mentioned here. The mixing inlet should impart low losses (less than a few percent [1,31]) and provide an undisturbed constant flow

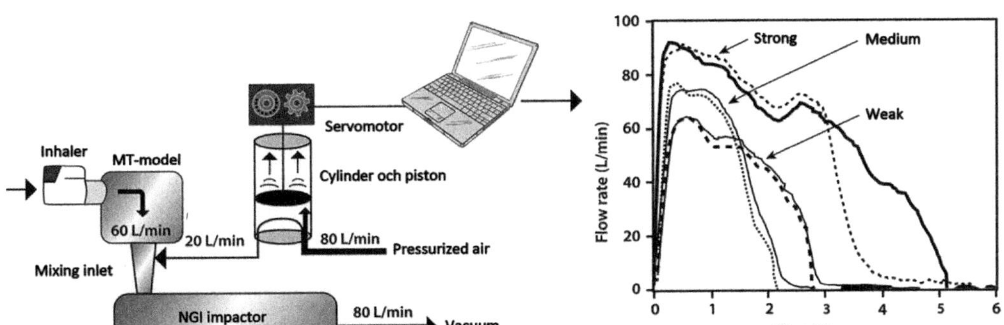

Figure 6.5 To the left the principle air flow set-up for withdrawal of doses for testing inhalers using realistic mouth throat models and flow profiles. To the right, three recorded (solid lines) and replayed (dashed lines) flow profiles are shown. *Adapted from B. Olsson, L. Borgström, H. Lundbäck, M. Svensson, Validation of a general in vitro approach for prediction of total lung deposition in healthy adults for pharmaceutical inhalation products, J. Aerosol Med. Pulm. Drug. Deliv. 26 (2013) 355–369.*

velocity of the air directed into the impactor. This is accomplished with the design proposed by Miller et al. [30] where the auxiliary air is entered in the outer part of a concentric design, thus double-acting as sheet-gas. The flow rate in the impactor should be unperturbed by varying pressure differentials created by the resistance of the device. This can be accomplished by using a critical-flow valve between the vacuum drain and the impactor outlet. The sonic flow in such a valve ensures constant velocity in the impactor which is the important attribute for maintaining the calibrated cut-off diameters of the stages [32]. Both Olsson et al. and Wei et al. showed that the quantity of API collected downstream the MT model was the same for collection on a filter and for collection in an impactor using the mixing inlet methodology [1,31].

The mixing-inlet methodology is today widely accepted and applied in inhalation research due to many favorable features (e.g., Refs. [1,4,16,25,33]). Since all critical components are now available commercially, Mitchell and Sugget [33] suggested that this approach could be possible to introduce in a pharmacopeial chapter after necessary general validation.

The Mixing inlet approach can also be applied to multi-breath nebulizers. Svensson et al. [34] modified and extended the methodology for pMDIs and DPIs to also cover testing of nebulizers by introducing three main modifications: (i) the breath simulator was programmed to generate a standard sinusoidal breathing pattern (standard in nebulizer testing), (ii) the impactor used in the testing was cooled according to pharmacopeial guidance (Ph. Eur. 2.9.44), and (iii) the pressurized air fed into the mixing inlet (via the breathing simulator) was humidified (> 90 %RH) (See Fig. 6.6). The reason for the latter modification was that the very dry pressurized air was significantly affecting the evaporation and thus the deposition pattern in the impactor. The setup basically combines two standard characterization tests that are described in the pharmacopeia, (i) the

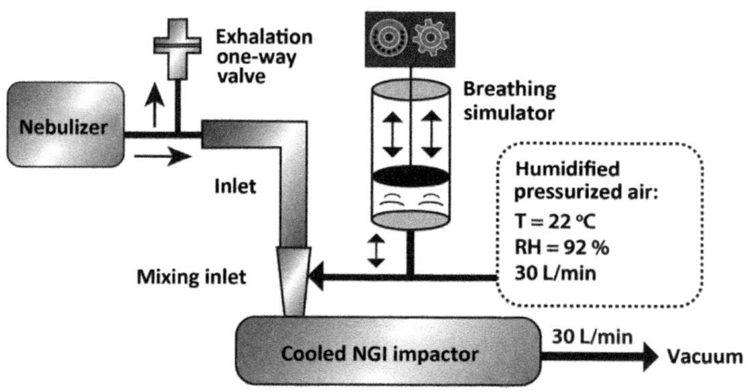

Figure 6.6 Adaptation of the mixing inlet approach for nebulizer testing. *Adapted from M. Svensson, E. Berg, J. Mitchell, D. Sandell, Laboratory study comparing pharmacopeial testing of nebulizers with evaluation based on nephele mixing inlet methodology, AAPS PharmSciTech 19 (2) (2017) 565–572.*

delivered dose testing using a breathing simulator (sinusoidal pattern) and (ii) APSD testing with a cooled impactor performed at constant air flow. The result from the two separate tests are usually combined to calculate a fine droplet dose less than a certain droplets size (a QC parameter), which is obtained directly with the modified setup. Replacing the pharmacopeial inlet in the described setup with a realistic MT model would turn it into a method for realistic estimation of total and regional lung dose for continuous nebulization.

6.5.1.1 Measuring the dose release process

The position of the aerosol bolus in the inhaled air may affect the regional lung deposition [35]. The drug release profile (i.e., drug air concentration as a function of inhaled volume) may thus be an important input to *in silico* modeling and for the development of a generic device and/or formulation. Ideally, the drug release profile should be measured using realistic inhalation profiles since these may affect the release profile.

An optical light scattering method monitoring the light intensity close to the exit of the mouthpiece of the inhaler during a simulated inhalation process is a fast and fairly simple screening method to study the dose emptying process. A high-speed camera in combination with a laser source may also be used. For passive DPIs it is favorable to use an upstream pressurized air method for dose release, eliminating any extra dead volume and avoiding optical interferences from aerosol particles deposited on, e.g., cuvette inner walls. These kinds of methods cannot discriminate between drug and excipient particles but may still be sufficiently informative regarding the dose release process, which could vary significantly between different DPIs, see Fig. 6.7.

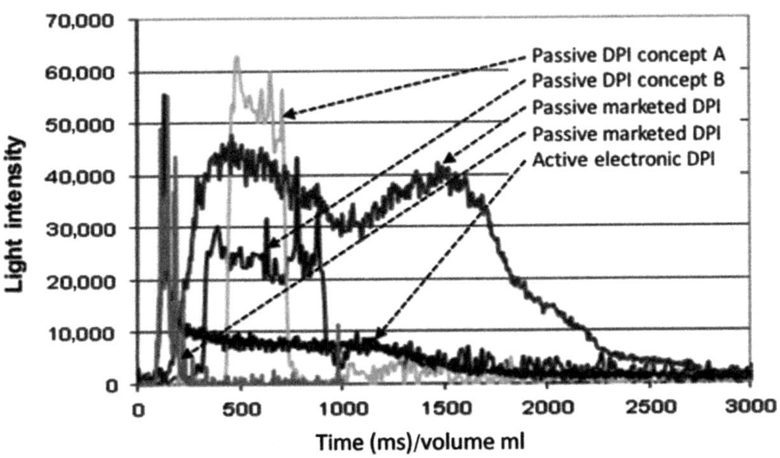

Figure 6.7 Timed dose release profiles from 5 different DPIs obtained with a laser beam at the mouthpiece exit and a high-speed camera equipment using a triggered pressurized air system to generate the flow through the inhaler.

Using more advanced laser diffraction particle size analyzers (e.g., Sympatec, Malvern) it is possible to continuously monitor the aerosolization process during dose release by repeatedly measuring the volume particle size distribution over time, which can be done with high frequency (e.g. 100 Hz, [36]). This kind of instruments are capable to qualitatively characterize both fine and coarse particles in a single measurement. Although they cannot discriminate between drug and excipient particles, a time phase shift of particles with significant differences in size, may indicate that drug and excipient release profiles are different. As a complement, for products where drug and excipient release profiles are different, the drug release process could be assessed using a dose collector with repetitive dose withdrawals with increasing sampling times and chemical analysis.

6.6 Data usage

6.6.1 Bioequivalence based on realistic estimates of lung doses

Estimating the relation of lung doses between two devices, batches or products is a much simpler problem than estimating the absolute value. The more similar the two entities, the easier. This is of course a consequence of the fact that when taking a ratio, an unknown or ill-determined proportionality factor will cancel out if, in reality, the factor affects both entities to the same extent (or at least, to a similar extent). An important practical problem for the pharmaceutical industry is to determine if the chance of demonstrating bioequivalence (BE) is high enough to risk the time and money associated with running a clinical study. Whether the characteristics of the test (T) and reference (R) products are sufficiently similar to each other are usually judged by comparing *in vitro* attributes. For inhaled products, arguably, the most important attribute is the TLD.

Standard *in vivo* measures of "extent and rate" of exposure at the target are the area under the plasma concentration versus time curve (AUC) and the maximal plasma concentration (C_{max}). (For locally-acting compounds, these are down-stream surrogate biomarkers and their ability to reflect events at the target may depend on the product and may need to be justified.) For compounds with non-negligible gastrointestinal absorption it is necessary to distinguish between contributions to AUC from pulmonary absorption (pAUC, surrogate for efficacy) and total AUC (tAUC, surrogate for systemic safety).

If it can be assumed that pulmonary bioavailability (BA) is complete or near complete then a reasonable assumption is that pAUC (from time 0 to infinity) is proportional to initial lung deposition, since [37]:

$$AUC_{0-inf} = [systemic\ dose]/[systemic\ clearance] \tag{6.1}$$

The gastrointestinal contribution to tAUC may be assumed to be the swallowed MT deposition scaled for oral BA (F_{oral}), which for established compounds typically is available in the literature.

Following our assumptions: [*systemic dose*] $= TLD + F_{oral}MT$.

Thus, for the safety surrogate:

$$\frac{tAUC_T}{tAUC_R} = \frac{TLD_T + F_{oral}MT_T}{TLD_R + F_{oral}MT_R} \tag{6.2}$$

By making (e.g., charcoal block) or intrinsically having $F_{oral} \approx 0$, we get for the efficacy surrogate

$$\frac{pAUC_T}{pAUC_R} = \frac{TLD_T}{TLD_R} \tag{6.3}$$

If it can be assumed that C_{max} is also proportional to initial total lung deposition, the T/R ratio for C_{max} is similar to Eq. 6.3 (if this, rather stretched, assumption is correct, it follows that C_{max} is proportional to pAUC, which possibly can be checked with literature data).

For many compounds, complete pulmonary BA cannot be assumed for reasons that include poor solubility and/or poor permeability, in which cases mucociliary clearance may translocate centrally deposited material from the lung to the gut in a process that is in kinetic competition with dissolution and absorption. The relative rates of the competing processes may be amenable to physiology-based pharmacokinetic modeling (PBPK, Chapter 12). For many compounds it is also reasonable to assume that absorption is most rapid from the alveolar space, and hence that alveolar deposition will govern C_{max}. An estimate of the T/R C_{max} ratio based on the alveolar dose ratio will for such compounds be sharper. For both cases the regional distribution of the lung dose is required as input, which in turn requires *in vitro* data obtained by the method illustrated in Fig. 6.1C.

6.6.2 *In-silico* modeling

One-dimensional (1D) algebraic filter-in-series type lung deposition models are covered in this book (Chapter 7) but merit a short discussion here. 1D models were initially developed many decades ago primarily for environmental aerosol protection purposes (e.g., ICRP and NCRP [38,39]). These models are fairly simple to use, produce instantaneous results, are accessible to the non-specialist, and are therefore attractive tools to convert realistic *in vitro* estimates of APSD into more useful *in vitro/in silico* estimates of regional lung deposition. Developed for ambient aerosols they were not considering the specific circumstances associated with forcefully inhaling a limited bolus aerosol from a narrow mouthpiece imparting considerable aerosol cloud velocity. Hence, the 1D models for MT deposition are usually not applicable to most pharmaceutical inhalers. One notable exception is the confined jet model recently developed for DPIs [40]. However, there are good reason to believe that when entering the trachea, most of the dynamics of the aerosol cloud has dissipated [41] and that therefore the 1D models for deposition in the trachea and downwards apply to a sufficient extent. Combined with realistic *in vitro* testing using MT replicas, where MT deposition is measured rather than ill modeled, the prospect for 1D lung deposition models to provide very useful estimates of regional lung deposition has greatly improved.

CFPD models can simulate the whole process of dose release, aerosol generation and subsequent interaction with the device and MT (Chapter 7), but this needs measurements or assumptions of initial and boundary conditions and models of multi-scale physics beyond airflow and particle transport. We argue that also CFPD may benefit from using realistic *in vitro* results from MT replicas, not least in validation exercises.

References

[1] B. Olsson, L. Borgström, H. Lundbäck, M. Svensson, Validation of a general in vitro approach for prediction of total lung deposition in healthy adults for pharmaceutical inhalation products, J. Aerosol Med. Pulm. Drug. Deliv. 26 (2013) 355–369.

[2] W. Azouz, P. Chetcuti, H. Hosker, D. Saralaya, J. Stephenson, H. Chrystyn, The inhalation characteristics of patients when they use different dry powder inhalers, J. Aerosol Med. Pulm. Drug. Deliv. 28 (1) (2015) 35–42.

[3] D. Prime, W. de Backer, M. Hamilton, A. Cahn, A. Preece, D. Kelleher, et al., Effect of disease severity in asthma and chronic obstructive pulmonary disease on inhaler-specific inhalation profiles through the ELLIPTA® dry powder inhaler, J. Aerosol Med. Pulm. Drug. Deliv. 28 (6) (2015) 486–497.

[4] M. Abadelah, H. Chrystyn, H. Larhrib, Use of inspiratory profiles from patients with chronic obstructive pulmonary disease (COPD) to investigate drug delivery uniformity and aerodynamic dose emission of indacaterol from a capsule based dry powder inhaler, Eur. J. Pharm. Sci. 134 (2019) 138–144.

[5] W. Azouz, Novel Methodology to Characterize How Asthma and Chronic Obstructive Pulmonary Disease Patients Use Their Inhalers and Methods to Improve the Inhaler Technique. Objective Assessment of How Patients Use Inhalers (Doctoral thesis), University of Huddersfield, 2012 <http://eprints.hud.ac.uk/17484/> (accessed 28.11.19).

[6] R.R. Delvadia, P.W. Longest, P.R. Byron, In vitro tests for aerosol deposition. I: Scaling a physical model of the upper airways to predict drug deposition variation in normal humans, J. Aerosol Med. Pulm. Drug. Deliv. 25 (2012) 32–40.

[7] P.R. Byron, X. Wei, R.R. Delvadia, P.W. Longest, J. Venitz, Breath profiles for testing new DPI devices in development, in: P.R. Byron, S.J. Farr, P.M. Young, J. Peart, J.D. Suman, D. Traini (Eds.), Respiratory Drug Delivery 2014, 1, Davis Healthcare International Publishing, LLC, River Grove, IL, 2014, pp. 295–302.

[8] R.R. Delvadia, X. Wei, P.W. Longest, J. Venitz, P.R. Byron, In vitro tests for aerosol deposition. IV: Simulating variations in human breath profiles for realistic DPI testing, J. Aerosol Med. Pulm. Drug. Deliv. 29 (2) (2016) 196–206.

[9] D. Sandell, Assessing in vitro BE using realistic inhalation profiles for regulatory approval of generic inhalers, in: R.N. Dalby, P.R. Byron, J. Peart, J.D. Suman, S.J. Farr, P.M. Young, et al. (Eds.), Respiratory Drug Delivery 2016, 1, Davis Healthcare International Publishing, LLC, River Grove, IL, 2016, pp. 133–146.

[10] D.L. Swift, Apparatus and method for measuring regional distribution of therapeutic aerosols and comparing delivery systems, J. Aerosol Sci. 23 (1992) S495–S498.

[11] D.L. Swift, The oral airway - a conduit or collector for pharmaceutical aerosols, in: P.R. Byron, R.N. Dalby, S.J. Farr (Eds.), Respiratory Drug Delivery IV, Interpharm Press, Buffalo Grove, IL, 1994, pp. 187–195.

[12] L. Thorsson, S. Edsbäcker, T.-B. Conradson, Lung deposition of budesonide from Turbuhaler is twice that from a pressurized metered-dose inhaler P-MDI, Eur. Respir. J. 7 (10) (1994) 1839–1844.

[13] B. Olsson, Aerosol particle generation from dry powder inhalers: can they equal pressurized metered dose inhalers? J. Aerosol Med. 8 (Suppl. 3) (1995) S13–S18.

[14] K.W. Stapleton, E. Guentsch, M.K. Hoskinson, W.H. Finlay, On the suitability of k- e turbulence modeling for aerosol deposition in the mouth and throat: a comparison with experiment, J. Aerosol Sci. 31 (6) (2000) 739–749.

[15] B. Grgic, A.F. Heenan, W.H. Finlay, In vitro intersubject and intrasubject deposition measurement in realistic mouth-throat geometries, J. Aerosol Sci. 35 (2004) 1025–1040.

[16] J.G. Weers, A.R. Clark, N. Rao, K. Ung, A. Haynes, S.K. Khindri, et al., In- vitro-in vivo correlations observed with indacaterol-based formulations delivered with the Breezhaler, J. Aerosol Med. Pulm. Drug. Deliv. 28 (4) (2015) 268–280.

[17] L. Golshahi, W.H. Finlay, An idealized child throat that mimics average pediatric oropharyngeal deposition, Aerosol Sci. Technol. 46 (5) (2012) i–iv.

[18] E. Javaheri, L. Golshahi, W.H. Finlay, An idealized geometry that mimics average infant nasal airway deposition, J. Aerosol Sci. 57 (2013) 14–21.

[19] C.A. Ruzycki, L. Golshahi, R. Vehring, W.H. Finlay, Comparison of in vitro deposition of pharmaceutical aerosols in an idealized child throat with in vivo deposition in the upper respiratory tract of children, Pharm. Res. 31 (6) (2014) 1525–1535.

[20] S. Pritchard, D. McRobbie, Studies of the human oropharyngeal airspaces using magnetic resonance imaging. II. The use of three-dimensional gated MRI to determine the influence of the mouthpiece diameter and resistance of inhalation devices on the airspace geometry, J. Aerosol Med. 17 (2004) 310–324.

[21] D. McRobbie, S. Pritchard, Studies of the human oropharyngeal airspaces using magnetic resonance imaging III. The effects of device resistance with forced maneuver and tidal breathing on upper airway geometry, J. Aerosol Med. 18 (2005) 325–336.

[22] P.K.P. Burnell, L. Asking, L. Borgström, S.C. Nichols, B. Olsson, D. Prime, et al., Studies of the human oropharyngeal airspace using magnetic resonance imaging IV-The oropharyngeal retention effect for four inhalation delivery systems, J. Aerosol Med. 20 (2007) 269–281.

[23] B. Olsson, L. Borgström, M. Svensson, H. Lundbäck, Modeling oropharyngeal cast deposition to predict lung delivery from powder inhalers, in: R.N. Dalby, P.R. Byron, J. Peart, J.D. Suman, S.J. Farr, P.M. Young (Eds.), Respiratory Drug Delivery VII, 1, Davis Healthcare International Publishing, River Grove, IL, 2008, pp. 197–205.

[24] R.R. Delvadia, M. Hindle, W. Longest, P.R. Byron, In vitro tests for aerosol deposition II: IVIVCs for different dry powder inhalers in normal adults, J. Aerosol Med. Pulm. Drug. Deliv. 26 (3) (2013) 138–144.

[25] X. Wei, M. Hindle, R.R. Delvadia, P.R. Byron, In vitro tests for aerosol deposition. V: Using realistic testing to estimate variations in aerosol properties at the trachea, J. Aerosol Med. Pulm. Drug. Deliv. 30 (5) (2017) 339–348.

[26] X. Wei, M. Hindle, A. Kaviratna, B.K. Huynh, R.R. Delvadia, D. Sandell, et al., In vitro tests for aerosol deposition. VI: Realistic testing with different mouth–throat model and in vitro—in vivo correlations for a dry powder inhaler, metered dose inhaler, and soft mist inhaler, J. Aerosol Med. Pulm. Drug. Deliv. 31 (2018). Available from: https://doi.org/10.1089/jamp.2018.1454.

[27] A. Brindley, B.S. Sumby, I.J. Smith, The characterisation of inhalation devices by an inhalation simulator: the Electronic Lung™, J. Aerosol Med. 7 (2) (1994) 197–200.

[28] P.K.P. Burnell, A. Malton, K. Reavill, M.H.E. Ball, Design, validation and initial testing of the Electronic Lung™ device, J. Aerosol Sci. 29 (1998) 1011–1025.

[29] M. Hamilton, R. Leggett, C. Pang, S. Charles, B. Gillett, D. Prime, In vitro dosing performance of the ELLIPTA dry powder inhaler using asthma and COPD patient inhalation profiles replicated with the Electronic Lung™, J. Aerosol Med. Pulm. Drug. Deliv. 28 (6) (2015) 498–506.
[30] N.C. Miller, M.J. Maniaci, S. Dwivedi, G.H. Ward, Aerodynamic sizing with simulated inhalation profiles: total dose capture and measurement, in: R.N. Dalby, P.R. Byron, S.J. Farr, J. Peart (Eds.), Respiratory Drug Delivery VII, 1, Serentec Press, Inc, Raleigh, NC, 2000, pp. 191–196.
[31] X. Wei, K. Bormann, P.R. Byron, Predicting variations in aerodynamic particle size distribution of the lung dose from budelin novolizer, Respiratory Drug Delivery Europe 2015, 2, RDD Online, Richmond, VA, 2015, pp. 533–536.
[32] B. Olsson, L. Asking, Methods of setting and measuring flow rates in pharmaceutical impactor experiments, Pharm. Forum 29 (3) (2003) 879–884.
[33] J.P. Mitchell, J.A. Suggett, Developing ways to evaluate in the laboratory how inhalation devices will be used by patients and care-givers: the need for clinically appropriate testing, AAPS PharmSciTech 15 (5) (2014) 1275–1291.
[34] M. Svensson, E. Berg, J. Mitchell, D. Sandell, Laboratory study comparing pharmacopeial testing of nebulizers with evaluation based on nephele mixing inlet methodology, AAPS PharmSciTech 19 (2) (2017) 565–572.
[35] E. Bondesson, T. Bengtsson, L. Borgström, L.-E. Nilsson, K. Norrgren, B. Olsson, et al., Dose delivery late in the breath can increase dry powder aerosol penetration into the lungs, J. Aerosol Med. 18 (1) (2005) 23–33.
[36] A. Dorosz, A. Penconec, A. Moskal, In vitro study on the aerosol emitted from the DPI inhaler under two unsteady inhalation profiles, J. Aerosol Sci. 101 (2016) 104–117.
[37] J. Gabrielsson, D. Weiner, Pharmacokinetic & Pharmacodynamic Data Analysis. Concepts and Applications, fourth ed., Swedish Pharmaceutical Press, Stockholm, 2000, p. 170.
[38] International Commission on Radiological Protection (ICRP), Human respiratory tract model for radiological protection, Ann. ICRP 24 (1994) 1–120. Publ. 66.
[39] NCRP Report 125, Deposition, Retention and Dosimetry of Inhaled Radioactive Substances, National Council on Radiation Protection and Measurements, Bethesda, MD, 1997, ISBN 0-929600-54-1.
[40] W.H. DeHaan, W.H. Finlay, Predicting extrathoracic deposition from dry powder inhalers, J. Aerosol Sci. 35 (3) (2004) 309–331.
[41] P.G. Koullapis, P. Hofemeier, J. Sznitman, S.C. Kassinos, An efficient computational fluid-particle dynamics method to predict deposition in a simplified approximation of the deep lung, Eur. J. Pharm. Sci. 113 (2018) 132–144.

CHAPTER 7

In silico methods to model dose deposition

Pantelis Koullapis[1,2], Fotos Stylianou[1,2], Ching-Long Lin[3,4,5], Stavros Kassinos[1,2] and Josué Sznitman[6]

[1]Department of Mechanical and Manufacturing Engineering, University of Cyprus, Nicosia, Cyprus
[2]Respiratory Hub (UCY RespiHub), University of Cyprus, Nicosia, Cyprus
[3]Department of Mechanical Engineering, The University of Iowa, Iowa, IA, United States
[4]Department of Radiology, The University of Iowa, Iowa, IA, United States
[5]Roy J. Carver Department of Biomedical Engineering, The University of Iowa, Iowa, IA, United States
[6]Department of Biomedical Engineering, Technion-Israel Institute of Technology, Haifa, Israel

7.1 Introduction

Determination of deposited aerosol dose in human airways can be accomplished *in vivo*, *in vitro* or *in silico*. *In vivo* techniques describe the real state, but their usage remains limited due to insufficient spatial resolution and concerns over patient exposure to radiation. *In vitro* methods allow systematic studies of particle size and flowrate effects and have proven effective for quantifying mouth-throat deposition. However, the *in vitro* measurement of regional deposition in replicas of the tracheobronchial tree tends to be costly and time-consuming and thus is not easily performed on a routine basis. *In silico* methods can complement *in vivo*/*in vitro* tests and provide detailed information on regional deposition patterns and airflow characteristics in the human airways.

In silico methods can be divided into two broad categories: algebraic whole-lung models, which historically were the first to be introduced primarily for environmental aerosol protection purposes, e.g. ICRP 1994 and NCRP 1997 [1,2], and three-dimensional Computational Fluid-Particle Dynamics (CFPD) simulations, which are now becoming increasingly prevalent. The schematic diagram in Fig. 7.1 presents the chronological development of *in silico* models. Algebraic whole-lung models provide deposition estimates obtained from analytical equations or empirical correlations [3]. These models are fairly simple to use, run on any current processor in a matter of seconds and can predict deposition throughout the entire lung. However, compared to 3D CFPD, they lack the ability to describe site-specific deposition within individual airways of the lung, and because they involve more simplifying assumptions, they can potentially lead to larger errors. Potential sources of uncertainty in the predictions of 1D models include the reliance on simple anatomic representations of the central and

Inhaled Medicines
DOI: https://doi.org/10.1016/B978-0-12-814974-4.00012-2

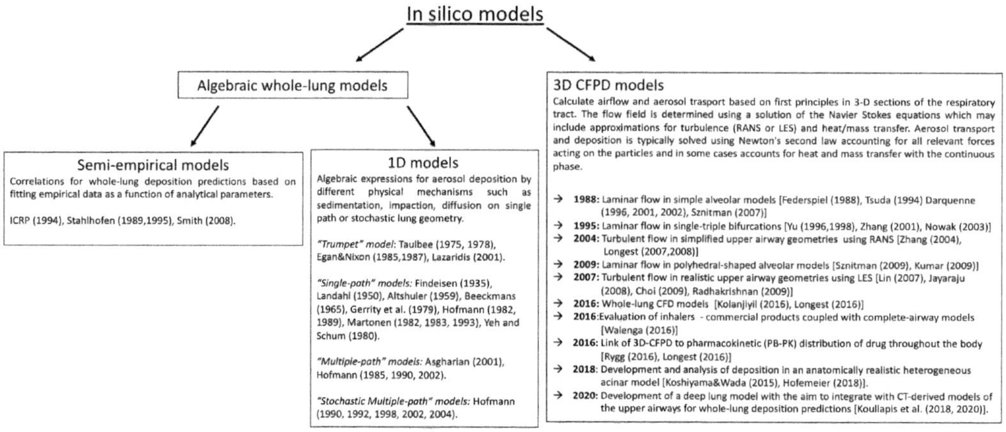

Figure 7.1 Schematic diagram showing the chronological development of in silico models. Terminology is explained in Sections 7.2 and 7.4.

peripheral airways, rather simplistic representation of structural changes due to airway disease and difficulty in capturing the effects of localized flow features on deposition.

Modern CFPD tools that have surfaced in the last couple of decades for lung applications allow for the prediction of deposition patterns within specific regions of interest in the respiratory tract [4–6]. The governing equations for the airflow and particle transport are solved numerically to simulate the flow aerodynamics and transport of inhaled aerosols in the airways. Complex effects such as geometric variability, breathing patterns and aerosol characteristics can be taken into account in CFPD models. Concerning pharmaceutical formulations, coupled inhaler–upper-airway simulations are nowadays possible and can account for the aerosol momentum as it is emitted from the inhaler into the mouth [7]. Highly realistic models of the pulmonary region, which include expansions and contractions of alveolar walls are also feasible [8]. Limitations of CFPD models include difficulties to account for complex phenomena related to aerosol physics (such as collisions and agglomeration/deagglomeration) and their high computational expense in resolving flow dynamics in the vast expanse of the human lung. As a consequence, the majority of existing CFPD models are limited to sections of the respiratory tract, for example from the oral cavity to the first 7–10 airway generations [9] or covering the terminal alveolar regions [5]. Nevertheless, CFPD models can provide valuable insights into the airflow and particle dynamics in the entire human lung.

7.2 The different roles of *in silico* methods

In silico tools can be used towards different objectives in investigating the human respiratory system. 1D models are mainly utilized to provide gross estimation of deposited dose that can then be used to assess the efficacy of inhaled medications. Less sophisticated, empirical, 1D models usually assume a relatively simple morphometric structure of the lung with only 4 regions (i.e. extrathoracic-ET, large Bronchial airways-BB, small bronchial airways-bb and alveolar region-Al), with a typical example shown in Fig. 7.2 [1,2]. These models run in rather simple computer programs and in principle can be used without specialized knowledge by anyone interested in total and regional deposition calculations (either open-source or commercial). Due to their simplicity, they quickly became popular tools for obtaining fast gross estimates of deposited dose whenever a more in-depth understanding is not crucial. Their main limitations are the greatly simplified morphometry and the lack of information about aerosol deposition within a given region, e.g. in single airway generations. More sophisticated 1D models, such as multiple- or stochastic- path models [10–12] employ more realistic lung structures in terms of dimensional variability, branching asymmetry,

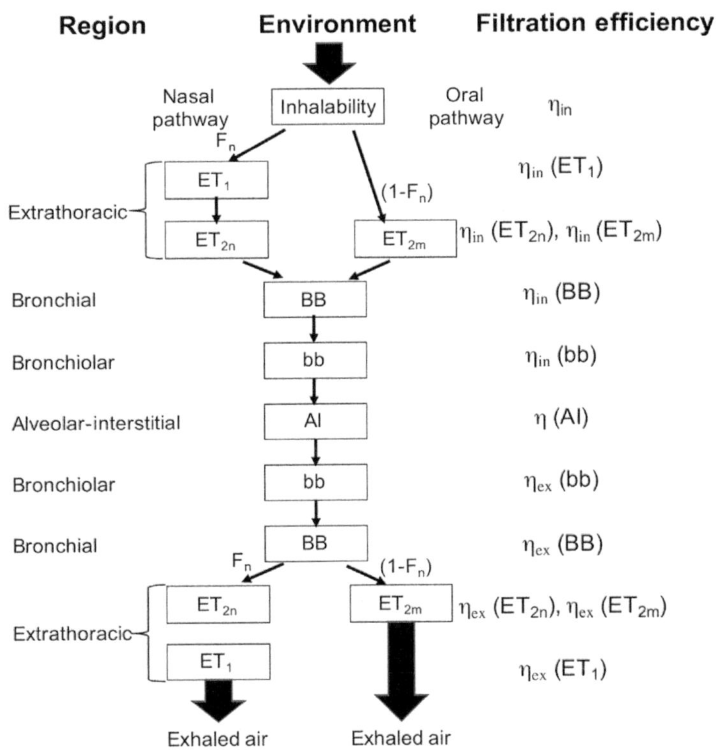

Figure 7.2 ICRP representation of inhalability of particles and their deposition in the extrathoracic, bronchial, bronchiolar and alveolar regions of the respiratory tract. This is the typical "series of filters" representation, adopted in 1D models. *Adapted from International Commission on Radiological Protection (ICRP), Human respiratory tract model for radiological protection, Ann. ICRP 24 (1994) 1–120 Publ. 66* [1].

and factors important for pharmaceutical aerosols such as bolus delivery and breath profiles. Currently they do not account for inter-subject variability.

High fidelity CFPD methods, on the other hand, have the ability to provide much more detailed insights on the airflow and particle deposition. In addition, they can be used to study portions of the airway tree that would not be accessible *in vitro*, for example, airways that are too small to be instrumented in replicas for direct airflow measurements. CFPD tools were initially used as means for understanding the fundamentals of airflow and aerosol transport. Focusing in the upper airways, CFPD were utilized to analyze the 3-Dimensional airflow features, such as the transition to turbulent flow in the extrathoracic region, a result of the oropharyngeal bend and the laryngeal jet formed at the glottis constriction. CFPD also revealed that these turbulent effects propagate into the first 3–5 generations of the tracheobronchial airways. Dean vortices and secondary flows due to curvature effects have been unveiled as well as regions with flow separation and recirculation. The range of information that can be extracted from 3D simulations is exemplified in Fig. 7.3, which showcases fully developed flow in a model of a human airway bifurcation during steady inhalation at Reynolds number 8500 in the parent branch [13]. The instantaneous velocity field, wall shear stresses and turbulent vortical structures can all be visualized in great detail.

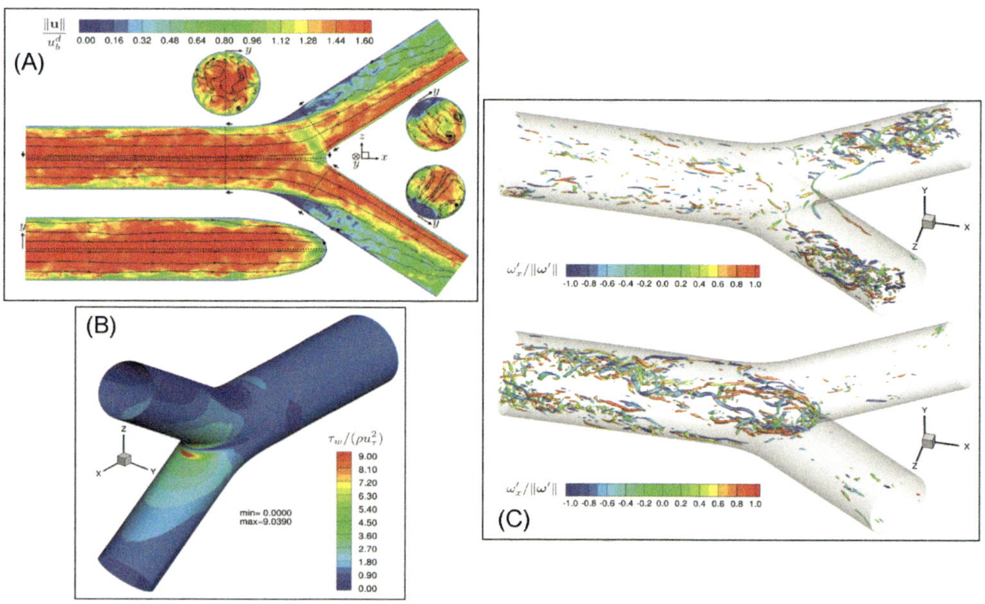

Figure 7.3 Turbulent flow in a human airway bifurcation model exemplifying the level of detail one can obtain from 3D simulations. (A) Instantaneous velocity magnitude contours. (B) Wall shear stresses. (C) Turbulent vortical structures identified by the Q-criterion. *Adapted from F.S. Stylianou, J. Sznitman, S.C. Kassinos, Direct numerical simulation of particle laden flow in a human airway bifurcation model, Int. J. Heat Fluid Flow 61 (2016) 677–710* [13].

Moreover 3D simulations have been used to determine locations of large pressure drops and wall shear stresses, typically found in airway disorders such as obstructive sleep apnea [14] and asthma [15]. The characteristics of heat and water vapor transfer during the inhalation of ambient air have been studied in detail using high-fidelity simulations [16]. Regarding the respiratory zone, CFPD simulations have been performed in 2D and 3D models of the microscopic alveolar structures, providing understanding of the physics in these low Reynolds number flows. Complex patterns, linked to the 3D nature of the flow, have been revealed with the aid of numerical simulations. Such patterns are largely determined by the interplay between recirculation in the cavity induced by ductal shear flow over the alveolar opening and radial flows induced by wall displacement [17]. Specifically, flows are dominated by recirculation patterns for alveoli located in the proximal acinar generations and become largely radial in the deeper acinar generations because of rhythmic wall motion and an increasing alveolus volume. Concerning the fate of inhaled aerosols, 3D simulations allow us to identify deposition hotspots and correlate deposition patterns to distinct airflow features. An example includes the enhanced deposition around the glottis and the sidewalls of the upper trachea due to inertial impaction arising from the laryngeal jet and the generated secondary motions. Moreover, 3D simulations can give insights on the transport characteristics of non-spherical particles, that are potentially attractive as airborne carriers for drug delivery [18], and thus assist the development of more effective drug aerosols.

In recent years, the use of numerical simulations in clinical practice has emerged as a credible tool, mainly propelled by the rapid increases in computational power and the ease of access to parallel computers [19,20]. In this respect, patient-specific simulations are employed in order to correlate structure with function or guide patient-tailored therapies. Medical-based applications usually combine imaging and computer simulations. For diagnostic purposes, imaging-based clinically focused CFPD is utilized to complement conventional lung function tests (e.g. spirometry) that can provide only limited regional and aggregate functional information. Imaging-based CFPD has shown the potential to provide more sensitive biomarkers of lung function than conventional spirometry metrics. An example of the application of CFPD in clinical practice has been showcased in the study of De Backer and co-workers [21]. In this study, CFPD calculations in airway geometries of asthmatic patients were capable of providing additional information about changes in overall airway resistance (R_{aw}) before and after acute bronchodilation compared to spirometry tests. Moreover, CFPD-based changes in R_{aw} were still detectable in some patients that presented normal FEV1 values. Besides diagnosis, *in silico* tools can assist in selecting the appropriate treatment and in the implementation of personalized medicine for improving the efficiency and efficacy of inhalation therapy. Specifically, CFPD simulations can provide a better understanding of aerosol deposition characteristics and resultant improvements or undertreatments following a prescribed medication. Examples of such applications include COPD and CF patients [19]. CFPD also finds application in areas such as understanding and analyzing different clinical scenarios during mechanical ventilation [22]. For example, CFPD has been used to simulate airflow during nasal high flow therapy [23,24]. In the future, imaging-based CFPD analyzes could further support clinical decision making through prediction of the consequence of therapeutic or surgical intervention on airway resistance and airflow structures.

While the personalized medicine approach to inhalation therapy could be attractive, the intrinsic inter-subject variability across lung anatomies is widespread across humankind [25,26], thus underlining the prodigious computational endeavors possibly ahead. Indeed, anatomical variability of the lungs influences aerosol deposition outcomes [27,28] and undeniably needs to be addressed when assessing general inhalation therapy. Rather than following the path of patient-specific CFPD tools, we argue here that the abovementioned multiscale *in silico* strategies can be particularly useful to undertake high-fidelity simulations representative across broad classes of human populations based on age, sex and disease status. The appeal of such simulation strategies would foremost lie at the level of pre-clinical *in silico* population studies and suited for exploring drug development and delivery methods, including new inhaler designs [29,30]. Indeed, the large anatomical variability in the upper bronchial generations is anticipated to produce different aerosol distributions entering the various lung lobes, even among healthy individuals inhaling under similar conditions, a point even more exasperated in the presence of respiratory diseases. Specifically, one embodiment of an *in silico* multiscale simulation strategy would take form in quantitatively mapping how much variability in lung anatomies influences the inhaled aerosol delivery endpoints (e.g. deposition predictions, local drug concentrations, etc.). This is a direct consequence of the minor effect that subject-specific MT anatomies have on the fate of the aerosol particles entering the tracheobronchial (TB) tract, having first escaped extra-thoracic (ET) filtering, as indicated in [9]. Instead the bulk of computational efforts could be directed towards modeling aspects in TB tree variability. In turn, findings from large-scale, parametric studies would be instrumental in understanding and thus predicting the distribution (e.g. mean, spread, etc.) in general human lung deposition data. In some sense, the advocated pipeline would be somewhat analogous to conducting pre-clinical studies using established *in vitro* impactors. With such results in hand, localized distribution characterizations of aerosols obtained from CFPD simulations could be fed for instance into existing pharmaco-kinetic (PK) models; a point that was recently highlighted [31] in delivering both regional lung tissue concentrations of a drug and established PK metrics (e.g. maximum blood concentration, area under the drug concentration curve). An ambitious, yet tangible, outcome would for example lie in improving current 1D model predictions and expanding existing commercial software to integrate CFPD-based benchmarks, not only for healthy populations but critically for diseased lung cases as well as pediatric populations.

These ideas are taken up again in Chapter 14, where we examine concrete examples of the application of *in silico* methods and machine learning for the identification of subpopulations of individuals with unique lung features. These approaches are emerging as powerful tools both for improving patient care in the clinic, but potentially also for designing more effective population-specific drug delivery strategies.

7.3 Choosing the appropriate *in silico* method based on lung region and underlying objective

Inhalation is initiated by the contraction of the diaphragm and intercostal muscles, which results in reduced pressure inside the thorax compared to atmospheric pressure. In exhalation, the lung and chest wall return to equilibrium position and shape, and the pressure increases to release the air from the lungs. Airflow in the respiratory tract is driven by the pressure difference between the oral opening and the alveoli, where the pressure, though time varying, is approximately spatially uniform. Under most circumstances, airflow in the lung can be reasonably approximated as incompressible [32]. The Reynolds number, representing the ratio of inertial to viscous forces, is used to classify the flow as laminar or turbulent. In a circular pipe, for Reynolds numbers below 2300 the flow is laminar and transitions to turbulence for $Re > 4000$. In the intermediate regime ($2300 < Re < 4000$), the flow will begin to transition from laminar to turbulent and then back to laminar at irregular intervals. Fig. 7.4 plots the variation of Reynolds number throughout the airway generations for three flowrates typically found during inhalation from an inhaler device.

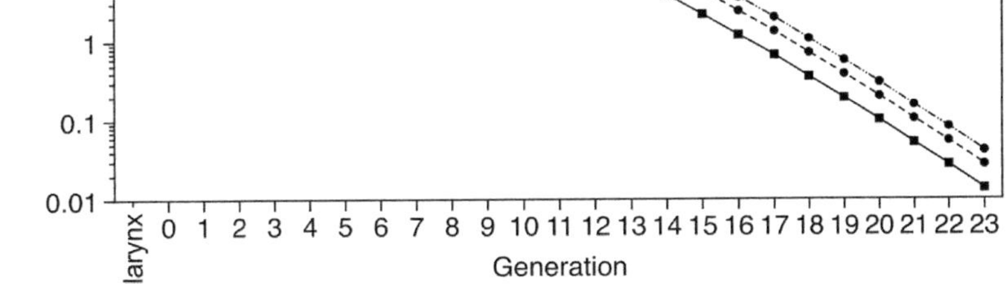

Figure 7.4 Reynolds number versus airway generation number for three inhalation flowrates, 30, 60 and 90 L/min.

At these flowrates, the Reynolds number in the larynx ranges between 3000 and 10,000. Even at the lower flowrates, and due to the complex geometry of the extrathoracic airways that includes bends, constrictions and expansions, airflow usually transitions to turbulence in the upper airways. The laryngeal jet formed at the glottis constriction produces much of this turbulence [33]. It's characteristics bear a resemblance to the flow through a constricted pipe, which can be classified as a free shear flow where the wall serves to confine the spreading of the jet rather than producing turbulence [34]. As we move deeper in the airways, Reynolds number decreases due to the overall increase of cross-sectional area that the air passes through. However, turbulent eddies generated in the upper airways may propagate into distal airways that would normally carry laminar flow based on their local Reynolds number. Zhang and Kleinstreuer [35] predicted numerically that turbulent fluctuations from the trachea can persist downstream to the third generation at inspiratory flowrates higher than 30 L/min. Similar observations were made in [33], using a patient-specific airway model and a more advanced flow solver. Turbulent effects eventually dissipate in the central airways, approximately at generations 4–6, and the flow relaminarizes. Reynolds number further decreases as we move deeper in the conducting airways and drops to about 1–10 in the respiratory region. In the acinus, Reynolds numbers span more than two orders of magnitude ($\sim 0.01-1$) with Poiseuille-like velocity profiles characterizing the flow patterns inside the acinar ducts. Hence, fluid inertia is anticipated to remain negligible in the alveolar region.

Concerning aerosol transport in the human airways, the determinant particle property is its aerodynamic size. Inhaled aerosols, either pollutants or therapeutics, typically have diameters in the range of 0.01–100 μm and they can be solid particles or droplets. In addition, the size of aerosols traveling in the human airways can change as a result of evaporation or condensation. Due to the high humidity in the lungs, powder particles inhaled from dry powder inhalers can grow in size as water condenses on their surface. Evaporation or condensation readily occurs for water droplets produced by nebulizers delivering aqueous drug formulations. Droplets have spherical shape whereas solid particles can typically be non-spherical. When traveling along an airway, particles will be exposed to different physical mechanisms, forcing them to diverge from the air streamlines and eventually deposit on the airway surfaces. The principal mechanisms acting upon inhaled aerosols are impaction due to inertial forces, sedimentation due to gravity and Brownian diffusion. Impaction is most effective in the upper airways, where air and particle velocities are higher than in the peripheral lung. On the other hand, particles in the alveolated region of the lung are preferentially deposited by diffusion and sedimentation due to smaller velocities and hence longer residence times. Small particles below 0.5 μm are deposited primarily by Brownian diffusion, while deposition by inertial impaction and sedimentation prevails for larger particles, producing the typical U-shape of the total deposition curve. Slow breathing is most effective for diffusion and sedimentation since it results in longer residence times, whereas impaction is higher for fast breathing due to higher velocities.

In conclusion, airflow in the upper airways is complex and transitions to turbulence. Therefore, high fidelity CFPD simulations are required to accurately capture these airflow characteristics and the ensuing particle transport and deposition, especially if regional deposition is of interest. As we move in the deeper airways, airflow relaminarizes and, as the Reynolds number decreases below unity it becomes mainly convective in the proximal alveolar cavities. Hence, in the deep lung, detailed deposition predictions (per segment) still requires the use of CFPD, but the prevailing low Reynolds numbers allow for a number of simplifications to be applied.

7.4 3D CFPD in the extrathoracic and conducting airways

There are three techniques for solving the Navier-Stokes equations for turbulent flow using a computer: Direct Numerical Simulations (DNS), Reynolds Averaged Navier-Stokes (RANS) and Large Eddy Simulations (LES). DNS tracks the details of the instantaneous turbulent fluctuations at all scales. However, it is exceedingly costly to implement and beyond routine use on current computers.

Presently, most CFPD simulations solve only for the mean flow using the RANS equations, resulting in a tremendous reduction in computational cost. However, airway curvature effects and the laminar-turbulent-laminar flow transition in the conducting airways is challenging for RANS and care must be exercised to choose validated RANS models [36]. In addition, dispersion of particles due to the turbulent velocity fluctuations is not well-captured with the classical Eddy Interaction Models (EIM) that are combined with RANS, since these models assume fluctuating velocities to be isotropic [37]. This assumption is not valid, especially near the walls where strong anisotropic turbulent structures develop. To overcome this drawback, correction functions for velocity fluctuations, obtained by curve fitting data from DNS duct flow, were proposed [38]. Although these correction functions improve deposition predictions compared to classical EIM assuming isotropy, the main shortcoming of this approach is that the correction functions were derived for ducted flow geometry. In addition, these corrections depend on the wall distance, which is usually difficult to estimate in complex geometries such as the human upper airway [39]. A more robust choice is the method of Large Eddy Simulations (LES), where only the smallest scales of motion (containing a small fraction of the kinetic energy) are discarded. The computational expense of LES is considerably higher than that of RANS, but it retains significantly more elements of the underlying turbulence physics than RANS [40,41][84,95]. With constant gains in computing power, LES has become affordable for routine use and recent LES-based deposition studies have established the trustworthiness of the method [42].

The above considerations highlight the need to exercise care when choosing turbulence models for application in CFPD simulations of flow and deposition in the extrathoracic and upper airways. Turbulence models need to perform reliably under time-varying flow conditions as well as during transitions between flow regimes, e.g. laminar-transitional-turbulent. For the first time, the SimInhale benchmark case consistently addressed the performance of

RANS and LES in capturing airflow and aerosol deposition characteristics in the extrathoracic and upper tracheobronchial (TB) airways [43]. Briefly, a number of independent research teams were solicited to simulate identical cases using both types of models implemented in their own custom numerical codes. Results were compared against *in vitro* flow (i.e. Particle Image Velocimetry - PIV [44]) and deposition measurements (i.e. Positron Emission Tomography - PET [45]) in corresponding 3D manufactured airway casts. Airflow results are demonstrated in Fig. 7.5 (normalized mean velocity and turbulent kinetic

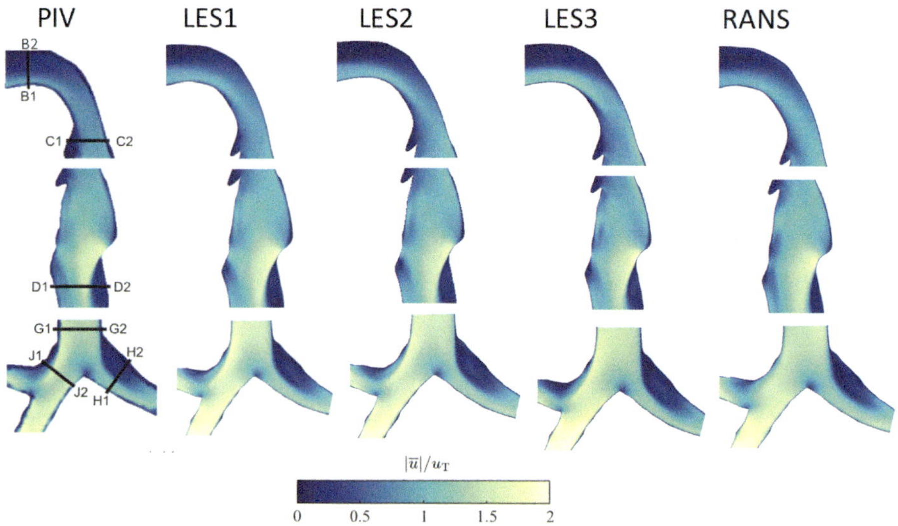

(A)

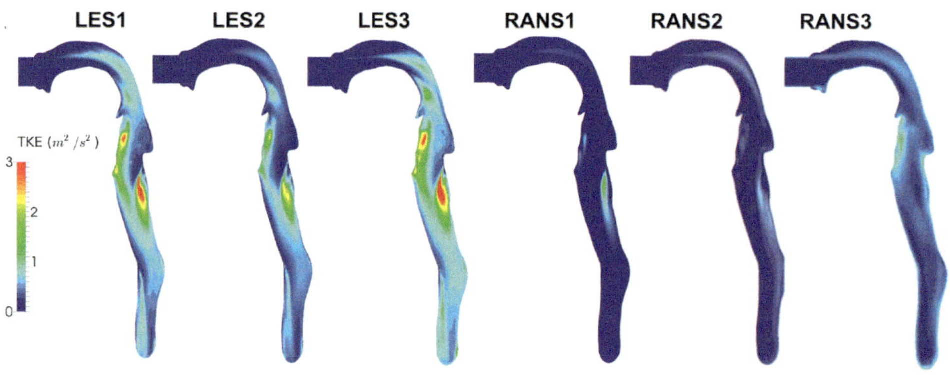

(B)

Figure 7.5 SimInhale benchmark case: (A) Comparison of normalized mean velocity contours between PIV, LES and RANS data; (B) Comparison of turbulent kinetic energy in the mouth, throat and trachea between three LES and three RANS simulations. *Adapted from P. Koullapis, et al., Regional aerosol deposition in the human airways: the SimInhale benchmark case and a critical assessment of in silico methods, Eur. J. Pharm. Sci. 113 (2018) and T. Janke, P. Koullapis, S.C. Kassinos, K. Bauer, PIV measurements of the SimInhale benchmark case, Eur. J. Pharm. Sci. 133 (2019)* [43,44].

energy contours). It was concluded that while RANS can perform acceptably when simulation conditions are properly setup, LES results exhibit considerably less variability and are generally in better agreement with *in vitro* measurements. Nevertheless, even in LES, results were observed to be sensitive to grid quality, design and resolution; grid resolution requirements were overall found to be higher than what is often reported in the literature and dependent on the specific simulation conditions (e.g. anatomy, flowrate, etc.). Thus, good practice is to undertake a grid independence study in any new case and to avoid relying on rules of thumb to forego this often time-consuming step. This is particularly important to bear in mind in clinical application scenarios, where the pressure for quick turnaround must often be balanced with computational trustworthiness considerations.

Recent studies have provided further evidence that the predicted respiratory airflows and deposition distributions in the upper TB tree are sensitive to the choice of outlet boundary conditions [46–48][85,101]; a general conundrum with *in silico* modeling approaches of respiratory transport phenomena in the lungs. Indeed, in the absence of complete patient-specific ventilation quantifications, a common practice is to impose uniform outlet pressures at the terminal sections of the bronchi. Yet, such strategy can significantly impact regional deposition estimates. Therefore, the specification of correct mass flowrate fractions, or alternatively pressure levels, at the outlets of an upper airway CFPD model requires that these be propagated from the alveolar regions upstream back to the distal ends of the 3D upper airway model. Several methods in recent years have been proposed to tackle this boundary condition challenge using either reduced dimensional models (e.g. typically based on impedance or resistive models [49]) or direct imaging methods [48,50]. Furthermore, the lack of detailed information on distal airway conditions complicates the simulation of deposition over complete breathing cycles in the upper airways. Inhaled aerosols that distally escape the TB model during the inhalation phase and exit into the deeper lungs cannot be tracked. This aerosol particle distribution will undergo further filtering and deposition in the deeper lung regions. As a result, the ensuing particle distribution that re-enters the upper bronchial segments during the exhalation phase is different from the one that escaped the TB model during inhalation.

A number of key points can be leveraged to limit the computational cost of simulations targeting the upper airways. For example, Koullapis et al. [9] have shown that regional deposition patterns in the upper TB tree, when expressed as segmental deposition efficiencies (DEs), are largely independent of the characteristics of the extrathoracic, MT region. This is demonstrated in Fig. 7.6, showing DEs in the first four generations (generation 0 is the trachea) for three models that have different mouth-throats and identical TB regions. In other words, the general morphological features of the MT region determine the amount of airborne aerosol filtering occurring in the extra-thoracic regions, and thereby the particle size distribution crossing distally into the main TB tree. In contrast, regional deposition across the upper TB region is specific to a particular TB tree morphometry [51] and is hence only weakly dependent on variations in incoming airflows from the trachea. This finding suggests that

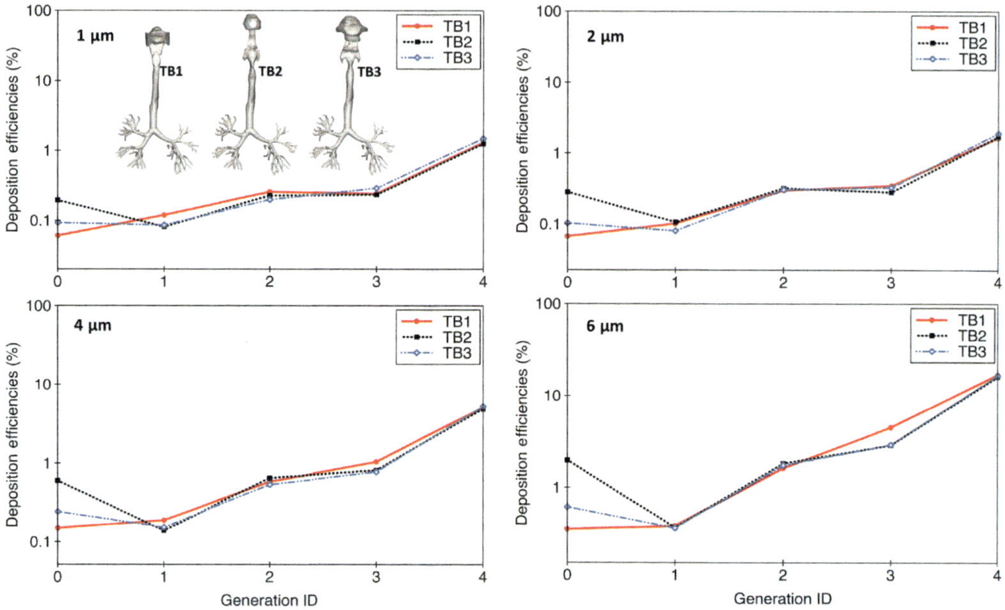

Figure 7.6 Deposition efficiencies in the first four generations (generation 0 is the trachea) for three models (TB1–3) with different mouth-throats and identical TB regions. *Adapted from P.G. Koullapis, L. Nicolaou, S.C. Kassinos, In silico assessment of mouth-throat effects on regional deposition in the upper tracheobronchial airways, J. Aerosol Sci. 117 (2018) 164–188* [9].

simulations of regional TB deposition can be conducted either using canonical *in silico* MT models (e.g. representing small, medium and large extra-thoracic volumes) or using previously-stored airflow fields and particle distributions. Such strategy offers considerable computational savings in the context of *in silico* population studies using large sample sizes; a point we will return to further below.

7.5 Modeling deposition in the acinus

The largest proportion of the human lung consists of the respiratory (or pulmonary) zone, where the gas-exchange takes place. Also referred to as the lung parenchyma, this region is located distal to the tracheobronchial region and includes all parts of the lung that contain alveoli. The term acinus (meaning berry in Latin) denotes all parts distal to a single terminal bronchiole and on average is beyond the sixteenth generation. The most proximal respiratory bronchioles, which originate from the terminal bronchioles, have relatively few alveoli attached on them. As we move deeper into the lung, each generation of respiratory bronchioles have increasingly more alveoli on them, until reaching the alveolar ducts, which are entirely covered with alveoli. The respiratory zone ends in the terminal alveolar sacs. A schematic of an acinus is shown in Fig. 7.7A,

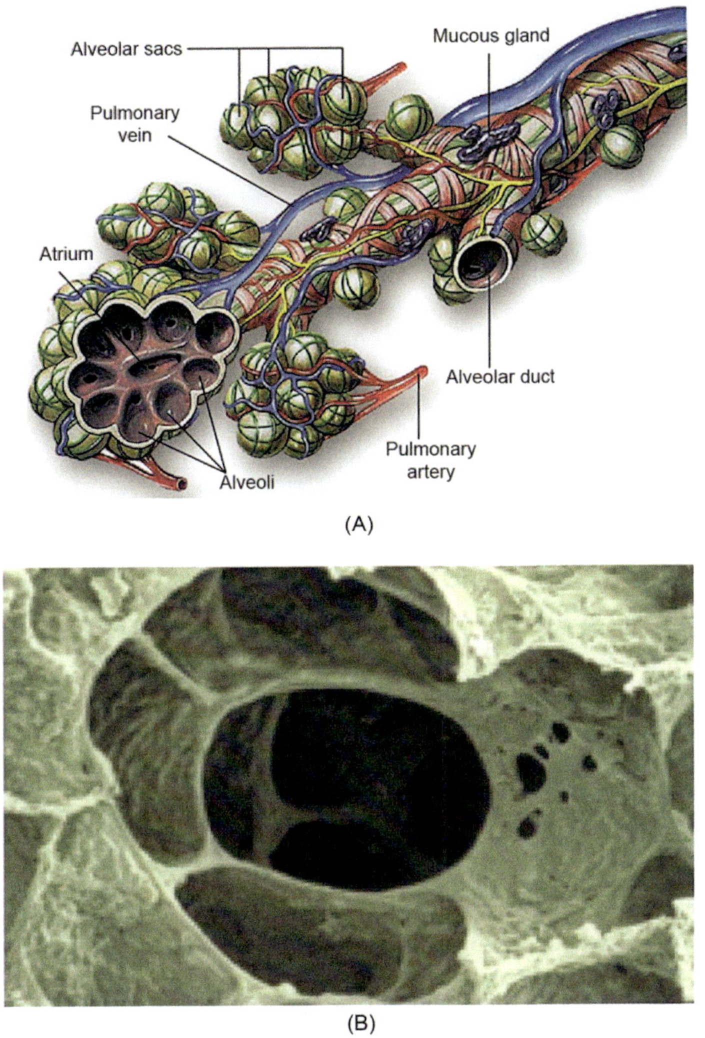

Figure 7.7 (A) Acinus region showing the alveolar ducts and sacs (original drawing courtesy of Patrick J. Lynch, medical illustrator). (B) Scanning electron micrograph of an alveolar duct surrounded by alveoli. *Adapted from P. Gehr, Annexe A. Anatomy and morphology of the respiratory tract, Ann. ICRP 24 (1–3) (1994) 121–166* [61].

whereas Fig. 7.7B shows an inside view of an alveolar duct from scanning electron micrograph.

In the absence of widely available *in vivo* imaging data for the respiratory airways, *in silico* models have offered an attractive gateway to explore respiratory airflows and aerosol transport in the depths of the lungs. Early models of the respiratory airways were made as rigid 2D ducts surrounded by dead-end air pockets [52][53]. Relatively

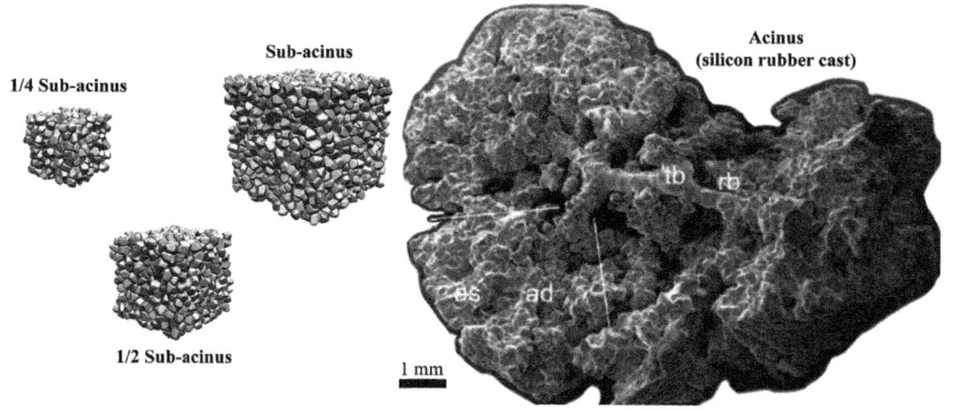

Figure 7.8 Heterogeneous sub-acinus models developed by Hofemeier et al. [8] using the mathematical model of Koshiyama and Wada [58]. A 1/4 sub-acinus, a 1/2 sub-acinus and a complete sub-acinus (i.e. 1/8 of a full acinus) are shown to scale next to the photograph of a cast of a full acinus (right side). *The full acinus cast is reproduced from B. Haefeli-Bleuer, E.R. Weibel, Morphometry of the human pulmonary acinus, Anat. Rec. 220 (4) (1988) 401–414* [84].

simple, these models were mainly used for understanding the most essential features of alveolar flow, that is strong recirculating flow in the proximal alveolar cavities and radial flow in the distal generations. However, these highly simplified models were missing an important feature of alveolar airways, namely, the rhythmical expansion and contraction of the acinar domain. The first alveolated duct CFPD model with non-rigid walls for studying aerosol transport was developed by Tsuda and co-workers [54]. More realistic 3-Dimensional models were developed in the past decade with the most commonly used model geometry being a bifurcating tree of circular pipes that are surrounded by truncated spheres [55]. Most advanced models employ space-filling geometries with alveoli of polyhedral-like shapes [56][5,57]. Despite significant progress, computational constraints have so far precluded the development of a complete acinar domain, since such a model would need to include around 10,000 alveolar cavities. Recently, Hofemeier et al. [8] conducted for the first time CFPD simulations in high-fidelity acinar models that capture average human morphometry and span up to the size of a characteristic sub-acinus, i.e. 1/8 of an acinus [58]. These are to date the largest domains to have ever been simulated. These models are illustrated and compared to a full acinus in Fig. 7.8. A few high-resolution 3D acinar imaging data have surfaced during the last years using micro-computed tomography (μCT) or scanning transmission X-ray microscopy [59,60][99,100]. However, the volumes of the reconstructed acinar models are still restricted, and such data have been confined to small animals rather than human acini.

The alveolar region of the deep lung, which presents the largest surface area and thinnest diffusion pathway into circulation for dissolved material, constitutes in many cases the premier target for drug delivery through the pulmonary route. In particular, the alveolar region is the target for the deposition and absorption of systemically acting inhaled medications such as proteins and peptides (inhaled insulin). It is also the target site for antibiotics such as anti-tuberculosis drugs. It is generally known that aerosols smaller than 2 μm, due to their low inertia, avoid deposition in the upper airways and penetrate in the deep lung generations where they can deposit in the respiratory zone. Since the alveolar airways have extremely small sizes (~300 μm) and are in general hard to access, computational methods are widely used to investigate deposition characteristics in the respiratory airways under various conditions. Due to the low air velocities in the deep alveolar region, deposition is governed by sedimentation (for particles above 1 μm) and diffusion (for particles smaller than 1 μm). Furthermore, aerosol deposition in deep regions of the lung can be influenced by complex pulmonary geometry. Deposition estimates in the acinus have been computed by 1D, 2D [62,63] and 3D [64] models. As noted in the previous paragraph, the latter typically include a few hundreds of alveoli and capture just a few percent of the volume of a single acinus as a result of computational constraints. Darquenne et al. [65] showed that the presence of wall motion significantly enhances deposition by using relative estimates with a stationary-wall model. Sera and co-workers [66,67] examined deposition in a murine pulmonary acinar model obtained from synchrotron micro-CT in a mouse. Under self-similar expansion and contraction, they identified the significant role of sedimentation on deposition of particles above 1 μm, with 3 μm particles having 100% deposition during a single breath. Concerning sub-micron particle deposition, particles in the range 0.1–0.4 μm were deposited in distal alveolar regions, whereas smaller particles were deposited widely throughout the acinus. Hofemeier et al. [8] employed their heterogeneous acinar domain, whose principles capture the space-filling property, to study deposition under realistic breathing conditions (i.e. quiet breathing and deep inhalation maneuver) and to investigate the role of the acinar domain size on particle transport and deposition outcomes. Their findings substantiate the general deposition trends under quiet breathing obtained with 1D models and underscore the significantly augmented deposition for all particle sizes during the deep inhalation maneuver. Regarding the effect of the acinar domain size on deposition outcomes, they found that smaller acinar domains (1/4 and 1/2 of a sub-acinus) yield slightly lower deposition efficiencies for particles in the range of 0.1–1 μm, as a result of the stronger ensuing convective flows carried along the acinar ducts in the larger domain.

An issue that remains to be tackled is the validation of *in silico* models of the respiratory region against *in vivo* data for lung deposition in humans. As suggested by Hofemeier et al. [8], and due to the ongoing absence of image-reconstructed human acinar data, one alternative would be to return to rodent-based heterogeneous models and in parallel conduct *in vivo* inhalation experiments in animals (e.g. rodents). A somewhat similar approach was conducted in [68], where respiration curves of ventilated rodents and particle properties were implemented to match experimental MRI data and explore *in silico* the deposition of 1 μm particles in polyhedral-based emphysematous acini models. While some encouraging agreement with experimental data was met, nevertheless such studies still fall short of a one-to-one comparison between experiments and simulations, and importantly do not go as far as translating directly to lung deposition in humans.

7.6 Towards integrated simulations covering the whole lung and combining more than one type of modeling

Existing computational studies of airflow and particle transport in the human respiratory tract mainly focus on truncated geometries of either the upper bronchial airways [40,69][84,93] or the terminal alveolar regions. Concerning the former, current studies of deposition in the central bronchial airways consider particle deposition only during the inhalation phase since particles that escape distally from the truncated geometry (i.e. the tree outlets) cannot be tracked back during the exhalation phase [70][71]. In order to account for the impact of exhalation on particle deposition in the human lungs, coupled simulations of bronchial and alveolar regions are required to close the system. In the case of the respiratory region, CFPD models have mainly been based on the so-called "bottom-up" approach, which considers models entirely void of the proximal, conducting regions, whereby information on the aerosol distribution crossing through the TB and entering the acinar region is in effect absent. One question lies, for example, in determining the size as well as spatial distribution of inhaled aerosols crossing through the central airways and entering into the alveolar regions. These are expected to be influenced primarily by particle size and airway orientation and thus to deviate from a simple uniform spatial distribution, commonly used in the majority of existing studies [5,72]. Deposition in the deeper alveolar regions can also be expected to be affected by the characteristics of transport and deposition of particles transiting through the proximal airways.

To resolve such shortcomings, recent advances have included efforts to couple conducting upper airway trees to breathing alveolar models and thus develop whole-lung CFPD models. Kleinstreuer and co-workers [73,74][75] documented a methodology for predicting particle deposition in a simplified 16-generation airway tree model, following a symmetric branching morphology. The tracheobronchial tree was geometrically decomposed into planar triple-bifurcation airway units (TBUs). Air-particle outflow conditions from an oral airway model were imported as inlet conditions for the first-level TBU. Overall, deposition statistics for the entire tree agreed rather well with those calculated using analytical models. Locally, however, deposition fractions based on analytical formulas differed greatly (from a few percent to 70% differences) from the simulation results. Differences were attributed to the local geometrical features as well as to ensuing flow characteristics and particle distributions. In a follow-up study, Kolanjiyil and Kleinstreuer [76] merged a realistic representation of the upper airways to the 16-generation simplified model and developed a model of the entire respiratory tract. The alveolar regions were modeled by adding spherical alveoli to the most distal triple-bifurcation airway units. Nanoparticle deposition at steady inhalation was modeled using the Eulerian-Eulerian approach. Shortcomings of the aforementioned studies include, among others, the use of planar triple-bifurcation airway models and limiting simulations to steady inhalation conditions only. In their latest study, Kolanjiyil and Kleinstreuer [77] improve their whole-lung airway model (WLAM) by using a subject-specific upper airways, from nose/mouth to generation 3, connected to adjustable TBUs to model generations 4 through 21. Spherical alveoli are introduced with increasing density from generations 16 to 21. Their whole lung model ends with a double bifurcation unit that represents the terminal alveolar sac (generations 22–23). They also incorporate physiologically realistic breathing conditions by applying a wall-displacement boundary condition on the alveolar tissue walls, making their model capable of capturing the transient particle trajectories during multiple breathing cycles. A dual-path whole lung model was utilized, where only two outlets of the upper airway model, one in the left and one in the right lung, were extended by attaching scaled TBUs in series. Limitations of the WLAM by Kleinstreuer et al. are the rather simplified acinar model with rigid alveolar ducts, the reinjections of particles into the next-level TBUs assuming uniform distributions and the hypothesis that the dual-path configuration can accurately capture deposition in the left and right lungs (quintuple-path WLAM are suggested as a further improvement).

In parallel to the abovementioned efforts, Longest and co-workers [78,79] published a series of studies on the development of the stochastic individual pathway (SIP) model. In this approach, individual continuous pathways beyond the third bifurcation (B3) of a mouth-throat to third generation (MT-B3) geometry are generated extending into each lobe of the lung through the terminal bronchioles (B15). Along each pathway, one daughter branch of each bifurcation is continued whereas the other is not. Their idea is to simulate a sufficient number of stochastically generated pathways until deposition results converge to an ensemble average. It was found that a single SIP model in the lower-left lobe can provide a representative average of total lung deposition [80][7] and, the number of SIP pathways required depends on the desired level of deposition resolution and the condition of the lung airways in terms of disease state. More recently, Tian et al. [81] integrated the SIP model with CFPD-based estimates of deposition in the alveolar regions in an effort to validate *in silico* predictions with *in vivo* deposition data. Namely, total lung deposition agreed within a relative error of 6% for the case of monodisperse aerosol with sizes of 1–7 μm. In the case of polydisperse aerosols released from a Dry Powder Inhaler and a Soft Mist Inhaler, CFPD predictions produced an average relative error of 10% for each inhaler when they directly compared the central, intermediary and peripheral scintigraphic regions of interest to calculated deposition in B1-B7 and B8-alveoli. Their study represents the first comparison of whole-lung CFPD predictions with regional *in vivo* deposition data of pharmaceutical inhalers, however, their choice of directly comparing certain generations from CFPD with scintigraphic regions of interest is problematic. A drawback of the SIP model is the assumption of symmetric outflow conditions at each bifurcation level (B4-B15) of the SIP model, which is valid only when the flow in the parent branch is fully developed and axi-symmetric (i.e. parabolic for laminar flow) such that the flow splits evenly in the subsequent daughter branches.

In these footsteps, and in view of delivering whole-lung simulations, Koullapis et al. [82,83] presented a computationally-efficient implementation of a deep lung model to predict aerosol deposition in the deep lung during full breathing cycles. Their model consisted of a simplified mid- to small-bronchial tree that represented the ten most distal generations of the conducting region combined with a heterogeneous acinar model (shown in Fig. 7.9); here, an Eulerian-Lagrangian approach was used to solve the airflow and aerosol equations, respectively, under sinusoidal breathing. The computational cost of the coupled simulation was decreased by taking advantage of the flow similarity across the central conducting regions in order to decompose the tree into representative subunits. The authors demonstrated resulting deposition estimates in rather strong agreement with classic deposition predictions using established 1D models. Limitations of the peripheral lung model are the rather simplified geometry of the conducting airways (repeated bifurcation in space), the lack of transitional region between conducting and respiratory region (transitional bronchioles) and the somewhat small number of alveoli in the respiratory region (sub-acinus model). Looking forward, integrating such deep lung models with LES simulations in the upper bronchial tree is anticipated to allow us to derive whole-lung deposition estimates during full breathing cycles, accounting for both the exhaled particle fraction and for information on the aerosol distribution crossing through the TB and entering the acinar region. Considering a step further, whole-lung CFPD models have the added benefit of offering the feasibility to emulate the effects of disease, including the uneven ventilation due to regional airway constriction in COPD or the destruction and remodeling of alveolar walls in emphysema. Hence, they represent promising tools that can be utilized to study deposition under such circumstances. In order to reduce computational costs to levels that are acceptable for routine use during drug development cycles, the outcomes and understanding derived from such CFPD simulations can eventually be used to derive

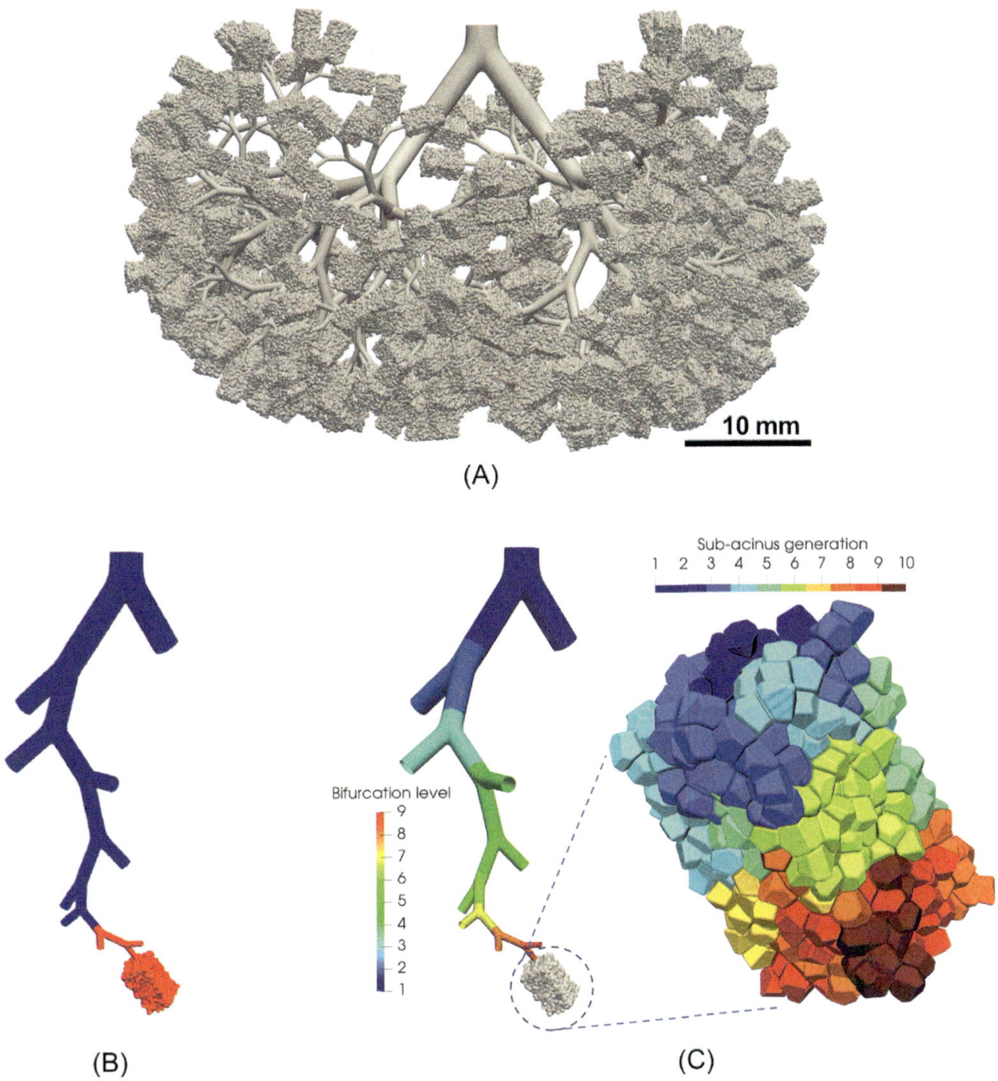

Figure 7.9 (A) Deep lung model developed in Koullapis et al. [82,83]. (B) Conducting and respiratory regions shown in blue and red, respectively, in a single path of the model. (C) Bifurcation levels and sub-acinus generations. *Adapted from P.G. Koullapis, P. Hofemeier, J. Sznitman, S.C. Kassinos, An efficient computational fluid-particle dynamics method to predict deposition in a simplified approximation of the deep lung, Eur. J. Pharm. Sci. 113 (June) (2018) 132–144 and P.G. Koullapis, F.S. Stylianou, J. Sznitman, B. Olsson, S.C. Kassinos, Towards whole-lung simulations of aerosol deposition: a model of the deep lung, J. Aerosol Sci. 144 (2020)* [82,83].

accurate correlations of deposition for a range of factors known to influence aerosol transport in the deep lung. These can then be incorporated in current analytical 1D models.

7.7 Simulations for the non-standard lung: Accounting for the effects of sex disease and age

There is large variability in lung morphology across subjects of different sex and age. In addition, airway diseases are accompanied by modifications of the airway anatomy. These geometric variations result in different airflow and aerosol deposition characteristics. Since, most of the existing models used for the estimation of regional drug deposition are based on data obtained from healthy subjects, they cannot capture the induced alterations in either flow or deposition. In addition, the vast majority of current inhaled pharmaceutical aerosols and delivery devices rely on "one size fits all" approach and do not account for the abovementioned variabilities. In the present section, we discuss how *in silico* tools can be utilized to help us understand and analyze the details of air and particle transport in the non-standard lung, and account for variability due to sex, disease and age.

Even among healthy subjects in the general population there is a substantial level of morphometric variability in the upper tracheobronchial airways. Morphometric measures, such as lumen areas, bifurcation angles and segmental lengths can vary remarkably. Biological sex accounts for a large fraction of these differences, but significant morphometric variability exists even among members of the same sex. The bar chart in Fig. 7.10 shows a comparison of the means and standard deviations of the cross-sectional areas of the larger airways from two different population pools (US and Cyprus), for men and

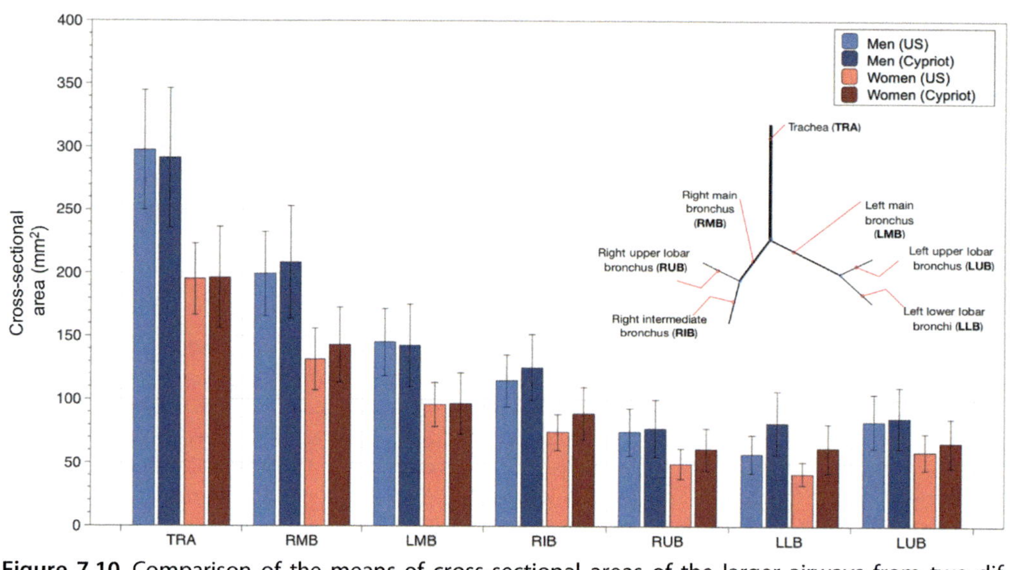

Figure 7.10 Comparison of the means of cross-sectional areas of the larger airways from two different population pools (US and Cyprus). Dark blue and dark red columns correspond to the mean values for men and women in the Cypriot population, while light blue and light red columns correspond to the means of the US population [25,26]. Bars denote the standard deviation.

women. It is clear that men have airways with larger cross-sectional areas in the first few lung generations [25,26].

A reasonable expectation is that the observed levels of morphometric variability in the upper tracheobronchial tree translate to significant variability in regional deposition of inhaled drugs even in the distal airways. It is worth noting for example the differences in the non-dimensionless Reynolds and Stokes numbers among the airways of male and female subjects. These numbers describe the airflow regime —laminar or turbulent— and the degree of inertial impaction, respectively. Due to the larger airway caliber in men (around 1.5 times larger cross-sectional area in trachea and large bronchi), the bulk velocities, Reynolds and Stokes numbers are smaller by as much as 1.5—5.5, 1.2—2.4 and 1.8—13 times, respectively, compared to the values found in women. These variations are anticipated to induce different flow and aerosol filtering characteristics in the large airways and eventually result in significant deposition variability in the more distal lung regions. However, while plausible this presumption has not been sufficiently quantified to date, mostly due to the difficulty of measuring local deposition in the conducting airways of generations 8—16 *in vivo*. Nevertheless, recent *in vivo* studies seem to confirm that patient-specific deposition hotspots in the central airways have a significant effect on lobar particle ventilation [85]. From the point of view of drug delivery, quantifying the effects of airway morphometry on regional delivery and deposition would be a worthwhile objective since it would contribute significantly in reducing the uncertainty associated with drug development. For example, once morphometric determinants of regional deposition are established, they could be used in the selection/exclusion of subjects enrolled in *in vivo* studies. Towards this goal, integrated simulations covering the whole lung such as those described in Section 6 could be used to perform *in silico* population studies that would help establish morphometric archetypes associated with certain patterns of regional deposition. This could be performed for healthy subjects (here healthy is taken to mean free of chronic lung disease) and then extended to account for the confounders of disease. Besides differences in lung morphology among men and women, sex-based disparities in respiratory disease are apparent and highly diverse [86]. For example, the year 2000 marked the first time that more women than men died from COPD. This trend is expected to continue and highlights the urgent need to better understand the potential mechanisms by which women are more susceptible to certain respiratory diseases than men.

Our current understanding of the dynamics of aerosol transport and deposition in diseased lungs remains limited, mainly due to our insufficient knowledge of the detailed geometry of remodeled airways and practical constraints in assessing deposition *in vivo* at an adequate level of detail. Airflow obstruction found in COPD or asthma can cause adverse pressure drops and high local velocities, which in turn can generate flow separation zones and enhanced impaction losses at deposition hotspots. Moreover, the increased resistance of the small airways and tissue compliance, results in longer time for the lungs to empty, which may lead to air trapping and alteration of ventilation distribution in

COPD patients. An obstruction in the peripheral lung for example is expected to reduce the amount of air reaching its region and, in the case of inhalation therapy, reduce the amount of drug aerosol depositing in the target site. Furthermore, when COPD patients use DPIs, the time of drug inhalation and the peak inspiratory flowrate decrease with the severity of disease [87]. As a result, DPIs operate at suboptimal flowrates and emit lower drug doses with particles becoming larger and larger due to insufficient de-agglomeration inside the inhaler at lower flowrates. This is highlighted in the study of Farkas et al. [87], who combined measurements of realistic inhalation profiles of mild, moderate, and severe COPD patients while inhaling through a commercial DPI (Symbicort Turbuhaler) and a stochastic airway model to estimate lung deposition. They found that while drug deposition in the lungs of mild COPD patients compared well with that of healthy subjects, lung deposition in patients with severe COPD was reduced by a factor of almost two. This implies that severe COPD patients receive a significantly lower lung dose than the desired.

For diseases of the upper airways, for which geometries can be reconstructed from medical imaging data (CT or MRI scans), CFPD can be applied directly in patient-specific models to help understanding airflow characteristics and correlate diseased sites to the induced wall shear stresses or deposition hotspots. Examples of applications include obstructive sleep apnea (OSA) and partial collapse of large airways that can occur during expiration in patients with lung diseases that are accompanied by abnormal pressure differences across the airway walls. They can also be applied to assist surgery planning [88] or to assess post-treatment outcomes. In the latter case, CFPD has been applied to study the effect of pulmonary lobectomy in treating lung cancer [89], for evaluating the effectiveness of operation in an OSA patient [14] and to quantify the airway pressure alteration and assessing the treatment outcome of the vascular ring surgery [90]. Simulation of deposition can be carried out in subject-specific models of diseased upper airways, in order to design the inhalation therapy in a way that maximizes the therapeutic outcome.

Since imaging-based models of the conducting airways with diameters less than 1 mm are currently unavailable due to resolution limitations, CFPD models of diseased airways basically consist of narrowed tubes that emulate the effects of asthma or COPD [91,92]. Although not fully realistic, these models are used to improve our understanding of the pathophysiology of lower airways accompanied by obstructive lung diseases. They can span multiple generations with regions of airflow obstruction distributed either symmetrically or randomly.

Another potential application of *in silico* tools concerns the emphysematous pulmonary acinus. Specifically, 3D CFPD simulations can be employed to shed light on alveolar flow mechanics and particle transport-deposition in diseased acini, at temporal and spatial resolutions that are beyond reach with current state-of-the-art imaging modalities. Oakes et al. [68] performed numerical simulations in polyhedral-based models of healthy and emphysematous sub-acini rat models. Emphysematous models were created by removing inter-septal alveolar walls and enhancing the alveolar volume in either a homogeneous or heterogeneous fashion. They found decreased deposition in the emphysematous models compared to the healthy one as well as increased dispersion in the diseased acini. In addition, particle deposition in emphysematous acini was found biased towards proximal acinar generations, while relative dispersion of particle concentrations was increased. Besides the study from Oakes et al. [68] dealing with rat acini, there is only a single study on simulating human emphysematous acini [93]. In this study, airflow patterns are investigated in a mathematically derived model that includes two generations of alveolar ducts. The effects of progressive emphysema were simulated by sequentially removing all alveolar septa within each alveolar duct and reducing the airway wall motion and flowrates. Their results show that septal destruction reduces airflow resistance through the alveolar ducts whereas the decrease in the oxygen transported to the acinus is attributed to the lower flowrates rather than septal destruction. Further *in silico* studies, combined with the limited *in vivo* data, can help us to understand the individual effects of emphysema.

Airway morphology changes considerably during growth from birth to adulthood [32]. As a result, deposition characteristics in children are different from those in adults. Despite the lack of experimental data on deposition in children, the very few available studies indicate higher total deposition in children by as much as twofold, compared to adults. Moreover, although inhalation therapies are widely used in children, treatment options and inhalation guidelines are basically derived from devices and protocols designed for adults [94]. Airway changes during growth, especially during the first 2–3 years, extend beyond airway caliper and thus we cannot treat the child lung as a miniaturized adult lung. Besides the smaller airway diameters, the child lung has fewer and smaller alveoli relative to the adult, and it also exhibits saccular-like architectures characterized by the absence of inter-alveolar septal walls [95]. During the first years of infancy, this delicate tissue gradually expands and evolves through a complex alveolarization process. Around the age of 2, the lungs start to resemble more closely the fully developed adult lung with space-filling structures. Apart from lung morphology, breathing parameters such as tidal volumes and frequencies also change with age up until adulthood. A better understanding of particle transport and deposition mechanisms within the developing lungs is essential in order to improve inhalation treatment in pediatric populations. *In vivo* investigations are typically limited due to ethical considerations whereas a few *in vitro* experiments were conducted in the large upper airways [96–98]. Application of *in silico* models in age-dependent studies have been initially limited to theoretical models due to the absence of widely-available imaging data in children [99]. Airflow and particle deposition simulations were recently carried out in idealized upper-airway models [92], a child-specific upper airway model [51] and the deep pulmonary acinar regions [100]. Das et al. [101] performed CFPD simulations of airflow and aerosol transport in an idealized but anatomically-faithful mouth-to-generation 7 airway geometry spanning a five year old to an adult. Choosing breathing conditions that mimic realistic age-specific inhalation maneuvers representative of DPI and nebulizer inhalation, they suggest the existence of an optimal aerosol size range for maximum deposition in the conducting airway that evolves with age and varies according to inhalation device. Although imaging-derived geometries of the child lung will remain limited in the coming years, *in silico tools* can be employed to examine the role of aerodynamic determinants in the fate of inhaled aerosols.

7.8 1D and reduced models

One-dimensional (1D) algebraic filter-in-series type lung deposition models were developed many decades ago for environmental aerosol protection purposes [1,2]. A comprehensive review of 1D models is given by [3]. These models are fairly simple to use, produce instantaneous results, are accessible to the non-specialist, and are therefore attractive tools to estimate regional lung deposition. Since they were initially developed for environmental aerosols, they were not adjusted to factors related to transport and deposition of inhaled therapeutic aerosols. Such an example concerns the increased spray momentum once the drug aerosol is emitted from the (usually) narrow mouthpiece of an inhaler that leads to high deposition losses in the oral cavity. In order to account for such effects, recent advances include combinations of 1D models with realistic in vitro testing using MT replicas, where 1D model predictions are basically corrected using the measured MT deposition. Since most of the dynamics of the aerosol cloud dissipate once it enters the trachea, 1D model predictions apply to a sufficient extent in the distal to MT airways.

As mentioned in Chapter 12, examples of software packages are the Multiple-Path Particle Dosimetry Model software (MPPD, freely available from Applied Research Associates Inc., USA), Mimetikos Preludium (available for licensing from Emmace Consulting AB, Sweden) and Gastroplus (Simulation Plus Inc., CA USA). The former package is not particularly addressing pharmaceutical aerosols, but contains many models based on the work of Asgharian and co-workers [10], including animal deposition models. Mimetikos Preludium is a package explicitly focused on pharmaceutical aerosols also including a pharmacokinetic (PK) module for mechanistic simulation of post-deposition drug disposition. Gastroplus, which accounts for additional Dosage Routes, is a commercial package that provides both deposition and PK predictions.

1D model predictions can be further improved by introducing corrections derived from CFPD simulations. For example, 3D CFPD methods can capture the effects of heterogeneous deviations from the standard lung (e.g. localized airway blockage, unevenly distributed emphysema etc.) and provide insights for 1D model improvements. Furthermore, CFPD simulations can shed light on anatomical effects (e.g. morphometry of the central airways, infant lung), which again can be used for enhancing 1D models.

7.9 Conclusions

This chapter introduced the range of *in silico* tools currently available for the prediction of the airflow and aerosol transport and deposition in the extrathoracic airways and the lung. The key features of the various modeling methods have been reviewed and areas where caution must be exercised have been identified. While the emerging role of *in silico* methods in the area of personalized medicine is an exciting development, we have argued that equally important, and potentially more impactful from the drug delivery perspective, is the application of these methods in large-scale population studies that are carried out *in silico*. The ultimate goal is to be identify subpopulations (clusters) of patients with unique lung features that might predispose to certain disease development scenarios. Equally important is the identification of patient clusters with morphometric and functional characteristics that predispose to identifiable drug deposition patterns. These ideas are explored at a more advanced level in Chapter 14, where concrete application examples are shown.

References

[1] International Commission on Radiological Protection (ICRP), Human respiratory tract model for radiological protection, Ann. ICRP 24 (1994) 1–120. Publ. 66.

[2] NCRP Report 125, Deposition, Retention and Dosimetry of Inhaled Radioactive Substances, National Council on Radiation Protection and Measurements, Bethesda, MD, 1997, ISBN 0-929600-54-1.

[3] W. Hofmann, Modelling inhaled particle deposition in the human lung—a review, J. Aerosol Sci. 42 (10) (2011) 693–724.

[4] A.R. Lambert, P.T. O'shaughnessy, M.H. Tawhai, E.A. Hoffman, C. Lin, Regional deposition of particles in an image-based airway model: large-eddy simulation and left-right lung ventilation asymmetry, Aerosol Sci. Technol. 45 (1) (2011) 11–25.

[5] P. Hofemeier, J. Sznitman, Revisiting pulmonary acinar particle transport: convection, sedimentation, diffusion, and their interplay, J. Appl. Physiol. (39)(2015) 1375–1385.

[6] P.G. Koullapis, S.C. Kassinos, M.P. Bivolarova, A.K. Melikov, Particle deposition in a realistic geometry of the human conducting airways: effects of inlet velocity profile, inhalation flowrate and electrostatic charge, J. Biomech. 49 (11) (2016).

[7] P.W. Longest, G. Tian, N. Khajeh-Hosseini-Dalasm, M. Hindle, Validating whole-airway CFD predictions of DPI aerosol deposition at multiple flow rates, J. Aerosol Med. Pulm. Drug. Deliv. 29 (0) (2016). p. jamp.2015.1281.

[8] P. Hofemeier, K. Koshiyama, S. Wada, J. Sznitman, One (sub-)acinus for all: fate of inhaled aerosols in heterogeneous pulmonary acinar structures, Eur. J. Pharm. Sci. 113 (2018) 53–63. June.

[9] P.G. Koullapis, L. Nicolaou, S.C. Kassinos, In silico assessment of mouth-throat effects on regional deposition in the upper tracheobronchial airways, J. Aerosol Sci. 117 (2018) 164–188.

[10] B. Asgharian, W. Hofmann, R. Bergmann, Particle deposition in a multiple-path model of the human lung, Aerosol Sci. Technol. 34 (4) (2001) 332–339.

[11] L. Borgström, B. Olsson, L. Thorsson, Degree of throat deposition can explain the variability in lung deposition of inhaled drugs, J. Aerosol Med. (2006) 473–483.

[12] W. Hofmann, B. Asgharian, R. Winkler-Heila, Modeling intersubject variability of particle deposition in human lungs, J. Aerosol Sci. 33 (2) (2002) 219–235.

[13] F.S. Stylianou, J. Sznitman, S.C. Kassinos, Direct numerical simulation of particle laden flow in a human airway bifurcation model, Int. J. Heat Fluid Flow 61 (2016) 677–710.

[14] M.Z. Lu, Y. Liu, J.Y. Ye, H.Y. Luo, Large eddy simulation of flow in realistic human upper airways with obstructive sleep, Procedia Comput. Sci. 29 (2014) 557–564.
[15] Á. Farkas, et al., The role of the combined use of experimental and computational methods in revealing the differences between the micron-size particle deposition patterns in healthy and asthmatic subjects, J. Aerosol Sci. (2020) 105582.
[16] D. Wu, M.H. Tawhai, E.A. Hoffman, C.-L. Lin, A numerical study of heat and water vapor transfer in MDCT-based human airway models, Ann. Biomed. Eng. 42 (10) (2014) 2117–2131.
[17] J. Sznitman, F. Heimsch, T. Heimsch, D. Rusch, T. Rösgen, Three-dimensional convective alveolar flow induced by rhythmic breathing motion of the pulmonary acinus, J. Biomech. Eng. 129 (5) (2007) 658–665.
[18] L. Shachar-Berman, Y. Ostrovski, A. De Rosis, S. Kassinos, J. Sznitman, Transport of ellipsoid fibers in oscillatory shear flows: implications for aerosol deposition in deep airways, Eur. J. Pharm. Sci. 113 (2018) 145–151.
[19] K.S. Burrowes, J. De Backer, H. Kumar, Image-based computational fluid dynamics in the lung: virtual reality or new clinical practice? Wiley Interdiscip. Rev. Syst. Biol. Med. 9 (6) (2017) 1–16.
[20] K. Poorbahrami, J.M. Oakes, Regional flow and deposition variability in adult female lungs: a numerical simulation pilot study, Clin. Biomech. Dec. (2018) 1–10.
[21] J.W. De Backer, et al., Computational fluid dynamics can detect changes in airway resistance in asthmatics after acute bronchodilation, J. Biomech. 41 (1) (2008) 106–113.
[22] L. Wiechert, A. Comerford, S. Rausch, W.A. Wall, Advanced multi-scale modelling of the respiratory system, Notes Numer. Fluid Mech. Multidiscip. Des. 116 (2011) 1–32.
[23] H. Kumar, C.J.T. Spence, M.H. Tawhai, Modeling the pharyngeal pressure during adult nasal high flow therapy, Respir. Physiol. Neurobiol. 219 (2015) 51–57.
[24] S.C. Van Hove, et al., An experimental and numerical investigation of CO_2 distribution in the upper airways during nasal high flow therapy, Ann. Biomed. Eng. 44 (10) (2016) 3007–3019.
[25] P.B. Dominelli, et al., Sex differences in large conducting airway anatomy, J. Appl. Physiol. 125 (3) (2018) 960–965.
[26] S. Christou, T. Chatziathanasiou, S. Angeli, P. Koullapis, F. Stylianou, J. Sznitman, Anatomical variability in the upper tracheobronchial tree: sex-based differences and implications for personalized inhalation therapies, J. Appl. Physiol. (2020). Available from: https://journals.physiology.org/doi/abs/10.1152/japplphysiol.00144.2020.
[27] J.K.F. Jakobsson, et al., Altered deposition of inhaled nanoparticles in subjects with chronic obstructive pulmonary disease, BMC Pulm. Med. 18 (1) (2018) 1–11.
[28] J. Rissler, A. Gudmundsson, H. Nicklasson, E. Swietlicki, P. Wollmer, J. Löndahl, Deposition efficiency of inhaled particles (15–5000 nm) related to breathing pattern and lung function: an experimental study in healthy children and adults, Part. Fibre Toxicol. 14 (1) (2017) 10.
[29] J. Choi, et al., Differences in particle deposition between members of imaging-based asthma clusters, J. Aerosol Med. Pulm. Drug. Deliv. 32 (4) (2019) 213–223.
[30] S. Miyawaki, E.A. Hoffman, S.E. Wenzel, C.L. Lin, Aerosol deposition predictions in computed tomography-derived skeletons from severe asthmatics: a feasibility study, Clin. Biomech. 66 (2019) 81–87.
[31] P.W. Longest, et al., Use of computational fluid dynamics deposition modeling in respiratory drug delivery, Expert. Opin. Drug. Deliv. 16 (1) (2019) 7–26.
[32] W.H. Finlay, The mechanics of inhaled pharmaceutical aerosols, Mech. Inhaled Pharm. Aerosols (2001) 175–220.
[33] C.L. Lin, M.H. Tawhai, G. McLennan, E.A. Hoffman, Characteristics of the turbulent laryngeal jet and its effect on airflow in the human intra-thoracic airways, Respir. Physiol. Neurobiol. 157 (2–3) (2007) 295–309.
[34] M.H. Tawhai, C.L. Lin, Airway gas flow, Compr. Physiol. 1 (3) (2011) 1135–1157.
[35] Z. Zhang, C. Kleinstreuer, Airflow structures and nano-particle deposition in a human upper airway model, J. Comput. Phys. 198 (1) (2004).
[36] P.W. Longest, J. Xi, Effectiveness of direct Lagrangian tracking models for simulating nanoparticle deposition in the upper airways, Aerosol Sci. Technol. 41 (4) (2007) 380–397.

[37] V. Agnihotri, G. Ghorbaniasl, S. Verbanck, C. Lacor, An eddy interaction model for particle deposition, J. Aerosol Sci. 47 (2012) 39–47.

[38] Y. Wang, P.W. James, On the effect of anisotropy on the turbulent dispersion and deposition of small particles, Int. J. Multiph. Flow 25 (3) (1999) 551–558.

[39] E.A. Matida, W.H. Finlay, C.F. Lange, B. Grgic, Improved numerical simulation of aerosol deposition in an idealized mouth-throat, J. Aerosol Sci. 35 (1) (2004) 1–19.

[40] J. Choi, M.H. Tawhai, E.A. Hoffman, C.L. Lin, On intra- and intersubject variabilities of airflow in the human lungs, Phys. Fluids 21 (10) (2009) 1–17.

[41] H. Radhakrishnan, S. Kassinos, CFD modeling of turbulent flow and particle deposition in human lungs, 2009 Annu, Int. Conf. IEEE Eng. Med. Biol. Soc. 2009 (2009) 2867–2870.

[42] S.T. Jayaraju, M. Brouns, C. Lacor, B. Belkassem, S. Verbanck, Large eddy and detached eddy simulations of fluid flow and particle deposition in a human mouth-throat, J. Aerosol Sci. 39 (10) (2008) 862–875.

[43] P. Koullapis, et al., Regional aerosol deposition in the human airways: the SimInhale benchmark case and a critical assessment of in silico methods, Eur. J. Pharm. Sci. 113 (2018).

[44] T. Janke, P. Koullapis, S.C. Kassinos, K. Bauer, PIV measurements of the SimInhale benchmark case, Eur. J. Pharm. Sci. 133 (2019).

[45] F. Lizal, M. Belka, J. Adam, J. Jedelsky, M. Jicha, A method for in vitro regional aerosol deposition measurement in a model of the human tracheobronchial tree by the positron emission tomography, Proc. Inst. Mech. Eng. Part H J. Eng. Med. 229 (10) (2015) 750–757.

[46] B. Asgharian, O. Price, Airflow distribution in the human lung and its influence on particle deposition, Inhal. Toxicol. 18 (10) (2006) 795–801.

[47] A. Comerford, C. Förster, W.A. Wall, Structured tree impedance outflow boundary conditions for 3D lung simulations, J. Biomech. Eng. 132 (8) (2010) 081002.

[48] Y. Yin, J. Choi, E.A. Hoffman, M.H. Tawhai, C.L. Lin, Simulation of pulmonary air flow with a subject-specific boundary condition, J. Biomech. 43 (11) (2010) 2159–2163.

[49] N. Pozin, S. Montesantos, I. Katz, M. Pichelin, I. Vignon-Clementel, C. Grandmont, A tree-parenchyma coupled model for lung ventilation simulation, Int. J. Numer. Method. Biomed. Eng. 33 (11) (2017) 1–30.

[50] J.W. De Backer, et al., Flow analyses in the lower airways: patient-specific model and boundary conditions, Med. Eng. Phys. 30 (7) (2008) 872–879.

[51] J.M. Oakes, S.C. Roth, S.C. Shadden, Airflow simulations in infant, child, and adult pulmonary conducting airways, Ann. Biomed. Eng. 46 (3) (2018) 498–512.

[52] M.R. Davidson, J.M. Fitz-Gerald, Flow patterns in models of small airway units of the lung, J. Fluid Mech. 52 (1) (1972) 161–177.

[53] W.J. Federspiel, J.J. Fredberg, Axial dispersion in respiratory bronchioles and alveolar ducts, J. Appl. Physiol. 64 (6) (1988) 2614–2621.

[54] A. Tsuda, F.S. Henry, J.P. Butler, Chaotic mixing of alveolated duct flow in rhythmically expanding pulmonary acinus, J. Appl. Physiol. 79 (3) (1995) 1055–1063.

[55] B. Ma, C. Darquenne, Aerosol deposition characteristics in distal acinar airways under cyclic breathing conditions, J. Appl. Physiol. 110 (5) (2011) 1271–1282.

[56] J. Sznitman, T. Heimsch, J.H. Wildhaber, A. Tsuda, T. Rösgen, Respiratory flow phenomena and gravitational deposition in a three-dimensional space-filling model of the pulmonary acinar tree, J. Biomech. Eng. 131 (2009) 031010.

[57] H. Kumar, M.H. Tawhai, E.A. Hoffman, C.-L. Lin, The effects of geometry on airflow in the acinar region of the human lung, J. Biomech. 42 (11) (2009) 1635–1642.

[58] K. Koshiyama, S. Wada, Mathematical model of a heterogeneous pulmonary acinus structure, Comput. Biol. Med. 62 (2015) 25–32.

[59] D.M. Vasilescu, et al., Assessment of morphometry of pulmonary acini in mouse lungs by nondestructive imaging using multiscale microcomputed tomography, Proc. Natl. Acad. Sci. U. S. A. 109 (42) (2012) 17105–17110.

[60] L. Xiao, T. Sera, K. Koshiyama, S. Wada, Morphological characterization of acinar cluster in mouse lung using a multiscale-based segmentation algorithm on synchrotron micro-CT images, Anat. Rec. 299 (10) (2016) 1424–1434.
[61] P. Gehr, Annexe A. Anatomy and morphology of the respiratory tract, Ann. ICRP 24 (1–3) (1994) 121–166.
[62] C. Darquenne, M. Paiva, Two- and three-dimensional simulations of aerosol transport and deposition in alveolar zone of human lung, J. Appl. Physiol. 80 (4) (1996) 1401–1414.
[63] C. Darquenne, G.K. Prisk, Effect of gravitational sedimentation on simulated aerosol dispersion in the human acinus, J. Aerosol Sci. 34 (4) (2003) 405–418.
[64] L. Harrington, G.K. Prisk, C. Darquenne, Importance of the bifurcation zone and branch orientation in simulated aerosol deposition in the alveolar zone of the human lung, J. Aerosol Sci. 37 (1) (2006) 37–62.
[65] C. Darquenne, L. Harrington, G.K. Prisk, Alveolar duct expansion greatly enhances aerosol deposition: a three-dimensional computational fluid dynamics study, Philos. Trans. Ser. A, Math. Phys. Eng. Sci. 367 (1896) (2009) 2333–2346.
[66] T. Sera, K. Uesugi, N. Yagi, H. Yokota, Numerical simulation of airflow and microparticle deposition in a synchrotron micro-CT-based pulmonary acinus model, Comput. Method. Biomech. Biomed. Eng. 18 (13) (2015) 1427–1435. Taylor & Francis.
[67] T. Sera, R. Higashi, H. Naito, T. Matsumoto, M. Tanaka, Distribution of nanoparticle depositions after a single breathing in a murine pulmonary acinus model, Int. J. Heat Mass. Transf. 108 (2017) 730–739.
[68] J.M. Oakes, P. Hofemeier, I.E. Vignon-Clementel, J. Sznitman, Aerosols in healthy and emphysematous in silico pulmonary acinar rat models, J. Biomech. 49 (11) (2016) 2213–2220.
[69] L. Nicolaou, T.A. Zaki, Direct numerical simulations of flow in realistic mouth-throat geometries, J. Aerosol Sci. 57 (2013) 71–87.
[70] D.K. Walters, W.H. Luke, A method for three-dimensional Navier–Stokes simulations of large-scale regions of the human lung airway, J. Fluids Eng. 132 (5) (2010) 051101.
[71] B. Soni, S. Aliabadi, Large-scale CFD simulations of airflow and particle deposition in lung airway, Comput. Fluids 88 (2013) 804–812.
[72] N. Khajeh-Hosseini-Dalasm, P.W. Longest, Deposition of particles in the alveolar airways: inhalation and breath-hold with pharmaceutical aerosols, J. Aerosol Sci. 79 (2015) 15–30.
[73] C. Kleinstreuer, Z. Zhang, An adjustable triple-bifurcation unit model for air-particle flow simulations in human tracheobronchial airways, J. Biomech. Eng. 131 (2) (2009) 021007.
[74] Z. Zhang, C. Kleinstreuer, C.S. Kim, Comparison of analytical and CFD models with regard to micron particle deposition in a human 16-generation tracheobronchial airway model, J. Aerosol Sci. 40 (1) (2009) 16–28.
[75] Z. Zhang, C. Kleinstreuer, C.S. Kim, Airflow and nanoparticle deposition in a 16-generation tracheobronchial airway model, Ann. Biomed. Eng. 36 (12) (2008) 2095–2110.
[76] A.V. Kolanjiyil, C. Kleinstreuer, Nanoparticle mass transfer from lung airways to systemic regions—Part I: Whole-lung aerosol dynamics, J. Biomech. Eng. 135 (2013) 121003.
[77] A.V. Kolanjiyil, C. Kleinstreuer, Computational analysis of aerosol-dynamics in a human whole-lung airway model, J. Aerosol Sci. 114 (2017) 301–316.
[78] P.W. Longest, G. Tian, R. Delvadia, M. Hindle, Development of a stochastic individual path (SIP) model for predicting the deposition of pharmaceutical aerosols: effects of turbulence, polydisperse aerosol size, and evaluation of multiple lung lobes, Aerosol Sci. Technol. 46 (12) (2012) 1271–1285.
[79] G. Tian, P.W. Longest, G. Su, R.L. Walenga, M. Hindle, Development of a stochastic individual path (SIP) model for predicting the tracheobronchial deposition of pharmaceutical aerosols: effects of transient inhalation and sampling the airways, J. Aerosol Sci. 42 (11) (2011) 781–799.
[80] P.W. Longest, G. Tian, R.L. Walenga, M. Hindle, Comparing MDI and DPI aerosol deposition using in vitro experiments and a new stochastic individual path (SIP) model of the conducting airways, Pharm. Res. 29 (6) (2012) 1670–1688.

[81] G. Tian, M. Hindle, S. Lee, P.W. Longest, Validating CFD predictions of pharmaceutical aerosol deposition with in vivo data, Pharm. Res. 32 (10) (2015) 3170–3187.
[82] P.G. Koullapis, P. Hofemeier, J. Sznitman, S.C. Kassinos, An efficient computational fluid-particle dynamics method to predict deposition in a simplified approximation of the deep lung, Eur. J. Pharm. Sci. 113 (June) (2018) 132–144.
[83] P.G. Koullapis, F.S. Stylianou, J. Sznitman, B. Olsson, S.C. Kassinos, Towards whole-lung simulations of aerosol deposition: a model of the deep lung, J. Aerosol Sci. 144 (2020).
[84] B. Haefeli-Bleuer, E.R. Weibel, Morphometry of the human pulmonary acinus, Anat. Rec. 220 (4) (1988) 401–414.
[85] S. Verbanck, M.F. Biddiscombe, O.S. Usmani, Inhaled aerosol dose distribution between proximal bronchi and lung periphery, Eur. J. Pharm. Biopharm. 152 (2020) 18–22.
[86] K.E. Pinkerton, et al., Women and lung disease. Sex differences and global health disparities, Am. J. Respir. Crit. Care Med. 192 (1) (2015) 11–16.
[87] Á. Farkas, F. Lizal, J. Jedelsky, J. Elcner, A. Horváth, M. Jicha, Simulation of airway deposition of an aerosol drug in COPD patients, Pharmaceutics 11 (4) (2019) 1–10.
[88] S. Ozlugedik, et al., Numerical study of the aerodynamic effects of septoplasty and partial lateral turbinectomy, Laryngoscope 118 (2) (2008) 330–334.
[89] Q. Gu, et al., Structural and functional alterations of the tracheobronchial tree after left upper pulmonary lobectomy for lung cancer, Biomed. Eng. Online 18 (1) (2019) 1–18.
[90] F.-L. Chen, T.-L. Horng, T.-C. Shih, Simulation analysis of airflow alteration in the trachea following the vascular ring surgery based on CT images using the computational fluid dynamics method, J. Xray. Sci. Technol. 22 (2) (2014) 213–225.
[91] F. Farkhadnia, T.B. Gorji, M. Gorji-Bandpy, Airflow, transport and regional deposition of aerosol particles during chronic bronchitis of human central airways, Australas. Phys. Eng. Sci. Med. 39 (1) (2016) 43–58.
[92] P.W. Longest, S. Vinchurkar, T. Martonen, Transport and deposition of respiratory aerosols in models of childhood asthma, J. Aerosol Sci. 37 (10) (2006) 1234–1257.
[93] A. Dutta, D.M. Vasilescu, J.C. Hogg, A.B. Phillion, J.R. Brinkerhoff, Simulation of airflow in an idealized emphysematous human acinus, J. Biomech. Eng. 140 (7) (2018).
[94] I. Amirav, M.T. Newhouse, Aerosol therapy in infants and toddlers: past, present and future, Expert. Rev. Respir. Med. 2 (5) (2008) 597–605.
[95] P.H. Burri, Structural aspects of postnatal lung development - alveolar formation and growth, Biol. Neonate 89 (4) (2006) 313–322.
[96] H.M. Janssens, J.C. de Jongste, W.J. Fokkens, S.G. Robben, K. Wouters, H.A. Tiddens, The Sophia Anatomical Infant Nose-Throat (Saint) model: a valuable tool to study aerosol deposition in infants, J. Aerosol Med. 14 (4) (2001) 433–441.
[97] K.G. Schuepp, et al., In vitro determination of the optimal particle size for nebulized aerosol delivery to infants, J. Aerosol Med. 18 (2) (2005) 225–235.
[98] L. Golshahi, M.L. Noga, W.H. Finlay, Deposition of inhaled micrometer-sized particles in oropharyngeal airway replicas of children at constant flow rates, J. Aerosol Sci. 49 (2012) 21–31.
[99] B. Asgharian, M.G. Ménache, F.J. Miller, Modeling age-related particle deposition in humans, J. Aerosol Med. 17 (3) (2004) 213–224.
[100] J.T. Katan, P. Hofemeier, J. Sznitman, Computational models of inhalation therapy in early childhood: therapeutic aerosols in the developing acinus, J. Aerosol Med. Pulm. Drug. Deliv. 29 (3) (2016) 288–298.
[101] P. Das, E. Nof, I. Amirav, S.C. Kassinos, J. Sznitman, Targeting inhaled aerosol delivery to upper airways in children: insight from computational fluid dynamics (CFD), PLoS One 13 (11) (2018) 1–20.

CHAPTER 8

Non-absorptive clearance from airways

Martin Donnelley[1], Mark Gardner[2], Kaye Morgan[3] and David Parsons[1,4]
[1]Adelaide Medical School and Robinson Research Institute, University of Adelaide, Adelaide, SA, Australia
[2]Australian Cancer Research Foundation Image X Institute, University of Sydney, Sydney, NSW, Australia
[3]School of Physics and Astronomy, Monash University, Clayton, VIC, Australia
[4]Respiratory and Sleep Medicine, Women's and Children's Hospital, North Adelaide, SA, Australia

8.1 Introduction

The health of the respiratory system is maintained via clearance mechanisms that propel inhaled debris and pathogens away from the lungs. Removal of particles that have been inhaled and deposited within the conducting airways begins with mucociliary clearance (MCC), a process that in healthy people is both effective and unnoticed. MCC works by trapping particles in mucus that coats the airway surface, and then moving this towards the mouth through the action of many ciliated cells. When disease is present, whether from systemic or other organ causes, or as a result of inhalation of pathogens, the lung can increase secretions to help improve clearance, and then recruit cough to further boost clearance [1]. Throughout these processes immune responses boost the numbers and capability of macrophages and neutrophils in the capture and killing or removal of the offending particles, particularly in the alveolar region [2].

Like the structure and function of the respiratory system itself, non-absorptive clearance mechanisms are complex, and their effectiveness depends on a number of parameters. These include the species, airway humidity, temperature, the physical, chemical and biological properties of the particles, and of course the health of the lungs. As a result, there can be variability in the measured clearance rates and behavior.

MCC rates can be used as a measure of airway health, and changes can indicate the effectiveness of any treatment that seeks to address compromised clearance. MCC is also important to consider when designing drug delivery methods, because these physiological processes that clear foreign substances from the lung may also result in drug clearance, and a reduction in efficacy.

There are several challenges associated with accurately measuring MCC, and a range of methods have been developed, the majority of which measure the transit time of a deposited marker substance. These methods cannot resolve individual structures within the lungs nor particles of inhalable size without restricting the field of view to a small part of the respiratory system. This means that existing approaches either capture bulk clearance or mass-transit at a whole-lung scale, or capture individual particle clearance

Inhaled Medicines
DOI: https://doi.org/10.1016/B978-0-12-814974-4.00002-X

behavior within a specific airway using high-magnification measurement methods. The continuous movement of the lungs restricts the time available to capture each measurement, and hence available methods.

This chapter begins by outlining the relevant anatomy and physiology of the respiratory system (Section 8.2), before focusing on measurement techniques in humans (Section 8.3) and in animal research studies (Section 8.4). Computational modeling of MCC is considered (Section 8.5), then the final Section 8.6 looks at future developments, focusing particularly on methods for measuring MCC and their applications.

8.2 Lung anatomy and physiology

In humans the lungs are the primary organ of the respiratory system, responsible for extracting oxygen from the atmosphere and transferring it to the blood, and returning carbon dioxide from the blood back to the atmosphere. The lungs are part of the lower respiratory tract, and are composed of a conducting zone and a respiratory zone (see Fig. 8.1). The conducting zone begins at the glottis and proximal trachea, branches into the bronchi and bronchioles (up to 23 generations), and is responsible for the transport of gas from the nose and mouth to the gas exchange regions. The respiratory zone is composed of alveolar ducts and alveoli, in which the oxygen and carbon dioxide gas exchange takes place. The adult lung contains ~500 million alveoli [3], ~2400 km of airways, and has a gas exchange surface area of ~70–100 m^2 [4].

The trachea and bronchi share a similar structure; they are tubular and have supporting cartilage rings to prevent collapse during respiration. The bronchioles are around 1 mm in diameter and do not have supporting cartilage, instead their walls are surrounded by smooth muscle. There are approximately 40 types of cells in the respiratory system [6]. The trachea, bronchi, and bronchioles are lined with ciliated pseudostratified columnar respiratory epithelium interspersed with mucus producing goblet cells, as well as club cells. Basal cells constitute approximately 30% of the airway epithelium and have been identified as the stem cells of the conducting airways [7]. In rodents, basal cells are only present in the trachea, but in humans they are present throughout the airway tree [8]. Proximally the airways are ciliated, but more distally the surface changes to a simple columnar epithelium lacking mucus producing goblet cells but containing secretory club cells [9]. Respiratory bronchioles contain occasional alveoli and have surface surfactant-producing cells.

The alveoli are comprised of two types of alveolar cells (type I and type II pneumocytes) that make up the walls and septa and together are responsible for gas exchange. The Type I cells are flat, make up 95% of the alveolar surface area, and have thin walls that facilitate gas exchange to and from the capillary beds that are as little as 0.1 μm from the alveoli. The Type II cells are larger, cubiodal, act as progenitor cells (of both type I and II cells), and release surfactant to lower the surface tension and prevent alveolar collapse

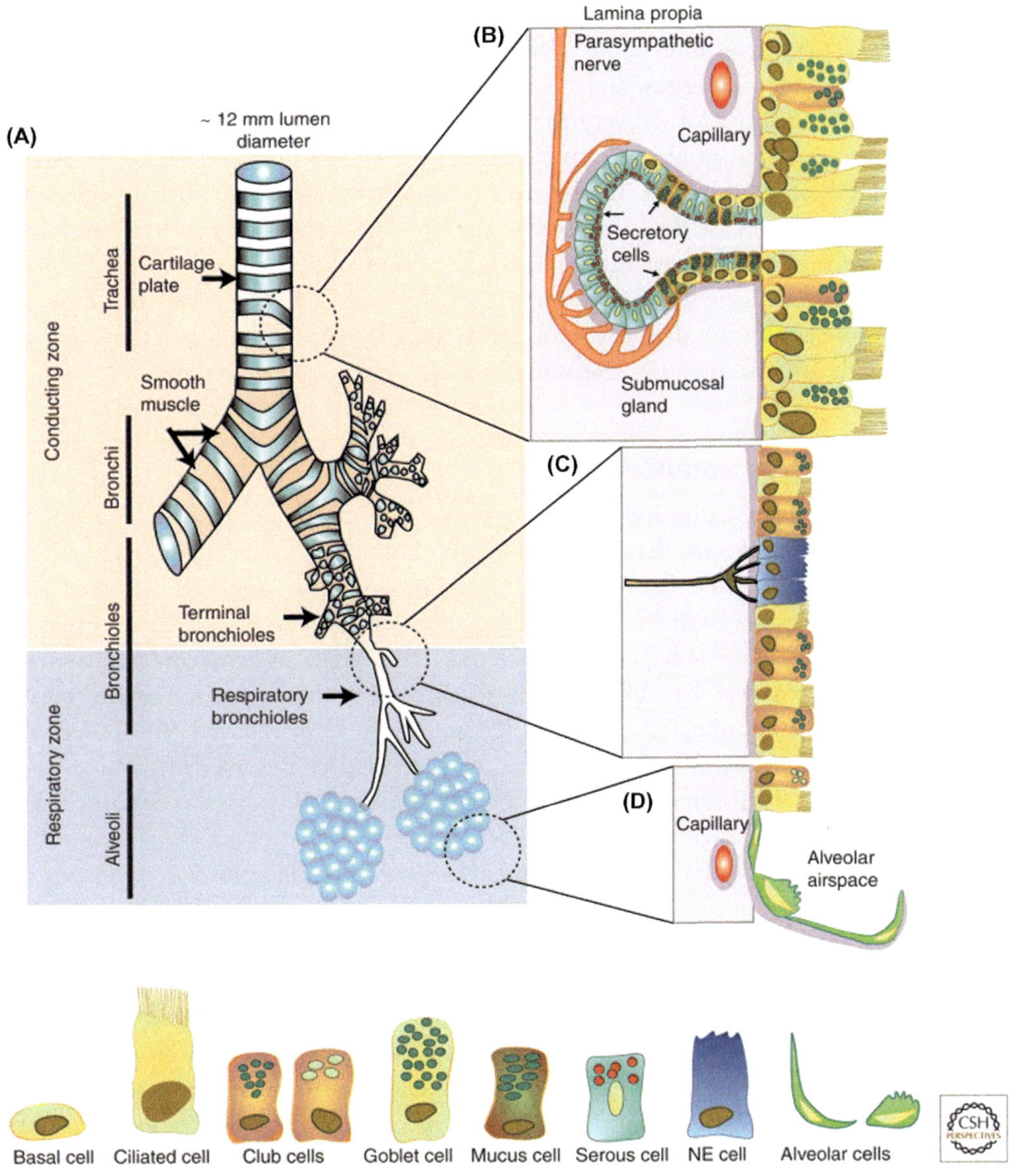

Figure 8.1 Structure of the respiratory system [5]. Included with permission from the copyright holder, Cold Spring Harbor Laboratory Press.

[10,11]. Despite taking up less surface area, there are more Type II cells than Type I cells in the lung. Alveoli also contain macrophages near the pneumocytes but separate from the alveolar walls. These cells have an important immunological role, engulfing and removing exogenous substances that deposit in the alveoli by phagocytosis.

Like our skin, the surfaces of the lung are exposed to the outside environment. On average, a person breathes more than 10,000 L of air every day, and that air often contains particulates, toxic gases, and microbial and viral pathogens. Inspired air can also deliberately contain drugs for delivery to the lungs. Upon inhalation, the high velocity of the airflow causes large particles to impact and deposit within the nose and larynx, and at the bifurcations of the airways. In the smaller lung airways where the air velocity is lower, particles fall out of the air stream by sedimentation and deposit on the airway walls. Any remaining particles in the airstream can make it into the alveoli where Brownian diffusion is also important for the smaller particles. However, the lung is a remarkably resilient organ that has evolved to handle these particles, toxic gases and pathogens with minimal lung or airway injury [12].

8.2.1 Mucociliary clearance

Lung defense involves anatomical barriers, aerodynamics that cause particulate impaction before the lung, immune mechanisms, and cough. However, the primary innate defense mechanism is Mucociliary Clearance (MCC) [5]. MCC is responsible for clearing inhaled debris from the bronchioles up the trachea, from where it can be expectorated or swallowed into the esophagus and excreted. The MCC system contains two key components: microscopic hair-like structures called cilia on the surface of the ciliated cells that beat in a coordinated fashion; and the airway surface liquid (ASL) layer that surrounds the cilia, which is comprised of two separate layers; the overlying mucus layer, and a distinct periciliary layer (PCL) near the cell surface [13]. Proper function of these components is vital for effective MCC.

The conducting airway epithelium contains a variety of different cell types, but it is the terminally differentiated ciliated cells [14] and secretory cells that contribute to MCC function [5]. Ciliated cells are easily identified microscopically by the presence of cilia on their apical surface [15]. Each cilium is 0.2–0.3 μm in diameter, and 6–7 μm in length in the upper airways, and ~4 μm in the smaller airways [16]. There are typically 50–100 cilia per cell, at a density of around 5–8 cilia/μm^2, with the number varying throughout the respiratory tract [17]. Cilia use adenosine triphosphate (ATP) as an energy source to sustain ciliary motion based on the motor activity of axonemal dynein [18]. Each cilium beats with a single waveform at frequencies of 10–20 Hz [19] in a phase-shifted manner with respect to its neighbor, creating a wave that travels across the epithelium, propelling the overlying mucus along the airway surface. Thus, for effective MCC the number of cilia, their structure, and their coordinated movement must all be correct. In addition to the conducting airways, ciliated cells are also present in the nasal passages and sinuses.

The ASL is composed of a protective mucus layer secreted by goblet cells, onto which inhaled particles, bacteria or viruses are trapped, and below it a low viscosity periciliary liquid (PCL) layer that provides lubrication and facilitates ciliary beating [20], enabling mucus clearance. Mucus is composed of ~98% water, ~0.9% salts and ~0.8% globular proteins, and 0.3% high molecular weight polymeric mucins [21]. The mucin glycoproteins are encoded by the *MUC* genes; in humans MUC5B is produced by goblet cells and submucosal glands, and MUC5AC by goblet cells [22]. MUC5B is the dominant mucin in the epithelium and glands, and the distal airways are a major site of expression [23]. MUC5B and MUC5AC are very large polymers (0.2–10 μm in length), and intertwine to form a mesh-like gel [24]. The mucus rheology is determined not only by its composition but also the level of airway surface hydration. The amount of water on the airway surface is osmotically altered by efflux of chloride ions by the cystic fibrosis conductance regulator (CFTR) and calcium activated chloride channels, and the influx of sodium ions by the epithelial sodium channel (ENaC) [25]. As a result, a 2–5 μm thick mucus layer (in the trachea) is maintained above the cilia to protect the epithelium [5].

The PCL is a gel containing the tethered mucins MUC1, MUC4 and MUC16 [26] and other molecules, and is ~7 μm thick (a similar length to the cilia). Like the mucus layer above it, the PCL hydration is altered by Cl^- and Na^+ ion transport [25]. The rate of MCC increases with greater hydration [27]. When the PCL is poorly hydrated or the mucus concentration increases (e.g. in cystic fibrosis) its depth reduces, causing the overlying mucus to compress the cilia, inhibiting MCC [20]. Severe mucus hyperconcentration—as seen in cystic fibrosis—can completely flatten the cilia causing mucus stasis, adhesion and eventually mucus plaque or plug formation [24].

Effective MCC therefore relies on the correct pattern and frequency of ciliary movement, as well as maintenance of the viscoelasticity and transportability of the mucus. Understanding these factors and the interaction between the mucus and the cilia is vital for measuring clearance of inhaled substances.

8.2.2 Alveolar clearance

The size of inhaled particles is the primary determinant of whether they are likely to deposit in the upper respiratory tract, upper bronchi, lower bronchi, alveoli, or be exhaled [28,29]. In general, smaller particles (i.e. <5 μm) are more likely to reach the alveoli where they cannot be cleared by MCC due to the absence of ciliated cells in those peripheral regions. Therefore, another method is required to clear the alveoli of infectious or toxic particles that evade the mechanical defense systems (including the MCC system). This is the job of alveolar macrophages (AM), which are the primary cellular defense of the innate immune system [30]. These cells secrete a number of products including oxygen metabolites, lysozyme (an antimicrobial enzyme), antimicrobial peptides and proteases. Combined with their phagocytic and intracellular killing ability, AM account for most of the clearance of microparticles and microorganisr from the distal airways and alveolar spaces [31]. When faced with large numbers of infectious particles, AM also produce an array of cytokines that initiate inflammatory responses and recruit neutrophils [30], a type of white blood cell that is part of the innate immune system.

8.2.3 Cough clearance

MCC via ciliary action is the primary clearance method in health, however when mucus is overproduced, clearance is supplemented by cough. A cough is a vital protective reflex, and consists of three phases: an inspiratory phase in which air is inhaled; a compressive phase characterized by fast closure of the glottis combined with a forced expiratory effort; and an expulsive phase in which air is rapidly released following glottis opening [32]. Cough can be initiated at the bronchi, trachea or larynx. Expiratory reflexes are similar to the cough reflex, but without the inspiratory phase. These two movements have different functions, with cough designed to promote clearance, and expiratory reflexes designed to prevent entry of substances into the lungs [32]. During a cough, the expired air hits the mucus layer, transferring part of the kinetic energy of the fast-moving air to the mucus, causing mucus to move toward the glottis.

8.2.4 Clearance in health and disease

In health, the MCC system operates to remove cellular debris as well as inhaled particles and pathogens that are deposited onto the airway surfaces, to keep the lungs relatively clean. Cough clearance serves as a backup when MCC is inadequate [33]; and alveolar macrophages remove insoluble particles that deposit in the alveoli. The failure of any of these can result in disease.

There are four well described muco-obstructive diseases: chronic obstructive pulmonary disease (COPD), cystic fibrosis (CF), primary ciliary dyskinesia (PCD), and non—cystic fibrosis bronchiectasis (bronchiectasis in the absence of this monogenetic cause) [24]. All four share clinical features of cough, sputum production, and episodic exacerbations. These result from the failure to correctly regulate the mucus concentration, producing mucus hyperconcentration (MUC5B is the dominant mucin by concentration [34]) that slows MCC and generates mucus plaques and plugs that adhere to airway surfaces [35]. Failure to clear these produces obstructions that predispose the lungs to chronic bacterial infection [20]. Although not considered a muco-obstructive disease, MCC is also severely impaired in asthmatics [36], even in patients with mild stable disease [37]. However, asthma has a distinct pathophysiological mechanism, with airway hyper-responsiveness that results in contraction of smooth muscle surrounding the airways in the bronchi and bronchioles that leads to reversible airway obstruction.

In studies examining MCC, fast- and slow-clearance phases have been observed, which is particularly important for understanding the kinetics of inhaled drug delivery. The fast-clearance phase has traditionally been interpreted as the initial, rapid clearance of particles from the larger tracheo-bronchial airways, whereas the slow-clearance phase is commonly attributed to the small airways and alveolar region [38]. The slow-clearance phase may also be caused by particles moving into a less-clearable compartment such as the PCL, the mucus layer, or epithelial cells. MCC rates vary between species, and are affected by age, humidity of the inspired air, the measurement location and the type of sedation used during measurement [39].

In normal subjects a wide range of tracheal mucus velocities (TMV) have been reported. Early studies suggested TMV was ~20 mm/min [40], but more recent studies report ~10 mm/min [41,42]. This variability likely results from the method chosen to measure TMV (see Section 8.3.2), and the fact that MCC is not a spatially uniform process. In disease, the TMV typically decreases, but this may be region dependent. For example, in patients with mild to moderate CF, whole-lung clearance may not be significantly different to healthy volunteers, but MCC in the small airways is significantly reduced [43]. Long-term studies (3 weeks) in patients with CF also show that more particles are retained in the airways compared to controls [44]. Together this data suggests that the MCC assessment method, the location in which MCC is measured, and the timescale over which measurements are made are all important factors.

8.3 Measuring clearance in humans

The primary motivations for measuring MCC are the understanding of disease pathophysiology, the assessment of disease progression and the effect of systemic or inhaled therapeutics on disease, and the understanding and quantification of the clearance of inhaled pharmaceuticals. For example, pharmaceuticals that successfully treat CF airway disease should rapidly improve airway surface hydration and mucus clearance. Over time these improvements should also result in reduced bacterial colonization, improved lung function (e.g. FEV1), fewer exacerbations, and improved quality of life, but all of these take substantially longer to be measurable. Thus, substantial work has attempted to use MCC as one of the primary biological outcome measures and tools for drug development, with measurements made using a range of techniques.

8.3.1 The history of MCC measurement

From the earliest studies to those most recently reported, almost all MCC measurements have been based on recording the transit time of particles artificially deposited onto the airway surfaces. This assumes that the marker particles move along the airway at the same rate as the airway secretions in which they are immersed. MCC was initially examined in the upper respiratory tract of animals and humans, and those techniques were later translated to assessing MCC in the lungs.

Quantitative *in vivo* measurement of MCC has been performed in humans for almost a century, beginning with studies directly observing the motion of India ink [45] or calcium phosphate powder [46] deposited onto nasal mucosa, and measuring their transit time to the oropharynx. Due to the challenge of visualizing the deposited ink or particles, Andersen developed a saccharine nasal MCC test in which the subject would tell the examiner when they tasted the sweet saccharine flavor on swallowing, allowing the transit time of a single saccharine particle from the nasal mucosa to the taste buds on the tongue be determined [47]. However, saccharine can alter the composition of the PCL, thereby changing the MCC behavior, so the method has been modified to utilize saccharine-loaded ion exchange resin particles [48]. Around the same time, radioactive particle tracking methods were developed that utilized an external gamma camera to measure the bulk transit of particles deposited into the nose [49].

To assess individual particle clearance a bronchoscopic method of measuring TMV based on tracking the motion of Teflon particles placed onto the tracheal surface was developed [40]. This method was able to demonstrate that in patients with obstructive lung disease there were many regions of the tracheal mucosa where MCC was completely absent. Later a similar radiographic method of tracking the motion of radiopaque Teflon discs through the nose was reported [50].

More recently, micro-optical coherence tomography (μOCT) with 1 μm resolution has been demonstrated to be capable of acquiring cross-sectional images of tissue reflectance in human tissue explants [51], and human nasal airways [52]. This system enables direct visualization of microscopic features, and extraction of image-based metrics relevant to MCC (refer to Section 8.4.3 for more details). The unique difference with this system is that mucus flow and MCC are measured directly, without the addition of tracking particles [53].

Each of these nasal MCC measurement methods has advantages and limitations. The saccharine test uses a single particle, so cannot examine spatial variation in MCC at various locations throughout the nose, cannot be frequently repeated, produced some discomfort for subjects, and is somewhat subjective [50]. However, its primary advantage is that it is easy and inexpensive to perform, with studies showing that the results are similar to those produced by radiotracer methods [54]. As a result, the saccharine test is still in use for some studies of nasal MCC. The advantage of radiotracer methods is that the particles are inert, the bulk MCC of particles can be more accurately and objectively tracked, and any treatment effects can be assessed. Radiographic methods for assessment of nasal MCC have not been widely reported, likely due to the radiation dose delivered to the brain. So far μOCT-based MCC assessments have not been reported in the human lung, likely due to challenges associated with respiration-induced motion [55]. However, μOCT probes designed for a standard bronchoscope working channel have recently been developed [56].

Tracheobronchial MCC is more difficult to measure than nasal MCC, primarily due to challenges with delivery and visualization due to the reduced accessibility of the trachea compared to the nose, and the inability to use taste as an outcome measure. Nonetheless, techniques developed in the nose have been adapted to the lung. The first *in vivo* assessments of lung MCC in humans were reported in the mid 1970s, and used two approaches. In the first, tantalum powder was insufflated into the lungs, and its clearance was tracked using serial chest X-rays [57]. Although these tantalum bronchograms could measure whole-lung clearance, technical issues meant it wasn't widely used [58]. The second method was based on inhalation of radio-labeled particles and gamma camera detection methods [59], a technique that has since become the most widely accepted technique for assessing lung MCC [38]. Nonetheless, significant variation in the characteristics of the particles, the method by which they are delivered to the airways, as well as the manner in which the results are interpreted and analyzed, can reduce the reliability of MCC as an outcome measure [38].

8.3.2 Modern clearance measurement in human lungs

Most modern human *in vivo* MCC assessments in the lung use an evolution of the methods first reported in the nose by Quinlan [49]. Inhaled particles are tagged with technetium (^{99m}Tc) and the radiation they emit is measured externally over a period of 1–24 hours [42,60], by placing the subject in front of a camera that records the emitted radiation. A range of ^{99m}Tc particles have been tested, but most studies now use a technetium sulfur colloid (Tc-SC) containing particles with a mean diameter of ~0.3 μm, which aggregate into larger droplets during aerosolization and inhalation [38]. More recently, dual-probe imaging methods have been developed, in which a small-molecule radio-labeled probe (Pentetate Indium Disodium In 111; In-DTPA) is added to the Tc-SC aerosol to measure paracellular absorption [61]. Tc-SC is cleared by MCC only, but In-DTPA is cleared by MCC and absorption through the epithelium, and can allow the local changes in ASL absorption and CFTR function in the CF lung to be measured [62].

The bulk clearance or retention of particles has been shown to be strongly influenced by their deposition location within the lung [63]. This deposition variation is characterized by the central to peripheral (C/P) ratio. C/P is determined by the particle characteristics (average size and distribution of size), breathing pattern (flow rate and tidal volume), and the status of the airways (lung size and amount of obstruction) [38]. In addition, the manner in which lung regions of interest are assigned as either central or peripheral varies [64]. These factors must be carefully controlled to achieve reproducible deposition both within and between patients. Standardized methods for measuring MCC and cough clearance have since been developed and validated to overcome these issues [60].

Generating reproducible MCC measurements is challenging, and has required the development of precision aerosol delivery systems and protocols that can improve the reproducibility of the particle deposition for the case of aerosol droplets. These consist of a metronome to give audio feedback about breath timing to the subject, combined with a pneumotach device that displays visual feedback about the tidal volume and flow rate, to aid them to maintain these parameters within a specific range. Aerosol delivery can be set to occur at particular phases of inspiration. Other factors such as the time between the delivery of the radiolabel and the onset of imaging are also important to consider and control for [38]. In many studies a measurement of cough clearance is also obtained by asking the subject to cough at a set time during the imaging period. Airflow during this maneuver is typically recorded using a pneumotach to measure the forcefulness of each cough.

In humans the clearance rate varies from 2 cm/min in the large airways, to 1 mm/min in the small airways, to months for macrophage clearance from the alveoli [65]. The particles remaining after 24 hours were originally thought to represent alveolar or non-ciliated deposition, but are now known to also be due to long-term airway retention [66]. The 24 hour percentage retention (R24) is an index of this airway versus alveolar initial deposition, and is typically inversely related to C/P, but can be altered by diseases such as CF and PCD [67]. In healthy human airways, almost all deposited particles greater than 6 μm are removed within 24 hours. However, as the particle size is reduced, greater fractions remain in the lung for more than 24 hours [68]. Magnetopneumographic methods can be used to assess the long-term clearance of ferrimagnetic iron oxide particles, without the burden of long-term radioactivity from radiotracers [69]. These methods have shown that clearance half-times can be as long as ~120 days for healthy airways, and longer in disease [70,71].

8.3.3 Measuring non-absorptive clearance of pharmaceuticals

The ability to detect radio-labeled particles has also facilitated the assessment of pharmaceutical deposition. Since the 1970s, studies have examined the deposition patterns produced by a range of devices including nebulizers, pressurized metered dose inhalers (pMDI's), and dry powder inhalers (DPI). These have helped elucidate the factors that control drug deposition within the lung [72]. Experimental measurements are also needed to inform simulations of airflow and deposition that utilize computational fluid particle dynamics [73,74]. However most work to date has focused on measuring or simulating the deposition of pharmaceuticals rather than the clearance of pharmaceuticals. Mucociliary clearance behaviors should be considered when predicting the bioavailability of dose and effectiveness of respiratory treatment in the lungs [75]. While clearance has been captured using radiotracer methods that track the signal from nanoparticles deposited within an aerosol [76], much more research could be done in this space.

8.4 Measuring clearance in animals

The motivations for measuring MCC in animal models are similar to those for humans. They include examining respiratory anatomy and physiology in normal animals; understanding disease pathogenesis in models of respiratory disease; and measuring the safety, efficacy, deposition and clearance of inhaled pharmaceutical and genetic therapies. Many of the methods and challenges are also similar, but the latter are exacerbated by the size differences between humans and small animal models.

8.4.1 Bulk clearance assessment in animal models

The first reports of ciliary motion were from Sharpey in 1830 [77], who injected powdered charcoal into rabbit nasal airways and described the spatial and temporal patterns of MCC that resulted. As in humans, most methods for measuring MCC in animals developed since that time have involved measuring the velocity of marker particles to infer the MCC behavior. *Ex vivo* studies in the 1950s examined MCC in airway tissues excised from animals [78], and these have continued for at least 50 years using a range of methodologies [79–81]. Since that time a variety of *in vivo* MCC assessment methods have been developed. For example, Grubb et al. developed a dye-based method for measuring the MCC rate in both the upper and lower airways of normal and CF mice [82]. A microdialysis probe was inserted into the measurement site, and the concentration of an injected dye was measured over time. When combined with the distance between the dye injection and the measurement site, the MCC rate could be calculated. A disadvantage of the dye method was that incisions had to be made in the tissue that is being measured to insert the microdialysis probe and to deliver the dye, which likely alters local MCC due to reduced airway hydration. Since then improved methods for delivering MCC marker particles into small animal airways have been developed to ensure that the particles are dispersed in the target area with minimal impact on airway physiology. These include aspiration [39,83,84], aerosolization [84,85], tracheal instillation via the oral route [84] and bronchoscopically. Endotracheal intubation approaches must be careful to not mechanically irritate the tracheal surface [86], as this is likely to influence MCC measurement.

Over a period of 30 years, a range of similar methods of measuring the MCC rate were developed in an effort to make MCC measurements in minimally-perturbed airways. These include using fluorescent microspheres between 200 nm up to 7 μm in diameter as MCC marker particles in transit-time measurement studies [83,85,87]. These methods required the trachea to be exposed by removing any muscle, skin and other surrounding tissue [83,85,87], with the fluorescent beads then visible through the tracheal wall using a dissection microscope or similar device. The primary weaknesses of this method are that only the trachea or nose can be examined and not the deeper conducting airways, the trachea must be exposed to visualize particle motion making the procedure terminal, and spatial variations in MCC cannot be quantified as individual particle behaviors cannot be resolved. Additionally, when particles are suspended in a carrier fluid, the deposition of bulk fluid into the trachea perturbs the MCC process being measured. Dry particle insufflation methods have now been developed to overcome this limitation [88,89].

Less invasive methods of MCC measurement were required for application to laboratory animal studies to enable long-term or repeated assessments of clearance, and to minimize the impact of the measurement technique itself on airway physiology. Assessment of MCC using radiotracers has been performed in the lungs of large animals such as dogs [90–92], sheep [93], and calves [94]. The small size of laboratory animal airways has made measurements of *in vivo* clearance using non-invasive radioactive particle tracking challenging [5]. Nonetheless, scintigraphic MCC assessment methods have been developed for use in mice, and are similar to those used clinically in humans and large animals [39,84,95]. As with the fluorescent bead methods, the radioactive sub-micron Tc-SC particles were prepared in a liquid that was then added to the airway. The motion of the radioactive particles was then tracked using a gamma-camera, with the image resolution enhanced by using a pinhole collimator. Typical image exposure lengths varied from 40 seconds to 10 minutes, depending on the amount of radiotracer present. The advantage of using gamma scintigraphy to measure MCC compared with using fluorescent beads is that it is relatively non-invasive, as surgical approaches are not required to expose the trachea to visualize particle motion. Gamma scintigraphy does require more specialized equipment (e.g. gamma camera, pinhole collimator, radiotracer) when compared to the fluorescent bead experimental setup. However, its major limitation is the much lower spatial and temporal resolutions achievable compared to other methodologies.

8.4.2 Local assessment of clearance in animal models

The methods described in the previous section focused on describing the bulk clearance behavior of many MCC tracking particles, and do not have the spatial or temporal resolution to resolve the behavior of individual particles or to examine local variations in MCC behavior. Approaches that allow for more local, high-resolution measurement of the MCC rate have the potential to provide a more detailed understanding of the MCC system, with improved temporal resolution enabling the effects of treatments on MCC to be detected as soon as they occur.

The first *in vivo* attempt to directly visualize individual tracking particle motion was via a bronchoscopic approach using Teflon particles in the trachea of dogs [96]. This method was then adapted to use radiopaque disks made of Teflon, mixed with a contrast agent such as bismuth trioxide, which allowed for radiographic assessment of MCC in the trachea of dogs [97] and sheep [93]. In this approach, 8–10 Teflon disks

~1 mm in diameter, 0.8 mm thick, and weighed between 1.5 and 2 mg were deposited and tracked. More recently, computed tomographic (CT) methods for measuring MCC rate in pigs *in vivo* using 350 × 25 μm tantalum microdisks were reported [98–100]. From the CT volumes the average microdisk speed was determined, along with the maximum particle speed, the percentage of time the particles were moving, and the relative and absolute position of the particles in the airway. Early efforts to quantify MCC discovered that mucus transport is complex and not a constant flow [83], so the ability to measure the instantaneous velocity of each particle has the potential to provide more information on the behavior of the MCC system than the bulk particle transport rate alone. Since CT imaging enables MCC to be measured in 3-dimensions, particle motion in both the ventral-dorsal and lateral planes can be assessed. Hoegger et al. used this method to demonstrate the preference of marker particles to migrate towards the ventral tracheal surface in pigs [99].

The primary disadvantage of these MCC imaging methods is the microdisks must be very large to be detectable radiographically. All of these studies use particles that are orders of magnitude larger than particles or drugs that could typically be inhaled. The CT imaging method also has a low temporal resolution (~8–15 seconds between scans [98,99]), due to the time required to acquire each volumetric scan.

To overcome the spatial and temporal resolution restrictions, an alternative approach has been developed to assess local clearance in animal models. This method involves using X-ray imaging at synchrotron or compact light sources [101]. The high X-ray coherence makes phase contrast X-ray imaging (PCXI) possible, enabling weakly-attenuating features to be detected, including small marker particles (See Fig. 8.2A) [102]. PCXI is sensitive to interfaces between soft tissue and air, so as a result these facilities are particularly well suited to high-resolution imaging of the lungs and airways. In addition, the very high X-ray flux provided by these sources enables the use of very short exposure times (10–500 ms), making dynamic imaging possible [103]. Together, these factors make PCXI ideal for the *in vivo* assessment of individual particle MCC in a variety of animal models—including mice [104], rats, and pigs [89]—using smaller particles than previously possible (10–200 μm). As with all clearance assessment methods, the particle choice is important, as surface properties such as electrical charge can impact the measured behavior [81]. As with the other particle-based MCC assessment methods, particles are deposited onto the airway surface, and their locations are tracked over successive X-ray images, allowing the instantaneous velocity of each particle to be measured. As well as measuring the mean marker particle speed at defined time points, Donnelley et al. have also created particle velocity heatmaps to better visualize the variability in the MCC behavior [105] (See Fig. 8.2B). Since the MCC system is complex—and it is well documented that the MCC measurements can be highly variable—these velocity heat maps allow for a greater *in vivo* understanding of the MCC system and may help begin to uncover why variations in MCC occur.

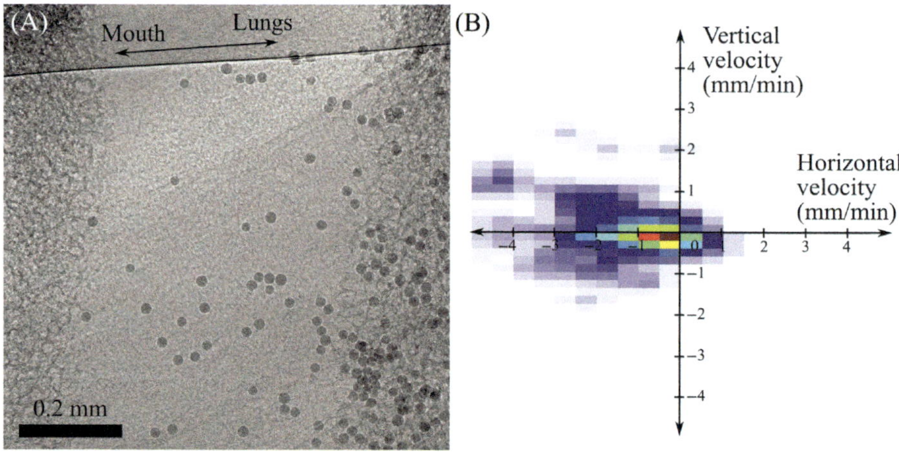

Figure 8.2 Local mucociliary clearance measured using synchrotron phase contrast X-ray imaging. (A) An in-vivo X-ray image of the tracheal surface of a normal wistar rat, containing 20 μm deposited COOH-coated high-refractive index glass beads. (B) 2D histogram showing the clearance velocity of these beads measured over a period of 15 s, 2 min after aerosolized hypertonic saline was delivered to accelerate clearance. Note that the positive 'horizontal velocity' is in the direction of the lungs (caudal) and the positive 'vertical velocity' is in the anterior/ventral direction. Images were acquired by the authors of this chapter at the SPring-8 synchrotron in Japan under proposal number 2017B1386.

The strength of these PCXI-based clearance assessment techniques is that they can assess individual particle behavior, and enable local spatial variations in MCC behavior to be quantified. For example, they have allowed visualization of how particles that move into clumps are most efficiently cleared; established that there are substantial local variations in clearance behavior along and across the airway; confirmed anecdotal reports of a small amount of MCC activity director towards the distal lung; and quantified whether pooled liquid influences the clearance of particles. Compared to the CT-based method, the time period between sequential image acquisitions can be two orders of magnitude shorter, enabling a more detailed assessment of the MCC behavior by making a larger number of measurements per particle in a given time period. In addition, depending on the animal model, the marker particle size can also be much smaller, and begin to more closely approximate the size of inhalable particles. Unlike gamma scintigraphy, which has proven challenging to adapt from humans down to mice, these PCXI approaches are scalable across a range of animal sizes, having been used in mice up to piglets [89].

The primary disadvantage of the PCXI-based methods is that they rely on being able to access specialized X-ray imaging facilities. This means that these studies can therefore only be performed at a few locations around the world such as the SPring-8 BL20XU beamline, the Australian Synchrotron Imaging and Medical Beamline, or the Munich Compact Light Source [106,107]. The requirement to travel to these facilities adds an array of logistical challenges including a number associated with animal model preparation and shipping [103]. This also makes frequent or longitudinal studies impossible. Furthermore, although PCXI-based experimental setups can be non-invasive and use shuttering approaches to minimize the radiation dose, the radiation could alter outcomes depending on the experiment design. Finally, the presence of many uniform particles in the acquired images can make linking their locations into trajectories difficult. This can be done manually, but automated approaches have been developed [108–110].

When smaller MCC tracking particles are used, a higher magnification is required to adequately resolve their location and behavior, reducing the available field of view. This means that a limitation of all of the individual particle tracking methods is that because of respiratory movements when imaging at very high magnification, it is not possible to resolve small particles when they are further into the airway tree than the trachea or mainstem bronchi. Therefore, at present these methods are essentially limited to producing measurements of TMV. Although TMV is regarded as being a reliable marker of mucus clearance in the airways, it may not represent true whole lung mucus clearance in the same manner as scintigraphic methods that capture the clearance behavior of the entire airway tree [93].

8.4.3 Direct assessment of clearance in animal models

The ability to assess clearance without the addition of trackable marker substances, whether delivered dry or as a liquid, has advantages. This is also vital for assessing any differences in the clearance of liquid droplets compared to discrete particles, which is an important feature given that drugs can be delivered in either form. Marker-free MCC measurements can now be achieved using an optical imaging method called micro optical coherence tomography (μOCT) [111], which has been applied to measuring a range of airway surface parameters such as airway surface liquid depth, ciliary beat frequency. This method has now been used to measure the MCC rate in *ex vivo* samples of pig [51,112], rat [113] and mouse [114] tissue. Although commonly applied to *ex vivo* tissue samples, μOCT has also been demonstrated *in vivo*, by fitting the μOCT sensor inside a probe placed into the trachea of an anaesthetized pig via an endotracheal tube [115]. A balloon on the end of the probe was inflated to keep the probe pressed against the airway surface tissue being imaged. The MCC rate was calculated by projecting a line parallel to the direction of mucus flow, and measuring the image intensity along the projected line over time. Compared to *ex vivo* imaging, the *in vivo* images contained more image artifacts, such as cardiac and respiratory motion artifacts, which may affect the MCC measurements.

The main limitation of this method is that the rigid probe limits access to the airway, so flexible probes must be developed [115]. Given the size of the probe and the difficulties in imaging swine trachea, more work is also needed for this method to be scaled down to smaller animals, such as mice and rats, in which MCC measurements must often be made for assessing the efficacy of therapeutics and for pharmacokinetics studies. Furthermore, when applied deeper into the lung tree it is likely that μOCT approaches will suffer from the same motion artifact challenges during respiration as the PCXI-based methods. This may mean that like the PCXI-based methods, μOCT currently remains limited to nasal and tracheal MCC assessments only.

8.5 Modeling airway clearance

The previous sections describing assessments in humans and animals show that MCC is a complicated process that involves the interaction of multiple physiological factors. Determining how each of these individually contributes to MCC, particularly in disease pathophysiology, is particularly challenging. As a result, efforts have been made to theoretically or computationally model ciliary action and MCC, to enable the effects of altering each of these factors to be assessed. Indeed, part of our understanding of MCC and ciliary motion is based on the results from these early models. MCC modeling is mathematically complicated, requires state-of-the-art computational techniques, and is itself a large field, so it will not be described in depth here. For a comprehensive review see Vanaki et al. [116].

Most ciliary beat models fit into one of two categories: discrete-cilia models and volume-force models. In the discrete models each individual cilium is modeled, and parameters are used to describe its shape throughout each stroke [117–119]. In the volume-force models MCC is modeled as a force distribution that varies both spatially and temporally as the cilia beat [120]. For examples that model particle clearance in human airways see the stochastic model from Hofmann et al. [65] or the approach via computational fluid dynamics from Kirch et al. [121]. Importantly, these studies enable the properties of micro- and nano-particles to be evaluated, to assess residence time, bioavailability and drug-release. More recent experimental and modeling approaches [122,123] have enabled the microscopic properties of the ciliary motion to be better understood, including the shear stress exerted by the cilia.

These studies suggest that modeling of individual cilia as well as MCC can provide important information about the contributions of a range of factors that influence clearance, and these are particularly powerful when combined with *ex vivo* and *in vivo* validations. Further development of these increasingly complex models will undoubtedly enhance our understanding of clearance in health and disease.

8.6 Future developments

Current techniques used for quantifying airway clearance in both humans and animals have a range of limitations. This means that there are significant opportunities for the further development of airway clearance measurement techniques, to facilitate improved spatial resolution, field of view, prediction of drug effects, and clinical viability.

While imaging modalities have greatly improved our understanding of other organs, a range of challenges associated with imaging the lung remain. Although radiotracer methods work well for assessing whole-lung clearance, the attempts to examine clearance in specific airways—to capture regional differences that align with regional lung diseases, such as the muco-obstructive diseases described earlier in this chapter—are poorly served by this technology. Challenges in imaging specific airways arise primarily from the constant breathing movement and the concomitant expansion and contraction of the airways and airspaces, which can result in image blurring. This is exacerbated when higher magnifications are used.

Although high magnification X-ray methods for assessing clearance developed at synchrotrons can provide finely-detailed high-resolution analyzes, they are inherently limited by their restricted field-of-view. Nevertheless, these novel high-resolution synchrotron analyzes will contribute to the understanding of local effects and the overall function of non-absorptive particulate clearance, in the same way that electron microscopy of cell organelles have greatly informed our understanding of higher level functioning of the relevant tissue and the organ. The benefits of individual particle imaging may also assist with a fuller understanding of the fast versus slow components of the clearance than is possible with global measurements by radiotracer methods. Now that particles can be visualized when they are located both on and within the ASL layer (See Fig. 23 in Lizal et al. [74]), the field can begin to address why such a disparate range of clearance rates and behaviors can be observed. The presence of static particles in the same locations as moving particles raises questions of how and why these differences appear, particularly when uniform particles with the same surface roughness and charge are used [81]. Factors such as ASL hydration, mucus thickness, localization to areas of poor or absent ciliary beating function, and cough will all influence particle capture or clearance, whether singly or together.

The accuracy of physiologically-based pharmacokinetic (PBPK) models commonly used for describing the fate of inhaled drugs depends on realistic MCC modeling. Mathematical models for MCC have been developed that can incorporate parameters like elasticity, viscosity, surface tension and sheer to describe fluid flows in the mucus and periciliary layers, and can model ciliary action either as a bulk force, an 'active porous medium' or as the sum of actions from many individual cilia [116,124]. A substantial amount of work has gone into modeling the interactions between these fluid flows and ciliary action to properly describe ciliary clearance on a range of airway surfaces. This progress in computational modeling of mucociliary clearance, combined with PBPK models that describe the effects of pharmaceutical agents on ciliary beat, allows overall MCC behavior and drug clearance to be described *in vivo*.

The primary driving forces for technical advancements are the need to better understand the key role that non-absorptive clearance plays in protecting the health of the lung by the efficient removal of foreign particles (physical, chemical or biological), and in drug design. Novel particles for therapeutics and biological-mechanisms discovery will be required in the future, and their interaction with the airways must be understood. The requirements for MCC measurement in research, clinical trials, and routine lung medicine must be clearly determined so that researchers and clinicians can take full advantage of these techniques. For future novel clearance measurement techniques to be valuable, they must be capable of directly addressing the diagnostic and physiological questions posed by researchers and clinicians. Furthermore, the data they provide must be reliable, accurate, and acquirable in real-life physiological settings.

With further development, clearance quantification methods could readily provide companion biomarkers for spirometric lung function measures such as FEV1 for the assessment of airway function in muco-obstructive diseases and other airway conditions like asthma. FEV1 is limited as a primary or sole outcome measure for assessing disease, with a typical within-subject variability of 6% in healthy subjects, which is worse in disease states and so reduces the discriminating power [125]. Reliance on FEV1 in clinical medicine also excludes children younger than 6 or 7 years of age as they cannot perform the breathing maneuvers required. As a result, lung function information is largely absent during the very period where disease prevention demands reliable lung health assessment to support the use of many available treatments. Unfortunately, studies of child MCC to date appear to have been primarily in children with cystic fibrosis (CF) [126], with limited work in non-CF children [127]. The need for radiotracers has limited the use of bulk MCC assessments in younger children, motivating the need for new methods.

8.6.1 What can new technology do?

A promising technology that may advance MCC assessment in human and animal research is OCT. Although there have been few reports of *in vivo* use in human airways, progress appears to be steady. Measurements reported so far include detail of airway surface MCC activity including visualization of ciliary beating, calculation of MCC rate, and the ability to track debris such as sloughed cells and mucus globules. These discernible but unidentifiable particles arise from the more distal airways and transit the field of view within the moving surface layer, and can provide a more biologically-relevant system for tracking MCC. OCT measurement currently uses an invasive probe-based system that may be difficult to place within the lung, especially in small animals. However, with miniaturization, OCT probe placement will likely be done bronchoscopically in the future, suggesting that a more controlled and routine method of assessment will become available.

The rapid advancement of sensor and sensing technologies is likely to change the opportunities for improved MCC measurement. With the miniaturization of wireless sensor systems (including wireless implantable microscopes), the development of a range of novel MCC sensing devices can be imagined. For future assessments of MCC health we envisage, for example, the detection of inhaled fluorescent or luminescent particles as they pass through the trachea, using a neck-mounted camera oriented towards the trachea and tuned to the relevant light frequencies.

8.7 Conclusions

The lung is a remarkably resilient organ that has evolved mechanisms to remove inhaled particulates and pathogens in order to maintain lung health. The main ways the respiratory system is cleared are via MCC, alveolar macrophage clearance and cough. These complex mechanisms must be understood and considered during the design of drugs and delivery methods for inhaled therapeutics. Methods for measuring clearance have been developed for human and animal populations, and most quantify the bulk or individual movement of deposited particles. Tracking particle detection has been performed by taste, radioactivity, fluorescence, X-rays, computed tomography and synchrotron phase contrast X-ray imaging. Since most methods for measuring MCC require an introduced tracer, these methods can make it difficult or impossible to capture airway surface behavior in an undisturbed system. However, more recently, optical coherence tomography (OCT) has been demonstrated to be a promising technology for assessing clearance without the addition of marker particles.

The opportunities and challenges that accompany the development of inhaled medicines are both varied and exciting. Existing measurement methods have limitations but can inform the growing number and complexity of computer simulations of MCC behavior. In reviewing this field, we now envisage increasingly more detailed questions about *in vivo* lung health can be posed and answered. With the rapid advances that have occurred in lung imaging, equipment miniaturization, novel assessment technologies, and data processing and analysis we can expect a steady improvement in the options and information that will be available to lung researchers and clinicians working to reduce the impact of respiratory diseases in our society.

References

[1] M. Munkholm, J. Mortensen, Mucociliary clearance: pathophysiological aspects, Clin. Physiol. Funct. Imaging 34 (3) (2014) 171–177. Available from: https://doi.org/10.1111/cpf.12085.

[2] A. Iwasaki, E.F. Foxman, R.D. Molony, Early local immune defences in the respiratory tract, Nat. Rev. Immunol. 17 (1) (2017) 7–20. Available from: https://doi.org/10.1038/nri.2016.117.

[3] M. Ochs, J.R. Nyengaard, A. Jung, L. Knudsen, M. Voigt, T. Wahlers, et al., The number of alveoli in the human lung, Am. J. Respir. Crit. Care Med. 169 (1) (2004) 120–124. Available from: https://doi.org/10.1164/rccm.200308-1107OC.

[4] E.R. Weibel, D.M. Gomez, Architecture of the human lung: use of quantitative methods establishes fundamental relations between size and number of lung structures, Science 137 (3530) (1962) 577–585. Available from: https://doi.org/10.1126/science.137.3530.577.

[5] X.M. Bustamante-Marin, L.E. Ostrowski, Cilia and mucociliary clearance, Cold Spring Harb. Perspect. Biol. 9 (4) (2017). Available from: https://doi.org/10.1101/cshperspect.a028241.

[6] T.J. Franks, T.V. Colby, W.D. Travis, R.M. Tuder, H.Y. Reynolds, A.R. Brody, et al., Resident cellular components of the human lung: current knowledge and goals for research on cell phenotyping and function, Proc. Am. Thorac. Soc. 5 (7) (2008) 763–766. Available from: https://doi.org/10.1513/pats.200803-025HR.

[7] J.R. Rock, M.W. Onaitis, E.L. Rawlins, Y. Lu, C.P. Clark, Y. Xue, et al., Basal cells as stem cells of the mouse trachea and human airway epithelium, Proc. Natl. Acad. Sci. 106 (31) (2009) 12771–12775. Available from: https://doi.org/10.1073/pnas.0906850106.

[8] M.J. Evans, L.S. Van Winkle, M.V. Fanucchi, C.G. Plopper, Cellular and molecular characteristics of basal cells in airway epithelium, Exp. Lung Res. 27 (5) (2001) 401–415. Available from: https://www.ncbi.nlm.nih.gov/pubmed/11480582.

[9] A. Wanner, M. Salathe, T.G. O'Riordan, Mucociliary clearance in the airways, Am. J. Respir. Crit. Care Med. 154 (6 Pt 1) (1996) 1868–1902. Available from: https://doi.org/10.1164/ajrccm.154.6.8970383.

[10] L.Y. Chang, J.D. Crapo, P. Gehr, B. Rothen-Rutishauser, C. Mühfeld, F. Blank, Alveolar epithelium in lung toxicology, Compr. Toxicol. 15 (2018) 50-77. https://doi.org/10.1016/B978-0-08-100601-6.00904-2.

[11] H.E. Ward, T.E. Nicholas, Alveolar type I and type II cells, Aust. N. Z. J. Med. 14 (5 Suppl 3) (1984) 731–734. Available from: https://www.ncbi.nlm.nih.gov/pubmed/6598039.

[12] W.E. Goldman, R.P. Dickson, G.B. Huffnagle, The lung microbiome: new principles for respiratory bacteriology in health and disease, PLoS Pathog. 11 (7) (2015). Available from: https://doi.org/10.1371/journal.ppat.1004923.

[13] M.R. Knowles, R.C. Boucher, Mucus clearance as a primary innate defense mechanism for mammalian airways, J. Clin. Invest. 109 (5) (2002) 571–577. Available from: https://doi.org/10.1172/jci0215217.

[14] E.L. Rawlins, B.L. Hogan, Ciliated epithelial cell lifespan in the mouse trachea and lung, Am. J. Physiol. Lung Cell Mol. Physiol. 295 (1) (2008) L231–L234. Available from: https://doi.org/10.1152/ajplung.90209.2008.

[15] A.E. Tilley, M.S. Walters, R. Shaykhiev, R.G. Crystal, Cilia dysfunction in lung disease, Annu. Rev. Physiol. 77 (2015) 379–406. Available from: https://doi.org/10.1146/annurev-physiol-021014-071931.

[16] M.M.J. Chang, L. Shih, R. Wu, Pulmonary epithelium: cell types and functions, Pulm. Epithelium Health Dis. 2008. https://doi.org/10.1002/9780470727010.ch1.

[17] S.H. Trindade, J.F. de Mello Jr., G. Mion Ode, G. Lorenzi-Filho, M. Macchione, E.T. Guimaraes, et al., Methods for studying mucociliary transport, Braz. J. Otorhinolaryngol. 73 (5) (2007) 704–712. Available from: https://www.ncbi.nlm.nih.gov/pubmed/18094814.

[18] M. Kikkawa, Big steps toward understanding dynein, J. Cell Biol. 202 (1) (2013) 15–23. Available from: https://doi.org/10.1083/jcb.201304099.

[19] P. Satir, S.T. Christensen, Overview of structure and function of mammalian cilia, Annu. Rev. Physiol. 69 (2007) 377–400. Available from: https://doi.org/10.1146/annurev.physiol.69.040705.141236.

[20] S.H. Randell, R.C. Boucher, Effective mucus clearance is essential for respiratory healthG. University of North Carolina Virtual Lung Am. J. Respir. Cell Mol. Biol. 35 (1) (2006) 20–28. Available from: https://doi.org/10.1165/rcmb.2006-0082SF.

[21] M.C. Rose, J.A. Voynow, Respiratory tract mucin genes and mucin glycoproteins in health and disease, Physiol. Rev. 86 (1) (2006) 245–278. Available from: https://doi.org/10.1152/physrev.00010.2005.
[22] L.S. Ostedgaard, T.O. Moninger, J.D. McMenimen, N.M. Sawin, C.P. Parker, I.M. Thornell, et al., Gel-forming mucins form distinct morphologic structures in airways, Proc. Natl. Acad. Sci. U. S. A. 114 (26) (2017) 6842–6847. Available from: https://doi.org/10.1073/pnas.1703228114.
[23] K. Okuda, G. Chen, D.B. Subramani, M. Wolf, R.C. Gilmore, T. Kato, et al., Localization of secretory mucins MUC5AC and MUC5B in normal/healthy human airways, Am. J. Respir. Crit. Care Med. 199 (6) (2019) 715–727. Available from: https://doi.org/10.1164/rccm.201804-0734OC.
[24] R.C. Boucher, J.M. Drazen, Muco-obstructive lung diseases, N. Engl. J. Med. 380 (20) (2019) 1941–1953. Available from: https://doi.org/10.1056/NEJMra1813799.
[25] R. Tarran, B. Button, M. Picher, A.M. Paradiso, C.M. Ribeiro, E.R. Lazarowski, et al., Normal and cystic fibrosis airway surface liquid homeostasis. The effects of phasic shear stress and viral infections, J. Biol. Chem. 280 (42) (2005) 35751–35759. Available from: https://doi.org/10.1074/jbc.M505832200.
[26] M. Kesimer, C. Ehre, K.A. Burns, C.W. Davis, J.K. Sheehan, R.J. Pickles, Molecular organization of the mucins and glycocalyx underlying mucus transport over mucosal surfaces of the airways, Mucosal Immunol. 6 (2) (2013) 379–392. Available from: https://doi.org/10.1038/mi.2012.81.
[27] J.V. Fahy, B.F. Dickey, Airway mucus function and dysfunction, N. Engl. J. Med. 363 (23) (2010) 2233–2247. Available from: https://doi.org/10.1056/NEJMra0910061.
[28] J. Heyder, Deposition of inhaled particles in the human respiratory tract and consequences for regional targeting in respiratory drug delivery, Proc. Am. Thorac. Soc. 1 (4) (2004) 315–320. Available from: https://doi.org/10.1513/pats.200409-046TA.
[29] S. Jabbal, G. Poli, B. Lipworth, Does size really matter?: relationship of particle size to lung deposition and exhaled fraction, J. Allergy Clin. Immunol. 139 (6) (2017) 2013–2014, e1. Available from: https://doi.org/10.1016/j.jaci.2016.11.036.
[30] J.B. Rubins, Alveolar macrophages: wielding the double-edged sword of inflammation, Am. J. Respir. Crit. Care Med. 167 (2) (2003) 103–104. Available from: https://doi.org/10.1164/rccm.2210007.
[31] Y. Sibille, H.Y. Reynolds, Macrophages and polymorphonuclear neutrophils in lung defense and injury, Am. Rev. Respir. Dis. 141 (2) (1990) 471–501. Available from: https://doi.org/10.1164/ajrccm/141.2.471.
[32] J. Widdicombe, Cough: what's in a name? Eur. Respir. J. 28 (1) (2006) 10–15. Available from: https://doi.org/10.1183/09031936.06.00096905.
[33] D.E. Leith, Cough, Phys. Ther. 48 (5) (1968) 439–447. Available from: https://doi.org/10.1093/ptj/48.5.439.
[34] M. Kesimer, A.A. Ford, A. Ceppe, G. Radicioni, R. Cao, C.W. Davis, et al., Airway mucin concentration as a marker of chronic bronchitis, N. Engl. J. Med. 377 (10) (2017) 911–922. Available from: https://doi.org/10.1056/NEJMoa1701632.
[35] M.A. Mall, H. Danahay, R.C. Boucher, Emerging concepts and therapies for mucoobstructive lung disease, Ann. Am. Thorac. Soc. 15 (Suppl. 3) (2018) S216–S226. Available from: https://doi.org/10.1513/AnnalsATS.201806-368AW.
[36] M. Del Donno, D. Bittesnich, A. Chetta, D. Olivieri, M.T. Lopez-Vidriero, The effect of inflammation on mucociliary clearance in asthma: an overview, Chest 118 (4) (2000) 1142–1149. Available from: https://doi.org/10.1378/chest.118.4.1142.
[37] J.R. Bateman, D. Pavia, N.F. Sheahan, J.E. Agnew, S.W. Clarke, Impaired tracheobronchial clearance in patients with mild stable asthma, Thorax 38 (6) (1983) 463–467. Available from: https://doi.org/10.1136/thx.38.6.463.
[38] S.H. Donaldson, T.E. Corcoran, B.L. Laube, W.D. Bennett, Mucociliary clearance as an outcome measure for cystic fibrosis clinical research, Proc. Am. Thorac. Soc. 4 (4) (2007) 399–405. Available from: https://doi.org/10.1513/pats.200703-042BR.
[39] X. Hua, K.L. Zeman, B. Zhou, Q. Hua, B.A. Senior, S.L. Tilley, et al., Noninvasive real-time measurement of nasal mucociliary clearance in mice by pinhole gamma scintigraphy, J. Appl. Physiol. (1985) 108 (1) (2010) 189–196. Available from: https://doi.org/10.1152/japplphysiol.00669.2009.

[40] R. Santa Cruz, J. Landa, J. Hirsch, M.A. Sackner, Tracheal mucous velocity in normal man and patients with obstructive lung disease: effects of terbutaline, Am. Rev. Respir. Dis. 109 (4) (1974) 458–463. Available from: https://doi.org/10.1164/arrd.1974.109.4.458.
[41] R.M. Goodman, B.M. Yergin, J.F. Landa, M.H. Golivanux, M.A. Sackner, Relationship of smoking history and pulmonary function tests to tracheal mucous velocity in nonsmokers, young smokers, ex-smokers, and patients with chronic bronchitis, Am. Rev. Respir. Dis. 117 (2) (1978) 205–214. Available from: https://doi.org/10.1164/arrd.1978.117.2.205.
[42] L. Morgan, M. Pearson, R. de Iongh, D. Mackey, H. van der Wall, M. Peters, et al., Scintigraphic measurement of tracheal mucus velocity in vivo, Eur. Respir. J. 23 (4) (2004) 518–522. Available from: https://www.ncbi.nlm.nih.gov/pubmed/15083747.
[43] S.H. Donaldson, W.D. Bennett, K.L. Zeman, M.R. Knowles, R. Tarran, R.C. Boucher, Mucus clearance and lung function in cystic fibrosis with hypertonic saline, N. Engl. J. Med. 354 (3) (2006) 241–250. Available from: https://doi.org/10.1056/NEJMoa043891.
[44] M. Lindstrom, P. Camner, R. Falk, L. Hjelte, K. Philipson, M. Svartengren, Long-term clearance from small airways in patients with cystic fibrosis, Eur. Respir. J. 25 (2) (2005) 317–323. Available from: https://doi.org/10.1183/09031936.05.00120103.
[45] A. Hilding, Ciliary activity and course of secretion currents of the nose, Mayo Clin. Proc. 6 (1931) 285.
[46] G.E. Tremble, Clinical observations on the movement of nasal cilia, An. Exp. Study, Laryngoscope 58 (3) (1948) 206–224. Available from: https://doi.org/10.1002/lary.5540580302.
[47] I. Andersen, G.R. Lundqvist, D.F. Proctor, Human nasal mucosal function in a controlled climate, Arch. Environ. Health 23 (6) (1971) 408–420. Available from: https://www.ncbi.nlm.nih.gov/pubmed/5133804.
[48] T. Deitmer, A modification of the saccharine test for nasal mucociliary clearance, Rhinology 24 (4) (1986) 237–240. Available from: https://www.ncbi.nlm.nih.gov/pubmed/3823746.
[49] M.F. Quinlan, S.D. Salman, D.L. Swift, H.N. Wagner Jr., D.F. Proctor, Measurement of mucociliary function in man, Am. Rev. Respir. Dis. 99 (1) (1969) 13–23. Available from: https://doi.org/10.1164/arrd.1969.99.1.13.
[50] B.M. Yergin, K. Saketkhoo, E.D. Michaelson, S.M. Serafini, K. Kovitz, M.A. Sackner, A roentgenographic method for measuring nasal mucous velocity, J. Appl. Physiol. Respir. Env. Exerc. Physiol. 44 (6) (1978) 964–968. Available from: https://doi.org/10.1152/jappl.1978.44.6.964.
[51] L. Liu, K.K. Chu, G.H. Houser, B.J. Diephuis, Y. Li, E.J. Wilsterman, et al., Method for quantitative study of airway functional microanatomy using micro-optical coherence tomography, PLoS One 8 (1) (2013) e54473. Available from: https://doi.org/10.1371/journal.pone.0054473.
[52] H.M. Leung, S.E. Birket, C. Hyun, T.N. Ford, D. Cui, G.M. Solomon, et al., Intranasal micro-optical coherence tomography imaging for cystic fibrosis studies, Sci. Transl. Med. 11 (504) (2019). Available from: https://doi.org/10.1126/scitranslmed.aav3505.
[53] A.L. Oldenburg, R.K. Chhetri, D.B. Hill, B. Button, Monitoring airway mucus flow and ciliary activity with optical coherence tomography, Biomed. Opt. Express 3 (9) (2012) 1978–1992. Available from: https://doi.org/10.1364/BOE.3.001978.
[54] E. Puchelle, F. Aug, Q.T. Pham, A. Bertrand, Comparison of three methods for measuring nasal mucociliary clearance in man, Acta Otolaryngol. 91 (3–4) (1981) 297–303. Available from: https://www.ncbi.nlm.nih.gov/pubmed/6266196.
[55] R.-J. Shei, J.E. Peabody, S.M. Rowe, Functional anatomic imaging of the airway surface, Ann. Am. Thorac. Soc. 15 (3) (2018) S177–S183. Available from: https://doi.org/10.1513/AnnalsATS.201806-407AW.
[56] D. Cui, K.K. Chu, B. Yin, T.N. Ford, C. Hyun, H.M. Leung, et al., Flexible, high-resolution micro-optical coherence tomography endobronchial probe toward in vivo imaging of cilia, Opt. Lett. 42 (4) (2017). Available from: https://doi.org/10.1364/ol.42.000867.
[57] G. Gamsu, R.M. Weintraub, J.A. Nadel, Clearance of tantalum from airways of different caliber in man evaluated by a roentgenographic method, Am. Rev. Respir. Dis. 107 (2) (1973) 214–224. Available from: https://doi.org/10.1164/arrd.1973.107.2.214.

[58] S.W. Clarke, D. Pavia, Lung mucus production and mucociliary clearance: methods of assessment, Br. J. Clin. Pharmacol. 9 (6) (1980) 537–546. Available from: https://doi.org/10.1111/j.1365-2125.1980.tb01078.x.

[59] I. Andersen, P. Camner, P.L. Jensen, K. Philipson, D.F. Proctor, A comparison of nasal and tracheobronchial clearance, Arch. Environ. Health 29 (5) (1974) 290–293. Available from: https://www.ncbi.nlm.nih.gov/pubmed/4472935.

[60] W.D. Bennett, B.L. Laube, T. Corcoran, K. Zeman, G. Sharpless, K. Thomas, et al., Multisite comparison of mucociliary and cough clearance measures using standardized methods, J. Aerosol Med. Pulm. Drug. Deliv. 26 (3) (2013) 157–164. Available from: https://doi.org/10.1089/jamp.2011.0909.

[61] T.E. Corcoran, K.M. Thomas, M.M. Myerburg, A. Muthukrishnan, L. Weber, R. Frizzell, et al., Absorptive clearance of DTPA as an aerosol-based biomarker in the cystic fibrosis airway, Eur. Respir. J. 35 (4) (2010) 781–786. Available from: https://doi.org/10.1183/09031936.00059009.

[62] T.E. Corcoran, A.S. Huber, M.M. Myerburg, D.J. Weiner, L.W. Locke, R.T. Lacy, et al., Multiprobe nuclear imaging of the cystic fibrosis lung as a biomarker of therapeutic effect, J. Aerosol Med. Pulm. Drug. Deliv. 32 (4) (2019) 242–249. Available from: https://doi.org/10.1089/jamp.2018.1491.

[63] J.S. Ilowite, G.C. Smaldone, R.J. Perry, W.D. Bennett, W.M. Foster, Relationship between tracheobronchial particle clearance rates and sites of initial deposition in man, Arch. Environ. Health 44 (4) (1989) 267–273. Available from: https://doi.org/10.1080/00039896.1989.9935893.

[64] M.F. Biddiscombe, S.N. Meah, S.R. Underwood, O.S. Usmani, Comparing lung regions of interest in gamma scintigraphy for assessing inhaled therapeutic aerosol deposition, J. Aerosol Med. Pulm. Drug. Deliv. 24 (3) (2011) 165–173. Available from: https://doi.org/10.1089/jamp.2010.0845.

[65] W. Hofmann, R. Sturm, Stochastic model of particle clearance in human bronchial airways, J. Aerosol Med. 17 (1) (2004) 73–89. Available from: https://doi.org/10.1089/089426804322994488.

[66] G.C. Smaldone, R.J. Perry, W.D. Bennett, M.S. Messina, J. Zwang, J. Ilowite, Interpretation of "24 hour lung retention" in studies of mucociliary clearance, J. Aerosol Med. 1 (1) (1988) 11–20. Available from: https://doi.org/10.1089/jam.1988.1.11.

[67] J.A. Regnis, K.L. Zeman, P.G. Noone, M.R. Knowles, W.D. Bennett, Prolonged airway retention of insoluble particles in cystic fibrosis versus primary ciliary dyskinesia, Exp. Lung Res. 26 (3) (2000) 149–162. Available from: https://www.ncbi.nlm.nih.gov/pubmed/10813088.

[68] W. Stahlhofen, R. Koebrich, G. Rudolf, G. Scheuch, Short-term and long-term clearance of particles from the upper human respiratory tract as function of particle size, J. Aerosol Sci. 21 (1990) S407–S410. Available from: https://doi.org/10.1016/0021-8502(90)90267-2.

[69] D. Cohen, S. Arai, J. Brain, Smoking impairs long-term dust clearance from the lung, Science 204 (4392) (1979) 514–517. Available from: https://doi.org/10.1126/science.432655.

[70] W. Moller, K. Haussinger, R. Winkler-Heil, W. Stahlhofen, T. Meyer, W. Hofmann, et al., Mucociliary and long-term particle clearance in the airways of healthy nonsmoker subjects, J. Appl. Physiol. (1985) 97 (6) (2004) 2200–2206. Available from: https://doi.org/10.1152/japplphysiol.00970.2003.

[71] W. Moller, K. Haussinger, L. Ziegler-Heitbrock, J. Heyder, Mucociliary and long-term particle clearance in airways of patients with immotile cilia, Respir. Res. 7 (2006) 10. Available from: https://doi.org/10.1186/1465-9921-7-10.

[72] A.R. Clark, Understanding penetration index measurements and regional lung targeting, J. Aerosol Med. Pulm. Drug. Deliv. 25 (4) (2012) 179–187. Available from: https://doi.org/10.1089/jamp.2011.0899.

[73] W. Hofmann, Modelling inhaled particle deposition in the human lung—a review, J. Aerosol Sci. 42 (10) (2011) 693–724. Available from: https://doi.org/10.1016/j.jaerosci.2011.05.007.

[74] F. Lizal, J. Jedelsky, K. Morgan, K. Bauer, J. Llop, U. Cossio, et al., Experimental methods for flow and aerosol measurements in human airways and their replicas, Eur. J. Pharm. Sci. 113 (2018) 95–131. Available from: https://doi.org/10.1016/j.ejps.2017.08.021.

[75] S. Edsbäcker, P. Wollmer, O. Selroos, L. Borgström, B. Olsson, J. Ingelf, Do airway clearance mechanisms influence the local and systemic effects of inhaled corticosteroids? Pulm. Pharmacol. Ther. 21 (2) (2008) 247–258. Available from: https://doi.org/10.1016/j.pupt.2007.08.005.

[76] R. Gracia, M. Marradi, U. Cossío, A. Benito, A. Pérez-San Vicente, V. Gómez-Vallejo, et al., Synthesis and functionalization of dextran-based single-chain nanoparticles in aqueous media, J. Mater. Chem. B 5 (6) (2017) 1143–1147. Available from: https://doi.org/10.1039/c6tb02773c.

[77] W. Sharpey, On a peculiar motion excited in fluids by the surfaces of certain animals, Edinb. Med. Surg. J. 34 (104) (1830) 113–122. Available from: https://www.ncbi.nlm.nih.gov/pubmed/30330224.

[78] A.C. Hilding, Ciliary streaming in the bronchial tree and the time element in carcinogenesis, N. Engl. J. Med. 256 (14) (1957) 634–640. Available from: https://doi.org/10.1056/NEJM195704042561403.

[79] J.L. Cooper, P.M. Quinton, S.T. Ballard, Mucociliary transport in porcine trachea: differential effects of inhibiting chloride and bicarbonate secretion, Am. J. Physiol. Lung Cell Mol. Physiol. 304 (3) (2013) L184–L190. Available from: https://doi.org/10.1152/ajplung.00143.2012.

[80] R. Francis, C. Lo, Ex vivo method for high resolution imaging of cilia motility in rodent airway epithelia, J. Vis. Exp. (78) (2013). Available from: https://doi.org/10.3791/50343.

[81] M. Gardner, A. McCarron, K. Morgan, D. Parsons, M. Donnelley, Particle coating alters mucociliary transit in excised rat trachea: a synchrotron X-ray imaging study, Sci. Rep. 9 (1) (2019) 10983. Available from: https://doi.org/10.1038/s41598-019-47465-1.

[82] B.R. Grubb, J.H. Jones, R.C. Boucher, Mucociliary transport determined by in vivo microdialysis in the airways of normal and CF mice, Am. J. Physiol. Lung Cell Mol. Physiol. 286 (3) (2004) L588–L595. Available from: https://doi.org/10.1152/ajplung.00302.2003.

[83] D.G. Brownstein, Tracheal mucociliary transport in laboratory mice: evidence for genetic polymorphism, Exp. Lung Res. 13 (2) (1987) 185–191. Available from: https://www.ncbi.nlm.nih.gov/pubmed/3665851.

[84] W.M. Foster, D.M. Walters, M. Longphre, K. Macri, L.M. Miller, Methodology for the measurement of mucociliary function in the mouse by scintigraphy, J. Appl. Physiol. (1985) 90 (3) (2001) 1111–1117. Available from: https://doi.org/10.1152/jappl.2001.90.3.1111.

[85] T.D. Rogers, L.E. Ostrowski, A. Livraghi-Butrico, B. Button, B.R. Grubb, Mucociliary clearance in mice measured by tracking trans-tracheal fluorescence of nasally aerosolized beads, Sci. Rep. 8 (1) (2018) 14744. Available from: https://doi.org/10.1038/s41598-018-33053-2.

[86] C.A. Puyo, T.E. Dahms, Innate immunity mediating inflammation secondary to endotracheal intubation, Arch. Otolaryngol. Head. Neck Surg. 138 (9) (2012) 854–858. Available from: https://doi.org/10.1001/archoto.2012.1746.

[87] B.R. Grubb, A. Livraghi-Butrico, T.D. Rogers, W. Yin, B. Button, L.E. Ostrowski, Reduced mucociliary clearance in old mice is associated with a decrease in Muc5b mucin, Am. J. Physiol. Lung Cell Mol. Physiol. 310 (9) (2016) L860–L867. Available from: https://doi.org/10.1152/ajplung.00015.2016.

[88] M. Donnelley, K.S. Morgan, K.K. Siu, D.W. Parsons, Dry deposition of pollutant and marker particles onto live mouse airway surfaces enhances monitoring of individual particle mucociliary transit behaviour, J. Synchrotron Radiat. 19 (Pt 4) (2012) 551–558. Available from: https://doi.org/10.1107/S0909049512018250.

[89] M. Donnelley, K.S. Morgan, R. Gradl, M. Klein, D. Hausermann, C. Hall, et al., Live-pig-airway surface imaging and whole-pig CT at the Australian Synchrotron Imaging and Medical Beamline, J. Synchrotron Radiat. 26 (1) (2019) 175–183. Available from: https://doi.org/10.1107/s1600577518014133.

[90] Y. Sakakura, D.F. Proctor, The effect of various conditions on tracheal mucociliary transport in dogs, Proc. Soc. Exp. Biol. Med. 140 (3) (1972) 870–879. Available from: https://www.ncbi.nlm.nih.gov/pubmed/5039386.

[91] S.K. Chopra, Effect of atropine on mucociliary transport velocity in anesthetized dogs, Am. Rev. Respir. Dis. 118 (2) (1978) 367–371. Available from: https://doi.org/10.1164/arrd.1978.118.2.367.

[92] J.C. Lay, M.R. Stang, P.E. Fisher, J.R. Yankaskas, W.D. Bennett, Airway retention of materials of different solubility following local intrabronchial deposition in dogs, J. Aerosol Med. 16 (2) (2003) 153–166. Available from: https://doi.org/10.1089/089426803321919915.

[93] J.R. Sabater, Y.M. Mao, C. Shaffer, M.K. James, T.G. O'Riordan, W.M. Abraham, Aerosolization of P2Y(2)-receptor agonists enhances mucociliary clearance in sheep, J. Appl. Physiol. (1985) 87 (6) (1999) 2191–2196. Available from: https://doi.org/10.1152/jappl.1999.87.6.2191.

[94] C.D. Jones, Mucociliary clearance from the calf lung, Can. J. Comp. Med. 47 (3) (1983) 265–269. Available from: https://www.ncbi.nlm.nih.gov/pubmed/6640409.

[95] J.L. Ortiz, A. Ortiz, J. Milara, M. Armengot, C. Sanz, D. Compan, et al., Evaluation of mucociliary clearance by three dimension micro-CT-SPECT in guinea pig: role of bitter taste agonists, PLoS One 11 (10) (2016) e0164399. Available from: https://doi.org/10.1371/journal.pone.0164399.

[96] M.A. Sackner, M.J. Rosen, A. Wanner, Estimation of tracheal mucous velocity by bronchofiberscopy, J. Appl. Physiol. 34 (4) (1973) 495–499. Available from: https://doi.org/10.1152/jappl.1973.34.4.495.

[97] M. Friedman, F.D. Stott, D.O. Poole, R. Dougherty, G.A. Chapman, H. Watson, et al., A new roentgenographic method for estimating mucous velocity in airways, Am. Rev. Respir. Dis. 115 (1) (1977) 67–72. Available from: https://doi.org/10.1164/arrd.1977.115.1.67.

[98] A.J. Fischer, M.I. Pino-Argumedo, B.M. Hilkin, C.R. Shanrock, N.D. Gansemer, A.L. Chaly, et al., Mucus strands from submucosal glands initiate mucociliary transport of large particles, JCI Insight 4 (1) (2019). Available from: https://doi.org/10.1172/jci.insight.124863.

[99] M.J. Hoegger, M. Awadalla, E. Namati, O.A. Itani, A.J. Fischer, A.J. Tucker, et al., Assessing mucociliary transport of single particles in vivo shows variable speed and preference for the ventral trachea in newborn pigs, Proc. Natl. Acad. Sci. U. S. A. 111 (6) (2014) 2355–2360. Available from: https://doi.org/10.1073/pnas.1323633111.

[100] M.J. Hoegger, A.J. Fischer, J.D. McMenimen, L.S. Ostedgaard, A.J. Tucker, M.A. Awadalla, et al., Impaired mucus detachment disrupts mucociliary transport in a piglet model of cystic fibrosis, Science 345 (6198) (2014) 818–822. Available from: https://doi.org/10.1126/science.1255825.

[101] Lyncean Technologies Inc. The Compact Light Source. http://www.lynceantech.com/, 2016 (accessed 22.10.19).

[102] M. Donnelley, K. Morgan, N. Farrow, K. Siu, D. Parsons, Non-invasive airway health measurement using synchrotron x-ray microscopy of high refractive index glass microbeads, AIP Conf. Proc. 1696 (1) (2016), https://doi.org/10.1063/1.4937505.

[103] K.S. Morgan, D. Parsons, P. Cmielewski, A. McCarron, R. Gradl, N. Farrow, et al., Methods for dynamic synchrotron X-ray imaging of live animals, J. Synchrotron Radiat. 27 (2019) 164-175. https://doi.org/10.1107/S1600577519014863.

[104] M. Donnelley, K.S. Morgan, K.K. Siu, A. Fouras, N.R. Farrow, R.P. Carnibella, et al., Tracking extended mucociliary transport activity of individual deposited particles: longitudinal synchrotron X-ray imaging in live mice, J. Synchrotron Radiat. 21 (Pt 4) (2014) 768–773. Available from: https://doi.org/10.1107/S160057751400856X.

[105] M. Donnelley, K.S. Morgan, M. Awadalla, N.R. Farrow, C. Hall, D.W. Parsons, High-resolution mucociliary transport measurement in live excised large animal trachea using synchrotron X-ray imaging, Respir. Res. 18 (1) (2017). Available from: https://doi.org/10.1186/s12931-017-0573-2.

[106] E. Eggl, M. Dierolf, K. Achterhold, C. Jud, B. Günther, E. Braig, et al., The Munich Compact Light Source: initial performance measures, J. Synchrotron Radiat. 23 (5) (2016) 1137–1142. Available from: https://doi.org/10.1107/s160057751600967x.

[107] R. Gradl, M. Dierolf, B. Gunther, L. Hehn, W. Moller, D. Kutschke, et al., In vivo dynamic phase-contrast X-ray imaging using a compact light source, Sci. Rep. 8 (1) (2018) 6788. Available from: https://doi.org/10.1038/s41598-018-24763-8.

[108] M. Gardner, D. Parsons, K.S. Morgan, A. McCarron, P. Cmielewski, R. Gradl, et al., Towards automated *in vivo* tracheal mucociliary transport measurement: detecting and tracking particle movement in synchrotron phase-contrast X-ray images, Phys. Med. Biol. (2020). Available from: https://doi.org/10.1088/1361-6560/ab7509.

[109] H.-W. Jung, S.-H. Lee, M. Donnelley, D. Parsons, I. Lee, Automated detection of circular marker particles in synchrotron phase contrast X-ray images of live mouse nasal airways for mucociliary transit assessment, Expert. Syst. Appl. 73 (2017) 57–68. Available from: https://doi.org/10.1016/j.eswa.2016.12.026.

[110] H.-W. Jung, S.-H. Lee, M. Donnelley, D. Parsons, V. Stamatescu, I. Lee, Multiple particle tracking in time-lapse synchrotron X-ray images using discriminative appearance and neighbouring topology learning, Pattern Recognit. 93 (2019) 485–497. Available from: https://doi.org/10.1016/j.patcog.2019.05.007.
[111] D. Huang, E.A. Swanson, C.P. Lin, J.S. Schuman, W.G. Stinson, W. Chang, et al., Optical coherence tomography, Science 254 (5035) (1991) 1178–1181. Available from: https://doi.org/10.1126/science.1957169.
[112] S.E. Birket, K.K. Chu, L. Liu, G.H. Houser, B.J. Diephuis, E.J. Wilsterman, et al., A functional anatomic defect of the cystic fibrosis airway, Am. J. Respir. Crit. Care Med. 190 (4) (2014) 421–432. Available from: https://doi.org/10.1164/rccm.201404-0670OC.
[113] K.L. Tuggle, S.E. Birket, X. Cui, J. Hong, J. Warren, L. Reid, et al., Characterization of defects in ion transport and tissue development in cystic fibrosis transmembrane conductance regulator (CFTR)-knockout rats, PLoS One 9 (3) (2014) e91253. Available from: https://doi.org/10.1371/journal.pone.0091253.
[114] L.A. Hancock, C.E. Hennessy, G.M. Solomon, E. Dobrinskikh, A. Estrella, N. Hara, et al., Muc5b overexpression causes mucociliary dysfunction and enhances lung fibrosis in mice, Nat. Commun. 9 (1) (2018) 5363. Available from: https://doi.org/10.1038/s41467-018-07768-9.
[115] K.K. Chu, C. Unglert, T.N. Ford, D. Cui, R.W. Carruth, K. Singh, et al., In vivo imaging of airway cilia and mucus clearance with micro-optical coherence tomography, Biomed. Opt. Express 7 (7) (2016) 2494–2505. Available from: https://doi.org/10.1364/BOE.7.002494.
[116] M.S. Vanaki, D. Holmes, S.C. Saha, J. Chen, R.J. Brown, P.G. Jayathilake, Muco-ciliary clearance: a review of modelling techniques, J. Biomech. 99 (2020) 109578. Available from: https://doi.org/10.1016/j.jbiomech.2019.109578.
[117] G.R. Fulford, J.R. Blake, Muco-ciliary transport in the lung, J. Theor. Biol. 121 (4) (1986) 381–402. Available from: https://doi.org/10.1016/s0022-5193(86)80098-4.
[118] W.L. Lee, P.G. Jayathilake, Z. Tan, D.V. Le, H.P. Lee, B.C. Khoo, Muco-ciliary transport: effect of mucus viscosity, cilia beat frequency and cilia density, Comput. Fluids 49 (1) (2011) 214–221. Available from: https://doi.org/10.1016/j.compfluid.2011.05.016.
[119] X. Yang, R.H. Dillon, L.J. Fauci, An integrative computational model of multiciliary beating, Bull. Math. Biol. 70 (4) (2008) 1192–1215. Available from: https://doi.org/10.1007/s11538-008-9296-3.
[120] D.J. Smith, E.A. Gaffney, J.R. Blake, Discrete cilia modelling with singularity distributions: application to the embryonic node and the airway surface liquid, Bull. Math. Biol. 69 (5) (2007) 1477–1510. Available from: https://doi.org/10.1007/s11538-006-9172-y.
[121] J. Kirch, M. Guenther, N. Doshi, U.F. Schaefer, M. Schneider, S. Mitragotri, et al., Mucociliary clearance of micro- and nanoparticles is independent of size, shape and charge—an ex vivo and in silico approach, J. Control. Rel. 159 (1) (2012) 128–134. Available from: https://doi.org/10.1016/j.jconrel.2011.12.015.
[122] M. Alber, M. Bottier, S. Blanchon, G. Pelle, E. Bequignon, D. Isabey, et al., A new index for characterizing micro-bead motion in a flow induced by ciliary beating: Part I, experimental analysis, PLOS Comput. Biol. 13 (7) (2017). Available from: https://doi.org/10.1371/journal.pcbi.1005605.
[123] M. Alber, M. Bottier, M. Peña Fernández, G. Pelle, D. Isabey, B. Louis, et al., A new index for characterizing micro-bead motion in a flow induced by ciliary beating: Part II, modeling, PLoS Comput. Biol. 13 (7) (2017). Available from: https://doi.org/10.1371/journal.pcbi.1005552.
[124] D.J. Smith, E.A. Gaffney, J.R. Blake, Modelling mucociliary clearance, Respir. Physiol. Neurobiol. 163 (1–3) (2008) 178–188. Available from: https://doi.org/10.1016/j.resp.2008.03.006.
[125] B.W. Dean, E.E. Birnie, G.A. Whitmore, K.L. Vandemheen, L.-P. Boulet, J.M. FitzGerald, et al., Between-visit variability in FEV1 as a diagnostic test for asthma in adults, Ann. Am. Thorac. Soc. 15 (9) (2018) 1039–1046. Available from: https://doi.org/10.1513/AnnalsATS.201803-211OC.

[126] B.L. Laube, G. Sharpless, K.A. Carson, A. Kelly, P.J. Mogayzel, Acute inhalation of hypertonic saline does not improve mucociliary clearance in all children with cystic fibrosis, BMC Pulm. Med. 11 (1) (2011). Available from: https://doi.org/10.1186/1471-2466-11-45.
[127] R. Boogaard, J.C. de Jongste, P.J.F.M. Merkus, Pharmacotherapy of impaired mucociliary clearance in non-CF pediatric lung disease. A review of the literature, Pediatric Pulmonol. 42 (11) (2007) 989–1001. Available from: https://doi.org/10.1002/ppul.20693.

CHAPTER 9

Dissolution and drug release

Elham Amini and Guenther Hochhaus
Department of Pharmaceutics, College of Pharmacy, University of Florida, Gainesville, FL, United States

9.1 Introduction

Successful inhalation therapy, namely achieving the desired pulmonary effects with minimum systemic side effects, depends on several drug/device/formulation properties that will determine the degree of lung selectivity. The term pulmonary targeting has been introduced to define these properties in a more quantifiable way, relating differences in the cumulative free drug concentrations in the lung to the free drug concentrations in the systemic circulation. Pharmacokinetic/pharmacodynamic simulations assessing factors important for achieving pulmonary targeting have identified key properties that are critical for this purpose. These include non-lung related factors such as low oral bioavailability and high systemic clearance; both factors limiting the systemic exposure of inhalation drugs. Properties that ensure a long residence time of a drug in the lungs are also crucial for pulmonary targeting. This means that drug/formulation/device properties prolonging the drug's stay in the lung enhance the pulmonary targeting of a given drug. An extended stay in the lung can be achieved through either slow dissolution or low permeability of the drug across pulmonary membranes [1], the latter being shown to be beneficial for long-acting beta-2-adrenergic drugs, e.g., olodaterol [2] or other highly soluble drugs such as tiotropium. The increased pulmonary residence time for corticosteroids, drugs generally crossing membranes easily, is driven by its high lipophilicity, low solubility in epithelial lining fluid, and consequently slow dissolution rates [3]. As a result of slow dissolution, pulmonary residence times of 2–7 hours [4,5] have been reported for inhaled corticosteroids such as budesonide, fluticasone propionate, and fluticasone furoate. Effect of delivered dose, excipients, particle size distribution, and other particle properties (amorphous vs. crystalline state), and their interplay with physiology related characteristics such as (I) membrane thickness at the site of deposition, and their relevance for sink or non-sink conditions, and (II) mucociliary clearance determining how much of slowly dissolving particles are removed, are parameters that need to be considered during development of new and generic orally inhaled drug products (OIDPs). These parameters are illustrated in Fig. 9.1.

Inhaled Medicines
DOI: https://doi.org/10.1016/B978-0-12-814974-4.00008-0

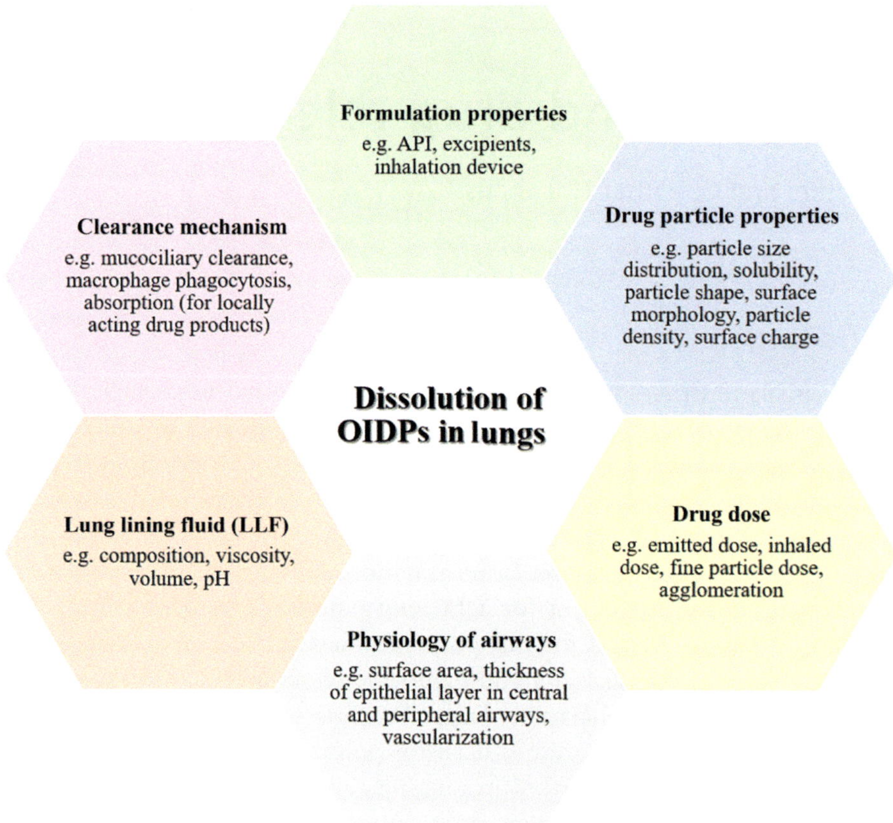

Figure 9.1 Overview of parameters affecting dissolution of OIDPs in lungs.

While dissolution studies of oral dosage forms are performed on a routine basis with validated methodology, there are currently no guidelines or pharmacopeia monographs for dissolution testing of OIDPs. An indication that, for a long time, most stakeholders thought the development of suitable dissolution techniques being of low priority is indicated by a statement from the Inhalation Ad Hoc Advisory Panel of the USP, which concluded in 2008 that there was no convincing indication that dissolution was "kinetically and/or clinically crucial for currently approved OIDPs" [6].

However, multiple studies demonstrated a strong relationship between dissolution/release rate and pharmacokinetic and pharmacodynamic properties [7,8] as these studies convincingly underlined that pulmonary targeting could be modulated by controlling the dissolution rate [9]. It might be speculated that the challenges involved in demonstrating pharmacokinetic bioequivalence of inhalation drugs might also be in part related to differences in the dissolution behavior of test and reference product and their effects on absorption rate. Techniques able to assess or predict the *in vivo* dissolution behavior of slowly dissolving inhalation drugs are therefore well needed.

9.2 Elemental concepts in dissolution process

9.2.1 Solubility

Solubility is defined as the capacity of a gaseous, liquid, or solid solute to dissolve in a particular solvent at a given temperature. Solubility of liquid and solid solutes depends on the balance between the free-energy state of solute-solute, solute-solvent, and solvent-solvent molecular interactions. The latter two are especially important for explaining the low water solubility of non-polar solutes that are unable to form hydrogen bonds with water. Given that the negative impact of a non-polar solute on water entropy state is diminished with temperature, water solubility of non-polar solutes normally increases with temperature. The units of solubility are reported as the amount of solute in a volume of solvent, e.g., Mol/L or mg/mL [10].

9.2.2 Dissolution

Dissolution is defined as the process by which a solute enters a solvent to yield a solution. All solid drug products, regardless of their route of administration, need to allow the active pharmacological ingredient (API) to dissolve in the body fluid at the site of administration to be absorbed and induce the physiological effect at the site of action [11].

Dissolution of a solid particle includes: (1) wetting of the solid particles by solvent displacing air from the surface of the particles, (2) breakdown of solid-state forces holding crystals, particles or granules, (3) bond formation and solvation, (4) diffusion of the dissolved molecules through the saturated layer around the particle surface, and (5) convection into the dissolution medium. Diffusion through the stagnant layer is considered as a rate-limiting step [12] (see Fig. 9.2).

Factors that affect the dissolution rate *in vitro* are [11,13]:

- Size, porosity, amorphous/crystalline state, and shape of the particles.
- Thickness of the stagnant layer.
- Solubility of the compound in the dissolution medium.
- Presence of some excipients.
- Difference between solubility and concentration of the dissolved drug.
- Stirring.
- Temperature.

9.2.3 The impact of particle size and shape on the dissolution process

The APIs particle size and its distribution (PSD) has been recognized as one of the most essential properties of an inhalation formulation, and it is usually expressed as the

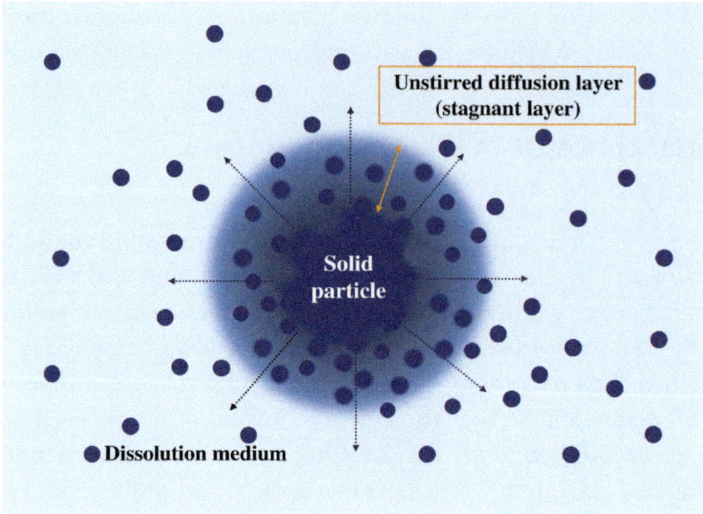

Figure 9.2 Schematic representation of the dissolution of a drug particle in the dissolution medium.

aerodynamic particle size distribution (APSD) of the emitted aerosol. PSD affects predeposition characteristics such as deposition in the mouth/throat region, lung dose, and regional deposition in central and peripheral regions of the lungs in addition to its effect on dissolution [14].

Concerning the dissolution process, particle size and shape will affect the surface area of the API accessible to the solvent and, therefore, will affect the dissolution rate. For a given shape of the particle, surface area per unit volume is inversely proportional to the size of the particles. A decrease in particle size will increase the specific surface area and lead to an increase in the dissolution rate [15]. Beside particle size, the thickness of the stagnant solution layer is important (Fig. 9.2) as based on the diffusion-controlled dissolution theory, particles are surrounded by a saturated stagnant layer in a bulk medium. Solute molecules traverse through this diffusion layer into the bulk dissolution medium. The thickness of this diffusion layer is directly dependent on the radius of particles. Smaller particles are surrounded by a thinner diffusion layer in the dissolution medium. Faster dissolution rates might be due to a higher fraction of smaller particles allowing molecules a faster diffusion into the dissolution medium. In a nutshell, reducing the particle size of API(s) will increase the dissolution rate of the formulation through an increase in surface area per unit of mass and a decrease in thickness of the stagnant layer around each particle [12,16]. In the case of very thin solvent films (e.g. epithelial lining fluid in the alveolar region) the stagnant layer might also be affected by the overall thickness of the solvent layer.

9.2.4 Sink vs. non-sink conditions

Based on the Nernst-Brunner equation (see Eq. 9.1), the dissolution rate is significantly affected by the difference between the solubility of the drug in the dissolution medium and the concentration of dissolved drug in the surroundings [15]. In the European Pharmacopeia, sink conditions are defined as "a volume of dissolution medium that is at least three to ten times the saturation volume" [17]. United States Pharmacopeia (USP) terms sink condition as "a volume of the medium at least three times that required in order to form a saturated solution of drug substance" [18]. Both regulatory and compendial guidelines agree on the statement that the maximum concentration of the dissolved drug substance in the dissolution medium should be less than 1/3 times the saturation solubility of that substance to have a sink condition. Deviations from this sink conditions can be categorized as non-sink conditions. Generally, dissolution testing in sink conditions has been recognized as a valuable assessment tool for formulation development and bioequivalence studies. US Food and Drug Administration's (FDA) guidance on dissolution testing has stated: "Sink conditions are desirable but not mandatory" [19]. Furthermore, USP's guidance on the dissolution procedure confirms this point by "a medium that fails to provide sink conditions may be acceptable, if it is shown to be more discriminative or otherwise appropriately justified" [18]. Dissolution testing should be performed under physiological conditions to reflect the *in vivo* performance of the product adequately. Depending on the extent of hydrophilicity/lipophilicity of the drug, non-sink conditions may exist in some regions of lungs. For lipophilic drugs sink conditions might be achievable in peripheral regions of the lungs (alveoli). Due to the large surface area, the thin epithelial cell monolayer, and the high blood flow of pulmonary circulation that allow a fast permeation and absorption [20,21]. While, in conducting airways with the smaller surface area, thicker epithelium and slower perfusion [22], there is the potential for non-sink conditions. The importance of non-sink conditions will be more pronounced for poorly soluble drugs when the delivered dose has access to a limited volume of fluid in lungs. Sink conditions might mask the potential formulation or batch to batch differences and mislead the *in vitro-in vivo* correlations. In other words, sink conditions may undermine discrimination for pulmonary drug delivery systems, especially poorly soluble drugs. Therefore, dissolution testing under perfect sink conditions may not be the most appropriate approach for all orally inhaled drug products. EMA recommends that the discriminatory power of the dissolution test for poorly soluble drugs should be the priority even if sink conditions criteria are not entirely met [23].

9.2.5 Surfactants and critical micelle concentration (CMC)

To achieve sink conditions for highly lipophilic inhalation drugs, such as corticosteroids, dissolution media often contain surfactants. Surfactants are amphiphilic molecules with a hydrophilic polar head and non-polar hydrocarbon tail. Surfactants can be classified according to the charge of their polar head group: cationic surfactants have a positively charged head group, anionic surfactants have a negatively charged head group, zwitterionic surfactants have a zwitterionic (both positive and negative charge) head group, and nonionic surfactants have an uncharged polar head group. Initially, when surfactants are added to water, they migrate to the air-water interface and orient themselves in a way that the hydrophobic part faces air, and the hydrophilic part is in water. This adjustment corresponds to the minimum surface tension. By increasing surfactant concentration, micelle formation occurs, which is another energetically stable structure. Micelles are spherical structures in which the hydrophobic parts of the surfactant molecule are pointing inwards the spherical structure and hydrophilic parts are towards the water. The critical micelle concentration (CMC) is an imperative characteristic of a surfactant and is defined as the concentration of surfactant at and above which micelles form [24,25]. In an aqueous dissolution medium, micelles can directly solubilize the solute by adsorbing the solute and remove it from the aqueous medium. Alternatively, the micelles can trap the solute inside the micelle's structure and keep it away from the aqueous phase to indirectly enhance the solubility [26]. In this scenario, due to the direct interaction of micelles with solute, the choice of a bio-relevant dissolution medium might be more important compared to the situation where the micelles would only act indirectly by reducing the dissolved drug concentration in the dissolution medium by removing the solute from the aqueous medium.

In contrast to the thoroughly characterized gastrointestinal fluids, in terms of their composition and structure, developing a bio-relevant lung lining fluid (LLF) in which drug solubility and dissolution needs to be investigated, is still in its infancy. Pulmonary surfactant is a lipoprotein mixture secreted by type II alveolar epithelial cells into the alveolar space. It is a surface-active complex, and its primary function is to reduce the surface tension at the air/liquid interface in the airways during the respiratory cycle and facilitate dissolution of particles. Dipalmitoyl phosphatidylcholine (DPPC) is the most abundant constituent of the lung surfactant. The selection of an appropriate surfactant with a suitable concentration is an integral part of developing a clinically relevant *in vitro* dissolution method, especially in the case of poor water-soluble drugs [27].

9.3 Dissolution of orally inhaled drug products (OIDPs)

9.3.1 Effects of drug formulation and excipients on dissolution rate

Interestingly, even formulations with similar particle size distribution of the API and aerodynamic performance may differ in dissolution profile. There is increasing evidence indicating that type and amount of excipients present in the formulation of OIDPs can affect the API dissolution rate. Excipients might affect the dissolution rate of an API through impacting the solvent properties and consequently its solubility. Moreover, excipients might change the surface properties of API particles present in a DPI or suspension-based MDIs, or even affect the particle formation/properties in solution-based MDIs. Increasing the ethanol content of a solution-based MDI formulation has been shown to affect size of the aerosols as well as the evaporation rate of these aerosols towards their residual particle sizes. The initial aerosol size is higher with increased ethanol concentrations in the formulation. Moreover, greater percent of ethanol in aerosols retards the evaporation of propellant and favors the generation of smoother particle. These alterations affecting the morphology and solvate/clathrate formation result in a notable slower dissolution rate of the API in a solution-based MDI [28,29]. The use of glycerol in solution-based pMDI formulations will restrict the water access for lipophilic APIs by concentrating the water molecules around its polar groups and subsequently hinder the dissolution process [30]. Spray-drying of poorly water-soluble azithromycin in the presence of L-leucin resulted in particles with substantially enhanced *in-vitro* dissolution rate. It seems that the dissolution of acidic L-leucine decreases the pH of the dissolution medium and causes an acidic microenvironment around the azithromycin molecules. The decreased pH increases the solubility of azithromycin and consequently the dissolution rate of this poorly water soluble compound [31]. Excipient effects have also been described for DPI formulations where it could be shown that the amount and characteristics of lactose fines modulated the dissolution behavior of poorly soluble APIs. Due to instant dissolution of lactose fines in an aqueous medium, agglomeration of lactose fines with API particles enhances the exposure of API to the dissolution medium enabling rapid dissolution. However, API-API agglomerates face a different situation in the medium since this type of agglomeration decreases the specific surface area and consequently delaying the dissolution rate [32–34].

9.3.2 Common dissolution media

During the past three decades, a variety of fluids have been proposed as dissolution media to study the dissolution behavior of the inhaled particles with specific modifications to be reflective of the physiology of the lungs (Table 9.1 and 9.2). While the composition of the epithelial lining fluid is rather complex, several developed dissolution media are based on simple inorganic salt mixtures in water or phosphate buffered saline (PBS) representative of physiological electrolyte levels. The original simulated lung fluid (SLF) was introduced as "Gamble's solution" by Moss in 1979 [35]. While Gamble's solution has a pH of 7.4, an acidic version of this solution was produced named artificial lysosomal fluid (ALF) as a representative of the lysosomal environment and simulation of the fate of particles after phagocytosis by macrophages in the lung [36]. Gamble's solution has also been modified by adding Mg^{2+}, Ca^{2+}, Na^{+}, and Cl^{-}, HCO_3^{-}, acetate, and citrate ions in different concentrations to mimic the interstitial fluid of the lung.

Besides, due to the presence of phospholipids and surfactants in LLF, some dissolution media were proposed to contain synthetic or natural surfactants such as polysorbate 80

Table 9.1 Composition of simple fluids used for dissolution studies of orally inhaled products.

Ingredients (%)	Water					PBS							
None	+					+							
DPPC								0.02			0.02		
SDS			0.3	0.5			0.5			0.2			0.1
SLS		0.3											
Tween 20									0.2				
Tween 80					0.01–0.5							0.02	
pH	–	1.2	1.2	–	–	7.4	7.4	7.4	7.4	7.4	7.4	7.4	7.4
References	[43,44]	[45]	[46]	[27]	[8]	[31,37,43,47–50]	[51]	[37]	[15]	[15]	[15]	[52]	[53]

Table 9.2 Composition of simulated lung fluids developed for *in-vitro* dissolution studies of orally inhaled compounds.

Composition	Original gamble's solution (g/L)	ALF[a] (g/L)	SILF[b] (g/L)	SSLF[c] (g/L)	Gamble's solution (g/L)	Gamble's solution (g/L)	Gamble's solution (g/L)	Modified gamble's solution (g/L)	Synthetic serum (g/L)	SELF[d] (g/L)	SLF[e] (g/L))	SLF (g/L)
Magnesium chloride	0.203	0.0106	0.203	0.203	0.095	–	–	0.212	–	0.2	–	–
Sodium chloride	6.019	3.21	6.019	6.019	6.019	6.779	6.400	6.415	6.779	6.02	6.8	–
Potassium chloride	0.298	–	0.298	0.298	0.298	–	–	–	–	0.298	–	–
Potassium hydrogen phthalate	–	–	–	–	–	–	–	–	–	–	0.2	
Monosodium phosphate	0.142	–	–	–	–	0.144	–	–	0.144	–	1.7	–
Disodium hydrogen phosphate	–	–	0.268	0.268	0.126	–	0.150	0.148	–	0.15	–	–
Sodium phosphate	–	0.179	–	–	–	–	–	–	–	–	–	–
Phosphoric acid	–	–	–	–	–	–	–	–	–	–	1.2	–
Sodium sulfate	0.071	0.039	0.071	0.071	0.063	–	–	0.079	–	0.072	–	–
Calcium chloride	0.368	0.097	0.368	0.368	0.368	0.022	0.255	0.255	0.022	0.256	0.29	–
Sodium acetate	0.952	–	0.952	0.952	0.574	–	–	–	–	–	0.58	–
Sodium bicarbonate	2.604	–	2.604	2.604	2.604	2.268	2.7	2.703	2.268	2.7	2.3	–
Sodium carbonate	–	–	–	–	–	–	–	–	–	–	0.63	–
Sodium citrate	0.097	0.077	0.097	0.097	0.097	0.0516	0.160	0.153	0.0516	–	0.59	–
Sodium hydroxide	–	6.00	–	–	–	–	–	–	–	–	–	–
Citric acid	–	20.8	–	–	–	–	–	–	–	–	0.42	–
Glycerin	–	0.059	–	–	–	0.375	0.190	0.118	0.45	0.376	0.45	–
Sodium tartrate	–	0.090	–	–	–	–	–	0.18	–	–	–	–
Sodium lactate	–	0.085	–	–	–	–	–	0.175	–	–	–	–
Sodium pyruvate	–	0.086	–	–	–	–	–	0.172	–	–	–	–
Formaldehyde	–	0.81	–	–		-	–	–	–	–	–	–
Ammonium chloride	–	–	–	–	–	0.535	0.118	–	0.535	–	5.3	–
Sulfuric acid	–	–	–	–	–	0.049	–	–	0.049	–	0.51	–
L-cysteine hydrochloride	–	–	–	–	–	0.121	–	–	–	0.122	–	–
HBSS[f]	–	–	–	–	–	–	–	–	–	–	–	775 (μL/mL)
DPPC[g]	–	–	–	0.02% (w/v)	–	–	0.02% (w/v)	–	–	0.01% (w/v)	–	4.8
DPPG[h]	–	–	–	–	–	–	–	–	–	–	–	0.5
Cholesterol	–	–	–	–	–	–	–	–	–	–	–	0.1

(Continued)

Table 9.2 (Continued)

Composition	Original gamble's solution (g/L)	ALF[a] (g/L)	SILF[b] (g/L)	SSLF[c] (g/L)	Gamble's solution (g/L)	Gamble's solution (g/L)	Gamble's solution (g/L)	Modified gamble's solution (g/L)	Synthetic serum (g/L)	SELF[d] (g/L)	SLF[e] (g/L))	SLF (g/L)
Ascorbic acid	–	–	–	–	–	–	–	–	–	0.018	–	0.025
Uric acid	–	–	–	–	–	–	–	–	–	0.016	–	0.016
Glutathione	–	–	–	–	–	–	–	–	–	0.03	–	0.52
Albumin	–	–	–	–	–	–	–	–	–	0.26	–	8.8
IgG	–	–	–	–	–	–	–	–	–	–	–	2.6
Transferrin	–	–	–	–	–	–	–	–	–	–	–	1.5
Mucin	–	–	–	–	–	–	–	–	–	0.5	–	–
DTPA[i]	–	–	–	–	–	0.079	–	–	–	–	–	–
Benzalkonium chloride (ABDAC)	–	–	–	–	–	0.050	–	–	–	–	–	–
pH		4.5	7.4	7.4	7.4	7.3	–	7.6	7.3	7.4	7.4	–
References	[35]	[36]	[54]	[54,55]	[56]	[57]	[58]	[59]	[60]	[41]	[61]	[27,42]

[a]Artificial Lysosomal Fluid.
[b]Simulated Interstitial Lung Fluid.
[c]Simulated Surfactant Lung Fluid.
[d]Simulated Epithelial Lung Fluid.
[e]Simulated Lung Fluid.
[f]Hanks' Balanced Salt Solution.
[g]1,2-dipalmitoyl-sn-glycero-3-phosphocholine.
[h]1,2-dipalmitoyl-sn-glycerol-3-phosphot-rac(1-glycerol).
[i]Diethylenetriaminepentaacetic acid.

(Tween 80), sodium dodecyl sulfate (SDS), Dipalmitoylphosphatidylcholine (DPPC), or Survanta® [8,15,27,37]. While addition of these surfactants have been shown to enhance solubility of poorly soluble compounds, the extent of this enhancement is not predictable and might differ based on the type of the surfactant and the interactions occurring between the API and surfactant [8,38]. Diluted solutions of commercially available natural surfactants (Survanta®, Curosurf®, Alveofact®) and bronchoalveolar lavage (BAL) from porcine or bovine lungs have been employed for *in vitro* dissolution studies [27,38,39]. Considering their cost, complex process of preparation, and limitation of only representing the surfactant component of alveolar lining fluids (in the case of commercial surfactants), further research is necessary to reveal whether these natural surfactants show any advantage over synthetic ones.

More complex matrixes have been designed to mimic the epithelial lining fluid (ELF) by adding albumin, cholesterol, IgG, mucin, and citrate ions to achieve desirable pH, viscosity, conductivity, surface tension, density, and stability profile. For instance, a PBS based solution modified by DPPC would be representative for the alveolar region, while a solution containing mucin has been proposed to reflect the lining fluid of the bronchiolar region [40]. Proteins might also be added to SLF to investigate the effect of protein binding on particles' toxicity. Furthermore, since the protein content of LLF alters in lung pathologies, e.g., increased levels of proteins in LLF of asthmatic patients, protein containing SLF might be more bio-relevant to elucidate the influence of protein content on the dissolution of delivered dose to the lung [41,42].

Dissolution media for *in vitro* dissolution testing should properly simulate the *in vivo* dissolution process in the lungs. Such media should also be simple, reproducible, stable, economical, and amenable to validation. Additionally, depending on the aim of the study, the discriminative power of the medium might be used as an evaluation criterion for finding the most appropriate dissolution medium. Use of a bio-relevant dissolution medium in which solubility of the target drug is similar to that of epithelial lining fluid might be of advantage when *in vitro* results are intended to be directly used for *in vivo* predictions. However, the choice of the surfactant type and its concentration might not be as important when the relative dissolution profiles of two formulations are assessed (e.g. during development of a generic product).

9.3.3 Special considerations in dissolution studies on orally inhaled drug products

There are several hurdles to overcome when developing a bio-relevant *in vitro* dissolution test for inhaled products. Primarily, as only the fraction of the aerosol that reaches the lungs is genuinely relevant for exploring post-deposition events, such as the dissolution of drug particles, a respirable fraction of the emitted dose needs to be collected from the inhaler for dissolution testing [62]. Additionally, the unique physiology of the lungs in terms of having a limited amount of aqueous fluid representing the epithelial lining fluid, and its special composition (e.g., presence of surfactants), should be considered when developing a bio-relevant *in vitro* dissolution method. These challenges necessitate special considerations for developing a robust and discriminate dissolution method for OIDPs [3].

9.3.4 Particle collection for dissolution studies

The first step towards the kinetic assessments of a dissolution process is the collection of particles on appropriate support to be transferred to a dissolution setup. Several approaches have been proposed which employ aerodynamic sizing apparatuses (Appendix 1) or alternative approaches to collect particles of inhaler formulations for dissolution testing. In general, the proposed particle collection approaches can be categorized into two classes:

9.3.4.1 Approach I. Collection of size-fractionated dose

The compendial aerodynamic sizing apparatuses such as the Next Generation Impactor (NGI), Andersen Cascade Impactor (ACI) and multi-stage liquid cascade impactor (MSLI), have been used to collect particles from a specific stage or a range of stages (see also Table 9.3). Particles are usually collected by placing one or several membranes onto a given stage [43,63]. A variety of membranes have been utilized for particle collection from these setups [64]. These collection membranes can be directly transferred to the dissolution apparatus or be sandwiched with an additional presoaked membrane and then placed into the dissolution apparatus using a filter cassette [63]. As an improvement, specially designed NGI plates with integrated impaction inserts were developed. These polycarbonate containing impaction inserts were then sandwiched and transferred into the USP dissolution vessel [37]. A few studies have also modified the multistage liquid impinger (MSLI) configuration to allow the collection of size-fractionated particles onto Calu-3 respiratory epithelial cell layers. A cell layer grown on a culture insert was placed directly under the second or third stage nozzle of a MSLI, while stages were flooded with a cell compatible buffer. Though the drug absorption was the main interest of these studies [65,66], the proposed modified MSLI can be adapted for dissolution studies, as well.

While these approaches can assess the sensitivity of a dissolution method to formulation properties and particle size differences, they are not necessarily informative for the overall dissolution behavior of the pulmonary deposited dose. Besides, there are some challenges associated with the use of cascade impactors for sample preparation. Several authors reported that the dissolution profiles of a given formulation were dependent on the amount of drug collected on a given membrane, resulting in a slower dissolution at higher deposited doses. It was suggested that the non-linearity in the dissolution might be due to the formation of drug piles on the collection membrane. When the mass of the particles increases on the collection membrane, the formation of drug agglomerates and piles close to the air jets will reduce the water-accessible surface area resulting in wetting problems that can affect the dissolution rate [15,47,64].

9.3.4.2 Approach II. Collection of samples representative of lung deposited particles

Efforts have been made to design approaches in which the particles are not sieved into the narrow size fractions and, thus, resemble the fraction of the dose that would deposit in the lung. Modified impactors/impingers and other methods collecting such fractions (e.g., collection of ex-throat doses by using anatomical mouth/throat replica) are examples of the second approach.

The twin impinger (TI) apparatus has been used as an aerosol collection method that divides the aerosol particles into two fractions. Particles collected in stage two represent the lung dose of a given inhaler formulation [29]. Son et al. modified the TI apparatus by adding an extra 300-mL reservoir flask to the base of the upper impinger chamber to function as a dissolution vessel. The modified setup was shown to successfully discriminate the drug release rates of different controlled-release DPI formulations [67].

By omitting the intermediate impaction plates from the ACI, abbreviated ACIs (aACI) allowed the collection of more bio-relevant samples with a broader particle size distribution [68]. To prevent the pile formation underneath the jet nozzles, approaches were set-up to collect aerosols directly after leaving the USP induction port using a specifically designed membrane holder [54]. For the same purpose, a cylindrical shaped stage extension spacer has also been introduced to be placed between stage 1 and the filter stage of the ACI. The insertion of the spacer made sedimentation the most dominant mechanism of deposition rather than impaction. Hence, a more evenly distributed particle layer on the membrane with less pile formation and agglomerates was achieved [15].

NGI apparatus can also be modified to collect the fine particle dose on a specific stage (typically stage 3). The outlet of NGI can be swapped to underneath of one of the collection plates to collect the particles landing in that specific plate [69]. A similar modification was recently proposed, which is incorporated into stage 2 of the NGI, allows the uniform deposition of the whole impactor stage mass (ISM) onto a single, high surface area membrane without the formation of drug piles. The proposed particle collection method has significantly reduced the "mass-effect" generally seen when particles are collected in standard cascade impactors [32].

In addition to the discussed modified aerodynamic sizing apparatuses that were adapted for dose collection purposes, there are a few devices/apparatuses explicitly designed and developed for dose collection from inhaler formulations. Bhagwat et al. used an anatomical throat model connected to a custom-made metal filter holder containing a 25 mm glass microfiber filter. The ex-throat particles deposited evenly on the filter paper without pile formation observed in the standard cascade impactor systems [8]. An anatomical mouth/throat model was also incorporated into a commercial sample collection system that collects particles evenly distributed across the surface of a filter insert. This insert can be directly transferred to a dissolution apparatus [70]. The sedimentation chamber is a different approach to deposit pharmacologically relevant aerosols onto cells cultured at the air/liquid interphase (e.g. Transwell® or similar filter supports). The Pharmaceutical Aerosol Deposition Device On Cell Cultures (PADDOCC) [71] and the Vitrocell Dry Powder Chamber are examples of this category that deposit aerosols based on the time of the flight and sedimentation. However, they are applicable to be implemented into *in vitro* dissolution studies, as well.

It is noteworthy to mention that dissolution testing can also be performed without a particle separation step. Airbrushing the particles onto the dissolution medium, manual sprinkling, using dry powder insufflators, or delivery systems such as the PreciseInhale aerosol generator have been employed for delivering aerosols to a dissolution apparatus [64].

9.3.5 Dissolution systems developed for orally inhaled drug products

A meticulous selection of dissolution methodology to provide reproducibility, robustness, and sensitivity involves optimizing dissolution medium, sampling schedule, and hydrodynamic conditions. Hydrodynamic conditions in an *in vitro* setting are controlled by stirring, agitation, flow rate, temperature, and viscosity of the dissolution medium [72]. Despite the necessity of establishing a bio-relevant *in vitro* dissolution method that can adequately characterize the *in vitro* properties of OIDPs to promote drug development phase or be qualitatively and quantitatively translated to *in vivo* performance of OIDPs, there is no well-standardized dissolution method approved by regulatory agencies and pharmacopeias. However, a variety of *in vitro* dissolution systems have been developed or modified over the past two decades.

9.3.5.1 USP apparatuses

9.3.5.1.1 USP apparatus V (paddle over disk apparatus)

USP apparatus V, which was originally developed for transdermal dosage forms, consists of a glass or any transparent and inert vessel with a paddle of a blade and the shaft utilized for stirring (Fig. 9.3). The volume of dissolution medium used in this apparatus can be varied from a minimum of 100 mL up to 1000 mL, depending on the structure of the vessel and physico-chemical properties of API being investigated [63]. Conventional dissolution media are listed in Tables 9.1 and 9.2. Sampling can be done manually or automated at predetermined time points. Using full flow filter tips will prevent undissolved particles from entering samples [73]. Drug dose can be directly collected on a stainless-steel support disk, or on a membrane which is attached to a disk assembly. Disk assembly is a membrane holder (stainless steel or watch glass) used

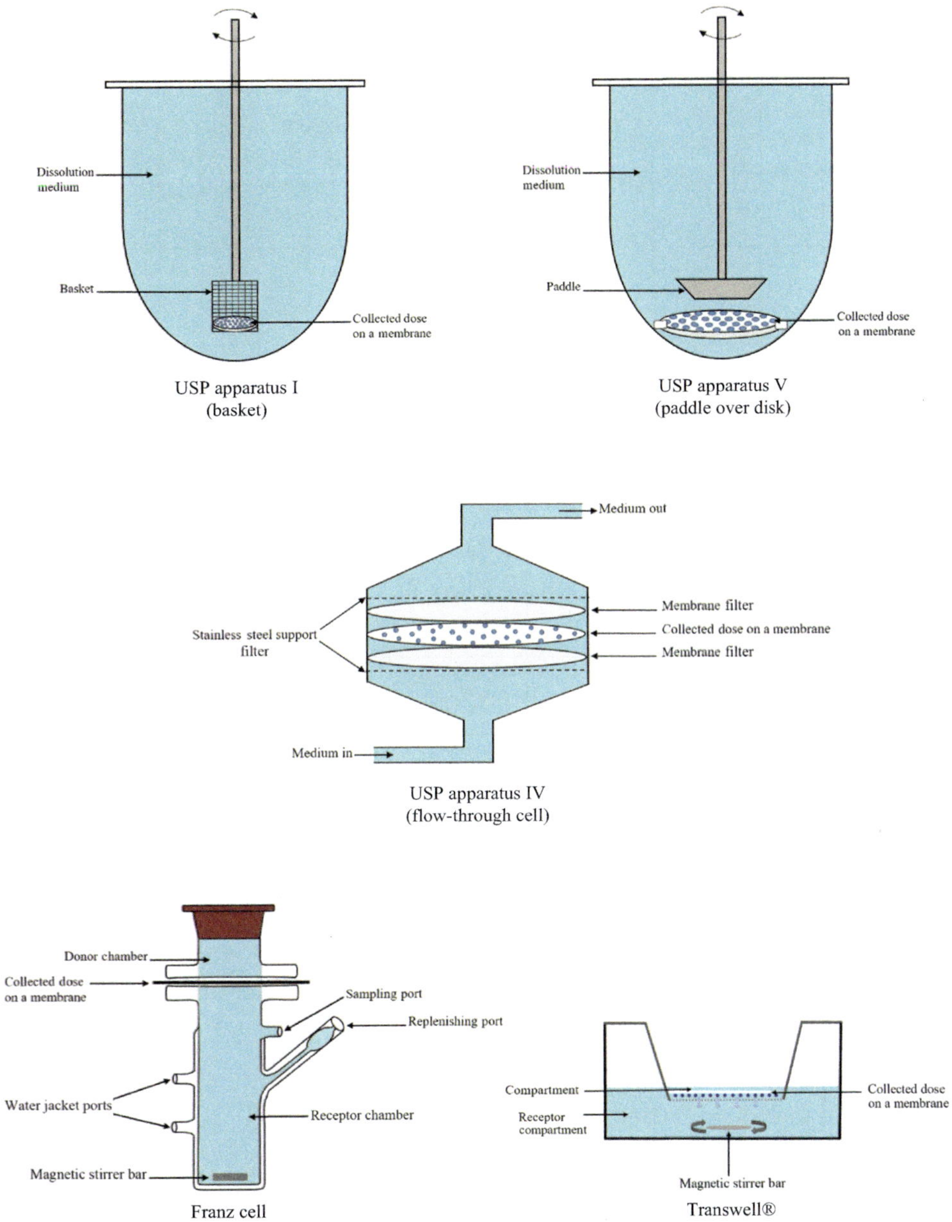

Figure 9.3 Schematic configuration of dissolution apparatuses adapted for dissolution studies of OIDPs.

as a sinker to keep the membrane with the collected dose flat and stable at the bottom of the vessel [47]. The distance between the bottom of the paddle and the membrane holder surface is recommended to be 20 ± 2 mm. This distance allows the paddle to

Table 9.3 Overview of dissolution studies developed for OIDPs.

Dissolution method	Dose collection method	Collection membrane	Dissolution medium	Agitation of medium	Temperature	Drug/compound	Mass effect	References
USP Apparatus V (Paddle over disk)	NGI	Disk insert	PBS	+	37 °C	Tobramycin, Clarithromycin, Insulin	Not evaluated	[79,80]
	aACI	Regenerated cellulose membrane	PBS ± DPPC	+	37 °C	Budesonide, Fenoterol	Observed	[15,47]
		Adhesive tape	mSLF with 0.2 v/v Tween 80	+	37 °C	Salbutamol Sulfate, Fluticasone Propionate, Salmeterol Xinafoate	Not evaluated	[81]
	mACI	Regenerated cellulose membrane	PBS ± DPPC	+	37 °C	Budesonide	Observed	[15]
		Whatman RC55 filters	0.5% SDS in PB	+	37 °C	Fluticasone Propionate, Fluticasone Furoate	Evaluated	[82]
	mNGI	Polycarbonate membrane (Cassette)	SLF, PBS, PBS ± 0.02% DPPC, PBS ± 0.02% Tween 80, PBS ± 0.2% Tween 80	+	37 °C	Budesonide, Salbutamol Sulfate	Observed	[37]
			SLF	+	37 °C	Temozolomide	Not evaluated	[83]
			Degassed water + SLS (pH = 1.2)	+	37 °C	Itraconazole	Not evaluated	[45]
			SLF, SLF + 0.02% DPPC	+	37 °C	Hydrocor tisone	Observed	[63]
			PBS, 0.2 m citrate buffer	+	37 °C	Rifampicin	Not evaluated	[84]
			PBS	+	37 °C	Budesonide	Not evaluated	[85]
	Weighting/ sprinkling	Regenerated cellulose membrane	0.05 M PB	+	37 °C	Disodium Cromoglycate (DSCG)	Not evaluated	[48]
		Whatman RC55 filters	0.5% SDS in PB	+	37 °C	Fluticasone Propionate, Fluticasone Furoate	Observed	[82]

USP Apparatus IV (Flow-through cell)	NGI	Whatman® Grade 2 filter paper	SLF	+	37 °C	Colistin, Rifampicin	Not evaluated	[86]
	aACI	Regenerated cellulose membrane	PBS	+	37 °C	Budesonide, Fenoterol	Observed	[47]
		Glass fiber filter	SLF, SLF + 0.02% DPPC	+	37 °C	Budesonide, Fluticasone Propionate, Triamcinolone Acetate	Not evaluated	[54]
	Weighting/sprinkling	Regenerated cellulose membrane	0.05 M PB	+	37 °C	Disodium Cromoglycate (DSCG)	Not evaluated	[48]
		Tuffryn membrane	PBS, SLF	+	37 °C	Budesonide	Not evaluated	[87]
Transwell®	ACI	PVDF filter membrane	PBS, DDW		37 °C	Budesonide, Fluticasone Propionate, Triamcinolone Acetonide, Flunisolide, Beclomethasone Dipropionate	Observed	[43]
		Glass microfiber filter (GF/C)	0.5% SDS in PBS	+	37 °C	Budesonide, Ciclesonide	Not evaluated	[51]
	NGI	Glass microfiber filter (GF/C)	PBS, 0.5% SDS	+	37 °C	Fluticasone Propionate	Not evaluated	[51]
	TI	Polyester membrane Transwell inserts	Gambles solution, SLF, or water with 0.5% SDS		Room temperature	Fluticasone Propionate, Beclomethasone Dipropionate	Not evaluated	[27]
	aACI	Polycarbonate Transwell inserts, Polyester Transwell inserts, Polycarbonate (Isopore) membrane	PBS	+	37 °C	Budesonide	Not evaluated	[49]
	mACI	Regenerated cellulose membrane	PBS	+	37 °C	Budesonide	Not evaluated	[49]
		Nitrocellulose membrane	Donor compartment: sLLF with 0.02% DPPC, Receptor compartment: sLLF ± D-αtocopheryl polyethylene glycol 1000 succinate (TPGS)	–	37 °C	Flunisolide, Triamcinolone Acetonide, Budesonide, Fluticasone Propionate, Beclomethason Dipropionate, Mometasone Furoate, Ciclesonide	Observed	[74]

(Continued)

Table 9.3 (Continued)

Dissolution method	Dose collection method	Collection membrane	Dissolution medium	Agitation of medium	Temperature	Drug/compound	Mass effect	References
		Glass microfiber filter (GF/C)	0.5% SDS in PB	+	Room temperature	Budesonide, Fluticasone Propionate, Fluticasone Furoate	Not evaluated	[82]
	Mouth-throat models	Glass microfiber filter (GF/C)	0.5% Tween 80 in water	+	37 °C	Budesonide, Fluticasone Propionate, Mometasone Furoate	Not evaluated	[8]
Franz cell	NGI	Nitrocellulose membrane	SLF	+	37 °C	Pyrazinamide, Rifampicin, Isoniazid	Not evaluated	[88]
		Whatman® Grade 2 filter paper	PBS	+	37 °C	Azithromycin Dihydrate	Not evaluated	[31]
			SLF	+	37 °C	Colistin, Rifampicin	Not evaluated	[86]
	TI	Nitrocellulose membrane	0.1 w/v SDS in PB	+	37 °C	Beclomethasone Dipropionate	Not evaluated	[53]
		Polycarbonate membrane	0.5% (w/v) SDS in SLF	+	37 °C	Beclomethasone Dipropionate, Formoterol Fumarate	Not evaluated	[29]
		Polycarbonate membrane	0.4% (w/v) SDS in SLF	+	37 °C	Beclomethasone	Not evaluated	[30]
	aACI	Regenerated cellulose membrane	PBS	+	37 °C	Budesonide, Fenoterol	Observed	[47]
	FSI	A/E glass fiber filter	PBS	+	37 °C	Salmeterol Xinafoate	Not evaluated	[89]
	Weighting/ sprinkling	Regenerated cellulose membrane	0.05 M PB	+	37 °C	Disodium Cromoglycate (DSCG)	Not evaluated	[48]
		High pure filter paper	Water	+	37 °C	Tobramycin	Not evaluated	[44]
		Regenerated cellulose membrane	PB, SLF	+	37 °C	Bovine Serum Albumin, Terbutaline Sulfate, Diprophylline	Not evaluated	[90]
		Cellulose acetate membrane	0.05 M PB, SLF	+	37 °C	Salbutamol Free Base, Salbutamol Sulfate	Not evaluated	[91]

		Disk of filter paper	PBS	+	37 °C	Salmeterol Xinafoate	Not evaluated	[92]
DissolvIt	PreciseInhale exposure system	Glass cover slip	Mucus simulant, Blood simulant	+	37 °C	Budesonide, Fluticasone Propionate	Evaluated	[78]
Beaker method	NGI	Whatman® Grade 2 filter paper	PBS	+	37 °C	Azithromycin Dihydrate	Not evaluated	[31]
			SLF	+	37 °C	Colistin, Rifampicin	Not evaluated	[86]
Dialysis bag	Weighting/ sprinkling	–	SLF	–	37 °C	Rifampicin, Rifabutin	Not evaluated	[93]
			0.1% Tween 80 in PBS	+	37 °C	Voriconazole	Not evaluated	[94]

effectively release drug particles from the exposed membrane surface and allow continuous circulation of media within the vessel. The paddle speed is being adjusted to 50–140 rpm [47,63]. Son et al. mentioned a dead volume between the membrane holder and the bottom of the vessel, which can disturb the circulation of the dissolution medium around the holder [37]. Hence, higher stirring speeds might be required to stir the dead volumes and maintain a homogenous circulation of dissolution medium in the vessel [47]. Albeit drug particles can be directly sprinkled into the vessel [48], as mentioned above, the dose can be introduced to this system through the attachment of the membrane to a sinker. The collected dose can be placed with the particles towards the watch glass or pre-soaked membrane into the membrane holder and released to the vessel [37,47]. In this case, drug particles might face poor wettability and need to diffuse through a diffusion barrier once they dissolve to reach to the bulk dissolution medium. Optimizing the pore size and material of the membrane can minimize this effect. Alternatively, the collected dose on the membrane or stainless-steel filter can face up to the dissolution medium to have a diffusion-free dissolution process [62].

As discussed in the particle collection section, pile formation and non-uniform distribution of drug particles collected on the membrane for dissolution studies affect the wetting process of particles by reducing the available surface area for dissolution [64] This mass-effect has also been described by several research groups when utilizing the paddle over disk apparatus [37,47,63]. Operation of the USP apparatus at large volume of media with respect to the saturation solubility of the target drug maintains sink conditions and ensures unimpaired dissolution. However, this type of mass-effect is caused due to the sample preparation methodology and not the USP dissolution methodology [32]. The paddle over disk apparatus has been successfully employed to discriminate between different compounds and different formulations of inhaled products [47]. Although, the use of large dissolution volumes and hydrodynamic conditions of this method has been questioned for inhalation products by several studies [48,49,74], a correlation between the mean dissolution time and the *in vivo* mean absorption time for a range of inhaled corticosteroids has been reported [32].

9.3.5.1.2 Apparatus IV (flow-through cell apparatus)

This apparatus consists of a dissolution medium containing the reservoir, a flow-throw cell, a pump, and a bath jacket. The membrane with the collected drug particles is placed in the cell (Fig. 9.3). The pump, which is usually an HPLC pump, causes a force to allow the medium to flow upwards through the flow-cell in a vertical manner. This pump allows for a continuous flow of the fresh medium. The flow rate is reported from 0.5 to 1.5 mL/min. Drug particles dissolve and pass the filter on the top of the cell to be collected for quantification. During this process, a water bath is used to maintain the temperature of the dissolution medium at 37 °C. Due to the continuous flow of fresh dissolution medium and adjustable flow rate, temperature, and pH sink conditions can be achieved. There are two different modes for this apparatus. The first mode is an open system (non-recycled system) that consists of a continuous flow of solvent passing through the cell from the reservoir. This mode is suitable for poorly soluble drugs because it provides favorable flowing fluid dynamics that are unlimited in volume for dissolution [54]. The second mode consists of a closed system that recirculates a fixed volume of the medium during the study time. The closed system approach is utilized when a small dissolution medium volume is preferable [48]. While providing the sink conditions and minimal influence of diffusion, this setup has been recounted to have a high fluid velocity in the middle of the vessel and a decreasing gradient towards the wall of dissolution vessel. This situation may cause a convection inside the cell and thus, question having the sink conditions in the apparatus. Dependency of dissolution kinetic on the flow rate of the passing medium is another concern in flow-through cell apparatus [54,62].

9.3.5.1.3 USP apparatus I (rotating basket apparatus)

USP apparatus I is not widely adapted for evaluating the dissolution profiles of inhaled products. A few studies have used this apparatus for testing controlled-released and nanoparticle formulations [71,72]. This apparatus consists of a vessel that is made of glass or other material that is transparent and inert, along with a basket in a cylindrical shape that is attached to the lower portion of the rotating stirrer (Fig. 9.3). Usually, the temperature in the basket is maintained at 37 °C. The speed of the rotation device has been adjusted from 50 to 100 rpm. Presumably, due to high variability in agitation conditions and interfering factors such as forming aggregates that get stuck in the basket mesh from stirring or floating particles at the surface of the medium this method might not be the best approach for inhaled formulations [37].

9.3.5.2 Diffusion-controlled apparatuses

Compared to gastrointestinal fluids, lung lining fluid is limited in volume and is much more stationary. Methods discussed above, may not be a true reflection of the actual *in vivo* dissolution process of inhaled particles in the limited and unstirred lung lining fluid. Franz cell and Transwell® system were developed to improve the non-physiologic conditions in the conventional dissolution setups. In these two apparatuses, the small volumes in the donor compartment mimic the limited lung lining fluid available for the dissolution of particles in respiratory airways. Furthermore, the presence of air-liquid interface in Franz diffusion cell and Transwell® system assure more bio-relevant conditions and can be an appropriate representative of lungs histology and physiology [48,49].

While the small volumes in these apparatuses may be deliberated as an asset, possible retention of drug particles in the membrane might be an interfering factor in these setups. Since diffusion of dissolved particles affects the rate of transfer from the donor to the receptor compartment, the diffusion coefficient and affinity of the compound to the membrane needs to be taken into account to ensure dissolution is the rate limiting step within these approaches [51,62].

9.3.5.2.1 Franz cell [75]

A Franz cell apparatus is a diffusion cell made of two glass compartments. The upper part is called the donor chamber and the bottom part the receptor. It has a semi-permeable membrane that separates donor and receptor chambers. Aerosol particles can directly be added on this membrane or be collected on a separate membrane that will be placed between the two donor and receptor chambers (Fig. 9.3). Drug particles in the donor chamber disintegrate, dissolve, and diffuse into the receptor side of the cell. On the receptor chamber, a sampling arm allows samples to be collected from under the semi-permeable membrane. The receptor medium is stirred with a small magnet bar, and has a temperature of 37 °C maintained with the help of a water jacket that surrounds the chamber [48,75]. The semi-permeable membrane separating the two chambers behaves as a diffusion barrier and has a profound effect on the observed dissolution rate in this method. The common membranes are cellulose acetate, polycarbonate, nylon, polysulfone, Teflon, and Tuffryn. These membranes differ in pore size, pore tortuosity, and membrane thickness [73]. The polycarbonate membrane has been shown as a suitable diffusion barrier in dissolution setups, due to the advantages of not swelling in contact with dissolution medium, lack of entrapped air, and allowing fast diffusion of dissolved drugs [63]. The presence of small air bubbles or wrinkles in the membrane can cause a non-homogenous contact area to dissolution medium under the membrane. This situation may lead to inconsistent wetting of particles [47]. However, pre-wetting the membrane, and degassing the dissolution medium might minimize this disturbing effect [76].

9.3.5.2.2 Transwell® system

Arora et al., in 2010, introduced a new application of Transwell® cell culture supports for dissolution studies of inhaled products [43]. Transwell permeable inserts are available in a range of pore sizes from 0.4μm to 8.0 μm and three different membranes: polycarbonate, polyester (PET), and collagen-coated polytetrafluoroethylene (PTFE) [77]. Aerosol particles can be collected directly on this membrane or on a separated membrane, which is transferred to the system facing up or down to the membrane of the Transwell® insert. The dissolution experiment is initiated by adding the dissolution medium into the insert as the donor compartment (Fig. 9.3). Experiments are usually performed at 37 °C and near 100% relative humidity to minimize the evaporation of medium. Samples are taken from the receptor compartment at predetermined time points. The removed volumes are replenished with fresh dissolution medium to maintain a consistent medium volume during the entire experiment [43,51]. To minimize fluid transfer between the compartments, it is pivotal to balance hydrostatic pressures by having equal levels of dissolution medium in the donor and receptor compartment [74]. Another critical parameter in this setup is the agitation of the medium. Stirring the dissolution medium in the receptor compartment causes a homogeneous concentration and increases the rate with which drug is diffusing across the membrane [49]. Similar to the Franz-cell, steps should be taken to ensure that the dissolution and not the diffusion is the rate limiting step in the transfer of dissolved particles into the receptor compartment [51].

One of the main criticism of the Transwell® set up is the lack of sink conditions and the dependency of the dissolution rate on the initial amount of drug delivered to the system. For water-soluble drugs, sink conditions are achievable even in this small volume of Transwell® setup, while for poorly soluble drugs maintaining sink conditions is a matter of debate. Due to small volumes used in this apparatus, overloading the set up with a high dose might lead to solubility-limited non-sink conditions and a significant decrease in the dissolution rate [74]. To overcome this problem, solubility of the target compound needs to be adjusted in the dissolution medium [8]. To illustrate, Sakagami et al. modified the dissolution medium by adding the solubilizer agent D-αtocopheryl polyethylene glycol 1000 succinate to enhance the solubility of poorly soluble corticosteroids. In this approach, drug concertation in the receptor was kept less than 1/3 of the solubility to ensured sink conditions throughout studies [74]. Likewise, May et al. reported having sink conditions (10% of saturation solubility) in their modified stirred Transwell® system [49]. The other concern regarding this apparatus is the mass-effect caused by the pile formation of particles collected on the membrane and the consequent wetting problems. Although the mass-effect dilemma can potentially affect the dissolution rate in USP vessels with larger volumes [37,47], it seems to be more challenging in volume-limited setups such as Transwell® [43,51]. Hence, it is vital to optimize the method with respect to the dissolution medium volume and the dose collection step to deliver a uniform and appropriate mass of drug to the apparatus.

9.3.5.2.3 Dissolvit®

The system was developed by Gerde et al. as a unique *in vitro* system to simulate the dissolution and absorption of the drug particles in the lungs. It simulates the physiological environment of the pulmonary system in terms of the air-blood barrier of the upper airways, mucus, lungs' blood flow, and the absorption of dissolved particles to the systemic circulation. Aerosols deposit uniformly on a glass coverslip by the PreciseInhale® aerosol generator. The particle mass is optimized to prevent the dose-effect and wetting problems, while high enough to be quantifiable after dissolution and absorption. In the dissolution chamber, the collected particles are in contact with the dissolution medium (mucus simulant). An optical microscope determines the dissolution of drug particles entering the dissolution medium based on the particle disappearance. Temperature is calibrated to 37 °C in the entire system. DissolvIt is considered to be a diffusion and flow-rate controlled apparatus. The feasibility of performing particle collection, dissolution, and quantification in a single apparatus is the greatest strength of this system. Pharmacokinetic assessment of two inhaled corticosteroids (fluticasone propionate and budesonide) in DissolvIt detected different dissolution/absorption profiles for compounds [78].

9.4 Mathematical description and statistical assessment of dissolution profiles

Several mathematical/statistical techniques have been used for assessing and describing the dissolution profiles to either characterize the behavior of a given formulation or identify differences or equivalence in the dissolution profile of different formulation. While these methods were initially developed for oral dosage forms and further extended to the other dosage forms, they can be adapted to describe and model the dissolution behavior of orally inhaled drug products. In general, dissolution profiles can be modeled by:

- Models linking dissolution rate to particle properties (e.g., Nernst-Brunner, and Noyes-Whittney).
- Model-Dependent Kinetic Approaches for describing dissolution/drug release-time profiles (e.g., First-order kinetics, without linking the behavior to physico-chemical properties).

A variety of statistical methods have also been used to test for statistically significant differences in drug dissolution/release profiles. These can be classified into the following categories:

- Model-independent methods (f1 and f2 tests).
- Analysis of variance:

  One-way analysis of variance (ANOVA) or t-student test to evaluate the difference between the means of two drug dissolution profiles in single time point dissolution or cumulative performance parameters (e.g., mean dissolution times; MDTs)
- Multivariate analysis of variance (MANOVA) assesses the difference between the means of two drug dissolution profiles across multiple time points. Statistical comparison of cumulative model parameter estimates [95].

Data analysis of dissolution/release profiles and linear/non-linear curve fitting can be performed using Excel add-in DDSolver, R software (e.g., R package deSolve or nlme), and SigmaPlot software [96,97].

9.4.1 Nernst-Brunner equation

The Nernst-Brunner equation is an adaptation of the Noyes-Whitney equation. It links the dissolution rate to particle and drug properties, such as surface area, and solubility. It integrates the diffusion layer concept of the Noyes-Whitney equation with Fick's 2nd law. This diffusion model considers a thin unstirred layer of the saturated solution surrounding the drug particles, from which diffusion takes place. Bisrat and Nystrom suggested that the diffusion layer of small particles might be smaller than that of large particles. This smaller diffusion layer results in a faster diffusion of the dissolved molecules from the surface of the particles to the bulk dissolution medium [98]. Consequently, the dissolution rate is described by the Nernst-Brunner equation [99,100]:

$$\frac{dM}{dt} = \sum_{i=1}^{n} \frac{DS_i(t)}{h_i(t)}(Cs - Ct) \tag{9.1}$$

where M is the total amount of undissolved drug; D is the diffusion coefficient; S_i is the surface area of particles; h_i is the diffusion layer thickness of the particles; C_s is the solubility of the drug the medium; and C_t concentration of the dissolved drug.

In this model, the shape of drug particles is considered to be spherical in geometry, and the overall surface area of particles can consequently be calculated for a given population of particles (e.g., those deposited on a defined stage during cascade impactor studies), from the associated particle radius (obtained from the particle size distribution) and the number of particles associated with a defined particle radius:

$$N = X_i(t=0)\left(\frac{4\pi r_i(t=0)^3 \rho}{3}\right)^{-1} \tag{9.2}$$

$$r_i(t) = \left(\frac{3X_i}{4\pi\rho N_i}\right)^{\frac{1}{3}} \tag{9.3}$$

$$S_i(t) = N4\pi r_i(t)^2 \tag{9.4}$$

where N is particle number at time t; X_i is the amount of undissolved drug; ρ is the density of drug particles; r_i is the radius of particles, and S_i denotes the surface area of particles at time t.

Additionally, considering that inhaled drug products are mostly non-ionized in the lung lining fluid and assuming the viscosity of the lung lining fluid is similar to that of the water, the diffusion coefficient (D) in Eq. 1.1 can be calculated by applying the Hayduk-Laudie equation as follows:

$$D = \frac{13.26 * 10^{-5}}{\eta_{water}^{1.4} * V_M^{0.589}} \tag{9.5}$$

where η_{water} is the dynamic viscosity of water at 37 °C, and V_M the molecular volume of the drug molecule.

The Nernst-Brunner equation describes dissolution kinetics throughout the dissolution process under the following assumptions: (1) A reduction in the particles' surface area during the dissolution process (2) All particles present in the medium will contribute to the total concentration of the dissolved drug. (3) The diffusion layer thickness of particles (if $r < 15$ μm radius) is related to the particle radius [101,102]:

$$h_i = r \tag{9.6}$$

As discussed in Section 3.4., for dissolution studies of orally inhaled drug products, a respirable dose of the drug is often collected on membrane. Having drug particles being captured on the surface or even embedded in the three-dimensional surface structure of a filter membrane might not allow using the above estimates of diffusion layer thickness (h_i) and effective surface area [13]. Likewise, stirring and agitation of the dissolution medium will alter the diffusion layer thickness (h_i) as well.

In the case of polydisperse drug particles, the particle size distribution of particles can be defined as the sum of discrete monodisperse fractions, e.g., those collected on a given bin during a cascade impactor experiment. Subsequently, the Nernst-Brunner equation can be used to describe the dissolution profile of each monodisperse fraction [103,104]. May et al. modeled the *in vitro* dissolution profiles of the USP paddle apparatus with the Nernst-Brunner equation to identify influencing factors on the dissolution rate of inhaled drugs. An abbreviated Andersen cascade impactor (aACI) and its modified version were used to collect respirable dose of inhalation powders. The obtained aerodynamic diameters were converted into geometric ones using the shape factor (k) and particle density (ρ) as following:

$$d_{aero} = d_{geo}\sqrt{\frac{\rho}{k}} \tag{9.7}$$

$$r_i = \frac{d_{geo}}{2} \tag{9.8}$$

The shape factor for spherical and cubic particles was considered 1 and 1.08, respectively. The surface area calculation was adapted for spherical and cubic particles, accordingly [15].

The Nernst-Brunner equation and its derivatives possess an advantage over model-independent kinetic functions in physiologically-based pharmacokinetic (PBPK) modeling approaches as they make allowance for physicochemical properties of the formulation. In this regard, some simulation software such as Mimetikos Preludium™ and GastroPlus™ have implemented the modified versions of Nernst-Bruner equation to model the *in vitro* dissolution data as an input for PBPK modeling [105−107].

Challenges with this approach are related to predicting the solubility in the epithelial lining fluid as it might differ from that observed in water. In addition, it is not trivial to account for the effects of formulation factors (e.g., particle/excipient interactions) on the active drug particle's surface area. Using cascade impactor studies to assess the aerodynamic particle size distribution of DPI formulations might also not allow determination of the primary geometric particle size of the API as API/carrier agglomerates might be responsible for the stage deposition. Lastly, the limited volume and resulting thinness of the alveolar lining fluid might affect the thickness of the diffusion layer [22].

9.4.2 Model-dependent kinetic functions [108,109]

Drug dissolution/release from solid dosage forms has also been described by kinetic models in which the dissolved amount of drug is expressed as a function of the time. A wide variety of mathematical models have been developed to fit the drug dissolution curves. Generally, upon applying a range of models, the values of the coefficient of determination (R^2) indicate which kinetic model is most appropriate for describing the dissolution profile of the drug. However, correlation coefficient (R), the sum of square residues (SSR), the mean square error (MS), or Akaike information criterion (AIC) might be used as the criterion for the most suitable model, as well [108]. Six commonly used drug release models will be discussed in this chapter.

9.4.2.1 Zero-order kinetics

Zero-order dissolution kinetics refers to the process of constant drug dissolution. In other words, the same amount of drug dissolves per unit of time. Low soluble drugs are more susceptible to exhibit a zero-order dissolution kinetic. However, having a mass-dependent dissolution process or permeation-controlled system can also lead to zero-order kinetics [62]. For instance, Riley et al., reported a zero-order dissolution kinetic for their flow-through cell apparatus; when the aerosolized dose was collected on a fiber filter and attached to a membrane filter embedded in a stainless-steel holder

[110]. Arora et al. described pseudo-zero-order kinetics for FP dissolution in Transwell® system due to its low aqueous solubility in distilled deionized water (DDW) [43]. Zero-order dissolution kinetics is expressed as:

$$Q_t = Q_0 + K_0 * t \tag{9.9}$$

where Q_t is the amount of drug dissolved in time t; Q_0 is the initial amount of the drug in the dissolution medium (it is usually zero); K_0 is zero-order release constant. Plotting the dissolution profile as the percent of drug dissolved versus time yields a straight line with a slope of K_0.

9.4.2.2 First-order kinetics

First-order kinetics implies where the dissolution rate is concentration-dependent, meaning the concentration of the dissolved drug in the bulk dissolution medium affects the dissolution rate. As the dissolved drug concentration increases in the bulk dissolution medium, dissolution will be slowed down, causing an exponential decay in the drug dissolution rate over time. First-order dissolution kinetics can be described as:

$$Q_t = Q_0(e^{-k_1 * t}) \tag{9.10}$$

where Q_t is the accumulated amount of drug dissolved in time t; Q_0 is the total amount of the drug delivered to the dissolution system at time $t = 0$; k_1 is the first-order dissolution constant. Plotting the dissolution profile as Ln % of drug undissolved vs. time yields a straight line with a slope of $-k_1$. May et al. remarked first-order kinetics model as the best descriptor of the obtained dissolution profiles with Franz cell and USP paddle apparatus [47].

9.4.2.3 Higuchi release model

This model describes drug release (dissolution and diffusion) from a dose collection unit as a diffusion dependent process based on Fick's law of diffusion and the square root of time. This model is based on the conditions that (i) drug particles are evenly distributed in the dose collection unit, (ii), dissolution of drug particles within the dose collection unit is rapid compared to the diffusion of dissolved drug molecules, (iii) the diffusion coefficient of the drug within the dose collection unit is constant and does not depend on time or the position of particles (iv) drug diffusion into the bulk dissolution medium takes place only in one dimension, (v), dissolved drug particles release into a perfect sink condition medium (vi) the dose collection unit does not swell or dissolve during drug release process [111].

Since the development of the Higuchi equation in 1961 [112], several mathematical rearrangements/modifications have been implemented to this equation. The simplified version of the Higuchi equation is presented as:

$$Q = Q_0 + K_H * t^{0.5} \tag{9.11}$$

Where Q is the amount of drug dissolved in time t; Q_0 is the initial amount of the drug dissolved in the dissolution medium (it is usually zero); K_H is the Higuchi dissolution constant. Plotting the dissolution profile as a cumulative percentage drug dissolved versus square root of time yields a straight line with a slope of K_H. The Higuchi dissolution constant (K_H) is associated to the diffusion coefficient of the drug (D), the total amount of the drug delivered to the dissolution system (A), and the saturated solubility of the drug (C_s) [111]:

$$K_H = A\,[2C_{init}DC_s]^{1/2} \tag{9.12}$$

Considering the conditions mentioned above, the Higuchi model seems to be a promising approach to modeling controlled-release dosage forms. For instance, Salama et al. modeled the experimental dissolution data of controlled release respiratory aerosols obtained from USP Apparatus 2, flow-through apparatus, and Franz cell apparatus with different kinetics models. Amongst the zero-order, first-order, Hixon–Crowell and Higuchi dissolution kinetic models, the Higuchi model described the data better, suggesting that wetting and diffusion are directing the dissolution rate of particles in these setups [48]. Interestingly, Son and McConville applied the Higuchi equation to model release profiles of hydrocortisone aerosolized particles from the membrane cassette in the mini-USP paddle apparatus. As a result, several unknown factors, such as the diffusion coefficient of the drug, initial loading concentration of the drug, and the volume of media inside the cassette were calculated [63].

9.4.2.4 Hixson-Crowell equation (cube-root law)

Similar to Nernst-Brunner tenets, Hixson and Crowell considered that the rate of dissolution is proportional to the available surface area, the diameter of the particles, and the concentration gradient. However, unlike the Nernst-Brunner equation, this approach addresses the time-dependent changes in the surface area of the dissolving particles in the dissolution medium. For instance, for spherical particles dissolving in a well-agitated bulk dissolution medium, the radius of the particle decreases continuously over time.

$$\sqrt[3]{M_t} = \sqrt[3]{M_0} - Kt \tag{9.13}$$

Where M_t is the undissolved mass of the particle at time t; M_0 is the total amount of the drug delivered to the dissolution system at time $t = 0$, and K is dissolution rate constant. Plotting the cube-root of the undissolved particle mass as a function of time yields a straight line with a slope of K, and the intercept will be the cube-root of the initial mass (M_0).

The cube-root law is based on three assumptions: (1) the concentration of dissolved drug in the bulk dissolution medium does not change significantly over time (probably due to perfect sink conditions), (2) particles are considered as spheres, and (3) the particles do not fragment into smaller pieces during dissolution process.

9.4.2.5 Korsmeyer-Peppas

Korsmeyer-Peppas, which is also known as the power law, is a semi-empirical release kinetic model. It is mostly used to characterize the drug release of polymeric dosage forms when the release mechanism is not clear, or more than one release mechanism could be involved. The exponential relationship between the release and the time is explained as:

$$\frac{M_t}{M_\infty} = k_{KP} * t^n \tag{9.14}$$

Where M_t is the mass of drug released at time t, M_∞ is the mass of drug released at infinite time; M_t/M_∞ is the fraction of drug released at time t; k_{KP} is the Korsmeyer-Peppas rate constant, and n is the parameter indicative of the drug release mechanism corresponding to Fickian or non-Fickian diffusion mechanism. Plotting the dissolution profile as log cumulative percentage drug release versus log time yields a straight line. Non-linear curve fitting of dissolution data up to where M_t/M_∞ is less than 60% will determine the exponent n.

Restani et al. developed a nano-in-micro DPI formulation to deliver chemotherapeutics to the lungs effectively. Nanoparticle vectors were loaded by paclitaxel and doxorubicin and micronized with chitosan to attain a controlled release drug delivery. *In-vitro* release studies were done by suspending the particles in citrate-phosphate buffer solution and sampling at pre-determined time points. The Korsmeyer-Peppas approach could perfectly capture the impact of different matrices on drug release [113].

9.4.2.6 Weibull

Weibull introduced the Weibull equation in 1951 as a distribution model [114]. It was adapted to the dissolution /release process by Langenbucher in 1972 [115]. This model can be applied to different forms of dissolution to describe the dissolution profile in terms of profile shape and time scale parameter. The Weibull equation expresses the accumulated amount of drug dissolved (M) as a function of time t:

$$M = M_0 * \left(1 - e^{\frac{-t^\beta}{\alpha}}\right) \tag{9.15}$$

This equation can be rearranged as:

$$\log\left[-\ln\left(1-\frac{M}{M_0}\right)\right]=\beta\log t-\log\alpha \tag{9.16}$$

where M_0 is the total amount of the drug delivered to the dissolution system at time $t = 0$; α is the scale parameter that defines the time scale of the process; β is the shape parameter which characterizes the curve as either exponential ($\beta = 1$), sigmoid, S-shaped, with upward curvature followed by a turning point ($\beta > 1$), or parabolic, with a higher initial slope followed by a consistent exponential phase ($\beta < 1$). Plotting the $-\ln(1 - M/M_0)$ vs. time (t) yields a straight line with the slope of shape parameter (β). The scale parameter is calculated from the ordinate value ($1/\alpha$) at time $t = 1$.

In the Weibull approach, the time required to dissolve 63% of the drug (t63) has been used as an applicable descriptor to compare dissolution rates. Bhagwat et al. used the Weibull probability distribution model to fit the dissolution data obtained with modified Transwell®. The t63 variable was utilized to assess the potential effects of Transwell® polycarbonate membrane and stirring of the medium on the dissolution rate of inhaled corticosteroids [116]. Another instance of this application was shown by Franek et al. Dissolution data obtained on a series of lipophilic compounds in the USP paddle apparatus, and Transwell® system were fitted to a Weibull model. To compare experimental- and Weibull-fitted dissolution profiles, the residual sum of squares (RSS) was computed in Excel. A one-way analysis of variance (ANOVA) was employed to compare the t63 of different compounds statistically. Correlation of the Weibull-fitted dissolution parameter (t63) to the literature reported mean pulmonary absorption time (MPAT) suggested that the t63 data indeed can be a bio-relevant indicator to differentiate between inhaled drug dissolution rates [82]. Hassoun et al. fitted the DissolvIt system dissolution data to a Weibull function. The shape and time scale parameters were estimated to model the dissolution of fluticasone propionate particles. The predicted dissolution curves were ultimately used as an input to the PBPK model [117].

The Weibull equation is a descriptive model and with no kinetic fundament to adequately characterize the dissolution kinetics of the drug. Furthermore, it does not consider a parameter indicative of the intrinsic dissolution rate of the drug. Hence, it is considered as an empiric model and has been the subject of some criticism due to this drawback.

9.4.3 Statistical methods for dissolution profile comparison

Several approaches have been proposed for assessing the differences between dissolution profiles. A model-independent mathematical approach was developed by Moore and Flanner [118] to compare dissolution profiles, and it is the recommended method by the FDA [19]. This approach, which is mainly used for comparison of dissolution profiles of the test (*T*) and reference (*R*) products, is based on a difference factor ($f1$) and a similarity factor ($f2$). The difference factor, $f1$, measures the percent error over all time points to determine if there is any evidence of a significant difference between the two dissolution profiles. While, the similarity factor, $f2$, uses an equivalence approach based on mean squared differences to determine if there is sufficient evidence of similarity between the two profiles. The mathematical approach is described as:

$$\text{Difference factor}, f1 = \left[\frac{\sum_{t=1}^{n} |R_t - T_t|}{\sum_{t=1}^{n} R_t}\right] * 100 \tag{9.17}$$

$$\text{Similarity factor}, f2 = 50 * log\left\{\left[1 + \frac{1}{n}\sum_{t=1}^{n}(R_t - T_t)^2\right]^{-0.5} * 100\right\} \tag{9.18}$$

where R_t and T_t are the mean percent drug dissolved/released at each time point for reference and test product, respectively, and n is the number of samples taken during the dissolution study. When $f2$ is equal to 100, the two profiles are deemed to be identical. Considering an average difference of 10% at all measured time points, the $f2$ value will be reflected as 50. FDA has set a standard that if the $f2$ value is greater than or equal to 50, this would indicate similarity between two dissolution profiles. FDA and EMA suggest the following acceptance criteria for solid oral dosage forms [19,119]:

- F1 values lower than 15 (i.e., 0–15) indicate no difference; there is no evidence of any difference.
- F2 values higher than 50 (i.e., 50–100) indicate similarity; there is evidence that there is no important difference.

When comparing dissolution profiles, it is recommended to have at least 12 individual dosage units of each of test and reference products. Since the mean data is used for the comparison, it is essential to ensure the percent coefficient of variation is less than 20% at the earlier time points and less than 10% at other time points. In the case of having a large variability in the data, utilizing a bootstrap approach can be helpful by providing a confidence interval. It is also recommended to utilize similar sampling time points between two dissolution/release profiles to ease the comparison of obtained data.

9.4.3.1 Mean dissolution time (MDT)

The mean dissolution time (MDT) is a model-independent parameter. It can be used as a metric to characterize and compare the dissolution behavior of inhalation products [32,47]. It can also be compared with non-compartmental pharmacokinetic parameters, such as the mean absorption time. Costa et al. proposed the following equation for calculating MDT [108]:

$$MDT = \frac{\sum_{j=1}^{n} \Delta M_j * t_j}{\sum_{j=1}^{n} \Delta M_j} \tag{9.19}$$

Where j is the sample number; n is the number of dissolution sample times; t_j is the midpoint between two consecutive time points, and ΔM_j denotes the additional amount of drug dissolved between two consecutive sampling points. MDT has been used in IVIVC approaches to probe for the correlation between the *in vitro* dissolution rate and the *in vivo* absorption rate [8].

9.5 Conclusion and regulatory considerations

A comprehensive understanding of drug product performance can be a game changing element for rational decision-making, facilitating the drug development phase, and eventually optimizing clinical study design strategies. Dissolution is not only a key tool in capturing the differences in formulation properties but a crucial input in IVIVR, IVIVC and PBPK studies to predict the *in vivo* performance of a product. The empirical approaches link the *in vitro* drug dissolution data to the *in vivo* PK data with the means of comparing MDT and MAT or correlating the dissolution rate to the absorption rate obtained from the deconvoluted systemic PK profile. More mechanistic models implement the dissolution kinetics as an input parameter alongside with other drug specific (e.g. PSD and solubility) and system specific (e.g. mucociliary clearance and permeability) parameters to predict the *in vivo* fate of a product.

While assessment of dissolution process and characterizing its kinetics is an integral part of the regulatory approval of orally administered drugs such as tablets and capsules, regulatory agencies have not provided any guidance on performing such studies for inhalation drugs. This issue might be related to the fact that the importance of the dissolution step for the pulmonary fate of lipophilic inhaled drugs has been recognized relatively late. For instance, the Inhalation Ad Hoc Advisory Panel of the USP in 2008 concluded that "there was no compelling evidence that dissolution was "kinetically and/or clinically crucial for currently approved" OIDPs" [6]. FDA realized the potential relevance of the dissolution studies around 2013 and provided funding for developing and evaluating a methodology for inhalation and nasal spray products in the second half of the last decade [120]. In the current regulatory landscape, the relevance of sensitive and robust dissolution tests in the regulatory area has been acknowledged for slowly dissolving inhalation products, however, future decisions need to be made by stakeholders on what methodology should be best employed. The selected approach might differ depending on whether the methodology is intended for

(I) assessment of new formulations in drug development phase, (II) batch release of products within the production phase or (III) is employed to compare test and reference products during the approval of generic formulations. A sample preparation step might not be as relevant for batch release purposes, while indeed, it should be integrated into a test that compares T and R products. Using the anatomical throat for sample preparation and dissolution experiments in either the Transwell® or one of the USP dissolution apparatuses might be advisable during the formulation and device development of the generic and new drug products. Within this context, the USP apparatus might have the advantage that dissolution profiles can be obtained under sink conditions in less than 3–5 hours, while Transwell® experiments generally take 24 hours, and sink conditions might not always be presented because of the small volumes employed.

Besides the implementation of dissolution studies for the regulatory purposes during the drug development and accordingly selection of an appropriate methodology, further clarification should be provided on what statistical tests are most appropriate to evaluate and compare inhalation profiles. Moreover, it needs to be rationalized for which compounds dissolution testing is relevant. Highlighting the importance of dissolution studies for specific compounds is another challenge that the currently ongoing activities in defining a biopharmaceutical classification system for inhalation drugs might be of great help.

References

[1] G. Hochhaus, H. Mollmann, H. Derendorf, R.J. Gonzalez-Rothi, Pharmacokinetic/pharmacodynamic aspects of aerosol therapy using glucocorticoids as a model, J. Clin. Pharmacol. 37 (1997) 881–892. Available from: https://doi.org/10.1002/j.1552-4604.1997.tb04262.x.

[2] J.M. Borghardt, B. Weber, A. Staab, C. Kunz, S. Formella, C. Kloft, Investigating pulmonary and systemic pharmacokinetics of inhaled olodaterol in healthy volunteers using a population pharmacokinetic approach, Br. J. Clin. Pharmacol. 81 (2016) 538–552. Available from: https://doi.org/10.1111/bcp.12780.

[3] J. Eriksson, E. Sjögren, H. Thörn, K. Rubin, P. Bäckman, H. Lennernäs, Pulmonary absorption - estimation of effective pulmonary permeability and tissue retention of ten drugs using an ex vivo rat model and computational analysis, Eur. J. Pharm. Biopharm. 124 (2018) 1–12. Available from: https://doi.org/10.1016/j.ejpb.2017.11.013.

[4] H. Mollmann, M. Wagner, S. Krishnaswami, H. Dimova, Y. Tang, C. Falcoz, et al., Single-dose and steady-state pharmacokinetic and pharmacodynamic evaluation of therapeutically clinically equivalent doses of inhaled fluticasone propionate and budesonide, given as Diskus or Turbohaler dry-powder inhalers to healthy subjects, J. Clin. Pharmacol. 41 (2001) 1329–1338. Available from: https://doi.org/10.1177/00912700122012913.

[5] A. Allen, P.J. Bareille, V.M. Rousell, Fluticasone furoate, a novel inhaled corticosteroid, demonstrates prolonged lung absorption kinetics in man compared with inhaled fluticasone propionate, Clin. Pharmacokinet. 52 (2013) 37–42. Available from: https://doi.org/10.1007/s40262-012-0021-x.

[6] V.A. Gray, A.J. Hickey, P. Balmer, N.M. Davies, C. Dunbar, T.S. Foster, et al., Erratum: the inhalation Ad Hoc advisory panel for the USP performance tests of inhalation dosage forms (Pharmacopeial Forum (2008) vol. 34 (4)), Pharmacopeial Forum 34 (2008) 1344.

[7] I. Coowanitwong, V. Arya, P. Kulvanich, G. Hochhaus, Slow release formulations of inhaled rifampin, AAPS J. 10 (2008) 342–348. Available from: https://doi.org/10.1208/s12248-008-9044-5.
[8] S. Bhagwat, U. Schilling, M.-J.J. Chen, X. Wei, R. Delvadia, M. Absar, et al., Predicting pulmonary pharmacokinetics from in vitro properties of dry powder inhalers, Pharm. Res. 34 (2017) 2541–2556. Available from: https://doi.org/10.1007/s11095-017-2235-y.
[9] J. Talton, J. , R. Singh, G. Hochhaus, Nanothin coatings for improved lung targeting of glucocorticoid dry powders: in vitro and in vivo characteristics, Proc. Respir. Drug Deliv., VII, Interpharm Press. Buffalo Grove, IL, 2000, p. 67. <http://faculty.virginia.edu/Nanoscale_Laser_Processing/AplandPDFs/RespiratoryDrugDelivery.pdf>.
[10] R. Baweja, The theory and practlce of industrial pharmacythird ed.J. Pharm. Sci. 76 (1987) 90–91. Available from: https://doi.org/10.1002/jps.2600760125.
[11] M.E. Aulton, K. Taylor, Part 1 Scientific principles of dosage form design, Aulton's Pharm. Des. Manuf. Med, Churchill Livingstone/Elsevier, Edinburgh, 2018, pp. 18–36.
[12] A.A. Noyes, W.R. Whitney, The rate of solution of solid substances in their own solutions, J. Am. Chem. Soc. 19 (1897) 930–934. Available from: https://doi.org/10.1021/ja02086a003.
[13] P. Bäckman, B. Olsson, Pulmonary drug dissolution, regional retention and systemic absorption: understanding their interactions through mechanistic modeling, in: Respir. Drug Deliv. 2020, 2020.
[14] P. Bäckman, U. Tehler, B. Olsson, P. Backman, U. Tehler, B. Olsson, Predicting exposure after oral inhalation of the selective glucocorticoid receptor modulator, AZD5423, based on dose, deposition pattern, and mechanistic modeling of pulmonary disposition, J. Aerosol Med. Pulm. Drug Deliv. 30 (2017) 108–117. Available from: https://doi.org/10.1089/jamp.2016.1306.
[15] S. May, B. Jensen, C. Weiler, M. Wolkenhauer, M. Schneider, C.-M. Lehr, Dissolution testing of powders for inhalation: influence of particle deposition and modeling of dissolution profiles, Pharm. Res. 31 (2014) 3211–3224. Available from: https://doi.org/10.1007/s11095-014-1413-4.
[16] P.J. Niebergall, G. Milosovich, J.E. Goyan, Dissolution rate studies II, J. Pharm. Sci. 52 (1963) 236–241. Available from: https://doi.org/10.1002/jps.2600520310.
[17] European Pharmacopoeia (Ph. Eur.), 5.17.1, Recommendations on dissolution testing, in: EDQM Council of Europe, 10th ed., 2019, p. 801.
[18] United States Pharmacopeia (USP), ⟨1092⟩ The dissolution procedure: volumetric apparatus, in: United States Pharmacopeial Convention, 2019, p. 7574.
[19] US Food and Drug Administration, Guidance for industry: dissolution testing of immediate release solid oral dosage forms, Cent. Drug Eval. Res. (CDER), US Dep. Heal. Hum. Serv. (1997).
[20] C.A.C. Ruge, J. Kirch, C.-M.M. Lehr, Pulmonary drug delivery: from generating aerosols to overcoming biological barriers-therapeutic possibilities and technological challenges, Lancet. Respir. Med. 1 (2013) 402–413. Available from: https://doi.org/10.1016/S2213-2600(13)70072-9.
[21] E. Boger, N. Evans, M. Chappell, A. Lundqvist, P. Ewing, A. Wigenborg, et al., Systems pharmacology approach for prediction of pulmonary and systemic pharmacokinetics and receptor occupancy of inhaled drugs, CPT Pharmacomet. Syst. Pharmacol. 5 (2016) 201–210. Available from: https://doi.org/10.1002/psp4.12074.
[22] J.M. Borghardt, C. Kloft, A. Sharma, Inhaled therapy in respiratory disease: the complex interplay of pulmonary kinetic processes, Can. Respir. J. 2018 (2018) 2732017. Available from: https://doi.org/10.1155/2018/2732017.
[23] European Medicines Agency/Committee for Medicinal Products for Human Use (CHMP), Reflection paper on the dissolution specification for generic solid oral immediate release products with systemic action, 2017. <www.ema.europa.eu/contact>.
[24] M.J. Rosen, J.T. Kunjappu, Characteristic features of surfactants, Surfactants Interfacial Phenom, fourth ed., John Wiley & Sons, Inc, Hoboken, NJ, 2012, pp. 1–38. Available from: https://doi.org/10.1002/9781118228920.ch1.
[25] M.J. Rosen, J.T. Kunjappu, Micelle formation by surfactants, Surfactants Interfacial Phenom, John Wiley & Sons, Inc, Hoboken, NJ, 2012, pp. 123–201. Available from: https://doi.org/10.1002/9781118228920.ch3.

[26] D. Sailaja, K.L. Suhasini, S. Kumar, K.S. Gandhi, Theory of rate of solubilization into surfactant solutions, Langmuir 19 (2003) 4014–4026. Available from: https://doi.org/10.1021/la0268698.

[27] A. Kumar, W. Terakosolphan, M. Hassoun, K.-K. Vandera, A. Novicky, R. Harvey, et al., A biocompatible synthetic lung fluid based on human respiratory tract lining fluid composition, Pharm. Res. 34 (2017) 2454–2465. Available from: https://doi.org/10.1007/s11095-017-2169-4.

[28] P.B. Myrdal, P. Sheth, S.W. Stein, Advances in metered dose inhaler technology: formulation development, AAPS PharmSciTech 15 (2014) 434–455. Available from: https://doi.org/10.1208/s12249-013-0063-x.

[29] F. Buttini, M. Miozzi, A.G. Balducci, P.G. Royall, G. Brambilla, P. Colombo, et al., Differences in physical chemistry and dissolution rate of solid particle aerosols from solution pressurised inhalers, Int. J. Pharm. 465 (2014) 42–51. Available from: https://doi.org/10.1016/j.ijpharm.2014.01.033.

[30] D.A. Lewis, P.M. Young, F. Buttini, T. Church, P. Colombo, B. Forbes, et al., Towards the bioequivalence of pressurised metered dose inhalers 1: design and characterisation of aerodynamically equivalent beclomethasone dipropionate inhalers with and without glycerol as a non-volatile excipient, Eur. J. Pharm. Biopharm. 86 (2014) 31–37. Available from: https://doi.org/10.1016/j.ejpb.2013.02.014.

[31] S. Mangal, H. Nie, R. Xu, R. Guo, A. Cavallaro, D. Zemlyanov, et al., Physico-chemical properties, aerosolization and dissolution of co-spray dried azithromycin particles with L-leucine for inhalation, Pharm. Res. 35 (2018) 28. Available from: https://doi.org/10.1007/s11095-017-2334-9.

[32] R. Price, J. Shur, W. Ganley, G. Farias, N. Fotaki, D.S. Conti, et al., Development of an aerosol dose collection apparatus for in vitro dissolution measurements of orally inhaled drug products, AAPS J. 22 (2020) 47. Available from: https://doi.org/10.1208/s12248-020-0422-y.

[33] G. Hochhaus, J. Bulitta, Using PBPK to link systemic PK to local delivery in the lung, in: ASCPT 2019 Pre-Conference Present, Washington, DC, 2019.

[34] D. Traini, P.M. Young, Formulation of inhalation medicines, in: P. Colombo, D. Traini, F. Buttini (Eds.), Inhal. Drug Deliv, John Wiley & Sons, Ltd, Chichester, 2013, pp. 39–40. Available from: https://doi.org/10.1002/9781118397145.

[35] O.R. Moss, Simulants of lung interstitial fluid, Health Phys. 36 (1979) 447–448. <http://www.ncbi.nlm.nih.gov/pubmed/489300>.

[36] W. Stopford, J. Turner, D. Cappellini, T. Brock, Bioaccessibility testing of cobalt compounds, J. Environ. Monit. 5 (2003) 675–680. Available from: https://doi.org/10.1039/B302257A.

[37] Y.-J. Son, M. Horng, M. Copley, J.T. McConville, Optimization of an in vitro dissolution test method for inhalation formulations, Dissolut. Technol. 17 (2010) 6–13. Available from: https://doi.org/10.14227/DT170210P6.

[38] S. Pham, T.S. Wiedmann, Note: dissolution of aerosol particles of budesonide in survanta™, a model lung surfactant, J. Pharm. Sci. 90 (2001) 98–104. Available from: https://doi.org/10.1002/1520-6017(200101)90:1<98::AID-JPS11>3.0.CO;2-5.

[39] B.B. Eedara, I.G. Tucker, S.C. Das, A STELLA simulation model for in vitro dissolution testing of respirable size particles, Sci. Rep. 9 (2019) 18522. Available from: https://doi.org/10.1038/s41598-019-55164-0.

[40] S. Radivojev, S. Zellnitz, A. Paudel, E. Fröhlich, Searching for physiologically relevant in vitro dissolution techniques for orally inhaled drugs, Int. J. Pharm. 556 (2019) 45–56. Available from: https://doi.org/10.1016/j.ijpharm.2018.11.072.

[41] N. Boisa, N. Elom, J.R. Dean, M.E. Deary, G. Bird, J.A. Entwistle, Development and application of an inhalation bioaccessibility method (IBM) for lead in the PM 10 size fraction of soil, Environ. Int. 70 (2014) 132–142. Available from: https://doi.org/10.1016/j.envint.2014.05.021.

[42] M. Hassoun, P.G. Royall, M. Parry, R.D. Harvey, B. Forbes, Design and development of a biorelevant simulated human lung fluid, J. Drug Deliv. Sci. Technol. 47 (2018) 485–491. Available from: https://doi.org/10.1016/j.jddst.2018.08.006.

[43] D. Arora, K.A. Shah, M.S. Halquist, M. Sakagami, In vitro aqueous fluid-capacity-limited dissolution testing of respirable aerosol drug particles generated from inhaler products, Pharm. Res. 27 (2010) 786–795. Available from: https://doi.org/10.1007/s11095-010-0070-5.

[44] F. Buttini, A.G. Balducci, G. Colombo, F. Sonvico, S. Montanari, G. Pisi, et al., Dose administration maneuvers and patient care in tobramycin dry powder inhalation therapy, Int. J. Pharm. 548 (2018) 182–191. Available from: https://doi.org/10.1016/j.ijpharm.2018.06.006.

[45] C. Duret, N. Wauthoz, T. Sebti, F. Vanderbist, K. Amighi, Solid dispersions of itraconazole for inhalation with enhanced dissolution, solubility and dispersion properties, Int. J. Pharm. 428 (2012) 103–113. Available from: https://doi.org/10.1016/j.ijpharm.2012.03.002.

[46] J.T. McConville, K.A. Overhoff, P. Sinswat, J.M. Vaughn, B.L. Frei, D.S. Burgess, et al., Targeted high lung concentrations of itraconazole using nebulized dispersions in a murine model, Pharm. Res. 23 (2006) 901–911. Available from: https://doi.org/10.1007/s11095-006-9904-6.

[47] S. May, B. Jensen, M. Wolkenhauer, M. Schneider, C.M. Lehr, Dissolution techniques for in vitro testing of dry powders for inhalation, Pharm. Res. 29 (2012) 2157–2166. Available from: https://doi.org/10.1007/s11095-012-0744-2.

[48] R.O. Salama, D. Traini, H.-K. Chan, P.M. Young, Preparation and characterisation of controlled release co-spray dried drug-polymer microparticles for inhalation 2: evaluation of in vitro release profiling methodologies for controlled release respiratory aerosols, Eur. J. Pharm. Biopharm. 70 (2008) 145–152. Available from: https://doi.org/10.1016/j.ejpb.2008.04.009.

[49] S. May, S. Kind, B. Jensen, M. Wolkenhauer, M. Schneider, C.-M. Lehr, Miniature in vitro dissolution testing of powders for inhalation, Dissolut. Technol. 22 (2015) 40–51. Available from: https://doi.org/10.14227/DT220315P40.

[50] G. Pilcer, R. Rosière, K. Traina, T. Sebti, F. Vanderbist, K. Amighi, et al., New co-spray-dried tobramycin nanoparticles-clarithromycin inhaled powder systems for lung infection therapy in cystic fibrosis patients, J. Pharm. Sci. 102 (2013) 1836–1846. Available from: https://doi.org/10.1002/jps.23525.

[51] M. Rohrschneider, S. Bhagwat, R. Krampe, V. Michler, J. Breitkreutz, G. Hochhaus, Evaluation of the transwell system for characterization of dissolution behavior of inhalation drugs: effects of membrane and surfactant, Mol. Pharm. 12 (2015) 2618–2624. Available from: https://doi.org/10.1021/acs.molpharmaceut.5b00221.

[52] M.C. Fontana, T.L. Durli, A.R. Pohlmann, S.S. Guterres, R.C.R. Beck, Polymeric controlled release inhalable powder produced by vibrational spray-drying: one-step preparation and in vitro lung deposition, Powder Technol. 258 (2014) 49–59. Available from: https://doi.org/10.1016/j.powtec.2014.03.011.

[53] C.I. Grainger, M. Saunders, F. Buttini, R. Telford, L.L. Merolla, G.P. Martin, et al., Critical characteristics for corticosteroid solution metered dose inhaler bioequivalence, Mol. Pharm. 9 (2012) 563–569. Available from: https://doi.org/10.1021/mp200415g.

[54] N.M. Davies, M.R. Feddah, A novel method for assessing dissolution of aerosol inhaler products, Int. J. Pharm. 255 (2003) 175–187. Available from: https://doi.org/10.1016/S0378-5173(03)00091-7.

[55] N.A. Dennis, H.M. Blauer, J.E. Kent, Dissolution fractions and half-times of single source yellowcake in simulated lung fluids, Health Phys. 42 (1982) 469–477. Available from: https://doi.org/10.1097/00004032-198204000-00007.

[56] C. Colombo, A.J. Monhemius, J.A. Plant, Platinum, palladium and rhodium release from vehicle exhaust catalysts and road dust exposed to simulated lung fluids, Ecotoxicol. Environ. Saf. 71 (2008) 722–730. Available from: https://doi.org/10.1016/j.ecoenv.2007.11.011.

[57] J. Wragg, B.E.N. Klinck, The bioaccessibility of lead from Welsh mine waste using a respiratory uptake test, J. Environ. Sci. Health A. Tox. Hazard. Subst. Environ. Eng. 42 (2007) 1223–1231. Available from: https://doi.org/10.1080/10934520701436054.

[58] C. Julien, P. Esperanza, M. Bruno, L.Y. Alleman, Development of an in vitro method to estimate lung bioaccessibility of metals from atmospheric particles, J. Environ. Monit. 13 (2011) 621–630. Available from: https://doi.org/10.1039/c0em00439a.

[59] M. Takaya, Y. Shinohara, F. Serita, M. Omo-Ogasawara, N. Otaki, T. Toya, et al., Dissolution of functional materials and rare earth oxides into pseudo alveolar fluid, Ind. Health 44 (2006) 639–644. Available from: https://doi.org/10.2486/indhealth.44.639.

[60] G.M. Kanapilly, G. Raabe, C.H.T. Goh, R.A. Chimentit, O.G. Raabe, C.H.T. Goh, et al., Measurement of in vitro dissolution of aerosol particles for comparison to in vivo dissolution in the lower respiratory tract after inhalation, Health Phys. 24 (1973) 497–507. Available from: https://doi.org/10.1097/00004032-197305000-00004.

[61] J.E. Gray, G.S. Plumlee, S.A. Morman, P.L. Higueras, J.G. Crock, H.A. Lowers, et al., In vitro studies evaluating leaching of mercury from mine waste calcine using simulated human body fluids, Environ. Sci. Technol. 44 (2010) 4782–4788. Available from: https://doi.org/10.1021/es1001133.

[62] T. Riley, D. Christopher, J. Arp, A. Casazza, A. Colombani, A. Cooper, et al., Challenges with developing in vitro dissolution tests for orally inhaled products (OIPs), AAPS PharmSciTech 13 (2012) 978–989. Available from: https://doi.org/10.1208/s12249-012-9822-3.

[63] Y.-J. Son, J.T. McConville, Development of a standardized dissolution test method for inhaled pharmaceutical formulations, Int. J. Pharm. 382 (2009) 15–22. Available from: https://doi.org/10.1016/j.ijpharm.2009.07.034.

[64] A. Floroiu, M. Klein, J. Krämer, C.-M. Lehr, Towards standardized dissolution techniques for in vitro performance testing of dry powder inhalers, Dissolut. Technol. 25 (2018) 6–18. Available from: https://doi.org/10.14227/DT250318P6.

[65] J. Fiegel, C. Ehrhardt, U.F. Schaefer, C.M. Lehr, J. Hanes, Large porous particle impingement on lung epithelial cell monolayers - toward improved particle characterization in the lung, Pharm. Res. 20 (2003) 788–796. Available from: https://doi.org/10.1023/A:1023441804464.

[66] M. Bur, H. Huwer, L. Muys, C.-M. Lehr, Drug transport across pulmonary epithelial cell monolayers: effects of particle size, apical liquid volume, and deposition technique, J. Aerosol Med. Pulm. Drug Deliv. 23 (2010) 119–127. Available from: https://doi.org/10.1089/jamp.2009.0757.

[67] J.T. McConville, N. Patel, N. Ditchburn, M.J. Tobyn, J.N. Staniforth, P. Woodcock, Use of a novel modified TSI for the evaluation of controlled-release aerosol formulations. I, Drug Dev. Ind. Pharm. 26 (2000) 1191–1198. Available from: https://doi.org/10.1081/DDC-100100991.

[68] J.P. Mitchell, S.C. Nichols, Meeting report: summary of Abbreviated Impactor Measurement Workshop organized by the European Pharmaceutical Aerosol Group, Ther. Deliv. 2 (2011) 307–310. Available from: https://doi.org/10.4155/tde.11.6.

[69] M. Svensson, E. Berg, Measuring the fine particle dose using inter-stage filters in the NGI: an overview of two methods, AIM Spec. Work. Drug Deliv. to Lung 21, The Aerosol Society, Edinburgh, 2010, pp. 382–385.

[70] Copley Scientific, Copley Scientific introduces a simple device for inhaled dose dissolution testing. <https://www.copleyscientific.com/news-events/copley-scientific-introduces-a-simple-device-for-inhaled-dose-dissolution-testing/>. 2020 (accessed 10.02.20).

[71] S. Hein, M. Bur, T. Kolb, B. Muellinger, U.F. Schaefer, C.-M. Lehr, The Pharmaceutical Aerosol Deposition Device on Cell Cultures (PADDOCC) in vitro system: design and experimental protocol, Altern. Lab. Anim. 38 (2010) 285–295. Available from: https://doi.org/10.1177/026119291003800408.

[72] S.P. Velaga, J. Djuris, S. Cvijic, S. Rozou, P. Russo, G. Colombo, et al., Dry powder inhalers: an overview of the in vitro dissolution methodologies and their correlation with the biopharmaceutical aspects of the drug products, Eur. J. Pharm. Sci. 113 (2018) 18–28. Available from: https://doi.org/10.1016/j.ejps.2017.09.002.

[73] Copley Scientific, Quality Solutions for the Testing of Pharmaceuticals [Brochure], Nottingham, 2016.

[74] M. Sakagami, H. Li, J.J. Venitz, In vivo-relevant transwell dish-based dissolution testing for orally inhaled corticosteroid products, Pharm. Res. 36 (2019) 95. Available from: https://doi.org/10.1007/s11095-019-2635-2.

[75] T.J. Franz, Percutaneous absorption on the relevance of in vitro data, J. Invest. Dermatol. 64 (1975) 190–195. Available from: https://doi.org/10.1111/1523-1747.ep12533356.

[76] M. Haghi, D. Traini, M. Bebawy, P.M. Young, Deposition, diffusion and transport mechanism of dry powder microparticulate salbutamol, at the respiratory epithelia, Mol. Pharm. 9 (2012) 1717–1726. Available from: https://doi.org/10.1021/mp200620m.

[77] Corning, Transwell® Permeable Supports, Fish. Sci. (2017). <https://beta-static.fishersci.com/content/dam/fishersci/en_US/documents/programs/scientific/brochures-and-catalogs/guides/corning-transwell-permeable-supports-guide.pdf>.

[78] P. Gerde, M. Malmlöf, L. Havsborn, C.-O.O. Sjöberg, P. Ewing, S. Eirefelt, et al., DissolvIt: an in vitro method for simulating the dissolution and absorption of inhaled dry powder drugs in the lungs, Assay. Drug Dev. Technol. 15 (2017) 77–88. Available from: https://doi.org/10.1089/adt.2017.779.

[79] G. Pilcer, R. Rosiere, K. Traina, T. Sebti, F. Vanderbist, K. Amighi, New co-spray-dried tobramycin nanoparticles-clarithromycin inhaled powder systems for lung infection therapy in cystic fibrosis patients, J. Pharm. Sci. 102 (2013) 1836–1846. Available from: https://doi.org/10.1002/jps.23525.

[80] F. Depreter, A. Burniat, D. Blocklet, S. Lacroix, M. Cnop, F. Fery, et al., Comparative pharmacoscintigraphic and pharmacokinetic evaluation of two new formulations of inhaled insulin in type 1 diabetic patients, Eur. J. Pharm. Biopharm. 80 (2012) 4–13. Available from: https://doi.org/10.1016/j.ejpb.2011.09.015.

[81] J.Y.S. Tay, C.V. Liew, P.W.S. Heng, Dissolution of fine particle fraction from truncated Anderson cascade impactor with an enhancer cell, Int. J. Pharm. 545 (2018) 45–50. Available from: https://doi.org/10.1016/j.ijpharm.2018.04.048.

[82] F. Franek, R. Fransson, H. Thörn, P. Bäckman, P.U. Andersson, U. Tehler, Ranking in vitro dissolution of inhaled micronized drug powders including a candidate drug with two different particle sizes, Mol. Pharm. 15 (2018) 5319–5326. Available from: https://doi.org/10.1021/acs.molpharmaceut.8b00796.

[83] N. Wauthoz, P. Deleuze, A. Saumet, C. Duret, R. Kiss, K. Amighi, Temozolomide-based dry powder formulations for lung tumor-related inhalation treatment, Pharm. Res. 28 (2011) 762–775. Available from: https://doi.org/10.1007/s11095-010-0329-x.

[84] Y.-J. Son, J.T. McConville, Preparation of sustained release rifampicin microparticles for inhalation, J. Pharm. Pharmacol. 64 (2012) 1291–1302. Available from: https://doi.org/10.1111/j.2042-7158.2012.01531.x.

[85] K. Šimková, B. Joost, G. Imanidis, Production of fast-dissolving low-density powders for improved lung deposition by spray drying of a nanosuspension, Eur. J. Pharm. Biopharm. 146 (2020) 19–31. Available from: https://doi.org/10.1016/j.ejpb.2019.11.003.

[86] W. Wang, Q.T. Zhou, S.-P. Sun, J.A. Denman, T.R. Gengenbach, N. Barraud, et al., Effects of surface composition on the aerosolisation and dissolution of inhaled antibiotic combination powders consisting of colistin and rifampicin, AAPS J. 18 (2016) 372–384. Available from: https://doi.org/10.1208/s12248-015-9848-z.

[87] M. Mezzena, S. Scalia, P.M. Young, D. Traini, Solid lipid budesonide microparticles for controlled release inhalation therapy, AAPS J. 11 (2009) 771–778. Available from: https://doi.org/10.1208/s12248-009-9148-6.

[88] J.G.Y. Chan, H.-K. Chan, C.A. Prestidge, J.A. Denman, P.M. Young, D. Traini, A novel dry powder inhalable formulation incorporating three first-line anti-tubercular antibiotics, Eur. J. Pharm. Biopharm. 83 (2013) 285–292. Available from: https://doi.org/10.1016/j.ejpb.2012.08.007.

[89] A.G. Balducci, H. Steckel, F. Guarneri, A. Rossi, G. Colombo, F. Sonvico, et al., High shear mixing of lactose and salmeterol xinafoate dry powder blends: Biopharmaceutic and aerodynamic performances, J. Drug Deliv. Sci. Technol. 30 (2015) 443–449. Available from: https://doi.org/10.1016/j.jddst.2015.07.010.

[90] K. Möbus, J. Siepmann, R. Bodmeier, Zinc–alginate microparticles for controlled pulmonary delivery of proteins prepared by spray-drying, Eur. J. Pharm. Biopharm. 81 (2012) 121–130. Available from: https://doi.org/10.1016/j.ejpb.2012.01.018.

[91] S. Scalia, R. Salama, P. Young, D. Traini, Preparation and in vitro evaluation of salbutamol-loaded lipid microparticles for sustained release pulmonary therapy, J. Microencapsul. 29 (2012) 225–233. Available from: https://doi.org/10.3109/02652048.2011.646326.

[92] A.G. Balducci, H. Steckel, F. Guarneri, A. Rossi, G. Colombo, F. Sonvico, et al., High shear mixing of lactose and salmeterol xinafoate dry powder blends: biopharmaceutic and aerodynamic performances, J. Drug Deliv. Sci. Technol. 30 (2015) 443–449. Available from: https://doi.org/10.1016/j.jddst.2015.07.010.

[93] R.V. Pai, R.R. Jain, A.S. Bannalikar, M.D. Menon, Development and evaluation of chitosan microparticles based dry powder inhalation formulations of rifampicin and rifabutin, J. Aerosol Med. Pulm. Drug Deliv. 29 (2015) 179–195. Available from: https://doi.org/10.1089/jamp.2014.1187.

[94] S. Arora, M. Haghi, C.-Y. Loo, D. Traini, P.M. Young, S. Jain, Development of an inhaled controlled release voriconazole dry powder formulation for the treatment of respiratory fungal infection, Mol. Pharm. 12 (2015) 2001–2009. Available from: https://doi.org/10.1021/mp500808t.

[95] T. Riley, D. Christopher, IPAC-RS Conference: Bringing Value to the Patient in a Changing World, in: Dissolution Test. Inhaled Prod., Washington DC, 2011.

[96] Y. Zhang, M. Huo, J. Zhou, A. Zou, W. Li, C. Yao, et al., DDSolver: an add-in program for modeling and comparison of drug dissolution profiles, AAPS J. 12 (2010) 263–271. Available from: https://doi.org/10.1208/s12248-010-9185-1.

[97] Y.B. Wang, A.B. Watts, J.I. Peters, S. Liu, A. Batra, R.O. Williams, In vitro and in vivo performance of dry powder inhalation formulations: comparison of particles prepared by thin film freezing and micronization, AAPS PharmSciTech 15 (2014) 981–993. Available from: https://doi.org/10.1208/s12249-014-0126-7.

[98] M. Bisrat, C. Nyström, Physicochemical aspects of drug release. VIII. The relation between particle size and surface specific dissolution rate in agitated suspensions, Int. J. Pharm. 47 (1988) 223–231. Available from: https://doi.org/10.1016/0378-5173(88)90235-9.

[99] E. Brunner, Reaktionsgeschwindigkeit in heterogenen Systemen, Zeitschrift Für Phys. Chemie 47U (1904) 56. Available from: https://doi.org/10.1515/zpch-1904-4705.

[100] A. Dokoumetzidis, P. Macheras, A century of dissolution research: from Noyes and Whitney to the biopharmaceutics classification system, Int. J. Pharm. 321 (2006) 1–11. Available from: https://doi.org/10.1016/j.ijpharm.2006.07.011.

[101] G. Sertsou, Analytical derivation of time required for dissolution of monodisperse drug particles, J. Pharm. Sci. 93 (2004) 1941–1944. Available from: https://doi.org/10.1002/jps.20119.

[102] K. Sugano, Theoretical comparison of hydrodynamic diffusion layer models used for dissolution simulation in drug discovery and development, Int. J. Pharm. 363 (2008) 73–77. Available from: https://doi.org/10.1016/j.ijpharm.2008.07.002.

[103] J.B. Dressman, D. Fleisher, Mixing-tank model for predicting dissolution rate control of oral absorption, J. Pharm. Sci. 75 (1986) 109–116. Available from: https://doi.org/10.1002/jps.2600750202.

[104] R.J. Hintz, K.C. Johnson, The effect of particle size distribution on dissolution rate and oral absorption, Int. J. Pharm. 51 (1989) 9–17. Available from: https://doi.org/10.1016/0378-5173(89)90069-0.

[105] B. Olsson, E.C. Ab, About the PK module, Mimetikos Preludium TM - PK Modul. User Man, Emmace Consulting AB, Lund, 2018, pp. 4–5.

[106] Simulations Plus Inc, 4.2.4.2 Dissolution, in: GastroPlus™ Manual, Version 9.7, Lancaster, CA, 2019, p. 170.

[107] A.T. Lu, M.E. Frisella, K.C. Johnson, Dissolution modeling: factors affecting the dissolution rates of polydisperse powders, Pharm. Res. An. Off. J. Am. Assoc. Pharm. Sci. 10 (1993) 1308–1314. Available from: https://doi.org/10.1023/A:1018917729477.

[108] P. Costa, J.M. Sousa Lobo, Modeling and comparison of dissolution profiles, Eur. J. Pharm. Sci. 13 (2001) 123–133. Available from: https://doi.org/10.1016/S0928-0987(01)00095-1.

[109] J. Siepmann, F. Siepmann, Mathematical modeling of drug dissolution, Int. J. Pharm. 453 (2013) 12–24. Available from: https://doi.org/10.1016/j.ijpharm.2013.04.044.

[110] T. Riley, A. Jones, M.B. Huescar, T. Roche, In vitro method for determining the dissolution rate of inhalation aerosols, RDD2008 2 (2008).

[111] J. Siepmann, N.A. Peppas, Higuchi equation: derivation, applications, use and misuse, Int. J. Pharm. 418 (2011) 6–12. Available from: https://doi.org/10.1016/j.ijpharm.2011.03.051.

[112] T. Higuchi, Rate of release of medicaments from ointment bases containing drugs in suspension, J. Pharm. Sci. 50 (1961) 874–875. Available from: https://doi.org/10.1002/jps.2600501018.

[113] R.B. Restani, R.F. Pires, A. Tolmatcheva, R. Cabral, P.V. Baptista, A.R. Fernandes, et al., POxylated dendrimer-based nano-in-micro dry powder formulations for inhalation chemotherapy, ChemistryOpen 7 (2018) 772–779. Available from: https://doi.org/10.1002/open.201800093.

[114] W. Weibull, Wide applicability, J. Appl. Mech. 103 (1951) 293–297.

[115] F. Langenbucher, Linearization of dissolution rate curves by the Weibull distribution, J. Pharm. Pharmacol. 24 (1972) 979–981. Available from: https://doi.org/10.1111/j.2042-7158.1972.tb08930.x.

[116] S. Bhagwat, M. Rohrschneider, L. Sandmi, G. Hochhaus, S. Alfadehl, G. Hochhaus, Development of an in vitro dissolution test method for inhaled corticosteroids, JAMPD 26 (2013) A58–A59.

[117] M.L. Tan, P. Zhao, L. Zhang, Y.F. Ho, M.V.S. Varma, S. Neuhoff, et al., Use of physiologically based pharmacokinetic modeling to evaluate the effect of chronic kidney disease on the disposition of hepatic CYP2C8 and OATP1B drug substrates, Clin. Pharmacol. Ther. 105 (2019) 719–729. Available from: https://doi.org/10.1002/cpt.1205.

[118] J.W. Moore, H.H. Flanner, Mathematical comparison of dissolution profiles, Pharm. Technol. 20 (1996) 64–75.

[119] European Medicines Agency/Committee for Medicinal Products for Human Use (CHMP)/EWP/QWP/1401/98 Rev.1, Guideline on the investigation of bioequivalence, Eur. Med. Agency (2010).

[120] US Food and Drug Administration, FYs 2013-2017 Regulatory Science Report: Locally-Acting Orally Inhaled and Nasal Drug Products, 2017. <https://www.fda.gov/drugs/resourcesforyou/consumers/buyingusingmedicinesafely/genericdrugs/ucm592245.htm>.

Appendix 9.A1 Schematic configuration of compendial particle sizing apparatuses

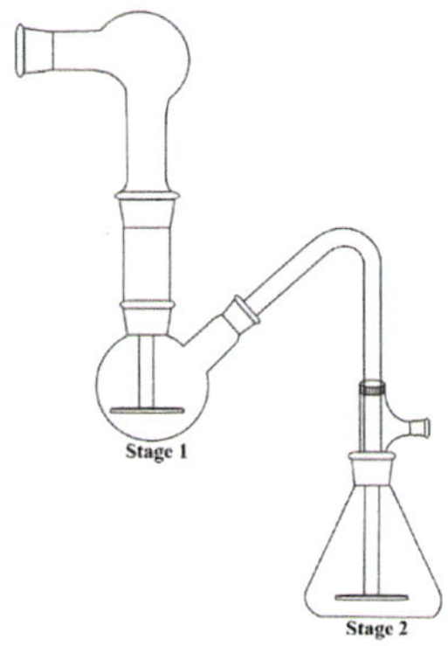

Twin impinger (TI)

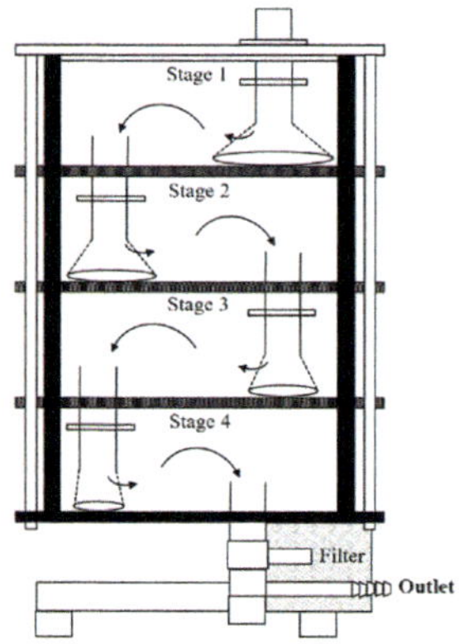

Multi-stage liquid impinger (MSLI)

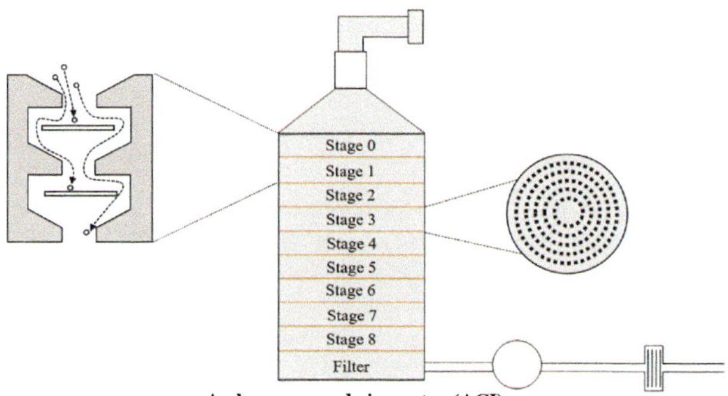

Andersen cascade impactor (ACI)

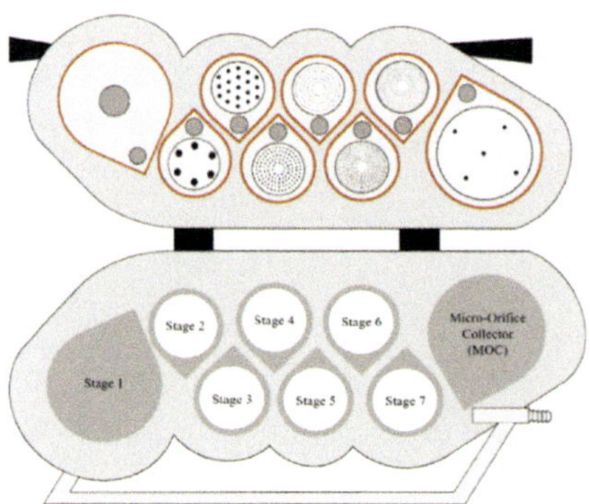

Next generation impactor (NGI)

CHAPTER 10

Epithelial permeability and drug absorption in the lungs

Zachary Enlo-Scott, Magda Swedrowska and Ben Forbes
Institute of Pharmaceutical Science, King's College London, London, United Kingdom

10.1 Absorptive clearance from the lungs

Absorption is one of the routes by which inhaled drugs are cleared from the lungs. Although some inhaled drugs have a site of action at the mucosal surface, e.g. mucolytic agents or antibiotics, most inhaled drugs require an absorption step into or across the respiratory epithelium to reach their site of action. For respiratory medicines, the site of action is in the lung tissue. Alternatively, the lungs can be used as a port of entry to deliver drugs for action elsewhere in the body. If drug is delivered in solid particle form, dissolution in lung lining fluid is a pre-absorptive step. Before and after the drug is in solution, absorptive clearance is in competition with non-absorptive clearance mechanisms such as metabolism, uptake by macrophages and mucociliary clearance [Chapter 8 "Non-absorptive clearance from airways"].

For inhaled medicines that are delivered for therapeutic action in the lungs, direct delivery to the target organ is beneficial for fast onset of therapeutic activity. Direct access to the target organ for labile molecules avoids systemic degradative losses that reduce bioavailability and enables delivery of drugs which are poorly absorbed when delivered via the oral route. The rate and extent of absorption from the lungs determines the bioavailability of drugs that are inhaled for systemic activity. For example, insulin absorption after inhalation is faster or comparable to delivery by subcutaneous injection. Although the respiratory epithelium is less permeable to large peptide or protein drugs than small molecules, absorption is sufficient for inhalation to be a promising route of delivery for systemic delivery of biopharmaceuticals.

The principal barrier to absorption of inhaled drugs is the respiratory epithelium, which transitions markedly in cell types and structure from the airways (trachea and bronchi) to the alveoli (Fig. 10.1). Highly permeable drugs are generally absorbed from the lungs rapidly and exhibit good bioavailability. The volume and type of fluid surface, area of the epithelium, the thickness of the epithelium, tightness of the intercellular junctions and cell phenotype (including transporter expression) all affect the permeability barrier presented by the epithelium. The physicochemical properties of the drug also determine

Inhaled Medicines
DOI: https://doi.org/10.1016/B978-0-12-814974-4.00004-3

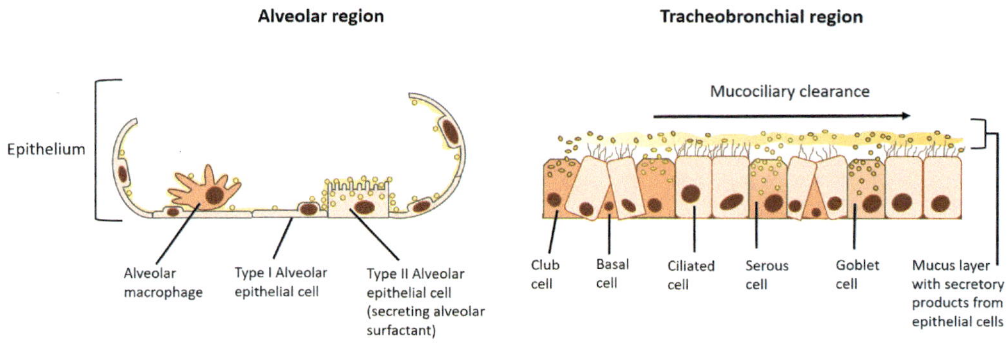

Figure 10.1 Schematic representation of the airway epithelium.

permeability [see Chapter 2 "The API"], including molecular size, lipophilicity, polarity (hydrogen bonding, charge), the affinity of the compound for plasma proteins and lung tissue. Small, nonpolar and lipophilic molecules are absorbed across the epithelium transcellularly and are highly permeable in the lungs [1].

10.2 Epithelial drug transport

The transport of molecules across epithelial barriers can occur via one or more of the following mechanisms: passive paracellular or transcellular transport, carrier-mediated uptake or efflux transport or vesicular mechanisms (Fig. 10.2) [2,3].

The paracellular route of drug transport is the permeation of drug between the cells that form the continuous epithelial barrier. The lung epithelium is a layer of cells interconnected by tight and more loosely adherent junctions that acts as a barrier to solute transfer and regulates the transport of molecules by paracellular route [4]. Structurally, tight junctions between adjacent cells consist of more than 40 proteins such as actin-binding proteins, cytoplasmic and adhesive transmembrane proteins. One of the most important protein families in the transmembrane proteins group is claudin, which is responsible for the selectivity of the intercellular junction. As the transport is limited by the size of the intercellular pores, and the relatively small proportion of epithelial surface area that these constitute, only small hydrophilic compounds use the paracellular route as their main route of transepithelial transport, with transfer in absorptive and secretory directions via diffusion according to their concentration gradient [5].

The transcellular route of drug transport is available to lipophilic compounds that are able to traverse lung epithelial cells by partition into the plasma membrane. Many compounds exhibit weak basic or acidic characteristics that determine the proportion of drug existing in the unionized form that can partition into the membrane lipid bilayer according to pH. Most compounds permeate biological membranes

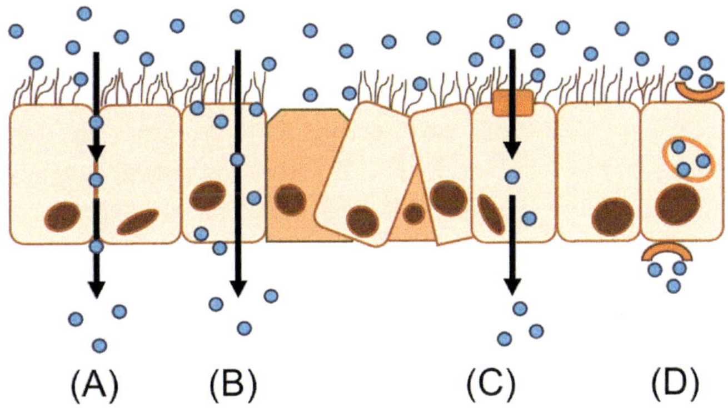

Figure 10.2 Schematic diagram of pathways for drug absorption across lung epithelial monolayer. Passive diffusion can occur via (A) the paracellular or (B) the transcellular route, (C) active transport and (D) transcytosis.

under passive diffusive mechanisms dictated by the concentration gradient as described by Fick's first law of diffusion. When the concentration on one side of the cell membrane is higher than the other side, net drug movement occurs by diffusion in an energy-free process [6]. When transport depends on partition and diffusion, the rate of drug flux is dictated by size, charge, lipophilicity and concentration of the active molecules [7]. For oral drug absorption, Lipinski and colleagues have described limiting physicochemical characteristics factors as a 'Rule of Five'. Accordingly, most small lipophilic compounds are well able to cross epithelia. Other compounds may require a drug delivery system to enhance uptake across cell membranes [1,4].

Drug transporters are present in epithelial cell membranes and provide an energy-dependent pathway for molecules to pass the hydrophobic lipid bilayer of cell membranes. The membrane transport proteins are specific to particular classes of compounds [8]. The protein transporters that are likely to influence the disposition of inhaled compounds belong to two protein superfamilies: (i) the ATP-binding cassette (ABC) superfamily (P-glycoprotein (P-gp), multidrug resistance-associated proteins (MRP), and breast cancer resistance protein (BCRP)) and (ii) the solute linked carrier (SLC) superfamily (organic anion/cation transporters and peptide transporters). Protein transporters (ABC and SLC) have specific bindings sites and outer or inner gates that can be opened to allow transport [3,9]. Active transport mediated by protein transporters requires a contribution of metabolic energy to enable directional transport of molecules in an energetically antagonistic direction and are subject to saturation when all binding sites are occupied, leading to a maximal transport rate. Other transporters can facilitate solute transport down a concentration gradient without spending energy (known as facilitated diffusion) for example glucose, oxygen, carbon dioxide and amino acids [10].

The expression of protein transporters within the lung tissue may have an impact on the pulmonary disposition and pharmacokinetics of inhaled drugs [11,12]. Drug transporters may affect the rate and extent of distribution of compounds to the target site, accumulation in specific cell types and retention of the drug in the lung, as well as absorption into the systemic circulation [11,13]. In addition, drugs may affect the transport of endogenous substances across biological membranes in the lungs [9,14]. As ABC and SLC transporters have been identified in human lungs (Table 10.1), it is important

Table 10.1 Summary of ABC and SLC transporters in human lung tissue.

Protein	Localization	Possible substrates	References
ABC family			
P-gp	Bronchial epithelial cells • Alveolar macrophages • Alveolar epithelium • Serous cells of bronchial mucosa • Bronchial capillaries	Broad range of substrates; corticosteroids (e.g. budesonide, beclomethasone dipropionate), Chemotherapeutics	[13,15–19]
MRP1	• Bronchi/bronchiolar epithelium • Alveolar macrophages • Bronchial ciliated epithelial cells • Mucus secreting cells of bronchial	Doxorubicin Pacitaxel	[9,20–22]
MRP2	• Primary bronchial and epithelial cells	Cisplatin Clarithromycin	[9,21,23]
BCRP	Bronchial epithelial cells and seromucinous glands • Small endothelial capillaries of the lung • Alveolar pneumocytes	Cisplatin	[15,21,24]
SLC family			
OCT1	• Bronchial ciliated cells • Airway smooth muscle cells	Salbutamol Beclomethasone dipropionate Budesonide Formoterol Pentamidine Salmeterol xinafoate Para-amino-salicylic acid	[9,25]

(*Continued*)

Table 10.1 (Continued)

Protein	Localization	Possible substrates	References
OCT2	Bronchial ciliated cells • Basal cells	Beclomethasone dipropionate Budesonide Fluticasone propionate Ipratropium bromide Levofloxacin Pentamidine Tiotropium bromide Para-amino-salicylic acid	[9,25]
OCT3	• Bronchial basal cells • Bronchial intermediate cells • Bronchial epithelial ciliated cells • Pulmonary blood vessels • Airway smooth muscle cells	Salbutamol Budesonide Ciprofloxacin Fluticasone propionate Formoterol Pentamidine Salmeterol xinafoate	[9,25]
OCTN2	Airway epithelial cells	Ciprofloxacin Formoterol Ipratropium bromide Tiotropium bromide	[9,26]

to investigate their role in drug transport across epithelium after inhalation. Transporters in the lung can also mediate uptake of drugs from the systemic circulation causing local drug accumulation with consequences for pulmonary targeting or toxicity.

Vesicle-mediated endocytosis and transcytosis provide alternative transport mechanisms across cell layers. In particular, the type I alveolar epithelial cells and the endothelial cells, which lie at an interface between the airspace and blood environments, are very thin and have an ability to convey molecule transcellularly in a passive vesicular formation process [27]. The process commences with the induction of membrane curvature by specific coat proteins (clathrin and caveolin) to form a vesicle at the mucosal surface that encapsulates drug-containing extracellular fluid [28]. The vesicles are then transported across the cytoplasm and fuse with basolateral cell membrane releasing the internal contents on the serosal side [29].

Drug permeability is based on the transport rate (flux) of the drug across the epithelium, which is a composite measure taking into account all routes of transepithelial transport. In the absence of saturable mechanisms, permeability is not concentration dependent and can be calculated as an apparent permeability coefficient (P_{app}), such that P_{app} = drug flux $\times$ 1/concentration $\times$ surface area.

10.3 Lung retention

Lung retention may be defined as localized accretion of inhaled drugs, leading to significantly elevated or prolonged drug concentrations within the lungs. Retention of drugs within the lungs is beneficial because it increases lung exposure and reduces systemic concentrations, although excessive lung accumulation may be a source of toxicological concern. Lung retention mechanisms may occur in extracellular or intracellular lung compartments, thereby encompassing effects including low solubility/slow dissolution rate, tissue binding, ion trapping within the cytosol or lysosomes, active drug transport, molecular drug interactions with airway surface liquid or surfactant lipids, and evasion of non-absorptive clearance processes.

10.3.1 Extracellular interactions

Within the extracellular environment of the lungs, interaction between the drug and the mucus or lung surfactant that lines the mucosal surface may influence drug retention. Airway mucus may bind drug or constitute a significant physical barrier. Negatively charged lipids within lung surfactant lipids may interact with drugs via molecular interactions. The site of drug deposition in the lungs will determine the nature of the mucosal environment, which is dominated by mucus in the airways and lung surfactant in the alveolar region.

Within the conducting airways of the respiratory tract, the respiratory epithelium is ciliated, with the cilia immersed in a periciliary liquid layer, that resides beneath a more viscous protective gel layer of mucus. The function and mechanism of mucociliary clearance is described in Chapter 8 [Chapter 8 "Non-absorptive clearance from airways"], and its effects on drug absorption are discussed in Section 10.4.1. Evasion of mucociliary clearance provides a mechanism for enhancing lung retention. After deposition, slow dissolution increases the probability of particle clearance by mucociliary clearance. However, if dissolution and mucus penetration is rapid or mucociliary clearance can be slowed then retention in the lung may be increased [30]. The use of mucoadhesive particles has been extensively researched. Mucoadhesion has historically been explored as a method of increasing particle residence time within the lungs for pulmonary drug delivery, however the adhesive trapping of particles within mucus may increase elimination by mucociliary clearance [31]. Based on this, there is evidence that non-adhesive particles capable of penetrating mucus (possibly through mucolytic abilities) increase lung retention. It has been shown that mucus layer thickness, which ranges from 2 to 30 μm in the lungs of healthy individuals, may be tenfold as thick in patients with cystic fibrosis, which may have implications for drug delivery in obstructive airway disease [32,33].

Molecular interactions between drug and respiratory mucus also affect penetration and lung retention. An example of this is the antibiotic amikacin, which has limited diffusion in mucus due to electrostatic interactions with mucin fibers [33], which necessitates the use of a liposomal formulation for this drug to reach its target. Alternative methods to increase mucus penetration have focused on the functionalization of carriers with 2 or 5 kDa polyethylene glycol (PEG), to reduce adhesive interactions [33,34]. Following penetration of the mucus gel layer, interactions with the periciliary liquid, may also lead to drug retention. *Ex vivo* studies suggest that particles coated with endogenous phospholipids may lead to retention before gradually being displaced into the mucus [35].

Interactions with phospholipids in surfactant secreted from type II pneumocytes occur for particles deposited in the alveolar region. The association of phospholipids with hydrophobic cationic drugs provides a mechanism for drug retention in the lungs [36]. Phospholipid interactions may also prolong lung residence of hydrophobic proteins and polymeric nanoparticles [37,38].

10.3.2 Cell and tissue sequestration

In addition to retention of drugs within the extracellular environment of the lung, there is also the potential for drugs to be retained or "trapped" within the intracellular environment, which may occur through active transport or passive mechanisms. Passive drug sequestration within lung cells may be the result of ion trapping within the cytosol or lysosomes [39]. Ion trapping is the process by which high concentrations of a chemical may accumulate within cells based on differences between intracellular and extracellular pH and the pKa of the xenobiotic [40]. Non-ionized basic drugs may penetrate the cell membrane and become ionized in the lower pH cytosolic environment and are thereby "trapped" [40]. The pH in the extracellular environment is pH 7.4 in healthy lungs compared to pH 7.2 intracellularly [41]. Ion trapping occurs as the cell membrane is permeable to non-ionized lipid soluble molecules and poorly permeable to ionized molecules. Upon entering a reducing environment, a basic molecule may be protonated by accepting an H^+ ion leading to ion trapping, while the trans-membrane equilibrium is maintained for non-ionized molecules which continue to enter the cell and become trapped.

Ion trapping may also occur within membranous organelles such as mitochondria or vesicles, although the most notable example of ion trapping is within lysosomes. Lysosomal trapping occurs by the same process described above, however as lysosomes are acidic organelles (pH 4–5) the effect is much more pronounced, especially for cationic or lipophilic/amphiphilic amine drugs (Fig. 10.3). Lysosomal trapping restricts drug diffusion back into the cytosol or extracellular environment [9] and there is *in vitro* and *in vivo* evidence of this being a relevant mechanism of lung retention of inhaled β-adrenergic compounds such as formoterol and salmeterol [39]. Lysosomal trapping has also been suggested as a drug retention mechanism for accumulation of

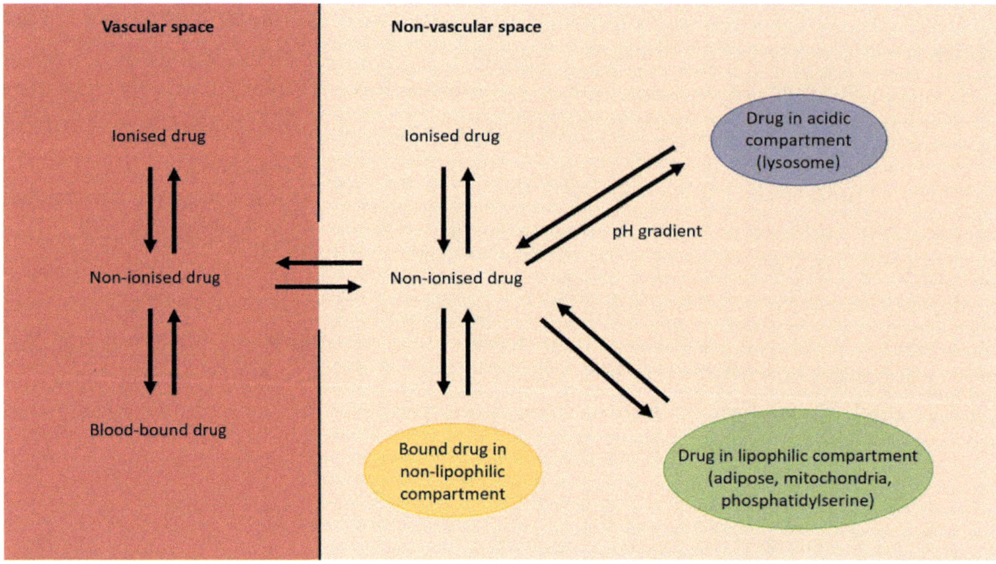

Figure 10.3 Mechanisms of drug trapping, partitioning and binding that contribute to retention in lung tissue.

respiratory drugs in human alveolar macrophages [42]. Lysosomal trapping may have toxicological implications if high concentrations of lysosomotropic drugs increase lysosomal pH, reduce lysosomal function and adversely affect cell health.

Finally, non-specific binding to lung lipids and proteins is a significant mode of drug retention within the lungs, and in some circumstances may influence the drug absorption. It has been predicted that for some drugs with high tissue binding coefficients, as much as 50% of the inhaled dose may be retained by smooth muscle in the tracheobronchial airways, or up to 5% within the alveolar epithelium [43]. Fluticasone propionate shows a high affinity to the human lung glucocorticoid receptor and has also shown to have a high degree of non-specific binding in lung tissue [44], leading to lung retention which has been demonstrated *in vitro* and clinically.

10.4 Experimental models for lung permeability

10.4.1 Mucus models

Drug disposition in the lung is complex and the fate of the inhaled particles depends on their solubility and deposition site [45]. Drug absorption is in competition with non-absorptive clearance mechanisms (Fig. 10.4).

A significant proportion of the respirable particles reaching lungs deposit in the mucus in the conducting zone, which acts as first biological barrier for drug permeability. The volume and the composition of the mucus depends on the location in the lungs, with

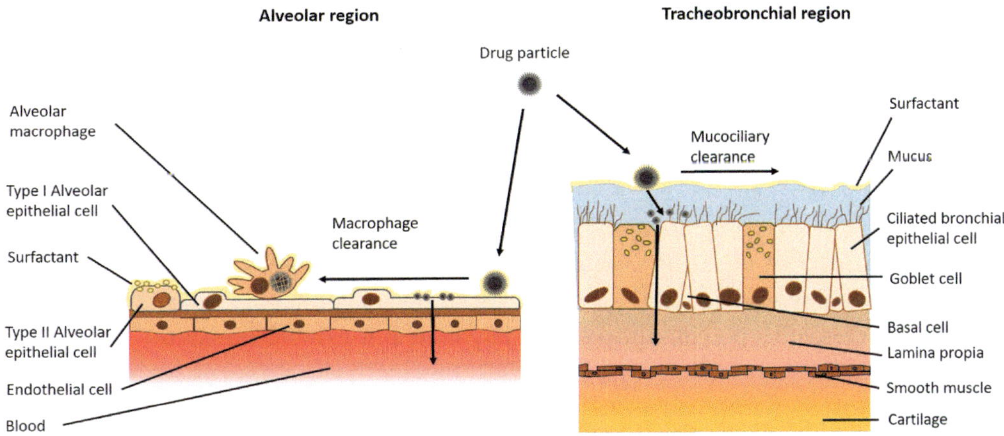

Figure 10.4 Pathway to drug absorption in the alveoli and tracheobronchial region with competing clearance mechanisms by macrophages and mucociliary clearance, respectively.

a thickness of 10–30 μm in the trachea, 2–5 μm in the bronchi [46–48] and gradually diminishes in depth along the length of airways [46]. In contrast, the alveolar epithelium surface-lining layer is much thinner in the absence of mucus and ranges from 0.1 μm in the respiratory bronchioles to 0.05 μm in the alveoli [46]. In healthy airways, mucus is a complex hydrogel composed mainly of water (~96%), electrolytes, non-mucin proteins, phospholipids and mucins with a pH of ~6.6 in healthy individuals [49]. Mucins are encoded by different *muc* genes and currently 13 (out of 21) have been detected in the pulmonary system [50]. These *muc* genes can be divided into three subgroups: (i) gel-forming mucins (MUC5AC, MUC5B, MUC2, MUC8, MUC19), (ii) membrane-associated mucins (MUC1, MUC4, MUC11, MUC13, MUC15, MUC16, MUC20) and (iii) secreted but not polymerized (MUC7). In healthy airways, the MUC5AC is typically expressed by the goblet cells, whereas mucosal cells of the submucosal glands express in majority MUC5B [50,51]. Overproduction and overexpression of mucins is a key element of many chronic pulmonary diseases, including cystic fibrosis, asthma and chronic obstructive pulmonary disease [52].

In healthy lungs, the mucus layer is a dynamic barrier that covers epithelial cells, providing a selective permeability barrier for drugs. The ability of particles to penetrate mucus depends on the charge, size, solubility and lipophilicity of the molecule [53,54]. The gel forms polyvalent adhesive interactions with deposited particles as powerful trapping mechanism in which the negative charges on the glycosylated parts of mucins fibers bind the positive charges on the surface of particles [55]. In addition to the ionic interactions, mucin fibers can also interact with hydrophobic parts on the surface of particles to form the multiple low-affinity adhesive interactions.

The potential role of airway mucus in the dissolution and permeability of inhaled drugs has not been fully investigated and a limited number of studies report respirable particle interactions with airway mucus. As drug permeability through the mucus layer is particularly difficult to investigate *in vivo*, *in vitro/ex vivo* models are more commonly used to investigate the parameters influencing the disposition of inhaled compounds following deposition on the airway mucosal surface.

Mucus can be collected from tissue and used for permeability studies in a variety of experimental configurations (e.g. Ussing chamber, Transwell setup), but mostly it is used to study mucus-drug interactions. While the native respiratory mucus represents the complex structure of mucus *in vivo* and can be collected using an endotracheal tube for use in permeability studies [56,57] it is difficult to obtain and highly variable in composition. As an alternative porcine mucus is widely used as it exhibits similarities with human mucus and its more readily accessible [58,59]. Porcine tracheal mucus has similar rheological properties and structure to human airway secretions [60]. Porcine mucus has been used to assess the penetration of nanocarriers designed for inhaled delivery [59] and the permeability of two compounds with different physico-chemical properties (salbutamol sulfate and indomethacin) is significantly impaired by mucus [60]. A limitation of many studies is that purified mucin gels lack the structure and barrier properties (e.g. gel-forming properties) of native mucus [61].

Mucus-secreting cell models can also be used to study particle permeability and impact of drugs on mucus secretion. The most commonly used cell culture models rely on the use of chamber system in which a donor and a receptor chamber are separated by a cell layer. Cell lines that secrete mucus can be grown on cell culture inserts (e.g. Transwell inserts) or Ussing chambers (vertical or horizontal set up) or Franz cells. Bronchiolar epithelial cells from a variety of origins can be used for permeability studies, however the majority of them do not secrete airway mucins [34,62]. The bronchial cell line Calu-3 is one of the few respiratory cell lines that forms tight junctions and secretes mucin (MUC5AC) in an air-liquid interface culture (AIC). The culture conditions are very important as cells grown in AIC secrete more mucus and exhibit a more physiological transepithelial electrical resistance (TEER) compared to cells grown using liquid covered culture (LCC) [60,63,64].

The impact of mucus on the permeability of selected compounds (testosterone, diazepam, propranolol, mannitol) has been investigated using Calu-3 cells grown at LCC and AIC [64]. The study showed that the transport of the most lipophilic compound (logP 5.5) was completely reduced across AIC Calu-3 cells. Drugs with logP 3–4 had significantly decreased transport across AIC compared to LCC cells. Whereas, the transport of hydrophilic compounds with low logP was similar across both systems. Another study has shown that drug permeability across Calu-3 cells correlates well with apparent permeability values obtained in primary cultured rabbit tracheal epithelial cells which secrete mucus and drug absorption measured *in vivo* using rats [65]. Nonetheless, primary cells from healthy donors are used as the gold standard, as these contain a heterogenous cell population including secretory, ciliated, and basal cells that secrete airway tissue specific mucin [66]. Primary bronchial cells can also be harvested from patients with pulmonary conditions to incorporate the disease phenotype in the culture model [67]. However, access to primary cells is limited, the variability between donors is high, cell culture is expensive, and the cells can be passaged only a few times. Recent advances in organ on-chip microfluidic models allow drug permeability across mucus and epithelial layers to be studied in a system that aims to capture the complexity of the 'whole organ'. One airway organ on-chip model is composed of human bronchial epithelial cells that were cultured for 14 days in AIC conditions. The cultured cells expressed barrier function (cell polarity and formation of tight junction) and mucus secretion rate similar to *in vivo* respiratory epithelium [68,69]. While all above models may be used to increase understanding of the role mucus plays in drug permeability, they do not represent the full range of complex interactions between the mucus layer and epithelium that occur *in vivo*.

10.4.2 *In vitro* cell models

Drug permeability is commonly measured using epithelial cells cultured *in vitro* as permeability barriers, the best example of this being the intestinal Caco-2 cell line used for predicting permeability within the gastrointestinal tract [70]. With regards to permeability within the lung, *in vitro* models have also been developed by culturing various cells as epithelial permeability barriers, with varying success depending on the cell type and culturing conditions. For this purpose, cells are typically cultured on a semi-permeable polycarbonate or polyester membrane, supporting cell growth whilst also having the capacity for xenobiotics to diffuse through membrane pores, e.g. Transwell®, Snapwell® and ThinCert® cell culture inserts (Fig. 10.5). Cells may be grown either directly on the Transwell membrane or the membrane may be precoated with a solution of collagen, fibronectin, basement membrane extract, vitronectin or other coating solutions to aid cell adhesion or mimic the extracellular matrix [71,72]. The epithelial cells may be cultured using LLC or AIC, as described in the

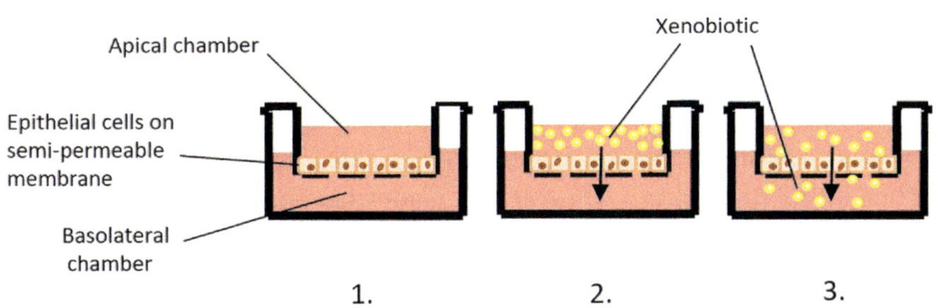

Figure 10.5 Diagram showing lung epithelial cells cultured on a transwell filter (1), the addition of drug to the apical chamber (2), and the permeation of drug across the epithelial barrier into the basolateral chamber (3).

preceding section, with the culture method having implications for cell differentiation and polarization of the membranes. Additionally, cells can be cocultured either on the apical side, or by adding at least one cell type to either side of the membrane e.g. epithelial and endothelial/fibroblasts/dendritic cells. Regardless of the culturing method, cells must reach confluence and form a permeability barrier which depends on expression of functional tight junction proteins (e.g. zonula occludens-1, claudins, e-cadherin). Cell layer barrier properties may be assessed by measuring TEER values (Ω/cm^2) or transepithelial potential difference (mV), where higher values indicate the formation of a greater barrier to solute flux [73,74]. The growth of cells on culture inserts like these allows for the direct measurement of xenobiotic transport from one side of the membrane to the other.

Drugs may be delivered to cell layers using an aerosol if at air-liquid interface, or more commonly by introducing the xenobiotic in solution to the apical chamber [75,76]. Whilst use of aerosols is more physiologically relevant, solutions are easier to apply, do not require specialist equipment and can maintain the "infinite" dose which is required for sink conditions and calculation of P_{app} values. Alternatives to cell layers are a variety of newer systems models involving 3D hydrogels, spheroid/organoid cultures and microfluidic models. A wide variety of respiratory epithelial cell types have been investigated as barrier-formers including bronchial and alveolar cell lines, primary cells and cocultures, the most prominent of which are described below.

10.4.3 Bronchial cell lines

Various bronchial cell lines have been explored as permeability models for the tracheobronchial region of the respiratory tract, under the rationale that using respiratory epithelial cells derived from a particular region of the lungs can model passive permeability along with active transport mechanisms, metabolism and potentially mucus-interactions that operate within that region. Drug transport mechanisms are the most studied feature and Calu-3 and 16HBE14o- cells are the most well characterized models [73,74].

10.4.3.1 Calu-3 cells

Of the commercially available human bronchial cell lines, Calu-3 is the most well characterized as a drug permeability model and the most widely used due to its suitability for use in drug transport experiments. Calu-3 is an adenocarcinoma-derived lung epithelial cell line from a 25 year old Caucasian male, established in 1975 [73]. The cell line is suitable as a permeability model due to its expression of functional tight junction proteins such as zonula occludens-1, e-cadherin and claudin-3 [63]. Calu-3 also produce secretions containing mucins also found *in vivo* such as mucin 5a. TEER values for the cell line vary depending on culturing conditions, but several researchers have reported values of 300–800 Ω/cm^2 for AIC and 600–2500 Ω/cm^2

for LLC [63,65,69]. The high TEER values are indicative of the robust permeability barrier formed, which has been shown to restrict transport of paracellular permeability markers such as mannitol, atenolol, sodium fluorescein and FITC-dextran similarly to the respiratory epithelium *in vivo* [63,65,69]. The correlation of Calu-3 P_{app} values with effective permeability (P_{eff}) data from isolated perfused lung (IPL) experiments and Caco-2 P_{app} data highlight the utility of this cell line as a permeability model [45,65,74]. Calu-3 are sometimes cited as expressing cilia, but this is not well established [63,77]. Another limitation is low expression of drug transporters such as P-glycoprotein [73,78], although Calu-3 has been used as an *in vitro* model to study active ion transport as the cell lines expresses significant amounts of the cystic fibrosis transmembrane conductance regulator and mechanisms such as endocytosis have also been shown to occur within this cell line [79].

10.4.3.2 16HBE14o- cells

The 16BHE14o- cell line is derived from a 1 year old male heart and lung patient, and was established from normal bronchial epithelial cells which were immortalized with a pSVori- plasmid [74]. The cells are commercially available and together with Calu-3 represent one of the most common cell lines used as a bronchial epithelial permeability model. 16BHE14o- cells form a functional polarized epithelial barrier with a "cobblestone" appearance consistent with the morphology of primary bronchial epithelial cells. As a permeability model, 16HBE14o- cells have been shown to form functional tight junctions, including expression of zonula occludens-1, e-cadherin and claudin-3, and produce typical TEER values of 500 Ω/cm^2 when cultured under submerged conditions [76]. Researchers have generally reported significantly lower TEER values for 16HBE14o- when under AIC [76]. A variety of compounds with different permeability across 16HBE14o- cells have been studied and a correlation between 16HBE14o- P_{app} values and IPL P_{eff} values has been shown [74,80]. Studies have shown that 16HBE14o- cells possess active transport mechanisms mediated by CFTR and P-glycoprotein [81].

Limitations of 16HBE14o- cells include generally lower TEER values and higher permeability than Calu-3 cell layers, a requirement for longer culturing (up to 21 days) and that the cells have not been shown to produce significant volumes of mucus. Benefits of the 16HBE14o- cell line are its non-cancer phenotype and expression of drug transporters.

10.4.3.3 Other bronchial cell lines

Several other human bronchial cell lines are commonly used in *in vitro* research, including BEAS-2B, NCI-H292, H460 and H727, but evidence suggests that they are limited in their suitability to model drug transport in the respiratory epithelium. Generally, these cells produce low TEER values under LLC or AIC conditions consonant with a relatively low expression of functional tight junctions. BEAS-2B cells are popular in biomedical research, but poor cell layer barrier formation is the key reason that the cell line is not commonly used for permeability studies [69,82,83]. There is continuing interest in developing immortalized cell lines with specific phenotypes which brings the prospect that future bronchial epithelial cell lines may be optimized for permeability modeling.

10.4.4 Alveolar cell lines

In comparison to bronchial cell lines, there are limited *in vitro* models of the alveolar epithelial permeability barrier. This is due to challenges with isolation, purification and differentiation of lung cells that have a Type I alveolar cell phenotype and the subsequent development of cell lines that reflect this phenotype.

10.4.4.1 A549 cells

Of the commercially available alveolar cell lines, A549 is by far the most widely used in pharmaceutical research. This is primarily due to its ease of use, affordability, ready availability and lack of alternative alveolar-like cell lines. A549 cells have been explored by several researchers as a model of alveolar permeability, either as a monoculture or as a coculture including fibroblasts, macrophages or dendritic cells. However, whilst A549 has proved invaluable as an *in vitro* model for studying drug effects in applications such as lung cancer, lung toxicity and tuberculosis, it has been shown to be unsuitable as a permeability model [72,84,85]. A549 has repeatedly been shown to produce low TEER values, little functional tight junctions and to be highly permeable to paracellular markers of transport (such as atenolol, FITC-Dextran, sodium fluorescein or mannitol) in stark contrast to primary human or rat alveolar cells which consistently produce significantly higher permeability barriers [69,86]. The TEER values for A549 are typically reported as $<100\ \Omega/cm^2$ under both AIC and LLC conditions, and whilst higher TEER values may be achieved these are often the result of the formation of a multi-layer of cells rather than the monolayer of epithelial cells that exist *in vivo*.

The inability for A549 to form an appropriate permeability barrier may relate to the cells being derived from a lung adenocarcinoma and diverging from normal alveolar epithelial cell phenotype in terms of barrier formation. A549 cells produce various phospholipids associated with surfactant, which is typical of Type II alveolar cells, but do not differentiate into Type I alveolar cells which represent the ~95% of the surface area of the alveolar region and thereby constitute the majority of the permeability barrier.

10.4.4.2 TT1 cells

Whilst not commercially available, the non-cancer derived alveolar cell line TT1 has been investigated as a permeability barrier. TT1 has the benefit of being an immortalized non-cancer derived cell line, that thereby may possess a phenotype more similar to a "normal" alveolar cell [85,87]. Additionally, TT1 displays the phenotype of a Type I like alveolar cell, in contrast to A549 that displays the phenotype of a Type II alveolar cell. The cells were produced by the Tetley group at Imperial College London, following the protocol described by Kemp et al. [87]. Several studies have been performed investigating their use as permeability model, in comparison to A549. Whilst published data shows that they develop low TEER values similar to A549 under AIC or LCC conditions [72], more recent work has shown that slightly higher TEER values may be achieved by altering the culturing conditions (>140 Ω/cm^2) with paracellular permeability of sodium fluorescein being similar to Calu-3 under certain experimental conditions. Despite this, the cell line still generates a significantly lower permeability barrier that what is observed using primary alveolar cells and therefore currently has limited use as an alveolar permeability model [72].

10.4.4.3 hAELVi cells

One of the more recently generated alveolar cell lines used to model the alveolar epithelium *in vitro* are hAELVi cells. Immortalized from primary alveolar cells using a proprietary method, these commercially available alveolar cells have a type I alveolar cell phenotype and have been shown to form a permeability barrier reflective of the alveolar epithelium [88]. As it is a newer model, less data is available, but it has been shown to express the tight junction protein zonula occludens-1, generate TEER values >1000 Ω/cm^2 and significantly exclude paracellular transport of sodium fluorescein [89], when cultured under either AIC or LCC conditions. One of the limitations with this cell line in comparison to those typically used is cost and the requirement for special culturing medium and coating solutions.

10.4.4.4 NCI-H441 cells

NCI-H441 cells have also been used as a model of the alveolar epithelial permeability barrier, with some researchers highlighting their utility for transport studies [90]. Variable TEER values have been reported, ranging from 100 to 1000 Ω/cm^2, however there is relatively consistent evidence of functional Zonula occludens-1, E-cadherin, claudin-1 and claudin-3 expression when visualized using immunohistochemistry. The variability in TEER values likely relates to the culturing conditions used, with different researchers highlighting that the use of the corticosteroid dexamethasone is required to achieve TEER values $\geq$300 Ω/cm^2 [90,91]. Under these conditions, NCI-H441 has been shown to significantly exclude paracellular permeability markers such as sodium fluorescein and FITC-Dextran (4–70 kDa). NCI-H441 cells have been shown to have similar expression to primary human alveolar cells of several drug transporters, including P-gp, OCT1, OCT2, OCT3, OCTN1, and OCTN2 [90]. Other researchers have shown paracellular permeability of NCI-H441 to be more similar to Calu-3 than A549 and the cell line has been used to investigate alveolar fluid homeostasis, another useful consideration in any alveolar permeability model [92]. Potential limitations with this cell line are its variable phenotype (similarities to club cells and type II alveolar cells) and its origin from a papillary adenocarcinoma within pericardial fluid [90].

10.4.5 Primary cell models

Although bronchial and alveolar cell lines are more widely used as *in vitro* lung permeability models due to their ease of use, experimental reproducibility, lack of genetic variation and amenability to high throughput assays, primary cells are also commonly used and provide several advantages. The main benefit of primary bronchial and alveolar cells as *in vitro* permeability models is their greater similarity to the epithelium *in vivo*. This includes the expression of tight junction proteins, drug transporters, ion channels and the production of biorelevant airway surface secretions. General limitations when using primary cells apply to such models, including ethical approval, sourcing donor tissue, limited cell viability and loss of relevant protein expression after subsequent passages.

Models utilizing primary cells from several species have been reported, including human, dog, mouse, rat, guinea pig, rabbit, cow, sheep and pig. Of these, the most commonly used are human bronchial and alveolar cells, and rat alveolar cells.

10.4.5.1 Primary human bronchial epithelial cells (HBECs)

As an *in vitro* model of lung permeability, primary human bronchial epithelial cells (HBECs) are often considered to represent the gold standard. The key benefit of these cells is the apparent physiological relevance and normal bronchial epithelial phenotype, complete with the expression of tight junction proteins and drug transporters required to effectively make predictions of *in vivo* lung permeability. HBECs are commercially available and may be derived from either healthy or diseased donors (e.g. asthma, COPD, cystic fibrosis, smokers). Whilst it is evident that variable results may be obtained in different laboratories, under controlled conditions TEER values of $\geq 1000\ \Omega/cm^2$ may be achieved using AIC or LCC conditions [93]. Cultures produce a ciliated pseudostratified columnar epithelium with goblet cells and functional ion channels have also been reported by several researchers [93].

10.4.5.2 Primary human alveolar epithelial cells (HAECs)

Similarly to HBEC's, primary human alveolar epithelial cells (HAECs) represent the gold standard for *in vitro* modeling of the epithelial permeability barrier of the distal region of the lungs. Whilst these cells are also commercially available, they are more difficult to obtain experimentally. TEER values of $\geq 2000\ \Omega/cm^2$ have commonly been reported [89] with formation of tight junctions and desmosomes consonant with results showing the significant exclusion of paracellular permeability markers [94,95].

Electron microscopy has been used to confirm the formation of a monolayer containing both Type I and Type II alveolar cells in a simple squamous epithelium.

10.4.5.3 Primary rat alveolar epithelial cells (RAECs)

Due to the limited availability of human primary tissue, rat alveolar epithelial cells (RAECs) are commonly used to form *in vitro* alveolar permeability models. Extensive studies using RAECs have shown a good correlation with *in vitro* and *in vivo* human data, including similar TEER ($\geq$2000 Ω/cm^2) and size exclusion of varying molecular weights of FITC-dextran [86]. Limitations with this model are those associated with interspecies differences, such as differences in drug transporter expression and metabolism within rats compared to humans [96].

10.4.5.4 Complex primary cell models

The use of primary human epithelial cells as *in vitro* lung permeability models also includes the development of complex commercially available tissue models, the most common of which are MucilAir (Epithelix) and EpiAirway (Mattek). Both these models have the advantages that the cells may be obtained from either healthy or diseased donors (e.g. smoker, asthmatic, COPD, cystic fibrosis), dependent on the field of interest. One of the key benefits of these models is that the cells remain viable and can be cultured for longer periods of time than is typical for primary cells, thereby allowing the study of chronic/subchronic exposures [97,98]. Current limitations include the high cost compared to other models, and the relative lack of alveolar permeability models (currently only nasal, bronchial and small airway models are available for studying lung permeability).

10.4.5.5 Cell co-cultures

One common method used for forming *in vitro* lung permeability barriers, includes the coculture of either bronchial or alveolar cells with other relevant cell types, to create a double or triple coculture instead of the more typically used epithelial monoculture. Whilst the alveolar/bronchial cell is usually primarily responsible for barrier formation, researchers may include other cell types to increase the physiological relevance of the model or study mechanisms such as inflammation, the effect of phagocytosis by alveolar macrophages, or how the inhaled xenobiotic may affect fibroblasts.

The typical method for coculture depends on the second or third cell type to be introduced, (Fig. 10.6). In the case of fibroblasts, dendritic cells or endothelial cells, the Transwell® is usually inverted so that the cells may be pipetted onto the basolateral side of the Transwell®, allowed to attach over a few hours, before replacing the Transwell® upright, and culturing the cells under submerged conditions before pipetting the bronchial/alveolar onto the apical side of the Transwell® [99].

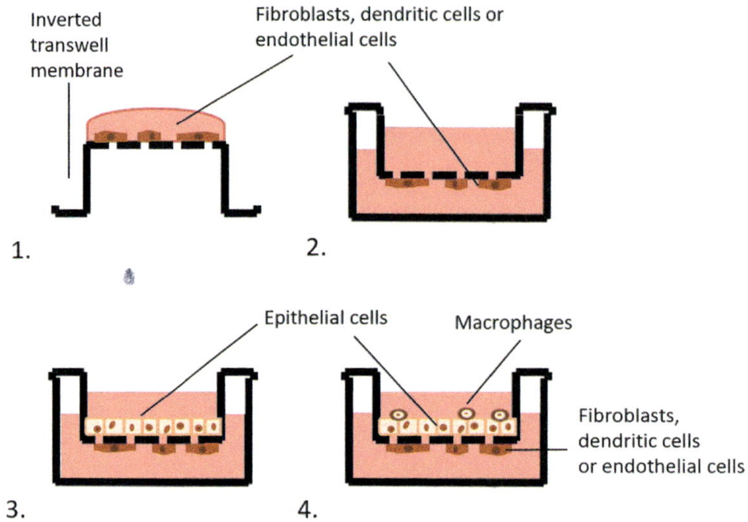

Figure 10.6 Diagram adapted from Rothen-Rutishauser et al. [99], showing a method for triple co-culture of cells as a complex in vitro permeability model. Fibroblasts, dendritic or endothelial cells adhere to the inverted basolateral side of a Transwell insert (1 & 2), the Transwell insert is replaced into the receiver well so that epithelial cells may be cultured on the apical side (3), macrophages may also be added to apical side of the Transwell insert (4).

Dendritic cells are typically obtained as primary cells or by differentiating the monocytic cell line THP-1. Fibroblasts, may be obtained as primary cells (several species, including human, rat, guinea pig and mouse have been used) or by using the human lung fibroblast cell lines MRC-5 and WI-38 or the widely available murine fibroblast cell line 3T3 [97]. In the case of macrophages, these are typically added to the apical side of the Transwell insert containing pre-cultured alveolar epithelial cells under AIC or LCC conditions. For this purpose, macrophages are usually sourced by differentiating monocytes obtained from blood or by differentiating monocytic cell lines such as THP-1 or U937 [88].

Although coculture methods have typically aimed to address research questions related to potential xenobiotic toxicity, there is increasing evidence to suggest other cell types may also significantly influence xenobiotic permeability within the lung, based on drug sequestration within cells or phagocytosis of nanoparticles [42].

10.5 Measures of absorptive transport

10.5.1 *In vitro* models

In vitro absorption models are widely used due to advantages over other models, such as being amenable to high throughput screening of several compounds, reduced cost over other more advanced models, the ability to elucidate specific absorption mechanisms and ethical considerations in comparison to *in vivo* studies. Whilst the main disadvantages include reduced physiological or clinical relevance in comparison to *ex vivo* or *in vivo* absorption models, there have been several advances made in optimizing and validating the use of *in vitro* absorption models. Additionally, for the assessment of dosimetry, deposition, dissolution and absorptive transfer, use of *in vitro* models is useful for investigating the effect of physicochemical properties of the drug and drug formulation on lung permeability. Particular benefits of *in vitro* absorption models are that they provide an early indication of biopharmaceutical performance before moving into *ex vivo* studies or pre-clinical stages of drug development. *In vitro* absorption models also allow mechanistic investigation of absorptive processes within the lungs that are difficult to study in more complex systems.

Most *in vitro* models are based on the cultivation of lung epithelial cells as previously described, but are adapted to investigate absorptive drug transport by exposing air interfaced cells to a drug aerosol using an impinger or impactor or newer bespoke equipment such as PreciseInhale™ or VitroCell Cloud™ systems [100]. Although these methods are non-standardized, they have the advantage of providing a relevant exposure mode and allowing drug to be followed through integrated deposition, dissolution and absorptive transport processes. Other models focus on using microfluidic approaches or in-line cells, with both allowing flow-through of receiver fluid, modeling respiratory perfusion, adjacent to the air interfaced membrane [101]. Aerosol delivery is a key factor as drug absorption characteristics within the respiratory tract vary according to epithelial and airway surface liquid depth, epithelial permeability, tissue depth and surface area, tissue perfusion and non-absorptive clearance mechanisms. Whilst aerodynamic particle size data provides a general guide to regional deposition patterns, there are various other particle properties that may affect deposition-dissolution rates and availability of drug in absorption models.

Some *in vitro* dissolution-absorption models rely on the use of an artificial membrane. A recently developed method is the use of the PreciseInhale™ device, alongside the "DissolvIt" artificial air blood barrier membrane [102], which has the benefit that absorptive drug transfer can be monitored in addition to dissolution of aerosol particles. Using this device, a precise dose of the drug formulation may be delivered to the membrane, particle dissolution is monitored by microscopic optical measurements, whilst drug that undergoes absorptive transport across the membrane may be quantified in a perfusate.

10.5.2 Isolated perfused lungs

Ex vivo models have the potential to help elucidate physiological processes within specific organs in a controlled environment without the complications of first pass metabolism. The anatomy and physiology of the isolated organ is maintained including; (i) structural and cellular integrity, (ii) function of permeability barriers,

(iii) inter- and intracellular interactions, and (iv) biochemical activity [103]. IPL is a well-established *ex vivo* organ model which enables study of the mechanisms of drug disposition in the lungs. The IPL has been previously adapted for various species of animals, such as mice, rats [104,105], guinea pigs, rabbits [106], dogs. While the utilization of human lungs is limited by availability, this is also possible [107,108]. The IPL has been employed mainly in pharmaceutical research to study drug dissolution and absorption [109–111], disposition [103], and metabolism [112,113]. The IPL set up allows administration of compounds with control of parameters such as ventilation rates, respiratory patterns, lung volume, temperature, pH and easy mass balance recovery. It is also possible to collect multiple samples from one experiment and limit the use of animals. Limitations of the IPL method are the complexity in experimental manipulations, high variability in individual lung samples and viability of tissues over 2–3 hours (maximum 5 hours) as well as the absence of tracheobronchial circulation. These matters coupled with the total costs, make the IPL model unsuitable for high throughput experimentation.

The considerations for selection of species for IPL study are the ethics, availability, cost of animals and maintenance and the type of experiment, drug administration and available apparatus. It is recommended to use the same species to evaluate pharmacodynamic and toxicological studies to examine PK/PD relation and to evaluate *in vitro – in vivo* correlations. Each species has unique anatomic differences including the branching pattern, diameter of the airways, arrangements of the lung lobes, and different physiological parameters such as respiratory rate or lung volume [109]. The most common species used for IPL are rats, followed by rabbits and guinea pigs [103]. Animal size is another factor to consider as the mouse model might be too small to studying drug absorption, whereas dog or non-human primate lungs require larger apparatus, are more expensive and raise greater ethical issues [114].

There are different surgical approaches that can remove lungs from the donor, however it should be performed within 10–15 min [45], with special care to avoid any contact with tissue. After surgical removal the lungs are connected to an artificial ventilation system [115]. The lungs are then exposed to the compounds of interest or formulations through the perfusate or directly to the lungs, with samples of perfusate taken periodically and easily and lavage samples taken as a terminal end point [115]. As IPL models can be used to study the pharmacokinetics of inhaled pharmaceutical formulations, parameters and factors that might influence the results of the studies include: (i) method of drug administration (nebulization vs tracheal instillation), (ii) perfusion method (single-pass perfusion vs recirculated system and constant flow perfusion vs constant pressure perfusion), (iii) perfusate type (artificial perfusates vs autologous whole blood), (iv) ventilation method and ventilation rate.

Rat IPL model studies have been performed to study the mechanisms and factors involved in the absorption of compounds. The incorporation of kinetic modeling approaches to experiments has allowed differentiation of the contribution of absorptive (passive and active) and non-absorptive (mucociliary clearance, phagocytosis and metabolism) processes involved in the disposition of drugs in the lungs. The absorption data can be fitted across doses using different models and the rate constants are obtained. A first-order model can be used for passive absorption and non-absorptive clearance, whereas active transport is modeled using Michaelis-Menten kinetics [45]. IPL permeability measurements have been used to estimate pulmonary drug disposition after intratracheal drug delivery [45,80,110,116,117] and strong *in vitro* – *in vivo* correlation (r = 0.98) has been reported between the rat IPL drug absorption half-life and rat pulmonary absorption half-life measured *in vivo* [110].

The IPL preparation (Fig. 10.7) has been investigated as an *ex vivo* model for screening the pulmonary absorption of compounds by GlaxoSmithKline [118] and AstraZeneca [110]. There are a number of methodological variations in how the IPL technique is set up [109], including the approach of using a simple system at low cost that does not need a specialist equipment for maintaining lung viability [80]. Administration of compounds to the lungs also ranges from simple instillation [118] and fine sprays [110] to more complex aerosol administration [119]. Instillation gives precise control over dosimetry, but the dose might not penetrate the airways as fully as aerosol administration [25]. The drug transfer profiles from the airspace to the perfusate after instillation [82] have shown to be comparable to those reported after administration of compounds by nebulizer catheter to a more complex physiologically-controlled IPL system [110], and a similar correlation with *in vivo* pulmonary drug absorption was obtained.

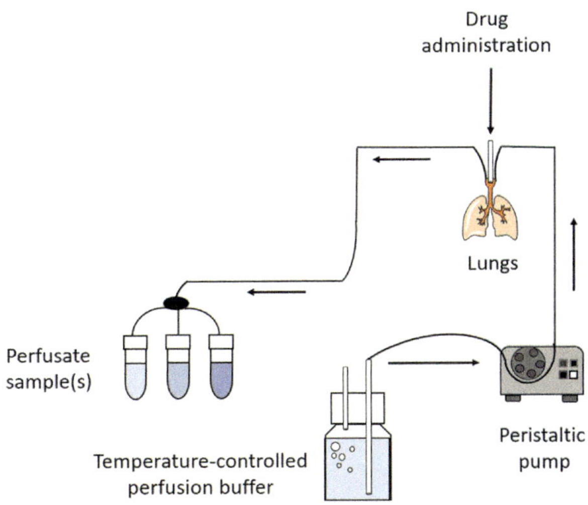

Figure 10.7 An illustrative isolated perfused (*ex vivo*) lung system. Many adaptations of this basic system are reported.

10.5.3 *In vivo* experiments

Pre-clinical drug development relies on a rodent species (e.g. rats or mice) and a non-rodent species (e.g. dog or monkey). Rodents are commonly used for preclinical studies despite being obligate nasal breathers. As most inhaled drugs are inhaled orally, tracheal cannulation is required if nasal filtering of an aerosol is to be avoided. Of the non-rodent species dog is most common, although several other models are used, including pigs, sheep, rabbits and primates where necessitated due to specific lung physiology, drug transporters or relevant receptors. Non-rodent species are capable of both passive oral and nasal inhalation which may complicate data based on the potential for more variable intraspecies drug deposition and subsequent absorption.

Multiple delivery methods have been investigated, but the most commonly used are endotracheal intubation (for intratracheal instillations or aerosols), or devices for passive inhalation of aerosols such as nose/head only or whole body devices (Fig. 10.8). Dose and regional deposition within the respiratory tract are highly method dependent and do not translate well to human deposition after use of inhaler devices, which is one of the challenges associated with the translation of pre-clinical drug absorption data to the clinic [120].

For the purpose of drug absorption studies endotracheal intubation may be used to deliver solutions/suspensions or aerosols to the lungs. For the delivery of aerosols with this method, a tube with a relatively large diameter is required to ensure secure contact between tube and trachea and prevent loss of the aerosol, but also to reduce the fraction of aerosol depositing in the tube. This method is rarely used in comparison to passive inhalation methods that are readily available, easier to use and less invasive. The most common form of endotracheal intubation is for intratracheal instillation, whereby a liquid solution or suspension is delivered by inserting a much narrower tube, with the rodent under anesthesia. A practical method for intratracheal instillation has been described by Lizio et al. [121].

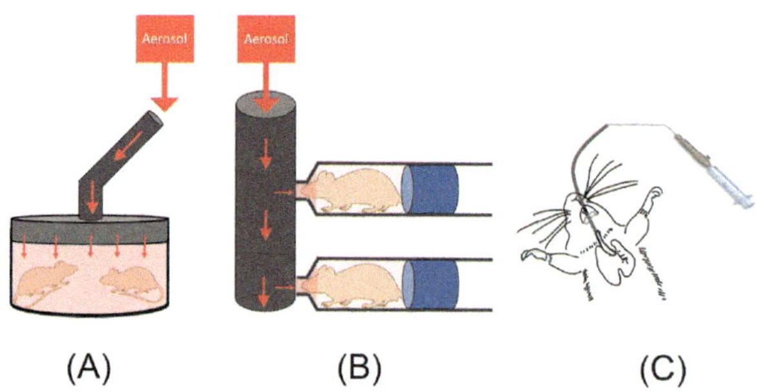

Figure 10.8 Diagram adapted from Price et al. [120], showing different preclinical methods for aerosol delivery. (A) Whole body passive inhalation, (B) Nose-only passive inhalation, (C) Direct delivery via endotracheal intubation.

Limitations with endotracheal tubes compared to other forms of delivery are the relatively narrow oral cavity of rats and experimental difficulty of visualizing the trachea even under appropriate anesthesia. Additionally, there is the increased risk of damage and inflammation to the trachea which may affect study outcomes. When performed correctly, this method has the advantage of precisely delivering a known dose directly to the lungs, especially of relevance when there is limited test material making it of great value to researchers studying the kinetics of novel investigative nanoparticles or siRNA coated polymers [122–124]. Another direct method of delivery is via tracheotomy, similar to the type standardly performed for bronchoalveolar lavage (BAL), however this is not suitable for repeated or long term dosing that may be required.

Drug absorption studies that use aerosol delivery methods for rodents often use nose/head restraining tubes as a gold standard. In comparison to the whole body devices that excessively distribute drug on the skin/fur, nose only devices mean that a greater percentage of the drug is targeted towards the respiratory tract and less drug material is required, additionally it is a method that easily allows for repeated dosing if required. However, due to the restraints there is increased stress on the animal, potential for heat build-up and it is more labor intensive than exposing rodents in a large whole body chamber suitable for long term exposures [120]. With all passive inhalation methodologies, it remains a challenge to characterize and quantify the deep lung dosing.

Overall, the value of passive nose-only inhalation systems outweighs the limitations. Many modern systems allow for the aerosolized drug to simultaneously be delivered to 12 ports, with the potential for this system to be stacked in a modular way so that as many as 96 animals may be dosed at one time in a "rodent nose-only inhalation tower", but also allowing ports to be plugged to reduce this number and prevent excess use of drug. Blood samples may be collected over a specific time course following the inhalation exposure, to give preclinical pharmacokinetic data. For similar non-rodent pharmacokinetic data to be obtained, this may be performed using anesthetized dogs intubated with cuffed endotracheal tubes and mechanically ventilated at a set tidal volume and breath/min rate (e.g. 10 mL/kg and 15 breaths/min) [125]. For preclinical drug absorption studies, where precise quantification of the delivered dose is also desired, the PreciseInhale® allows for both nose-only inhalation or tracheal intubation methods to be used in both rodents and dogs.

Species selection considerations for *in vivo* inhalation studies include the amount and cost of available drug material for preclinical absorption studies, with intratracheal instillation being favored if there is limited material. Intratracheal aerosol administration may be the method of choice if preclinical drug absorption data requires the characterization of deep lung or alveolar region dosing [120]. If this is not a requirement then passive methodologies are more likely to be favored, particularly if more data is to be collected after the exposure, large sample sizes are to be used or the use of anesthesia may influence the results.

10.5.4 *In vitro-in vivo* correlation

Based on an extensive *in vivo* data set generated in rats in the 1970s by Schanker and Co-workers, relationships have been reported between the physicochemical properties of drug compounds and drug absorptive clearance from the lungs *in vivo* [126]. Relationships have also been established correlating compound permeability in respiratory cell lines with absorptive clearance for the lungs *ex vivo* or *in vivo* [1,74,80]. Correlations have also been established between physicochemical properties of drug compounds and P_{eff} in isolated perfused lungs [110] and between P_{eff} in isolated perfused lungs and pulmonary absorption *in vivo* [110,127]. Current progress in mechanistic modeling of drug absorption in the lungs in humans [see below] utilizes permeability data from *in vitro* and *ex vivo* models and offers a promising approach to developing an enhanced understanding of how drug permeability measurements can be used to predict human lung absorption [128].

10.6 Mathematical modeling of pulmonary absorption

Modeling pulmonary absorption concerns the use of *in silico* or "computer" modeling techniques, to predict the pharmacokinetics of inhaled xenobiotics. This includes inhaled medicines, but there are also applications in applying absorption modeling to inhaled pollutants from environmental or occupational exposure. *In silico* prediction of inhaled drugs, allows the estimation of respiratory bioavailability in humans before and after clinical trial data is available, and is therefore of importance for optimizing drug formulations to achieve the required therapeutic dose (local or systemic) and interpreting study outcomes.

Physiologically based pharmacokinetic (PBPK) modeling software often uses a (semi-) mechanistic approach to simulating drug absorption from the lungs, based on regional deposition, dissolution, muciliary clearance or metabolism rate, permeability and perfusion into systemic circulation. This may be scaled depending on expected average lung volumes for an adult male, female or child or by user-supplied experimental data. This mechanistic approach contrasts with empirical pharmacokinetic modeling which focuses on compartmental parameters for lungs, systemic absorption/distribution and elimination.

Deposition or prediction of the fraction of drug deposited in different regions of the respiratory tract is most often the first step associated with absorption modeling, followed by consideration of dissolution rate which is usually predicted from user-supplied data or calculated based on known drug solubility and other physicochemical properties like lipophilicity. Following this various data for lung permeability must be considered. Whilst the focus of modeling lung absorption relies on estimates of transport mechanisms and permeability rates, these may be considered separately in different regions of the respiratory tract and require selective inputs for regional drug deposition. There is substantial evidence highlighting that both the mechanisms and rates of permeability vary significantly depending on whether the drug is deposited in the extrathoracic region, large and small airways, or the alveolar region. After accounting for drug deposition in the different regions of the lung, the focus of absorption modeling shifts to the different rates of dissolution, permeability and perfusion within the different lung regions. This is required in order to calculate respiratory bioavailability, temporal lung exposure/retention and non-absorptive clearance. Several commercially available PBPK modeling software incorporate these functions in some form, such as Gastroplus™ (Simulations-Plus), Mimetikos Preludium™ (Emmace), Simcyp Simulator™ (Certara) and PK-SIM™ (Bayer AG). Additionally, similar "in-house" PBPK models also exist such as Pfizer's PulmoSim™ or AstraZeneca's Lung-Sim.

The first transport mechanism considered is often non-absorptive clearance by mucociliary clearance, occurring in both the large and small airways of the bronchial tree. Estimated mucociliary clearance rates vary, dependent on the location but has been experimentally determined to occur at a moderately faster rate in the small airways than the large airways, with the former being capable of clearing up to approximately 95% of deposited drug if this clearance pathway is not saturated. To determine the rate, mucus velocity may be approximated e.g. 0.5 cm/min. Assumptions are then made on whether only solid drug material is transported in the mucus or also dissolved material. In addition to drug solubility, diffusivity can also be predicted, with the Hayduk-Laudie Diffusivity equation commonly used (Eq. 10.1).

Hayduk-Laudie Diffusivity equation (for diffusion of non-electrolytes in water):

$$D\left(cm^2 s^{-1}\right) = 1.326E^{-4}/\mu^{1.14} \times MVS^{0.598} \tag{10.1}$$

μ = dynamic viscosity of water (cp), MVS = molar volume of solute (cm^3/mol)

For epithelial permeability there are several possible transport mechanisms as previously described, frequently these may be assimilated in an overall rate based on *in vitro* P_{app} or *ex vivo* P_{eff} data. There has been some research performed that attempts to predict transport and distribution at a (sub)cellular level [129], however this is predominantly limited to interpreting mechanisms rather than predicting of lung permeability based on QSAR or mechanistic mathematical approaches. Despite this, computational approaches to predict or interpret "small scale" transport or distribution are highly relevant to understanding particular tissue retention mechanisms e.g. mitochondrial, nuclear binding or lysosomal trapping [130,131]. This may be of importance as non-specific binding may have a large capacity even with a low binding affinity, and lead to slow prolonged drug release [128]. However, rather than focusing on a cellular level, lung permeability descriptors in simulation programmes typically include parameters such as epithelium surface area and depth, airway surface liquid depth, tissue depth and perfusion (blood-tissue perfusion coefficient).

As *in vitro* permeability models correlate to *in vivo* permeability models, a scaling factor may be applied so that either Transwell derived P_{app} data or IPL derived P_{eff} data may be used to predict lung permeability. Using the P_{app} or P_{eff} data in this way, the permeability data may be optimized or scaled to give predictions more relevant to human lung physiology than if lung permeability/human pharmacokinetics are assumed to be similar to preclinical rodent pharmacokinetic data.

For the purposes of absorption modeling, P_{eff} may be defined as drug transport across the airway surface liquid, lumen, epithelial tissue (apical membrane, cytosol and basolateral membrane), interstitial fluid, extracellular matrices and capillary walls into systemic circulation. This definition includes many of the required considerations of a mechanistic mathematical approach to absorption modeling. P_{eff} may be explained mathematically as:

$$\frac{1}{P_{eff}} = \frac{1}{P_{mem}} + \frac{1}{P_{mem}}$$
$$P_{eff} = \frac{P_{mem}}{2} \tag{10.2}$$

where P_{mem} is cell membrane permeability.

Whilst P_{eff} values are determined experimentally, it is essentially a sum of permeability descriptors such as epithelium surface area and depth, airway surface liquid depth, tissue depth and perfusion (blood tissue perfusion coefficient), all of which will of course be species dependent. Due to the species variations, this makes it essential to incorporate human specific lung parameters alongside *in vitro* or *in vivo* permeability rate data for the drug/compound of interest.

Although P_{eff} values describe the rate of effective permeability or drug transport across the lung, K_a (association or binding constants) are required to determine the transport across specific lung or body compartments, based on whether the proportion of drug that is either bound or unbound (free).

$$K_a = \frac{k_{on}}{k_{off}} \tag{10.3}$$

The association constant, which is a first order rate constant, relates to several partition coefficients such as; the fraction unbound in airway surface liquid, the tissue-plasma partition coefficient, the fraction unbound in plasma and the blood-plasma partition coefficient. Each stage from association with the airway surface liquid to disassociation from plasma within the blood, is required for the drug to have a systemic availability following inhalation.

For a pharmacokinetic prediction, the transfer of drug from the lung to blood, the body may be divided into compartments, e.g. a central compartment, peripheral compartment(s), and may also include compartments for buccal/nasal/gastrointestinal absorption. Each compartment has an associated estimate for (re)distribution rate constants, clearance rates and systemic elimination rates, with clearance and absorption rates kinetically competing to provide a predicted overall pharmacokinetic curve of systemic drug concentration over time. By predicting the likely pharmacokinetic profile of an inhaled drug, respiratory bioavailability (F_{ab}) may be estimated, where

$$F_{ab} = \frac{[AUC]_{Inhaled} \times Dose_{Intravenous}}{[AUC]_{Intravenous} \times Dose_{Inhaled}} \tag{10.4}$$

One of the limitations with current *in silico* efforts to predict human lung permeability is the lack of extensive validation against human clinical data and the challenges of directly/indirectly measuring free drug concentrations within lung epithelium and tissue [128].

10.7 Conclusion

Most inhaled medicines are for action in the lungs and, unless the target is in the lumen, bioavailability is controlled by epithelial permeability. As drug concentrations in the lungs are very difficult to measure *in vivo*, clearance of drug from the lungs to the systemic circulation is commonly used as a measure of pulmonary absorption. A number of *in vitro*, *ex vivo* and *in vivo* models are available to measure drug permeability or airspace to blood transfer of drug. Data generated using these models can be used as pulmonary absorption parameters for *in silico* physiologically-based pharmacokinetic models, and have produced good fits with plasma pharmacokinetics of inhaled medicines in humans.

References

[1] N. Mathias, K.-J. Kim, V. Lee, Targeted drug delivery to the respiratory tract: solute permeability of air-interface cultured rabbit tracheal epithelial cell monolayers, J. Drug. Target. 4 (1996) 79–86.

[2] J.E. Hastedt, P. Bäckman, A.R. Clark, W. Doub, A. Hickey, G. Hochhaus, et al., Scope and relevance of a pulmonary biopharmaceutical classification system AAPS/FDA/USP Workshop March 16-17th, 2015 in Baltimore, MD, AAPS Open 2 (2016) 1–20.

[3] C. Bosquillon, Drug transporters in the lung—do they play a role in the biopharmaceutics of inhaled drugs? J. Pharm. Sci. 99 (2010) 2240–2255.

[4] M. Boegh, C. Foged, A. Müllertz, H. Mørck Nielsen, Mucosal drug delivery: barriers, in vitro models and formulation strategies, J. Drug. Deliv. Sci. Technol. 23 (2013) 383–391.

[5] J.M. Anderson, C.M. Van Itallie, Physiology and function of the tight junction, Cold Spring Harb. Perspect. Biol. 1 (2009) 1–16.

[6] Drug passage across the cell membrane, in: S.A. Hill, T.E. Peck (Eds.), Pharmacol. Anaesth. Intensive Care, fourth ed., Cambridge University Press, Cambridge, 2014.

[7] P.S. Burton, R.A. Conradi, A.R. Hilgers, Mechanisms of peptide and protein absorption: (2) Transcellular mechanism of peptide and protein absorption: passive aspects, Adv. Drug. Deliv. Rev. 7 (1991) 365–385.

[8] S. Chillistone, J.G. Hardman, Factors affecting drug absorption and distribution, Anaesth, Intensive Care Med. 18 (2017) 335–339.
[9] S. Nickel, C.G. Clerkin, M.A. Selo, C. Ehrhardt, Transport mechanisms at the pulmonary mucosa: implications for drug delivery, Expert. Opin. Drug. Deliv. 13 (2016) 667–690.
[10] F. Kreuzer, L. Hoofd, Facilitated diffusion of oxygen and carbon dioxide, Comprehensive Physiology, John Wiley & Sons, Inc, Hoboken, NJ, 2011, pp. 89–111.
[11] L. Gustavsson, C. Bosquillon, M. Gumbleton, T. Hegelund-Myrbäck, T. Nakanishi, D. Price, et al., Chapter 6. Drug Transporters in the Lung: Expression and Potential Impact on Pulmonary Drug Disposition, in: 2016: pp. 184–228.
[12] M. Gumbleton, G. Al-Jayyoussi, A. Crandon-Lewis, D. Francombe, K. Kreitmeyr, C.J. Morris, et al., Spatial expression and functionality of drug transporters in the intact lung: objectives for further research, Adv. Drug. Deliv. Rev. 63 (2011) 110–118.
[13] C. Ehrhardt, P. Bäckman, W. Couet, C. Edwards, B. Forbes, M. Friden, et al., Current progress toward a better understanding of drug disposition within the lungs: summary proceedings of the first workshop on drug transporters in the lungs, J. Pharm. Sci. 106 (2017) 2234–2244.
[14] D.J. Murphy, D. Desjardins, N. Dereuddre-Bosquet, P. Brochard, L. Perrot, A. Pruvost, et al., Preclinical development of a combination microbicide vaginal ring containing dapivirine and darunavir, J. Antimicrob. Chemother. 69 (2014) 2477–2488.
[15] H.C. Cooray, S. Shahi, A.P. Cahn, H.W. van Veen, S.B. Hladky, M.A. Barrand, Modulation of P-glycoprotein and breast cancer resistance protein by some prescribed corticosteroids, Eur. J. Pharmacol. 531 (2006) 25–33.
[16] K. Dilger, M. Schwab, M.F. Fromm, Identification of budesonide and prednisone as substrates of the intestinal drug efflux pump P-glycoprotein, Inflamm. Bowel Dis. 10 (2004) 578–583.
[17] L. Campbell, A.N. Abulrob, L.E. Kandalaft, S. Plummer, A.J. Hollins, A. Gibbs, et al., Constitutive expression of P-glycoprotein in normal lung alveolar epithelium and functionality in primary alveolar epithelial cultures, J. Pharmacol. Exp. Ther. 304 (2003) 441–452.
[18] P. Van der Valk, C.K. van Kalken, H. Ketelaars, H.J. Broxterman, G. Scheffer, C.M. Kuiper, et al., Distribution of multi-drug resistance-associated P-glycoprotein in normal and neoplastic human tissues: analysis with 3 monoclonal antibodies recognizing different epitopes of the P-glycoprotein molecule, Ann. Oncol. 1 (1990) 56–64.
[19] E. Lechapt-Zalcman, I. Hurbain, R. Lacave, F. Commo, T. Urban, M. Antoine, et al., MDR1-Pgp 170 expression in human bronchus, Eur. Respir. J. 10 (1997) 1837–1843.
[20] M.J. Flens, G.J. Zaman, P. van der Valk, M.A. Izquierdo, A.B. Schroeijers, G.L. Scheffer, et al., Tissue distribution of the multidrug resistance protein, Am. J. Pathol. 148 (1996) 1237–1247.
[21] G.L. Scheffer, A.C.L.M. Pijnenborg, E.F. Smit, M. Müller, D.S. Postma, W. Timens, et al., Multidrug resistance related molecules in human and murine lung, J. Clin. Pathol. 55 (2002) 332–339.
[22] J.M. Brechot, I. Hurbain, A. Fajac, N. Daty, J.F. Bernaudin, Different pattern of MRP localization in ciliated and basal cells from human bronchial epithelium, J. Histochem. Cytochem. 46 (1998) 513–517.
[23] G.E. Sandusky, K.S. Mintze, S.E. Pratt, A.H. Dantzig, Expression of multidrug resistance-associated protein 2 (MRP2) in normal human tissues and carcinomas using tissue microarrays, Histopathology 41 (2002) 65–74.
[24] K. Bleasby, J.C. Castle, C.J. Roberts, C. Cheng, W.J. Bailey, J.F. Sina, et al., Expression profiles of 50 xenobiotic transporter genes in humans and pre-clinical species: a resource for investigations into drug disposition, Xenobiotica 36 (2006) 963–988.
[25] K.S. Lips, C. Volk, B.M. Schmitt, U. Pfeil, P. Arndt, D. Miska, et al., Polyspecific cation transporters mediate luminal release of acetylcholine from bronchial epithelium, Am. J. Respir. Cell Mol. Biol. 33 (2005) 79–88.
[26] G. Horvath, N. Schmid, M.A. Fragoso, A. Schmid, G.E. Conner, M. Salathe, et al., Epithelial organic cation transporters ensure pH-dependent drug absorption in the airway, Am. J. Respir. Cell Mol. Biol. 36 (2007) 53–60.
[27] K.Y.Y. Fung, G.D. Fairn, W.L. Lee, Transcellular vesicular transport in epithelial and endothelial cells: challenges and opportunities, Traffic 19 (2018) 5–18.

[28] N.S. Parkar, B.S. Akpa, L.C. Nitsche, L.E. Wedgewood, A.T. Place, M.S. Sverdlov, et al., Vesicle formation and endocytosis: function, machinery, mechanisms, and modeling, Antioxid. Redox Signal. 11 (2009) 1301–1312.
[29] M. Takano, M. Kawami, A. Aoki, R. Yumoto, Receptor-mediated endocytosis of macromolecules and strategy to enhance their transport in alveolar epithelial cells, Expert. Opin. Drug. Deliv. 12 (2015) 813–825.
[30] J.D. Brain, P.A. Valberg, Models of lung retention based on ICRP, Arch. Environ. Heal. An. Int. J. 28 (1974) 1–11.
[31] C.S. Schneider, Q. Xu, N.J. Boylan, J. Chisholm, B.C. Tang, B.S. Schuster, et al., Nanoparticles that do not adhere to mucus provide uniform and long-lasting drug delivery to airways following inhalation, Sci. Adv. 3 (2017) 1–11.
[32] I. Roy, N. Vij, Nano-delivery in airway diseases: challenges and therapeutic applications, Nanomedicine 6 (2010) 237–244.
[33] C. Loira-Pastoriza, J. Todoroff, R. Vanbever, Delivery strategies for sustained drug release in the lungs, Adv. Drug. Deliv. Rev. 75 (2014) 81–91.
[34] H.H. Sigurdsson, J. Kirch, C.-M. Lehr, Mucus as a barrier to lipophilic drugs, Int. J. Pharm. 453 (2013) 56–64.
[35] P. Gehr, S. Schurch, Y. Berthiaume, V.I. Hof, M. Geiser, Particle retention in airways by surfactant, J. Aerosol Med. 3 (1990) 27–43.
[36] X. Liao, T.S. Wiedmann, Solubilization of cationic drugs in lung surfactant, Pharm. Res. 20 (2003) 1858–1863.
[37] S.M. McAllister, H.O. Alpar, Z. Teitelbaum, D.B. Bennett, Do interactions with phospholipids contribute to the prolonged retention of polypeptides within the lung? Adv. Drug. Deliv. Rev. 19 (1996) 89–110.
[38] R.P. Valle, C.L. Huang, J.S.C. Loo, Y.Y. Zuo, Increasing hydrophobicity of nanoparticles intensifies lung surfactant film inhibition and particle retention, ACS Sustain. Chem. Eng. 2 (2014) 1574–1580.
[39] E. Bäckström, E. Boger, A. Lundqvist, M. Hammarlund-Udenaes, M. Fridén, Lung retention by lysosomal trapping of inhaled drugs can be predicted in vitro with lung slices, J. Pharm. Sci. 105 (2016) 3432–3439.
[40] G.A. Siebert, D.Y. Hung, P. Chang, M.S. Roberts, Ion-trapping, microsomal binding, and unbound drug distribution in the hepatic retention of basic drugs, J. Pharmacol. Exp. Ther. 308 (2004) 228–235.
[41] S.C. Wood, K.E. Schaefer, Regulation of intracellular pH in lungs and other tissues during hypercapnia, J. Appl. Physiol. 45 (1978) 115–118.
[42] A. Ufuk, F. Assmus, L. Francis, J. Plumb, V. Damian, M. Gertz, et al., In vitro and in silico tools to assess extent of cellular uptake and lysosomal sequestration of respiratory drugs in human alveolar macrophages, Mol. Pharm. 14 (2017) 1033–1046.
[43] J. Yu, G.R. Rosania, Cell-based multiscale computational modeling of small molecule absorption and retention in the lungs, Pharm. Res. 27 (2010) 457–467.
[44] A. Valotis, P. Högger, Human receptor kinetics and lung tissue retention of the enhanced-affinity glucocorticoid fluticasone furoate, Respir. Res. 8 (2007) 54–63.
[45] M. Sakagami, In vivo, in vitro and ex vivo models to assess pulmonary absorption and disposition of inhaled therapeutics for systemic delivery, Adv. Drug. Deliv. Rev. 58 (2006) 1030–1060.
[46] J.S. Patton, Mechanisms of macromolecule absorption by the lungs, Adv. Drug. Deliv. Rev. 19 (1996) 3–36.
[47] N. Sanders, C. Rudolph, K. Braeckmans, S.C. De Smedt, J. Demeester, Extracellular barriers in respiratory gene therapy, Adv. Drug. Deliv. Rev. 61 (2009) 115–127.
[48] J.J. Wine, The genesis of cystic fibrosis lung disease, J. Clin. Invest. 103 (1999) 309–312.
[49] B. Olsson, E. Bondesson, L. Borgström, S. Edsbäcker, S. Eirefelt, K. Ekelund, et al., Pulmonary drug metabolism, clearance, and absorption, Control. Pulm. Drug Deliv., Springer, New York, 2011, pp. 21–50.
[50] J. Ma, B.K. Rubin, J.A. Voynow, Mucins, mucus, and goblet cells, Chest 154 (2018) 169–176.

[51] D.A. Groneberg, P.R. Eynott, S. Lim, T. Oates, R. Wu, I. Carlstedt, et al., Expression of respiratory mucins in fatal status asthmaticus and mild asthma, Histopathology 40 (2002) 367–373.
[52] M.C. Rose, J.A. Voynow, Respiratory tract mucin genes and mucin glycoproteins in health and disease, Physiol. Rev. 86 (2006) 245–278.
[53] P.G. Bhat, D.R. Flanagan, M.D. Donovan, The limiting role of mucus in drug absorption: drug permeation through mucus solution, Int. J. Pharm. 126 (1995) 179–187.
[54] B.K. Rubin, Therapeutic aerosols and airway secretions, J. Aerosol Med. 9 (1996) 123–130.
[55] S.K. Lai, Y.-Y. Wang, J. Hanes, Mucus-penetrating nanoparticles for drug and gene delivery to mucosal tissues, Adv. Drug. Deliv. Rev. 61 (2009) 158–171.
[56] B.S. Schuster, J.S. Suk, G.F. Woodworth, J. Hanes, Nanoparticle diffusion in respiratory mucus from humans without lung disease, Biomaterials 34 (2013) 3439–3446.
[57] B.K. Rubin, O. Ramirez, J.G. Zayas, B. Finegan, M. King, Collection and analysis of respiratory mucus from subjects without lung disease, Am. Rev. Respir. Dis. (1990) 1040–1043.
[58] T.T. Kararli, Comparison of the gastrointestinal anatomy, physiology, and biochemistry of humans and commonly used laboratory animals, Biopharm. Drug. Dispos. 16 (1995) 351–380.
[59] X. Murgia, P. Pawelzyk, U.F. Schaefer, C. Wagner, N. Willenbacher, C.-M. Lehr, Size-limited penetration of nanoparticles into porcine respiratory mucus after aerosol deposition, Biomacromolecules 17 (2016) 1536–1542.
[60] E. Cingolani, S. Alqahtani, R.C. Sadler, D. Prime, S. Stolnik, C. Bosquillon, In vitro investigation on the impact of airway mucus on drug dissolution and absorption at the air-epithelium interface in the lungs, Eur. J. Pharm. Biopharm. 141 (2019) 210–220.
[61] X. Murgia, B. Loretz, O. Hartwig, M. Hittinger, C.-M. Lehr, The role of mucus on drug transport and its potential to affect therapeutic outcomes, Adv. Drug. Deliv. Rev. 124 (2018) 82–97.
[62] J.Y. Lock, T.L. Carlson, R.L. Carrier, Mucus models to evaluate the diffusion of drugs and particles, Adv. Drug. Deliv. Rev. 124 (2018) 34–49.
[63] C.I. Grainger, L.L. Greenwell, D.J. Lockley, G.P. Martin, B. Forbes, Culture of Calu-3 cells at the air interface provides a representative model of the airway epithelial barrier, Pharm. Res. 23 (2006) 1482–1490.
[64] A. Stentebjerg-Andersen, I.V. Notlevsen, B. Brodin, C.U. Nielsen, Calu-3 cells grown under AIC and LCC conditions: implications for dipeptide uptake and transepithelial transport of substances, Eur. J. Pharm. Biopharm. 78 (2011) 19–26.
[65] N.R. Mathias, J. Timoszyk, P.I. Stetsko, J.R. Megill, R.L. Smith, D.A. Wall, Permeability characteristics of Calu-3 human bronchial epithelial cells: in vitro - in vivo correlation to predict lung absorption in rats, J. Drug. Target. 10 (2002) 31–40.
[66] M. Leslie Fulcher, S. Gabriel, K.A. Burns, J.R. Yankaskas, S.H. Randell, Well-differentiated human airway epithelial cell cultures, in: Human Cell Culture Protocols, Humana Press, Totowa, NJ, n.d., pp. 183–206.
[67] F. Carlini, C. Picard, C. Garulli, D. Piquemal, P. Roubertoux, J. Chiaroni, et al., Bronchial epithelial cells from asthmatic patients display less functional HLA-G isoform expression, Front. Immunol. 8 (2017) 1–11.
[68] M. Nikolic, T. Sustersic, N. Filipovic, In vitro models and on-chip systems: biomaterial interaction studies with tissues generated using lung epithelial and liver metabolic cell lines, Front. Bioeng. Biotechnol. 6 (2018) 120.
[69] B. Forbes, A. Shah, G. Martin, A.B. Lansley, The human bronchial epithelial cell line 16HBE14o − as a model system of the airways for studying drug transport, Int. J. Pharm. 12 (2003) 161–167.
[70] J.B. Lee, A. Zgair, D.A. Taha, X. Zang, L. Kagan, T.H. Kim, et al., Quantitative analysis of lab-to-lab variability in Caco-2 permeability assays, Eur. J. Pharm. Biopharm. 114 (2017) 38–42.
[71] J. Mantaj, T. Abu-Shams, Z. Enlo-Scott, M. Swedrowska, D. Vllasaliu, Role of the basement membrane as an intestinal barrier to absorption of macromolecules and nanoparticles, Mol. Pharm. 15 (2018) 5802–5808.
[72] E.H.J. van den Bogaard, L.A. Dailey, A.J. Thorley, T.D. Tetley, B. Forbes, Inflammatory response and barrier properties of a new alveolar type 1-like cell line (TT1), Pharm. Res. 26 (2009) 1172–1180.

[73] B. Forbes, Human airway epithelial cell lines for in vitro drug transport and metabolism studies, Pharm. Sci. Technol. Today 3 (2000) 18–27.
[74] F. Manford, A. Tronde, A.-B. Jeppsson, N. Patel, F. Johansson, B. Forbes, Drug permeability in 16HBE14o- airway cell layers correlates with absorption from the isolated perfused rat lung, Eur. J. Pharm. Sci. 26 (2005) 414–420.
[75] H.X. Ong, D. Traini, C.-Y. Loo, L. Sarkissian, G. Lauretani, S. Scalia, et al., Is the cellular uptake of respiratory aerosols delivered from different devices equivalent? Eur. J. Pharm. Biopharm. 93 (2015) 320–327.
[76] C. Ehrhardt, C. Kneuer, J. Fiegel, J. Hanes, U. Schaefer, K.-J. Kim, et al., Influence of apical fluid volume on the development of functional intercellular junctions in the human epithelial cell line 16HBE14o- : implications for the use of this cell line as an in vitro model for bronchial drug absorption studies, Cell Tissue Res. 308 (2002) 391–400.
[77] M.E. Kreft, U.D. Jerman, E. Lasič, N. Hevir-Kene, T.L. Rižner, L. Peternel, et al., The characterization of the human cell line Calu-3 under different culture conditions and its use as an optimized in vitro model to investigate bronchial epithelial function, Eur. J. Pharm. Sci. 69 (2015) 1–9.
[78] K.O. Hamilton, G. Backstrom, M.A. Yazdanian, K.L. Audus, P-glycoprotein efflux pump expression and activity in Calu-3 cells, J. Pharm. Sci. 90 (2001) 647–658.
[79] A. Swiatecka-Urban, C. Boyd, B. Coutermarsh, K.H. Karlson, R. Barnaby, L. Aschenbrenner, et al., Myosin VI regulates endocytosis of the cystic fibrosis transmembrane conductance regulator, J. Biol. Chem. 279 (2004) 38025–38031.
[80] C. Bosquillon, M. Madlova, N. Patel, N. Clear, B. Forbes, A comparison of drug transport in pulmonary absorption models: isolated perfused rat lungs, respiratory epithelial cell lines and primary cell culture, Pharm. Res. 34 (2017) 2532–2540.
[81] C. Ehrhardt, C. Kneuer, M. Laue, U.F. Schaefer, K.-J. Kim, C.-M. Lehr, 16HBE14o- human bronchial epithelial cell layers express P-glycoprotein, lung resistance-related protein, and caveolin-1, Pharm. Res. 20 (2003) 545–551.
[82] C.E. Stewart, E.E. Torr, N.H. Mohd Jamili, C. Bosquillon, I. Sayers, Evaluation of differentiated human bronchial epithelial cell culture systems for asthma research, J. Allergy (2012) 1–11. 2012.
[83] M. Le Vée, A. Bacle, E. Jouan, V. Lecureur, S. Potin, O. Fardel, Induction of multidrug resistance-associated protein 3 expression by diesel exhaust particle extract in human bronchial epithelial BEAS-2B cells, Toxicol. Vitr. 58 (2019) 60–68.
[84] K.A. Foster, C.G. Oster, M.M. Mayer, M.L. Avery, K.L. Audus, Characterization of the A549 cell line as a type II pulmonary epithelial cell model for drug metabolism, Exp. Cell Res. 243 (1998) 359–366.
[85] I.W.H. Jarvis, Z. Enlo-Scott, E. Nagy, I.S. Mudway, T.D. Tetley, V.M. Arlt, et al., Genotoxicity of fine and coarse fraction ambient particulate matter in immortalised normal (TT1) and cancer-derived (A549) alveolar epithelial cells, Environ. Mol. Mutagen. 59 (2018) 290–301.
[86] Y. Matsukawa, V.H.L. Lee, E.D. Crandall, K.-J. Kim, Size-dependent dextran transport across rat alveolar epithelial cell monolayers, J. Pharm. Sci. 86 (1997) 305–309.
[87] S.J. Kemp, A.J. Thorley, J. Gorelik, M.J. Seckl, M.J. O'Hare, A. Arcaro, et al., Immortalization of human alveolar epithelial cells to investigate nanoparticle uptake, Am. J. Respir. Cell Mol. Biol. 39 (2008) 591–597.
[88] S. Kletting, Co-culture of human alveolar epithelial (hAELVi) and macrophage (THP-1) cell lines, ALTEX (2018) 211–222.
[89] A. Kuehn, Human alveolar epithelial cells expressing tight junctions to model the air-blood barrier, ALTEX (2016) 251–260.
[90] J.J. Salomon, V.E. Muchitsch, J.C. Gausterer, E. Schwagerus, H. Huwer, N. Daum, et al., The cell line NCl-H441 is a useful in vitro model for transport studies of human distal lung epithelial barrier, Mol. Pharm. 11 (2014) 995–1006.
[91] F. Kielgast, H. Schmidt, P. Braubach, V.E. Winkelmann, K.E. Thompson, M. Frick, et al., Glucocorticoids regulate tight junction permeability of lung epithelia by modulating claudin 8, Am. J. Respir. Cell Mol. Biol. 54 (2016) 707–717.
[92] H. Ren, N.P. Birch, V. Suresh, An optimised human cell culture model for alveolar epithelial transport, PLoS One 11 (2016) 1–22.

[93] R.E. Rayner, P. Makena, G.L. Prasad, E. Cormet-Boyaka, Optimization of normal human bronchial epithelial (NHBE) cell 3D cultures for in vitro lung model studies, Sci. Rep. 9 (2019) 500.

[94] K.J. Elbert, U.F. Schäfer, H. Schäfers, K. Kim, V.H.L. Lee, C. Lehr, Monolayers of human alveolar epithelial cells in primary culture for pulmonary absorption and transport studies, Pharm. Res. 16 (1999) 601–608.

[95] I.R. Witherden, E.J. Vanden Bon, P. Goldstraw, C. Ratcliffe, U. Pastorino, T.D. Tetley, Primary human alveolar type II epithelial cell chemokine release, Am. J. Respir. Cell Mol. Biol. 30 (2004) 500–509.

[96] F. Oesch, E. Fabian, R. Landsiedel, Xenobiotica-metabolizing enzymes in the lung of experimental animals, man and in human lung models, Arch. Toxicol. 93 (2019) 3419–3489.

[97] U.G. Sauer, S. Vogel, A. Hess, S.N. Kolle, L. Ma-Hock, B. van Ravenzwaay, et al., In vivo–in vitro comparison of acute respiratory tract toxicity using human 3D airway epithelial models and human A549 and murine 3T3 monolayer cell systems, Toxicol. Vitr. 27 (2013) 174–190.

[98] A. Baxter, S. Thain, A. Banerjee, L. Haswell, A. Parmar, G. Phillips, et al., Targeted omics analyses, and metabolic enzyme activity assays demonstrate maintenance of key mucociliary characteristics in long term cultures of reconstituted human airway epithelia, Toxicol. Vitr. 29 (2015) 864–875.

[99] B. Rothen-Rutishauser, A newly developed in vitro model of the human epithelial airway barrier to study the toxic potential of nanoparticles, ALTEX (2008) 191–196.

[100] S. Ehrmann, O. Schmid, C. Darquenne, B. Rothen-Rutishauser, J. Sznitman, L. Yang, et al., Innovative preclinical models for pulmonary drug delivery research, Expert. Opin. Drug. Deliv. 17 (2020) 463–478.

[101] T.S. Frost, L. Jiang, R.M. Lynch, Y. Zohar, Permeability of epithelial/endothelial barriers in transwells and microfluidic bilayer devices, Micromachines 10 (2019) 1–18.

[102] P. Gerde, M. Malmlöf, L. Havsborn, C.-O. Sjöberg, P. Ewing, S. Eirefelt, et al., DissolvIt : an in vitro method for simulating the dissolution and absorption of inhaled dry powder drugs in the lungs, Assay. Drug. Dev. Technol. 15 (2017) 77–88.

[103] H.M. Mehendale, L.S. Angevine, Y. Ohmiya, The isolated perfused lung—a critical evaluation, Toxicology 21 (1981) 1–36.

[104] K. Nelson, C. Bobba, E. Eren, T. Spata, M. Tadres, D. Hayes Jr., et al., Method of isolated ex vivo lung perfusion in a rat model: lessons learned from developing a rat EVLP program, J. Vis. Exp. (2015).

[105] Å. Ryrfeldt, E. Nilsson, Uptake and biotransformation of ibuterol and terbutaline in isolated perfused rat and guinea pig lungs, Biochem. Pharmacol. 27 (1978) 301–305.

[106] J.U. Bleyl, A.R. Heller, A. Fehrenbach, M. Heintz, H. Fehrenbach, G. Klenz, et al., Pretreatment with perfluorohexane vapor attenuates fMLP-induced lung injury in isolated perfused rabbit lungs, Exp. Lung Res. 36 (2010) 342–351.

[107] A. Linder, G. Friedel, P. Fritz, K. Kivistö, M. McClellan, H. Toomes, The ex-vivo isolated, perfused human lung model: description and potential applications, Thorac. Cardiovasc. Surg. 44 (1996) 140–146.

[108] R.F. Minchin, M.R. Johnston, M.A. Aiken, M.R. Boyd, Pharmacokinetics of doxorubicin in isolated lung of dogs and humans perfused in vivo, J. Pharmacol. Exp. Ther. 229 (1984) 193–198.

[109] A. Tronde, C. Bosquillon, B. Forbes, The isolated perfused lung for drug absorption studies, Drug Absorpt. Stud., Springer US, Boston, MA, 2008, pp. 135–163.

[110] A. Tronde, B. Nordén, A.-B. Jeppsson, P. Brunmark, E. Nilsson, H. Lennernäs, et al., Drug absorption from the isolated perfused rat lung–correlations with drug physicochemical properties and epithelial permeability, J. Drug. Target. 11 (2003) 61–74.

[111] A. Tronde, E. Krondahl, H. von Euler-Chelpin, P. Brunmark, U. Hultkvist Bengtsson, G. Ekström, et al., High airway-to-blood transport of an opioid tetrapeptide in the isolated rat lung after aerosol delivery, Peptides 23 (2002) 469–478.

[112] M.J. Chiang, P. Whitney, D. Massaro, Protein metabolism in lung: use of isolated perfused lung to study protein degradation, J. Appl. Physiol. 47 (1979) 72–78.

[113] W. Dalbey, E. Bingham, Metabolism of trichloroethylene by the isolated perfused lung, Toxicol. Appl. Pharmacol. 43 (1978) 267–277.
[114] C. Biancosino, M. Albert, A. Linder, Acute toxicity of irinotecan in the ex-vivo isolated perfused human lung model high-dose therapy during isolated perfusion without acute toxic lung edema, Interact. Cardiovasc. Thorac. Surg. 6 (2007) 583–587.
[115] K. Nahar, N. Gupta, R. Gauvin, S. Absar, B. Patel, V. Gupta, et al., In vitro, in vivo and ex vivo models for studying particle deposition and drug absorption of inhaled pharmaceuticals, Eur. J. Pharm. Sci. 49 (2013) 805–818.
[116] J. Eriksson, E. Sjögren, H. Thörn, K. Rubin, P. Bäckman, H. Lennernäs, Pulmonary absorption – estimation of effective pulmonary permeability and tissue retention of ten drugs using an ex vivo rat model and computational analysis, Eur. J. Pharm. Biopharm. 124 (2018) 1–12.
[117] E. Selg, P. Ewing, F. Acevedo, C.-O. Sjöberg, Å. Ryrfeldt, P. Gerde, Dry powder inhalation exposures of the endotracheally intubated rat lung, *ex vivo* and *in vivo* : the pulmonary pharmacokinetics of fluticasone furoate, J. Aerosol Med. Pulm. Drug. Deliv. 26 (2013) 181–189.
[118] C.D. Edwards, C. Luscombe, P. Eddershaw, E.M. Hessel, Development of a novel quantitative structure-activity relationship model to accurately predict pulmonary absorption and replace routine use of the isolated perfused respiring rat lung model, Pharm. Res. 33 (2016) 2604–2616.
[119] P. Gerde, P. Ewing, L. Låstbom, Å. Ryrfeldt, J. Waher, G. Lidén, A novel method to aerosolize powder for short inhalation exposures at high concentrations: isolated rat lungs exposed to respirable diesel soot, Inhal. Toxicol. 16 (2004) 45–52.
[120] D.N. Price, N.K. Kunda, P. Muttil, Challenges associated with the pulmonary delivery of therapeutic dry powders for preclinical testing, KONA Powder Part. J. 36 (2019) 129–144.
[121] R. Lizio, A. Westhof, C.-M. Lehr, T. Klenner, Oral endotracheal intubation of rats for intratracheal instillation and aerosol drug delivery, Lab. Anim. 35 (2001) 257–260.
[122] W.G. Kreyling, U. Holzwarth, N. Haberl, J. Kozempel, A. Wenk, S. Hirn, et al., Quantitative biokinetics of titanium dioxide nanoparticles after intratracheal instillation in rats: Part 3, Nanotoxicology 11 (2017) 454–464.
[123] J. Lipka, M. Semmler-Behnke, A. Wenk, J. Burkhardt, A. Aigner, W. Kreyling, Biokinetic studies of non-complexed siRNA versus nano-sized PEI F25-LMW/siRNA polyplexes following intratracheal instillation into mice, Int. J. Pharm. 500 (2016) 227–235.
[124] J. Lipka, M. Semmler-Behnke, R.A. Sperling, A. Wenk, S. Takenaka, C. Schleh, et al., Biodistribution of PEG-modified gold nanoparticles following intratracheal instillation and intravenous injection, Biomaterials 31 (2010) 6574–6581.
[125] M.R. Corboz, Z. Li, V. Malinin, A.J. Plaunt, D.M. Konicek, F.G. Leifer, et al., Preclinical pharmacology and pharmacokinetics of inhaled hexadecyl-treprostinil (C16TR), a pulmonary vasodilator prodrug, J. Pharmacol. Exp. Ther. 363 (2017) 348–357.
[126] G. Taylor, The absorption and metabolism of xenobiotics in the lung, Adv. Drug. Deliv. Rev. 5 (1990) 37–61.
[127] J. Eriksson, E. Sjögren, H. Lennernäs, H. Thörn, Drug absorption parameters obtained using the isolated perfused rat lung model are predictive of rat in vivo lung absorption, AAPS J. 22 (2020) 1–12.
[128] P. Bäckman, S. Arora, W. Couet, B. Forbes, W. de Kruijf, A. Paudel, Advances in experimental and mechanistic computational models to understand pulmonary exposure to inhaled drugs, Eur. J. Pharm. Sci. 113 (2018) 41–52.
[129] K.A. Min, X. Zhang, J. Yu, G.R. Rosania, Computational approaches to analyze and predict small molecule transport and distribution at cellular and subcellular levels, Biopharm. Drug. Dispos. 35 (2014) 15–32.
[130] U.E. Honegger, R.D. Zuehlke, I. Scuntaro, M.H.A. Schaefer, H. Toplak, U.N. Wiesmann, Cellular accumulation of amiodarone and desethylamiodarone in cultured human cells, Biochem. Pharmacol. 45 (1993) 349–356.
[131] M. Duvvuri, Intracellular drug sequestration events associated with the emergence of multidrug resistance: a mechanistic review, Front. Biosci. 10 (2005) 1499–1509.

CHAPTER 11

Drug distribution in lung tissue

Erica Bäckström[1] and Markus Fridén[1,2]
[1]Drug Metabolism and Pharmacokinetics, Research and Early Development, Respiratory & Immunology, BioPharmaceuticals R&D, AstraZeneca, Gothenburg, Sweden
[2]Translational PKPD Group, Department of Pharmaceutical Biosciences, Uppsala University, Uppsala, Sweden

11.1 Introduction

Local treatment of the lung via the inhaled route revolutionized the treatment of asthma in the 1970s [1]. Inhalation is an attractive route of delivery due to the possibility to target the airways directly and thereby creating sufficient concentrations in the lung over an appropriate dosing interval. At the same time, inhalation minimizes systemic exposure and consequently reduces side effects [2]. Many different properties such as solubility, dissolution, basicity, metabolism and transporters can influence the lung retention of inhaled compounds. Over time, two main strategies for designing controlled absorption from the lung have emerged, where absorption rate is either limited by slow drug particle dissolution or by the affinity of the dissolved compound to lung tissue [3]. Deposition of dry powder material with poor aqueous solubility may lead to increased duration in the lungs as the inhaled particles slowly dissolve at the site of deposition [3]. Corticosteroids as fluticasone propionate (FP) and fluticasone furoate are examples of inhaled compounds that are believed to be retained in the lungs due to the dissolution rate being the rate limiting step [4].

As exemplified below it is generally held that drug distribution in lung tissue is a property of the drug that may determine the onset, intensity or duration of response to the inhaled drug. The concept of drug distribution in lung tissue relates to defining the location and state of the drug in lung tissue at several levels. At the regional level, one can consider how the drug is distributed across the central airways versus peripheral lung as result of regional differences in drug disposition processes including deposition, dissolution, permeation, interaction with tissue and transfer to blood. Within any of these defined regions of the lung, the drug is also distributed across distinct histological entities including the pulmonary epithelium, sub-epithelium, vascular walls and endothelium. Again, within each histological structure there are several different cell types, which may interact with the drug in their own way via known mechanisms of drug tissue distribution; non-specific binding, passive or carrier-mediated cellular uptake, sequestration in organelles and even in some cases specific binding to abundant

Inhaled Medicines
DOI: https://doi.org/10.1016/B978-0-12-814974-4.00007-9

target protein. As the primary objective of inhaled drug design is typically to optimize the local exposure of free drug at the lung target site, the tissue drug distribution between free (available) and bound (unavailable) becomes something that is essential to be able to measure, understand and potentially also modulate. Hence as introduced below, there has been substantial research and discussion into the relationship between drug properties, lung retention and duration of effect and how these may be linked to processes of tissue distribution. Ion class, i.e. the pKa of a compound, can have a profound influence on lung retention. Cooper et al. illustrated this by gathering of data from compounds dosed as solutions delivered via the intratracheal route. The amount in lung (as % dose) shows that compounds can be broadly grouped by ion class. Acidic, neutral and zwitterionic compounds have relatively short $t_{1/2}$ in lung, whereas mono-bases are intermediate and dibasic compounds have much longer $t_{1/2}$ in lung [3].

The microkinetic model was introduced in the 90s [5] to explain the prolonged action of long-acting β-agonists (LABAs). According to this model, the phospholipid membrane of cells acts as a compartment into which drugs can partition at various degrees [5,6] depending of their lipophilicity. Sykes et al. [7] suggest that the retention of β-agonists is partly due to phospholipid interaction that directly affects the kinetic association rate (k_{on}) and dissociation constant (K_d) and thereby produce a depot for maintenance of local efficacious drug concentrations around the target receptor [7]. Another theory for the long duration of action of the LABA salmeterol is the exo-site theory that postulates that the lipophilic tail of salmeterol binds to a second site, the so-called exo-site, within the receptor that functions as an anchor and provides persistent activation of the receptor by the molecule [8]. The mechanism of persistence of salmeterol receptor activation has been debated for nearly 3 decades. The question is whether microkinetics alone is enough to explain the duration of action or if there is validity to the exo-site theory. According to several review papers, the microkinetic theory is sufficient to prolong the duration of action and there is still no clear exo-site evidence [6,9].

However, the long duration of action of all inhaled LABAs and the multiphasic plasma concentration cannot be fully explained by the microkinetic model. For olodaterol, a LABA with only moderate lipophilicity ($\log D = 1.2$) in comparison to salmeterol ($\log D > 2.5$), the microkinetic model is highly unlikely as the moderate lipophilicity of olodaterol results in lower ability to accumulate in the lipid bilayer [10]. Borghardt et al. modeled the pharmacokinetic processes of olodaterol in the clinic and came to the conclusion that there are three parallel pulmonary absorption processes, the slowest of which ($t_{1/2}$ 21.8 h) was associated with 70% of the lung deposited dose and therefore suitable for once daily dosing [11]. Overall, absorption of dissolved drug is considered fast in the alveoli and slow in the conducting airways due to differences in surface area, perfusion, and epithelial thickness and the multiphasic PK can be explained with the parallel absorption processes with different rates. One additional theory is that multiphasic PK is connected to tissue distribution being in itself the rate limiting factor. A 5-compartment model has recently been developed, by which the multiphasic lung profiles of LABAs are described with a model structure containing both a shallow (rapidly equilibrating) and deep (slowly equilibrating) lung tissue compartment [12]. The lysosomes represent a plausible explanation for the deep reservoir for bases and di-bases. However, this theory would not explain the behavior of the quaternary amines (tiotropium, ipratropium, and glycopyrronium), which are devoid of any ionizable centers and possess a permanent positive charge.

11.2 Pharmacokinetic concepts of drug distribution in tissue

11.2.1 General concepts of drug distribution in tissue

In a general sense, drug distribution in tissue typically refers to the partioning of drug from the systemic circulation to the tissue of an organ, described by the steady-state tissue-to-plasma partition coefficient (K_p). K_p is known to mechanistically depend on the balance of affinity for plasma proteins versus 'tissue' and for most tissues it can be reasonably well predicted in silico from the physicochemical drug properties, knowing that free drug concentration rapidly equilibrates across fenestrated capillary beds [13,14]. For organ tissues like the brain with a tighter endothelium, K_p can be lower than expected from physicochemical properties if there is also carrier mediated drug efflux occurring at the level of the endothelial layer. For such tissues, and any slowly perfused tissue, one can experimentally observe relevant time-dependency of the K_p, as dependent on half-life of drug clearance from the organ tissue. Hence, in addition to the (steady-state) extent of tissue distribution (K_p), parameters describing the rate of transport have been introduced. In physiologically-based pharmacokinetic modeling, these rates are generally described as flow of plasma with units of volume plasma per unit time and denoted permeability surface area product (PS) [15] or influx clearance (CL_{in}) [16]. In the light of pharmacological activity being assumed to be driven by diffusible (unbound) drug in solution, a development of the K_p concept is the $K_{p,uu}$ describing the ratio of unbound organ interstitial fluid concentration $C_{u,ISF}$ to unbound plasma concentration $C_{u,p}$. As alluded to above, a drug being transported purely by passive diffusion across capillary wall into and out of an organ, $K_{p,uu}$ will be close to 1 even if the rate of transport (PS) would be slow. For a drug with predominant active efflux or influx, $K_{p,uu}$ will be respectively below and above 1 [16].

Whilst most organs do not have the type of capillary bed that allows $K_{p,uu} \neq 1$ for a small molecule, there are still conditions during which the K_p (note referring to total drug), is less predictive of physicochemical properties and assuming $K_{p,uu} = 1$. Such is the case for the liver, where the capillary bed transport is unrestricted but where hepatocytes express high levels of drug transporters that accumulate and enrich drug in intracellular compartments mediating their elimination by metabolic biotransformation or biliary excretion [17]. This points towards the importance of intra-tissue distribution, which occurs within the tissue by mechanisms unrelated to those that mediate blood-to-tissue transfer. As a quantity describing free drug partitioning between the interstitial space and the intracellular space, $K_{p,uu,cell}$ was defined for brain tissue [18,19]. As available bioanalytical methodology does not allow estimation of free drug concentration in the various intracellular compartments of organ cells, $K_{p,uu,cell}$ is estimated indirectly as described below, and must be practically seen as a weighted average representation of various organ cell types and intracellular sub-compartments, rather than as an explicit cytosol-to-interstitial free drug concentration ratio. The concept of $K_{p,uu,cell}$ has been applied to well defined *in vitro* cell systems as well [20], but free drug and total drug distribution between organelles remain to be elucidated.

Finally, it is conceivable and indeed observed in hepatocytes [21] that cellular distribution is not always instantaneous, and therefore drug distribution in a tissue (as lung) cannot be considered independent of time. Pharmacokinetic frameworks for non-instantaneous intra-tissue distribution are abound, but typically represent empirical arrangements to describe *in vivo* distribution data.

11.2.2 Lung specific considerations

When considering the specifics of drug distribution in lung tissue we first focus on the interface between the tissue and blood, as this drug transport is relevant for all routes of administration, especially in the light of the vast blood perfusion rate of this particular organ. Notably, the lung has two circulation systems: the pulmonary circulation that perfuses the peripheral parts of the lung to oxygenate the blood and the bronchial circulation which serves to provide oxygen and nutrient to the denser tissue of the airways, into which oxygen does not sufficiently diffuse from the airspace. Whilst, the characteristics of the capillary endothelium of the bronchial circulation is fenestrated in a similar manner to most other organs, the pulmonary capillary bed has relatively tightly associated endothelial cells, which prevents excess filtration of plasma protein into interstitial spaces [22]. From the perspective of drug distribution of small molecules however, the endothelial transport has so far been considered a rapid process [23], and not substantially impactful on the overall drug absorption rate.

Local drug delivery to an organ from a different route than blood introduces some fundamentally different processes to consider: for inhaled drugs, the biopharmaceutical aspects of deposition, particle dissolution etc., but also the additional transport barrier in the form of the pulmonary epithelium, which is generally considered the predominant rate-limiting step to drug absorption of dissolved drug. Furthermore, as the point of entry (via epithelial layer) is not the same as the point of exit (via endothelial layer) there will inevitably exist local concentration gradients in the lung with spatial heterogeneity - even upon continuous dosing to pharmacokinetic steady-state. This makes spatial aspects of drug distribution much more complex for inhaled delivery compared to systemic delivery where one can reasonably assume homogenous drug distribution within the interstitial spaces at steady-state.

11.3 Mechanisms of pulmonary drug distribution

11.3.1 Trans-epithelial flux

The epithelium of the lungs needs to be considered to play a major part in the tissue distribution of inhaled compounds as the large surface area of the epithelium, and its associated volume, provide a vast opportunity for absorption and distribution. Transcellular and paracellular diffusion are the major pathways of transport across the epithelial barrier. Several drug transporter genes are widely expressed in the lung including organic cation transporters (OCTs), organic anion transporting polypeptides (OATPs), and transporters of the ATP binding cassette family including the multidrug resistance proteins (e.g. P-glycoprotein (P-gp)) [24]. β-agonists such as salbutamol, formoterol, and salmeterol are substrates for OCTs, but the fraction that is actively transported into cells is expected to be minor [25,26]. However, drug transporter expression and function in the lung is still an emerging area and little is known of the implications for the biopharmaceutics of inhaled drugs [24,27].

Isolated human ATI-like cells in primary culture (hAEpC) are to date the most used model as it reflects the *in vivo* situation of the air-blood barrier in the alveolar bed due to their ability to form tight junctions and hence, exhibiting high trans-epithelial electrical resistance (TEER, a parameter for tightness of epithelium). The hAEpC cultures are especially used for studies of absorption and transport of xenobiotics in the lung [28–30]. When it comes to cell lines, there is currently only one cell line of alveolar origin available forming tight junctions and hence being suitable for transport and absorption experiments, the immortalized cell line called human alveolar epithelial lentivirus immortalized (hAELVi) cells [31]. The human alveolar cell line A549, derived from an adenocarcinoma does not exhibit high TEER values and therefore is it not well suited for drug absorption studies [32], but it is on the other hand commonly used in toxicity studies. There are several different *in vitro* models based on bronchial cells available, with 16HBE and Calu-3 being among the most commonly used. A more advanced cell culture model is the 3D culture with primary airway epithelial cells cultured at air-liquid interphase represent physiologically relevant models of the human airway consisting of ciliated cells, mucus secreting goblet cells and basal cells [33,34], and are now commercialized under trade names such as MucilAir and EpiAirway by Epithelix Sàrl and MatTek Corporation, respectively.

An alternate approach to study trans-epithelial flux is to use the well-established Caco-2 cell line (derived from a human colon carcinoma) that is frequently used to predict human intestinal permeability [35]. Values of Caco-2 intrinsic permeability (P_{app}) were compared to the *ex vivo* effective permeability (P_{eff}) from the isolated perfused rat lung (IPL) model and were found to be generally well correlated. This data suggests that intrinsic Caco-2 permeability has the potential to be used for early predictions of passive transcellular permeability across the lung epithelium [36].

11.3.2 Cellular uptake and distribution

Drug availability for the target is often referred to as tissue binding and the drug being either 'free' or 'bound' where the free form is considered pharmacologically active and the bound is not. Although physical interaction with tissue constituents (non-specific binding) does occur at any place, drug availability also depends on other processes such as membrane transport and compartmentation of the tissue and target as discussed above. A practical and yet physiologically relevant parameter to quantify the extent of tissue distribution is the unbound volume of distribution in the lung ($V_{u,lung}$) [37]. This is the proportionality constant between the amount of drug in tissue and the free drug concentration in the lung tissue interstitial space. The ratio of total lung and unbound plasma concentration at steady-state ($K_{p,u}$) and $V_{u,lung}$ is expected to be closely related as $V_{u,lung}$ represents overall tissue binding.

Precision cut lung slices, i.e. slices of fresh viable agarose filled lung tissue, are utilized in the estimation of $V_{u,lung}$. The ideal lung slice contains alveolar tissue, airways and blood vessels in a morphological organization close to the *in vivo* situation, and fully operational transporters. Hence, slices can be used to study retention of compounds due to lysosomal trapping and carrier-mediated transport. The cationic compounds ipratropium, tiotropium, and MPP^+ are substrates of OCTs and organic cation/carnitine transporters (OCTNs) and carrier-mediated transport have been demonstrated for ipratropium and MPP^+ in the lung slice system [37]. From the profiling of inhaled compounds, it was evident that drugs have very different tissue distribution and thereby different $V_{u,lung}$. LABAs had an average $V_{u,lung}$ of 1000 mL/g whereas short-acting β-agonist had a $V_{u,lung}$ of 2 mL/g, these suggest that a large $V_{u,lung}$ is associated with slower absorption kinetics from the lung to the systemic circulation. This slow absorption of drug through pulmonary tissue seems to be effectively prolonging the effect-duration of bronchodilators.

The unbound drug partition coefficient of the cell ($K_{p,uu,cell}$) describes the intracellular to extracellular unbound drug concentration ratio. If the only distribution mechanism is binding to tissue, $K_{p,uu,cell}$ will be equal to one, and in such cases, $V_{u,lung}$ can be expected to be equal to 1/fraction of unbound drug lung in homogenate ($1/f_{u,lung}$). $K_{p,uu,cell}$ was estimated high in the lung slice system for cations MPP^+ (130) and ipratropium (7.1), bases propranolol (12), formoterol (6.0), salmeterol (2.4), and salbutamol (2.2) and dibase AZD3199 (34) indicating active uptake and/or lysosomal trapping for these compounds (Fig. 11.1).

Lysosomal trapping has been reported to play a major role in the accumulation and retention of bases [38]. Lysosomes, which are particularly abundant in lung tissue [39], are

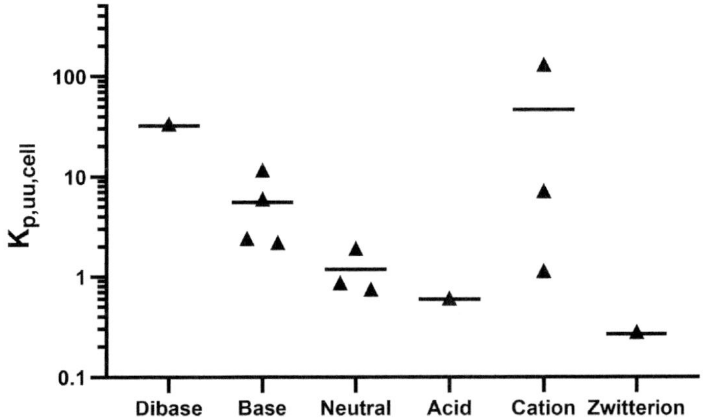

Figure 11.1 Experimental $K_{p,uu,cell}$ values of compounds grouped by ion class. The mean $K_{p,uu,cell}$ value was high for cations, bases, and the di-base, whereas the mean $K_{p,uu,cell}$ value for neutrals, the acid, and the zwitterions was close to unity [37].

acidic organelles with pH 4–5 that play a key role in various metabolic processes in the cells [40]. Lysosomal trapping results from the diffusion of basic compounds from cytosol to lysosomes, where the compound becomes charged and hence a non-permeable ionized species. The restricted back-diffusion into the cytosol leads to an accumulation of compounds in lysosomes. The trapping is energy-dependent and most importantly a reversible process. Uptake of one base into lysosomes may be decreased by the presence of another base as the intra-lysosomal pH increases with a higher lysosomal concentration of bases. This increased pH results in a reduced capacity to accumulate bases as a shift towards neutral, and more permeable, species occur. This phenomenon has been demonstrated in isolated liver lysosomes [41], in alveolar macrophages [42], as well as in precision-cut rat lung slices [37]. Lysosomal trapping can be studied in more detail via co-incubation with monensin. Monensin is an antibiotic able to transport protons across lipid membranes of cells and therefore has the capacity to raise the intra-lysosomal pH and hence reduce the lysosomes ability to trap basic compounds [43,44]. The presence of monensin reduced the uptake of LABAs formoterol and salmeterol and dibasic ultralong-acting β-agonist AZD3199 into precision cut rat lung slices by approximately 70%, whereas the uptake of short-acting β-agonist salbutamol was unaffected (Fig. 11.2) [38].

The redistribution from lysosomes causes slowness in the distribution kinetics for the LABAs and ultralong-acting β-agonist, whereas the distribution and kinetics of the short-acting β-agonist salbutamol does not appear to involve lysosomal trapping [38]. The concept of the lysosomal sub-compartment of the cell representing the most slowly equilibrating, and thus the rate-limiting process of β-agonist distribution, can be understood by considering the mechanism by which lysosomal trapping occurs. The slow kinetics of lysosomal trapping is a key mechanism by which retention in the

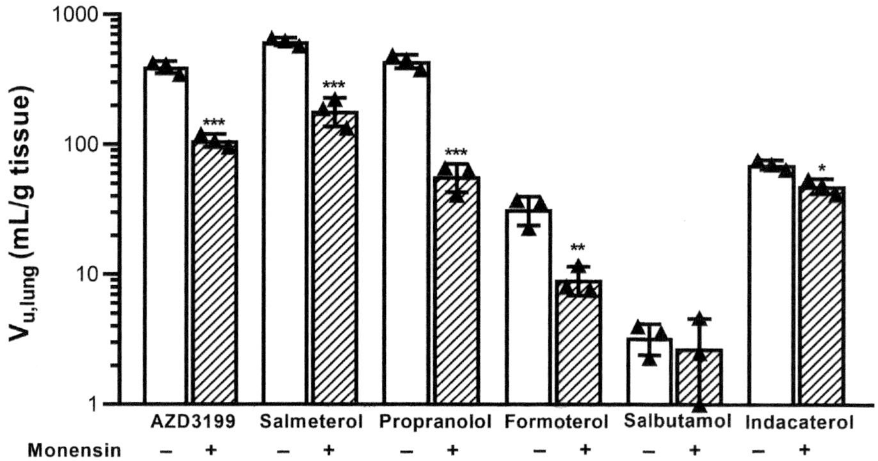

Figure 11.2 Contribution of lysosomal trapping to lung tissue uptake. Lung slices were incubated in the absence or presence of monensin to determine the contribution of lysosomal trapping to lung tissue uptake. Monensin reduced partitioning to various extents for all compounds except salbutamol n = 3, mean ± SEM, *$P \leq 0.05$, **$P \leq 0.01$, ***$P \leq 0.001$, [38].

lung and the effect duration of inhaled β-adrenergic bronchodilators are prolonged. These results are in agreement with the 5-compartment model which explains the multiphasic lung profile of LABAs with a rapidly and a slowly equilibrating compartments where the lysosomes represent the slow compartment [12]. Interestingly, in experiments with basic amines in isolated perfused lung experiments, a fraction of the dose appears to be associated with a 'slowly eluting pool' [45] suggesting that there is an intrinsically slow component to the tissue distribution of basic drugs, which conceivably represents lysosomal trapping.

However, lung slices do not specifically address the first cellular barrier of the airway epithelium that inhaled drugs encounter. For studies to gain a deeper understanding of the cellular and subcellular trafficking, one can use cell lines cultured at an air-liquid interface such as Calu-3 cells. The contribution of lysosomal trapping as a mechanism driving retention of different bronchodilators have been investigated with Calu-3 cells [46]. The data indicate that the LABAs formoterol and salmeterol were trapped in lysosomes whereas the short-acting β-agonist salbutamol was not [46], all in agreement with what was observed in slices.

Determining the extent to which a molecule binds non-specifically to proteins (free fraction, f_u) is critical as it influences compound dosing, drug efficacy, clearance rate and potential for drug interactions. Approaches to measure non-specific binding in tissue, equilibrium dialysis and ultrafiltration, utilize tissue homogenates [47,48]. One major disadvantage with homogenization of lung tissue is the disruption of the normal drug compartmentalization in the cells, including the pH gradients, thereby precluding the possibility of lysosomal trapping. The use of equilibrium dialysis or ultrafiltration of lung homogenates are not standard practices in PK/PD evaluation of inhaled compounds because of the potentially large errors in the estimates of free drug concentration [47]. As mentioned earlier, if the only distribution mechanism is binding to tissue constituents $V_{u,lung}$ will be expected to equal $1/f_{u,lung}$. However, if compounds are trapped in lysosomes the free fraction in lung tissue, $f_{u,lung}$, will be incorrect. For compounds that are involved in active uptake by transporters or trapping in lysosomes the free fraction estimated with lung homogenate will be an overestimation.

Structure-activity research during 1970–80s focused on lipophilic modifications of inhaled corticosteroids to achieve lung retention after inhalation. Extended dwell time in the lungs was attained by increased lipophilicity and consequently improved tissue binding as well as enhanced hepatic first pass inactivation by CYP3A [49]. Other chemical modifications such as reversible esterification of compounds have also been shown to affect both the duration of action and therapeutic ratio compared to other routes of administration. Budesonide forms reversible fatty acid esters within the cells of the airway tissue resulting in a formation of an intracellular depot of inactive drug. Over time, the budesonide esters hydrolyze back to their active state [49,50]. This reversible process extends budesonides anti-inflammatory effect and increase its airway selectivity.

11.3.3 Target mediated drug disposition

Levy introduced the term target-mediated drug disposition (TMDD) as a possible mechanism responsible for non-linear pharmacokinetic profiles [51]. TMDD corresponds to a special case wherein a significant proportion of a drug (relative to dose) is bound with high affinity to a pharmacological target, to such extent that this interaction is reflected in concentrations of the drug. Few small molecular weight compounds have been identified to exhibit TMDD, but as larger molecules such as peptides, proteins and antibodies are developed for inhalation, the incidence of TMDD is likely to increase [52]. Biologics differ from small molecules not only in matters of their size, but they have also slower absorption rates, different elimination routes, and high affinity for specific targets. The binding to target with high affinity and subsequent turnover of the drug-target complex can contribute significantly to the disposition of biologics. However, this elimination by binding to a target is saturable because of the finite number of targets on the cell surface. This saturability causes the non-linearity in pharmacokinetic profiles, especially at low doses of a drug, which is often the case for drug administered by inhalation.

Interestingly, in a systems pharmacology approach to mechanistically describe lung disposition in rats, inclusion of receptor binding was necessary for accurate predictions of spleen concentrations [23], which verifies that FP has a high receptor-bound fraction previously observed in target occupancy studies [53]. This elucidates the potential pitfall of only relying on K_p-values when predicting tissue concentrations after low doses of highly potent compounds. Under such circumstances, underpredictions are inevitable, as K_p-values do not account for receptor binding. In general, one can assess the likelihood of seeing target-mediated drug distribution by calculating the target-bound fraction of drug (f_{tb}, Eq. 11.1) as a function of the target density in relevant tissue (B_{max}), the drug affinitiy for the target (K_d) and the non-specific distribution (binding) of drug in the tissue ($V_{u,lung}$) determined at saturating concentrations [53].

$$f_{tb} = \frac{1}{1 + \frac{V_{u,lung} * K_d}{B_{max}}} \tag{11.1}$$

11.3.4 Metabolism

Most xenobiotics are metabolized by phase I (oxidative) enzymes, such as cytochrome P450 (CYP), flavin containing monooxygenases (FMO), monoamine oxidase (MOA), xanthine oxidase/aldehyde oxidase (XO/AO) and epoxide hydrolase (EH) [54] with CYP being the most important family of enzymes accounting for about 75% of the total human drug metabolism [55]. Multiple studies have shown the presence (mRNA expression or protein) of CYP1A1, CYP1B1, CYP2A6, CYP2A13, CYP2B6, CYP2C8/18, CYP2D6, CYP2E1, CYP2F1, CYP2J2, CYP2S1, CYP3A4/5, CYP3A43, CYP4B1, EHs and FMOs as the major drug metabolizing enzymes present in different pulmonary cells including alveolar type I (ATI) and type II (ATII) cells, Clara cells, ciliated columnar epithelial cells and macrophages [56–58]. So, even though the liver is the major site of metabolism, other tissues such as the lung should not be ignored. Microsomes are typically employed to study phase I drug metabolism. However, at the cellular level the lung is much more heterogeneous than the liver and consequently microsomes prepared from whole lung tissue may dilute out the drug metabolizing activity concentrated in a few cell types. A recent study by Rubin et al. compared the activity of drug metabolizing enzymes *in vitro* (microsomes from rat and human lung, human hepatocytes, and human type II alveolar cells) via incubations with specific substrates [59]. The study found less metabolic activity in incubations with human ATII cells when compared to isolated hepatocytes and higher activity in rat lung microsomes compared with human lung microsomes for all reactions selective for FMO, CYP1B1, CYP2C9, CYP2J2 and CYP3A4. The data indicates that isolated ATII cells do not offer more than lung microsomes for studying pulmonary drug metabolism and that rat lung microsomes can be used to investigate the potential metabolism in the lungs [59].

Drug metabolism can also be studied with lung slices and the use of rat lung slices for drug metabolism investigations was first reported in 1977 [60]. As slices contain a variety of different cell types with differing metabolic activity and tissue architecture is intact both phase I and phase II processes are fully represented. More recently, lung slices have been used to investigate the pulmonary drug metabolism of ciclesonide, mavoglurant (AFQ056), and benzydamine [61–63]. However, the potential differences in metabolism between species need to be considered when using for example rat lung slices. The metabolism of a range of phase I and phase II probe substrates have previously been assessed in both rat and human lung preparations and the data indicates that pulmonary CYP activity is relatively low in general, but that there are significant differences in enzyme activity between rat and human lung [64].

In contrast to traditional low molecular weight compounds, larger molecules as peptides, proteins and antibodies can be metabolized via different enzymes e.g. proteases and peptidases. There is a lack of mechanistic knowledge about the details of the processes involved especially around the localization and activity of proteolytic enzymes in the different parts of the lung and most importantly the possible differences in proteolytic activity in pathological conditions. Baginski et al. [65] investigated expression patterns of proteolytic enzymes in human respiratory cell types (human bronchial epithelial cells (hBEpC, Calu-3, and 16HBE14o) and human alveolar epithelial cells (A549)) on mRNA level and found marked differences between the expression pattern of the different cells. Further studies are needed to fully understand the impact of proteolytic enzymes on inhaled large molecule drugs. In addition, due to differences in enzyme expression and activity across animal species, conclusions drawn from animal studies may not be representative and predictive of what might occur in humans [28].

11.4 Spatial distribution of compounds in lung tissue

11.4.1 Mass spectrometry imaging

Due to the complexity of the lung with over 40 different cell types in various structures, the local pharmacokinetic drug properties and the spatial distribution of compounds needs to be taken into consideration. Depending on the specific location of a respiratory disease process the pharmacological target sites can be either centrally (tracheobronchially) or peripherally located. Hence spatial information can be critical to have. Mass spectrometry imaging (MSI) is a technique that enables mapping of the local distribution of label-free molecular species in tissue sections at micrometer scale. MSI has been applied to study the spatial distribution of compounds in lungs in multiple studies [66–73]. The resolution of the MSI images has previously been the limiting factor, but with advances made with the technique image resolution on a single micrometer scale can now be produced. One major advantage with MSI is that several compounds can be simultaneously detected in the same tissue, which allows for comparison in the spatial distribution of various drugs or after different routes of delivery. As the compounds are detected by their mass, the distribution of a compound (delivered via one route of delivery) and a deuterated version of the same compound (delivered via another route) can be detected in the same section of a rat lung to allow direct comparison of the spatial distribution between routes of delivery. This dual-isotope approach has been used to reveal the distribution patterns after nebulized inhalation and intravenous (IV) delivery of salmeterol to rats. Inhalation led to deposition of compound in the entire lung but with several smaller areas with higher intensities and retention in bronchioles, whereas systemic delivery resulted in a more homogenous distribution of compound [72].

MSI can also be used to describe the morphology of the lung based on the molecular profile of tissue sub-regions such as alveoli, airways or blood vessels [74,75]. By combining the information of drug distribution with spatial clustering of the tissue based on the presence of specific molecular species, mean intensities in respective region can be extracted and a so-called lung targeting factor can be calculated. The lung targeting factor was introduced by Bäckström et al., and it describes the advantage of going inhaled in comparison to systemic administration at equivalent plasma concentrations. Inhaled salmeterol is reported to have a 31- and 45-fold targeting in the sub-epithelial and epithelial region at 30 min after administration, respectively [72]. However, MSI images do not reflect the free concentration of a compound but rather the total (including undissolved particles).

Co-administration of drugs of different chemotypes allow for comparison how physicochemical properties effect the spatial distribution. Hamm et al. investigated the two approaches to achieve lung retention, via slow drug particle dissolution or via high tissue affinity, with MSI after delivery via IV and nebulized inhalation. At 30 min after delivery, it was evident that the poorly soluble molecule FP had a different retention pattern and it was present in both alveolar and bronchiolar region whereas the soluble bases salmeterol and salbutamol was preferentially retained in bronchioles (Fig. 11.3).

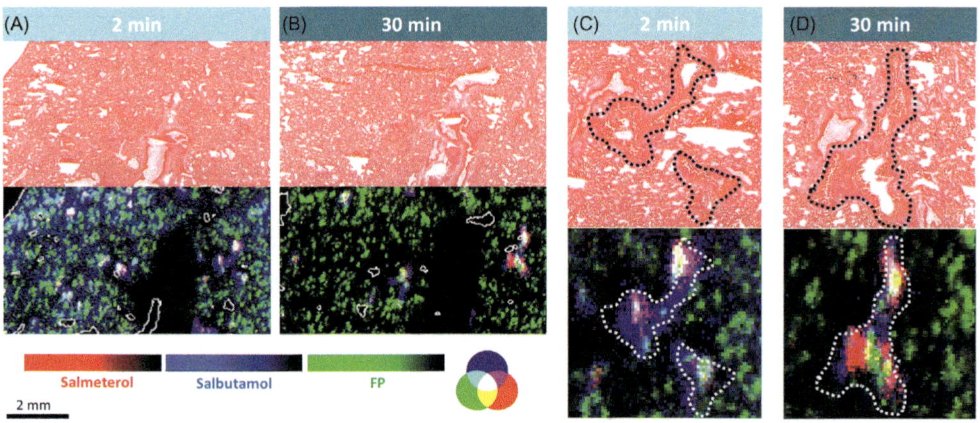

Figure 11.3 Matching lung histology with high spatial resolution DESI MS images. (A and B) H&E stained lung for 2 and 30 min after administration via inhaled nebulization and overlaid molecular distribution of (red) salmeterol, (blue) salbutamol and (green) FP from MSI. (C and D) Inserts showing two regions including a bronchiole (dashed lines) and corresponding H&E and MS images. Intensity scale is fixed for each molecular species independently and monochromatic lighter colors correspond to higher relative abundance and darker to lower abundance. Tissue area is outlined in solid white line [73].

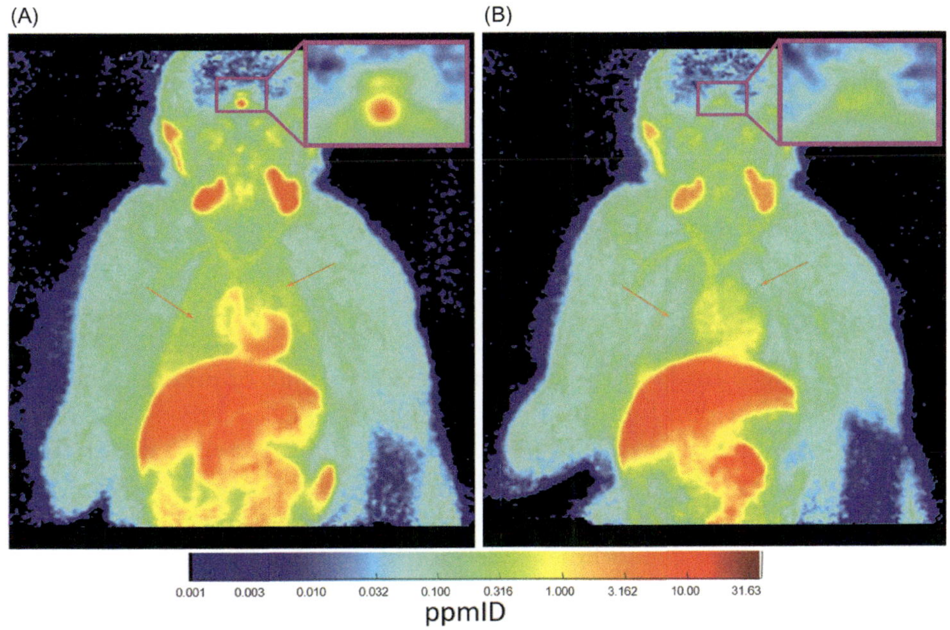

Figure 11.4 PET images of the distribution of radioactivity after IV injection of ^{11}C-VC-002 at (A) baseline and (B) after inhalation of ipratropium (150 μg/kg). Red arrows denote the lung and the inserts show the pituitary gland. The color scale is logarithmic, [76].

11.4.2 Positron emission tomography

The non-invasive external molecular imaging technique positron emission tomography (PET) is increasingly used in translational biomedical research and for clinical diagnoses. A key strength with PET is that it permits quantification of drug binding to their respective target proteins *in vivo*. i.e. it reflects the free concentration of the compound and not the total. PET has been applied to test the concept of estimating drug-induced target occupancy of a bronchodilator (ipratropium) in the non-human primate lung after inhalation and IV administration. The target occupancy in the lung lungs at 30 min after inhalation was one order of magnitude higher in comparison to after IV, consistent with the view that inhalation provides locally higher concentrations in lung tissue (Fig. 11.4) [76].

11.5 Summary

It has been learned from the experience of developing inhaled medicines that modulation of the drug's interaction with the tissue can be critical for determining the onset, intensity and duration of local drug response. These interactions include but are not limited to non-specific and hydrophobically driven interaction with tissue constituents.

Other specific processes such as lysosomal trapping, carrier-mediated transport, metabolism and even drug binding to the target itself are important. Furthermore, drug distribution in lung tissue is multi-dimensional and goes far beyond considering the drug as being 'free or bound'; the exposure to locally administered drug should be expected to, and has been demonstrated, to distribute unevenly across airways of different sizes, across histological structures of the larger airways and most likely across the different cell-types that reside in and traffic to the lung.

11.6 Outlook

Advances have been made in the field and the knowledge of different mechanisms and how they affect distribution in the lungs has greatly increased, but the complexity and heterogeneity of the respiratory system still represent a major challenge for the development of efficacious inhaled drugs. As the field is moving towards precision medicine, targeting specific diseased sub-structures of the lung and away from treating the lung as a whole, there are more knowledge gaps to fill. Most importantly, there is a need for functional readouts to define the free drug at the target sites in the intact tissue where the spatial resolution is kept. Assessment of target engagement markers through gene expression with *in situ* hybridization techniques such as RNAscope [77], or assessment of translation of proteins downstream from the target with imaging mass cytometry [78,79], could potentially be applied. In addition, the impact of severe lung disease with extracellular matrix remodeling and infiltration of inflammatory cells may potentially have a large impact on distribution and retention of inhaled drugs. However, a recent clinical inhalation study with idiopathic pulmonary fibrosis (IPF) patients by Usmani et al. showed that inhaled drugs can be optimized to reach the peripheral areas of the lung where the active scarring occurs in IPF patients [80]. The effect of different respiratory diseases on distribution and tissue affinity is an area that require further investigation, especially in fibrotic disease where both tissue constituents and local blood flow will be regionally altered. However, in terms of implications for inhaled product development it appears likely that mechanisms related to regionally altered deposition and dissolution will have a more profound effect on therapeutic performance and/or plasma pharmacokinetics. Currently, the plasma-concentration time profile, supported by physiologically-based pharmacokinetic modeling is used to indirectly and qualitatively make inferences of all these aspects and how they might impact therapeutic performance. In the future, with developing techniques such as receptor occupancy of inhaled drug by PET imaging [81] or bronchosorption [82] to sample the inhaled drug, it is conceivable that refined practices to ensure product consistency can evolve.

References

[1] S.W. Stein, C.G. Thiel, The history of therapeutic aerosols: a chronological review, J. Aerosol Med. Pulm. Drug. Deliv. 30 (1) (2017) 20–41.

[2] P. Backman, et al., Advances in inhaled technologies: understanding the therapeutic challenge, predicting clinical performance, and designing the optimal inhaled product, Clin. Pharmacol. Ther. 95 (5) (2014) 509–520.

[3] A.E. Cooper, D. Ferguson, K. Grime, Optimisation of DMPK by the inhaled route: challenges and approaches, Curr. Drug. Metab. 13 (4) (2012) 457–473.

[4] E. Selg, et al., Dry powder inhalation exposures of the endotracheally intubated rat lung, ex vivo and in vivo: the pulmonary pharmacokinetics of fluticasone furoate, J. Aerosol Med. Pulm. Drug. Deliv. 26 (4) (2013) 181–189.

[5] G.P. Anderson, A. Linden, K.F. Rabe, Why are long-acting beta-adrenoceptor agonists long-acting? Eur. Respir. J. 7 (3) (1994) 569–578.

[6] G. Vauquelin, S.J. Charlton, Long-lasting target binding and rebinding as mechanisms to prolong in vivo drug action, Br. J. Pharmacol. 161 (3) (2010) 488–508.

[7] D.A. Sykes, et al., Observed drug-receptor association rates are governed by membrane affinity: the importance of establishing "micro-pharmacokinetic/pharmacodynamic relationships" at the beta2-adrenoceptor, Mol. Pharmacol. 85 (4) (2014) 608–617.

[8] M. Johnson, et al., The pharmacology of salmeterol, Life Sci. 52 (26) (1993) 2131–2143.

[9] R.A. Coleman, On the mechanism of the persistent action of salmeterol: what is the current position? Br. J. Pharmacol. 158 (1) (2009) 180–182.

[10] P. Casarosa, et al., Functional and biochemical rationales for the 24-hour-long duration of action of olodaterol, J. Pharmacol. Exp. Ther. 337 (3) (2011) 600–609.

[11] J.M. Borghardt, et al., Model-based evaluation of pulmonary pharmacokinetics in asthmatic and COPD patients after oral olodaterol inhalation, Br. J. Clin. Pharmacol. 82 (3) (2016) 739–753.

[12] R. Hendrickx, et al., Translational model to predict pulmonary pharmacokinetics and efficacy in man for inhaled bronchodilators, CPT Pharmacomet. Syst. Pharmacol. (2017).

[13] T. Rodgers, D. Leahy, M. Rowland, Physiologically based pharmacokinetic modeling 1: predicting the tissue distribution of moderate-to-strong bases, J. Pharm. Sci. 94 (6) (2005) 1259–1276.

[14] T. Rodgers, M. Rowland, Physiologically based pharmacokinetic modelling 2: predicting the tissue distribution of acids, very weak bases, neutrals and zwitterions, J. Pharm. Sci. 95 (6) (2006) 1238–1257.

[15] Y. Takasato, S.I. Rapoport, Q.R. Smith, An in situ brain perfusion technique to study cerebrovascular transport in the rat, Am. J. Physiol. 247 (3 Pt 2) (1984) H484–H493.

[16] M. Hammarlund-Udenaes, et al., On the rate and extent of drug delivery to the brain, Pharm. Res. 25 (8) (2008) 1737–1750.

[17] H. Kusuhara, Y. Sugiyama, Pharmacokinetic modeling of the hepatobiliary transport mediated by cooperation of uptake and efflux transporters, Drug. Metab. Rev. 42 (3) (2010) 539–550.

[18] M. Friden, et al., Measurement of unbound drug exposure in brain: modeling of pH partitioning explains diverging results between the brain slice and brain homogenate methods, Drug. Metab. Dispos.: Biol. Fate Chem. 39 (3) (2011) 353–362.

[19] M. Friden, et al., In vitro methods for estimating unbound drug concentrations in the brain interstitial and intracellular fluids, Drug. Metab. Dispos.: Biol. Fate Chem. 35 (9) (2007) 1711–1719.

[20] A. Mateus, P. Matsson, P. Artursson, Rapid measurement of intracellular unbound drug concentrations, Mol. Pharm. 10 (6) (2013) 2467–2478.

[21] P. Nordell, et al., Predicting metabolic clearance for drugs that are actively transported into hepatocytes: incubational binding as a consequence of in vitro hepatocyte concentration is a key factor, Drug. Metab. Dispos. 41 (4) (2013) 836–843.

[22] W.C. Aird, Phenotypic heterogeneity of the endothelium: II. Representative vascular beds, Circ. Res. 100 (2) (2007) 174–190.

[23] E. Boger, et al., Systems pharmacology approach for prediction of pulmonary and systemic pharmacokinetics and receptor occupancy of inhaled drugs, CPT: Pharmacomet. Syst. Pharmacol. (2016).

[24] T. Berg, et al., Expression of MATE1, P-gp, OCTN1 and OCTN2, in epithelial and immune cells in the lung of COPD and healthy individuals, Respir. Res. 19 (1) (2018) 68.

[25] A.J. Dudley, K. Bleasby, C.D. Brown, The organic cation transporter OCT2 mediates the uptake of beta-adrenoceptor antagonists across the apical membrane of renal LLC-PK(1) cell monolayers, Br. J. Pharmacol. 131 (1) (2000) 71−79.

[26] J.J. Salomon, et al., Beta-2 adrenergic agonists are substrates and inhibitors of human organic cation transporter 1, Mol. Pharm. (2015).

[27] C. Bosquillon, Drug transporters in the lung—do they play a role in the biopharmaceutics of inhaled drugs? J. Pharm. Sci. 99 (5) (2010) 2240−2255.

[28] B. Forbes, C. Ehrhardt, Human respiratory epithelial cell culture for drug delivery applications, Eur. J. Pharm. Biopharm. 60 (2) (2005) 193−205.

[29] S. Endter, et al., RT-PCR analysis of ABC, SLC and SLCO drug transporters in human lung epithelial cell models, J. Pharm. Pharmacol. 61 (5) (2009) 583−591.

[30] M. Bur, et al., Assessment of transport rates of proteins and peptides across primary human alveolar epithelial cell monolayers, Eur. J. Pharm. Sci. 28 (3) (2006) 196−203.

[31] A. Kuehn, et al., Human alveolar epithelial cells expressing tight junctions to model the air-blood barrier, Altex 33 (3) (2016) 251−260.

[32] K.A. Foster, et al., Characterization of the A549 cell line as a type II pulmonary epithelial cell model for drug metabolism, Exp. Cell Res. 243 (2) (1998) 359−366.

[33] D. Balharry, K. Sexton, K.A. BeruBe, An in vitro approach to assess the toxicity of inhaled tobacco smoke components: nicotine, cadmium, formaldehyde and urethane, Toxicology 244 (1) (2008) 66−76.

[34] S. Huang, et al., Potential of in vitro reconstituted 3D human airway epithelia (MucilAir) to assess respiratory sensitizers, Toxicol. Vitro 27 (3) (2013) 1151−1156.

[35] E.H. Kerns, et al., Combined application of parallel artificial membrane permeability assay and Caco-2 permeability assays in drug discovery, J. Pharm. Sci. 93 (6) (2004) 1440−1453.

[36] J. Eriksson, et al., Pulmonary absorption - estimation of effective pulmonary permeability and tissue retention of ten drugs using an ex vivo rat model and computational analysis, Eur. J. Pharm. Biopharm. 124 (2018) 1−12.

[37] E. Backstrom, et al., Development of a novel lung slice methodology for profiling of inhaled compounds, J. Pharm. Sci. 105 (2) (2016) 838−845.

[38] E. Backstrom, et al., Lung retention by lysosomal trapping of inhaled drugs can be predicted in vitro with lung slices, J. Pharm. Sci. 105 (11) (2016) 3432−3439.

[39] A.C. MacIntyre, D.J. Cutler, The potential role of lysosomes in tissue distribution of weak bases, Biopharm. Drug. Dispos. 9 (6) (1988) 513−526.

[40] C. de Duve, et al., Commentary. Lysosomotropic agents, Biochem. Pharmacol. 23 (18) (1974) 2495−2531.

[41] J. Ishizaki, et al., Uptake of imipramine in rat liver lysosomes in vitro and its inhibition by basic drugs, J. Pharmacol. Exp. Ther. 294 (3) (2000) 1088−1098.

[42] R.E. Vestal, D.M. Kornhauser, D.G. Shand, Active uptake of propranolol by isolated rabbit alveolar macrophages and its inhibition by other basic amines, J. Pharmacol. Exp. Ther. 214 (1) (1980) 106−111.

[43] D. Aowicki, A. Huczynski, Structure and antimicrobial properties of monensin A and its derivatives: summary of the achievements, Biomed. Res. Int. 2013 (2013) 742149.

[44] G.A. Siebert, et al., Ion-trapping, microsomal binding, and unbound drug distribution in the hepatic retention of basic drugs, J. Pharmacol. Exp. Ther. 308 (1) (2004) 228−235.

[45] R.N. Upton, D.J. Doolette, Kinetic aspects of drug disposition in the lungs, Clin. Exp. Pharmacol. Physiol. 26 (5−6) (1999) 381−391.

[46] V. Panduga, M.J. Stocks, C. Bosquillon, Cellular and subcellular drug traficking in bronchial epithelial cells: mechanisms controlling drug disposition, Respir. Drug. Deliv. (2018) 37−44.

[47] B. Forbes, et al., Challenges in inhaled product development and opportunities for open innovation, Adv. Drug. Deliv. Rev. 63 (1−2) (2011) 69−87.

[48] K. Wu, et al., Budesonide and ciclesonide: effect of tissue binding on pulmonary receptor binding, Drug. Metab. Dispos.: Biol. Fate Chem. 37 (7) (2009) 1421−1426.

[49] S. Edsbacker, R. Brattsand, Budesonide fatty-acid esterification: a novel mechanism prolonging binding to airway tissue. Review of available data, Ann. Allergy Asthma Immunol. 88 (6) (2002) 609–616.

[50] R. Brattsand, A. Miller-Larsson, The role of intracellular esterification in budesonide once-daily dosing and airway selectivity, Clin. Ther. 25 (Suppl. C) (2003) C28–C41.

[51] G. Levy, Pharmacologic target-mediated drug disposition, Clin. Pharmacol. Ther. 56 (3) (1994) 248–252.

[52] P. Dua, E. Hawkins, P.H. van der Graaf, A tutorial on target-mediated drug disposition (TMDD) models, CPT Pharmacomet. Syst. Pharmacol. 4 (6) (2015) 324–337.

[53] E. Boger, et al., A novel in vivo receptor occupancy methodology for the glucocorticoid receptor: toward an improved understanding of lung pharmacokinetic/pharmacodynamic relationships, J. Pharmacol. Exp. Ther. 353 (2) (2015) 279–287.

[54] A. Parkinson, *Biotransformation of xenobiotics*, in *Casarett & Doull's*, in: C.D. Klaassen (Ed.), Toxicology: The Basic Science of Poisons, McGraw-Hill, Inc, New York, 2001. 1363-224.

[55] F.P. Guengerich, Cytochrome p450 and chemical toxicology, Chem. Res. Toxicol. 21 (1) (2008) 70–83.

[56] J.Y. Zhang, Y. Wang, C. Prakash, Xenobiotic-metabolizing enzymes in human lung, Curr. Drug. Metab. 7 (8) (2006) 939–948.

[57] H. Raunio, et al., Expression of xenobiotic-metabolizing CYPs in human pulmonary tissue, Exp. Toxicol. Pathol. 51 (4–5) (1999) 412–417.

[58] T. Berg, et al., Gene expression analysis of membrane transporters and drug-metabolizing enzymes in the lung of healthy and COPD subjects, Pharmacol. Res. Perspect. 2 (4) (2014) e00054.

[59] K. Rubin, et al., Pulmonary metabolism of substrates for key drug-metabolizing enzymes by human alveolar type II cells, human and rat lung microsomes, and the isolated perfused rat lung model, Pharmaceutics 12 (2) (2020).

[60] J.J. O'Neil, et al., Metabolism in rat lung tissue slices: technical factors, J. Appl. Physiol. Respir. Env. Exerc. Physiol. 43 (5) (1977) 902–906.

[61] Y. Yilmaz, et al., Functional assessment of rat pulmonary flavin-containing monooxygenase activity, Xenobiotica 49 (5) (2019) 503–512.

[62] Y. Yilmaz, et al., Assessment of the pulmonary CYP1A1 metabolism of mavoglurant (AFQ056) in rat, Xenobiotica 48 (8) (2018) 793–803.

[63] R. Nave, R. Fisher, K. Zech, In Vitro metabolism of ciclesonide in human lung and liver precision-cut tissue slices, Biopharm. Drug. Dispos. 27 (4) (2006) 197–207.

[64] Y. Yilmaz, et al., Comparison of rat and human pulmonary metabolism using precision-cut lung slices (PCLS), Drug. Metab. Lett. 13 (1) (2019) 53–63.

[65] L. Baginski, et al., Reverse transcription polymerase chain reaction (RT-PCR) analysis of proteolytic enzymes in cultures of human respiratory epithelial cells, J. Aerosol Med. Pulm. Drug. Deliv. 24 (2) (2011) 89–101.

[66] A. Nilsson, et al., Fine mapping the spatial distribution and concentration of unlabeled drugs within tissue micro-compartments using imaging mass spectrometry, PLoS One 5 (7) (2010) e11411.

[67] G. Marko-Varga, et al., Drug localization in different lung cancer phenotypes by MALDI mass spectrometry imaging, J. Proteom. 74 (7) (2011) 982–992.

[68] B. Prideaux, et al., High-sensitivity MALDI-MRM-MS imaging of moxifloxacin distribution in tuberculosis-infected rabbit lungs and granulomatous lesions, Anal. Chem. 83 (6) (2011) 2112–2118.

[69] N. Sun, et al., Pharmacokinetic and pharmacometabolomic study of pirfenidone in normal mouse tissues using high mass resolution MALDI-FTICR-mass spectrometry imaging, Histochem. Cell Biol. 145 (2) (2016) 201–211.

[70] T. Matsumoto, et al., Distribution analysis via mass spectrometry imaging of ephedrine in the lungs of rats orally administered the Japanese Kampo medicine maoto, Sci. Rep. 7 (2017) 44098.

[71] R. Zecchi, et al., Impact of drug administration route on drug delivery and distribution into the lung: an imaging mass spectrometry approach, Eur. J. Mass. Spectrom. (Chichester) 19 (6) (2013) 475–482.

[72] E. Backstrom, et al., Uncovering the regional localization of inhaled salmeterol retention in the lung, Drug. Deliv. 25 (1) (2018) 838–845.

[73] G.R. Hamm, et al., Revealing the regional localization and differential lung retention of inhaled compounds by mass spectrometry imaging, J. Aerosol Med. Pulm. Drug. Deliv. (2019).
[74] K.A. Berry, et al., MALDI imaging mass spectrometry of phospholipids in the mouse lung, J. Lipid Res. 52 (8) (2011) 1551–1560.
[75] K.A. Zemski Berry, et al., Lipidomic characterization and localization of phospholipids in the human lung, J. Lipid Res. 58 (5) (2017) 926–933.
[76] M. Schou, et al., Pulmonary PET imaging confirms preferential lung target occupancy of an inhaled bronchodilator, EJNMMI Res. 9 (1) (2019) 9.
[77] Y.B. Wang, et al., The impact of pulmonary diseases on the fate of inhaled medicines--a review, Int. J. Pharm. 461 (1–2) (2014) 112–128.
[78] C. Giesen, et al., Highly multiplexed imaging of tumor tissues with subcellular resolution by mass cytometry, Nat. Methods 11 (4) (2014) 417–422.
[79] Q. Chang, et al., Imaging mass cytometry, Cytometry A 91 (2) (2017) 160–169.
[80] O.S. Usmani, et al., The topical study of inhaled drug (salbutamol) delivery in idiopathic pulmonary fibrosis, Respir. Res. 19 (1) (2018) 25.
[81] T.M. Maher, et al., A positron emission tomography imaging study to confirm target engagement in the lungs of patients with idiopathic pulmonary fibrosis following a single dose of a novel inhaled $\alpha v \beta 6$ integrin inhibitor, Respir. Res. 21 (1) (2020) 75.
[82] M.W. Sadiq, et al., Late Breaking Abstract - spatial pharmacokinetics of inhaled drugs in human lung – evaluation of regional lung targeting by direct sampling of epithelial lining fluid, Eur. Respir. J. 54 (Suppl. 63) (2019) OA2103.

CHAPTER 12

Physiologically-based pharmacokinetic modeling after drug inhalation

Anneke Himstedt[1,2], Per Bäckman[3] and Jens Markus Borghardt[1]
[1]Drug Discovery Sciences, Research DMPK, Boehringer Ingelheim Pharma GmbH & Co. KG, Biberach, Germany
[2]Department of Clinical Pharmacy, Institute of Pharmacy, University of Hamburg, Hamburg, Germany
[3]Emmace Consulting AB, Lund, Sweden

12.1 Introduction

With increased access to computer-based mathematical modeling tools as well as to *in vitro, ex vivo,* and *in vivo* data, the relevance of pharmacometrics increased in all stages of drug discovery and development [1–3]. Today, modeling approaches are broadly applied to investigate the pharmacokinetics (PK) and/or the relation between the pharmacokinetics and pharmacodynamics (PK/PD) of drugs in humans or preclinical species. Available pharmacometric approaches range from applying empirical to mechanistic models. While empirical models use available PK and/or PD data (e.g. plasma concentration-time profiles) to parameterize mathematical models of the drug PK (compartmental PK models), mechanistic models are typically based on available equations describing specific PK processes. Therefore, empirical models are often more descriptive and typically do not provide the same extent of mechanistic insights as mechanistic models. However, many modeling approaches are neither fully empirical nor fully mechanistic, but contain elements of both empirical and mechanistic modeling. This might allow to investigate specific PK processes in more detail while containing a meaningful complexity of the PK or PK/PD model.

Mechanistic PK approaches are typically referred to as physiologically-based PK (PBPK) models. In these models, relevant physiology, drug, and product attributes are mechanistically linked to specific PK processes. PBPK modeling is already frequently applied for orally, intravenously or subcutaneously administered drugs, for which systemic exposure in blood or plasma is considered an adequate surrogate (also representing the relevant tissue concentrations) to determine efficacy [4–6]. In contrast, fewer PBPK modeling approaches have been reported for local drug administration, for which the target organ is located even before drug absorption to blood. Therefore, local drug concentrations at the absorption site drive the efficacy. For this reason, and as drug concentrations in blood might not be a good surrogate for locally-acting

Inhaled Medicines
DOI: https://doi.org/10.1016/B978-0-12-814974-4.00009-2

inhaled drugs [7], PBPK modeling offers unique opportunities to infer on the local PK and PK/PD, as will be outlined later in this chapter.

As mentioned before, essential for applying PBPK models is to link the PK to a mechanistic understanding of involved processes, i.e., after drug inhalation this would mean the pulmonary PK processes. While the specific pulmonary PK processes are described in more detail elsewhere in this book, this book chapter will cover the following aspects:

1. Features of empirical and mechanistic pharmacometric approaches.
   a. Structure and building blocks of a general PBPK model.
   b. Structure and building blocks of PBPK models for orally inhaled drugs.
2. A summary of the current state-of-the-art PBPK modeling, based on published PBPK models evaluating the (pulmonary) PK after oral drug inhalation.
3. An outline and discussion of potential future applications, opportunities and (current) limitations of PBPK modeling for orally inhaled drugs.

12.2 Features of empirical and mechanistic pharmacometric approaches

As outlined, pharmacometric approaches range from empirical to mechanistic modeling approaches. All have in common that they are applied to better understand the PK or PK/PD characteristics of administered drugs.

Empirical modeling approaches are developed based on available PK data – normally plasma concentration-time profiles following the administration of a drug (also named top-down approach). From this data, PK parameters can be estimated, which describe the absorption of the drug, the distribution of the drug across the body (i.e. the volume of distribution) or the elimination of the administered drug (i.e. the clearance). To describe these processes, standard empirical models range from one-compartment PK models (three estimated parameters) to slightly more complex three-compartment PK models (seven estimated parameters).

Adjusting the standard model structures allows incorporating non-linear drug PK or more complex (pulmonary) absorption processes. Identifying the right model structure is one of the key challenges and the first step towards developing a compartmental model. For example, models with complex parallel (pulmonary) absorption processes [8–11], models with parallel pulmonary metabolic elimination [12], or with separate pulmonary dissolution and absorption of dissolved drug were described for orally inhaled drugs [13]. Estimating the PK parameters based on available PK data allows a broad application of these empirical models, as no *prior* mechanistic knowledge on the physiologically relevant PK processes of a drug is required. In general terms, empirical models do not mechanistically link the plasma PK to drug or formulation characteristics. However, even an empirical modeling approach allows to learn about the underlying principles determining the pulmonary PK. For example, performing an *in vitro in vivo* correlation (IVIVC) between the estimated absorption rates of different inhaled drugs to the respective *in vitro* dissolution rates allows to demonstrate the *in vivo* relevance of *in vitro* dissolution setups [14]. Furthermore, in a drug discovery setting, applying empirical modeling allows one to select the drug candidate with the best PK characteristics based on comparing estimated PK parameters.

In a clinical setting, applying non-linear mixed-effects modeling (i.e., integrating statistical elements such as inter-individual variability or residual variability in the compartmental model), allows simultaneous estimation of individual and population PK parameters [15]. These so-called population models are often applied to correlate the estimated individual PK parameters to patient-specific characteristics, such as age or body weight ("covariate analysis") [16]. Another application of these models is to predict plasma concentration-time profiles for new dosing strategies or for specific patient populations. In addition, empirical PK models are often applied to investigate the link between PK and PD by linking (plasma) concentration-time profiles either directly to effect readouts (e.g., E_{max} functions) or alternatively to include effect or turnover compartments [17,18].

In contrast to empirical approaches, mechanistic modeling approaches attempt to describe the drug PK based on the current understanding of all relevant PK processes. This means that both the model structure as well as the parameter values should be based on physiological or physicochemical data (bottom-up approach) instead of selecting the model structure and estimating the PK parameters based on the available PK data (top-down approach). The categorization of pharmacometric models into empirical and mechanistic models is not always possible. Often models include both empirical and mechanistic elements [19,20] and are therefore called semi-mechanistic or semi-physiological models. For example, semi-mechanistic models can provide a mechanistic implementation of relevant PK processes (e.g., a mechanistic representation of the target organ), while estimating all other PK parameters for the systemic PK based on available concentration-time profiles. These semi-mechanistic PK models are sometimes also referred to as minimal PBPK models [21,22].

PBPK modeling is a valuable approach in drug discovery, drug development, and regulatory assessment [22–31]. To allow an efficient use of PBPK modeling, software applications have emerged (for example Open Systems Pharmacology [32], SimCyp [33]). In addition to these software tools, additional commercial PBPK models with a stronger focus on oral drug inhalation, emerged (for example Mimetikos Preludium [34] and GastroPlus [35], for a detailed review consider [19,20]). These tools aim towards including drug-, disease- and formulation-specific aspects and relate these to the pulmonary PK [36,37]. Furthermore, custom-build PBPK modeling approaches became available, which extended pulmonary PBPK models by including the link between the pulmonary PK to the pulmonary PD or pulmonary target engagement (receptor occupancy) [38,39].

12.2.1 Structure and building blocks of a general PBPK model

While the basic structure of a PBPK model is – as in empirical models - compartmental in nature, each compartment has a physiological counterpart. Typically, whole-body PBPK models include compartments representing the most relevant organs (or groups of kinetically comparable organs, so-called lumping [21]). The whole-body PBPK model can be further divided on the organ level, for example into interstitial and intracellular space [40–42].

The organs, which are explicitly considered in the compartmental structure of a PBPK model, are selected based on the weight and function of the organ [43]. The heart and the lung are typically included due to their importance for the blood circulation, whereas liver, kidney and intestine are critical in their function as eliminating organs. Large organs, such as the muscle or the fat tissues, have a strong impact on the systemic PK of drugs and are therefore also included in the standard PBPK models. In contrast, smaller organs are typically not included in the standard PBPK models. The reason may be that even though these small organs can be kinetically quite different compared to the plasma / blood compartments, they generally do not influence the systemic PK to a relevant magnitude. A typical structure of a generic whole-body PBPK model is outlined in Fig. 12.1

Input parameters determining the mass transfer between the physiological compartments and therefore the drug PK can be attributed to three categories (Fig. 12.2). The

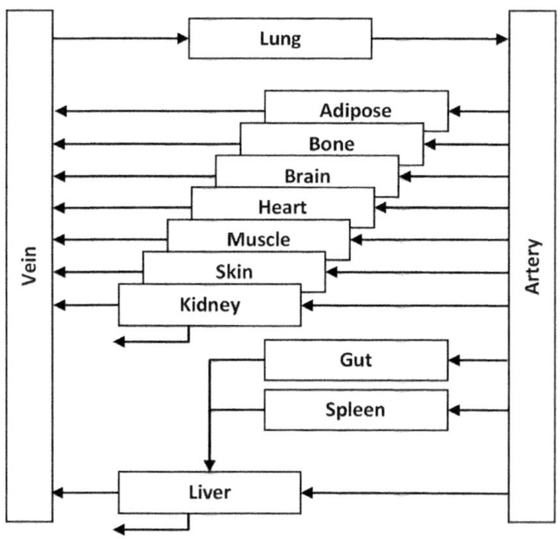

Figure 12.1 Organ and tissue topology of a generic 13-compartment PBPK model. *Adapted and modified from S. Pilari, W. Huisinga, Lumping of physiologically-based pharmacokinetic models and a mechanistic derivation of classical compartmental models, J. Pharmacokinet. Pharmacodyn. 37 (2010) 365–405.*

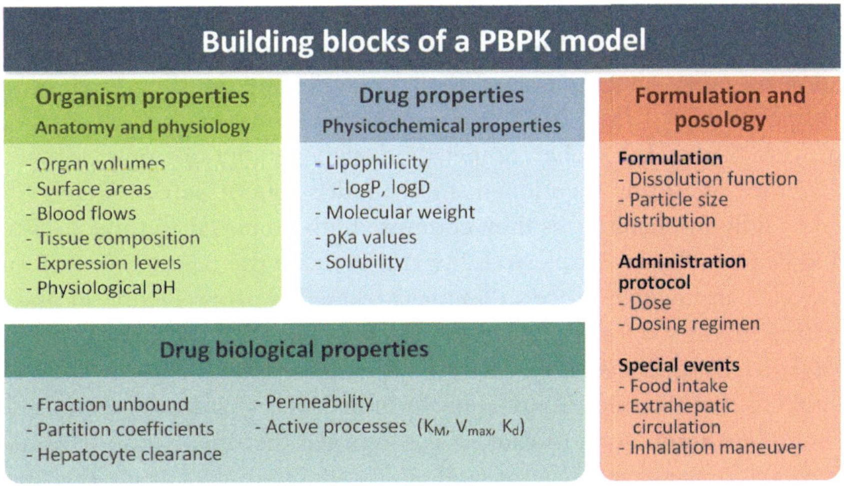

Figure 12.2 Basic building blocks of a PBPK model. Depending on the model and or the drug of interest, some of these components are optional. *Adapted and modified from L. Kuepfer, C. Niederalt, T. Wendl, J.F. Schlender, S. Willmann, J. Lippert, et al., Applied concepts in PBPK modeling: how to build a PBPK/PD model, CPT: Pharmacomet. Syst. Pharmacol. 5 (2016) 516–531.*

first category are '*organism properties*', given by the anatomy and physiology of the organism (including e.g. organ volumes, blood flow and protein expression levels). The second category are '*drug properties*' (e.g., lipophilicity, molecular weight and pK_a values) and the third category represents '*drug biological properties*' depending on both physiology and drug properties (e.g., fraction unbound, tissue-partition coefficients, permeability, active transport processes and drug metabolism). Parameters attributed to the third category can theoretically be calculated based on parameters from categories one and two. Nevertheless, the experience is that the '*drug biological properties*' should be measured whenever possible with *in vitro* and/or *in vivo* experiments as these experimental values appear to be more reliable (e.g., *in vitro* plasma protein binding, *in vitro* hepatocyte assays). Therefore, all input parameters should be - whenever possible - chosen based on physiological knowledge or experimental data. Some PBPK models also allow incorporating formulation characteristics, administration protocols, and different routes of administration. This '*formulation and posology*' information can be considered as a fourth category, as illustrated in Fig. 12.2.

Due to the implementation of physiological databases including all '*organism properties*' [44], models to predict '*drug properties*' based on the chemical structure, as well as regression-based models [45–48] to predict '*drug biological properties*', PBPK models enable prospective predictions of drug PK, even before conducting the respective *in vivo* and *in vitro* PK experiments. Examples include extrapolating to diseased/special populations based on alterations in physiology or even predicting the PK of new drugs without conducting any *in vivo* experiments [49]. However, for example, to perform an extrapolation from normal patients to elderly required collecting detailed *prior* knowledge about anatomy and physiology in these populations, including quantitative information on every single relevant PK process affecting the drug (such as perfusion, tissue composition etc.) [50,51]. This amount of information is rarely (if ever) available, and lack of data has to be compensated with assumptions or parameter estimation. Therefore, as already mentioned, most models cannot be considered either fully empirical or fully mechanistic, as they comprise both empirical and mechanistic aspects to varying degrees. To increase credibility and evaluate the descriptive performance of the PK model, an iterative process ('*learn-and-confirm*') with predicting of and comparing with (preclinical and/or clinical) data is recommended [25,52,53].

PBPK models for drugs given orally or by intravenous administration often focus on quantifying the systemic PK to evaluate both efficacy and safety. Typically, when considering these administration routes, it is assumed that free concentrations in tissue and plasma are similar at steady state (and at fast equilibrium). Hence, the systemic PK is considered as a good surrogate for target site concentrations. While this might be a fair assumption for organs with a high perfusion, this assumption might not hold true for either organs with a slow equilibrium due to slow perfusion with plasma, or for organs, from which the drug is absorbed [21].

To account for this, PBPK models allow predicting local drug concentrations in the relevant tissue based on mechanistic inclusion of relevant physiological characteristics (perfusion, surface area etc.). As measuring local (free) drug concentrations is often not feasible, this model-based prediction of the local tissue concentration-time profiles can be a relevant advantage in cases, for which the local target concentrations may differ from the systemic concentrations (e.g., after local administration such as oral drug inhalation).

12.2.2 Structure and building blocks of a PBPK model for orally inhaled drugs

As the name suggests, the efficacy of locally-acting drugs is driven by local drug concentrations whereas potentially dose-limiting adverse effects can be correlated with systemic drug concentrations, local pulmonary drug concentrations or even particle-related. Hence, modeling of orally inhaled drugs requires an adequate prediction of both pulmonary and systemic PK processes to evaluate pulmonary efficacy and systemic safety simultaneously.

Applying PBPK modeling to understand the local PK of locally administered drugs requires an understanding of the key processes determining the local pharmacokinetics: release, local clearance, including local metabolism as well as tissue interaction of the administered drug. In case of orally inhaled drugs, this is considered even more complex compared to other routes of administration due to the heterogeneity of the lung (regional differences in physiology and the presence of non-absorptive, local clearance mechanisms such as the mucociliary clearance) [37,54,55]. As a result of this complexity, the deposition patterns, including the lung dose and deposited fractions in different areas of the lung, of inhaled drug formulations are difficult to evaluate. This may result in high uncertainties related to predictions of pulmonary target-site concentrations. Furthermore, it is challenging to validate (and therefore to improve) PBPK-based predictions of local pulmonary concentration-time profiles in a clinical setting, given that the systemic concentration is generally not reflective of the pulmonary situation.

Most PBPK models, which are not specifically adapted to account for oral drug inhalation, describe the lung as a single uniform organ - which is certainly a strong simplification of reality. The physiology of the alveolar space is different compared with other parts of the lungs, i.e., the perfusion of the alveolar space is much higher [44,56,57], the endothelial and epithelial surface areas are higher, and finally also the constitution is different [58,59]. Assuming a uniform distribution of the drug into the different lung tissues might not have a relevant impact on adequately predicting the systemic PK of orally or intravenously administered drugs (due to the low weight of the conducting airways and therefore low impact on the total volume of distribution). This assumption however might not be adequate when considering pulmonary drug administration; the physiological differences between the different pulmonary compartments can be expected to result in different local pulmonary PK profiles. In agreement, it was demonstrated for neutral and basic drugs that drug distribution to and drug absorption from the alveolar space is faster compared to other parts of the lung [60]. Therefore, the assumption of a uniform lung cannot be considered adequate to evaluate the systemic and especially the local PK of inhaled drug formulations with a relevant deposition in the conducting (central) airways. In conclusion, these simplified PBPK models should be considered inadequate for evaluation of the local and systemic PK following inhalation. A schematic depiction that illustrates the differences between central and peripheral regions of the lung is provided in Fig. 12.3. Even though this illustration is still a simplification of the pulmonary PK processes, it might provide a reasonable basis for generic PBPK models to predict the (pulmonary) PK of orally inhaled drugs.

A PBPK model, which can be used to predict the (pulmonary) PK of a broad range of orally inhaled drugs should include several pulmonary PK processes, which are specific for oral drug inhalation and thus not relevant for systemic drug administration. The first inhalation-specific process a PBPK model should account for is the deposition pattern of the inhaled aerosol. As illustrated in Fig. 12.3, the fate of a drug particle or droplet will be very different depending on whether it deposits in the respiratory region, the conducting airway region or in the mouth throat region. Following deposition, solid drug particles will start to dissolve in the epithelial lining fluids (ELF). While this step is relevant for inhaled particle formulations or suspensions, it is not relevant for drugs inhaled as a solution. In the conducting airways, undissolved drug particles are transported towards the mouth-throat region via the mucociliary clearance (MCC) and are subsequently swallowed, whereas particles deposited in the alveolar-interstitial area may be cleared by pulmonary macrophages [61–63]. Dissolved

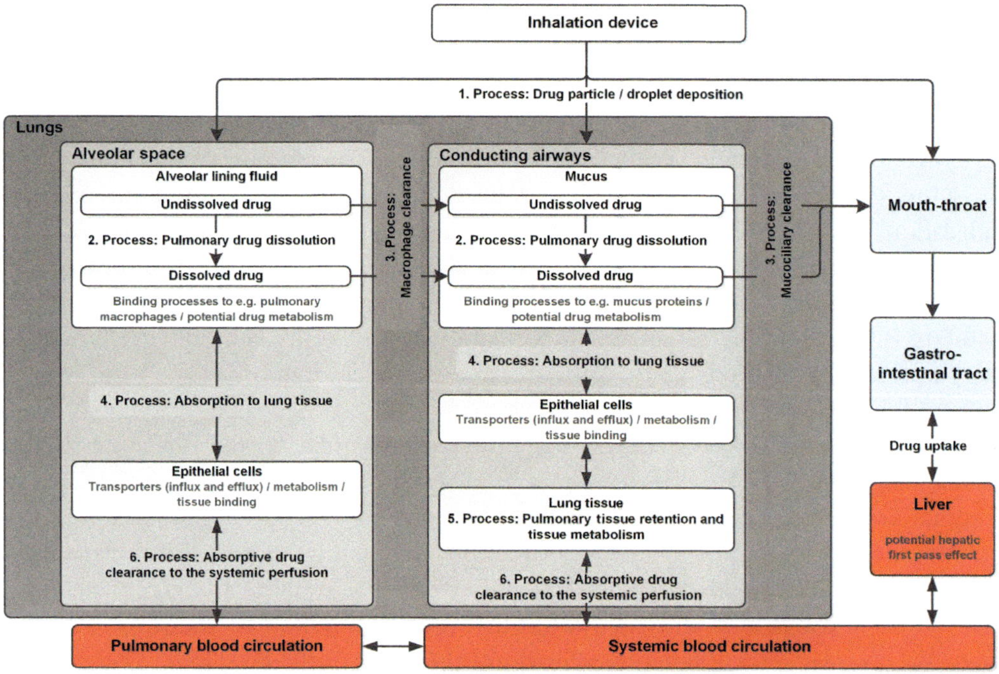

Figure 12.3 Schematic depiction of PK processes after inhalation. *Adapted and modified from J.M. Borghardt, C. Kloft, A. Sharma, Inhaled therapy in respiratory disease: the complex interplay of pulmonary kinetic processes, Can. Respir. J. 2018 (2018).*

unbound drug in the ELF may permeate into the epithelial cells from where it can distribute across the lung tissues and be absorbed into the systemic circulation. Drug molecules within the lung may also be subject to pulmonary metabolism [64–66]. While all these processes can occur in parallel, their relative impact on local and systemic PK and PD depends on the properties of the investigated drug.

The physicochemical properties of inhaled drugs vary as a result of the chemical structure; the optimal properties can be dependent on the target location (e.g., intra- vs. extracellular) or dependent on the desired efficacy (e.g., short- vs. long acting). In general, even though currently this evaluation is still based on a small data set of inhaled drugs, the characteristics of inhaled drugs are different compared to orally administered drugs with a trend towards a higher molecular weight as well as a higher polar surface area of inhaled drugs [67,68]. Based on the different physicochemical properties, the relevance of the individual pulmonary PK processes will vary for different drugs. As suggested by e.g. Hastedt et al [70], inhaled drugs can be grouped analogous to the biopharmaceutical classification system (BCS) applied for orally administered drugs [69] depending on their solubility and permeability (Fig. 12.4). However, as the characteristics of the lung and the GI tract as absorption sites strongly differ, one may expect that

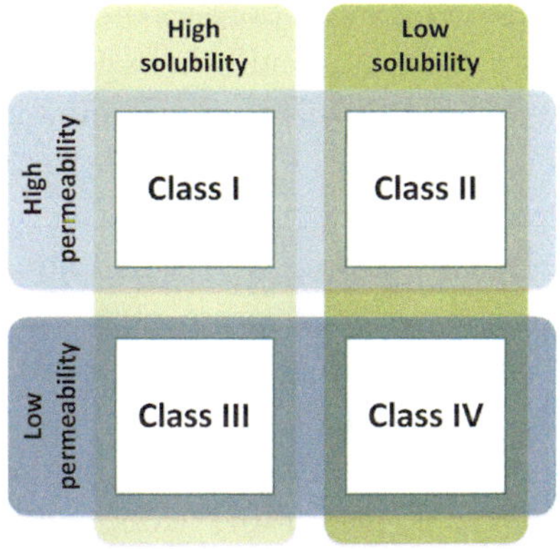

Figure 12.4 Characteristics of orally inhaled drugs based on permeability and solubility. Scheme based on considerations for the Biopharmaceutic Drug Classification System (BCS) for orally administered drugs, originally published by Amidon et al. [67].

class characteristics relevant for oral drugs do not necessarily apply to inhaled drugs. For example, low solubility combined with low permeability might reduce the oral bioavailability for orally administered drugs, and can therefore be considered a non-optimal PK profile. In contrast, for inhaled drugs, this physicochemical profile might result in a desired long-lasting pulmonary drug retention, as discussed for e.g., Fluticasone propionate [9]. Nevertheless, the same principles may apply for classification of both oral and inhaled drugs. For instance, most inhaled glucocorticosteroids are lipophilic drugs characterized by low solubility and high permeability and may therefore belong to a tentative class II (Fig. 12.4). Such drugs, would be characterized by slow dissolution and fast permeation through pulmonary membranes resulting in prolonged residence time of particles in lumen as the main mechanism prolonging effect duration [13]. Long luminal residence time of solid drug particles also increases the relevance of the MCC, which can result in a reduced pulmonary bioavailability. Hence, a good mechanistic representation and a good understanding of the interplay of pulmonary deposition, dissolution and MCC would be critical for adequately predicting the rate and the extent of drug absorption for these specific drugs with a PBPK model.

Other drugs, such as inhaled bronchodilators, are characterized by relatively high permeability and good solubility, these drugs could be considered Class I, compare Fig. 12.4 [71]. These drugs would be expected to rapidly dissolve and permeate into lung tissue with rapid absorption from the lung surfaces. Duration of effect and lung selectivity can, however, be achieved through high tissue binding, lysosomal trapping, or slow receptor-off kinetics [72–75]. The PK of these drugs will likely not be affected to a relevant extent by dissolution and the MCC and could therefore be assumed to be perfusion-limited.

Finally, drugs such as long-acting muscarinic-receptor antagonists are characterized by low permeability and fast dissolution and could be assigned to Class III (see Fig. 12.4). In contrast to inhaled corticosteroids or inhaled sympathomimetic drugs, these drugs show low permeability through cell membranes. Hence, while dissolution is rather fast, low permeability slows down absorption into pulmonary tissue, resulting in potentially prolonged lung retention. A PBPK model for this drug type would not necessarily be sensitive to dissolution and MCC, but it requires an adequate representation of permeability-limited absorption and distribution processes. The typically applied perfusion-limited absorption model might not be adequate for these kind of drugs.

Recent approaches aimed for combining the slow dissolution kinetics with a high tissue affinity, resulting in overall even more extended pulmonary residence times, which is essential for effective pulmonary targeting. Such drugs would require including all processes depicted in Fig. 12.3 and potentially even the employment of a permeability-limited absorption and distribution model. Table 12.1 summarizes critical pulmonary PK processes and the relevance of their inclusion in PBPK models depending on drug class.

Besides the pulmonary PK processes mentioned in Table 12.1, which may only be relevant for drugs with specific characteristics, additional processes such as pulmonary metabolism, binding to the mucus, drug absorption from the gastro intestinal tract, and the systemic PK should always be considered when modeling the PK of orally inhaled drugs. In the following sections, each of the pulmonary PK processes depicted in Fig. 12.3 will be discussed related to the experimental characterization techniques providing input data to models, as well as available mechanistic and empirical models that were already incorporated into PBPK models for orally inhaled drugs.

12.2.2.1 Drug deposition

Understanding the lung dose and how it distributes in the lung following oral drug inhalation is an important aspect, as an adequate evaluation of lung dose as well as the local deposition patterns provides the basis for a mechanistic evaluation of subsequent pulmonary processes such as dissolution, MCC and permeation into tissue. Drug aerosols can deposit in the inhalation device, in the mouth throat area, or in the lung. The deposited aerosol fraction in the lung can then be further differentiated based on regional deposition patterns, for instance aerosol fractions deposited in the large airways, the small airways and the respiratory region (see Chapters 6 and 7 for more details). At the most basic level, drug deposition in PBPK models can be accounted for by dividing the delivered dose into a few PK dose compartments. This means that the inhaled dose is distributed between physiological compartments representing the mouth-throat area and the lung. In the (PB)PK model, the lung dose can be further divided into deposition in the central and peripheral lung regions to account for regional differences in the pulmonary PK [13]. The total lung dose is derived from the

Table 12.1 Relevance of physiological PK processes for different drug characteristics.

Drug characteristics	Deposition 1st process#	Dissolution 2nd process#	MCC 3rd process#	Absorption into lung tissue 4th process#	Pulmonary tissue binding 5th process#	Absorptive clearance from the lung tissue 6th process#
Class I: High solubility, high permeability	+	–	–	–	(+)*	(+)*
Class II: Low solubility, high permeability	+	+	+	–	(+)*	(+)*
Class III: High solubility, low permeability	+	–	–	+	(+)*	(+)*
Class IV: Low solubility, low permeability	+	+	+	+	(+)*	(+)*

#more details on the different processes are provided in Fig. 12.3. ' + ' indicates that for these drug characteristics the respective pulmonary PK process should be included in the PBPK model, whereas '–' indicates that the impact of the respective pulmonary PK process can be expected negligible and therefore does not have to represented for the respective drug.

*For drugs with high pulmonary tissue affinity, including a mechanistic representation of the tissue retention might be additionally required.

delivered dose and the mouth-throat deposition, which can be experimentally determined using physical mouth-throat models (see Chapter 6). Experimental data on regional lung deposition patterns (e.g. ratio of central to peripheral deposition (C/P)) can be obtained from 2- or 3-dimensional gamma scintigraphy studies [76–80]. These C/P ratios may be useful to understand differences between formulations, but are challenging to interpret due to a significant overlap between airway and respiratory tissue in the central region.

Another method to obtain deposition patterns as input for mechanistic PBPK models are mathematical deposition models such as the 3-dimensional fluid particle dynamics (CFPD) models or 1-dimensional (1-D) algebraic engineering models [81]. Here, the deposition model is applied to predict deposition patterns based on aerosol characteristics such as aerodynamic particle size distribution, anticipated inhalation maneuver and expected lung physiology. All these properties are experimentally measurable and could vary between patients and as a result of instructions and applied formulation/device characteristics. However, validating the lung dose and its distribution is challenging and any predicted deposition patterns should be considered carefully. Ideally, lung deposition models should be combined with experimental data. As this data is unfortunately rarely available (on an individual level), sometimes these 1-D algebraic models have to be used even without systematic evaluation of the results.

Several types of mathematical deposition models are available in literature. Most often, 1-D algebraic models are incorporated in PBPK models [34,82–84], such as the NCRP model [81] or stochastic models such as the multiple path particle deposition model (MPPD [85,86]). Typically, these deposition models are based on branched-tube airway geometries published by Weibel et al. [87,88]. These models characterize the airway geometries by the number of airway generations, number of parallel airways in each generation and the respective airway diameter and length. Models such as NCRP predict deposition in these geometries based on 3 different deposition mechanisms, namely impaction, sedimentation, and diffusion [88]. The deposition pattern is usually predicted for each pulmonary generation (24 in the standard Weibel model) and for one extra thoracic region (i.e., the mouth-throat). However, to enable a reasonable level of complexity for a PBPK model, which includes MCC, permeation, and tissue affinity, the predicted deposition patterns are typically reduced in complexity. This means that the predicted deposition patterns for e.g., 24 airway generations are lumped into PK compartments representing different lung regions rather than specific airway generations. These compartments typically are one extrathoracic compartment; one or two conducting airway regions (usually defined as Weibel generations 0–15); and the respiratory region (Weibel generations 16–23). The reason for this simplification is that generations within these regions share some common characteristics such as presence of the MCC in the conducting airways (generations 0–15) or a high surface area and high perfusion in the respiratory region (generations 16–23) or that the deposited dose in the mouth-throat area is swallowed and enters the GI tract (unless expectorated, generation 0).

Several applications of 1-D deposition models are described in the literature or as part of commercial PBPK modeling software. For instance, a derivative of the empirical ICRP66 model [89] is the deposition model available in the PCAT module of the SimulationsPlus GastroPlus® generic inhalation PBPK model. Other available inhalation PBPK models, such as Mimetikos Preludium™ apply a selection of 1-D models including the empirical ICRP66 model and the more mechanistic NCRP model [34]. Another example of such a mechanistic model is the use of the MPPD model by Gaz et al. [84].

Recently, examples have emerged in which computational fluid dynamics (CFD) models were applied to predict the deposition in the mouth throat area and the first airway generations and combined with 1-D models to predict the deep lung deposition. Vulovic et al. [90], for instance, employed CFD simulations to predict the ex-mouthpiece fraction of the dose and combined these with predictions performed with the ICRP66 model. So far, no systematic comparison of the different implementations (e.g., CFPD versus 1-D model based predictions) is available. Thus, it remains to be demonstrated, which level of complexity is meaningful and represents a good compromise between complexity and quality of PK predictions (Fig. 12.5).

12.2.2.2 Pulmonary drug dissolution

As mentioned above, dissolution of solid drug in lung lining fluid may represent the rate-limiting step for drug absorption into the lung tissue for many poorly soluble inhaled drugs (e.g. some inhaled glucocorticosteroids). For these drugs, an adequate characterization and modeling of pulmonary dissolution is necessary to understand the *in vivo* performance of an inhaled drug product [13].

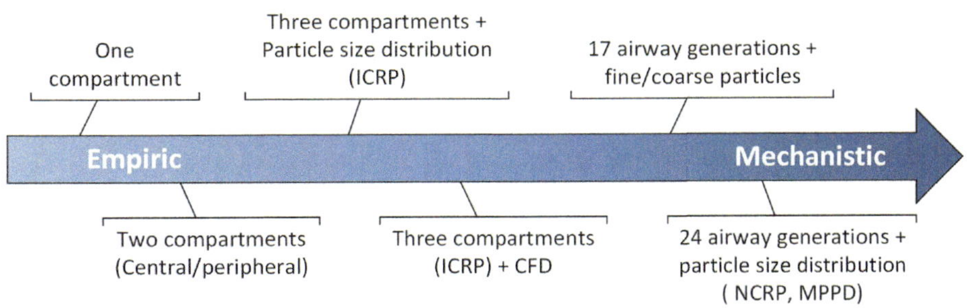

Figure 12.5 Modeling approaches for drug deposition ordered from empirical to mechanistic modeling. The number of compartments here refers to the number of pulmonary compartments, excluding the mouth-throat compartment.

Dissolution kinetics can be incorporated into PBPK models for orally inhaled drugs via two distinct approaches: as empirically measured rate constants derived from biorelevant dissolution assays (often utilizing dissolution on a surfactant coated semipermeable membrane [14]) or using a mechanistic (*in silico*) dissolution model (also see Chapters 9). Applying the empirical approach has some advantages as it theoretically allows for a direct determination of dissolution kinetics at conditions resembling those in the lung lining fluid. However, the complex nature of the *in vitro* setup (and *in vivo* dissolution) is also associated to challenges as it makes standardization of the methods difficult.

Instead of defining the dissolution kinetics based on *in vitro* data, a derivation of the Nernst-Brunner equation [91] could be applied. This would even allow scaling dissolution kinetics for a polydisperse particle size formulation [92]. A combination of *in vitro* dissolution rates and a mathematical dissolution model was included in the Mimetikos Preludium™ model. In a first step, a dissolution profile is determined *in vitro* and subsequently fitted to a Johnson model [92] to generate a particle-specific parameterization of the dissolution model. These parameters are in a second step used in to predict the *in vivo* dissolution kinetics. Additional inputs to mechanistic dissolution models are typically drug or formulation properties such as; drug solubility, diffusivity, density and the particle surface area. Both approaches require knowledge of additional input parameters such as the volumes of the endothelial lining fluid in the different airway regions [38].

Two of the most challenging aspects when modeling the pulmonary dissolution is the limited availability of high-quality input data and the lack of standardized experiments. Critical parameters comprise capturing the relevant aerosol fraction for testing, transfer of this aerosol fraction into a dissolution setup, selection of a relevant dissolution medium and dissolution test equipment. Especially, capturing the aerosol can result in significant experimental errors, as the specific surface area of the captured fraction determines the dissolution kinetics. For instance, excessive agglomeration or de-agglomeration of aerosol drug-excipient co-agglomerates can result in clinically irrelevant experimentally measured dissolution profiles [93]. Velaga et al published a more systematic review on different dissolution methods [94] (Fig. 12.6).

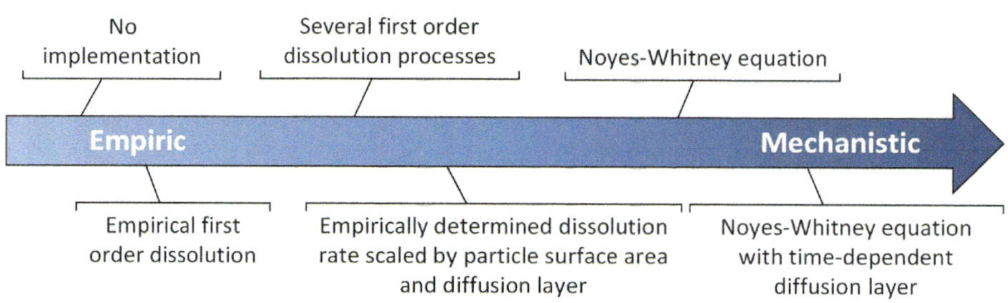

Figure 12.6 Modeling approaches for drug dissolution ordered from empirical to mechanistic modeling.

12.2.2.3 Mucociliary and macrophage clearance

Non-absorptive mucociliary clearance (MCC) is a process, which transports solid drug particles that deposit on the airway mucosa upwards from the conducting airways into the throat area from which the drug is subsequently swallowed. The MCC can thus significantly reduce both the pulmonary bioavailability and the luminal residence time, particularly for poorly soluble or potentially for mucin-bound drugs (e.g., colistin [95]). For these drugs, MCC should be incorporated in any predictive PBPK model [36]. Therefore, it can be considered important to understand how the MCC varies throughout the lung, the factors that influence the MCC such as the impact of respiratory disease on the mucociliary clearance [96,97] (see Chapter 8). As mentioned before, the MCC does not significantly affect the PK of rapidly absorbed drugs. For these drugs, the MCC is often neglected in drug-specific inhalation models [39,84]. If the MCC is expected to affect the PK to a relevant degree, it is most often implemented as one or more first-order clearance processes from the tracheobronchial region, depending on the compartmental model structure. For a PBPK (including the deposition) model separating the lungs into central and peripheral compartments, the MCC is typically represented as a single first-order clearance of undissolved drug from the central lung [13,38]. If the PBPK model structure accounts for more than one conducting airway compartment, the MCC can be implemented as two or up to four first-order processes, each moving the drug to the adjacent higher airway compartment and finally the first gastrointestinal tract compartment [34,83]. In PBPK models that further divide the airway compartments into endothelial lining fluid and tissue compartments, only the amount of solid drug located in the ELF would be subject to MCC.

Hofmann and Sturm developed a stochastic model for MCC, calculating the mucus velocity in each airway generation based on airway diameter and length [98,99]. Their model results in faster MCC in the upper airways (e.g., the trachea) compared to the terminal bronchioles. This approach has been used in the model by Cabal et al. [82,100], to fit the generational structure of their Lung Modeling Platform model.

As of now, experimental data on mucus velocity and therefore MCC rates is only available as total clearance from the airways. However, if the assumption that the regional MCC differs between the airway generations should be correct, this may be contradictory to the implementation of a (single) first-order clearance process. Another approach, which could account for the non-linear MCC, is the use of time-dependent MCC model, i.e. a high mucociliary clearance in the first minutes representing the fast MCC from the trachea followed by a slower mucociliary clearance at later time points representing the slow MCC from the periphery of the lung. The mechanistic implementation of the MCC model (combined with the deposition model) can be evaluated based on retention data from pulmonary clearance studies conducted with insoluble particles, like gold or Teflon [101]. So far, the authors are however not aware that this data was used to adequately evaluate a PBPK model for orally inhaled drugs. Alternatively,

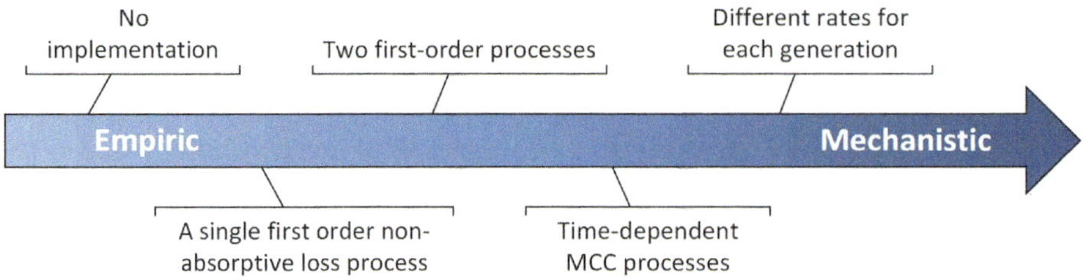

Figure 12.7 Modeling approaches for mucociliary clearance (MCC) ordered from empirical to mechanistic modeling.

since the pulmonary bioavailability (especially for poorly soluble drugs) is the result of the interplay between the pulmonary deposition, the MCC, as well as the pulmonary dissolution, the predicted pulmonary bioavailability for poorly soluble drugs could be used to evaluate PBPK models for orally inhaled drugs [36] (Fig. 12.7).

A second non-absorptive clearance mechanism is the removal of solid drug particles from the alveolar space to the lymph system by alveolar macrophages [54,61–63,102]. These cells also degrade specific drug molecules, such as macromolecules [54,102]. Even though it was demonstrated that clearance by alveolar macrophages can affect the pharmacokinetics of macromolecules, it is generally not believed to have a significant impact on the overall rate of absorption of small inhaled drug molecules and is therefore typically omitted in PBPK models [20]. However, even though the overall absorption rate from the lung tissue might not be affected by lymphatic drug clearance, this specific elimination pathway may result in higher than expected drug levels in e.g. the spleen [104].

12.2.2.4 Absorption into lung tissue

Mechanistic modeling of absorption of dissolved drug in ELF into pulmonary tissue requires a PBPK model, with (at a minimum) separate PK compartments representing lung lining fluid and tissue. Pharmacokinetic models without this level of detail combine all processes, namely the pulmonary dissolution, the drug absorption into the lung tissue, and the absorption from the lung tissue to the systemic circulation in one or more absorption rate constants [13,71]. While these PK models might still adequately describe the plasma PK of orally inhaled drugs, they only provide limited information on local pulmonary concentrations and their relation to product attributes such as dissolution.

If the PBPK model differentiates between pulmonary dissolution, absorption into lung tissue and absorptive clearance from the tissue to plasma, the passive absorption from the lung surface would be determined by the permeability of the drug, scaled with the surface area of the respective tissue [105]. This effective permeability (P_{eff}) can be determined by *in vitro* or *ex vivo* experiments (see Chapter 10) [105]. Most PBPK models with dedicated (sub-)models for orally inhaled drugs further account for differences in pulmonary absorption between alveolar and tracheobronchial epithelium by either a predefined scaling factor [39] or based on the epithelial thickness [34,83]. In absence of experimental data, passive diffusion of unionised (neutral) drug molecules can be calculated by employing the Nernst-Planck equation and Fick's law [106] in combination with physicochemical drug properties such as pKa and logD [82].

For some drugs, there might be additional information on active drug transport through membranes available, i.e., active influx or efflux processes mediated by transport proteins. Whenever quantitative information, such as the pulmonary expression levels and localization of the respective (transport) protein and drug-specific parameters describing the interaction between the drug and the respective protein (K_m, v_{max}), is available, the active transport may be incorporated into the PBPK model. More details on transporters in the lung are provided in Chapter 10.

Gaohua et al. [107] developed a PBPK model for several antituberculotic drugs administered by oral administration (not inhalation). This model included active transport mechanisms, as inclusion of transporters resulted in better predictions of plasma and ELF concentrations. They performed a sensitivity analysis regarding the effect of unspecific uptake and/or efflux transporters at the ELF-lung and lung-blood barriers on the ELF-to-blood ratios of the drugs. Based on this, it was concluded that for targeting the bacteria in the ELF, including the active transporters would be relevant. However, as many targets of inhaled drugs are located in the respective pulmonary tissues rather than on the surface of the lungs, transporters on the epithelial site might not be as relevant for other inhaled drugs as in this example (Fig. 12.8).

Furthermore, due to the lack of quantitative studies demonstrating an effect of active transport mechanisms on pulmonary drug PK in humans [20], these processes are rarely included in PBPK models.

12.2.2.5 Tissue retention and pulmonary metabolism

Understanding retention of drug in lung tissue, also on a regional level such as comparing retention in the conducting airways to retention in the alveolar space, is a critical aspect as the lung tissue represents the target site of many inhaled

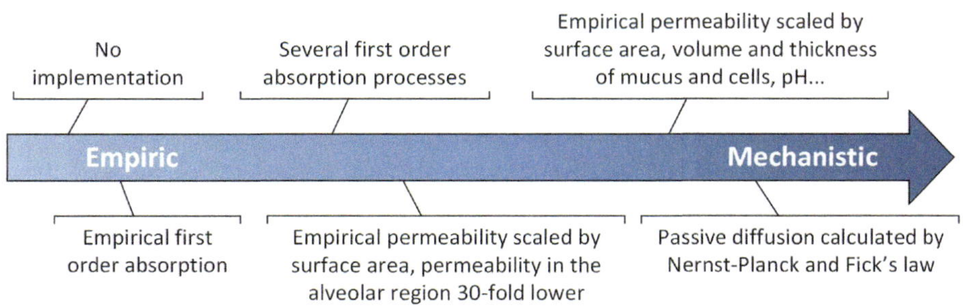

Figure 12.8 Modeling approaches for drug absorption into lung tissue ordered from empirical to mechanistic modeling.

drugs. Without pulmonary retention by e.g., slow dissolution or relevant tissue affinity, achieving long-lasting efficacy or pulmonary targeting would not be feasible [108].

The residence time of drug in lung tissues is determined by the specific tissue perfusion and the partitioning of drug between tissue and plasma (tissue partition coefficient, Kp). Lower blood flow and higher Kp results in longer retention of drug in tissue and, potentially, longer duration of effect. In line with this, most PBPK models incorporate the rate of exchange by considering both the tissue affinity in the form of a Kp and the bronchial and/or pulmonary blood flow.

Experimental determination of Kp values for the lung has been described in detail in Chapter 11. If no prior information on tissue affinity or on the lung retention in general is available, Kp values can be predicted *in silico* based on the physicochemical properties of a drug and the respective tissue composition [45–48,109]. These Kp prediction methods incorporate the octanol/water partitioning (logP), the fraction unbound (fu), pKa values and the blood-to-plasma ratio to predict the tissue affinity.

Kp prediction methods, accounting also for ionization of the drug and for interactions between the drug and acidic phospholipids provide significantly better predictions compared to methods accounting only for membrane partitioning and non-specific binding to albumin [45]. Predicting the tissue affinity with these *in silico* based methods represents the default for most generic PBPK platforms (GastroPlus, Mimetikos Preludium). More complex tissue interaction models, such as sequestration into lysosomes cannot be accounted for with the here described methods. It should be noted that, even though these *in silico* predictions are more mechanistic (see Fig. 12.9), this does not mean that they are considered more accurate than measured Kp values, therefore whenever experimental Kp values, e.g., from preclinical studies are available, these represent clearly better input parameters.

Depending on the *prior* information that is available, pulmonary metabolism, including prodrug activation [110] or ester formation [111], can be incorporated into

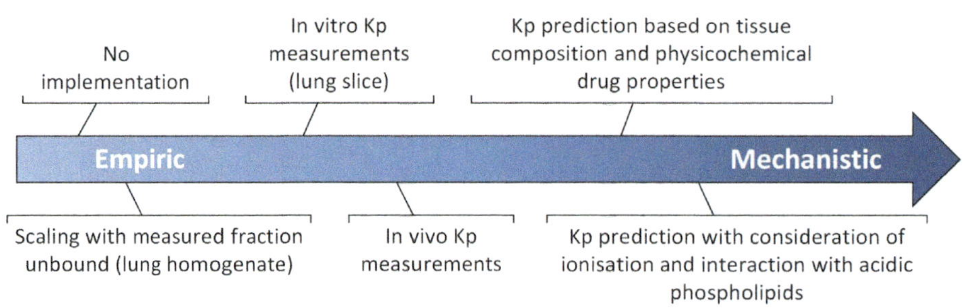

Figure 12.9 Modeling approaches for tissue retention ordered from empirical to mechanistic modeling. Kp: tissue to plasma partition coefficient.

PBPK models in two different ways. First, an unspecific metabolic clearance, characterized by Michaelis-Menten kinetics, can be estimated based on *in vitro or ex vivo* experimental data (e.g., lung slices or incubations with lung tissue homogenate). Alternatively, if the specific metabolizing enzymes are known, metabolic rates can be predicted based on pulmonary expression levels of the respective metabolizing enzyme and drug-specific parameters (K_m, v_{max}).

Since, with the exception of prodrugs, the relevance of pulmonary metabolism on the PK of most inhaled small molecule drugs is considered negligible [20], this process is typically omitted from PBPK models. Prodrugs, such as ciclesonide and beclomethasone dipropionate are metabolized in the lung by pulmonary enzymes into their active forms. In those cases the inclusion of pulmonary metabolism into the model is considered necessary [112].

12.2.2.6 Absorptive clearance from the lung tissue to the systemic perfusion

As mentioned before, most empirical or semi-mechanistic models use empirical rate constants that condense several pulmonary PK processes in one or more first-order absorption rates estimated based on systemic drug concentration measurements. The absorptive clearance from the tissue to the systemic perfusion should not be misunderstood as the same process governing the absorption of dissolved drug from the ELF to the lung tissue. To account for this, PBPK models describe the absorptive clearance from the tissue either by perfusion- or permeability-limited absorption kinetics.

The absorptive clearance involving perfusion-limited kinetics is solely governed by the organ perfusion, while permeability-limited absorption kinetics consider the membrane permeation as the rate-limiting step. This process can be described either by scaling the experimental value for the apparent permeability with the surface area of the blood vessels, or if no experimental data should be available by predicting the permeability based on passive diffusion by applying the principles of Nernst-Planck and Fick's law [106]. Which of the options shown in Fig. 12.10 can be considered optimal depends on the drug characteristics. For most well permeable drugs, the perfusion-limited absorption model would be adequate to represent the exchange process between tissue and blood,

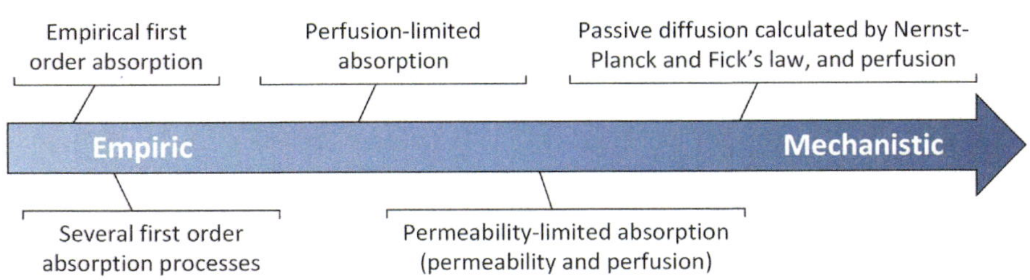

Figure 12.10 Modeling approaches for absorptive clearance from the lung ordered from empirical to mechanistic modeling.

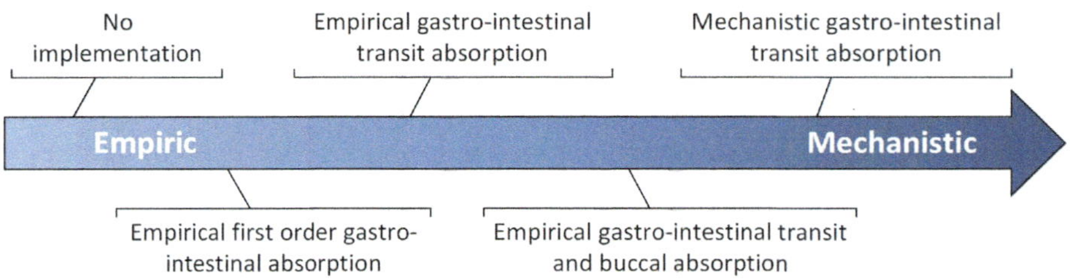

Figure 12.11 Modeling approaches for parallel absorption ordered from empirical to mechanistic modeling.

whereas for most poorly permeable drugs, the permeability-limited absorption model can be considered the best choice. One additional aspect discriminating PBPK models from many empirical PK models is the inclusion of backflow from the systemic circulation into the lung tissues.

12.2.2.7 Parallel absorption from the mouth throat and the GI tract

The majority of drug reaching the mouth-throat area by deposition or by the MCC is swallowed and, if the respective drug should be orally bioavailable, can be absorbed in the gastro intestinal tract [55]. The inclusion of this process can range from an empirical first-order absorption process [39] to a fully mechanistic physiologically-based transit absorption model [83,113] (compare Fig. 12.11). Other processes that possibly affect the fate of drugs in the mouth-throat region are expectoration of drug and buccal drug absorption. Both of these processes are usually deemed negligible and are therefore not accounted for in most PBPK models. An exception to this are Mimetikos Preludium and GastroPlus, which allow accounting for the buccal absorption of drugs.

12.2.2.8 Systemic pharmacokinetics

The systemic PK of a drug, including the drug clearance, but also the (re-) distribution of drug molecules to the lung, can be included in PBPK models with varying complexity (see Fig. 12.12). The simplest way to include the systemic PK is to "attach" an empirical

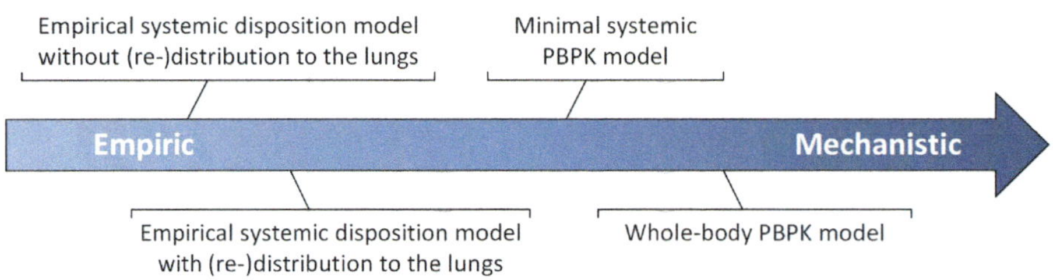

Figure 12.12 Modeling approaches for systemic PK ordered from empirical to mechanistic modeling.

PK model to a (semi-)mechanistic pulmonary PK model via (parallel) pulmonary first-order absorption processes [13]. Since this empirical model structure does not include the backflow of drug from the systemic circulation into the lung, it does not allow evaluating e.g., the lung selectivity for different routes of administration.

Even for more mechanistic inhalation PBPK models the systemic PK model can be simplified to an empirical systemic PK model [34] or substituted with a minimal or whole-body PBPK model [39,114]. As these more mechanistic models typically also include the backflow of drug to the lungs, they can be applied for evaluating the pulmonary PK for any administration route (e.g., oral, intravenous and inhalation).

In theory, these systemic PBPK models allow evaluating the pulmonary selectivity (i.e. pulmonary exposure vs. systemic exposure). Boger et al. applied PBPK models for fluticasone propionate and salbutamol to evaluate the pulmonary receptor occupancy versus the systemic receptor occupancy over time [38], and the plasma concentration-effect relationship after oral administration versus oral inhalation [39], respectively. In addition, simultaneously modeling the pulmonary and systemic PK allows evaluating the impact of systemic PK parameters on pulmonary selectivity. For example, to illustrate the importance of systemic PK parameters for oral drug inhalation, the exchange between lung tissue and the systemic compartments was added by Himstedt et al. in a mechanistic way to the semi-mechanistic model by Weber and Hochhaus [13,115]. A sensitivity analysis based on this model for three inhaled drugs indicated for example that the systemic clearance is one of the three most important determinants for selectivity in the conducting airways (Fig. 12.13). Therefore, the systemic PK model should be considered as important as the pulmonary PK model, when evaluating the

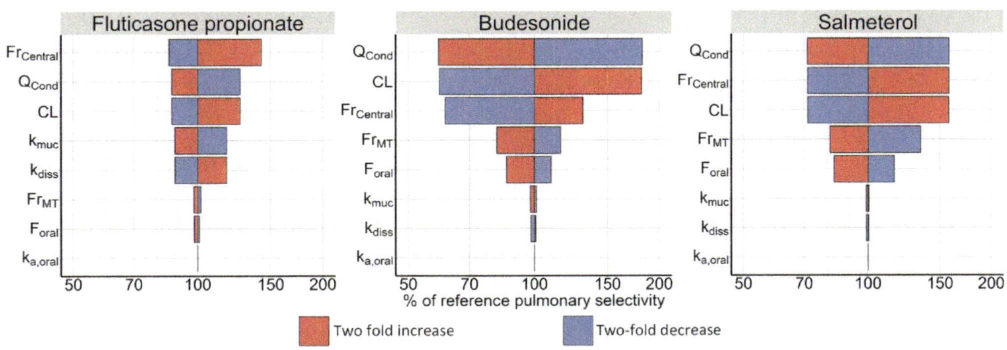

Figure 12.13 Predicted impact of PK parameters on the AUC-based selectivity in the conducting airways at steady state. $Fr_{Central}$: Fraction of the lung dose deposited in the conducting airways, k_{muc}: mucociliary clearance constant, k_{diss}: dissolution rate constant, F_{oral}: oral bioavailability, $k_{a,oral}$: oral absorption rate constant, Q_{Cond}: conducting airway blood flow, CL: systemic clearance. *Adapted and modified from A. Himstedt, S.G. Wicha, J.M. Borghardt, Model-based evaluation of pulmonary pk selectivity – towards a feasibility assessment of targeting the lung by oral drug inhalation, in: P.R. Byron (Ed.), Respiratory Drug Delivery, Davis Healthcare International Publishing, Moore, CA, 2020.*

pulmonary selectivity after oral drug inhalation. This also means that every good PBPK model for orally inhaled drugs should be evaluated based on PK data after intravenous administration and not only on data after oral drug inhalation.

12.3 Published PBPK models for orally inhaled drugs

Published PK models for orally inhaled drugs range from semi-mechanistic modeling approaches to whole-body PBPK models. In this section, we want to give an overview of PBPK models describing the pulmonary and/or systemic drug PK after oral inhalation. Furthermore, as the purpose of any model-based analysis should not only be the model building process, but also to apply the developed model to investigate research or development questions, the following section will additionally illustrate the purpose of the reviewed PBPK models. It has to be mentioned that the discussed models are merely examples and a systematic review of existing PBPK models is out of scope for this book chapter. A more systematic review with less focus on PBPK modeling was e.g. published by Borghardt et al. [19].

12.3.1 Semi-mechanistic models

A five-compartment model was developed by Hendrickx et al. [71], who applied a semi-mechanistic modeling approach, combining an empirical systemic PK model with two lung compartments ("shallow and deep tissue"). These pulmonary compartments were characterized by physiological lung volumes and the fraction unbound in the lung for several bronchodilators. The lung dose was assumed to be deposited entirely in the shallow lung compartment and distribution rates between the shallow and deep tissue compartments were estimated based on experimental plasma and time-resolved lung concentration data. Because of the high solubility of the investigated drugs, the MCC and the pulmonary dissolution were not included in this model. The predicted pulmonary concentration-time profile was linked to a sigmoidal maximum effect (E_{max}) model predicting the inhibition of histamine- or methacholine-induced bronchoconstriction as shown by change in the forced expiratory volume in 1 second (FEV1). The intent of this analysis was to predict the human pulmonary PK and corresponding pulmonary efficacy based on available data from rats and dogs. The published model framework was validated for several compounds using both plasma and lung concentration-time profiles in rats and dogs. Efficacy predictions for human correlated well with observed FEV1 data from patients with chronic obstructive pulmonary disease (COPD).

Another semi-mechanistic model was introduced by Weber and Hochhaus [13], providing a simulation framework for inhaled corticosteroids. This model consists of a compartmental model separating the central and peripheral lung, and combining this with an empirical systemic PK model. The deposited fractions of the lung dose in the central and the peripheral lung were fixed to 0.5, due to lack of more reliable information. Dissolution and subsequent absorption into the systemic circulation were described by first-order rate constants estimated based on clinical PK data, while the MCC rate constant was taken from a publication by Byron [116]. This PK model was developed as a freely available tool to enable clinical trial simulations of inhaled corticosteroid PK studies, accounting for within-subject and between-subject variability. In a follow up analysis, the applicability of the PK model was demonstrated by evaluating the impact of different parameters on bioequivalence trials [117]. In this analysis, the purpose was to evaluate the sensitivity of plasma PK metrics (area under the plasma concentration-time curve and maximal concentration in plasma) to detect differences in formulation characteristics, namely lung dose, central to peripheral deposition ratios and dissolution characteristics.

12.3.2 Drug-specific PBPK models for orally inhaled drugs

Boger et al. [39] built an inhalation PBPK model to investigate advantages of pulmonary versus intravenous administration of salbutamol in rats and subsequent translation from rat to human. Drug deposition patterns after intratracheal instillation (rats) and oral drug inhalation (humans) were predicted based on morphometric lung models [59,89]. A complete particle size distribution was used to predict an airway generation-dependent deposition pattern [118]. Every airway generation was characterized by specific PK compartments representing the ELF, the epithelium and sub-epithelium. Due to the high solubility of salbutamol, dissolution processes and the MCC were considered negligible. The absorption of drug into the lung tissue was calculated from *in vitro* experiments and airway-specific surface areas. The effective permeability in the generations 17–25 (the alveolar region) was assumed to be 30-fold lower than in the tracheobronchial region (generations 1–16), based on the permeability of mannitol, a marker for para-cellular permeation [119]. Tissue affinity was incorporated as Kp values, which were calculated from plasma and lung concentration-time profiles after intravenous administration of salbutamol in rats. The Kp values were adapted for predicting the human PK by accounting for differences in the free fraction in plasma. Absorptive clearance into the blood compartment of the whole-body PBPK model was assumed perfusion-limited and thus governed by the blood flow. Since salbutamol shows an oral bioavailability of 39% in man, absorption from the gastro-intestinal tract was included as an empirical first-order absorption (parameters empirically estimated based on oral PK data). Model-based predictions of local and systemic concentrations were evaluated with observed concentrations in the ELF, lung tissue and plasma of rats.

By linking the PBPK model to a sigmoidal E_{max} model, the developed PBPK model was applied to understand the relation between systemic concentrations and pulmonary efficacy after both inhaled and oral administration. Oral inhalation provided efficacy at lower systemic concentrations than after oral administration, showing the advantage of inhaled administration over oral administration for salbutamol. In addition, drug concentrations in the ELF of a specific airway generation were used as input for the PD model to predict the time-dependent change in FEV1. Overall, the predicted FEV1 profiles after orally inhaled delivery of salbutamol were considered to show good agreement with observed clinical data.

Gaz et al. [84] built a PBPK/PD model for a hypothetical inhaled bronchodilator to investigate its impact on different airway obstruction patterns and FEV1. The inhaled dose was split into three fractions, namely drug deposited in the mouthpiece, the mouth-throat region and the lung. The lung was described in more detail, namely PK compartments for different airway generations. Each airway generation was characterized by compartments representing the bronchial mucosa, the bronchial muscle, connected to a single bronchial vasculature compartment. However, in contrast to the model developed by Boger et al, this model only included the airways up to generation 17 (trachea = generation 0) and excluded the alveolar region, as the model focussed on characterizing the bronchodilation. Particle deposition in the lung was characterized by two probability density functions, which depend on the aero- and hydrodynamics of the respective particle bin. To account for the assumption that the aerodynamic particle size has an influence on the likelihood of depositing in the lung or the mouth-throat region, the probability density function was defined separately for fine and coarse particles. As validation, the resulting deposition patterns were compared with predicted deposition patterns generated with the MPPD model [85,86]. Dissolution and MCC were not included in the PK model, due to the administration of a droplet formulation. By assuming different diffusivities through the bronchial mucus and cell layers as well as a generation-specific epithelial thickness, absorption from each airway generation was characterized by a different rate constant. The absorptive clearance from the bronchial muscle compartments was described by first-order rate constants scaled with the bronchial blood flow. Parallel absorption from the gut was modeled as a separate empirical first-order process. The purpose of Gaz et al.'s work was to build a model framework allowing the prediction of bronchodilation caused by drugs based on local pulmonary drug concentrations. The course of FEV1 over time was predicted by correlating the amount of drug in the muscle compartments with the expected bronchodilation and the resulting total airway resistance. This PBPK model was not evaluated with clinical data, but the predicted FEV1 profiles were found to reasonably agree with clinical FEV1 readouts. According to the authors, the model may be adapted for other bronchodilators. However, this would require PK and PD data for every new drug.

12.3.3 "Generic" PBPK models for orally inhaled drugs

12.3.3.1 Mimetikos Preludium

The Mimetikos Preludium PBPK model (Emmace Consulting AB, Lund, Sweden) is a commercially available model specifically targeting orally and nasally inhaled drugs [34].

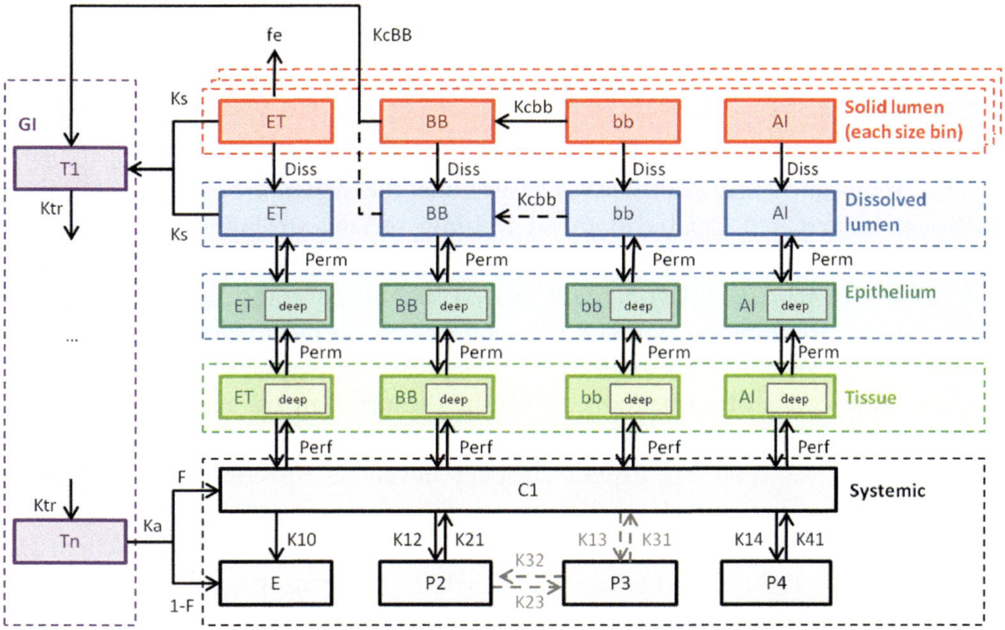

Figure 12.14 Schematic representation of the Mimetikos Preludium Model. Airway regions ET (extra thoracic), BB (large bronchi), bb (bronchiolar) and AI (alveolar interstitial) are subdivided into physiological compartments representing the ELF, the epithelium and lung tissue. Arrows represent transport processes, which are mechanistically included in the respiratory tract and empirically included in the systemic PK model.

As shown in Fig. 12.14, the Preludium model can be considered a semi-mechanistic framework, as it provides a mechanistic description of all pulmonary PK processes (including pulmonary drug deposition, pulmonary dissolution, MCC, absorption into the lung tissues, tissue binding and perfusion into the system), whereas the systemic PK is represented by an empirical compartmental PK model.

The Preludium model allows choosing between different algebraic 1-D deposition models, including the NCRP [80] and the ICRP models [89]. The user can manually define the lung geometry or alternatively can select standard deposition models including disease specific characteristics for asthma patients and COPD patients. Input parameters to calculate the deposition patterns include the inhalation maneuver as well as data from *in vitro* impactor experiments. The aerosol is characterized by a lognormal distribution of the aerodynamic diameter, as well as a fraction of large particles. Large particles are assumed to deposit in the mouth-throat region (ET).

The mucociliary clearance is characterized as two first-order rate constants specifying the transport rate from bronchi (BB) to the first gastro intestinal compartment and from bronchiolar (bb) to bronchi (BB), respectively. Dissolution in ELF is mechanistically included by using a modified Johnson model [37]. The parameterization of the dissolution model can be derived from dissolution experiments using a built-in regression software. Permeation into airway tissue is simulated according to Fick's law, using a first-order rate constant representing effective permeability. The permeability value can either be obtained from an *ex vivo* model [105] or calculated from standard *in vitro* permeability experiments.

The removal of drug from airway tissues into the systemic circulation is assumed perfusion limited, but can be modified by drug specific attributes such as tissue to plasma partition coefficient (Kp). The model also enables parameterization of deep tissue binding to represent physiological process such as lysosomal sequestration of dibases. Finally, an empirical systemic PK model is connected to the mechanistic lung model.

One purpose of analyzes performed with the Preludium model was to understand the link between *in vitro* aerosol properties and clinically observed batch variability [120]. Furthermore, it was applied to explain variability in clinically observed PK parameters for fluticasone propionate by batch-specific data on dissolution and aerosol characteristics (mass median aerodynamic diameter, the distribution of particles, and the coarse fraction) [37]. Currently, the Preludium model is applied to support developing an inhaled biopharmaceutical classification system (iBCS).

12.3.3.2 SimulationsPlus GastroPlus PCAT

The GastroPlus Pulmonary Compartmental Absorption and Transit module (PCAT™) (Simulations Plus, Lancaster, CA) is one of the few commercially available generic PBPK models for oral inhalation. Pulmonary deposition is based on the ICRP66 model, dividing the lung into the extrathoracic region, the tracheobronchial and bronchiolar regions, and the alveolar-interstitial space [35,83]. As depicted in Fig. 12.15, these pulmonary regions are further divided into compartments representing the ELF (solid and dissolved drug) and the lung tissue. The lung tissue compartments are connected to the lymphatic system (which is unique across all PBPK models) and a systemic PK model, which can be an empirical PK model or a whole-body PBPK model.

The PCAT module can be used to predict the PK after pulmonary administration in rat, mouse, dog, and human. As inhalational administration is rather unusual in rodents, the model also supports intra-tracheal administration. In addition to the ICRP66 model, the model allows user-defined deposition patterns, enabling the use of alternative deposition models.

The MCC is implemented as two first-order processes from the bronchiolar and tracheobronchial regions to the extrathoracic region, where the drug is swallowed and transferred to the GastroPlus model's ACAT module for oral absorption [113]. The pulmonary dissolution of solid drug particles in the ELF is characterized based on particle size distribution, water solubility and the diffusion rate. Absorption of dissolved drug

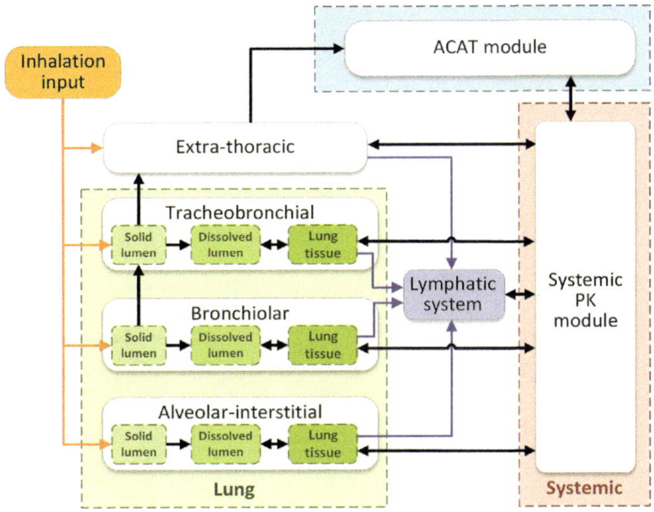

Figure 12.15 Structure of the GastroPlus PCAT module (green). *Adapted and modified from SimulationsPlus(R), GastroPlus(R): Additional dosage routes. https://www.simulations-plus.com/software/gastro-plus/additional-dosage/; S.R. Chaudhuri, V. Lukacova, Simulating delivery of pulmonary (and intranasal) aerosolised drugs, Orally Inhaled Nasal Drug Products (2010) 26–30. www.ondrugdelivery.com.*

into the lung tissues is based on the alveolar permeability, which is anticipated based on the molecular weight (or user-defined). The alveolar permeability is scaled for the tracheobronchial and bronchiolar regions to account for the increase in epithelial thickness [36]. Metabolism can be defined in any of the lung compartments. The absorptive clearance from the lung tissue compartments is considered diffusion-limited, i.e. governed by the blood flow and the blood-tissue partitioning. The respective partitioning coefficient can either be experimentally determined or predicted *in silico*.

Different working groups have applied the PCAT module from GastroPlus® to predict the pulmonary and systemic PK of orally inhaled drugs. Chaudhuri and Lukacova [82] predicted plasma concentration-time profiles of budesonide without fitting any parameters of the model. According to the authors, the predictions provided a reasonable agreement to observed concentration-time profiles. Likewise, Bäckman et al. [36] used this model to investigate systemic exposure of the selective glucocorticoid receptor modulator AZD5423 after administration of different formulations and different devices (after the deposition patterns were predicted with an alternative deposition software).

12.3.3.3 Lung Modeling Platform

Another generic PBPK platform for orally inhaled drugs has been presented by the working group around Cabal and Caniga [81,99]. This PBPK modeling framework was built to translate systemic and pulmonary PK between rats, dogs, and human. Their model consists of five to six independent modules (see Fig. 12.16). Modules for

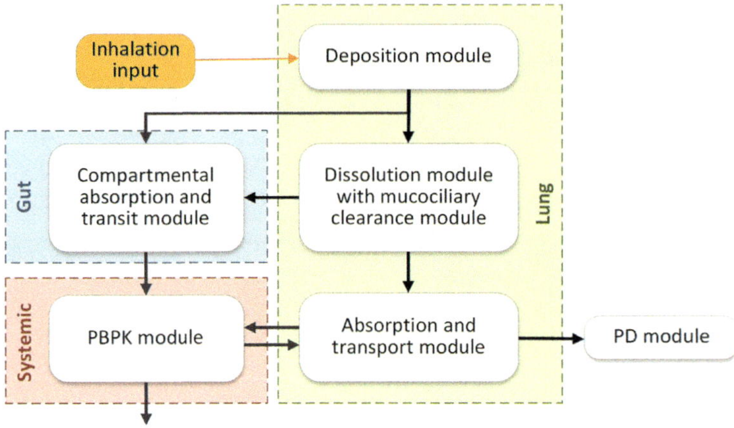

Figure 12.16 Model framework of the Lung Modeling Platform [81].

deposition, dissolution and MCC, absorption and transport, as well as an optional PD module represent the inhalation-specific PK processes. All modules are connected to two additional modules representing the systemic PK (whole-body PBPK model) as well as parallel transit absorption from the gastro intestinal tract.

The pulmonary deposition is predicted based on the typical path model by Yeh and Schum [121] and is therefore comparable to the MPPD model (here applied to monodisperse particles). The MCC and dissolution are competing processes removing the undissolved drug from the epithelial lining liquid. The velocity of the mucus clearance is specifically calculated for each species [98]. The parallel dissolution rate is proportional to the difference in amounts of solid drug and its concentration in the solution (saturation-limited dissolution).

Absorption and transport is characterized by mass flow between seven different lung tissue compartments (ELF, epithelium, interstitial space, immune cells, smooth muscle, endothelium, and macrophages). The respective rate constants are calculated by applying a cell-based model by Yu and Rosania [122], which differentiates between the mouth-throat, tracheobronchial, and alveolar-interstitial regions. Based on physicochemical drug properties, Nernst-Planck's and Fick's equations are implemented to describe the rate of mass transport of charged and neutral species of molecules across each of the lipid bilayers. The predicted concentration in each of the cellular compartments can be used as input into the optional PD module (Fig. 12.17).

12.3.4 Purpose and applicability of reviewed models

All previously described models differ in the implementation of inhalation-specific processes, namely the six pulmonary processes (see Fig. 12.3), as well as parallel absorption from the gastro intestinal tract, the mouth-throat, and the systemic PK. Fig. 12.18

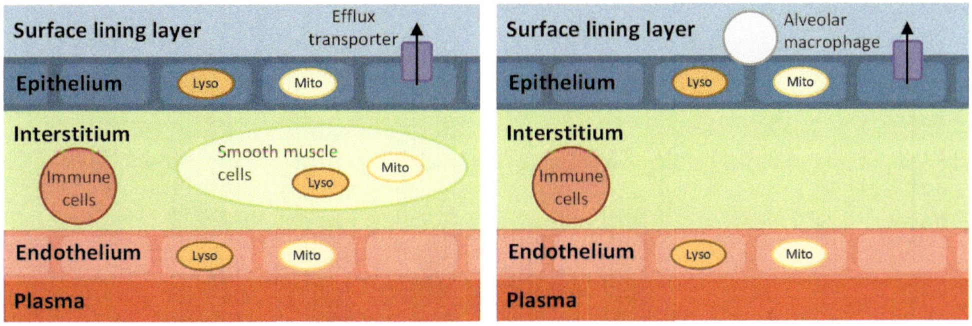

Figure 12.17 Compartments implemented in the absorption and transport module in the tracheobronchial (left panel) and the alveolar-interstitial region (right panel). Cell structures include two organelle compartments (lysosomes and mitochondria). *Adapted from M. Caniga, A. Cabal, K. Mehta, D.S. Ross, M.A. Gil, J.D. Woodhouse, et al., Preclinical experimental and mathematical approaches for assessing effective doses of inhaled drugs, using mometasone to support human dose predictions, J. Aerosol Med. Pulm. Drug Deliv. 29 (2016) 362–377.*

shows a direct comparison of all seven models regarding the mechanistic degree of the implemented pulmonary (and systemic) PK processes. The mechanistic degree was defined based on the arrow diagrams, which can be found in Figs. 12.5–12.12. As discussed before, a higher mechanistic degree does not necessarily provide a better predictive performance. Depending on the intent of the modeling analysis as well as the characteristics of the analyzed drug, an empirical model or at least less mechanistic implementation of single pulmonary processes may provide comparable predictions, while maintaining a reasonable complexity of the PBPK model.

The generic PBPK models (Preludium, GastroPlus and the Lung Modeling Platform) tend to be more mechanistic in nature, as these models have to be applicable to many different drugs. Drug-specific models typically only provide a mechanistic representation of processes that are relevant for the investigated drug, as can be seen for the models by Hendrickx, Boger and Gaz et al. [39,71,84]. The exclusion of certain PK processes is justified, as an inclusion would needlessly complicate the analysis without adding a better prediction quality. However, it prevents that these models can easily be adapted for drugs, for which other (pulmonary) PK processes are relevant due to different physicochemical drug properties.

Table 12.2 summarizes how the models can be applied for the following investigations: (1) extrapolation to other drugs, (2) comparison of different formulations, (3) translation between species and (4) to the diseased state as well as (5) the ability to link the model output to a PD model.

In order to get a " + " for category "Extrapolation to other drugs", the PBPK model has to be applicable to other drugs without any additional *in vivo* data. This means that the PK can be adjusted entirely based on *in vitro* data, without re-

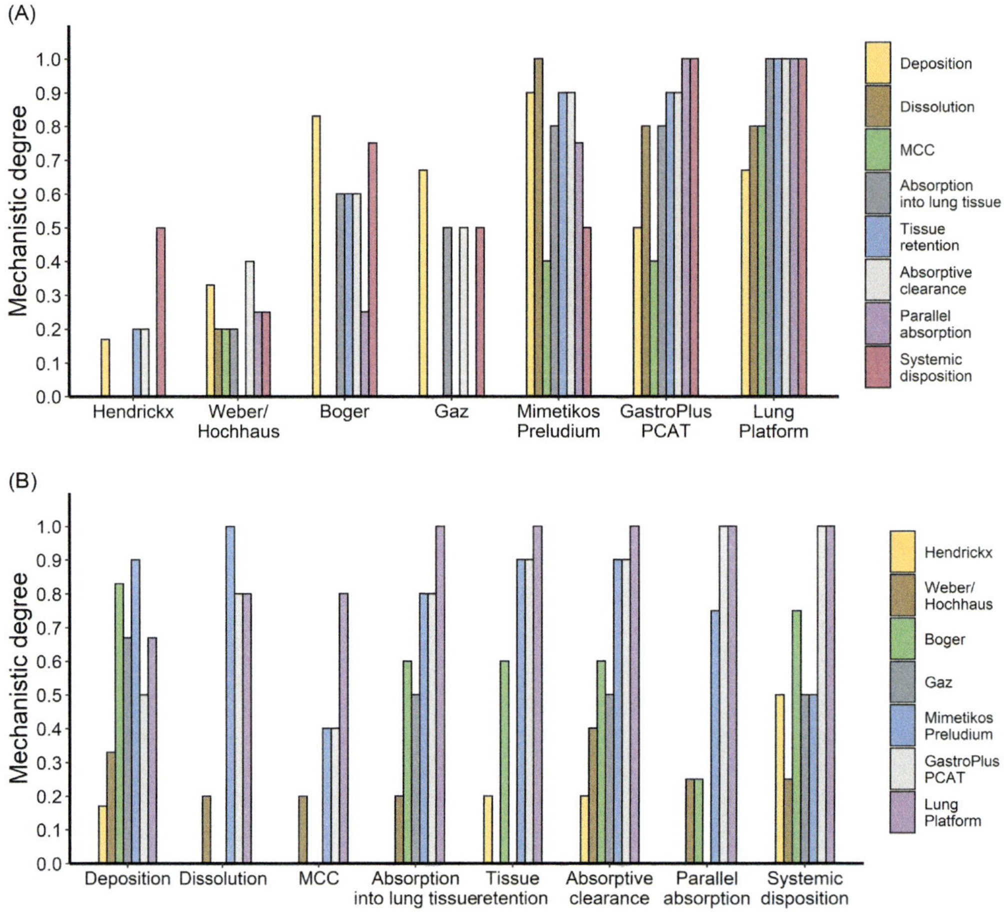

Figure 12.18 Height of the bars corresponds to the model's position on the process-specific arrow scales above (Figs. 12.5–12.12). Top panel: mechanistic degree of the different models stratified by the PK model, Bottom panel: mechanistic degree of different processes stratified by pulmonary PK process. The mechanistic degree in this figure represents a ranking of different approaches and should not be considered as a continous scale i.e., a mechanistic degree of 1.0 is not necessarily "twice as mechanistic" as a mechanistic degree of 0.5.

estimation of PK parameters, and that each of the discussed pulmonary and systemic PK process can be included without manually adapting the model. The model by Boger et al. is characterized by a " ± ", because even though the MCC and dissolution were not included, making the model unsuitable for low solubility compounds, it can be applied for other drugs that are highly soluble. Nevertheless, Boger et al. have shown in a previous publication [114] that a mechanistic representation of the MCC and pulmonary dissolution can be included in this modeling framework. This would however require adapting the structure of the current model.

Table 12.2 Applicability of discussed semi-mechanistic and PBPK models.

		Hendrickx	Weber & Hochhaus	Gaz	Boger	Mimetikos Preludium	GastroPlus PCAT	Lung Modeling Platform
1	Extrapolation to other drugs	–	–	–	±	+	+	(+)§
2	Comparison of formulations	–	±	±	+	+	+#	(±)§
3	Translation between species	+ (rat, dog, human)	–	–	+ (rat, human)	+*	+ (mouse, rat, dog, human)	(+)§ (rat, dog, human)
4	Translation to diseased state	–	–	±	–*	+	–	(+)§
5	Linking pulmonary PK and PD	+	–	+	+	+	+	(+)§

All applications were evaluated ranging from "–" to " + " based on defined criteria, " + " indicating that the model is fully applicable, while "–" means it is not suited for this specific investigation. A " ± " indicates that the model may be applicable, when certain prerequisites are fulfilled.
#external deposition data required to compare different formulations,
*not parameterized in software, but adaptable. The evaluation for the Lung Modeling Platform is shown in brackets, since this model is not publicly available.
§The evaluation for the Lung Platform is shown in brackets, since this model is not publicly available.

The PBPK models were judged suitable for "Comparison of formulations", if they account for different particle size distributions and if these were used to mechanistically predict the respective pulmonary drug deposition. Both models from Weber and Hochhaus and Gaz et al. are rated " ± ", as these models do not allow PK predictions based on a particle size distribution. Instead, they only distinguish between the central and peripheral lung and fine and coarse particles, respectively. The same reasoning applies to the Lung Modeling Platform, as this PBPK model assumes monodisperse particles to predict the respective deposition patterns. Therefore, these models cannot be applied to perform a model-based comparison of different inhaled formulations that are characterized by different particle size distributions.

"Translation between species" requires the inclusion of physiological information about lung anatomy and morphometry (provided by the model), which is true for four of the seven models. "Translation to the diseased state", i.e., predicting the PK in asthma or COPD patients is only possible if the model itself allows for modifying specific parts of lung anatomy. For example, it is known that in asthma or COPD airway constrictions narrow the conducting airways and thereby alter the deposition patterns. An alternative to adapting the lung geometry would be manually including quantitative deposition data, which is not readily available in patients.

The criteria for "linking the pulmonary PK and PD" are first a predicted pulmonary concentration-time profile with the option of calculating the unbound tissue concentration (inclusion of fraction unbound in tissue, or plasma protein binding in combination with Kp values), and second an incorporation of backflow of drug from the systemic circulation into the lung. Neglecting the latter would result in an underestimation of pulmonary drug concentrations at later time points.

12.4 Future applications of PBPK modeling for inhaled drugs - opportunities and limitations

Until today, PBPK modeling was mainly applied for retrospective analyzes. However, the real strength of PBPK models is to prospectively predict or investigate scenarios, *prior* to cost-intensive *in vivo* studies. As PBPK modeling for orally inhaled drugs is a relatively young discipline, only few examples exist in the public domain. In the future, it can be expected that PBPK modeling for orally inhaled drugs will become more often applied. Furthermore, based on the experience with other routes of administration, it can also be anticipated that PBPK modeling can improve the mechanistic understanding of orally inhaled drugs.

Potential opportunities of a well-trained PBPK model range from the preclinical up to the late clinical stage:

1. To perform sensitivity analyzes aiming at identifying the most relevant pulmonary PK parameters, which drive pulmonary efficacy and/or pulmonary

targeting. Based on this analysis, for example, it might be possible to optimize the most relevant drug properties and drug product characteristics at early stages of drug discovery.

2. To better understand the quality of a drug candidate; i.e., what is the expected pulmonary PK and PD selectivity as well as the duration of pulmonary efficacy achieved after oral drug inhalation,
3. To predict the efficacious human inhaled dose, also for unknown modes of action. This includes translating between different preclinical species and human, or even between different administration methods. For example, a human efficacious dose might have to be predicted based on data after intratracheal instillation or after nasal inhalation in rats.
4. To bridge the pharmacokinetics and the (pulmonary) target engagement between healthy volunteers investigated in Phase 1 clinical trials and patients, which are typically not investigated before a Phase 2 study,
5. To bridge between different inhaled particle/droplet formulations and/or inhalation devices. For example to predict the PK of the final inhalation device in a Phase 2 clinical trial based on PK data from a Phase I study (combined with *in vitro* data), which was performed with a preliminary nebulizer formulation,
6. To perform sensitivity analyzes with respect to identify how PK is responding to variations in product and batch attributes such as dose, dose deposition pattern and dissolution rate. This could for instance, support clinically relevant specifications and also clinically relevant design targets.
7. To provide a framework, which allows the development of an inhaled biopharmaceutical classification system (iBCS).

Even though the future opportunities for PBPK modeling are manifold, it remains a challenge to develop fully generic PBPK models for inhaled drugs. The most obvious reason is the limited number of publically available training data sets. Furthermore, even for drugs, such as fluticasone propionate or salbutamol, for which most pulmonary processes have intensively been studied, it remains challenging to combine the available *in vitro* and *in vivo* data. For example, different methods to investigate the pulmonary dissolution might result in different PK predictions, and a good IVIVC still has to be demonstrated.

12.5 Conclusions and outline

PBPK modeling can be a strong and powerful approach to better understand the pulmonary fate of inhaled drugs. It offers unique opportunities, which cannot be achieved with the standard analyzes. However, a fully generic mechanistic PBPK model for inhaled drugs remains to be developed and even more importantly, to be evaluated for a wide range of inhaled drugs.

Acknowledgments

We would like to thank Achim Sauer, Günther Hochhaus, and Bo Olsson for carefully reviewing the book chapter and providing valuable suggestions to improve this chapter.

References

[1] J.Y. Lee, C.E. Garnett, J.V. Gobburu, V.A. Bhattaram, S. Brar, J.C. Earp, et al., Impact of pharmacometric analyses on new drug approval and labelling decisions, Clin. Pharmacokinet. 50 (2011) 627–635.
[2] E. Manolis, S. Rohou, R. Hemmings, T. Salmonson, M. Karlsson, P. Milligan, The role of modeling and simulation in development and registration of medicinal products: output from the EFPIA/EMA Modeling and Simulation Workshop, CPT Pharmacomet. Syst. Pharmacol. 2 (2013) 1–4.
[3] S. Marshall, R. Madabushi, E. Manolis, K. Krudys, A. Staab, K. Dykstra, et al., Model-informed drug discovery and development: current industry good practice and regulatory expectations and future perspectives, CPT Pharmacomet. Syst. Pharmacol. 8 (2019) 87–96.
[4] K.L. Gill, I. Gardner, L. Li, M. Jamei, A bottom-up whole-body physiologically based pharmacokinetic model to mechanistically predict tissue distribution and the rate of subcutaneous absorption of therapeutic proteins, AAPS J. 18 (2016) 156–170.
[5] M. Jamei, Recent advances in development and application of physiologically-based pharmacokinetic (PBPK) models: a transition from academic curiosity to regulatory acceptance, Curr. Pharmacol. Rep. 2 (2016) 161–169.
[6] E. Luzon, K. Blake, S. Cole, A. Nordmark, C. Versantvoort, E.G. Berglund, Physiologically based pharmacokinetic modeling in regulatory decision-making at the European Medicines Agency, Clin. Pharmacol. Ther. 102 (2017) 98–105.
[7] M.L. Rizk, L. Zou, R.M. Savic, K.E. Dooley, Importance of drug pharmacokinetics at the site of action, Clin. Transl. Sci. 10 (2017) 133–142.
[8] J.M. Borghardt, B. Weber, A. Staab, C. Kunz, S. Formella, C. Kloft, Investigating pulmonary and systemic pharmacokinetics of inhaled olodaterol in healthy volunteers using a population pharmacokinetic approach, Br. J. Clin. Pharmacol. 81 (2016) 538–552.
[9] G. Hochhaus, M. Chen, J. Shur, A. Kurumaddali, U. Schilling, Y. Jiao, et al., Unraveling the pulmonary fate of fluticasone and friends: meeting the physiologic and pharmacokinetic challenges, Respir. Drug Deliv. 1 (2020) 139–146. 2020.
[10] J. Melin, S. Prothon, C. Kloft, A. Cleton, C. Amilon, C. Jorup, et al., Pharmacokinetics of the inhaled selective glucocorticoid receptor modulator AZD5423 following inhalation using different devices, AAPS J. 19 (2017) 865–874.
[11] C. Bartels, M. Looby, R. Sechaud, G. Kaiser, Determination of the pharmacokinetics of glycopyrronium in the lung using a population pharmacokinetic modelling approach, Br. J. Clin. Pharmacol. 76 (2013) 868–879.
[12] M. Sakagami, Insulin disposition in the lung following oral inhalation in humans: a meta-analysis of its pharmacokinetics, Clin. Pharmacokinet. 43 (2004) 539–552.
[13] B. Weber, G. Hochhaus, A pharmacokinetic simulation tool for inhaled corticosteroids, AAPS J. 15 (2013) 159–171.
[14] M. Rohrschneider, S. Bhagwat, R. Krampe, V. Michler, Jr. Breitkreutz, Gn. Hochhaus, Evaluation of the transwell system for characterization of dissolution behavior of inhalation drugs: effects of membrane and surfactant, Mol. Pharm. 12 (2015) 2618–2624.
[15] P.L. Bonate, Pharmacokinetic-Pharmacodynamic Modeling and Simulation, Springer, 2011.

[16] K. Dykstra, N. Mehrotra, C.W. Tornøe, H. Kastrissios, B. Patel, N. Al-Huniti, et al., Reporting guidelines for population pharmacokinetic analyses, J. Clin. Pharmacol. 55 (2015) 875–887.

[17] M. Danhof, E.C.M. de Lange, O.E. Della Pasqua, B.A. Ploeger, R.A. Voskuyl, Mechanism-based pharmacokinetic-pharmacodynamic (PK-PD) modeling in translational drug research, Trends Pharmacol. Sci. 29 (2008) 186–191.

[18] R. Upton, D. Mould, Basic concepts in population modeling, simulation, and model-based drug development: Part 3—Introduction to pharmacodynamic modeling methods, CPT Pharmacomet. Syst. Pharmacol. 3 (2014) 88.

[19] J.M. Borghardt, B. Weber, A. Staab, C. Kloft, Pharmacometric models for characterizing the pharmacokinetics of orally inhaled drugs, AAPS J. 17 (2015) 853–870.

[20] P. Backman, S. Arora, W. Couet, B. Forbes, W. de Kruijf, A. Paudel, Advances in experimental and mechanistic computational models to understand pulmonary exposure to inhaled drugs, Eur. J. Pharm. Sci. 113 (2018) 41–52.

[21] S. Pilari, W. Huisinga, Lumping of physiologically-based pharmacokinetic models and a mechanistic derivation of classical compartmental models, J. Pharmacokinet. Pharmacodyn. 37 (2010) 365–405.

[22] J.E. Sager, J. Yu, I. Ragueneau-Majlessi, N. Isoherranen, Physiologically based pharmacokinetic (PBPK) modeling and simulation approaches: a systematic review of published models, applications, and model verification, Drug Metab. Dispos. 43 (2015) 1823–1837.

[23] C. Wagner, P. Zhao, Y. Pan, V. Hsu, J. Grillo, S. Huang, et al., Application of physiologically based pharmacokinetic (PBPK) modeling to support dose selection: report of an FDA public workshop on PBPK, CPT Pharmacomet. Syst. Pharmacol. 4 (2015) 226–230.

[24] L. Zhang, Y.D. Zhang, P. Zhao, S.-M. Huang, Predicting drug–drug interactions: an FDA perspective, AAPS J. 11 (2009) 300–306.

[25] P. Zhao, L. Zhang, J.A. Grillo, Q. Liu, J.M. Bullock, Y.J. Moon, et al., Applications of physiologically based pharmacokinetic (PBPK) modeling and simulation during regulatory review, Clin. Pharmacol. Ther. 89 (2011) 259–267.

[26] H.M. Jones, M. Dickins, K. Youdim, J.R. Gosset, N.J. Attkins, T.L. Hay, et al., Application of PBPK modelling in drug discovery and development at Pfizer, Xenobiotica 42 (2012) 94–106.

[27] H.M. Jones, N. Parrott, K. Jorga, T. Lavé, A novel strategy for physiologically based predictions of human pharmacokinetics, Clin. Pharmacokinet. 45 (2006) 511–542.

[28] C. Hartmanshenn, M. Scherholz, I.P. Androulakis, Physiologically-based pharmacokinetic models: approaches for enabling personalized medicine, J. Pharmacokinet. Pharmacodyn. 43 (2016) 481–504.

[29] F.-P. Theil, T.W. Guentert, S. Haddad, P. Poulin, Utility of physiologically based pharmacokinetic models to drug development and rational drug discovery candidate selection, Toxicol. Lett. 138 (2003) 29–49.

[30] M. Chetty, R.H. Rose, K. Abduljalil, N. Patel, G. Lu, T. Cain, et al., Applications of linking PBPK and PD models to predict the impact of genotypic variability, formulation differences, differences in target binding capacity and target site drug concentrations on drug responses and variability, Front. Pharmacol. 5 (2014) 258.

[31] M. Chenel, F. Bouzom, L. Aarons, K. Ogungbenro, Drug–drug interaction predictions with PBPK models and optimal multiresponse sampling time designs: application to midazolam and a phase I compound. Part 1: comparison of uniresponse and multiresponse designs using PopDes, J. Pharmacokinetics Pharmacodyn. 35 (2008) 635–659.

[32] J. Lippert, R. Burghaus, A. Edginton, S. Frechen, M. Karlsson, A. Kovar, et al., Open systems pharmacology community—an open access, open source, open science approach to modeling and simulation in pharmaceutical sciences, CPT Pharmacomet. Syst. Pharmacol. 8 (2019) 878.

[33] M. Jamei, S. Marciniak, K. Feng, A. Barnett, G. Tucker, A. Rostami-Hodjegan, The Simcyp® population-based ADME simulator, Expert. Opin. Drug Metab. Toxicol. 5 (2009) 211–223.

[34] B. Olsson, P. Bäckman, in: R.N. Dalby, P.R. Byron, M. Hindle, J. Peart, D. Traini, P.M. Young, S.J. Farr, J.D. Suman, A. Watts (Eds.), Respiratory Drug Delivery, 1, Davis Healthcare International Publishing, River, Grove, IL, 2018, pp. 103–111.

[35] SimulationsPlus(R), GastroPlus(R): Additional dosage routes. https://www.simulations-plus.com/software/gastroplus/additional-dosage/, 2020 (accessed 31.01.20).

[36] P. Bäckman, U. Tehler, B. Olsson, Predicting exposure after oral inhalation of the selective glucocorticoid receptor modulator, AZD5423, based on dose, deposition pattern, and mechanistic modeling of pulmonary disposition, J. Aerosol Med. Pulm. Drug Deliv. 30 (2017) 108–117.

[37] P. Bäckman, B. Olsson, Drug dissolution, regional retention and system ic absorption: understanding their interactions though mechanistic modelling, in: P.R. Byron (Ed.), Respiratory Drug Delivery, Davis Healthcare International Publishing, River Grove, IL, 2020.

[38] E. Boger, N. Evans, M. Chappell, A. Lundqvist, P. Ewing, A. Wigenborg, et al., Systems pharmacology approach for prediction of pulmonary and systemic pharmacokinetics and receptor occupancy of inhaled drugs, CPT: Pharmacomet. Syst. Pharmacol. 5 (2016) 201–210.

[39] E. Boger, M. Fridén, Physiologically based pharmacokinetic/pharmacodynamic modeling accurately predicts the better bronchodilatory effect of inhaled versus oral salbutamol dosage forms, J. Aerosol Med. Pulm. Drug Deliv. 32 (2019) 1–12.

[40] L. Kuepfer, C. Niederalt, T. Wendl, J.F. Schlender, S. Willmann, J. Lippert, et al., Applied concepts in PBPK modeling: how to build a PBPK/PD model, CPT: Pharmacomet. Syst. Pharmacol. 5 (2016) 516–531.

[41] H.M. Jones, K. Mayawala, P. Poulin, Dose selection based on physiologically based pharmacokinetic (PBPK) approaches, AAPS J. 15 (2013) 377–387.

[42] L.T. Baxter, H. Zhu, D.G. Mackensen, R.K. Jain, Physiologically based pharmacokinetic model for specific and nonspecific monoclonal antibodies and fragments in normal tissues and human tumor xenografts in nude mice, Cancer Res. 54 (1994) 1517–1528.

[43] S.A. Peters, Physiologically-Based Pharmacokinetic (PBPK) Modeling and Simulations: Principles, Methods, and Applications in the Pharmaceutical Industry, John Wiley & Sons, 2012.

[44] R.P. Brown, M.D. Delp, S.L. Lindstedt, L.R. Rhomberg, R.P. Beliles, Physiological parameter values for physiologically based pharmacokinetic models, Toxicol. Ind. Health 13 (1997) 407–484.

[45] V. Lukacova, T. Lave, G. Fraczkiewicz, M. Bolger, W. Woltosz, General approach to calculation of tissue: plasma partition coefficients for physiologically based pharmacokinetic (PBPK) modeling, in: Poster Session presented at: 2008 AAPS National Annual Meeting and Exposition, 2008.

[46] T. Rodgers, D. Leahy, M. Rowland, Physiologically based pharmacokinetic modeling 1: predicting the tissue distribution of moderate-to-strong bases, J. Pharm. Sci. 94 (2005) 1259–1276.

[47] T. Rodgers, M. Rowland, Physiologically based pharmacokinetic modelling 2: predicting the tissue distribution of acids, very weak bases, neutrals and zwitterions, J. Pharm. Sci. 95 (2006) 1238–1257.

[48] W. Schmitt, General approach for the calculation of tissue to plasma partition coefficients, Toxicol. Vitro 22 (2008) 457–467.

[49] P. Zhao, Md.L. Vieira, J.A. Grillo, P. Song, T.C. Wu, J.H. Zheng, et al., Evaluation of exposure change of nonrenally eliminated drugs in patients with chronic kidney disease using physiologically based pharmacokinetic modeling and simulation, J. Clin. Pharmacol. 52 (2012) 91S–108S.

[50] J.-F. Schlender, M. Meyer, K. Thelen, M. Krauss, S. Willmann, T. Eissing, et al., Development of a whole-body physiologically based pharmacokinetic approach to assess the pharmacokinetics of drugs in elderly individuals, Clin. Pharmacokinet. 55 (2016) 1573–1589.

[51] J.-F. Schlender, V. Vozmediano, A.G. Golden, M. Rodriguez, T.S. Samant, C.V. Lagishetty, et al., Current strategies to streamline pharmacotherapy for older adults, Eur. J. Pharm. Sci. 111 (2018) 432–442.

[52] L.B. Sheiner, Learning versus confirming in clinical drug development, Clin. Pharmacol. Ther. 61 (1997) 275–291.

[53] P. Zhao, M. Rowland, S.M. Huang, Best practice in the use of physiologically based pharmacokinetic modeling and simulation to address clinical pharmacology regulatory questions, Clin. Pharmacol. Ther. 92 (2012) 17–20.

[54] J.S. Patton, P.R. Byron, Inhaling medicines: delivering drugs to the body through the lungs, Nat. Rev. Drug Discov. 6 (2007) 67–74.

[55] J.M. Borghardt, C. Kloft, A. Sharma, Inhaled therapy in respiratory disease: the complex interplay of pulmonary kinetic processes, Can. Respir. J. 2018 (2018).

[56] S.L. Bernard, R.W. Glenny, N.L. Polissar, D.L. Luchtel, S. Lakshminarayan, Distribution of pulmonary and bronchial blood supply to airways measured by fluorescent microspheres, J. Appl. Physiol. 80 (1996) 430–436.
[57] M.S. Dunnill, G.R. Massarella, J.A. Anderson, A comparison of the quantitative anatomy of the bronchi in normal subjects, in status asthmaticus, in chronic bronchitis, and in emphysema, Thorax 24 (1969) 176–179.
[58] R.A. Parent, Treatise on Pulmonary Toxicology: Comparative Biology of the Normal Lung, CRC press, 1992.
[59] H. Yeh, G. Schum, M. Duggan, Anatomic models of the tracheobronchial and pulmonary regions of the rat, Anat. Rec. 195 (1979) 483–492.
[60] A. Himstedt, C. Braun, S.G. Wicha, J.M. Borghardt, Towards a quantitative mechanistic understanding of localized pulmonary tissue retention—a combined in vivo/in silico approach based on four model drugs, Pharmaceutics 12 (2020) 408.
[61] B.E. Lehnert, Pulmonary and thoracic macrophage subpopulations and clearance of particles from the lung, Environ. Health Perspect. 97 (1992) 17–46.
[62] B.E. Lehnert, Y.E. Valdez, G.L. Tietjen, Alveolar macrophage-particle relationships during lung clearance, Am. J. Respir. Cell Mol. Biol. 1 (1989) 145–154.
[63] M. Geiser, M. Casaulta, B. Kupferschmid, H. Schulz, M. Semmler-Behnke, W. Kreyling, The role of macrophages in the clearance of inhaled ultrafine titanium dioxide particles, Am. J. Respir. Cell Mol. Biol. 38 (2008) 371–376.
[64] J. Hukkanen, O. Pelkonen, J. Hakkola, H. Raunio, Expression and regulation of xenobiotic-metabolizing cytochrome P450 (CYP) enzymes in human lung, Crit. Rev. Toxicol. 32 (2002) 391–411.
[65] T. Shimada, H. Yamazaki, M. Mimura, N. Wakamiya, Y.F. Ueng, F.P. Guengerich, et al., Characterization of microsomal cytochrome P450 enzymes involved in the oxidation of xenobiotic chemicals in human fetal livers and adult lungs, Drug Metab. Dispos. 24 (1996) 515–522.
[66] J. Campbell, C. Van Landingham, S. Crowell, R. Gentry, D. Kaden, S. Fiebelkorn, et al., A preliminary regional PBPK model of lung metabolism for improving species dependent descriptions of 1,3-butadiene and its metabolites, Chem. Biol. Interact. 238 (2015) 102–110.
[67] Y.B. Choy, M.R. Prausnitz, The rule of five for non-oral routes of drug delivery: ophthalmic, inhalation and transdermal, Pharm. Res. 28 (2011) 943–948.
[68] T.J. Ritchie, C.N. Luscombe, S.J. Macdonald, Analysis of the calculated physicochemical properties of respiratory drugs: can we design for inhaled drugs yet? J. Chem. Inf. Modeling 49 (2009) 1025–1032.
[69] G.L. Amidon, H. Lennernäs, V.P. Shah, J.R. Crison, A theoretical basis for a biopharmaceutic drug classification: the correlation of in vitro drug product dissolution and in vivo bioavailability, Pharm. Res. 12 (1995) 413–420.
[70] J.E. Hastedt, P. Bäckman, A.R. Clark, W. Doub, A. Hickey, G. Hochhaus, et al., Scope and relevance of a pulmonary biopharmaceutical classification system AAPS/FDA/USP Workshop March 16-17th, 2015 in Baltimore, MD, AAPS Open 2 (2016) 1–30. Available from: https://doi.org/10.1186/s41120-015-0002-x.
[71] R. Hendrickx, E.L. Bergström, D.L.I. Janzén, M. Fridén, U. Eriksson, K. Grime, et al., Translational model to predict pulmonary pharmacokinetics and efficacy in man for inhaled bronchodilators, CPT: Pharmacomet. Syst. Pharmacol. 7 (2018) 147–157.
[72] D. Lombardi, B. Cuenoud, S.D. Krämer, Lipid membrane interactions of indacaterol and salmeterol: do they influence their pharmacological properties? Eur. J. Pharm. Sci. 38 (2009) 533–547.
[73] M. Johnson, P. Butchers, R. Coleman, A. Nials, P. Strong, M. Summer, et al., The pharmacology of salmeterol, Life Sci. 52 (1993) 2131–2143.
[74] P. Casarosa, I. Kollak, T. Kiechle, A. Ostermann, A. Schnapp, R. Kiesling, et al., Functional and biochemical rationales for the 24-hour-long duration of action of olodaterol, J. Pharmacol. Exp. Ther. 337 (2011) 600.
[75] G. Pelaia, A. Vatrella, M.T. Busceti, L. Gallelli, C. Calabrese, R. Terracciano, et al., Pharmacologic rationale underlying the therapeutic effects of tiotropium/olodaterol in COPD, Ther. Clin. Risk Manag. 11 (2015) 1563–1572.

[76] S. Newman, G. Pitcairn, P. Hirst, et al., Scintigraphic comparison of budesonide deposition from two dry powder inhalers, Eur. Respir. J. 16 (2000) 178–183.
[77] S. Newman, K. Steed, G. Hooper, A. Källén, L. Borgström, Comparison of gamma scintigraphy and a pharmacokinetic technique for assessing pulmonary deposition of terbutaline sulphate delivered by pressurized metered dose inhaler, Pharm. Res. 12 (1995) 231–236.
[78] G. Taylor, S. Warren, S. Dwivedi, M. Sommerville, L. Mello, C. Orevillo, et al., Gamma scintigraphic pulmonary deposition study of glycopyrronium/formoterol metered dose inhaler formulated using co-suspension delivery technology, Eur. J. Pharm. Sci. 111 (2018) 450–457.
[79] J. Weers, B. Metzheiser, G. Taylor, S. Warren, P. Meers, W.R. Perkins, A gamma scintigraphy study to investigate lung deposition and clearance of inhaled amikacin-loaded liposomes in healthy male volunteers, J. Aerosol Med. Pulm. Drug Deliv. 22 (2009) 131–138.
[80] M.F. Biddiscombe, S.N. Meah, S.R. Underwood, O.S. Usmani, Comparing lung regions of interest in gamma scintigraphy for assessing inhaled therapeutic aerosol deposition, J. Aerosol Med. Pulm. Drug Deliv. 24 (2011) 165–173.
[81] NCRP, Deposition, retention and dosimetry of inhaled radioactive substances, NCRP Report No. 125 1996.
[82] A. Cabal, K. Mehta, P. Guo, A. Przekwas, In-silico lung modeling platform for inhaled drug delivery, Proc. Drug Deliv. Lungs 27 (2016) 82–86.
[83] S.R. Chaudhuri, V. Lukacova, Simulating delivery of pulmonary (and intranasal) aerosolised drugs, Orally Inhaled Nasal Drug Products (2010) 26–30. Available from: www.ondrugdelivery.com.
[84] C. Gaz, G. Cremona, S. Panunzi, B. Patterson, A. De Gaetano, A geometrical approach to the PKPD modelling of inhaled bronchodilators, J. Pharmacokinet. Pharmacodyn. 39 (2012) 415–428.
[85] F.J. Miller, B. Asgharian, J.D. Schroeter, O.T. Price, Improvements and additions to the Multiple Path Particle Dosimetry model, J. Aeorosol Sci. 99 (2016) 14–26.
[86] National Institute for Public Health and the Environment (RIVM), Multiple Path Particle Dosimetry Model (MPPD v 1.0): A Model for Human and Rat Airway Particle Dosimetry, Bilthoven, The Netherlands, 2002.
[87] C.P. Yu, C.K. Diu, A comparative study of aerosol deposition in different lung models, Am. Ind. Hyg. Assoc. J. 43 (1982) 54–65.
[88] E.R. Weibel, D.M. Gomez, Architecture of the human lung, Science 137 (1962) 577–585.
[89] International Commission on Radiological Protection, ICRP Publication 66 Human Respiratory Tract Model for Radiological Protection, Elsevier, New York, 1994.
[90] A. Vulović, T. Šušteršič, S. Cvijić, S. Ibrić, N. Filipović, Coupled in silico platform: computational fluid dynamics (CFD) and physiologically-based pharmacokinetic (PBPK) modelling, Eur. J. Pharm. Sci. 113 (2018) 171–184.
[91] W. Nernst, Theorie der Reaktionsgeschwindigkeit in heterogenen Systemen, Z. für physikalische Chem. 47 (1904) 52–55.
[92] A.T. Lu, M.E. Frisella, K.C. Johnson, Dissolution modeling: factors affecting the dissolution rates of polydisperse powders, Pharm. Res. 10 (1993) 1308–1314.
[93] R. Price, G. Farias, W. Ganley, J. Shur, Demonstrating Q3 structural equivalence of dry powder inhaler blends: new analytical concepts and techniques, in: R.N. Dalby, P.R. Byron, M. Hindle, J. Peart, D. Traini, P.M. Young, S.J. Farr, J.D. Suman, A. Watts (Eds.), Respiratory Drug Delivery, DHI Publishing, Glendale, AZ, 2018, pp. 265–276.
[94] S.P. Velaga, J. Djuris, S. Cvijic, S. Rozou, P. Russo, G. Colombo, et al., Dry powder inhalers: an overview of the in vitro dissolution methodologies and their correlation with the biopharmaceutical aspects of the drug products, Eur. J. Pharm. Sci. 113 (2018) 18–28.
[95] J.X. Huang, M.A. Blaskovich, R. Pelingon, S. Ramu, A. Kavanagh, A.G. Elliott, et al., Mucin binding reduces colistin antimicrobial activity, Antimicrob. Agents Chemother. 59 (2015) 5925–5931.
[96] E. Houtmeyers, R. Gosselink, G. Gayan-Ramirez, M. Decramer, Regulation of mucociliary clearance in health and disease, Eur. Respir. J. 13 (1999) 1177–1188.

[97] G.C. Smaldone, W.M. Foster, T.G. O'Riordan, M.S. Messina, R.J. Perry, E.G. Langenback, Regional impairment of mucociliary clearance in chronic obstructive pulmonary disease, Chest 103 (1993) 1390–1396.

[98] W. Hofmann, B. Asgharian, The effect of lung structure on mucociliary clearance and particle retention in human and rat lungs, Toxicolo. Sci. 73 (2003) 448–456.

[99] W. Hofmann, R. Sturm, Stochastic model of particle clearance in human bronchial airways, J. Aerosol Med.: Off. J. Int. Soc. Aerosols Med. 17 (2004) 73–89.

[100] M. Caniga, A. Cabal, K. Mehta, D.S. Ross, M.A. Gil, J.D. Woodhouse, et al., Preclinical experimental and mathematical approaches for assessing effective doses of inhaled drugs, using mometasone to support human dose predictions, J. Aerosol Med. Pulm. Drug Deliv. 29 (2016) 362–377.

[101] J.R.H. Smith, M.R. Bailey, G. Etherington, A.L. Shutt, M.J. Youngman, Effect of particle size on slow particle clearance from the bronchial tree, Exp. Lung Res. 34 (2008) 287–312.

[102] M. Lohmann-Matthes, C. Steinmuller, G. Franke-Ullmann, Pulmonary macrophages, Eur. Respir. J. 7 (1994) 1678–1689.

[103] C. Lombry, D.A. Edwards, V. Préat, R. Vanbever, Alveolar macrophages are a primary barrier to pulmonary absorption of macromolecules, Am. J. Physiol. Lung Cell. Mol. Physiol. 286 (2004) L1002–L1008.

[104] J. Shao, J. Talton, Y. Wang, L. Winner, G. Hochhaus, Quantitative assessment of pulmonary targeting of inhaled corticosteroids using ex vivo receptor binding studies, AAPS J. 22 (2020) 39.

[105] J. Eriksson, E. Sjogren, H. Thorn, K. Rubin, P. Backman, H. Lennernas, Pulmonary absorption - estimation of effective pulmonary permeability and tissue retention of ten drugs using an ex vivo rat model and computational analysis, Eur. J. Pharm. Biopharm. 124 (2018) 1–12.

[106] A. Fick, Ueber Diffusion, Annalen der Physik 170 (1855) 59–86.

[107] L. Gaohua, J. Wedagedera, B.G. Small, L. Almond, K. Romero, D. Hermann, et al., Development of a multicompartment permeability-limited lung PBPK model and its application in predicting pulmonary pharmacokinetics of antituberculosis drugs, CPT Pharmacomet. Syst. Pharmacol. 4 (2015) 605–613.

[108] G. Hochhaus, H. Möllmann, H. Derendorf, R.J. Gonzalez-Rothi, Pharmacokinetic/pharmacodynamic aspects of aerosol therapy using glucocorticoids as a model, J. Clin. Pharmacol. 37 (1997) 881–892.

[109] P. Poulin, F.P. Theil, Prediction of pharmacokinetics prior to in vivo studies. 1. Mechanism-based prediction of volume of distribution, J. Pharm. Sci. 91 (2002) 129–156.

[110] K.D.R.E.A. Keller, Ciclesonide: an on-site-activated steroid, New Drugs for Asthma, Allergy and COPD 31 (2001) 91–93.

[111] A. Tunek, K. Sjödin, G. Hallström, Reversible formation of fatty acid esters of budesonide, an antiasthma glucocorticoid, in human lung and liver microsomes, Drug. Metab. Dispos. 25 (1997) 1311–1317.

[112] J. Malmborg, B.A. Ploeger, Predicting human exposure of active drug after oral prodrug administration, using a joined in vitro/in silico–in vivo extrapolation and physiologically-based pharmacokinetic modeling approach, J. Pharmacol. Toxicol. Methods 67 (2013) 203–213.

[113] B. Agoram, W.S. Woltosz, M.B. Bolger, Predicting the impact of physiological and biochemical processes on oral drug bioavailability, Adv. Drug Deliv. Rev. 50 (Suppl. 1) (2001) S41–S67.

[114] E. Boger, O. Wigström, A partial differential equation approach to inhalation physiologically based pharmacokinetic modeling, CPT: Pharmacomet. Syst. Pharmacol. 7 (2018) 638–646.

[115] A. Himstedt, S.G. Wicha, J.M. Borghardt, Model-based evaluation of pulmonary PK selectivity – towards a feasibility assessment of targeting the lung by oral drug inhalation, in: P.R. Byron (Ed.), Respiratory Drug Delivery, Davis Healthcare International Publishing, Moore, CA, 2020.

[116] P.R. Byron, Prediction of drug residence times in regions of the human respiratory tract following aerosol inhalation, J. Pharm. Sci. 75 (1986) 433–438.

[117] B. Weber, G. Hochhaus, A. Systematic analysis of the sensitivity of plasma pharmacokinetics to detect differences in the pulmonary performance of inhaled fluticasone propionate products using a model-based simulation approach, AAPS J. 17 (2015) 999–1010.

[118] D. Lee, A.S. Wexler, Particle deposition in juvenile rat lungs: a model study, J. Aerosol Sci. 42 (2011) 567–579.
[119] B. Forbes, Human airway epithelial cell lines for in vitro drug transport and metabolism studies, Pharm. Sci. Technol. Today 3 (2000) 18–27.
[120] P. Bäckman, B. Olsson, De-risking inhalation product development using predictive model, in: R. N. Dalby, J. Peart (Eds.), Respiratory Drug Delivery Asia, Davis Healthcare International Publishing, LLC, Kerela, 2018, pp. 83–90.
[121] H.-C. Yeh, G. Schum, Models of human lung airways and their application to inhaled particle deposition, Bull. Math. Biol. 42 (1980) 461–480.
[122] J.Y. Yu, G.R. Rosania, Cell-based multiscale computational modeling of small molecule absorption and retention in the lungs, Pharm. Res. 27 (2010) 457–467.

CHAPTER 13

Inhaled aerosols: Emerging clinical methods

Joy Conway[1,2], Martyn Biddiscombe[3] and Omar Usmani[3]
[1]Brunel University London, London, United Kingdom
[2]Southampton NIHR Biomedical Research Centre for Respiratory and Critical Care, Southampton, United Kingdom
[3]National Heart and Lung Institute (NHLI), Imperial College London & Royal Brompton Hospital, London, United Kingdom

13.1 Impact of disease on the deposition and disposition of inhaled drugs

Targeting inhaled drugs to the lung is not easy. The lungs have a highly complex structure which has evolved to repel foreign airborne substances. Inhaled medication must first traverse the sharp bend of the upper airways and then follow the inhaled airstream to the bronchial region without significant impaction losses. This is much harder in obstructive airways diseases such as asthma and chronic obstructive pulmonary disease (COPD) which are chronic inflammatory disorders characterized by airflow limitation. This can create obstruction and ventilation heterogeneities due to airway narrowing and chronic hypersecretion preventing the medication penetrating freely to the site of action. This results in non-uniform distributions of aerosol with, perversely, diseased regions often receiving less medication than healthy regions. Breathing patterns are altered and hyperinflation is often a characteristic of more severe disease. The patient's inability to use the inhaler correctly, particularly during an exacerbation, when their inhalation flow rate might be significantly reduced, can also lead to poor efficacy.

The physical characteristics of the aerosol are critical in order to overcome airways obstruction in diseases such as asthma and COPD. Particle size is the most important physical determinate of how deep a dose can be delivered into the airways. It is important for the dose to reach all parts of the lung including the more distal small airways where much of the disease is located. It has been shown that small particles and droplets are better able to negotiate narrow airways than larger ones [1]. An aerosolized drug is often defined by its fine-particle dose (FPD). This represents the proportion of the aerosol dose comprising particles smaller than 5 μm. These particles are considered to have the greatest potential for penetrating into the adult lungs, however inhaler designers try to achieve sizes of 2−3 μm as smaller particles and droplets are less likely to be affected by airways narrowing and reduced inhalation flow in disease [1] (Fig. 13.1).

Inhaled Medicines
DOI: https://doi.org/10.1016/B978-0-12-814974-4.00014-6

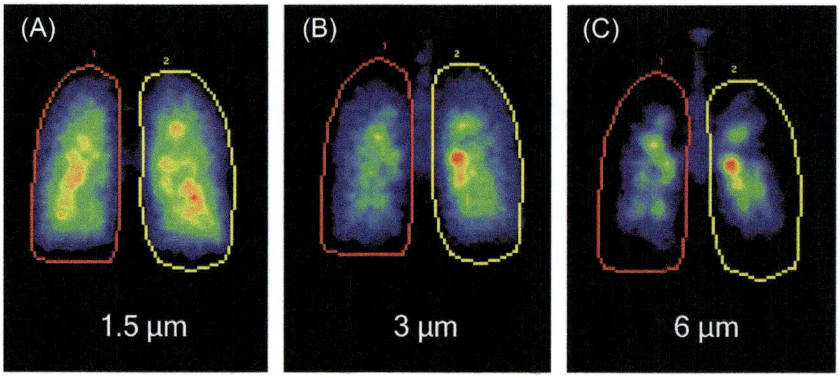

Figure 13.1 Lung deposition images, obtained using gamma scintigraphy, illustrate how aerosol particle size influences lung deposition. Deposition within the whole lung is circled in red (left lung) and yellow (right lung). Density of deposition is displayed as a color scale with red indicating greatest deposition and dark blue least deposition. These images of repeat inhalations for the same individual show uniform deposition with a fine inhaled aerosol (A) (1.5 μm MMAD) through to heavy centralized deposition with a coarse inhaled aerosol (C) (6 μm MMAD) (B) shows the deposition pattern of an intermediate size aerosol (3 μm MMAD). *Adapted with permission of the American Thoracic Society. Copyright © 2020 American Thoracic Society. All rights reserved. O.S. Usmani, et al., Am. J. Respir. Crit. Care Med., 172 (12) (2005) 1497–1504. The American Journal of Respiratory and Critical Care Medicine is an official journal of the American Thoracic Society. Readers are encouraged to read the entire article for the correct context at https://doi.org/10.1164/rccm.200410-1414OC. The authors, editors, and The American Thoracic Society are not responsible for errors or omissions in adaptations.*

Interstitial lung disease (ILD) is an example of restrictive lung disease and covers a range of disorders that cause scarring (fibrosis) of the lung parenchyma. This leads to stiffness in the lungs making it difficult to breathe. Little has been done to deliver inhaled medication in ILD as current medication has not been effective by this route of administration. One recent study has investigated the delivery of aerosolized medications to the lungs of patients with idiopathic pulmonary fibrosis (IPF), a form of ILD [2]. It was expected that airway distortion caused by traction bronchiectasis of the surrounding lung may detrimentally influence airway flow leading to poor penetration of aerosols to areas of scarring. However, the study showed that small (1.5 μg) particles were able to penetrate to the site of disease in the lungs of patients with IPF suggesting that the development of inhaled medication to treat the disease might be an option. Currently the only approved medications for IPF are pirfenidone (Esbriet®) and nintedanib (Ofev®), which only have conditional recommendations and limited tolerability [3].

13.2 Clinical markers (non-imaging) used to investigate small airway disease

Lung function testing is crucial for investigating diseased lungs and their response to treatment. However, while simple measurements of flow and lung volume are central to lung function testing, they are not ideal for the assessment of disease in the peripheral airways. The small peripheral/airways extend from generation 8 to the alveoli [4] and have an internal diameter less than 2 mm and do not contain cartilage in their walls. They are a major site of early pathology in lung disease and widespread disease may accumulate there well before it is noticed by the patient or detected using conventional lung function tests. It may be at a relatively advanced stage by the time it is detected. Lung function tests such as spirometry are far more sensitive to disease present in the large airways. The lack of sensitivity in the small airways is a consequence of their large cumulative cross-sectional surface area and airway volume which only contributes a fraction of the total airway resistance of the lungs [5].

The small airways are also relatively inaccessible to biopsy and because of the scarcity of information coming from this region they have often been referred to as the "quiet zone" [6]. However, in recent years, more specialized non-invasive tests, which offer the ability to detect early changes due to disease in the peripheral airways, have become available to clinical practice. These tests have the advantage that they don't put excessive demands on the patient apart from relaxed tidal breathing and therefore do not modify the airway smooth muscle tone or stress the patient. Impedance oscillometry is one such technique. It applies an oscillating pressure-flow signal at the open mouth during tidal breathing. The signal travels into the airways and is reflected back to a detector at the mouth allowing the derivation of parameters of respiratory mechanics for both the central and peripheral regions. These parameters include respiratory impedance (Z) and its associated components resistance (R) and reactance (X). Oscillation signals at 20 Hz reflect values in the central airways while signals at 5 Hz reflect values throughout the airways. Parameters reflecting respiratory mechanics in the peripheral airways can easily be derived from these values by subtracting one from the other, i.e. R5−R20 gives the airways resistance for the small airways. The technique has more recently been called impulse oscillometry (IOS) and is widely available for clinical use through the development of easy to operate commercially made machines. IOS has been shown to be a reliable and sensitive technique for assessing bronchial hyper-responsiveness in adults and children [7]. It has also been shown to be as sensitive as spirometry in detecting smoking-related lung function impairments or those due to exposure to occupational hazards.

Inert gas washout tests measure the efficiency of gas mixing in the lungs and are able to derive information from both the central and peripheral airways. The multiple breath washout test is the most common employed technique and even though gas washout techniques have been around for more than 60 years they have only recently found their way into the arsenal of the clinician largely due to the lack of commercially made devices. The technique involves washing a tracer gas, with low solubility in blood and tissues, from the lungs by continuous breathing of another gas which replaces it. Inert gases that can be washed out include sulfur hexafluoride (SF_6) and helium in diluted form. However, these gases must first be washed into the lungs before they can be washed out again using air. When the tracer gas is Nitrogen (N_2) it is called the multiple-breath nitrogen washout (MBNW) test. The advantage of the MBNW is that the nitrogen is already resident in the lungs, as air is 78% N_2, and can be washed out to below 2% by repeated breaths of 100% oxygen (O_2). If the airways are damaged gas mixing becomes impaired leading to ventilation heterogeneity in the region of damage. Disease progression can be seen through changes in the washout curve, which can be repeated at regular time intervals. Parameters derived from the MBNW test include the lung clearance index (LCI), which is a measure of gas mixing in the whole lung, S_{acin} and S_{cond}, which are measures of heterogeneity in the acinar and conducting airways respectively [8,9]. Importantly, MBNW can provide evidence of the presence of peripheral airways disease much earlier than conventional lung function tests [10] (Fig. 13.2).

Fractional exhaled nitric oxide (FeNO) is another non-invasive method that can detect the effect of disease in the peripheral airways. Nitric oxide (NO) is produced by cells throughout the airways and can be measured in exhaled breath. It has been shown to be raised above normal levels in the presence of airway inflammation [11]. FeNO is easy to measure and requires just one breath during tidal breathing. In asthma, it can detect eosinophilic inflammation moderately well in central and peripheral airways. A two-compartment model has been developed that can help to localize the site of inflammation with FeNo using different flow rates [12]. Under low flow conditions, FeNO reflects central airways inflammation while at higher flows it represents alveolar inflammation.

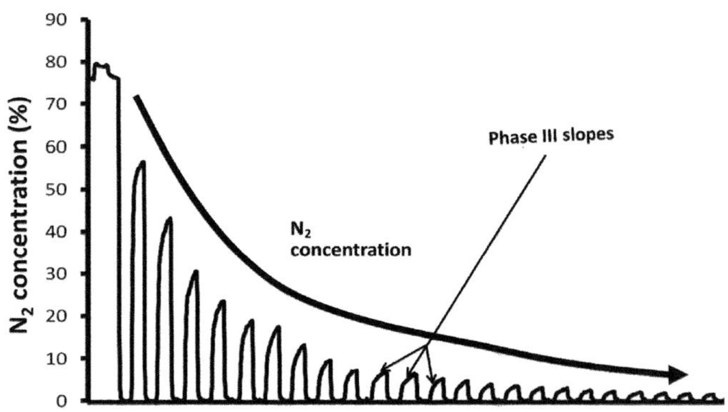

Figure 13.2 Typical multiple breath N_2 washout trace. The N_2 concentration of exhaled air is reduced with each breath of oxygen. Participants inhale 1 L tidal breaths until the N_2 content has been reduced to <2%. The lung-clearance index is derived directly from the washout curve. Phase III slopes are derived from each exhaled breath of N_2 and used to calculate Sacin and Scond, which are measures of the ventilation inhomogeneity in the acinar and conducting airways, respectively.

13.3 Imaging methods: Scintigraphy, SPECT, CT, PET, MRI, CT-CFPD

Imaging techniques have provided a wealth of knowledge regarding *in vivo* deposition of inhaled aerosols. They have also allowed the visualizing of regional aerosol distribution. This has led to improvements in the delivery of inhaled medications to patients with asthma, cystic fibrosis, and chronic obstructive pulmonary disease, where the lung is the target. Imaging methods can also be applied to the comparison of two aerosolized products in terms of whole-lung dose and deposition pattern and also have potential for the assessments of bioequivalence.

Of the imaging methods, **2D planar gamma scintigraphy** is the most widely accessible method to measure pharmaceutical compounds in the lungs and studies date back to the late 1970s. The main requirement is access to suitable imaging equipment, usually a gamma camera, and radiopharmaceuticals. *In vivo* measurements of regional deposition require trace amounts of gamma-emitting radionuclides to be added to the aerosol formulation to enable the camera to form an image of the distribution of radiolabeled compound in the lungs. However, it is hardly ever possible to incorporate a gamma-emitting radionuclide into the active molecular structure of the drug compound. Many of the early studies radiolabeled an inert substitute that was added to the inhaler instead of the drug or in addition to it [13,14]. Strict *in vitro* quality control procedures were necessary to ensure that the substitute behaved aerodynamically similar to the drug. A major methodological step forward in the late 1980s allowed a type of "direct" radiolabelling method of aerosol drug formulations in MDIs, [15] which can also be adapted for DPIs [16] removing the need for a substitute. However, rather than a chemical bond this method only provides a physical association between the radionuclide and drug during inhalation with the two rapidly disassociating once in the lung environment limiting imaging times to a few minutes. Despite this, the method is the basis for most of the 2D gamma scintigraphy studies to the present day. However, it has often been a challenge for investigators to develop methods to quantitate what is observed visually and compare data obtained from different laboratories. The main disadvantage with planar gamma scintigraphy is that the 3D Lung structure is 'compressed' into two dimensions which makes it difficult to relate the aerosol deposition patterns to specific airways (Fig. 13.3).

Single-photon emission computed tomography (SPECT) is a three-dimensional imaging modality that can be used to image inhaled medication in the lungs. The scanner comprises two or three gamma camera heads which rotate around the supine patient providing multiple images of the in-vivo distribution of gamma-emitting radionuclides acquired from different camera angles. These images are then combined and reconstructed to display a three-dimensional image of the radionuclide distribution within the lungs. The camera software is able to display transverse, coronal and sagittal slices of the lungs [17].

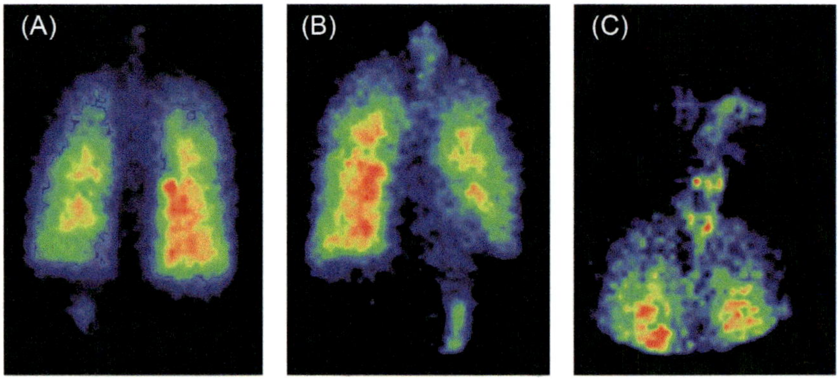

Figure 13.3 Lung images obtained using planar gamma scintigraphy of the same individual, from different views, (A) posterior thorax, (B) anterior thorax, and (C) oropharyngeal. Red areas indicate regions of highest radioactivity and dark blue of least radioactivity. *Adapted with permission of the American Thoracic Society. Copyright © 2020 American Thoracic Society. All rights reserved. O.S. Usmani, et al., Am. J. Respir. Crit. Care Med., 172 (12) (2005) 1497–1504. The American Journal of Respiratory and Critical Care Medicine is an official journal of the American Thoracic Society. Readers are encouraged to read the entire article for the correct context at https://doi.org/10.1164/rccm.200410-1414OC. The authors, editors, and The American Thoracic Society are not responsible for errors or omissions in adaptations.*

Most modern SPECT cameras combine SPECT and CT allowing both imaging modalities to be used during the same session without the patient altering position. This offers the potential to combine high-resolution anatomical detail (CT) with the functional distribution of a radiotracer (SPECT). The CT element can also be used for attenuation and scatter correction of the SPECT data, which will improve the accuracy of the reconstructed SPECT image. The advantages of SPECT imaging compared to planar scintigraphy are more accurate delineation of regional anatomy and function, better separation of overlying segments or sections of the lung, greater ability to combine with other data, e.g., CT, MRI, etc., and better ability to differentiate small from large airways (Fig. 13.4).

Positron emission tomography (PET) is another three-dimensional functional imaging technique which uses positron-emitting radionuclides to form images of the aerosol distribution [18]. A number of positron-emitting radionuclides are available for lung imaging including ^{11}C-Carbon, ^{13}N-Nitrogen, ^{15}O-Oxygen and ^{18}F-Flourine. The most commonly used molecule is ^{18}F-fluorodeoxyglucose (18F-FDG). PET imaging depends on the coincidence detection of two gamma photons which are the by-products of the annihilation of a positron with an ordinary electron, found in tissue. The two photons that are emitted travel in opposite directions and are detected by radiation detectors mounted in a ring within the scanner. Unlike planar scintigraphy and SPECT, no collimator is necessary to form the images allowing for improved sensitivity compared to the other two methods. The chief advantage of PET for

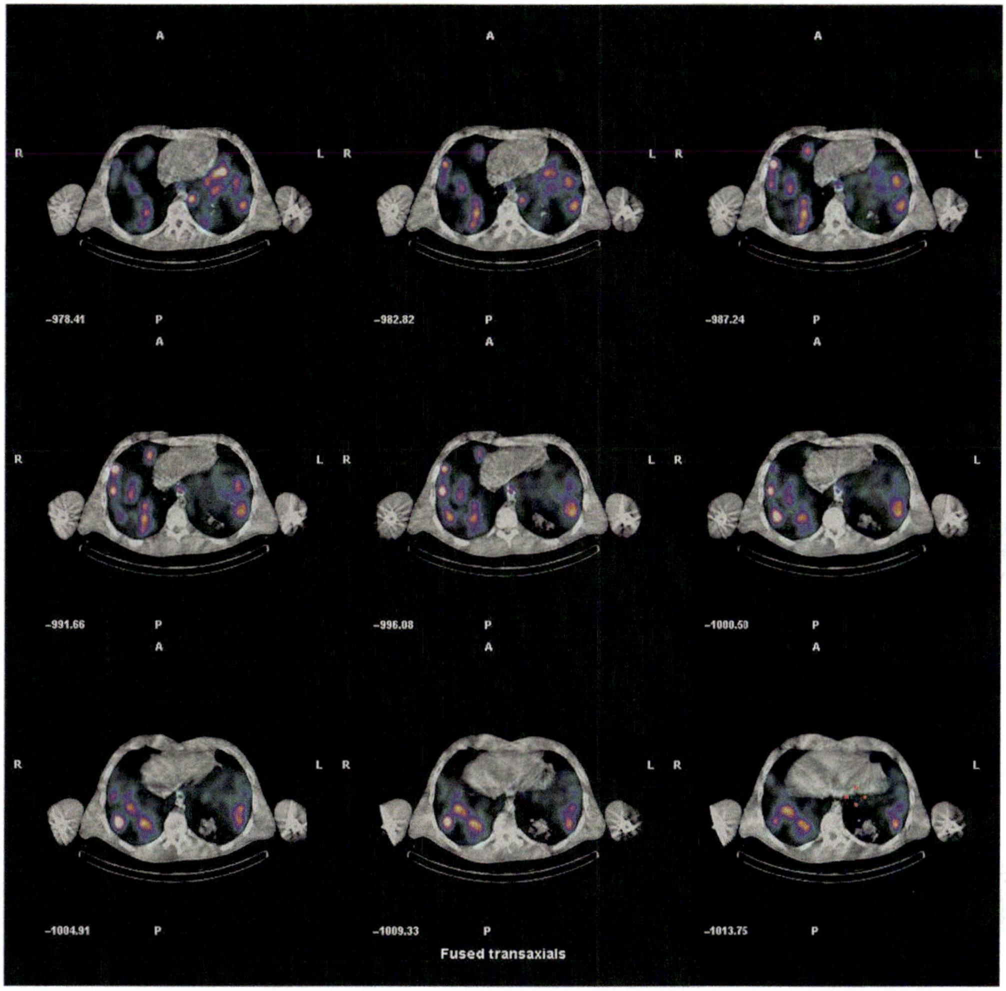

Figure 13.4 SPECT-CT images of aerosol deposition (inhaled, technetium-labeled, freeze-dried, micro-colloid of human serum albumin) in moderate airway obstruction. Aerosol deposition (in color) can be viewed as transverse slices through the thorax with the relevant anatomy from CT images (gray scale) aligned to allow anatomical reference points for the deposition. Density of deposition is displayed as a color scale with areas of greatest deposition displayed as bright yellow through to areas of least density as dark green.

imaging aerosol deposition in the lungs is that the radionuclide is incorporated into the drug molecule unlike, SPECT and planar imaging. This allows longer imaging times. As with SPECT, PET can be combined with CT or MRI in the same scanner to provide both functional and anatomical information. The main disadvantages are costs and the availability of a cyclotron needed to produce positron-emitting radionuclides.

High Resolution Computed Tomography (HRCT) provides images that are three-dimensional maps of tissue density. They are, therefore, different to SPECT and PET, which are 3D maps of the distribution of a radiopharmaceutical. HRCT provides images of lung structure and the airways can be clearly seen making it useful for characterizing disease [19]. It can also be combined with a contrast agent, such as xenon, to provide information on lung ventilation. However, HRCT is unable to directly visualize aerosol deposition in the lungs but data from HRCT can be used to create models of the central airways which can be used for the mathematical modeling of aerosol deposition [20]. It has been used to demonstrate regional deposition including inequalities in deposition between the left and right lungs and the simulation of points of large eddies [21]. HRCT density measurements have been used to quantitatively assess lung structure in a range of respiratory conditions, especially in emphysema.

CT-CFPD Imaging-based Modeling The combination of lung CT images with Computational Fluid and Particle Dynamics (CFPD) simulations has led to the development of personalized functional modeling of the airways to investigate disease in the small and large airways, such as Functional Respiratory Imaging (FRI) [22].

FRI is a proprietary technology that combines high-resolution CT scans with computer-based flow simulations. A Patient specific 3D visualization and quantification of their lung structure and lung function can be generated. FRI is capable of producing highly clinically relevant patient specific biomarkers, presenting 3D visualization of the patient's airway and lung geometry, regional airway resistance and aerosol deposition patterns. Low dose HRCT scans are taken at inspiration and expiration. From the HRCT scans patient-specific airway and lung structures are segmented, and 3D reconstructed

Magnetic resonance imaging (MRI) has one distinct advantage over all the other methods in that no ionizing radiation is used. The use of radiation in infants, children or pregnant women is typically not authorized by ethics review boards, unless there are exceptional circumstances. MRI uses the nuclear magnetic resonance properties of the soft tissue of the body to form images. It has good spatial and temporal resolution. Most clinical MRI is based on imaging the proton of the hydrogen atoms found in water, which is the most abundant substance in living tissues. However, as most of the lungs are air rather than water, proton density is low. MRI on its own is not suitable for imaging the lungs directly. Ventilation contrast agents are used to measure gas distribution in the lungs and produce high-resolution images of the airspaces highlighting regions of airflow obstruction as ventilation defects and heterogeneity in disease distribution. Hyperpolarized ^{3}He produces a large MRI signal due to the alignment of its atomic nuclei spin prior to imaging in the MRI scanner. It has a far higher sensitivity than unpolarized ^{3}He atoms and enables imaging with a spatial resolution similar to conventional ^{1}H water imaging. Other functional MRI contrast agents such as ^{129}Xe and oxygen with enhanced MRI signal are also available [23].

13.3.1 Limitations of current imaging methods

Each of these imaging methods have their strengths and limitations. Some are more suitable to measure lung structure (HRCT) while others are better able to measure ventilation (MRI) or visualize the distribution of inhaled aerosols (planar, SPECT, PET). However, the main limitations in common with current imaging methods are temporal and spatial resolution. Even the best HRCT MRI scanners are still unable to directly visualize small airways. The combination of CFPD and HRCT imaging can potentially provide a better understanding of the effect of airway geometry effect, including lung disease influence aerosol deposition in the lungs.

13.4 Lack of meta-analysis – need for standardized approaches to imaging studies and correlation to clinical outcome

Despite the wealth of deposition data accumulated over the past 40 years from centers world-wide, until 2012 there were no common standards for performing deposition studies. This may have hindered the development of inhaled products as data from different centers were not completely comparable. This in turn led regularity agencies to question the value of imaging data since each center had their own standards. In order to combat this the International Society for Aerosols in Medicine (ISAM) Regulatory Affairs Networking Group convened the Sub-Committee for the Standardization of Lung Imaging Techniques in early 2010. The intention was to standardize the techniques for aerosol deposition assessment of orally inhaled products, using Planar, SPECT and PET imaging. They aimed to identify key areas in radionuclide imaging that could be standardized in order to determine the essential information to allow standardization in each area and to publish a consensus statement that incorporated practical recommendations for standardization of each of the imaging modalities [24].

Similar issues of comparability exist in the standardization of quantitative HRCT metrics between different centers [25]. Multicenter trials are often hindered by differences in scanner equipment and protocols used. The choice of reconstruction algorithm influences image resolution and density histogram parameters. Regular quality assurance by scanning phantoms at all collaborating sites is important but not always possible.

13.5 Importance of small airways disease and our inability to direct visualize this peripheral zone

The small airways are an important delivery site in the treatment of asthma and COPD. The inflammation associated with these diseases is present in both the distal small airways and the proximal large airways. The small airways also contribute to hyper-responsiveness and airway remodeling as well as emphysematous destruction of the lung parenchyma.

Imaging techniques have been used to assess lung morphology but it has been difficult to directly visualize the peripheral airways because of the low resolution of the scanners available. However, recent technological advances have led to improved spatial resolution in imaging modalities such as HRCT, allowing a more detailed assessment of small airways structure. Novel MRI imaging methods, and micro-CT in combination with HRCT and histology, have also provided new insights into the development of disease in the peripheral airways and its progression [26].

13.6 Emergence of MRI

MRI has not previously allowed the acquisition of images of lungs, or aerosol deposition within the lungs, of sufficient quality or resolution [27]. Hyperpolarized helium (^{3}He) MRI has been developed over the past decades and has become an established technique, allowing high-resolution images of ventilation distribution. There have been numerous reported studies using his technique to investigate obstructive lung diseases such as COPD, asthma and CF [28–30] and to investigate the effect of therapeutic intervention such as the use of ivacaftor for CF [31].

Other hyperpolarized gases are used such as Xenon but this is associated with a reduced signal [32]. The production of hyperpolarized gases is complex and there is the potential shortage of world-wide supplies of helium. Centers using hyperpolarized gases also need to have immediate access to a cyclotron which tends to limit its use to specialist centers.

Novel MRI methods have potential for future use as outcome measures for trials involving lung disease and inhaled therapeutics. There have been advances made for both Fourier decomposition (FD-MRI) methods as well as oxygen enhanced MRI (OE-MRI) [33,34]. These techniques do not use hyperpolarized gases, which makes their application more widely accessible. The development of novel MRI methods can allow detail on structure and function of the lungs without the need for a radiation dose. This allows repeat imaging which may be of particular importance in life cohorts of pediatric lung disease.

13.7 Combining HRCT and micro CT

HRCT of the lungs offers qualitative description of disease and also allows quantitative measurement of indices such as density of tissue per voxel. This can give a description of density changes throughout the lung fields. Although direct measurement of the small airways is beyond current HRCT imaging resolution, indirect assessment of the effects of disease includes quantification of gas trapping on expiratory HRCT scans. Recent methods of quantification of HRCT images of lung disease include parametric response mapping (PRM), which matches inspiratory and expiratory lung scans to examine local changes in density. The use of this technique, when image registration of inspiratory and expiratory CT images is combined with CT density thresholds, gives a description of functional small airway disease (PRM^{fSAD}, a measure of non-emphysematous air trapping) and emphysema (PRM^{emph}) [35]. These methods are being developed alongside clinical trials using HRCT to look at small airway dysfunction and to further understand correlations between HRCT indices and clinical/functional outcome measures. These methods do require standardization and correlation with clinical outcome measures and lung function indices [35].

HRCT images can also be used to establish mathematical modeling of inhaled flow patterns and aerosol deposition. One example of this approach is the use of data from HRCT combined with CFPD to create simulations of functional changes within the airways and predict deposition pattern of inhaled drugs [36,37].

Tanabe and colleagues [38] used micro-computed tomography (micro-CT), HRCT and histology to show that the progression of COPD was characterized by a decrease in the number of terminal bronchioles. Small airway disease occurs early in the life-course of COPD. Inhaled formulations that produce a greater percentage of fine particles have therefore been directed at delivering therapy to the small airways in those with COPD.

13.8 Using imaging to look at pediatric lung disease

Imaging pediatric lung disease has several difficulties not least of which is the need to minimize radiation dose in early life. This is complicated further when considering the need to monitor pediatric lung disease throughout the life course of the disease into adulthood. Cumulative radiation dose over a life course raises obvious ethical concerns. Computational models have been built using anatomical information relating to the lungs during childhood. These can then be used to model particle deposition mechanisms. There are a number of anatomical models of different age ranges and different aspects of anatomy. Issues unique to children in pulmonary drug delivery include their lower tidal volume and highly variable breathing.

In vitro or *ex vivo* anatomical models offer an interesting alternative. Recent work describes an *ex vivo* infant-like respiratory model of bronchopulmonary dysplasia. This model is composed of a 3D-printed head connected to a sealed enclosure containing a leporine thorax. Physiological data and pleural-mimicking depressions were measured for chosen respiratory rates. Homogeneity of ventilation was assessed by ^{81m}krypton scintigraphies. Regional radioaerosol deposition was quantified with ^{99m}technetium-diethylene triamine pentaacetic acid after jet nebulization [39].

13.9 Handling errors

A note must be made here that all of the work described in this chapter is of little use if inhaler technique is not taken into account. A study by Melzer et al [40] reported, that in a cohort of 688 individuals with COPD, 65% had poor technique for at least one device. Another study of 2935 patients with COPD found over 50% of their cohort had critical handling errors for their inhaler devices [41]. There is a significant relationship between poor inhaler use and symptom control in patients with COPD [41]. Education and re-checking of technique is essential.

13.10 Conclusion

Current methods for assessing aerosol deposition *in vivo* have been summarized. Current and emerging imaging techniques have enabled insight into the fate of inhaled aerosols in health and disease. Data from such trials have been related to other measures of lung function and to clinical outcome. Data from imaging has also been used to inform physical models of airways for *in vitro* experiments and to build a structure for CFPD studies. The design improvements for inhalers and formulations and the reported clinical trials have allowed description and targeting of aerosol deposition within the lung. There remain many challenges including the need for an imaging method suitable for life cohorts of diseases such as CF and primary ciliary dyskinesia.

There have been multiple improvements in measures of aerosol deposition *in vivo*. Imaging has helped to identify the efficiency of inhaled drugs. Small airway disease is an important component of several lung diseases but we are, at present, unable to directly visualize the small airways *in vivo*. Developments using micro-CT have allowed the description of small airway destruction and the importance of small airways disease in the pathological development of COPD. Developments on all fronts may allow further understanding of inhaled aerosol deposition and the relationship between deposition and clinical effect.

References

[1] O.S. Usmani, M.F. Biddiscombe, P.J. Barnes, Regional lung deposition and bronchodilator response as a function of beta2-agonist particle size, Am. J. Respir. Crit. Care. Med. 172 (12) (2005) 1497–1504. Available from: https://doi.org/10.1164/rccm.200410-1414OC.

[2] O.S. Usmani, M.F. Biddiscombe, S. Yang, S. Meah, E. Oballa, J.K. Simpson, et al., The topical study of inhaled drug (salbutamol) delivery in idiopathic pulmonary fibrosis, Respir. Res. 19 (1) (2018) 25. Available from: https://doi.org/10.1186/s12931-018-0732-0.

[3] P. Rogliani, L. Calzetta, F. Cavalli, M.G. Matera, M. Cazzola, Pirfenidone, nintedanib and N-acetylcysteine for the treatment of idiopathic pulmonary fibrosis: a systematic review and meta-analysis, Pulm. Pharmacol. Ther. 40 (2016) 95–103. Available from: https://doi.org/10.1016/j.pupt.2016.07.009.

[4] E.R. Weibel, Morphology of the Human Lung, Academic Press, New York, 1963. Available from: https://www.springer.com/gp/book/9783642875557.

[5] J.C. Hogg, P.T. Macklem, W.M. Thurlbeck, Site and nature of airway obstruction in chronic obstructive lung disease, N. Engl. J. Med. 278 (25) (1968) 1355–1360. Available from: https://www.nejm.org/doi/full/10.1056/NEJM196806202782501.

[6] J. Mead, The lung's "quiet zone", N. Engl. J. Med. 282 (23) (1970) 1318–1319. Available from: https://www.nejm.org/doi/full/10.1056/NEJM197006042822311.

[7] E. Oostveen, D. MacLeod, H. Lorino, R. Farre, Z. Hantos, K. Desager, et al., The forced oscillation technique in clinical practice: methodology, recommendations and future developments, Eur. Respir. J. 22 (6) (2003) 1026–1041. Available from: https://doi.org/10.1183/09031936.03.00089403.

[8] A. Larsson, C. Jonmarker, O. Werner, Ventilation inhomogeneity during controlled ventilation. Which index should be used? J. Appl. Physiol. 65 (1988) 2030–2039. Available from: https://www.physiology.org/doi/pdf/10.1152/jappl.1988.65.5.2030.

[9] S. Verbanck, D. Schuermans, A. Van Muylem, C. Melot, M. Noppen, W. Vincken, et al., Conductive and acinar lung-zone contributions to ventilation inhomogeneity in COPD, Am. J. Respir. Crit. Care. Med. 157 (5) (1998) 1573–1577. Available from: https://doi.org/10.1164/ajrccm.157.5.9710042.

[10] S. Verbanck, D. Schuermans, M. Meysman, M. Paiva, W. Vincken, Noninvasive assessment of airway alterations in smokers: the small airways revisited, Am. J. Respir. Crit. Care Med. 170 (4) (2004) 414–419. Available from: https://doi.org/10.1164/rccm.200401-037OC.

[11] P.J. Barnes, R.A. Dweik, A.F. Gelb, P.G. Gibson, S.C. George, H. Grasemann, et al., Exhaled nitric oxide in pulmonary diseases a comprehensive review, Chest 138 (3) (2010) 682–692. Available from: https://doi.org/10.1378/chest.09-2090.

[12] N.M. Tsoukias, S.C. George, A two-compartment model of pulmonary nitric oxide exchange dynamics, J. Appl. Physiol. 85 (2) (1998) 653–666. Available from: https://doi.org/10.1152/jappl.1998.85.2.653.

[13] S.P. Newman, D. Pavia, F. Moren, N.F. Sheahan, S.W. Clarke, Deposition of pressurised aerosols in the human respiratory tract, Thorax 36 (1) (1981) 52–55. Available from: https://doi.org/10.1136/thx.36.1.52.

[14] B.M.X. Zainudin, S.E.J. Tolfree, M. Biddiscombe, M. Whitaker, M.D. Short, S.G. Spiro, An alternative to direct labelling of pressurised bronchodilator aerosol, Int. J. Pharm. 51 (1989) 67–71. Available from: https://doi.org/10.1016/0378-5173(89)90076-8.

[15] D. Köhler, W. Fleischer, H. Matthys, New method for the easy labelling of beta-2-agonists in the metered dose inhaler with technetium99m, Respiration 53 (2) (1988) 65–73. Available from: https://doi.org/10.1159/000195399.

[16] R. Melchor, M.F. Biddiscombe, V.H.F. Mak, M.D. Short, S.G. Spiro, Lung deposition patterns of directly labelled salbutamol in normal subjects and in patients with reversible airflow obstruction, Thorax 48 (5) (1993) 506–511. Available from: https://doi.org/10.1136/thx.48.5.506.

[17] J. Fleming, D.L. Bailey, H.K. Chan, J. Conway, P.J. Kuehl, B.L. Laube, et al., Standardization of techniques for using single-photon emission computed tomography (SPECT) for aerosol deposition assessment of orally inhaled products, J. Aerosol. Med. Pulm. Drug. Deliv. 25 (S1) (2012). Available from: https://doi.org/10.1089/jamp.2012.1Su5.

[18] M.B. Dolovich, D.L. Bailey, Positron emission tomography (PET) for assessing aerosol deposition of orally inhaled drug products, J. Aerosol. Med. Pulm. Drug. Deliv. 25 (S1) (2012) S52–S71 (2012). Available from: https://doi.org/10.1089/jamp.2012.1Su6.

[19] G.G. King, Current and emerging imaging in relation to drug discovery in airways disease, Pulm. Pharmacol. Ther. 24 (5) (2011) 497–504. Available from: https://doi.org/10.1016/j.pupt.2011.07.003.

[20] M. Castro, S.B. Fain, E. Hoffman, D.S. Gierada, S.C. Erzurum, S. Wenzel, Lung imaging in asthmatic patients: the picture is clearer, J. Allergy Clin. Immunol. 128 (3) (2011) 467–478. Available from: https://doi.org/10.1016/j.jaci.2011.04.051.

[21] A.R. Lambert, P.O. Shaughnessy, M.H. Tawhai, E.A. Hoffman, C.-L. Lin, Regional deposition of particles in an image-based airway model: large-eddy simulation and left-right lung ventilation asymmetry, Aerosol Sci. Technol. 45 (1) (2011) 11–25. Available from: https://doi.org/10.1080/02786826.2010.517578.

[22] L.A. De Backer, W.G. Vos, R. Salgado, J.W. de Backer, A. Devolder, S. Verhulst, et al., Functional imaging using computer methods to compare the effect of salbutamol and ipratropium bromide in patient-specific airway models of COPD, Int. J. Chron. Obstruct. Pulm. Dis. 6 (1) (2011) 637−646. Available from: https://doi.org/10.2147/COPD.S21917.

[23] W. Zha, S.K. Nagle, R.V. Cadman, M.L. Schiebler, S.B. Fain, Three-dimensional isotropic functional imaging of cystic fibrosis using oxygen-enhanced MRI: comparison with hyperpolarized 3 He MRI, Radiology 290 (1) (2018) 229–237, https://doi.org/10.1148/radiol.2018181148.

[24] B.L. Laube, T.E. Corcoran, S.G. Devadason, M.B. Dolovich, J. Fleming, S. Newman, Standards for lung imaging techniques, J. Aerosol. Med. Pulm. Drug. Deliv. 25 (Suppl. 1) (2012) 1−3. Available from: https://doi.org/10.1089/jamp.2012.1Su1.

[25] N.D. Weatherley, J.A. Eaden, N.J. Stewart, B.J. Bartholmai, A.J. Swift, S.M. Bianchi, et al., Experimental and quantitative imaging techniques in interstitial lung disease, Thorax 74 (6) (2019) 611−619. Available from: https://doi.org/10.1136/thoraxjnl-2018-211779.

[26] J.C. Hogg, J.E. McDonough, M. Suzuki, Small airway obstruction in COPD: new insights based on micro-CT imaging and MRI imaging, Chest 143 (5) (2013) 1436−1443. Available from: https://doi.org/10.1378/chest.12-1766.

[27] M.F. Biddiscombe, O. Usmani, The importance of imaging and physiology measurements in assessing the delivery of peripherally targeted aerosolized drugs, Ther. Deliv. 3 (11) (2012) 1329−1345. Available from: https://doi.org/10.4155/tde.12.113.

[28] A. Ouriadov, E. Lessard, K. Sheikh, G. Parraga, Pulmonary MRI morphometry modelling of airspace enlargement in chronic obstructive pulmonary disease and alpha-1 antitrypsin deficiency, Magn. Reason. Med. 79 (1) (2018) 439−448. Available from: https://doi.org/10.1002/mrm.26642.

[29] D. Leary, S. Svenningsen, F. Guo, S. Bhatawadekar, G. Parraga, G.N. Maksym, Hyperpolarised 3He magnetic resonance imaging ventilation defects in asthma: relationship to airway mechanics, Physiol. Rep. 4 (7) (2016) e12761. Available from: https://doi.org/10.14814/phy2.12761.

[30] M. Kolodziej, M.J. de Veer, M. Cholewa, G.F. Egan, B.R. Thompson, Lung function imaging methods in cystic fibrosis pulmonary disease, Respir. Res. 18 (1) (2017) 96. Available from: https://doi.org/10.1186/s12931-017-0578-x.

[31] T.A. Altes, M. Johnson, M. Fidler, M. Botfield, N.J. Tustison, C. Leiva-Salinas, et al., Use of hyperpolarised helium-3 MRI to assess response to ivacaftor treatment in patients with cystic fibrosis, J. Cyst. Fibros. 16 (2) (2017) 267−274. Available from: https://doi.org/10.1016/j.jcf.2016.12.004.

[32] H.F. Chan, N.J. Stewart, G. Norquay, G.J. Collier, J.M. Wild, 3D diffusion-weighted 129Xe MRI for whole lung morphometry, Magn. Reson. Med. 79 (6) (2018) 2986−2995. Available from: https://doi.org/10.1002/mrm.26960.

[33] G. Bauman, O. Pusteria, O. Bieri, Ultra-fast steady-state precession pulse sequence for fourier decomposition pulmonary MRI, Magn. Reson. Med. 75 (4) (2016) 1647−1653. Available from: https://doi.org/10.1002/mrm.25697.

[34] O. Pustera, G. Bauman, O. Bieri, Three-dimensional oxygen-enhanced MRI of the human lung at 1.5T with ultra-fast steady-state free precession, Magn. Reson. Med. 79 (1) (2018) 246−255. Available from: https://doi.org/10.1002/mrm.26665.

[35] K. Gove, T. Wilkinson, S. Jack, K. Ostridge, B. Thompson, J. Conway, Systematic review of evidence for relationships between physiological and CT indices of small airways and clinical outcomes in COPD, Respir. Med. 139 (2018) 117−125. Available from: https://doi.org/10.1016/j.rmed.2018.05.005.

[36] P. Koullapis, B. Ollson, S. Kassinos, J. Sznitman, Multiscale *in silico* lung modeling strategies for aerosol inhalation therapy and drug delivery, Curr. Opinion. Biomed. Eng. 11 (2019) 130−136. Available from: https://doi.org/10.1016/j.cobme.2019.11.003.

[37] I. Katz, M. Pichelin, S. Montesantos, A. Murdock, S. Fromomt, J. Venegas, The influence of lung volume during imaging on CFD within realistic airway models, Aerosol. Sci. Tech. 51 (2) (2017) 214−223. Available from: https://doi.org/10.1080/02786826.2016.1254721.

[38] N. Tanabe, D.M. Vasilescu, M. Kirby, H.O. Coxson, S.E. Verleden, B.M. Vanaudenaerde, et al., Analysis of airway pathology in COPD using a combination of computed tomography, micro-computed tomography and histology, Eur. Respir. J. 51 (2) (2018) 1701245. Available from: https://dx.doi.org/10.1183/13993003.01245-2017.

[39] Y. Montigaud, S. Perinel, J.C. Dubus, L. Lecler, M. Suau, C. Goy, et al., Development of an ex vivo respiratory pediatric model of bronchopulmonary dysplasia for aerosol deposition studies, Sci. Rep. 9 (2019) 5720. Available from: https://doi.org/10.1038/s41598-019-42103-2.

[40] A.C. Melzer, B.J. Ghassemieh, S.E. Gillespie, P.K. Lindenauer, M.A. McBurnie, R.A. Mularski, et al., Patient characteristics associated with poor inhaler technique among a cohort of patients with COPD, Respir. Med. 123 (2017) 124–130. Available from: https://doi.org/10.1016/j.rmed.2016.12.011.

[41] M. Molimard, C. Raherison, S. Lignot, A. Balestra, S. Lamarque, A. Chartier, et al., Chronic obstructive pulmonary disease exacerbation and inhaler device handling: real-life assessment of 2935 patients, Eur. Respir. J. 49 (2017) 1601794. Available from: https://doi.org/10.1183/13993003.01794-2016.

CHAPTER 14

Machine learning and *in silico* methods

Ching-Long Lin[1,2,3], Eric A. Hoffman[2,3,4] and Stavros Kassinos[5]

[1]Department of Mechanical Engineering, The University of Iowa, Iowa City, IA, United States
[2]Department of Radiology, The University of Iowa, Iowa City, IA, United States
[3]Roy J. Carver Department of Biomedical Engineering, The University of Iowa, Iowa City, IA, United States
[4]Department of Internal Medicine, The University of Iowa, Iowa City, IA, United States
[5]Computational Sciences Laboratory (UCY-CompSci), Mechanical and Manufacturing Engineering, University of Cyprus, Nicosia, Cyprus

14.1 Introduction

14.1.1 Machine learning and big data

Machine learning is a data-driven technology in the field of artificial intelligence to extract insightful information from heterogeneous data sets [1]. Each data set used in machine learning algorithms is represented by a set of features. The features may be continuous or categorical. A supervised learning algorithm learns from features assigned with labels. On the other hand, an unsupervised learning algorithm learns features from unlabeled data and uses the learned features to recognize the class of new data. Decision tree, naïve Bayes and support-vector machine are common supervised-learning algorithms. Clustering methods, such as k-means, hierarchical model and Gaussian mixture models, are unsupervised learning algorithms. Deep learning is a sub-field of machine learning that uses artificial neural networks to extract features.

Over the past decade, the National Institutes of Health (NIH) in the United States has sponsored multicenter trials for lung diseases. These trials include the Severe Asthma Research Program (SARP) [2], the SubPopulations and InteRmediate Outcome Measures in Chronic Obstructive Pulmonary Disease (COPD) Study (SPIROMICS) [3], the COPD Genetic Epidemiology (COPDGene) [4] and the Multi-Ethnic Study of Atherosclerosis-Lung (MESA Lung) [5–7]. SARP aims to identify phenotypes that differentiate severe asthma from those with mild-moderate asthma. The rationale behind SARP is that severe asthma represents approximately 10% of the total asthma population, but accounts for about 50% of the disease-associated costs [8]. Since the population of severe asthma is relatively small, a collaborative approach that shares protocols and data by multiple sites is a necessity to gather sufficient numbers of subjects for any meaningful powered studies [2]. Thus, SARP allows for a comprehensive phenotyping with clinical, biologic, genetic and imaging data. Due to the scope of the study, there are several funding cycles of SARP I, II and III. The lessons learned from the previous funding cycle enable refinement of protocols and methods for acquisition and analysis of data, and

Inhaled Medicines
DOI: https://doi.org/10.1016/B978-0-12-814974-4.00013-4

incorporation of new ideas, hypotheses and goals into the renewal of SARP. For example, with SARP III [9], longitudinal data have been collected with standardized protocols [10], e.g. for consistent data sets and computed tomography (CT) imaging data quality.

Similarly, in order to study COPD, which was the third leading cause of morbidity and mortality in the United States [11], SPIROMICS was established to identify and validate surrogate markers of disease severity for intermediate outcome measures. These rich sets of clinical, biological, genetic, and quantitative CT data on large cohorts of asthma and COPD patients and healthy subjects enable the identification of homogeneous subpopulations of patients (clusters), interrogating phenotype-disease relationships in subpopulations, and further understanding why some patients are unresponsive to standard therapies to improve treatment outcomes. Thus, these studies offer tremendous opportunities and challenges to the communities of machine learning and *in silico* methods for research, such as CFPD simulations of airflow and particle deposition in subject-specific human lungs [12–22]. Due to highly dynamic characteristics of the human lungs, machine learning and *in silico* methods can be applied to investigate intra-subject, inter-subject and inter-cluster variations. CFPD-derived variables that are difficult to measure *in vivo* and *in vitro*, such as regional ventilation and hot spots with high aerosol deposition, can be used to better understand structure-function relationships as well as inhaled aerosol distributions. Ultimately, subject-specificity may be adequately achieved by cluster-specificity to bridge individual and population scales, moving toward precision medicine [23,24].

14.1.2 Clinical, molecular and imaging phenotyping and clustering

The clinical, biologic, genetic and imaging data collected by the above multicenter studies have shed light on several important findings and led to new insights on the heterogeneity of asthma and COPD. These studies have also enabled employment of machine learning techniques and development of new phenotyping variables and novel methodologies. For example, Moore et al. [25] used clinical data from 726 SARP subjects for cluster analysis. The data included demographic data (sex, race, age), age of onset, asthma duration, symptoms, health care use (HCU), smoke exposure, physiologic measures [pulmonary function tests (PFTs), atopy], amounting to a total of 628 clinical variables. These variables were reduced to 34 core variables for unsupervised hierarchical cluster analysis, identifying five clinical clusters with distinct clinical characteristics. Wu et al. [26] expanded Moore's study by including blood and bronchoscopic inflammatory and fractional exhaled nitric oxide data (FeNO, a surrogate biomarker of eosinophilic airway inflammation to predict corticosteroid response) from 378 SARP I and II asthmatic and healthy control subjects. They derived ten variables clusters and six clinical clusters. They also found that a total of 51 (or 112) nonredundant variables were required to achieve an accuracy of 88% (or 93%) in supervised classification. Moore et al. [27] conducted a new cluster analysis on 423 SARP subjects by using blood and sputum inflammatory cell assessments in addition to clinical data. They identified four sputum clusters, such as moderate-to-severe asthma with neutrophil-predominant or mixed granulocytic inflammation. Modena et al. [28] used bronchial airway epithelial cell (BAEC) gene expression and FeNO to study 129 asthma patients and 26 healthy control subjects from SARP. They first identified a sub-set of 549 genes whose expression correlated with FeNO from a total of 1384 genes, and then performed k-means to the expression of these genes to identify five molecular clusters in which they found unknown and novel molecular pathways. The use of CT imaging-based variables for phenotyping is considered as a major advance due to its quantitative, non-invasive characteristics, but its application was in its infancy until recent years [29]. For example, Gupta et al. [30] conducted a pioneering asthma study using only three CT-based variables, including lumen and wall volumes in a segmental bronchus and air trapping, to derive three imaging clusters. Choi et al. [31] developed a unique set of CT imaging-based variables for asthma subjects using pairs of lung CT inspiration and expiration scans to identify four imaging clusters [32].

14.1.3 Physics-based learning

Complementary to machine learning, physics-based learning seeks to identify novel disease features (risk factors) and associated subgroups via clinical notions of disease manifestations. For example, a recent physics-based study on a genetic risk factor associated with genetically-determined airway variation has probed the very etiology of the COPD disease process. Airway alteration may lead to differential deposition patterns of particulate matter that could affect disease risk or therapeutic response. Smith et al. [33] found two major lower lobe segmental airway branch variants that exist within families. Among them, 74% had standard segmental anatomy, 16% had an accessory sub-superior segmental airway with overall shorter segmental lengths and higher percentage of emphysema-like lung, and 6% had an absent right medial-basal segmental airway and smaller CT-resolved airway lumen areas throughout the lung. Shorter airway lengths may lead to more generations of airway branches and bifurcations, where inhaled particles tend to deposit more. Smaller lumen areas could result in increased airway resistance, reflecting on lung function. Subjects with an accessory segmental airway had higher odds of COPD among non-smokers and smokers, whereas subjects with absence of a right medial-basal segmental airway had higher odds of COPD among smokers. Airway branch variation was associated with genetic polymorphisms within FGF10, and FGF10-haploinsufficient mice exhibited a similar airway phenotype with fewer airways and increased airways resistance. These findings suggest that airway branch variants, detectable by CT, could serve as heritable biomarkers of widely altered lung structure and function as well as a COPD susceptibility factor. Physics-based learning may be a powerful complement to machine learning by allowing interrogation of the yet-to-be recognized interplays between novel risk factors and clinical, biological, genetic and radiologic phenotypes.

This chapter reviews the status of machine learning of quantitative CT imaging-based variables, the notion of cluster-guided imaging-based *in silico* lung models and the prospect of using physics-based learning for novel risk-factor identification and deep learning for automatic feature extraction together with machine learning to better understand the structure and function relationships in subpopulations for the design of future drug delivery. Alterations of lung structure and function are multi-scale, reflecting phenotypes of the lungs at different stages of the pathologic process. Thus, it is essential to examine variables at both local (segmental/parenchymal) and global (lobar/lung) scales to capture a wide spectrum of pathologic states. In addition, some *in vivo* and *in vitro* data are difficult to measure; but they are important to explain the correlations between structural and functional alterations and their implications on inhaled drug delivery. *In silico* lung models can predict some missing data. While building individualized CFPD lung models for a few subjects can be done, generation of CFPD-based variables for a large population is difficult, if not impossible, due to high computational time and cost. To bridge individual and population scales, identification of clusters characterized by distinct structural and functional variables and clinical characteristics can greatly facilitate the design of cluster-specific drug delivery and the assessment of therapeutic-intervention outcomes.

This chapter is organized as follows. Section 14.2 reviews CT imaging-based metrics defined at both local and global scales. Section 14.3 presents imaging clusters for asthma and COPD patients and their association with clinical characteristics. Section 14.4 discusses *in silico* methods and the strategy of using cluster membership to guide CFPD analysis for assessment of cluster-specific particle deposition patterns. Section 14.5 presents the prospect of utilizing physics-based learning and deep learning complementarily with machine learning. Finally, section 6 discusses future work in regard to utilization of longitudinal data to further advance precision medicine.

14.2 CT imaging-based metrics

CT imaging provides the best resolution among all imaging modalities. Some CT scanners can resolve in-plane detail of 0.5 mm × 0.5 mm or better, resolving up to about 10 generations of the airways. The lungs, lobes, airways and vasculatures can be segmented from volumetric CT images via an imaging processing approach. Structural and functional imaging-based metrics, such as one-dimensional (1D) airway skeleton (tree), luminal area, airway diameter, wall thickness, air and tissue volumes of the lungs, lobes among others, can be extracted along with anatomical information and labeling, such as airway generation and name. If two or more static CT images of the same subject are acquired at different lung volumes, such as inspiratory scans at total lung capacity (TLC) and expiratory scans at functional residual capacity (FRC) or residual volume (RV), functional variables, such as regional lung deformation and air volume changes, can be generated by image registration methods [34–37]. The registration-derived functional variables can be used for machine learning and for specifying subject-specific boundary conditions for CFPD lung models.

As a demonstration, using the automated segmentation software Apollo (VIDA Diagnostics) [38], four local structural variables including branching angle (θ), airway circularity (Cr), wall thickness (WT) and hydraulic diameter (D_h) are extracted from TLC scans as illustrated in Fig. 14.1. The variables of θ, Cr, WT and D_h are phenotypes of

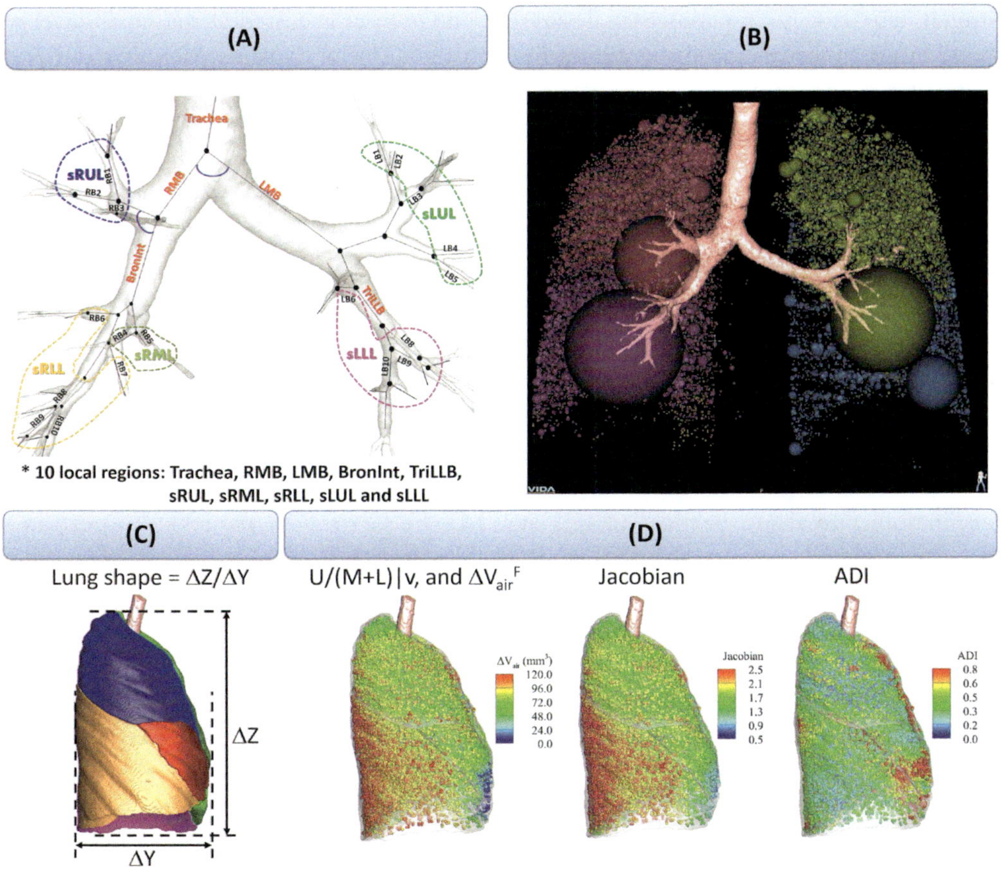

Figure 14.1 Multiscale imaging-based variables employed for the cluster analysis of asthma subjects [32], including structural and functional variables at local (segmental or parenchymal) and global (lobar or lung) scales. sRUL: sub-grouped right upper lobe (RUL) with branches of RB1; sRML: sub-grouped right middle lobe (RML) with branches of RB4; sRLL: sub-grouped right lower lobe (RLL) with branches of RB6; sLUL: sub-grouped left upper lobe (LUL) with branches of LB1; sub-grouped left lower lobe (LLL) with branches of LB6 and LB8. (A) Inspiration image-based local structures: θ, Cr, WT* and D_h*. (B) Expiration image-based global and lobar function: AirT%. (C) Global structure. (D) Registration-based global and lobar functions.

altered skeletal structure, heterogeneous airway cross-sectional shape, airway wall thickening (or thinning) and airway luminal narrowing, respectively. In order to capture regional alterations, these variables are extracted from 10 segmental airways. Percentage of air-trapped voxels (AirT%) at FRC or RV can also be extracted to measure tissue alteration and lung function. Additionally, the lung shape at TLC is a measure of global lung structure. Choi et al. [31,32] obtained three functional variables including fractional regional air-volume change (ΔV_{air}^{F}), regional volume change (Jacobian) and an anisotropic deformation index (ADI) between TLC and FRC (or RV). The ΔV_{air}^{F}, Jacobian and ADI indicate preferential air-volume change, local expansion and non-uniform stretch, respectively, in parenchymal regions. The metrics acquired at the voxel level can be reduced to lobar metrics by taking fraction (ΔV_{air}^{F}) or medians (Jacobian and ADI) in five lobes and a whole lung, resulting in a total of 6 regions. All of the imaging-based metrics at both local (segmental/parenchymal) and global (lobar/lung) scales are illustrated in Fig. 14.1. A total of 57 imaging-based metrics are constructed for the study of asthma patients [32], including 32 local (θ, *Cr*, WT* and D_h* in various regions), 20 lobar (ΔV_{air}^{F}, AirT%, Jacobian and ADI in five lobes) and 5 global variables (lung shape, U/(M + L)|v, AirT%, Jacobian and ADI). U/(M + L)|v is the ratio of the air flow distribution to the upper (U) lobe over that of the middle (M) and lower (L) lobes. These multiscale metrics aim to capture distinct phenotypes at different stages of disease progression.

For COPD subjects, additional imaging-based variables shall be included, such as functional small airways disease percentage (fSAD%) to quantify diseased small airways at expiration, emphysema percentage (Emph%) to quantify emphysematous tissues at inspiration, and tissue fraction (β_{tissue}) at TLC, FRC or RV, namely the portion of tissue volume in each voxel, to assess a possible alteration of local tissue. A parametric response map (PRM) based on fSAD% and Emph% [39] can be used to characterize COPD patients at various severity stages.

In machine learning, factors causing data bias need to be addressed. In learning CT imaging-based metrics over a large cohort, inter-subject and inter-site variabilities are two major bias factors. New normalization schemes for WT and D_h [31] have been developed to account for inter-subject variability due to sex, age, and height. An unbalanced number of samples due to sex, age and other variables can potentially cause large variations within groups, masking disease-related airway alterations. Employing a cohort of healthy subjects, Choi et al. [31] applied multiple linear regression with given sex, age and height to derive predicted values of tracheal diameter and wall thickness. These quantities are then used to normalize WT and D_h, denoted as WT* and D_h*. The normalization step allows dissociation from the effects of wall thickening (a phenotype for inflammation) and luminal narrowing (hyper-responsiveness). Differentiation of the two effects is important because diseased lungs are characterized by distinct phenotypes including airflow obstruction, bronchial hyper-responsiveness and airway inflammation.

Additionally, a new fraction-threshold measure for density-based assessment has been developed to account for inter-site variability due to protocol differences in association with scanners and coaching methods [40]. Specifically, Choi et al. [40] demonstrated the effect of using different CT scanners at three different imaging centers on air-trapping measures, concluding that use of different CT scanners causes significant variation by data distribution which goes beyond actual patient differences.

14.3 Imaging clusters and clinical characteristics

Due to the large number of imaging-based metrics, dimensional reduction such as principal component analysis (PCA) can be employed to assist with data analysis. For example, Choi et al. [32] analyzed a total of 61 healthy subjects (59% females), 106 non-severe (64% females) and 142 severe (63% females) asthmatic subjects. They applied PCA to reduce 57 imaging-based metrics to 7 principal components (PCs), which were then used to perform a k-mean clustering analysis. The number of clusters was determined by a cluster stability analysis. Each cluster exhibited strong association with distinct clinical characteristics, including asthma severity, gender, body mass index (BMI), onset of asthma, atopy, asthma quality of life questionnaire (AQLQ), asthma control questionnaire (ACQ), bronchial challenge (PC20), sputum induction, blood sample and bronchial alveolar lavage (BAL) tests (see Fig. 14.2). Specifically, Cluster 1

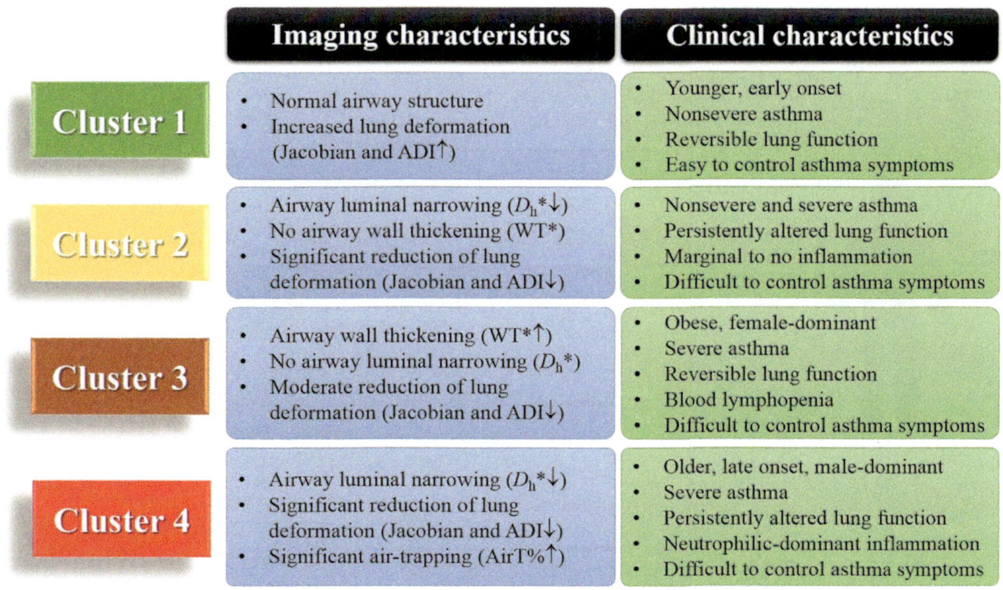

Figure 14.2 Summary of four asthmatic imaging clusters along with associated clinical characteristics. Both Cluster 3 and Cluster 4 were severe asthmatic patients [32].

was characterized by normal airway structure with hyper-inflation measured by Jacobian and ADI. Cluster 1 subjects were early-onset younger non-severe asthmatics with reversible lung function. Cluster 2 exhibited airway narrowing and persistently reduced lung deformation and function. Cluster 2 was composed of non-severe and severe asthmatics with marginal-to-no inflammation and difficult-to-control asthma symptoms. Cluster 3 had significant airway wall thickening without airway narrowing. Cluster 3 subjects were severe asthmatics dominated by obese females with reversible lung function, along with a lack of lymphocytes. Cluster 4 exhibited airway narrowing, wall thickening, air-trapping and reduced lung deformation. Cluster 4 subjects were severe asthmatics dominated by late-onset older males with a neutrophil-dominant signature. It is noted that both Cluster 3 and Cluster 4 were severe asthmatics, however they had distinct structural and functional characteristics, such as airway luminal area.

Based on the above clustering analysis, a simple tree-decision model [32] could be developed for classification using only two local structural (D_h*, WT*) and two global functional (Jacobian, AirT%) variables as illustrated in Fig. 14.3. The simple cluster model enables bridging individual and population scales for potential clinical applications in that a pair of CT scans acquired for a new patient can be processed to extract the four imaging-based metrics for classification, and the cluster-associated clinical characteristics and CFPD-derived data can be used to predict lung function and guide tailored treatment for that patient.

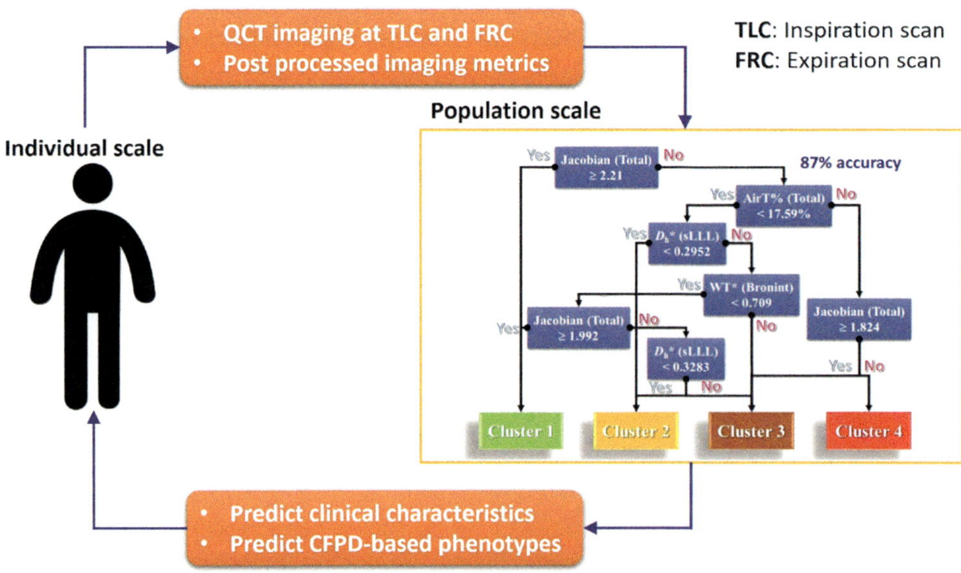

Figure 14.3 Bridging individual & population scales: a simple predictive model for cluster classification with four imaging-based variables that achieves an accuracy of 87% [32].

For the analysis of COPD patients, the set of imaging-based metrics shown in Fig. 14.1 are expanded by including fSAD%, Emph% and β_{tissue}. Due to the confounding factor of smoking status (behavioral risk factor), current smokers and former smokers were analyzed separately. Using a batch of current smokers (N = 284) from SPIROMICS, four statistically stable clusters were identified [41]. Cluster 1 had relatively normal airway structures. Cluster 2 had an increase of wall thickness and fSAD%. Cluster 3 exhibited airway wall thinning and luminal narrowing. Cluster 4 had a significant increase of emphysema and a decrease of luminal diameter along with significant elevation of small airways disease (increased fSAD%) and significant reduction of lung deformation. Association tests of imaging-based clusters with clinical characteristics were performed. Cluster 4 showed a relatively low FEV_1/FVC ratio (FEV_1, forced expiratory volume in one second; FVC, forced vital capacity), which is used in the diagnosis of obstructive lung disease. In contrast, Cluster 1 showed normal FEV_1/FVC with younger age. Cluster 2 had the highest BMI among the four clusters. Haghighi et al. [42] then applied the same analysis to a cohort of former smokers (N = 406) from SPIROMICS and identified four statistically stable imaging clusters. Cluster 1 showed normal airway structure and lung function. Cluster 2 was dominated with obese females with an increase of tissue fraction at inspiration. Cluster 3 was populated with older males exhibiting small airway narrowing. Cluster 4 was severe COPD subjects with the highest progression rate of emphysema.

Gibson and Simpson [43] and De Marko et al. [44] reported that about 15%–45% of patients with COPD may have asthma-COPD overlap, so-called ACO. It suggests that the two respiratory diseases may share common characteristics and they are difficult to differentiate by using clinical measures. Thus, accurate diagnosis of these diseases is essential for proper treatments. Choi et al. [45] mixed SARP asthma and SPIROMICS COPD data sets together to determine the ability of employing the above imaging-based metrics to differentiate between them. They found that asthma and COPD patients exhibit similar alterations of Cr and D_h^*. On the other hand, density-based measures between asthma and COPD are significantly different. For example, fSAD% and Emph% are elevated in asthma and COPD but more prominently in COPD subjects. β_{tissue} is significantly increased in asthma and decreased in COPD subjects as compared with healthy subjects. Their study suggests that imaging-based variables can sensitively discriminate different respiratory diseases that exhibit similar spirometry-measured lung functions.

14.4 *In silico* methods and cluster-guided CFPD analysis

Subject-specific CT-based CFPD lung models [12–22] can be employed to study the effects of imaging-based structural and functional metrics, e.g. airway constriction and air volume change, on regional ventilation, flow resistance and particle deposition.

Regional air volume change between CT image volumes at TLC and FRC (or RV), can be obtained by calculating the Jacobian of the transformation field using image registration [34–36]. By overlapping regional air volume change with the entire 1D airway tree, the flow rate fractions for the parenchymal units that enclose terminal bronchioles can be derived. The subject-specific CFPD boundary conditions imposed at the 3D ending branches are more heterogeneous than the common assumptions, such as uniform pressure, uniform mass flow or uniform velocity. For healthy subjects, the 3D flow boundary conditions can then be determined via tree connectivity with 1D airway tree and mass conservation [19]. For asthma and COPD subjects, a 1D flow resistance model [20] could be used to predict regional ventilation for boundary conditions. Heat and water vapor transfer in the human airways could be modeled by a 3D-1D coupled thermo-fluid model [18, 21], and a mathematical epithelial cell model for airway surface liquid regulation [22] could be integrated with 3D CFPD lung models for simulation of mechanotransduction to predict the periciliary liquid (PCL) height on the airway wall. Automatic geometric modeling algorithms enable the airway geometry beyond the CT resolution limit to be extended, to create paths of the 3D airway from the trachea to peripheral airways labeled with anatomical information [17]. Building a CT-based CFPD lung model is computationally expensive due to the complexity of airway structure and inherent feature of turbulent flows, thus applying such a model to a large cohort of subjects is challenging. A strategy to overcome this issue is using the cluster membership to identify representative subjects for CFPD analysis and then characterizing distinct *in silico* archetypes by interrogating the CFPD-derived features of particle deposition patterns in subpopulations. For a comprehensive review of *in silico* CFPD models, please refer to Chapter 7.

For example, Choi et al. [46] used the cluster membership identified for asthma patients [32] to guide CFPD analysis, aiming to explain cluster-specific structure and function relationships and improve drug administration to asthmatics. By studying only small numbers of cluster subjects characterized by distinct imaging and clinical features, the efforts for CFPD analysis can be reduced considerably. It is noted that both Cluster 3 and Cluster 4 were severe asthma (see Fig. 14.2), but only Cluster 4 had constricted airways. Choi et al. [46] showed that CFPD-predicted deposition fractions in Cluster 4 were higher than those of Cluster 3 for 1, 2, 4 and 8 μm particles. Fig. 14.4 compares the particle deposition densities in a Cluster 3 subject exhibiting normal airway luminal area, with a Cluster 4 subject having constricted airways in the lower left lobe. The hot spot of high particle deposition density (color-coded red) on the downstream bifurcation is caused by the impact of a high-speed jet flow caused by the constricted LLB airway segment. Rajaraman et al. [47] further studied the effect of hygroscopicity on deposition of particles in Cluster 3 and Cluster 4 asthmatic subjects. This information may assist with development of strategies using cluster-specific drug size to improve deposition targeting severe asthma with distinct features.

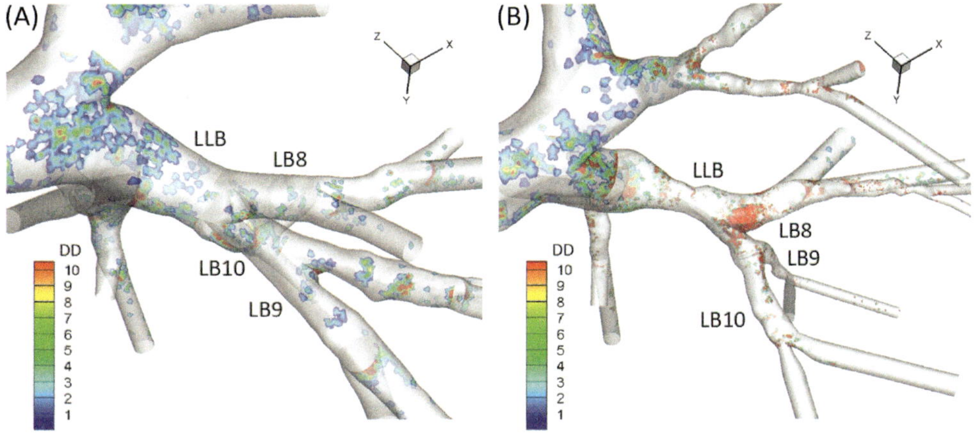

Figure 14.4 Deposition density (DD, particle number/mm^2) of 4 μm particles in (A) a Cluster 3 subject with normal airway structure and (B) a Cluster 4 subject with LLB constriction [46].

14.5 From machine and physics-based learning to deep learning

Physics-based learning seeks to identify novel features in association with environmental (PM2.5), behavioral (smoking, e-vaping), genetic (airway variant) and other risk factors. Subpopulations can then be defined and labeled with these novel features. In conjunction with machine learning, one can interrogate the interplay between imaging and clinical variables and the progression of clusters in subpopulations labeled with these novel features. Using genetically-determined airway variants [33] as an illustration, the airway shortening in a smoker subject with an accessory sub-superior airway (found in about 16% of the population) yields 6 more generations and 8 times more conducting airway branches to fill the lung (see Fig. 14.5) [48], leading to increased pressure drop to alveolar regions and higher airway resistance [20,48]. Thus, one could first classify the subjects into subpopulations by genetically-determined airway anatomy – standard vs variant – and then apply clustering to these subpopulations and compare clusters in subpopulations to assess the effect of the genetic risk factor on lung function and its interplay with other risk factors.

Machine learning requires extraction of imaging-based metrics from CT images (see Fig. 14.1) based on prior knowledge of lung physiology and pathophysiology – a process called feature engineering. This process is time consuming and cannot be used for detecting new phenotypes. Thus, some unknown novel features and phenotypes at early stages of lung disease progression may not be accounted for. In contrast, deep learning relies on artificial neural networks to extract features automatically. Thus, computer-aided diagnosis systems using convolutional neural networks (CNN) have been extensively developed to quantify the amount and position of the textural patterns of an image. González et al. [49]

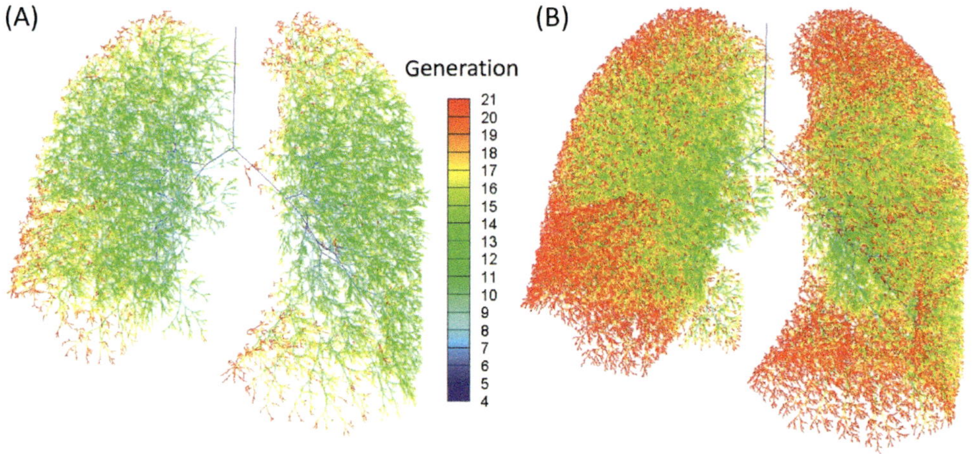

Figure 14.5 3D map of airway generation distributions in the entire 1D conducting airway models for (A) a subject with standard airway anatomy and (B) a subject with an accessory subsuperior airway and shorter branches [48].

developed a CNN to classify smokers with COPD by stage, and to predict those who are likely to have exacerbations and mortalities, using inputs of 4 slices of 3D CT scans at TLC for each subject from a total of 7983 COPDGene subjects. Ardila et al. [50] proposed a deep learning algorithm that uses a patient's current and prior 3D low-dose CT (LDCT) scans to predict the risk of lung cancer.

Fig. 14.6 shows the schematic of a convolutional autoencoder (CAE) model developed to identify lung tissue patterns from the CT lung images of Korean subjects exposed to humidifier disinfectants (HD) [51], a potential environmental risk factor for lung disease in Korea. These tissue patterns were used to build a logistic regression model for sensitive detection of HD-associated lung injury. The CAE model was trained to learn 1D representations of the 3D regions of interest (ROIs) extracted from the inspiratory CT images. The 1D ROI representations were then used to identify tissue pattern clusters. The pattern clusters were subsequently grouped into four factors with the assumption that pattern clusters in the same factor are strongly correlated with similar latent traits. Using these factors, a logistic regression model with factor scores as predictors was built to evaluate signs of underlying diseases. Thus, CNNs in conjunction physics-based learning and machine learning can potentially aid investigation of the effect of unknown or poorly defined lung diseases.

14.6 Conclusions

This chapter has reviewed the collaborative efforts of acquiring huge heterogeneous data sets for healthy subjects, asthma and COPD patients, extracting multiscale

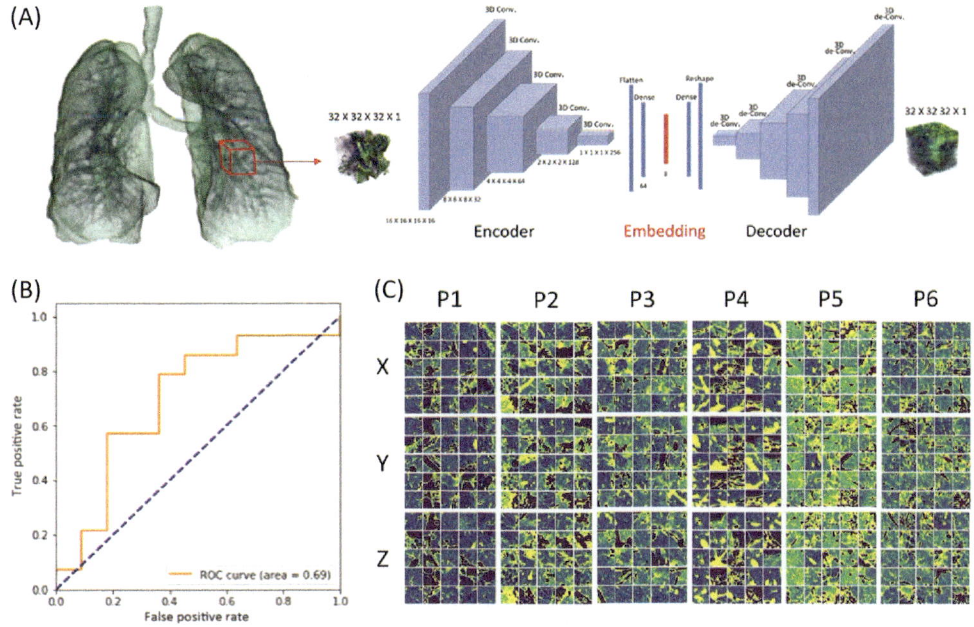

Figure 14.6 (A) A schematic of ROIs extracted randomly from the lungs and fed into a CAE to learn the 1D representations (embeddings) of the ROIs. (B) The receiver operation characteristic (ROC) curve of the logistic regression model trained on the latent variables. The entire dataset was split in a 75–25 ratio for training and testing data. An accuracy of 68% and area under the curve of 0.69 was achieved. (C) Pattern-clusters with large contributions in the most important latent variable in predicting signs for a HD-exposed lung. The images were shown in transverse (X), coronal (Y), and sagittal (Z) planes [51].

imaging-based metrics, identifying imaging clusters, and using cluster membership to guide CFPD analysis for assessment of inhaled aerosol delivery. The ultimate goal is to advance precision medicine. Both imaging-based metrics and CFPD models are multiscale in nature, within and between individuals, respectively. Machine learning of imaging-based metrics over a large cohort of asthma and COPD patients enabled imaging clusters to be identified and their associations with clinical characteristics to be established. The cluster membership allowed identification of cluster archetypes for *in silico* CFPD analysis. CFPD-derived variables, such as airway resistance and deposition fraction, can be used to assess regional distributions of particles in subjects with severe lung functions but distinct imaging-based metrics in a cluster-specific manner.

Moving forward, it is essential to employ longitudinal data to assess stability and transition of cluster membership over time for outcome assessment. The aforementioned imaging-based metrics were based on cross-sectional data. To identify longitudinal clusters characterized by disease progression, the changes in these metrics over time should be added into learning algorithms. In addition, deep learning techniques that use neural networks to extract features should be employed to capture non-linear features of the data for more sensitive clustering. Furthermore, physics-based learning based on novel risk factors could clearly differentiate subpopulations and should be used together with machine learning and deep learning to further advance precision medicine.

Acknowledgments

This work was supported in part by NIH grants U01 HL114494, R01 HL094315, R01 HL130506, R01 HL112986, S10 RR022421, S10 OD018526 and T32 HL144461, FDA grant U01 FD005837 as well as the Korea Environmental Industry & Technology Institute (KEITI) grant RE201806027 funded by Ministry of Environment (MOE) as "The Environmental Health Action Program". The authors also thank the Extreme Science and Engineering Discovery Environment (XSEDE) (allocation MCA07S015) sponsored by the National Science Foundation for computational time at San Diego Supercomputer Center (SDSC) and the Texas Advanced Computing Center (TACC).

References

[1] R.C. Deo, Machine learning in medicine, Circulation 132 (20) (2015) 1920–1930.
[2] S.E. Wenzel, W.W. Busse, Severe asthma: lessons from the Severe Asthma Research Program, J. Allergy Clin. Immunol. 119 (1) (2007) 14–21.
[3] D. Couper, et al., Design of the subpopulations and intermediate outcomes in COPD Study (SPIROMICS), Thorax 69 (5) (2013) 491–494.
[4] E.A. Regan, et al., Genetic epidemiology of COPD (COPDGene) study design, COPD 7 (1) (2010) 32–43.
[5] D.E. Bild, et al., Multi-ethnic study of atherosclerosis: objectives and design, Am. J. Epidemiol. 156 (9) (2002) 871–881.
[6] B.M. Smith, et al., Comparison of spatially matched airways reveals thinner airway walls in COPD. The Multi-Ethnic Study of Atherosclerosis (MESA) COPD Study and the Subpopulations and Intermediate Outcomes in COPD Study (SPIROMICS), Thorax 69 (11) (2014) 987–996.
[7] E.A. Hoffman, et al., Variation in the percent of emphysema-like lung in a healthy, nonsmoking multiethnic sample. The MESA lung study, Ann. Am. Thorac. Soc. 11 (6) (2014) 898–907.
[8] S. Sullivan, et al., Extent, patterns, and burden of uncontrolled disease in severe or difficult-to-treat asthma, Allergy 62 (2) (2007) 126–133.
[9] W.G. Teague, et al., Baseline features of the Severe Asthma Research Program (SARP III) cohort: differences with age, J. Allergy Clin. Immunol. Pract. 6 (2) (2018) 545–554. e4.
[10] J.P. Sieren, et al., SPIROMICS protocol for multicenter quantitative computed tomography to phenotype the lungs, Am. J. Respir. Crit. Care Med. 194 (7) (2016) 794–806.
[11] R. Lozano, et al., Global and regional mortality from 235 causes of death for 20 age groups in 1990 and 2010: a systematic analysis for the Global Burden of Disease Study 2010, Lancet 380 (9859) (2013) 2095–2128.
[12] C.L. Lin, M.H. Tawhai, E.A. Hoffman, Multiscale image-based modeling and simulation of gas flow and particle transport in the human lungs, Wiley Interdiscip. Rev. Syst. Biol. Med. 5 (5) (2013) 643–655.
[13] S. Miyawaki, et al., A 4DCT imaging-based breathing lung model with relative hysteresis, J. Comput. Phys. 326 (2016) 76–90.
[14] S. Miyawaki, E.A. Hoffman, C.-L. Lin, Effect of static vs. dynamic imaging on particle transport in CT-based numerical models of human central airways, J. Aerosol Sci. 100 (2016) 129–139.
[15] S. Miyawaki, E.A. Hoffman, C.-L. Lin, Numerical simulations of aerosol delivery to the human lung with an idealized laryngeal model, image-based airway model, and automatic meshing algorithm, Comput. Fluids 148 (2017) 1–9.

[16] S. Miyawaki, et al., Effect of carrier gas properties on aerosol distribution in a CT-based human airway numerical model, Ann. Biomed. Eng. 40 (7) (2012) 1495–1507.

[17] S. Miyawaki, et al., Automatic construction of subject-specific human airway geometry including trifurcations based on a CT-segmented airway skeleton and surface, Biomech. Model. Mechanobiol. (2016) 1–14.

[18] D. Wu, et al., A numerical study of water loss rate distributions in MDCT-based human airway models, Ann. Biomed. Eng. 43 (11) (2015) 2708–2721.

[19] Y. Yin, et al., Simulation of pulmonary air flow with a subject-specific boundary condition, J. Biomech. 43 (11) (2010) 2159–2163.

[20] S. Choi, et al., 1-D network simulations for evaluating regional flow and pressure distributions in the healthy and asthmatic human lungs, J. Appl. Physiol. (1985) 2019.

[21] D. Wu, et al., A numerical study of heat and water vapor transfer in MDCT-based human airway models, Ann. Biomed. Eng. 42 (10) (2014) 2117–2131.

[22] D. Wu, et al., An integrated mathematical epithelial cell model for airway surface liquid regulation by mechanical forces, J. Theor. Biol. 438 (2018) 34–45.

[23] B. Mesko, The role of artificial intelligence in precision medicine, Exp. Rev. Precis. Med. Drug. Dev. 2 (5) (2017) 239–241.

[24] V.S. Parekh, M.A. Jacobs, Deep learning and radiomics in precision medicine, Exp. Rev. Precis. Med. Drug. Dev. 4 (2) (2019) 59–72.

[25] W.C. Moore, et al., Identification of asthma phenotypes using cluster analysis in the Severe Asthma Research Program, Am. J. Respir. Crit. Care Med. 181 (4) (2010) 315–323.

[26] W. Wu, et al., Unsupervised phenotyping of Severe Asthma Research Program participants using expanded lung data, J. Allergy Clin. Immunol. 133 (5) (2014) 1280–1288.

[27] W.C. Moore, et al., Sputum neutrophil counts are associated with more severe asthma phenotypes using cluster analysis, J. Allergy Clin. Immunol. 133 (6) (2014) 1557–1563. e5.

[28] B.D. Modena, et al., Gene expression in relation to exhaled nitric oxide identifies novel asthma phenotypes with unique biomolecular pathways, Am. J. Respir. Crit. Care Med. 190 (12) (2014) 1363–1372.

[29] N.N. Jarjour, et al., Severe asthma: lessons learned from the National Heart, Lung, and Blood Institute Severe Asthma Research Program, Am. J. Respir. Crit. Care Med. 185 (4) (2012) 356–362.

[30] S. Gupta, et al., Quantitative computed tomography-derived clusters: redefining airway remodeling in asthmatic patients, J. Allergy Clin. Immunol. 133 (3) (2014) 729–738.

[31] S. Choi, et al., Quantitative assessment of multiscale structural and functional alterations in asthmatic populations, J. Appl. Physiol. (2015). p. jap. 01094.2014.

[32] S. Choi, et al., Quantitative computed tomographic imaging-based clustering differentiates asthmatic subgroups with distinctive clinical phenotypes, J. Allergy Clin. Immunol. 140 (3) (2017) 690–700. e8.

[33] B.M. Smith, et al., Human airway branch variation and chronic obstructive pulmonary disease, Proc. Natl. Acad. Sci. U.S.A. 115 (5) (2018). p. E974-e981.

[34] Y. Yin, E.A. Hoffman, C.L. Lin, Mass preserving nonrigid registration of CT lung images using cubic B-spline, Med. Phys. 36 (9) (2009) 4213.

[35] N.D. Ellingwood, et al., Efficient methods for implementation of multi-level nonrigid mass-preserving image registration on GPUs and multi-threaded CPUs, Comput. Methods Prog. Biomed. 127 (2016) 290–300.

[36] B. Haghighi, et al., A GPU-based symmetric non-rigid image registration method in human lung, Med. Biol. Eng. Comput. 56 (3) (2018) 355–371.

[37] S. Choi, et al., Registration-based assessment of regional lung function via volumetric CT images of normal subjects vs. severe asthmatics, J. Appl. Physiol. 115 (5) (2013) 730–742.

[38] E.A. Hoffman, et al., The comprehensive imaging-based analysis of the lung: a forum for team science, Acad. Radiol. 11 (12) (2004) 1370.

[39] C.J. Galbán, et al., Computed tomography-based biomarker provides unique signature for diagnosis of COPD phenotypes and disease progression, Nat. Med. 18 (11) (2012) 1711–1715.

[40] S. Choi, et al., Improved CT-based estimate of pulmonary gas trapping accounting for scanner and lung volume variations in a multi-center study, J. Appl. Physiol. 117 (6) (2014) 593–603.

[41] B. Haghighi, et al., Imaging-based clusters in current smokers of the COPD cohort associate with clinical characteristics: the SubPopulations and Intermediate Outcome Measures in COPD Study (SPIROMICS), Respir. Res. 19 (1) (2018) 178.
[42] B. Haghighi, et al., Imaging-based clusters in former smokers of the COPD cohort associate with clinical characteristics: the SubPopulations and Intermediate Outcome Measures in COPD Study, Respir. Res, Revis. Rev. (2019).
[43] P. Gibson, J. Simpson, The overlap syndrome of asthma and COPD: what are its features and how important is it? Thorax 64 (8) (2009) 728–735.
[44] R. De Marco, et al., The coexistence of asthma and chronic obstructive pulmonary disease (COPD): prevalence and risk factors in young, middle-aged and elderly people from the general population, PLoS One 8 (5) (2013) e62985.
[45] S. Choi, et al., Differentiation of quantitative CT imaging phenotypes in asthma versus COPD, BMJ Open. Respir. Res. 4 (1) (2017).
[46] J. Choi, et al., Differences in particle deposition between members of imaging-based asthma clusters, J. Aerosol Med. Pulm. Drug. Deliv. (2019).
[47] P.K. Rajaraman, et al., Transport and deposition of hygroscopic particles in asthmatic subjects with and without airway narrowing, J. Aerosol Sci. (2020) 105581.
[48] C. Zou, et al., Characteristics of airflow and particle deposition in airway variants among smokers and non-smokers, B64. COPD: Mechanism and Treatment, American Thoracic Society, 2019, p. A3867.
[49] G. González, et al., Disease staging and prognosis in smokers using deep learning in chest computed tomography, Am. J. Respir. Crit. Care Med. 197 (2) (2018) 193–203.
[50] D. Ardila, et al., End-to-end lung cancer screening with three-dimensional deep learning on low-dose chest computed tomography, Nat. Med. (2019).
[51] F. Li, et al., Identification of lung tissue patterns in subjects exposed to humidifier disinfectants using a convolutional deep learning model. American Thoracic Society International Conference, May 15–20, 2020, Philadelphia, pp. A7907–A7907.

CHAPTER 15

The emerging state of the art

Stavros Kassinos[1,2], Per Bäckman[3] and Anthony J. Hickey[4]
[1]Computational Sciences Laboratory (UCY-CompSci), Mechanical and Manufacturing Engineering, University of Cyprus, Nicosia, Cyprus
[2]Respiratory Hub, University of Cyprus, Nicosia, Cyprus
[3]Emmace Consulting AB, Lund, Sweden
[4]RTI International, Research Triangle Park, NC, United States

15.1 Introduction

Despite a continuous improvement in our understanding of inhalation therapies, reliable and accurate prediction of the *in vivo* performance of drugs based on first principles is still challenging. Perhaps the single most important impediment to rapid progress in this regard has been the inaccessibility of the distal lung to direct observation. For example, as discussed in Chapters 6−7, direct assessment of lung dose deposition in intermediate and peripheral lung regions remains beyond the resolution of even modern pulmonary imaging and beyond replication via *in vitro* approaches. Furthermore, our understanding of target receptors in the large expanse of the distal lung is far from precise, as is our mechanistic understanding of the local PK processes occurring post-deposition leading up to target exposure, as discussed in Chapters 8−11. Consequently, correlating key product *in vitro* attributes such as aerodynamic particle size distribution, dissolution, and drug physicochemical properties with local action, or even with the more generalizable plasma concentration profiles, remains challenging. This is obviously not made any easier by the diversity of inhaled products as outlined in Chapters 1−5.

Key areas for development include understanding the fate of the aerosol, understanding drug tissue interactions and, ultimately, drug target interactions in the lung. In the remainder of this short chapter we will outline a vision for how a coordinated integration of *in vivo*, *in vitro* and *in silico* approaches can provide better insights into the first of these key improvement areas, the regional deposition of the inhaled aerosols.

15.2 The potential of *in silico* aerosol deposition methods and current issues

In Chapter 7, we have seen that *in silico* methods fall in two broad families, algebraic 1D models and 3D Computational Fluid Particle Dynamics (CFPD) models. 1D models are the primary *in silico* tool currently in use for drug development by virtue of their speed and ease of use. CFPD tools carry significant computational expense but

Inhaled Medicines
DOI: https://doi.org/10.1016/B978-0-12-814974-4.00015-8

have the benefit of providing results with an unprecedented level of detail. The family of CFPD models is not monolithic, rather itself is further divided into models of varying complexity, fidelity and expense.

In recent years, several groups worldwide are pushing towards the development of "whole lung" CFPD simulation strategies [1–3]. The methods pursued vary significantly, but all efforts are driven by the benefits of integrated simulations that can track the flow and particle transport over complete inhalation cycles and over the entire complex expanse of the lung airways. These benefits include the ability to apply realistic breathing patterns without the need to impose artificial boundary conditions in any segment of the simulated domains; the ability to account for the air flow being driven by the deforming acinar regions; the possibility to track particles not only during inhalation, but during entire complex maneuvers including breath holds and exhalation. Furthermore, given reliable information from medical imaging and other *in vivo* methods [4,5], the underlying three-dimensional topology used in such integrated CFPD lung simulations can be modified to reflect various non-standard lung topologies with relative ease. For example, infant lungs or lungs at various stages of COPD emphysema and asthma can be represented [6–8].

When thinking about the emerging role of *in silico* methods, it is useful to distinguish between patient-specific applications and pre-clinical population studies relevant to drug development. The former require use of CFPD methods with patient-specific geometries including the extrathoracic and central tracheobronchial regions. The latter, as explained in Chapter 7 and in Koullapis et al. [9], can be based on representative information for the dose escaping filtering in the extrathoracic region and entering the tracheobronchial tree reconstructed from chest CT-scans and merged with models of the peripheral lung. This information must include the aerodynamic particle size distribution and bolus arrival times. In our view, the most impactful prospect in the context of inhaled drug development is the area of *in silico* population studies and in what follows we outline this vision.

One of us (SK) has recently completed a relatively large population study including 185 healthy adults, which has established the impressive level of morphometric variability of the central tracheobronchial airways in the general population, even among healthy individuals of the same sex [10].

Differences become even larger when comparing women to men. For example, Fig. 15.1 shows the impressive difference in the diameter of the tracheobronchial airways between two heathy adults, 14.58 mm for a 50-year-old female on the left vs 22.05 mm for a 45-year-old male on the right. Other morphometric features, such bifurcation angles and segment lengths exhibit significant variability as well. Based on preliminary *in silico* results, we have been arguing that this large morphometric variability of the central airways is bound to also induce significant

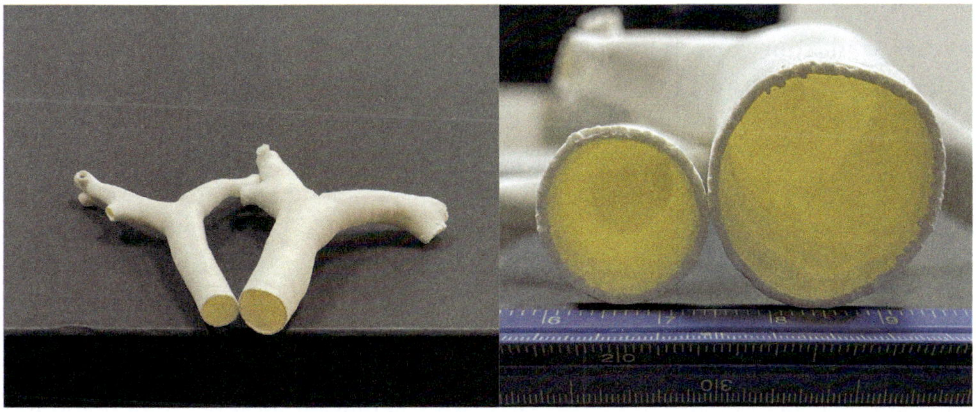

Figure 15.1 Trachea and main bronchi of two healthy subjects reconstructed from chest CT-scans and 3D printed, showcasing the impressive difference in airway diameters. In each panel, placed on the left are the airways of a 50-year-old female (14.58 mm trachea diameter) and on the right those of a 45-year-old male (22.05 mm trachea diameter).

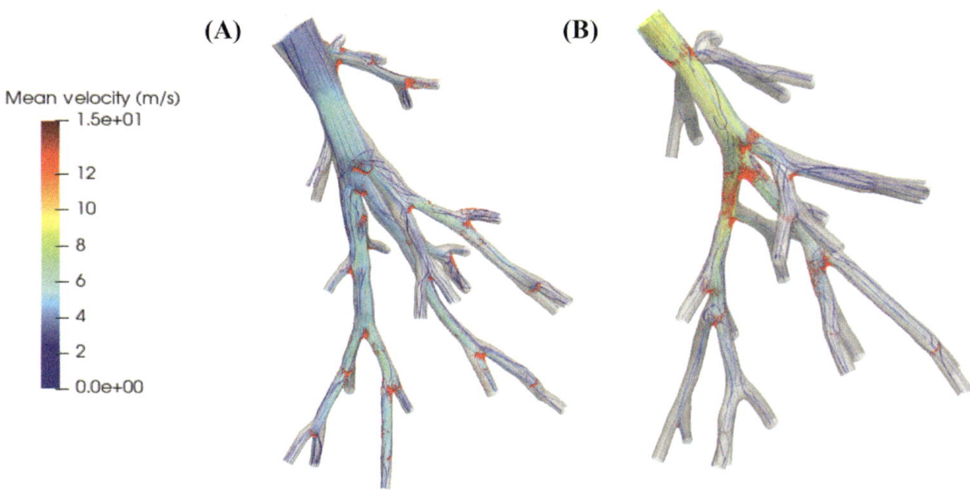

Figure 15.2 In silico deposition hotspots for 6 μm particles in the promixal bonchi of the Left Lower Lobe in two patient-specific geometries sharing the same mouth-throat geometry and comparable tracheal lumen areas. Inhalation rate is at 30 L/min. On the left (A) the case of a 68-year-old female with tracheal lumen area of 244 mm^2 and main bifurcation angle of 70 degrees. On the right (B) the case of a 28-year-old male of tracheal lumen area of 241 mm^2 and main bifurcation angle of 101 degrees.

differences in the distribution of particle ventilation among the five lobes in the distal lung.

Shown in Fig. 15.2 are the mean velocity levels and deposition hotspots for 6 μm particles in the proximal airways of the lower left lobe of two different individuals for an inhalation rate of 30 L/min. The tracheobronchial trees of the two subjects were reconstructed from chest CT-scans and merged with the same extrathroracic airways (mouth-throat down to just below the glottis). The two subjects had comparable tracheal diameters but significant differences in the main bifurcation angle. There is significant difference in the local velocity levels between the two cases, and more importantly, in the localization of deposition hotspots. These are more evenly distributed in one case (case A on left) but are concentrated in one central region in the other (case B on right). Similar differences between the two subjects were found in the proximal airways of all lobes.

The recent *in vivo* study of Verbanck et al. [11] provides direct evidence in support of this approach. Using 2D planar scintigraphy, they identified hotspots in the central tacheobornhial airways that were associated with significant local deposition and found them to induce significant differences in lobar particle ventilation. These results point to a promising line of research. While it might be impractical to subject large numbers of patients to scintigraphy studies in order to explore further these morphometric effects, a more promising strategy is to carry a small number of coordinated *in vivo* and *in silico* studies to establish correlations between the two, and then, proceed with large population studies *in silico* that will leverage the large numbers of chest CT-scans that are available at various medical databases (Fig. 15.3).

Computational efficiency will be of paramount importance in the context of such large-scale population studies. Based on the conclusions of Koullapis et al. [9], we argue that each patient has his/her own characteristic deposition efficiency map for the central tracheobronchial airways. This efficiency map is important for the particle ventilation of the distal lobes, but it is largely independent of the extrathoracic airways. Thus, in the envisioned *in silico* population studies, CFPD methods are applied only to the thoracic airways and appropriate bolus profiles at the entrance of the tracheobronchial geometries will be provided via a combination of *in vitro* and *in silico* data generated beforehand. Not

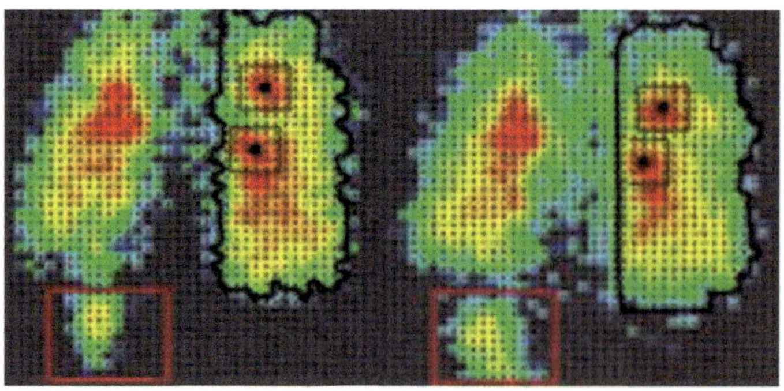

Figure 15.3 2D scintigrams showing deposition hot spots in the central right lung (black single pixels surrounded by squares) following inhalation of 3 μm particles at 30 L/min (left) and 60 L/min (right). Thick black lines delineate the lung reach. *Adapted from Verbanck et al. [11].*

having to simulate the extrathoracic airways leads to significant savings in computational effort, allowing one to instead channel resources to the simulation of the central and distal lung.

As explained in Chapters 6 and 7, realistic *in vitro* methods utilizing mouth-throat replicas and careful instrumentation to monitor drug release from different types of devices can provide valuable data to inform the boundary conditions to be used *in silico* methods. The envisioned procedure relies on carrying *in vitro* measurements in mouth-throat (MT) geometries, selected so as to capture geometric variability in the population, while also using a range of inhalation profiles, again designed to capture the variability of maneuvers used by different classes of patients. These same cases can be simulated via 3D CFPD methods and once good correlation is achieved, 3D flowfields and particle distributions can be archived to be used as inflow conditions for the simulations during the *in silico* population studies. Since the deposition efficiencies of the central airways are in effect the morphometric signature of the central airways, using a library of inflow conditions that captures variability in the extrathoracic airways allows one to reproduce scenarios that cover the overall variability that can be expected in the population.

Focusing on whole lung simulations, there are several simulation strategies being pursued by a number of groups as outlined in Section 7. Our own vision centers on using high-fidelity LES-based approaches in the central tracheobronchial airways. The same 3D CFPD methods are used for the deep lung as well, but the simulation strategy is optimized for computational efficiency by taking advantage of the low Reynolds number regime that prevails in the distal lung [1,12]. Regardless of the specific whole lung model one chooses to adopt, there are certain key ingredients that should be included to achieve a good level of realism. These include a realistic representation of the effects of gravity, which is necessary since sedimentation becomes an increasingly important mode of deposition as airborne particles move from the central to the distal lung. Airflow must be consistent with, and ideally the product of, the motion of the acinus. While simulations utilizing coupled flow structure interactions are being considered as research topics, it is unlikely that they can be applied in large population studies in the immediate future as a result of the added computational cost. Nevertheless, a viable approach is to prescribe a motion of the acinus that reproduces the desired inhalation profile. This is the approach we have been following in [1,12,13]. In this regard, it is important to introduce flexible walls both for the alveolar cavities and the acinar ducts.

The future success of *in silico* methods rests to a large extent on gaining the acceptance and confidence of stakeholders and end users, i.e. regulatory agencies and the pharmaceutics development community. To achieve this, the predictions of 3D CFPD whole lung models must be tied to *in vivo* results. As discussed earlier, our current reliance primarily on 2D planal scintigrams to probe *in vivo* deposition patterns is problematic because of information loss as data in folded (projected) onto planes. Nevertheless, one can conceive of methods to map 3D CFPD results onto planes, allowing at least the projected version of *in silico* predictions to be compared directly to planar scintigrams. Using this approach in a series of carefully designed *in vivo* and *in silico studies* for selected patient groups will allow the establishment of correlations between 3D CFPD results and scintigrams. The main benefit of this effort will be the gain of trust in such validated *in silico* methods. Once 3D CFPD whole lung models gain wider acceptance, which will be based on track record, the flow of information could be reversed and 2D planar scintigrams could be unfolded onto 3D deposition maps *in silico* using validated mapping methods.

As described in Chapter 14, *in silico* methods using 3D CFPD whole lung models can be used in conjunction with machine learning and artificial intelligence methods. Such integration becomes meaningful in the context of large population studies, where simulation results, processed with artificial intelligence tools, can be used to detect particular regional deposition patterns that are associated with certain anatomical features, but potentially also with particular genotypes.

15.3 Synthesis of the emerging state of the art

The preceding discussion leads to the point where we can synthesize a vision for an emerging state of the art that fully leverages the potential of *in silico* methods in product development. This vision is summarized in Fig. 15.4 and further explained below.

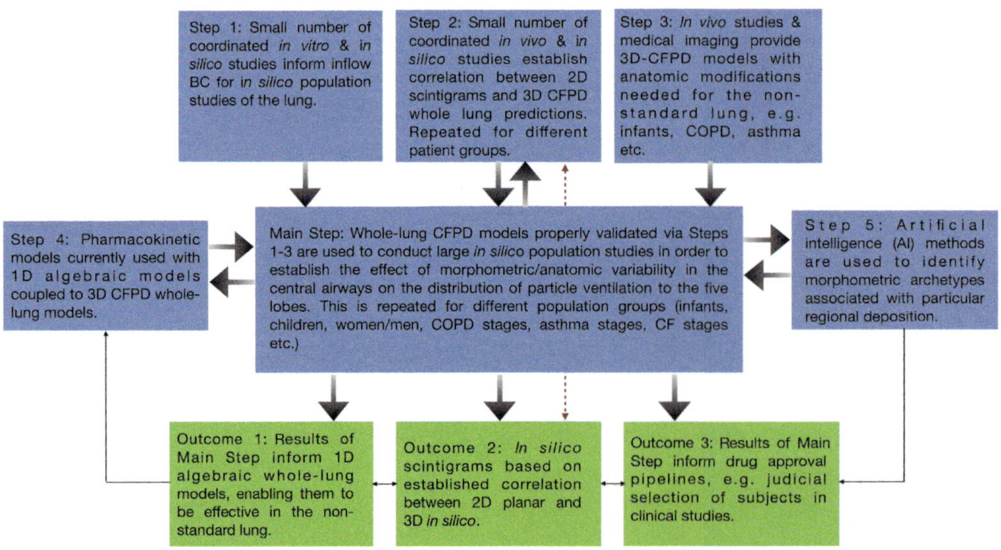

Figure 15.4 Diagram providing a synopsis of the vision for an emerging state of the art.

The first three steps concern the use of *in vivo* and physiologically relevant *in vitro* methods to inform *in silico* methods and to establish validated *in vivo* - *in silico* correlations. In Step 1, we envision carefully designed, combined *in vitro* and *in silico*, studies aiming to provide validated inflow boundary conditions for use with 3D CFPD lung simulations. Such boundary conditions will need to capture population variability in the extrathoracic (MT) deposition. They can take various forms; an appealing approach is to store such validated flow and particle-distribution and arrival-time histories in databases. This will have to be conducted for a series of flowrates and inhalation maneuvers, which is a time-consuming process, but will only be done once.

Step 2 involves the parallel study of regional deposition (central and distal lung) in carefully selected groups of patients. A prerequisite is to obtain both 2D planar scintigrams and high-resolution CT-scans for each subject. The CT-scans will be used to reconstruct the central airways in 3D and then extend them *in silico* to fill the lobal surfaces. Recorded inhalation flow profiles will be used to predict *in silico* regional deposition patters over the entire lung. The 2D planar projections (folding) of the 3D *in silico* regional deposition patterns for various particle sizes can then be analyzed to establish correlations between 2D scintigrams and projected *in silico* results. Studying and understanding these correlations will establish the level of trust needed before embarking on large-scale population studies *in silico*, as foreseen in the Main Step. In the longer term, and as *in silico* methods become established and trusted by stakeholders, the flow information could be reversed. One could imagine using validated *in silico* tools to unfold 2D planar scintigrams onto 3D deposition patterns or in some cases even replacing *in vivo* scintigrams with *in silico* 3D deposition results.

A key contribution of *in silico* tools is that they provide an effective way for studying deposition in non-standard lungs, where morphometric deviations from an "ideal mean lung" can arise as a result of age, sex or disease status. Before such non-standard populations can be studied *in silico*, a coordinated effort among many centers will be needed, in order to come to a consensus about the most significant morphometric variations. Building such a consensus it is important because it will establish a common reference point for comparisons and cross-validation across different *in silico* approaches and efforts, much as there have been multi-center efforts to standardize protocols for chest CT-scans. *In vivo* and imaging methods can help quantify anatomic modifications.

With input from the first three steps, *in silico* population studies can be initiated. In parallel, *in silico* tools can start to be integrated with state-of-the-art pharmacokinetic (PK) models currently in use with 1D algebraic models. Such models are in general based on just a few lung compartments and thus are not designed to take full advantage of the detailed information that 3D CFPD methods can generate. Nevertheless, as in the case of 2D scintigrams, a stepping down of 3D CFPD outputs is a useful strategy here as well. Agglomerating 3D CFPD deposition results to the lung compartments of PK models, will tie the output of the emerging methods with the results of simpler but established methods that have been studied for a longer time and are relatively well understood and trusted. Validation of PK-enabled 3D CFPD can be carried out by comparing, for example, predicted plasma profiles against *in vivo* results and also to the predictions of PK-enabled 1D models, such as the Mimetikos Preludium (available for licensing from Emmace Consulting AB, Sweden) or the Gastroplus (Simulation Plus Inc., CA, USA). In the longer term, as trust in 3D CFPD whole-lung models become established, and as improved understanding of the regional variability of dissolution, clearance and absorption in the lung becomes available, the flow information can again be reversed as was the case for scintigrams. By default, 3D CFPD whole-lung models can take into account this new information as it becomes available in the future and produce results that reflect the improved understanding, which in turn can be fed into improved PK modeling for 1D models. As described in Chapters 8–11, new knowledge on disease-induced alterations of epithelial integrity, modified clearance capacity and inflammatory response can be integrated in such CFPD-augmented PK models to yield *in silico* tools capable for addressing specific target population groups with modified lung pathophysiology.

With the accumulation of data generated via the *in silico* population studies of the Main Step (Fig. 15.4), it will eventually become possible to start applying the machine learning and AI tools described in Chapter 14 to hunt for particular morphometric clusters that are linked to specific regional deposition patterns. Going beyond deposition patterns, and as these methods become established, such population clusters could be linked to expected therapeutic outcomes.

There are three main outcomes of this emerging vision that are likely to have significant impact on the development of new inhalation therapeutics. Improved 1D algebraic models, informed by the output of PK-enabled 3D CFPD *in silico* studies. In effect this amounts to distilling the improved knowledge that will be generated into a form that can be used effectively and quickly in drug development cycles. The second outcome concerns 2D planar scintigraphy. While at the beginning scintigraphy will be used as an enabler of *in silico* methods by providing the necessary reference for validation, eventually *in silico* methods can return the favor by allowing 2D planar scintigrams to be unfolded into 3D deposition patterns.

All these developments will unfold over several years and will require open cooperation among many different academic, medical and industry groups. Several examples exist where such open cooperation has been achieved, including COST Action MP1404 – "SimInhale", and this offers an optimistic note that all the key players can come together to make this emerging vision a reality. This is not an individual, or small group activity, it has to be a joint research community effort. Eventually, if this vision meets its potential, it would ideally be recognized and integrated in to drug product regulation and approval process to assure quality, safety and efficacy in a timely and efficient manner.

References

[1] P.G. Koullapis, F.S. Stylianou, J. Sznitman, B. Olsson, S.C. Kassinos, Towards whole-lung simulations of aerosol deposition: a model of the deep lung, J. Aerosol Sci. 144 (2020).

[2] A.V. Kolanjiyil, C. Kleinstreuer, Computational analysis of aerosol-dynamics in a human whole-lung airway model, J. Aerosol Sci. 114 (2017) 301–316.

[3] P.W. Longest, G. Tian, N. Khajeh-Hosseini-Dalasm, M. Hindle, Validating whole-airway CFD predictions of DPI aerosol deposition at multiple flow rates, J. Aerosol Med. Pulm. Drug Deliv. 29 (0) (2016). p. jamp. 2015.1281.

[4] J.K.F. Jakobsson, J. Hedlund, J. Kumlin, P. Wollmer, J. Löndahl, A new method for measuring lung deposition efficiency of airborne nanoparticles in a single breath, Sci. Rep. 6 (2016) 36147. Available from: 10.1038/srep36147.

[5] J.K.F. Jakobsson, H.L. Aaltonen, H. Nicklasson, A. Gudmundsson, J. Rissler, P. Wollmer, et al., Altered deposition of inhaled nanoparticles in subjects with chronic obstructive pulmonary disease, BMC Pulm. Med. 18 (2018) 129.

[6] J.M. Oakes, S.C. Roth, S.C. Shadden, Airflow simulations in infant, child, and adult pulmonary conducting airways, Ann. Biomed. Eng. 46 (3) (2018) 498–512.

[7] P. Das, E. Nof, I. Amirav, S.C. Kassinos, J. Sznitman, Targeting inhaled aerosol delivery to upper airways in children: insight from computational fluid dynamics (CFD), PLoS One 13 (11) (2018) 1–20.

[8] J.M. Oakes, P. Hofemeier, I.E. Vignon-Clementel, J. Sznitman, Aerosols in healthy and emphysematous in silico pulmonary acinar rat models, J. Biomech. 49 (11) (2016) 2213–2220.

[9] P.G. Koullapis, L. Nicolaou, S.C. Kassinos, In silico assessment of mouth-throat effects on regional deposition in the upper tracheobronchial airways, J. Aerosol Sci. 117 (2018) 164–188.

[10] S. Christou, T. Chatziathanasiou, S. Angeli, P. Koullapis, F. Stylianou, J. Sznitman, et al., Anatomical variability in the upper tracheobronchial tree: sex-based differences and implications for personalized inhalation therapies, J. Appl. Physiol. (2020). Available from: https://journals.physiology.org/doi/abs/10.1152/japplphysiol.00144.2020.

[11] S. Verbanck, M.F. Biddiscombe, O.S. Usmani, Inhaled aerosol dose distribution between proximal bronchi and lung periphery, Eur. J. Pharm. Biopharm. (2020). in press.

[12] P. Hofemeier, K. Koshiyama, S. Wada, J. Sznitman, One (sub-)acinus for all: fate of inhaled aerosols in heterogeneous pulmonary acinar structures, Eur. J. Pharm. Sci. 113 (2018) 53–63.

[13] P.G. Koullapis, P. Hofemeier, J. Sznitman, S.C. Kassinos, An efficient computational fluid-particle dynamics method to predict deposition in a simplified approximation of the deep lung, Eur. J. Pharm. Sci. 113 (2018) 132–144.

Editorial closing remarks

The mission of this book has been to synthesize a vision of upcoming developments in the field of inhalation. It was argued that over the next decade the field is likely to undergo a transformation where *in vivo*, *in vitro* and *in silico* methods will be integrated much more closely together. It is expected that instead of being viewed as alternative options, these methods will evolve towards becoming linked in a unified approach, each complementing the others, allowing obstacles and bottlenecks to be more effectively circumvented towards rapid new drug discovery efforts. For such an integrated view to be appreciated, a thorough understanding of the current state of the art, encompassing past achievements but also the open issues that frustrate further progress, is necessary. In its first two sections, the book provided this critical review of the current state of the art, while the last section concluded with a view of the emerging evolution over the next decade.

As outlined in the opening chapter, drug inhalation differs from oral administration in two key aspects, physiology and delivery. In selecting API characteristics for safe and effective therapy, the unique lung physiology and biochemistry, which sets inhaled products apart from their oral counterparts, must be kept in mind. The location of the target tissue with respect to lung physiology, but also that of the target cell within the tissue, is critical and needs to be accounted for in the selection of a candidate molecules. Tissue properties of the different generations of the lung vary significantly. The upper airways have relatively thick walls with normal cell membranes and present a much larger barrier to the permeation of small molecules than the very thin membranes of the alveoli where gas exchange occurs. Beyond generational tissue variability, the location of the target cells within the tissue is also important. Microbiome and macrophages are found in the lung lumen, adrenergic and muscarinic receptors are found on the cell walls of the bronchial sub-epithelium whilst other targets are found within cells in the sub-epithelium and thus create additional challenges for molecules to reach their site of action. Going to the cell level, intracellular targets require membrane permeability for the drug to access the target; in contrast membrane-bound targets may well favor drugs that have high affinities for membranes, such as lipophilic amines. The discussion of API was covered in depth in Section 2 (Chapters 8–12), where the fate of the drug once it has landed on the lung tissue is examined through the scope of the competing mechanisms of dissolution, clearance and absorption. The latest developments in our understanding of the physicochemical and physiological processes that underpin these competing mechanisms was presented, leading to a discussion of physiologically-based pharmacokinetic modeling in Chapter 12.

Inhalation differs from oral delivery in one other critical aspect, that of delivery. Oral administration involves simple delivery that provides a single path for the drug to reach the target system, thus ensuring good control of the delivered dose. On the contrary, during inhalation the dose emitted by the device has to negotiate its way through complex anatomical features and a vast network of airways with varying local aerodynamics. This single fact complicates both efforts to achieve controlled delivery to specific targets and to predict the regional deposition of the delivered dose. It also impacts the selection of physicochemical properties for the drug formulation. To answer these challenges there have been continued efforts to improve device design over the last 70 years or so. Three main types of devices are currently in use, namely nebulizers, metered dose inhalers and dry powder inhalers, each imparting different physicochemical properties to the emitted drug, with important implications for the fate of the emitted dose. The relative strengths and weaknesses of each device type were explained along with critical assessment of expected developments (Chapters 3–5).

The relatively poor accessibility of the distal lung introduces another challenge to understanding and assessing drug delivery. Despite ongoing progress in the area of high-resolution medical imaging and lung-function tests in the clinic (Chapter 13), deposition information generated by these *in vivo* modalities suffers of poor spatial and temporal resolution. Traditionally, the incomplete picture available *in vivo* has been complemented with an array of *in vitro* and *in silico* approaches.

In vitro methods to study dose deposition of inhaled medication can provide clinically relevant information about inhaler and nebulizer performance if conducted under patient realistic conditions, i.e., using realistic flow profiles, mouth-throat models, and handling, which was reviewed and discussed (Chapter 6). Depending on the properties of the inhalation product, and the question at hand, *in vitro* methods may simply involve a filter measurement to estimate total lung deposition or may require more complicated techniques to decouple variable flow in the inhaler and mouth-throat model with constant flow in a cascade impactor, as well as assessment of the time resolved dose release process to provide input data to *in silico* modeling of regional deposition.

The range of *in silico* tools currently available for the prediction of the airflow and aerosol transport and deposition in the extrathoracic airways and the lung allows further probing of aerosol behavior (Chapter 7). 1D models for MT deposition are usually not applicable to most pharmaceutical inhalers. One notable exception is the confined jet model recently developed for DPIs. However, there are good reasons to believe that when entering the trachea, most of the dynamics of the aerosol cloud has dissipated and that therefore 1D models for deposition in the trachea and downwards apply to a sufficient extent. Combined with realistic *in vitro* testing using MT replicas, where MT deposition is measured rather than ill modeled, the prospect for 1D lung deposition models to provide very useful estimates of regional lung deposition has greatly improved. 3D Computational Fluid Particle Dynamics (3D-CFPD) is emerging as a powerful tool that can potentially be a game changer if properly coupled with *in vivo* and *in vitro* methods. 3D-CFPD models can simulate the whole process of dose release, aerosol generation and subsequent interaction with the device and MT (Chapter 7), but this needs measurements or assumptions of initial and boundary conditions and models of multi-scale physics beyond airflow and particle transport. We argue that also 3D-CFPD may benefit from using realistic *in vitro* results from MT replicas, not least in validation exercises. The key features of the various CFD modeling methods have been reviewed and areas where caution must be exercised have been identified. The emerging trend towards integrated whole-lung 3D-CFPD models has been explained. It has been argued that, while the emerging role of *in silico* methods in the area of personalized medicine is an exciting development, potentially more impactful, from the drug delivery perspective, is the application of these methods in large-scale population studies that are carried out *in silico*. The ultimate goal is to identify subpopulations (clusters) of patients with unique lung features that might predispose to certain disease development scenarios. Equally important is the identification of patient clusters with morphometric and functional characteristics that predispose to identifiable drug deposition patterns. Along with the push towards whole-lung simulations, the coupling of 3D-CFPD models with AI tools (Chapter 14) is another exciting development that is likely to further enhance the impact of *in silico* populations studies.

As acknowledged in Chapter 15, despite a continuous improvement in our understanding of inhalation therapies, reliable and accurate prediction of the *in vivo* performance of drugs based on first principles is still challenging. Perhaps the single most important impediment to rapid progress in this regard has been the inaccessibility of the distal lung to direct observation. The *in vivo* assessment of lung dose deposition in intermediate and peripheral lung regions remain beyond the resolution of even modern pulmonary imaging and beyond replication via *in vitro* approaches. Furthermore, our understanding of target receptors in the large expanse of the distal lung is far from precise, as is our mechanistic understanding of the local PK processes occurring post-deposition leading up to target exposure. Consequently, correlating key product *in vitro* attributes such as aerodynamic particle size distribution, dissolution, and drug physicochemical properties with local action, or even with the more generalizable plasma concentration profiles, remains challenging. The diversity of inhaled products adds to the challenge. Understanding drug tissue interactions and, ultimately, drug target interactions in the lung are key areas of development for the coming years. Nevertheless, the emergence of 3D-CFPD *in silico* methods is likely to have the greatest impact in improving our understanding and ability to predict regional deposition. The alignment of *in vivo*, *in vitro* and *in silico* methods proposed in Chapter 15 is likely to benefit all three modes of inquiry through complementarity and ultimately produce gains in understanding, speed and effectiveness during product design.

Index

Note: Page numbers followed by "*f*" and "*t*" refer to figures and tables, respectively.

B

E

F

J

K

L

M

N

O

P

Q

R

S

T

U

V

W

X

Z

9780128149744